MEETING THE CHALLENGE

Mark, a high school sophomore, spent many frustrating hours reading and studying biology, but he failed every biology test. He could not understand or remember the content well enough to participate in class discussions. Mrs. Reed, the biology teacher, was also frustrated because she knew that he was a hard-working student who diligently studied the assigned material. When she checked his permanent record, she found he had average grades with a B– or C+ average. She spoke with his other teachers and learned that he was a hard-working, but struggling, student in most of his classes.

Mark reached total frustration when Mrs. Reed assigned the biology unit on heredity. After struggling with the text material, he asked for assistance. Mrs. Reed suggested that he write an outline of the chapter and make a vocabulary notebook for the terms that troubled him. After two weeks, he showed no progress toward understanding genes, chromosomes, and so on, so Mrs. Reed asked for a conference with the reading teacher. Mrs. Reed and

"Meeting the Challenge" excerpts in each chapter show secondary school content area teachers in action.

To locate them, use your Table of Contents.

Mark met with the reading teacher after school. After considerable discussion, the reading teacher realized that Mark was attempting to memorize each of the terms (concepts) as a separate entity because he did not understand the interrelationships among them and could not relate these ideas to his own experiences. The reading teacher showed Mark how to use the table of contents as an overview or outline of the important ideas in the chapter and as a guide to superordinate ideas and subordinate ideas. Mrs. Reed explained the connection between the heredity chapter and the preceding chapter, as well as the conceptual relationships of the terms in the text. Jointly, they created the semantic map shown in Figure 3.2. As a result of these experiences, Mark began to conceptualize the terms as interrelated concepts rather than trying to remember each one as a separate entity.

A teacher may help a student *see* the connections among concepts in a content area chapter.
(© Robert Finken/The Picture Cube)

This "Meeting the Challenge" example appears in Chapter 3 "A Conceptual Approach to Developing Meaningful Vocabulary"

FIGURE **3.2**

Semantic Map

Heredity

Physical traits   Mental traits

Chromosomes

Genes

DNA   RNA

Secondary School Literacy Instruction

The Content Areas

■ ■ ■ ■ ■ ■ ■ ■ ■ ■ ■ ■ ■ ■ ■

Secondary School Literacy Instruction
The Content Areas

SIXTH EDITION

Betty D. Roe
Tennessee Technological University

Barbara D. Stoodt
*Visiting Professor at Northern Kentucky University and
Adjunct Instructor at the University of Cincinnati*

Paul C. Burns
Late of University of Tennessee at Knoxville

Houghton Mifflin Company   Boston   New York

*To Mike Roe, with appreciation and thanks for all his help on this project,
and*
To Linda and Susan

Senior Sponsoring Editor: Loretta Wolozin

Associate Editor: Lisa Mafrici

Senior Project Editor: Susan Westendorf

Senior Production/Design Coordinator: Jill Haber

Senior Manufacturing Coordinator: Priscilla Bailey

Marketing Manager: Pamela Laskey

Cover design: Catherine Hawkes, Cat and Mouse

Cover image: Elmer Bischoff, *Orange Sweater*, 1955, oil on canvas, 48½ x 57."
San Francisco Museum of Modern Art, Gift of Mr. and Mrs. Mark Schorer.

Printed in the U.S.A.

Library of Congress Catalog Card Number: 97-72537

ISBN: 0-395-872413

1 2 3 4 5 6 7 8 9-DC-01 00 99 98 97

Brief Table of Contents

Contents

Preface

Secondary school teachers use textbooks and other printed materials extensively as vehicles to convey content area information to their students. Content area teachers often discover, however, that their students are not maximizing their learning potential and do not read at levels necessary for understanding the types of printed material the teachers would like to use. Students also do not use such strategies as writing to learn in the content areas or reading/study strategies. This situation can frustrate teachers who do not know how to help their students learn literacy strategies to support their students' understanding in domain-specific material.

This book offers all content area teachers detailed and practical explanations of reading, writing, and study strategies needed by students to acquire and use new information. Techniques for teaching these strategies in a broad range of disciplines are included. Teachers thus help their students become more efficient, effective readers of their content materials and facilitate their students' learning of the subject matter content.

Audience and Purpose

Secondary School Literacy Instruction: The Content Areas, Sixth Edition, has been written primarily for preservice teachers preparing for secondary school certification in teacher education programs and for experienced secondary school teachers who want to help their students read content assignments with more understanding. Neither group is likely to have substantial background knowledge in literacy instruction. This book has thus been written at an introductory level, with the needs and concerns of these teachers in mind. The text also contains information that is useful for reading specialists who work cooperatively with content teachers in helping secondary students with reading difficulties and for secondary school administrators who must know about the reading needs of secondary school students if they are to set school policies appropriately.

This book provides a strategy-based approach to content reading. Much secondary content area material is written at a high difficulty level and students are required to read extensively. Teachers who know how to teach the reading and study skills strategies appropriate to their content area enhance their students' success in the classroom.

■ ■ Revisions in This Edition

The sixth edition of *Secondary School Literacy Instruction: The Content Areas* has been thoroughly updated and revised. A revised part and chapter organization places background information in the first two chapters, so that students can build appropriate schemata for understanding ensuing chapters. A new chapter has been added on "Literature-Based and Thematic Approaches to Content Area Teaching," and an all-new Afterword addresses "Use of Technology for Literacy Learning in a Technological Age." There are several new "Meeting the Challenge" features to show how teachers in secondary schools have applied the ideas presented in the chapters. These vignettes can make the information in the chapters easier to understand because they are placed in the context of real situations. New examples from secondary-level textbooks are located in various chapters throughout the text. Also, new pedagogical questions have been added in the margins throughout the text to call attention to important terminology and concepts.

Every chapter has been reworked to reflect the latest developments in reading instruction. Chapter 1, "Literacy in the Secondary School," has a heavily updated section on the National Assessment of Educational Progress.

Chapter 2, "Secondary School Reading Programs," stresses involvement of all school personnel in creating schoolwide reading programs.

Chapter 3, "A Conceptual Approach to Developing Meaningful Vocabulary," has been reorganized and updated extensively. A notable addition is a section on multiple intelligences and vocabulary learning. It is closely related to reading comprehension and leads naturally into the next two chapters.

Chapter 4, "The Process of Constructing Meaning in Texts," and Chapter 5, "Strategies for Constructing Meaning in Texts," cover the area of reading comprehension as a cognitive process based on integrating data from the reader, the text, and the context. Chapter 5 examines strategic processing of text, along with the strategies and skills that facilitate this processing. In this chapter we emphasize modeling, demonstrating, coaching, and guided practice.

Chapter 6, "Location and Organization of Information," and Chapter 7, "Reading-Study Strategies for Textbook Use," present useful strategies for all content areas. Chapter 6 has added information on computer applications, such as Internet searches, and on the Cornell Note-taking System and I-Charts, another system for note taking. Chapter 7 has a number of new examples from content area textbooks.

Four chapters that focus more specifically on instruction in content area classes come next. Chapter 8, "Writing in the Content Areas," has added information about on-line writing conferences, character journals, social justice notebooks, and pen pals. Chapter 9, "Literature-Based and Thematic Approaches to Content Area Teaching," is nearly all new, except for the material on thematic units that was in the last edition. Chapter 10, "Reading in the Content Areas: I," and Chapter 11, "Reading in the Content Areas: II," feature updated content area examples.

Chapter 12, "Diversity in the Secondary School Classroom," addresses strategies for helping exceptional students and students from diverse social, cultural, and economic backgrounds.

Expanded coverage of classroom-based assessment is included in Chapter 13, "Classroom Literacy Assessment." More information on portfolio assessment and performance-based assessment has been added, and test-review sources have been updated.

An entirely new section on technology, "Afterword: Use of Technology for Literacy Learning in a Technological Age," ends the text. This section covers a range of technological tools from overhead projectors, televisions, and audiotape recorders to computers and multimedia applications to education.

Features of the Text

This text presents a balance of theory and applications related to secondary school literacy. *Secondary School Literacy Instruction: The Content Areas*, Sixth Edition, provides unique emphasis on the content areas with practical strategies and illustrations of content materials from all high school subject areas. In all chapters, extensive use is made of actual secondary school material to explicitly bring theory into practice. A major strength of this book is the guidance it provides teachers in helping students improve their reading performance through the application of reading and study skills. To help the reader gain a more complete understanding of content, each text chapter contains the following features:

Overview A brief description of the most important concepts and themes of each chapter. Readers can use the overview to provide a mental set for reading the chapter.

Purpose-Setting Questions Purpose-setting questions focus readers' attention on the important aspects of chapter content.

Meeting the Challenge These vignettes and examples illustrate how teachers have used the ideas discussed in the chapter to meet their teaching challenges. They put the concepts from the chapter into realistic contexts for the students and help answer the question that content teachers often ask: How will I use this information on reading in my future classroom teaching?

Margin Questions These questions focus attention on important terminology and concepts in the material.

Summary The summary pulls together the main ideas of the chapter. Readers can use the summary to review their own knowledge and reinforce chapter content.

Discussion Questions Higher-level essay questions that instructors can use as homework assignments or as the basis of class discussion are provided for each chapter.

Enrichment Activities Application activities that go beyond chapter content provide students with opportunities to practice what they have learned in each chapter. These range from ideas for research papers to creating lesson plans and using strategies.

In addition, the *Instructor's Resource Manual with Test Questions* offers learning objectives, suggested teaching and learning strategies, instructional materials, and assessment techniques and materials for each chapter. Sets of examination items provided for chapters include multiple-choice, true-false, and essay questions. Appropriate performance-based assessment activities are also included for each chapter. Model syllabi that could be used for a course in secondary school reading instruction and a study skills learning activity packet are provided in this manual, along with a transition guide that outlines the changes from the fifth edition to the sixth edition.

Acknowledgments

We are indebted to many people for their assistance in the preparation of our manuscript. Although we would like to acknowledge the many teachers and students whose inspiration was instrumental in the development of this book, it is impossible to name them all. Particular appreciation is due Toni Fortune Anderson, Karen Claud, Katherine M. Dooley, Rory Lewelyn, Cathy McCurdy, and Bryce Stevens. Grateful recognition is also given to our developmental editor, Merryl Maleska Wilbur, and the following reviewers whose constructive advice and criticism helped greatly in the writing and revision of the manuscript.

Suellen Alfred, Tennessee Technological University
Mary Ann Dzama, George Mason University

Karen Fitzpatrick, Delaware State University
Nancy Gibney, University of Detroit Mercy
Rosalind B. Green, Xavier University
Sharon Kraus, Glenville State College
Candace Poindexter, Loyola Marymount University
Frank Serafini, Arizona State University

In addition, appreciation is expressed for those who have granted permission to use sample materials or citations from their respective works.

Betty D. Roe, *Tennessee Technological University*

Barbara D. Stoodt, *Visiting Professor at Northern Kentucky University* and *Adjunct Instructor at the University of Cincinnati*

Secondary School Literacy Instruction

The Content Areas

Contexts of Literacy Instruction for Content Area Teachers

Literacy in the Secondary School

Overview

This chapter opens with a discussion of the nature of reading, followed by a look at the literacy demands on secondary school students. Next is an overview of secondary school students' reading needs, including a discussion of the relationship of reading instruction to the secondary school curriculum. Then faulty assumptions about teaching reading are examined, and reading achievement levels of students and minimum competency requirements for students are addressed.

Purpose-Setting Questions

As you read this chapter, try to answer these questions:

1 What occurs during the reading process?
2 What literacy demands do secondary school students face?
3 What are secondary school students' reading needs?
4 What are some faulty assumptions about teaching reading in secondary schools?
5 What are some concerns about reading achievement levels of secondary school students?
6 What is the purpose of minimum competency testing?

MEETING THE CHALLENGE

"**M**y students aren't doing their reading assignments for my class. I don't know whether they *can't* or just *won't* read the material. Either way, my lessons haven't been going smoothly," a new secondary school teacher complained to a colleague.

A librarian can help locate reading materials for students to augment the regular class texts. (© Susie Fitzhugh)

"First, you need to find out if they *can* read the material," the colleague replied. "Do you know how to construct a *cloze test* or a *group reading inventory?*"

"No. Are they hard to do?" the new teacher responded.

"Cloze tests are easier to construct. However, you may feel that you get more specific information from the inventory," the colleague answered.

"Will you show me how to make these assessments?" asked the new teacher. "And will you help me interpret the results?"

"I'll lend you a book that describes them," the colleague said. "I got it for a college methods course. I'm sorry that I don't have more time to help, but you might ask the special reading teacher or the reading consultant for some assistance too."

"I didn't think of that," the new teacher admitted. "Thanks for your advice."

After studying the book's description of the two assessment measures, the teacher chose to prepare and administer a cloze test to the students. The results surprised her. Only a small number of the students appeared to be capable of reading the text independently. The majority could read it with teacher assistance, but some could not read it with understanding, even with teacher assistance.

"Thank goodness for the independent level group," she thought, "but what can I do to help the others?"

She returned to her colleague with her new question. He replied, "Check out that book some more. It suggests strategies that help prepare students for reading, guide them through reading, and direct them in analysis after reading. It describes study methods and ideas for study guides and other instructional activities for those students who can learn from the text with help. It suggests alternative materials and strategies for the other less capable readers, but I still think you should talk to the reading specialists about this as well."

The teacher examined more sections of the recommended book and gained ideas from it. Then she talked to the reading staff in her school. She now had a better idea of what she needed to do, and she had more specific questions to ask them.

"Where can I locate lower-level reading material for the students who can't read this text?" she asked.

"Enlist the help of the media specialist," she was told. "Also make some transcripts of class discussions that can be duplicated and used as reading material for these students."

"Oh, yes. I remember that idea," she said. "The book called it use of language experience materials. What would you suggest that I do to prepare the ones who can read the text with help for successful reading?"

"For *all* your students, try developing the new vocabulary through semantic webs or semantic feature analysis. Provide purposes for their reading that involve higher-level thinking. Perhaps use anticipation guides," she was told.

"The book explains all those activities," she said with relief. "I guess I had better get busy."

"If you need help when you get into the process, call me," the reading consultant said. "I'll be glad to lend a hand with specifics."

"It's sure good to have some direction for this," the teacher sighed. "Who would have thought I'd be so concerned about *reading?* I'm a *science* teacher."

Although this scenario is not based on the experience of a single teacher, the situation depicted is a common one. Teachers who have not had courses in secondary reading methods often find themselves in this situation. It would be good if they could all find colleagues with the right books and advice to offer! This text is designed to help teachers know what to do about their students' reading problems and whom to ask for assistance when it is needed. All the techniques and activities mentioned in the scenario are explained in detail in later chapters. "Meeting the Challenge" sections in the remainder of this book are usually based on the experiences of individual teachers in various school settings, rather than being composite depictions.

■ ■ What Is Reading?

How would you define reading?

Reading is described in many ways by different people. Some describe it as a thinking process. Others say that it is the reconstruction and interpretation of meanings behind printed symbols or that it is the process of understanding written language. Still others say that it is a transaction between the reader and the text. All of these explanations are accurate. Despite continuing disagreement about the precise nature of the reading process, there are points of general agreement among reading authorities. One such point is that comprehension of written material is the purpose of reading instruction. In fact, we consider *reading comprehension* and *reading* to be synonymous, because when understanding breaks down, reading actually has not occurred.

The word identification skills of sight word recognition, use of context clues, structural analysis, phonic analysis, and use of the dictionary's respellings for pronunciation facilitate understanding by helping readers associate printed words with the words in their oral and listening vocabularies. Readers who lack word identification abilities are not able to make these associations; thus, they require assistance with reading.

During the reading process, there is an interplay between the reader's preexisting knowledge and the written content. Competent reading is an active process in which the reader calls on experience, language, and schemata (theoretical constructs of knowledge related to experiences) to anticipate and understand the author's written language. Therefore, readers both bring meaning to print and take meaning from print. It is, as Rosenblatt (1989) and Goodman (Aaron et al., 1990b) would say, transactive.

The nature of the reading process alters as students mature. In the early stages of reading, word identification requires a reader's concentration. Eventually, however, readers are able to use their reading ability (ability to interpret written language) for pleasure, appreciation, knowledge acquisition, and functional purposes. Thus, reading competence has many faces. Competent readers locate materials and ideas that enable them to fulfill particular purposes, which may be to follow directions, to complete job applications, or to appreciate Shakespearean plays. In addition, competent readers adjust their reading style as they move from narrative to expository content. Finally, they read with various types of understanding—literal, interpretive, critical, and creative.

The terms *literal, interpretive (inferential), critical,* and *creative* refer to the types of thinking that are commonly associated with reading comprehension. *Literal understanding* refers to the reader's recognizing or remembering ideas and information that are explicitly stated in printed material. *Interpretive comprehension* occurs when the reader synthesizes ideas and information from printed material with knowledge, experience, and imagination to form hypotheses. Interpretive comprehension requires that the reader use ideas and information that are not stated on the printed page; that is, the reader must "read between the lines," use deductive reasoning, and make assumptions based on the facts given. *Critical comprehension (evaluation)* requires that the reader make judgments about the content of a reading selection by comparing it with external criteria. The reader may have developed these criteria through experience, through reference to resource materials, or through access to information provided by authorities on the subject. *Creative understanding (reading beyond the lines)* has to do with the reader's emotional responses to printed material (appreciation) and his or her ability to produce new ideas based on the reading experience. Creative understanding is built on literal, inferential, and critical understanding. A reader's intellectual understanding provides a foundation for his or her emotional reaction. For example, a reader may respond to an author's style or may identify with a certain character, story incident, or the author's use of symbolism.

Good readers exercise comprehension monitoring (metacognitive) strategies as they read. They constantly ask if the material they are reading makes sense, and if not, what they should do to remedy their lack of understanding.

■ ■ ■ Literacy Demands on Secondary School Students

How will the levels of literacy that your secondary school students have affect their content area learning?

The term **literacy** refers to the ability to read and write. Au (1993, p. 20) defines it as "the ability and willingness to use reading and writing to construct meaning from printed text, in ways which meet the requirements of a particular social context." Taber (1987, p. 458) says that "literate people can respond to whatever daily reading tasks they face." We would extend that statement to include the writing tasks they face as well.

Secondary school students have to read content textbooks and supplementary materials in school and for homework outside of school. This reading may include electronically transmitted text read from a computer monitor. Some of the material is likely to be highly technical in nature. Students also need to write in-class and homework papers and to write responses to test questions, study questions, and assigned readings. However, they have even more varied literacy needs in their activities outside school.

Even if students ignore purely recreational reading, they need to read signs found in their environment, recipes, menus, manuals for operating equipment, instructions for assembling items, job applications, television schedules, transportation schedules, road maps, labels on food or medicine, newspapers, public notices, advertisements, bank statements, bills, and many other functional materials. Failure to read some of these materials with adequate understanding can result in their commission of traffic violations, becoming lost, having unpleasant reactions to food or medicine, being ejected from unauthorized areas, missing desirable programs, failing to make connections with needed transportation, losing employment opportunities, and other undesirable outcomes.

Secondary students also need to write letters to family and friends, instructions to people who are doing things for them (such as feeding their pets), notes to themselves about tasks to be completed, phone messages for other members of their households, responses to a multitude of forms, and many other items. Mistakes in these activities can also have potentially bad results. For example, an inaccurately written phone message may cause someone to fail to pick up a young child at school on time. Our culture places a high value on literacy, and we are inundated with reading and writing demands in order to carry out everyday tasks.

The job market also affects students' literacy needs. Research shows that the number of low-literacy jobs has decreased, and even jobs considered to be low in literacy demands may require the ability to read such materials as manuals for operating equipment. Mikulecky (1996, p. 155) says that "the ability to set purposes, self-question, summarize information, monitor comprehension, and make useful notes distinguishes superior job performers from merely adequate job performers." Workers have to put together information from a variety of sources to solve problems and perform job requirements. High school students may or may not have opportunities to practice such uses of printed material.

Good literacy skills are especially important to students who plan to attend college. Whimbey (1987) says that reading at grade level is not good enough for these students because students entering college are expected to be able to read at higher than twelfth-grade level, as determined by a traditional reading test.

In everyday situations, all people, secondary students included, must identify and seek the information that they need. Therefore, in a model secondary classroom, much instruction would center on issues and problems that are relevant to the students in everyday life, providing instruction in finding and understanding information, comparing and evaluating sources of the information, and going beyond the printed material by interpreting, generalizing, synthesizing, and applying the information (Feathers and Smith, 1987).

Secondary school teachers can think about how students need the material from their classes in everyday life. Then, in many cases, they can plan instruction designed to help the students apply this information to real-life situations. To accomplish this goal, a variety of supplementary reading sources need to be incorporated into the lessons, and teachers need to offer the students guidance in reading both the textbook and the supplementary materials, and in integrating the information gained from these sources with information from lectures, demonstrations, discussions, and audiovisual presentations. Teachers also need to offer instruction that would allow students to record such material in a meaningful way. Note taking, organizational skills, and other tasks important in writing information for use by the student and others would be included.

Providing a variety of reading and writing experiences using varied materials can help students develop the backgrounds to read material needed in the real world and the skill to express themselves in clear and functional ways. Reading short textbook assignments to answer factual checkup questions and writing single word or phrase answers to questions or circling correct responses are not sufficient.

Secondary School Students' Reading Needs

In recent years the need to provide well-conceived secondary school reading programs has grown as the population in secondary schools has increased and the importance of comprehensive curricula has been recognized. Comprehensive programs for reading instruction at the secondary level are described in detail in Chapter 2. This section serves as a brief orientation to these programs.

The population being served in secondary schools today is diverse in a variety of ways: culturally, linguistically, mentally, physically, and economically. Teachers must try to reach *all* students, not just the advantaged and gifted ones, who are the easiest to teach. See Chapter 12 for more on the diversity of students.

How Does Reading Instruction Fit into the Secondary School Curriculum?

This section explains the general relationship of reading/study skills to content reading and shows the content area teacher's position in the overall picture. It also shows the general organization and approach of this text. The concepts discussed here are analyzed in greater detail in later chapters.

Word Identification

Do students need to be able to use all of the different word identification skills and strategies? Why, or why not?

Word identification skills and strategies include sight word recognition, contextual analysis, structural analysis, phonic analysis, and use of the dictionary's respellings to determine pronunciation. The goal of word identification instruction is to develop students' independence in identifying words.

Sight words are words students have memorized and are able to identify immediately. Secondary students usually have a good store of sight words that help them read content materials with understanding. Each time a content teacher introduces a new technical or specialized term that is important to understanding the content area, the teacher hopes to turn the new word into a sight word for the students; the study of the subject would be inefficient if many of the important words had to be analyzed carefully before recognition occurred. The content teacher can help impress new words on the students' memories, and thus turn them into sight words, by writing them on the chalkboard, pronouncing them, and discussing them with the students. Knowledge of sight words also enables students to use contextual analysis.

Contextual analysis is use of the context (surrounding words and sentences) in which an unknown word occurs to identify the word. Contextual analysis skills are powerful tools for secondary students to use in reading content area materials, and content area teachers will benefit from helping students become aware of the usefulness of context in word identification. Contextual analysis not only plays a role in word identification but also is an important tool for determining word meaning.

Structural analysis involves the use of word parts such as affixes, root words, syllables, and smaller words that are joined to form compound words to help in the identification of unfamiliar words. Structural analysis is extremely helpful in analysis of content area words because in many cases certain prefixes, suffixes, and root words appear repeatedly in the related technical terms of a discipline. Learning to recognize these word parts can be very helpful in decoding the vocabulary of the discipline.

Phonic analysis involves breaking words into basic sound elements and blending these sounds together to produce spoken words. Phonic analysis is not taught by the content area teacher but lies in the province of the special reading teacher.

Use of the dictionary's respellings to determine pronunciation is an important skill for students to master. Many students need lessons in using the dictionary's pronunciation key to help them decode the respellings.

Comprehension

Why is reading comprehension a central concern of a content area teacher?

Reading comprehension is an interactive process of meaning construction. The reader's background knowledge structures (schemata), the information in the text, and the context in which the reading takes place all interact to produce comprehension. Schemata related to the reading material must be activated if students are to comprehend material as fully as possible.

Word identification skills and strategies help students pronounce words, but word meanings must be understood before reading comprehension can occur. Many of the words that content readers encounter represent labels for key concepts in the content areas. A reader learns word meanings through experience, word association, discussion, concept development, contextual analysis, structural analysis, and use of a dictionary and a thesaurus. Content teachers can help students comprehend content materials by teaching them the meanings of key vocabulary terms. Structural analysis plays an important part in the determination of word meaning in content area classes. Morphemes, the smallest meaningful units of a language, include prefixes, suffixes, and root words. Each content area has common word parts such as these that are frequently found in instructional materials for the class. Analogy exercises, semantic feature analysis, word sorts, and words webs (or semantic webs or arrays) are all good vocabulary development activities. These activities are explained in detail in Chapter 3.

To read with comprehension, readers must also be able to perceive the internal organization of reading materials, understand the various writing patterns used to structure content materials, and understand the material at the appropriate cognitive levels.

A reader's perception of the internal organization of a selection is based on the ability to identify main ideas and supporting details as well as on familiarity with various organizational writing patterns. Expository writing patterns may include cause-effect, comparison-contrast, sequence of events, or one or more of a variety of other organizations. For narrative materials, knowledge of story grammar (or story structure) is important. Readers understand content better when they are able to follow the particular writing pattern and organization used. Content area teachers need to be familiar with the types of writing patterns encountered frequently in their particular disciplines, so that they can help students to understand these patterns.

When reading, students must comprehend material literally, interpretively, critically, and creatively, as each type of comprehension is appropriate. Modeling, discussion, a problem-solving approach to reading, comprehension monitoring, visualization strategies, judicious use of questioning techniques, use of writing to learn, use of study guides, and directed reading lessons serve as vehicles for developing these types of understanding. Chapters 4 and 5 address comprehension instruction.

Content reading requires flexible use of reading rate. The concept of rate can be examined best as it relates to comprehension. Rate is governed by purpose for reading, type of comprehension desired, familiarity with content, and type of content. Content area teachers need to help students learn to vary their reading rates to fit particular instructional materials and different purposes for reading. Chapter 7 discusses reading rate.

Study Skills

How can poor study skills affect content area learning?

In the secondary school, students are expected to become more independent in applying their reading skills and strategies in work-study situations. **Study skills** involve application of reading skills and strategies to learning written content area material. There are three basic types of study skills: those that involve locating information through reading; those that are concerned with understanding and remembering content; and those that are concerned with the organization of information once it has been located and read. Content area teachers need to help students learn to use these study skills efficiently, so that they can study the content assignments more effectively. Teaching study skills in the situations in which they are expected to be used is more effective than teaching them in isolation. Examples of study skills can be found in Chapters 6 and 7, and application of these skills to particular content areas is discussed in Chapters 10 and 11.

■ Some Faulty Assumptions About Teaching Reading

Several faulty assumptions about the teaching of reading should be considered.

1. Teaching reading is a concern only in the elementary school. In many school systems, formal reading instruction ends at the sixth grade. The idea that a child who has completed the sixth grade should have mastered the complex process of reading fails to take into account that learning to read is a continuing process. People learn to read over a long period of time, attempting more-advanced reading materials as they master easier ones. Even after encountering all the reading skills through classroom instruction, readers continue to refine their use of them, just as athletes first learn the techniques of a sport and then practice and refine their abilities with time.

2. Teaching reading in the content areas is separate and distinct from teaching subject matter. Teaching reading and study skills is an integral part of teaching any content area, and content teachers' efforts to do so are important to the success of any secondary school reading program. A teacher is obligated to teach students how to use the printed materials that are assigned. When a teacher employs printed materials to teach a content area, that teacher is using reading as a teaching aid—and should use it for maximum effectiveness. Teaching reading in subject matter areas is a complementary learning process, inseparable from the particular subject matter.

3. Reading needs in the secondary school can be met through remedial work alone. Some schools fail to make an essential distinction between *developmental reading,* which is designed to meet the needs of all students, and *corrective reading* or *remedial reading,* which both provide specific assistance to readers who are having difficulties. Not only should developmental (as well as remedial) classes be made available, but also within each class the content teacher can promote developmental reading by helping students learn the concepts and vocabulary of that content area, and they can enhance their students' reading comprehension by assisting them in interpreting and evaluating the text material. Corrective reading assistance can also be given within each class, as needed.

Additionally, teachers can help students develop better reading study skills and other specialized skills associated with the particular content areas. For example, reading and understanding written directions is a skill that is needed in every secondary classroom. Other universally needed skills include reading to discover main ideas, details, and inferences. Even more important than absorbing the vast amount of printed material that they encounter every day is the secondary school students' development of critical reading ability. Before they leave secondary school, students should know how to sort out fact from opinion, truth from half-truth, information from emotion.

4. A reading specialist or an English teacher should be responsible for the teaching of reading.   Reading specialists have distinct responsibilities in secondary reading programs, but the results of their efforts are negligible without the help of classroom teachers. Responsibility for teaching reading cannot be delegated solely to English teachers. Reading as a tool for learning is no more important in English class than it is in most other classes, and English teachers do not necessarily have any better preparation for teaching reading skills than do other teachers. All content teachers (English, science, health, social studies, mathematics, computer science, home economics, business education, industrial arts, agriculture, physical education, music, art, and others) have a responsibility to teach the language and organization of their particular content areas, and to do so they must help students read that content.

5. The teaching of reading and the teaching of literature are one and the same.   Reading skills are important to the study of literature, as they are to the study of every content area. It should be understood, however, that teaching literature should not consist merely of having students read stories and then giving vocabulary drills and exercises to find details and main ideas. It is dangerous to assume that a student will improve content reading skills by practicing with only literature selections, for reading in other content areas involves primarily expository, rather than narrative, selections and requires integration of information gained from graphic aids such as pictures, maps, graphs, charts, and diagrams with the written text.

Reading Achievement Levels and Minimum Reading Competency

There is much concern in our country about the reading achievement levels of secondary students. This concern has manifested itself in much testing.

Reading Achievement Levels

The wide range in reading abilities among secondary school students presents their teachers with a difficult problem. For example, in a group classified as seventh graders, there may be boys and girls whose reading skills equal those of many tenth or eleventh graders. Some twelfth graders may have a fifth- or sixth-grade reading ability, whereas others may read at the level of college seniors. In addition to having students with a wide range of reading abilities, secondary schools often have large numbers of remedial readers. Thus, teachers in secondary schools should know that a student's grade placement may not reflect his or her reading ability. Teaching reading in the secondary schools includes strengthening the performances of students who are reading well for their grade placements *and* giving more basic assistance to students who are reading at levels significantly below their grade placements.

The National Assessment of Educational Progress (NAEP) is a study to determine competence in a number of learning areas, including reading. NAEP assessments in reading involve nationally representative samples of students in the fourth, eighth, and twelfth grades. Currently, overall assessment results are analyzed by placement on a single proficiency scale, showing the kinds of tasks the students can perform at different achievement levels (*Reading Today*, 1993).

Beginning in 1992, the NAEP has reported results in terms of three achievement levels. Those students scoring at the *basic* level showed "partial mastery of the knowledge and skills fundamental for proficient work at each grade" (Mullis, Campbell, and Farstrup, 1993, p. 12). Those scoring at the *proficient* level exhibited "solid academic performance and demonstrated competence over challenging subject matter" (Mullis et al., 1993, p. 12). Students who scored at the *advanced* level displayed even higher levels of performance, including the ability to integrate prior knowledge with text information at the eighth-grade level and the ability to integrate text and document directions to accurately complete a task at the twelfth-grade level (Mullis et al., 1993).

In 1994 the percentage of twelfth graders who reached the proficient level declined in comparison to the 1992 results. In addition, a smaller percentage of twelfth graders were at or above the basic level. Twelfth graders in three regions—Northeast, Central, and West—showed lower average reading proficiency than did the twelfth graders in the 1992 assessment. The decline was attributed to the performance of the students with lower proficiency (those at the 10th, 25th, and 50th percentiles) and "was evident for all three assessed purposes for reading: *reading for literary experience, reading to gain information,* and *reading to perform a task.*" These results indicate much room for improvement.

Some educators have questioned the use of NAEP results. For example, Harste asserted that "standardized tests that reduce literacy to a single scale are, put bluntly, invalid, and invalid, generic tests of literacy have zero instructional usefulness" (Farstrup, 1989–1990, p. 12).

To improve the assessment, beginning in 1992, test developers incorporated longer, more realistic reading selections than were previously used and had students construct written responses. Data were collected related to instructional practices and background information about students ("Analyzing the NAEP Data," 1993/1994). This is an encouraging development. Educators, however, still have some concerns about the assessment. One is that some information included in the NAEP report reflected interviews with teachers and students, and the interviews produced conflicting information in response to some questions. Another concern is that the standards may have been set too high. Additionally, some educators wonder if the "NAEP achievement levels are valid measures of what students should know" ("Analyzing the NAEP Data," 1993/1994, p. 1). The National Academy of Education has produced a report claiming that the NAEP achievement levels were set by a fundamentally flawed process, and a report by the Technical Review Panel has questioned the adequacy of the test questions and complained about the overlapping definitions of the achievement levels ("NAEP Achievement Standards Draw Criticism," 1993/1994). Further analysis and clarification of the validity of the findings will emerge with further study. For now, teachers should be cautious in interpreting information from these test results.

Other 1994 findings of the NAEP merit mention. Students who had more literacy materials in the home and did more recreational reading had higher average reading proficiency than did those who read less frequently, but there were declines in the reported presence of literacy materials in the home and of recreational reading for twelfth-grade students between 1992 and 1994. Students who had frequent home discussions about their studies had higher average reading proficiency than students who did not, but twelfth graders' reports indicated a decline in such activity between 1992 and 1994. Students who watched less than four hours of television a day scored higher on reading proficiency than did those who watched more. Both eighth and twelfth graders who read more than five pages each day for school and homework had higher reading proficiencies than those who read less. Unfortunately, according to NAEP data: "Since 1992, there was an increase in the percentage of twelfth graders who reported reading five or fewer pages each day, and a decline in the percentage who reported reading 11 or more pages." Also, although eighth and twelfth graders who reported being asked to explain what they read and to discuss various interpretations of what they read at least once a week had higher reading proficiencies, twelfth graders reported being asked to explain what they read less often in 1994 than in 1992, and both eighth and twelfth graders reported fewer discussions of interpretations of their reading ("Results from the NAEP 1994 Reading Assessment," 1994).

■ Minimum Competency Programs

What are the implications of having a minimum competency test as a requirement for graduation?

A development stemming from students' failure to achieve minimum reading competencies is the requirement by some state boards of education that students must acquire certain measurable abilities before they can be awarded a high school diploma. A number of states now have published minimum requirements for graduation. Oescher and Kirby (1989) reported that seventeen states require students to "pass" a **minimum competency test** in order to graduate from high school. Such tests are generally of two types: one is a "survival skills" reading test, asking the student to read such things as a schedule or a medicine bottle label; the other is a "basic skills" test in which reading skills such as identifying meanings of prefixes or making inferences are tested. Both types assess specific skills and are scored on the basis of specific cutoff points, but there is frequent disagreement as to what cutoff point should be set as "passing."

Competency tests have been developed at the state level in some states and at the local level in others. Instructional objectives commonly included on these tests are identifying main ideas and details, finding sequence and cause-and-effect patterns, making inferences, following written directions, using an index and table of contents, using a dictionary, extracting information from graphic aids, and interpreting and completing common forms. Some secondary schools use a commercially available standardized survey reading test (such as the *Gates-MacGinitie Reading Test: Survey*); other schools use commercially available standardized reading tests that measure survival reading skills or basic skills.

In some cases, students who fail the tests must take remedial classes; in others, no remedial program is required. Singer and others (1988) studied the results of two types of placement on high school students who failed their district's reading competency test but were reading at grade 5.5 or higher as assessed by a standardized reading test. They found that these students were "more likely as a group to benefit from placement in a regular English class than in a remedial reading class that does not provide diagnostically based instruction" (p. 519). The researchers believed that the students benefited more from the regular English class because they were beyond the stage of reading acquisition and into a stage of reading to learn from text; thus, they needed more stress on metacognitive strategies, higher-level reasoning skills, abstract vocabulary, and knowledge of things beyond their immediate experiences.

One concern about minimum competency testing is that teachers may just teach to have students pass the test, which would provide only *minimum* competency for everyone, rather than helping students reach their full potentials (Oescher and Kirby, 1989). Another concern is that failure on minimum competency tests may have adverse psychological effects on students. Richman and others (1987) found that, when high-academic-risk students failed a minimum competency test, their self-esteem was adversely affected and neuroticism and apprehension increased. Catterall (1989) found that there was a strong association between failure on the competency test and reduced belief by the students that they would finish school.

Some educators have felt that minimum competency tests are unfair to some subgroups of our population. Some teachers feel that standardized curricula, brought about because of minimum competency testing requirements, impair their ability to match learning objectives to particular student needs. They worry about covering all the skills with all the students, even though some students have not mastered the skills already presented. Such concerns often result in inappropriate instructional pacing, which, according to research, accounts for poor reading performance on the part of students of low socioeconomic levels (Rosenholtz, 1987).

Ellman (1988) feels that the tests used are not valid for testing verbal skills. He points out such problems with all standardized tests that focus on speed, remarking that some students work more slowly than others and are adversely affected by the timing of the tests. He also believes that the test producers overlook individual differences in students' development of skills and knowledge, assuming that they all should have mastered the same material or skills by the same date. He states that the tests discourage holistic teaching approaches because isolated factors are easier to test, and that generally such tests do not attempt to test for creativity and higher-order thinking skills.

Making important decisions based on a single test score is not wise. Multiple sources of assessment data, such as teacher observation, student work samples, and tests, collected over a period of time, are essential to informed decision-making.

Summary

Knowledge and understanding of the reading process enable teachers to develop effective reading instruction. Reading is a complex process with many facets.

There are a number of misconceptions about the teaching of reading at the secondary school level. These faulty assumptions include the notions that (a) teaching reading is a concern only in the elementary school; (b) teaching reading in the content areas is separate and distinct from teaching subject matter; (c) reading needs can be met through remedial work alone; (d) a reading specialist or English teacher should be totally responsible for the teaching of reading; and (e) the teaching of reading and the teaching of literature are one and the same.

Factors that influence secondary reading programs include the wide range in reading ability among secondary school students and dissatisfaction with school reading achievement levels and the resulting trend toward minimum competency testing.

Discussion Questions

1 Which "faulty assumptions" seem most evident in your school situation?

2 Do you believe that it is possible to increase learning in the content areas by providing appropriate help to students in their study of printed materials? Give as many examples as possible to support your position.

3 What factors account for many secondary school graduates' inability to read well enough to cope with basic reading requirements? Give reasons for your answer.

4 What factors account for the wide range of reading ability of secondary school students? Defend your answer.

Enrichment Activities

*1   What do you think are the most important things about reading that a content area teacher should know? Interview a content area teacher about this question. Compare the findings with your own views.

2   Keep a log of your literacy activities for a week. What do your findings suggest about reading and writing to meet the daily needs of young adults?

*3   Interview three students, one of each of the following types: (a) accelerated reader, (b) average reader, and (c) remedial reader. Try to learn each student's perspective as to the effect of his or her reading ability on school achievement, self-image, and life goals. Share your findings with the class.

4   Visit a secondary classroom. Try to identify the range of reading abilities. Compare your impressions with those of the teacher.

---

*Activities with asterisks are designed for in-service teachers, student teachers, and practicum students.

CHAPTER 2

Secondary School Reading Programs

In this chapter we consider the personnel who are responsible for reading instruction, the components and development of total-school reading programs, and choosing materials for secondary school programs. The total-school organization for reading requires much special planning. Responsibility for execution of the various aspects of the program must be assigned. Cooperation of staff members is essential, as is in-service training for them. Program goals and instructional techniques must be determined cooperatively by the involved personnel, materials for the program must be chosen carefully, and the program must be evaluated thoughtfully.

Purpose-Setting Questions

As you read this chapter, try to answer these questions:

1 What responsibilities for reading instruction in the secondary school belong to the content area teacher, the administrator, the reading consultant, the special reading teacher, and the librarian or media specialist?
2 What are necessary activities related to the development of a total-school reading program?
3 What are some questions that a teacher should ask about materials being evaluated for use in a secondary school reading program?

■ ■ Personnel Responsible for Reading Instruction

The secondary school reading program is the responsibility of a number of individuals. Those responsible for various portions of the program include content area teachers, administrators, reading consultants, special reading teachers, and librarians or media specialists.

■ Content Area Teachers

How does the content area teacher's responsibility for his or her students' reading skill differ from that of the special reading teacher?

The content area teacher's responsibility is to help students *read* their textbooks and supplementary materials more effectively in order to *learn* the content more effectively. **Content area teachers** need to know what reading skills are necessary for successful reading of the materials in their particular disciplines, and they need to be capable of assisting students in applying these skills as they complete their content area assignments. In most cases, such as in teaching technical vocabulary, reading instruction and content instruction are identical. Content teachers may often find that minilessons in a particular reading strategy will pay large dividends in the students' understanding of an assignment.

Content area teachers do not have the *primary* responsibility for teaching reading strategies. The responsibility for helping students with significantly impaired reading abilities belongs to a special reading teacher. However, content teachers do have to adjust assignments for these students. It may be necessary to provide alternate materials and teaching methods for these students if their content learning is to be successful.

Following are the requirements for content area teachers that will enable them to meet their students' needs and the goals of the reading program:

1. Knowledge of the reading skills that are needed by secondary students in order to read content materials in their disciplines.
2. Knowledge of assessment measures that can help them identify students who cannot read the standard assignments, students who can read the assignments only with much assistance, or those who can read the assignments with ease.
3. Ability to identify specific learning problems that should be referred to a specialist in order to provide appropriate help for students who require it.
4. Knowledge of ways to help students learn specific skills and strategies needed for their content areas.
5. Knowledge of study aids and procedures that can help students achieve success in content area reading.
6. Knowledge of effective ways to differentiate assignments for students reading at different levels of proficiency.
7. Willingness to cooperate with other school personnel, such as the special reading teacher, in helping students reach their full potential in content reading.

Even though content area teachers may initially be hesitant about reading strategy instruction, they often change their attitudes when they learn useful strategies. Poindexter (1994) found that four strategies—the jigsaw method, anticipation/reaction guides, What I Know (essentially K-W-L), and self-questioning—helped students in her content area reading class to see that they could teach reading strategies successfully and thereby enhance comprehension of their content area material. (See Chapter 12 for a description of the jigsaw method and Chapter 5 for an explanation of the other three strategies.)

■ Special Reading Teacher

What kinds of interactions do the special reading teacher and the content area teacher need to have?

The **special reading teacher** generally works directly with students. This person should have a graduate degree in reading or the equivalent, have several years of teaching experience, and be certified as a reading specialist. *Standards for Reading Professionals* (1992), developed by the Professional Standards and Ethics Committee and the Advisory Group to the National Council of Accreditation of Teacher Education Joint Task Force of the International Reading Association, provides an outstanding set of criteria for reading educators and indicates degrees of competence needed in various categories that are listed.

Although the specific responsibilities of the reading specialist may vary from locale to locale, the following are fairly typical:

1. Uses a variety of methods to teach reading strategies, administers and interprets formal and informal reading assessments, and knows and uses appropriate materials for reading instruction.
2. Plans and teaches reading classes for average readers, accelerated readers, and/or disabled readers.
3. Works with paraprofessionals and parents who may assist with the reading program.
4. Works with content area teachers whose students are in reading classes; assists content area teachers in selecting instructional materials to meet the needs of students; when called upon, helps content teachers develop and utilize reading instruction within content classrooms; provides suggestions on establishing learning centers within content classrooms, especially involving use of specialized instruction for the reader who is severely disabled.
5. Assists the reading consultant as a demonstration teacher and resource person.

Jaeger (1996) makes the case that reading specialists should spend more time working with school personnel, rather than working directly with children for all, or the large majority, of their time. She believes that they would have more impact working with curriculum development (e.g., helping teachers incorporate literature-based instruction), instructional problem solving (observing classes, helping teachers to adjust instructional activities, doing demonstration teaching, and/or providing professional resources and consultation), assessment (including translating assessment results into instructional plans), and parent liaison activities, essentially serving as a reading consultant at the building level. This change in emphasis may be more appropriate as more schools adopt an inclusion model for dealing with special needs students. (Information about inclusion is located in Chapter 12.)

Reading Consultant

What are the main differences between the jobs of the reading consultant and the special reading teacher?

The **reading consultant** works with administrators and other school personnel to develop and coordinate schoolwide reading programs. The reading consultant may work from the central office with more than one school. This person is freed from classroom teaching and instruction of special reading classes. He or she should have a high degree of professional skill and knowledge, have had formal study in reading and related areas and several years successful teaching experience, and have met certification qualifications as a special teacher of reading. The *Standards for Reading Professionals* (1992), mentioned earlier, provides criteria for these reading educators.

Again, although the specific responsibilities of the reading consultant may vary somewhat from locale to locale, the following are typical:

1. Studies the populations to be served—both students and teachers—and assists principals/supervisors/administrators in planning comprehensive reading programs.
2. Orients beginning teachers to philosophy, procedures, and materials for the school reading program and keeps all school staff informed about new developments in reading.
3. Evaluates programs, making recommendations for changes as needed.
4. Provides in-service instruction, conducting workshops, seminars, conferences, and minilessons on topics such as informal reading inventories and construction of teaching or study guides.
5. Evaluates and recommends reading materials.
6. Works as resource person with special cases when difficulty or complexity requires a high degree of professional competence.
7. Keeps the school community informed about the purposes and progress of the reading programs.

Principal or Administrator

A most significant prerequisite for a good secondary reading program is administrative direction. The administrator alone possesses the prestige and authority to carry through a sound reading program. He or she must encourage the staff and ensure that the reading philosophy is implemented in logical ways. He or she needs to initiate the definition of the reading program's philosophy and must facilitate that philosophy by extending it to the entire school.

The administrator has nine major functions in the reading program:

1. Knowing about reading and students.   The administrator increases his or her knowledge by taking formal courses in reading, attending reading workshops and conferences, visiting often with outstanding reading teachers, studying the reading materials used in the school, and/or maintaining a professional reading library. The effective administrator understands the complexity of the reading act; that "reading" implies understanding meanings, not just decoding; that secondary students are continuing to develop their reading proficiency at ever higher levels; and that reading is an integral part of all content area instruction.

Ward and Bradford (1983) found that achievement of junior high school students is positively influenced when they are taught under the supervision of an administrator who is eligible for certification in reading or who has earned additional college credits in reading. If the teachers of these students perceive the supervisor to have reading expertise, the effect on students' reading achievement is also positive.

2. Stimulating improvement opportunities.   The administrator can accomplish this goal by evaluating the present program with teachers and observing classrooms for reading instruction practices. Reading topics of interest to many teachers—such as methods of grouping students, classroom analysis of reading needs, methods of improving comprehension and retention, methods of teaching study and research skills, and ways of individualizing instruction in the various content areas—provide critical issues for consideration at faculty meetings, workshops, and conferences.

3. Enhancing teaching/learning environment.   Three contributions that the administrator can make in this area are reducing pupil-teacher ratio; meeting and exceeding requirements for library resources; and involving parents, paraprofessionals, and students in the reading program.

Sanacore (1988) believes that the school principal should support schoolwide independent reading, since it can have a positive effect on students' reading habits and achievement. He laments the fact that some principals see independent reading as frivolous and delegate it to time after skills instruction, ignoring the fact that it provides prior knowledge of content that will be studied, helps students build reading interests, allows students to apply skills in realistic text, and helps students develop a love of reading. Sanacore believes that in each subject area five weeks of independent reading could be offered to students, allowing exposure to independent reading in at least one class throughout most of the school year without sacrificing content instruction in any one class. This approach would, of course, require large numbers of books appropriate to the different instructional areas from which students could choose their independent reading. Sanacore's position is congruent with that of Hillerich (1983, p. 100), who has stated that "independent reading should be half of the total program in reading instruction."

4. Selecting effective materials. To avoid inappropriate purchases, administrators must see that valid standards and procedures for selection of superior materials are developed. Many schools have in their storerooms materials and learning aids that never should have been bought, but that were purchased hastily when money suddenly became available from an unexpected source. The best way to avoid such mistakes is to pre-evaluate materials. Tentative decisions should be reached by a group that includes people who are knowledgeable about local resources, available alternatives, and potential users' opinions and preferences. Potential users should be a part of the group. Final decisions about major purchases should come only after tryouts on a limited scale.

Assistance in choosing appropriate materials may also be obtained from sources such as university faculty. Some universities have entire courses devoted to materials selection. (More on selection of materials is included later in this chapter.)

5. Creating appropriate organizational plans. In organizing for reading instruction, the administrator should be aware of important guidelines: (a) vast differences exist among the instructional needs of students of similar age/grade placement; (b) organizational patterns should be flexible and altered as better ways are discovered; (c) more emphasis should be placed on methods of providing for individual differences by teachers than on methods of grouping; and (d) organization is not a "method of instruction"—it can only facilitate or hinder effective instruction.

6. Helping to collect and interpret assessment information. The school needs to maintain appropriate reading assessment information in the student's permanent record. The administrator realizes that reading survey tests indicate the range of reading achievement in the class, whereas diagnostic reading tests help teachers to locate specific reading strengths and weaknesses. He or she should be sensitive to the fact that the best standardized tests are those that are valid and reliable and for which the norming population for the test resembles the class to be tested. The administrator also values informal assessments, including informal reading inventories, informal skills checks, and observation. He or she understands the advantages of portfolio assessment and encourages its use. He or she also realizes that a single measure is never sufficient for assessment decisions. (See Chapter 13 for a detailed description of assessment tools.)

7. Providing corrective/remedial services. The administrator (a) understands the need for corrective or remedial reading instruction; (b) realizes that some students need more assistance than is possible in a regular classroom to reach their reading potential; (c) is alert for possible instructional weaknesses throughout the curriculum, such as failure to adjust content material to fit students' needs and ineffective motivation for developing reading interests; (d) provides appropriate materials; and (e) wisely utilizes the reading specialist and the reading consultant for this service.

8. Communicating about the reading program. The administrator should be aware of the following questions frequently posed by parents and be prepared to answer them reasonably: How is reading taught in the school? What can I do to help my child like reading? What can we do to help our child who is a poor reader? Should I hire a tutor for my child who is having trouble with reading? What special programs do you have for poor readers? How fast should my teenager be able to read?

9. Hiring capable personnel. All teachers are expected to understand reading difficulties that may occur in their content area assignments and to adjust assignments to fit the students' reading capabilities. The administrator should give special consideration to candidates who have had courses in reading methods.

Teachers who are hired specifically as reading personnel should meet the guidelines established by the International Reading Association (Professional Standards and Ethics Committee, 1992). Teachers should also exhibit personal characteristics that enhance their effectiveness in interactions with students, such as empathy, patience, and positive attitudes.

Obviously, administrators can have a major impact on the reading program and its effectiveness for students. They need feedback about their performance so that they will be able to improve continuously (Sanacore, 1994).

■ Librarian or Media Center Specialist

The librarian or media center specialist provides assistance to the special reading teacher and the content area teacher alike by locating books and other printed materials on different subjects and reading levels, making available audiovisual aids that can be used for motivation and background building, and providing students with instruction in location strategies related to the library or media center, such as doing on-line computer searches for information or searching electronic or printed reference books. The librarian may set up special displays of printed materials or create specialized bibliographies or lists of Internet addresses on specific subjects at the request of the teachers and may provide students with direct assistance in finding and using appropriate materials. Recreational reading may be fostered by the librarian's book talks or attractive book displays on high-interest topics.

■ Teamwork

The content area teacher is a part of a team concerned with the development of secondary school students' reading skills. He or she is concerned with reading proficiency largely because it can enhance or adversely affect the learning of content.

Content area teachers may ask for the reading consultant's assistance in identifying approaches that will best meet the special reading needs of their students. They may send students who are reading far below the level of the instructional materials assigned for the grade to the special reading teacher for assessment and remedial instruction, or the special reading teacher may come into the content classrooms to provide assistance. Content teachers should work closely with the special reading teacher in planning reading assignments for students who are receiving remedial assistance; they should consult with the special reading teacher about instructional materials to meet the reading needs of their students; and they may ask the special reading teacher to teach lessons in some aspects of reading.

Content area teachers should expect to work hand in hand with the librarian and/or media center specialist when assembling materials for teaching units and when teaching library skills. Content magazines, print and electronic reference materials, and recreational reading materials should be a part of the library's yearly budget allocation, and content teachers should be the ones who recommend appropriate materials.

Content teachers find that assistance from reading specialists/consultants benefits their programs. Particularly useful are services in conducting class presentations on various topics, acting as mentors for new teachers, preparing study guides for content texts, diagnostic testing, locating appropriate materials, determining readability levels of materials, and conducting in-service sessions on reading components (Colt, 1990; Woods and Topping, 1986).

The principal sets the tone of the school's reading program. The content area teacher should be able to approach the principal for funding for instructional materials that are needed to meet the diverse reading needs of the students in content classes and for help with organizational arrangements, such as special grouping practices that will enhance the content area reading program.

When the principal or administrator, reading consultant, special reading teacher, and librarian or media specialist collaborate with the content area teachers to produce a good reading program for a school, success for the program is likely. When staff members understand one another's roles and responsibilities, cooperation is enhanced.

■ ■ Total-School Reading Programs

A total-school reading program is one in which all school personnel cooperate and all students are offered reading instruction according to their needs. Reading instruction is generally offered in special reading classes and is also a priority in content area classes, although, as Barry (1994) points out, some schools appear to be moving away from special reading classes. The specialist may come into content classrooms and offer assistance there instead. Reading strategies and skills are taught as they are needed, facilitating meaningful application of the instruction. In such a program, all components of reading instruction are included:

Why is developmental reading instruction needed in secondary school?

1. **Developmental reading** is taught to students who are progressing satisfactorily in acquiring reading proficiency. The *developmental component* of the program is for average and above-average readers. A special reading teacher, who directs the program, helps students to develop further comprehension skills and strategies, vocabulary knowledge, rate of reading, and study skills.

How does reading in content area materials pose special problems for students?

2. **Content area reading** is taught. In the *content area component* of the program the students are helped to comprehend specific subject matter. Reading skills and strategies required for effective reading of the content area material are considered. Within each content area—English, mathematics, social studies, science, and so forth—reading materials with which students can experience reading success must be used. Such materials may include multilevel texts, materials from library sources with lower levels of reading difficulty, interactive computer programs, videos or films, and tapes.

Why should content teachers be concerned with recreational reading?

3. **Recreational reading** is encouraged. The *recreational component* is an important, although frequently neglected, aspect of the comprehensive reading program, since the ultimate goal of all reading instruction is to develop good lifelong reading habits. Although English teachers and reading specialists have particularly strong reasons for motivating students to read for pleasure, everyone involved with students should actively encourage recreational reading.

How do corrective and remedial reading instruction differ?

4. **Corrective and remedial reading** instruction are offered to students who are experiencing difficulties. The *corrective and remedial component* of the program are for students who are reading at levels that are below their potential reading levels. Corrective readers generally read from six to eighteen months below potential. They are generally served by the regular classroom teacher through in-class adjustments to assignments and materials.

Remedial readers may have gaps of two or more years between instructional and potential levels. These students usually need to work on basic word recognition and comprehension strategies and skills. Good comprehenders, in general, tend to use more strategies and be more flexible in their use than do poor comprehenders (Kletzien, 1991), so developing strategies and the ability to use them is very important to these students. As their fluency improves, the students can learn how to apply general study skills. This part of the program is directed primarily by the special reading teacher, generally in a separate class.

Implementing a total-school reading program is a difficult, demanding assignment, but the energy invested in it is well spent. The process of implementation can be diagrammed as shown in Figure 2.1.

Figure 2.1 shows a sequence of activities through which a school's staff can move in developing a total-school reading program, from defining a reading philosophy to evaluating the program. Throughout the entire sequence, constant in-service training is offered to the staff involved in the program development. Suggestions provided during in-service activities will be most helpful if they address current needs and can be implemented immediately. Results of each step in the sequence provide input, which may affect subsequent in-service sessions for the director(s) of the in-service training.

FIGURE 2.1

Implementation of a School Reading Program

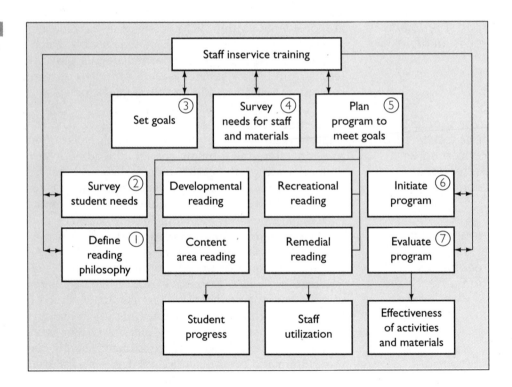

■ Staff In-Service Training

What kind of in-service training is most helpful to content area teachers?

A first reaction to this implementation plan may be that **in-service training** is overemphasized. Careful consideration, however, reveals that this is not the case. Many secondary teachers (in some schools, most teachers) and administrators have little background knowledge concerning the nature of reading, the reading strategy needs of students, available formal tests of reading progress, informal measures of reading achievement, reading interests of adolescents, and other topics related to helping secondary students progress in reading. In addition to this lack of knowledge, some of the teachers are opposed to the idea of teaching reading strategies. They often fail to realize that helping their students *read* the subject matter with more understanding will help these students *learn* subject matter concepts more effectively.

The initial in-service training sessions should be designed to help the school's staff members recognize not only the need for reading instruction in the school but also the benefits to them as subject matter specialists if this need is adequately met. In-service sessions should involve the entire school staff—administrators, faculty members from all departments, media specialist(s), and guidance personnel.

Subsequent in-service sessions may deal with such topics as

1. Setting realistic program objectives
2. Determining reading strategy and skill needs of students
3. Locating and using appropriate materials for meeting student needs
4. Learning techniques for teaching specific strategies
5. Teaching directed reading lessons in content areas
6. Differentiating instruction in content area classes
8. Using the library or media center to full advantage
9. Evaluating the program's effectiveness

The in-service training may take a variety of forms, including the following:

1. Workshops in the school, conducted by the school's reading consultant or reading teacher or by an outside expert on the topic under consideration
2. Reading conferences and conventions
3. Demonstration lessons
4. Faculty planning sessions (teachers working together to plan implementation of the program in their special areas using the resources available in the school)
5. Teachers observing the teaching of innovative peers
6. Consultants teaming with individual teachers or small groups of teachers to solve teacher-identified instructional problems
7. University courses

Any in-service session should include practical suggestions of immediate usefulness in addition to necessary theoretical background. Demonstrations of techniques, handouts, and displays of useful materials are more effective than mere "pep talks." Teachers should have input into the planning of the in-service activities.

■ Reading Committee

Although all staff members need to believe in the concept of a schoolwide program and need to be willing to cooperate in implementing it, a small staff group or reading committee can do much program planning and submit ideas to the entire staff for input, endorsement, and implementation. The reading committee should be composed of people with the ability and enthusiasm to offer effective guidance of the program. A good composition for such a committee might be the principal, the reading consultant, all special reading teachers, a representative from each department, the media specialist, a guidance counselor, and perhaps a school board member or representative from a parent group.

Defining Reading Philosophy

The reading committee elicits ideas from the other members of the staff concerning the nature of reading, the reading abilities that are necessary for comprehending printed material in the respective subject areas, the importance of recreational reading, and other similar areas. Then committee members integrate these ideas with published research and expert opinion to produce a statement of the school's reading philosophy, which they share with the entire staff. Representative statements from such a document might include:

1. Reading is the process of getting meaning from printed symbols.
2. Secondary school students need reading instruction, although the type of instruction needed may differ from student to student.
3. Students need help in learning to read printed materials before they can read these materials to learn concepts.
4. Special reading skills are needed to read certain content area materials with understanding.

Surveying Student Needs

The stimulus for developing a total-school reading program may be low student scores on standardized reading achievement tests or student reading deficiencies detected by faculty members. If test results have motivated the effort, these results may be used as a beginning for surveying student needs. Reading achievement tests generally reveal the students' accomplishments in broad areas of reading (comprehension, vocabulary, rate). If an achievement test in reading has not previously been administered, the reading committee can choose an appropriate test for administration. After broad areas of reading difficulty have been identified, the committee may choose either standardized or informal assessment measures to pinpoint specific difficulties. Measures of reading interests and attitudes toward reading also may be administered at this time to help the staff clarify student needs.

Setting Goals

When embarking on an all-school reading program, it is helpful to have some goals in mind. The reading committee can identify goals for the program and submit them to the rest of the faculty for input and approval. All faculty members need to have a part in deciding on goals because these goals will influence each teacher's classroom activities. Some goals that might be stated include the following:

1. All students will be offered an opportunity to develop and refine their reading strategies and skills through special reading classes.
2. All students will be helped to develop reading strategies and skills specific to particular content areas during the content area classes.
3. Each student will be offered reading assignments that are appropriate to his or her reading achievement level.
4. All students will be encouraged to read for recreation in a variety of interest areas.
5. All students will be given opportunities to use the resources of the school's media center.
6. All students who need special instruction by a qualified specialist will receive it.

Surveying Needs for Staff and Materials

The reading committee can analyze the needs of the school relative to meeting the goals of the reading program. For example, the committee may discover that another qualified reading teacher will be needed if each student who needs special help is to receive it. The total implementation of this portion of the program may have to be postponed until funding is acquired; however, the program goal will at least clarify existing needs.

If each student in the school is going to be offered an opportunity to develop and refine basic reading skills, the committee may find that rooms are needed for reading laboratories. In addition, the laboratories require staff, materials, and equipment suitable for students who are reading on a wide variety of levels and who need help with many different skills.

Considering the amount of money available for implementing the program, the committee members may study catalogs of materials and equipment, may preview or examine available items, and may choose the items needed most to implement the program. The committee may preview promising materials on an ongoing basis during the program's implementation, or the reading consultant and reading teachers may assume that responsibility. Naturally, all staff members should be encouraged to suggest appropriate materials, especially those related closely to particular disciplines.

Planning a Program to Meet Goals

When the committee has obtained information about the skill needs of the students and the goals of the program, it can make specific program plans. Plans may center around the four major aspects of reading instruction—developmental reading, content area reading, recreational reading, and remedial reading.

Developmental Reading.   Developmental reading involves the teaching of basic reading strategies and skills. Developmental readers at the secondary level generally have good backgrounds in word recognition skills and general comprehension skills of a literal nature, but they often have room for improvement in interpretive, critical, and creative reading skills, as well as in reading/study skills. Students who have a firm foundation in basic word recognition and comprehension skills and strategies are ready for some emphasis on rate and flexibility of rate, but basic strategies and skills should be emphasized first.

Developmental reading classes also may go beyond basic skills instruction and offer help with special reading problems in the content areas, in cooperation with the content area teachers, who also will stress such assistance. To teach these skills, instructors often use demonstrations, lectures, class discussion, worktexts, computer programs, and mechanical equipment. Demonstrations of the application of reading strategies are perhaps the most effective approach to use in developmental classes. Teacher modeling of the strategies for the students through think-aloud presentations allows students to see what they are expected to do. Such demonstrations should be followed by guided practice and independent practice of the strategies presented.

Using integrated units centered around a theme can be particularly effective in encouraging purposeful reading and writing activities in a developmental reading class, as well as in any content class (Lipson et al., 1993; Smith and Johnson, 1993). Smith and Johnson (1993) formed literature-based response groups, based on the students' choices of adolescent novels related to the selected theme. Students wrote in journals, participated in whole-class and small-group discussions, worked on group projects, and did individual response papers. The teacher and students decided together "what to study, how to study it, and how to assess their progress" (p. 29). Lipson and others (1993) recommended that teachers use frequent explicit instruction to help the students develop the higher-order thinking skills needed to apply the knowledge learned from the theme. Stewart and associates (1996) also found that a literature-based developmental reading program in a junior high school resulted in improved reading and attitudes toward reading. This program offered choice in reading material, reading in a variety of genres, reading at their own paces, writing in response journals, writing letters to authors, participating in whole-class reading of a book and in thematic units along with free reading, and use of skills packets. Students said that choice of reading material, interesting reading material, time provided for reading, and practice were beneficial to them in the reading class and in their reading for their content classes.

Developmental reading classes frequently feature group instruction. However, some programs are individualized: teachers may assign materials on different levels to different students or make use of individual student contracts. The individualized programs may utilize a laboratory setting.

Lecture presentation of material on how to improve reading proficiency is likely to elicit questions from the students, and the ensuing discussion can be valuable to the whole class. Moreover, some students are auditory learners—they learn better through hearing. Lecture-demonstration combinations are especially effective for helping students acquire techniques for increasing rate of reading.

Many developmental reading programs make use of worktexts either as the basic texts for the programs or as supplementary materials. Some programs use a number of different textbooks, and instructors assign appropriate sections to individual students. Some are now using computer programs instead of textbooks.

Some developmental reading programs employ mechanical devices, such as computers (with appropriate software) and other rate improvement devices. These machines help students learn to read faster in a variety of ways. However, they are not essential to the development of a good program, even though they function as motivational devices for some students.

Computer software designed to promote speed reading often contains exercises in phrase reading, rather than word-by-word reading, and scanning for key words. The program may show students text—one word or one phrase or one line at a time—presented at rates that the teacher or the student users predetermine. The rate chosen can be varied to fit the needs of the individual user. Sometimes related comprehension checks are provided. Some of this software is not very effective, so teachers should preview all software designed for rate improvement before using it with students. At present, not all schools have a sufficient number of computers available for wide use of these programs.

The various devices for increasing rate are adjustable to speeds appropriate for different individuals. Controlled reading devices in general can help individuals realize that it is possible for them to read faster. However, the skills so acquired must be transferred from machine-assisted reading to reading without assistance before the student will have truly acquired a useful reading technique.

Recreational reading is also frequently emphasized in developmental reading classes. Time in class is often utilized for recreational reading activities, and teachers may use many motivational techniques to encourage reading for pleasure, both in class and outside of class.

Farrell (1982) described a junior high reading class that was based on sustained silent reading (SSR), a procedure in which students read self-selected material silently while the teacher also reads. Some techniques other than SSR were also used in the class, including vocabulary development activities and discussion and writing of reports on material read. Students were graded on vocabulary tests, class reading, number of books read and reported on, and special forms of book reports. All students in the program gained in their reading levels as indicated by a standardized reading test (90 percent between one and two years) during the year. By May all students were reading above grade level.

Content Area Reading.   All of the basic areas of reading discussed earlier—vocabulary, general comprehension, critical reading, study skills, appreciation, and rate—are necessary to understanding content area material. A competent content teacher will address these areas when students need them to understand particular content. Thus, the strategies and skills are taught as a means to the end of better content understanding. The developmental reading teacher, on the other hand, has as his or her main goal the teaching of the reading strategies and skills themselves.

Each content teacher is especially concerned with the specific applications and reading strategies and skills that are particular to his or her content area. For instance, the social studies teacher will be very attentive to the cause-and-effect and chronological order patterns of organization, whereas the science teacher must be especially concerned with the classification pattern, the cause-and-effect pattern, and the following of directions. Although the special reading teacher will also work on these patterns, it is the content teacher who can observe the students' ability or inability to understand a particular pattern within the actual content materials and can provide instruction as needed to facilitate the learning of the content. Since many content area teachers have had no previous training in helping students with reading strategies, these teachers may need in-service training to help them prepare for these tasks. (See Chapters 10 and 11 for more elaboration on how these content area teachers provide reading help to benefit their own content areas.)

Sanacore (1990) suggests that social studies teachers can encourage lifetime literacy activities by using literature, as well as textbooks, paperbacks, magazines, and newspapers, in classes and by reading aloud to students. Sanacore (1992) also stresses providing time for independent reading. Such activities would be positive ones for use by all content area teachers. Independent reading from self-selected books helps students improve their reading fluency as they apply reading strategies and skills to reading meaningful texts, and it helps them build background knowledge that will enhance subsequent reading.

Recreational Reading. Recreational reading is reading for pleasure. Many secondary school students today do not read recreationally. Alternate high-interest activities, such as movies, television, and readily available cars, are partially responsible for the fact that many young people do not read for pleasure. Also, some students lack adult role models who read for pleasure and may never have been exposed to enjoyable reading materials. All teachers and other school staff members—principals, librarians, and guidance counselors—can encourage recreational reading. They can provide reading materials and information about reading materials and can act as positive role models by reading recreationally in the presence of students. Newman (1982) suggested having a readers' club to encourage recreational reading. The club can meet to discuss interesting books, to develop a list of recommended books, and to participate in interesting activities (e.g., book parties and guest authors).

Content area teachers should encourage recreational reading for three major reasons:

1. The content area teacher may have a special rapport with some students who do not like to read and with whom no other secondary teacher has established this special relationship.
2. A certain content area may be the only one that holds a student's interest at a particular time. For example, a physical education teacher might be able to motivate a particular boy or girl to read extracurricular books on sports.
3. Particular subject matter becomes more "real" as a reader experiences events through imaginative literature. For example, the topic of the American Revolution, which might take up only one chapter in a social studies textbook, will be more meaningful to a student who reads Esther Forbes's *Johnny Tremain* and becomes involved in Johnny's experiences of that period's political intrigue and his preparation for war. *Across Five Aprils* by Irene Hunt gives students broadened perspectives on the Civil War, and students who read James Watson's *Talking in Whispers,* a novel set in Chile, will have a better idea of what can happen to civil rights in a military dictatorship. Good nonfiction selections can also add interest to the study of history. Teachers may want to recommend *The Eagle and the Dragon* (about the United States' relationship with China) by Don Lawson and *Eyes on the Prize: America's Civil Rights Years, 1954–1965* by Juan Williams. Science teachers can enrich their programs by supplementing course material with readings in nonfiction—for example, *The Quest for Artificial Intelligence* by Dorothy Hinshaw Patent. Teachers of agriculture can use literature to sustain student interest; for example, Henry Billings's *All Down the Valley* is an interesting story of the Tennessee Valley Authority. Teachers of composition may find Lois Duncan's *Chapters: My Growth as a Writer* useful, and music teachers may want to suggest *Nothing but the Best: The Struggle for Perfection at the Juilliard School* by Judith Kogan. Extra effort by each content area teacher to find interesting supplementary reading material may lead to enduring reading habits and tastes in the students.

Remedial Reading.   Remedial instruction is generally designed for those students who read two or more years below the level at which they could be expected to read with understanding. Such instruction is given by a reading specialist in a special reading class or a reading laboratory and is based on assessment of individual strengths and weaknesses.

Assessment of needs for remedial readers is generally quite extensive, with both formal and informal measures being utilized. Attitude, interest, and personality inventories are frequently used to supplement the reading test information, and counseling personnel are often involved in the testing and advisement of the students. (See Chapter 13 for a discussion of formal and informal tests that may be used.)

Ideally, remedial reading classes should be small, and the work should be conducted in small groups and on a one-to-one basis. As Kress (1989, p. 370) points out, "Individualized instruction based on individualized diagnosis has long been acknowledged as the best in remediation, but . . . it is not the predominant delivery for remediated readers at present." Remedial programs are generally individualized as much as staffing will allow. To offer more individual and small-group help than a single teacher can manage, schools often use paraprofessionals in addition to the regular instructor. The assessment and program planning for each remedial student are done by the reading teacher. Then the teacher shows each paraprofessional how to conduct help sessions with a specific student or a small group of students. Paraprofessionals are shown how to help students use the printed materials and equipment needed for the students' individual programs; how to offer encouragement and reassurance; how to help the students correct poor reading habits; how to monitor attendance; and how to keep the reading teacher apprised of either positive or negative changes in the subjects' reading performances. While paraprofessionals work with individuals and small groups, the reading teacher is free to offer intensive individual and small-group help to students who have problems that the paraprofessionals are not qualified to handle. The instructor also must continuously monitor the activities of the paraprofessionals.

Other attempts at individualization have some students working on computer programs to meet their particular needs while the teacher works directly with other students. Some programs have a management component that records scores and/or errors for each student, which can be examined by the teacher later, and these programs are particularly useful in this type of situation.

Computer-assisted instruction has entered the remedial reading scene for several reasons: the computer is a patient dispenser of information, not showing irritation at slow responses or the need for repetition; the computer offers interactive instruction—the student responds to prompts and receives feedback from the computer; feedback offered about correctness of responses can be immediate; and some programs can branch to explanations and additional practice for students who are having problems. Computers are not enough for a complete remedial program, however, because they cannot observe student behavior in ways that teachers can, and they cannot administer responses that are as individualized to a particular student's needs (Kress, 1989).

Remedial readers often lack interest in conventional "reading resource room" activities because they have been exposed to these activities so often throughout their school years. Secondary level remedial reading programs, therefore, have to offer students more than special instruction and materials designed for their ability levels. They have to motivate the students to want to improve their reading and get the students actively involved in reading for real purposes. Use of literature-based response groups with carefully selected adolescent novels can help to meet this challenge.

Remedial reading instruction needs to be as practical as possible. The students need to be able to see how it is going to help them cope with real-life needs. Therefore, reading instructors should confer with each student about his or her personal concerns and try to tailor the remedial program to reflect the perceived needs of the individual.

In many cases, a remedial reader has never been successful in reading activities. Since success is a powerful motivator, the reading teacher should plan some activity that is designed to allow the student to experience success with each session. Teachers try to use high-interest materials of appropriate difficulty levels with remedial readers. Care must be taken to avoid choosing materials that are obviously written for much younger readers. When high-interest materials of appropriate levels are not available, teachers may use the language experience approach described in Chapter 8.

One way to point out success to the students is to show them concrete indications of progress. Graphing their comprehension scores from week to week may help them to see that they are improving as they apply themselves to their reading activities. Keeping a record of books read and satisfactorily reported on to the teacher provides another visible sign of progress.

Because of repeated failures in the past, remedial students often enter reading programs with extremely poor self-concepts. These students need a stress-free, nonintimidating environment for learning (Wolak, 1990). Every effort must be made to avoid embarrassing the students. Counseling, along with help in improving reading strategies, may be needed for these students.

Remedial students often need initial instruction in, or reteaching of, basic word recognition and comprehension strategies and skills. Therefore, decoding skills, vocabulary building, and comprehension are generally stressed in remedial programs, whereas little attention is given to rate. The basic skills are necessary prerequisites to programs for increasing rate, but in a remedial program some attention may be given to developing flexibility of rate. The students may have fallen into the trap of plodding word-by-word through all reading materials, even those that only need to be skimmed.

Since improvement is the aim of remedial reading classes, these classes are a means to an end, not an end in themselves. Ideally, students will increase their reading ability through participation in these classes and will move on to more developmental reading activities and full participation in the regular reading assignments for content classes. Placement in a remedial reading class should not constitute a "life sentence" to such classes.

Facilities for the Program.   Much reading instruction in the secondary school takes place within the regular content classroom. However, developmental and remedial reading classes sometimes are held in standard classrooms and sometimes in reading laboratories. Developmental and remedial reading classes as described earlier can be held in reading laboratories, where the pupils work more independently than in a typical class situation. Reading laboratories are generally equipped with a wide variety of materials and equipment designed for individual student use. Computers may be available for tutorial and drill-and-practice programs. The laboratory instructors administer assessment instruments and plan special individualized programs for all students who attend. The students follow these plans independently to overcome their reading difficulties. Although many of the materials are self-scoring, the laboratory instructor is available to help students when needed. It is important for the laboratory instructor to monitor the students' activities and progress constantly. Otherwise, a student can become locked into an unsuitable program that lacks challenge or is frustrating.

Initiating the Program

Initiating a total-school program is a difficult undertaking. For this reason, some schools initiate such a program gradually. One possible method of gradual initiation might take place over a two-year period, as shown in Table 2.1. Another approach might be to initiate the program one or more grade levels at a time over a period of years.

TABLE 2.1

Plan for Initiating Program

	Developmental Reading	Content Reading	Recreational Reading	Remedial Reading
1st year	9th-grade, developmental classes	Content teachers teach study methods; use DRA; emphasize vocabulary	Media center Reading clubs	9th-grade remedial classes (voluntary)
2nd year	9th-grade classes plus voluntary 10th to 12th-grade classes	Content teachers learn and emphasize, when applicable, a reading skill each month	Media center English class time Reading clubs	9th to 12th-grade remedial classes (voluntary)

Evaluating the Program

A total-school reading program must constantly be evaluated in three areas—student progress, staff utilization, and effectiveness of activities and materials.

1. Student progress can be evaluated through standardized and informal achievement tests, as well as through teacher observation. Teacher observation may serve to help evaluate progress in areas rarely covered by tests. For example, students' attitudes toward, and interests in, reading can often be detected through observation, whereas tests may give no information about these areas. If progress has been unsatisfactory, reasons for the situation must be investigated.

2. The staff members need to look at the functions that are being performed by different people to determine whether there is unwarranted overlap of responsibility, inadequate coverage of some area or areas by qualified personnel, or insufficient staff to handle the needs of the students in some areas (perhaps remedial reading). If any inadequacies are detected, the staff members need to make plans to alleviate the problems in the future.

3. Teachers can keep records of the activities and materials that seem to be most effective in meeting the objectives of the program. Use of ineffective activities and materials should be discontinued, and the advice of the reading consultant should be sought about other possible approaches to the students' problems.

A program should be evaluated regularly throughout the school year, not only at the end of the year, although the end of the year is generally one good checkpoint for evaluation. Periodic evaluation sessions can help keep teachers aware of the need for continuous assessment of progress toward program goals.

A school's evaluation of its established reading programs can take the form of a "needs assessment." Basically, a needs assessment is an attempt to measure the gap between "what is" and "what should be." Such an evaluation overlaps program planning, implementation, and periodic checkups by internal or external personnel. When a needs assessment is done, student performance, personnel, the present reading program, the school plant, fiscal resources, and professional resources are all examined.

MEETING THE CHALLENGE

The way one school developed a total-school reading plan to meet specific goals is shown in the sample case described next.

Introduction

The school's faculty has recognized that all the students in the school can improve their basic reading skills in some way. They wish to offer possibilities for improvement to students who are reading above grade level, as well as students who are reading at grade level and students who are reading below grade level. They realize that many students have the capacity to read much better than they do, even though they are reading at grade level or above, and that some students reading below grade level are making satisfactory progress when their capacity levels are taken into consideration.

Inservice training for teachers is needed if a total-school reading program is to be successful. (© Michael Zide)

Area One: Developmental Reading

To meet the basic skills needs of the students, the faculty decides to include in each ninth-grade student's schedule one semester of reading instruction. Since there are approximately 200 ninth graders in the school, about 100 students are assigned to reading classes each semester. A special reading teacher is designated to teach five classes of approximately 20 students each semester. Because the students within each class vary greatly in reading achievement and needs, the class is conducted as a laboratory with individual and small-group instruction, rather than whole-class instruction. The teacher studies assessment results for each student and plans an individual course of study for each one, based on the student's current achievement level and needs. If several members of a class have similar needs, the teacher plans small-group sessions. Otherwise, the students work independently with materials on appropriate reading levels and meet regularly with the teacher for teacher-pupil conferences concerning the assignments. During the conferences, the teacher sometimes gives specific strategy or skill instruction, but conferences are also used to help students choose reading materials from a pool of appropriate ones, to check on word recognition and comprehension skills, and to help students plan ways to share their reading experiences with their classmates.

On Friday of each week, five or more of the students share with the rest of the class something they have read. The sharing may take a number of forms: oral reading of episodes from a book, illustrations of scenes from a book, panel discussions presented by several students who have read the same book, skits presented by students who have read the same book, and many others.

Plans are made to develop a second reading laboratory for students in the tenth, eleventh, and twelfth grades who are developmental readers but want to improve their basic reading skills and are willing to attend the laboratory during their regularly assigned study periods or free periods. Setting up this second laboratory has to be postponed until the second year of the program because another qualified reading teacher will be needed to provide specialized help for the students.

Area Two: Content Area Reading

The reading committee members identify reading strategies and skills that they feel are vital for content understanding. Then they arrange for in-service training sessions to help the content teachers learn to teach these strategies and skills. A particular strategy or skill is emphasized each month of the year. At the beginning of each month, in-service training for the selected strategy or skill is offered to the teachers for whom the training is appropriate. This approach gradually introduces the content teachers to the application of appropriate instruction, since in-service training about, and application of, instruction in all reading strategies and skills at once could be overwhelming for content teachers. Once teachers learn a technique, they are expected to continue to use it as it is needed. Teachers who already use the strategy or skill being taught in a particular in-service session are encouraged, but not required, to attend sessions to refresh their knowledge and perhaps acquire some new ideas for presentation. Sometimes these teachers are enlisted to help with the in-service presentations.

The ideas identified for focus are vocabulary building; recognizing and understanding prefixes and suffixes; using study methods; recognizing main ideas; following directions; locating information in textbooks and in the library; developing flexibility of rate; detecting sequence; using context clues; drawing conclusions and making inferences; reading maps, tables, charts, and graphs; detecting propaganda; recognizing facts and opinions; and detecting the author's motives or biases. During the first year, the faculty has chosen the following nine areas for emphasis: study methods, prefixes and suffixes, main ideas, sequence, context clues, following directions, flexibility of rate, locating information in textbooks, and reading maps.

The content area teachers also learn how to teach directed reading lessons in their respective content classes. They learn to utilize study guides to direct the silent reading portions of the directed reading lessons.

The job of the media specialist is defined as helping the teachers locate appropriate materials for use in their subject areas. These materials include books, magazines, and pamphlets written on a variety of reading levels. The teacher attempts to match the materials to the students' abilities.

The reading consultant is available to help content area teachers in planning reading instruction related to each content area. The consultant is available to teach specific demonstration lessons in the content area classes at the teachers' request.

Area Three: Recreational Reading

All content area teachers are encouraged to inform students about materials available for leisure-time reading in their respective disciplines. The English teachers have decided to make one class period a week available for recreational reading and sharing of pleasure reading materials. In addition, all students are encouraged to use the media center during their free periods.

The reading consultant and special reading teacher sponsor a reading club that meets during the homeroom/club period. Members read books on areas of mutual interest and discuss them with fellow club members.

Area Four: Remedial Reading

The faculty has decided that all students reading two years or more below capacity level should be offered individual or small-group (ten or fewer students) assistance by a qualified reading specialist. For ninth graders, this instruction is in addition to the special reading class provided in basic skills and is offered during the semester when the basic reading class is not scheduled. For tenth through twelfth graders, instruction is offered two days a week during the study period. No student is forced to enroll in the remedial course, but conferences are held with students who need help, and they are invited to take part.

Choosing Materials for a Secondary School Reading Program

A wide variety of reading materials is available for use in secondary school reading programs. Some materials are printed; others are audiovisual. Some are intended to teach strategies and skills; others are designed primarily to offer practice in strategies and skills already taught. Selection of the best materials for a particular situation is of primary importance. The burden of selection should not rest on one individual; instead, materials should be chosen through the cooperative efforts of a variety of people, including school administrators, reading consultants, special reading teachers, and content area teachers.

■ Evaluating Materials for Secondary School Reading Programs

Following are some of the questions that should be asked about materials being considered:

1. Is the philosophy behind the material sound?
2. Is the material designed to teach the strategies and skills the students in this school need?
3. Is the material appropriate to the maturity levels of the students with whom it is to be used? (Childish material must be avoided when choosing material for secondary school students.)
4. Is the material appropriate to the backgrounds of experience of the students for whom it is intended?
5. Is the material interesting to the students who will be using it?
6. Are provisions made to encourage application of strategies and skills taught by the material to reading situations outside the reading class, including reading in the content areas?
7. Is the material free from role stereotypes (of different nationalities, ethnic groups, sexes)?
8. Is the material up to date?
9. Is proper emphasis given to all components of the reading process?
10. Does the material provide for continuous assessment of reading ability?
11. Does the material include an adequate teacher's manual?
12. What kinds of written material are covered? Poetry? Prose? Nonfiction? Fiction?
13. Does the material have a good format (e.g., easy-to-read print, adequate margins, good quality paper)?
14. If the material is audiovisual, can it be operated independently by the students?
15. Is the material easy to use with students?
16. Is audiovisual material technically acceptable (good sound, color, etc.)?
17. Does multilevel material make provisions for placing students appropriately within a sequence?
18. Are all directions clearly given in written or oral form?
19. Does the material have pretest and posttest activities available?
20. Is the material adaptable to groups of students with different needs?
21. Does the material suggest follow-up activities to help reinforce the strategies and skills presented?
22. Has the material been field tested? With what results?
23. Have controlled research studies shown this material to be effective in teaching strategies and skills?
24. Is the cost of the material reasonable?

■ Evaluating Textbooks for Use in Content Classrooms

In addition to the general questions that should be asked about all materials in a secondary school reading program, some specific things about textbooks need to be considered. When evaluating a textbook for use in any content classroom, educators must decide what role that textbook is expected to play. Will it be a reference manual for the teacher or students, the basis for instruction, or the entire curriculum for the course? Without knowing the role of the textbook, a decision about its use may not be appropriate (Muther, 1985). If the text is to serve primarily as a reference manual for the teacher in the content area, it may be written at a higher readability level, have fewer motivational materials included, and have a greater concept density than if it is to serve as a reference manual for the students. A reference manual for the students or a text that is the basis for instruction should be written at a readability level that is accessible to a majority of the students (100 percent is unlikely) and should be designed to interest the students in the material. The content density of a text that is to be the basis of instruction should be lower than that of one that is a reference manual. A text that forms the entire curriculum for a course should be comprehensive in coverage of topics important to the subject, whereas a reference manual may have less comprehensive coverage and still be useful.

For each textbook adoption decision, of course, a key consideration is how well the book fits the course for which it will be used. Are important topics included and covered thoroughly rather than simply being mentioned? Bernstein (1985, p. 464) has pointed out that "textbooks in nearly every category tackle too many subjects and cover them so superficially that the students have difficulty understanding what is being said." Important and trivial material may be given equal attention.

Content should be checked for accuracy and currency. Treatment of controversial issues should be handled fairly. The representation of various segments of society should be handled fairly in textbooks. Segments of the population should not be treated as stereotypes in the material.

If the coverage of material is good, there is still the concern that students need to be able to understand the material. Texts with short, choppy sentences and stilted language patterns should be avoided, because students are not as likely to comprehend them as they are well-constructed text.

Farr and Tulley (1985) point out the importance of logical organization, as well as clarity, in textbooks. Osborn and others (1985) suggest the need for advance organizers and other devices to highlight the structure of the text. They indicate that researchers have found that students learn best from organized and readable text, sometimes referred to as "considerate" text. Text that is not considerate "requires the reader to organize its content and establish relationships between parts of the content" (p. 12). Deficiencies that have been cited in some textbooks are inadequate tables of contents, not enough chapter headings, and chapter subheadings that are cute, rather than informative (Bernstein, 1985).

The background experiences of the audience for the textbook should be considered when choices are made (Osborn et al., 1985). The material should provide sufficient information for the development of concepts but should not be repetitious in presenting material that is likely to be generally known by the target audience. In addition, Armbruster and Anderson (1981, p. 46) point out that "analogies, metaphors, and other types of figurative language should be used only if their referents are well known by the reader." Adults often overlook the fact that their students' backgrounds of experiences may not have included the referents necessary for understanding such material.

Pedagogical aids, such as chapter overviews, chapter and unit objectives, chapter summaries, discussion questions, and practice activities should be well designed and well written, focusing on important material. Discussion questions should include higher-order questions, as well as literal-level ones. Practice activities should be directly tied to chapter content and should be extensive enough to enhance learning.

Textbook format should also be considered in an evaluation. The format should be attractive and should enhance the readability through adequate white space, appropriate text size and style, good quality paper, and clarity of organization through headings and subheadings.

Teachers' editions of textbooks should give teachers ideas about how to build prerequisite knowledge for studying a topic, how to activate the students' prior knowledge before the instruction begins, and how to present certain material in a way that will encourage students to integrate the prior knowledge with the new material in the chapter (Osborn et al., 1985). The teachers' editions should provide teaching ideas that encourage students to read the textbooks for meaning and to search for supplementary information. They should provide teachers with questions on various cognitive levels that are appropriate for purpose-setting, discussion, and testing purposes. They should have suggestions for adjusting textbook use for different types of learners. Ways to arouse interest in the content should also be included in the teachers' editions, and teachers should be provided with thematic lists of supplementary reading material for them and their students.

Guzzetti and associates (1995) studied what students liked and did not like about their physical science texts. Students preferred refutational text (text that both gives a correct concept and refutes common incorrect information about the concept) to nonrefutational text. Although they liked narrative text, they preferred expository text for the presentation of physical science concepts. The students reported difficulty with unfamiliar noncentral concepts, unnecessarily complex examples, imprecise language, and lack of explicit statements in the text. They disliked "fancy" language. Sometimes they felt that the text did not give them enough background information and required too many inferences. Some females thought the texts were sexist, favoring males in illustrations. Students liked cross-references, numbered steps, illustrations, boxed or highlighted formulas, and glossaries. These areas of concern should be considered when evaluating textbooks in any content area.

Summary

Among the personnel responsible for the development of reading ability at the secondary school level are the content area teacher, the school administrator, the special reading teacher, the reading consultant, and the librarian or media center specialist. It is essential that all content teachers understand the reading act, since such understanding helps to facilitate the teaching of their particular subjects.

A total-school reading program involves all school personnel in a cooperative effort. Much in-service training is necessary for the program's implementation, and it is important to have a carefully chosen reading committee. All aspects of reading are considered in a total-school reading program: developmental reading, content area reading, recreational reading, and remedial reading.

Choice of materials for a secondary reading program is important and should be the result of the cooperative efforts of all personnel involved with the school's reading program.

Discussion Questions

1　After a total-school reading program has been initiated, what evaluation procedures should be utilized to determine its effectiveness? When should evaluation of the program take place? Who should be responsible for the evaluation?

2　How do remedial reading classes differ from developmental reading classes? Why do these differences exist?

3　What are some advantages of reading laboratories for improving reading skills?

4　What is the best procedure for choosing materials for use in a secondary school reading program?

5　Do you agree with the list of seven requirements for content area teachers presented at the beginning of this chapter? Why, or why not? Be specific.

6　How does the principal of a secondary school influence the reading program?

7　What factors are most important in evaluating content area textbooks?

Enrichment Activities

1　List the duties that a member of a school reading committee might be expected to perform. Compare your list with the lists your classmates have developed. Discuss differences of opinion.

*2　Report to the class on the provisions for reading instruction in your school.

*3 Check with your principal and fellow teachers about reading problems of students in your school. After identifying the two most common problems perceived by the educators in your school, write a plan for solving each problem. Share your findings and your plan.

4 Examine some reading material that could be used in a secondary school reading program. Ask yourself the questions presented in the section of this chapter entitled "Choosing Materials for a Secondary School Reading Program." Share your evaluation with your teacher and classmates.

*5 List the personnel in your school who are concerned with reading instruction. Briefly describe the responsibilities of each.

6 Interview a reading consultant and a special reading teacher. What are their functions and roles? Share your findings with the class.

7 With a partner, examine a secondary level textbook for your content area. Evaluate it, and report to the class on your findings.

---

*These activities are designed for in-service teachers, student teachers, or practicum students.

Strategies for Learning: Constructing Meaning and Studying

CHAPTER 3

A Conceptual Approach to Developing Meaningful Vocabulary

Overview

Concepts are the major focus of content reading instruction. Students who acquire content concepts can comprehend trade books, textbooks, newspapers, magazines, and other pertinent material; moreover, they can tell and write their own thoughts. Since the majority of words found in printed materials for content classes are labels for concepts, this chapter introduces a *conceptual, contextualized* approach to cultivating vocabulary growth.

Contextual strategies are integrated with instruction to guide students toward content concepts. In this chapter, we present strategies that will provide many meaningful and concrete experiences with words and concepts, with the ultimate goal of developing students' resources for learning words independently. Teachers are encouraged to focus on significant words for vocabulary instruction. This chapter is closely integrated with Chapters 4 and 5 because word meanings are important to reading comprehension.

Purpose-Setting Questions

As you read this chapter, try to answer these questions:

1 How are experiences, concepts, and words interrelated?
2 Why teach word meanings within the context of content area materials?
3 Why do students need multiple encounters with vocabulary?

■ ■ The Importance of Knowing Concepts and Words

*What are
schemata?*

*How are concepts
and categories
related?*

*How are words
and concepts
related?*

We build our understanding of words on concepts. Countless concepts are at work for each of us every conscious moment of our lives. Networks of interlocking concepts, or **schemata,** structure our minds. As we learn and experience new things, we both draw upon and increase our conceptual banks. In a sense, concepts are "hooks" on which we hang new experiences. When we encounter a novel situation for which we lack hooks, we create them. The chain of concept acquisition, usage, revision, and consolidation is continuous. **Concepts** can be described as *the categories into which our experiences are organized and the related web of ideas brought about through categorization* (Cooper et al., 1994).

Words, labels for concepts, shape meaning in oral and written language. Both word knowledge and conceptual development are connected to readers' experiences. Word meanings and concepts contribute a large part of the background knowledge that readers use for understanding print. Word knowledge and the ability to apply it are significantly related to reading comprehension, intelligence, thinking abilities, and academic achievement (Freebody and Anderson, 1983; Nagy and Herman, 1987). Students who know the important words in a reading assignment are better able to learn new concepts and ideas from written content (McKeown and Curtis, 1987; Nagy, 1988; Anderson and Nagy, 1993).

On the other hand, students who are having reading difficulties have more trouble learning new words (Sheffelbine, 1984). Text analysis reveals that in a school year students read between a half million and a million running words of text (Baumann and Kameenui, 1991). They encounter eight to fifteen new words every day, adding up to a yearly total of 3,000 to 5,000 new words (Nagy and Herman, 1987; White, Graves, and Slater, 1990). Clearly, students and teachers face a daunting task in dealing with the many words in written materials.

■ Conceptual Knowledge

Perhaps the most important aspect of concepts and vocabulary is the way they simplify and streamline communication. When people share similar concepts and vocabulary, they can easily communicate without any need to explain every idea, event, or object. Each new concept builds on preceding ones; their cumulative pattern makes extended descriptions unnecessary. When communication falters, one person probably lacks the concepts basic to the discussion. This problem occurs in textbooks when the author incorrectly assumes students know certain concepts. Communication is most efficient among individuals who are at similar stages of conceptual learning, because they are on the "same wavelength."

Concepts are the products of experience; they are the abstracted and cognitively structured mental experiences acquired by individuals in the course of

What processes are involved in conceptualizing?

their lives. The process of **conceptualizing** involves grouping specific objects, experiences, or information with common features into categories. The learner compares and contrasts new information with familiar data to identify appropriate categories for new examples. For example, John Kennedy, Lyndon Johnson, Dwight Eisenhower, and Harry Truman can be classified under the category of "U.S. presidents." Concepts are a mental filing system for sorting and organizing relationships among specific items and instances.

Many concepts and their word labels embrace a group of referents. The word *measurement* can include the referents *meter, ounce, gram,* and *inch,* each of which represents a concept. A word also can refer to a number of different referents. For example, the word *butterfly* can represent a *monarch,* a *painted lady,* a *kallima,* or even the opera *Madame Butterfly.* In this instance, the context helps readers know whether the author is talking about the insect or the opera.

■ Contextual Knowledge

How do readers use context to increase their various vocabularies?

Context analysis is a powerful aid to vocabulary expansion because students can often discern word meanings from the *context* in which they occur. Nagy, Herman, and Anderson (1985) found that eighth graders learned a statistically significant number of words when they analyzed context. Through analyzing context, students increase both listening and reading (*receptive*) vocabularies and speaking and writing (*expressive*) word knowledge (Sinatra and Dowd, 1991). However, receptive vocabularies are substantially larger than expressive vocabularies because learners have to know a word rather well before using it (Baumann and Kameenui, 1991). Readers and listeners use a word's verbal context to delimit its meaning by connecting it to their conceptual understandings.

Moreover, the verbal context determines how much prior knowledge the reader needs to infer meaning. This principle is illustrated in a discussion of the Fourth Amendment of the Constitution from a social studies text:

> The police must swear under oath that they have *probable cause,* a reasonable belief that a particular crime has been or is being committed.*

In this instance, *probable cause* is defined in context, but additional concepts complicate the reader's task. Phrases like *a reasonable belief, particular crime,* and *is being committed* may be unfamiliar, or the reader may have heard these terms but lack conceptual knowledge. Complex concepts are the least likely to be learned from context due to the textual demands illustrated in the preceding example (Nagy and Herman, 1987). Context can play an important role in vocabulary and conceptual development, but context use depends on the reader's prior knowledge.

---

*Source: Richard J. Hardy, *Government in America* (Boston: Houghton Mifflin Company, 1993), p. 171.

How Do Students Learn Words and Concepts?

What are aspects of associative learning?

Students learn words and concepts gradually through experiences within a broad context as they acquire knowledge structures, or schemata (Nagy and Herman, 1987; Sternberg, 1987). The importance of *meaningfulness, concreteness, and elaboration* (aspects of **associative learning**) is well documented in developing knowledge structures and vocabulary (Scruggs and Mastropieri, 1989). *Meaningfulness is grounded in the number and frequency of associations that a learner has with the word.* Familiarity is an acceptable synonym for meaningfulness (Scruggs and Mastropieri, 1989).

Concreteness is characterized as the degree to which a particular word, experience, or concept can evoke a specific picture or image for the student. Pictured concrete information is more memorable than verbally presented concrete or abstract information (Dale, 1969; Scruggs and Mastropieri, 1989).

What are the three levels of elaboration?

Elaboration is *building associations between words and meanings.* Students who have many associations have richer vocabularies. Word knowledge is most effectively elaborated through meaningful, concrete experiences (Scruggs and Mastropieri, 1989). Deliberate, planned instruction helps students develop successively deeper levels of word knowledge. The initial level of elaboration is **association,** wherein the reader associates the term with other words that are often synonyms, which indicates that he or she has some sense of the word's meaning. The second level is **comprehension;** at this level the reader recognizes the word and understands its meaning when encountering it in a reading context. **Generative processing** is the most sophisticated level of word understanding, one that reflects a deep level of cognitive processing. At this level the reader is fluent enough to produce the target word in a novel context and can use the word to express thoughts in oral and written language (Stahl 1985, 1986). Association, comprehension, and generative processing involve active processing and transfer of knowledge.

Multiple Intelligences and Vocabulary Learning

What can the seven intelligences be categorized as?

Gardner (1993) has identified seven types of intelligence and speculates there are additional ways of knowing; schools, however, tend to focus on only two, word intelligence and math, or logic, intelligence. These **seven intelligences,** which are characterized in Figure 3.1, are pathways for learning that can be applied to vocabulary. Every person has these intelligences, although individuals have different preferred intelligences. For example, some individuals use their visual intelligence more than other intelligences, whereas others may use their intrapersonal abilities as a primary avenue of learning. Students can use all seven intelligences to broaden and deepen their knowledge base.

1. Word intelligence
(verbal / linguistic)
Write, speak, read, tell

2. Math or logic intelligence
(logical / mathematical)
Solve problems, calculate,
question, experiment

3. Picture intelligence
(visual / spatial)
Paint, draw, read maps and figures,
make patterns and designs

4. Body intelligence
(bodily / kinesthetic)
Dance, exercise, move
around, play sports

5. Musical intelligence
(Musical / rhythmic)
Sing, listen to music, play
instrument, perform rhythmic
activities

6. Social intelligence
(interpersonal)
Do group work, mediate,
present demonstrations, sense
others' moods and feelings

7. Intrapersonal intelligence
Think deeply, set goals,
daydream, stay alone

FIGURE 3.1

Intelligence Type Characteristics

Each of the seven pathways (intelligences) can be implemented to reinforce word meanings. This approach is illustrated with the term *circumpolar* in Example 3.1.

■■ ■ EXAMPLE 3.1   *Employing Seven Intelligences to Learn Vocabulary*

Verbal	Logical	Body	Visual	Musical	Inter-personal	Intra-personal
Identify the prefix and root word in *circumpolar*.	Think: From where on Earth could you see the most circumpolar stars?	Walk the path that you think a circumpolar star would follow. Then mark it with sidewalk chalk.	On a star map, draw the 24-hour path of five circumpolar stars. Use a different color for each one.	Select music that creates the mood of circumpolar stars.	Explain circumpolar stars to a partner.	Think of your own explanation for the place where you would see the largest number of circumpolar stars.

■■ ■ Creating Effective Vocabulary Instruction

Creating effective vocabulary instruction includes various components that are common to reading, such as building interest and stimulating active learning. In addition, important procedures for developing vocabulary include: building conceptual relationships, integrating word meaning with particular contexts to facilitate word use, providing reinforcement to help students build associations between words and meaning, and offering instruction focused on specific words important to comprehension, including study of dennotative and connotative meanings. Readers usually need contextual information to connect with the concept appropriate to the reading selection. Therefore, the strategies, activities, and examples provided in this chapter often incorporate several aspects of word meaning.

Although vicarious experiences can support vocabulary development, learning is more effective when it is attached to real experience. A student who encounters the term *intersect* in a mathematics text will understand it better because of his or her familiarity with street intersections. However, students cannot have direct experience with every concept they encounter in reading. Thus, teachers must help students build both direct and indirect experience through field trips, exhibits, dramatizations, videos, television, resource persons, and pictures. They can help students relate their own experiences to the passages they read. Computerized encyclopedias such as the interactive multimedia Encarta® enable students to hear different languages, the sounds of musical instruments, and so forth, which enrich conceptual understanding. Moreover, the networking of concepts in multimedia materials enhances conceptual development. Of course, there are many multimedia programs that enhance learning in diverse areas of study. For example, the Microsoft program *Dangerous Creatures* explores the endangered world of wildlife, while *Golf* gives students ways of refining their golf game.

How does discussion contribute to vocabulary development?

Discussion is another means of exploring new words. Discussion helps students associate word pronunciation and meaning. Vocabulary discussions can be conducted in large- or small-group sessions. Students may brainstorm word associations for key words the teacher has identified and write down the words and phrases. They may identify synonyms and antonyms and create networks for target words. Many of the vocabulary activities in this chapter can be used orally in groups.

According to research, deliberate, planned instruction produces greater student growth in word knowledge than incidental instruction (McKeown et al., 1985; Anders and Bos, 1986; Graves and Prenn, 1986; Stahl, 1986; Duin and Graves, 1988; Baumann and Kameenui, 1991). Eeds and Cochrum (1985) emphasized activating students' prior knowledge (e.g., What do you know about _____?) when implementing vocabulary instruction. Thus, in all the discussions that follow you will see that we do not advocate leaving vocabulary instruction to chance. Instead, the many instructional ideas we discuss represent procedures and methods that you should build into your content area instruction in a deliberate, planned way. First, we discuss instructional ideas that center on developing conceptual relationships; next, methods for helping students use context clues; and third, ways in which you should choose and teach specific key words and terms for selections that students are reading. Finally, we discuss additional strategies that your students will learn to use independently. As with all vocabulary instruction and development, overlap occurs between and among these procedures.

Also, as with all vocabulary instruction, the overall goal is students' autonomy in word work. As you model and demonstrate the various word strategies and ways of figuring out word meanings and associations, your underlying goal is to help your students internalize these strategies for eventual independent use in their own reading.

■ Conceptual Relationships

How is conceptual learning different from learning facts?

Conceptual learning is based on understanding relationships among ideas rather than on lists of independent facts. Students can be overwhelmed by the constant learning required when responding to each incident, object, or idea as unique. For example, developing a concept of *river* would include linking it to other related concepts such as *waterway, transportation, tributaries,* and *recreation.* This illustrates the interlinking relationships among concepts that contribute to learning efficiency.

Conceptual relationships are illustrated in semantic maps such as the one shown in Figure 3.2 on page 62. These maps are important in content area study because the goal of such study is developing concepts. According to Simpson (1987), conceptual understanding evolves from four mental operations, which are emphasized in the reinforcement activities of this chapter. These mental operations are discussed in the conceptual reinforcement ideas section. Reinforcement activities to build vocabulary should incorporate these mental operations:

1. Recognizing and generating critical attributes—both examples and nonexamples—of a concept.
2. Seeing relationships between the concept to be learned and what is already known.
3. Applying the concept to a variety of contexts.
4. Generating new contexts for the learned concept.

■ Conceptual Reinforcement Instructional Activities

How do learners use attribute relations?

What is the purpose of a semantic feature analysis?

Attribute relations provide an organizational network focusing on concept characteristics. Students use their existing concepts to learn new concepts and conceptual relationships. For example, students know about horses, which helps them acquire a connected concept, unicorns. Related concepts can be compared using **semantic feature analysis.** Semantic feature analysis works best with related words, such as those connected to a specific concept or within a content area. Using some familiar words in a feature analysis gives students a basis for comparison with the new words. For example, in the following semantic feature analysis (Example 3.2), students could begin with the more familiar sports of football and baseball and then add a less familiar sport, such as rugby, later. The teacher might develop the grid of vocabulary words and features, or attributes, related to them and let the students complete the grid by putting Xs in appropriate cells—the ones in which the rows for specific

■ ■ ■ EXAMPLE 3.2   *Physical Education Attributes*

	Bases	Basket	Yard lines	Inflated ball	Round ball	Officials	Court	Field
Football			x	x		x		x
Baseball	x				x	x		x
Basket-ball		x		x	x	x	x	

How can conceptual relationships be organized?

terms intersect with columns that represent features related to the terms—or the students and teacher could develop the grid together as the terms are discussed.

Conceptual relationships can be organized in various ways, such as **class relations** and **examples** and **nonexamples.** *Class relations* are hierarchical networks. Words are related to one another by superordinate and subordinate concepts. For example, chromosomes are a part of the hereditary material in cells, and genes are found within chromosomes. *Examples* demonstrate a concept, whereas *nonexamples* demonstrate what the concept is not; both facilitate learning. For example, both dominant genes and recessive genes are examples of genes. Chromosomes are nonexamples of genes.

The Frayer model (Frayer, Frederick, and Klausmeier, 1969) was developed to create a more complete understanding of all the facets of a newly acquired concept. This model calls for inclusion of both examples and nonexamples to extend learning. In developing a concept of democratic government, for example, students can identify governments that are not democratic as well as ones that are democratic and explain why a particular government is an example or nonexample. Schwartz and Raphael (1985) developed a word map based on categories devised by Frayer and others (1969); Example 3.3 illustrates a variation of this activity. Example 3.4 illustrates another activity based on the Frayer model. Example 3.5 illustrates an example and nonexample activity.

■ ■ ■ EXAMPLE 3.3   Word Map

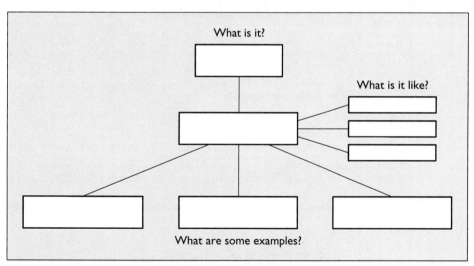

Source: R. M. Schwartz, and T. Raphael, "Concept of Definition: A Key to Improving Students' Vocabulary." Reading Teacher, 39 (1985), p. 201. Reprinted with permission of Robert M. Schwartz and the International Reading Association.

■ ■ ■ EXAMPLE 3.4   Frayer Model

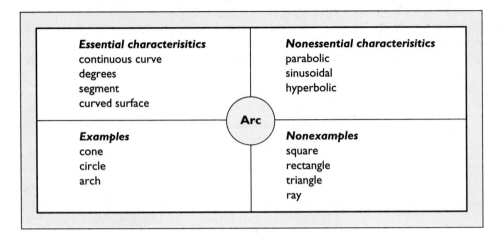

Essential characterisitics	Nonessential characterisitics
continuous curve	parabolic
degrees	sinusoidal
segment	hyperbolic
curved surface	
Arc	
Examples	Nonexamples
cone	square
circle	rectangle
arch	triangle
	ray

■ ■ ■ EXAMPLE 3.5   Mathematics Examples

Directions: Place a + on the line before each example and a – on the line before each nonexample. Be prepared to explain your answers.

The concept is *triangle*.

_____ scalene
_____ adjacent
_____ isosceles
_____ equilateral
_____ left
_____ vertical
_____ acute
_____ right
_____ obtuse

■ Contextual Connections

Context clues can help a learner predict the meaning of a word. Context clues improve overall comprehension because they help students to understand and to process text on a deep level (Sinatra and Dowd, 1991; Tipton, 1991). Context narrows a word's field of reference and helps specify its meaning, as well as building connections between known and new information (Sinatra and Dowd, 1991). Instructing students in the use of context strategies can increase their independent acquisition of vocabulary (Nagy, Herman, and Anderson, 1985; Jenkins, Matlock, and Slocum, 1989).

Although context may help students understand text, context alone may not provide enough clues to word meaning. Some context clues are contrived, neatly providing information about an unfamiliar word. However, in content reading, students also read long selections that rarely contain neat contextual explanations (Blachowicz and Zabroske, 1990). After all, authors write to transmit ideas rather than to define vocabulary (Sinatra and Dowd, 1991). Context is most useful when students are fluent readers who automatically recognize most of the words in a sentence, because this enables them to use the surrounding words to determine the meaning of an unknown word. They also need background information about the topic. A reader who knows a great deal about cars, for example, will be better able to read and understand words like *generator, transmission, chassis, accelerator, gasket, lubrication,* and *ignition system* and even more technical terms like *bore, stroke, displacement, valve, compression, drive shafts, axle, distributor, plug thread,* and *exhaust system.*

MEETING THE CHALLENGE

Mark, a high school sophomore, spent many frustrating hours reading and studying biology, but he failed every biology test. He could not understand or remember the content well enough to participate in class discussions. Mrs. Reed, the biology teacher, was also frustrated because she knew that he was a hard-working student who diligently studied the assigned material. When she checked his permanent record, she found he had average grades with a B– or C+ average. She spoke with his other teachers and learned that he was a hard-working, but struggling, student in most of his classes.

Mark reached total frustration when Mrs. Reed assigned the biology unit on heredity. After struggling with the text material, he asked for assistance. Mrs. Reed suggested that he write an outline of the chapter and make a vocabulary notebook for the terms that troubled him. After two weeks, he showed no progress toward understanding genes, chromosomes, and so on, so Mrs. Reed asked for a conference with the reading teacher. Mrs. Reed and

Mark met with the reading teacher after school. After considerable discussion, the reading teacher realized that Mark was attempting to memorize each of the terms (concepts) as a separate entity because he did not understand the interrelationships among them and could not relate these ideas to his own experiences. The reading teacher showed Mark how to use the table of contents as an overview or outline of the important ideas in the chapter and as a guide to superordinate ideas and subordinate ideas. Mrs. Reed explained the connection between the heredity chapter and the preceding chapter, as well as the conceptual relationships of the terms in the text. Jointly, they created the semantic map shown in Figure 3.2. As a result of these experiences, Mark began to conceptualize the terms as interrelated concepts rather than trying to remember each one as a separate entity.

A teacher may help a student *see* the connections among concepts in a content area chapter. (© Robert Finken / The Picture Cube)

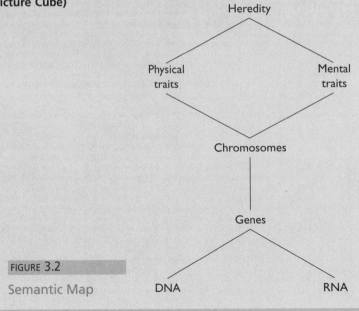

FIGURE 3.2

Semantic Map

Kinds of Context Clues

What are two types of context clues?

Syntactic context clues are derived from the grammatical function of the unfamiliar word in the sentence. **Semantic** context clues are derived from the meanings of the other words in the sentence. The most useful kinds of syntactic and semantic context clues are illustrated in the following list.

1. Definitions or direct explanations provide both semantic and syntactic clues, as illustrated in this sentence: He called this home *Monticello,* which means "little mountain" in Italian.

2. The appositive, or restatement clue, also offers both a semantic and a syntactic clue as illustrated in this sentence: The manatee, *an endangered mammal,* must be protected.

3. An adjective structure, which is a syntactic clue, is shown in this sentence: His *truculent* criticism of the demonstration revealed his feelings. The position of *truculent* in the sentence reveals that it is an adjective.

4. Comparison/contrast is a type of semantic clue that is illustrated in these examples: A *machete,* like a sword, must be very sharp. In bright light, the pupils of the eyes contract; in the dark, they *dilate.*

5. Synonyms/antonyms are semantic clues as illustrated in these examples: The *mercury* in the thermometer was dropping—the *quicksilver* was contracting.
   The *acid,* not the *base,* reddened the litmus paper.

6. Experience context clues give semantic information as shown in this sentence: *Artificial respiration* was applied to the nearly drowned man.

7. Cause and effect provides a semantic clue as shown in this example: She pushed the wrong computer key and *deleted* the only copy of the file.

8. Reflection of mood is a semantic clue to meaning as illustrated in these sentences: All alone, Jim heard the creaking sound of the opening door and saw a shadowy figure standing suddenly before him. Jim was literally *stupefied.*

9. Summary statements are semantic clues as shown in this example: Even though he was sixty-five years old, he continued to love sports. He played a skillful game of tennis and seldom missed his daily swim. He was very *athletic.*

How does figurative language provide context clues?

10. **Figurative language**—which includes personification, similes, metaphors, hyperbole, euphemisms, and allusions—provides context clues by making abstract and uncommon ideas more concrete.
    a. *Personification.* Human or personal qualities are given to inanimate things or ideas. Katherine Paterson used personification in *Bridge to Terabithia.* "Through his top ear came the sound of the Timmonses' old Buick—'Wants oil,' his dad would say—"(Paterson, 1987, p. 7)
    b. *Simile.* A direct comparison is made between things. The words *like, as . . . as,* and *so . . . as* are frequently used in making the comparisons

in similes. Similes are useful because they help us illustrate our thoughts and ideas. An example of a sentence containing a simile is "The thunder reverberated like an entire corps of bass drums."

c. *Metaphor.* This figure of speech also helps writers and speakers create clearer pictures through comparisons. These comparisons, however, do not use clue words such as *like* or *as.* Bruce Brooks used the following metaphor to describe music in *Midnight Hour Encores.* "Just give me the equivalent of antiseptic kitchens in which crew-cut husbands eat lime Jell-O with banana slices and miniature marshmallows suspended in it, served by perky housewives who got the recipe from a television commercial earlier in the day. 'I get it. The Fifties.'" (Brooks, 1986, p. 68)

d. *Hyperbole.* This is an exaggeration used for effect. Katherine Paterson used hyperbole to describe a girl in *Bridge to Terabithia.* "And the littlest one cried if you looked at her cross-eyed." (Paterson, 1987, p. 2)

e. *Euphemism.* Euphemism is used to express disagreeable or unpleasant facts indirectly. Death is often described as "passing away," "going to one's reward," or "going to the final rest."

f. *Allusion.* Allusions are references to information believed to be common knowledge. They may refer to Greek and Roman mythology, current or historical characters or events, or literature. Allusions are based on the assumption that the reader knows the characters, that the allusions will cause the reader to make associations, and that the allusions will clarify a point. Mary Ryan used the following allusion in *The Trouble with Perfect.* "Brian started making ravenous gurgling sounds and lurching around the kitchen like the Hunchback of Wheaton." (Ryan, 1995, p. 9)

Context Clue Strategies

Students need to develop a general idea of the kinds of clues that content can offer. For students who need greater support in using context clues, teacher-made wall charts showing these types of clues are useful. In using context clues, students can read backward and forward to locate clues and to generate hypotheses about word meaning; then they can test alternative possibilities to see if their predicted meaning makes sense. They can consider whether any other words might fit into that slot in the sentence. To refine word meaning, readers can use context clues in combination with the dictionary. An activity like sentence completion can be used in discussion groups. For example, if students were studying the words *bizarre, beguiling, astounding,* and *illustrious,* they might choose the appropriate word to complete this sentence: "She was a(n) _____ young woman." Then they could explain their choices.

Activities that include more extensive context or description help students enrich their use of inference. For example, the context in the earlier sentence could be extended to explain that the young woman in question had gained notoriety by going over Niagara Falls in a barrel.

Blachowicz and Zabroske (1990) found that students must know how to look for and use context clues and developed the following strategy to help students develop and test hypotheses about word meanings.

Look—before, at, after the word
Reason—to connect what they know with what the author tells them
Predict—a possible meaning
Resolve or redo—decide if they know enough, should try again, or consult an
     expert or reference

They discovered that weekly lessons focusing on two words found in regular instructional materials helped students establish the why, what, and how of context use in less than three months. Example 3.6 illustrates discussion questions to explore contextual understanding. This example is based on business concepts.

■ ■ ■ EXAMPLE 3.6   *Business Concepts*

How does the author help you understand the nature of the business cycle?

If prosperity is the high point in the business cycle, what do you think the low point in the business cycle is called?

A *cycle* is a repeating period or time. The term we use to describe how the economy moves from good times to bad times and back again is **business cycle.** Sometimes this series of changes is like a roller coaster. For a while, everything seems to be going very well. Jobs are plentiful, and anyone who wants to work can find a job. People feel good about the economy and are willing to spend their money. Because people are buying, business is good. And when business is good, we say we are enjoying prosperity. **Prosperity** is the high point of a business cycle. Sometimes it's called a *boom.* Employment is way up, the demand for goods and services is high, and businesses are turning out goods and services as fast as they can.

Source: Betty J. Brown and John Clow, General Business: Our Business and Economic World *(Boston: Houghton Mifflin Company, 1982), p. 144. Reprinted by permission of Houghton Mifflin Company.*

■ ■ A Conceptual, Contextualized Approach to the Instruction of Specific Words

Effective vocabulary instruction provides for repeated exposures to important words and concepts. This approach is especially valuable with subject matter reading and literature that requires specialized knowledge, such as a deep-sea adventure where water pressure and technical equipment are central to the plot (Smith, 1988). After carefully determining which concepts are necessary for student comprehension, the teacher can develop these concepts and the related words. In the following two sections, we first look at how teachers should go about selecting the specific words they wish to focus on and then examine instructional activities for teaching these selected words.

■ Choosing Words

Teachers should examine content reading materials to identify potentially difficult words before giving reading assignments. In time, their experience will enable them to recognize words that give students problems year after year. Teachers should also decide which vocabulary development technique is most likely to help students learn the identified words. Some words are best learned through context clues, whereas others must become sight words, and others are learned best with morphemic analysis (i.e., based on word roots and affixes). Example 3.7 shows a page from a content textbook with troublesome words underlined by the teacher.

How are technical vocabulary, specialized vocabulary, and general vocabulary different from one another?

In general, learners need three categories of words. The first is **general vocabulary,** consisting of common words that have generally accepted meanings. These words appear in both content reading materials and general reading materials. Words such as *neutral* and *mobilize* are in this group. The second category, **specialized vocabulary,** consists of words having both general and specialized meanings. The word *matter* is in this group. In general use, *matter* has the meaning reflected in the sentence "What is the matter?" The word *matter* also has a specialized meaning in science content. The last category is **technical vocabulary,** consisting of words representing specific concepts that are applicable to specific content subjects. *Photosynthesis* is an example of a technical word used in scientific content. The vocabulary in all these categories appears not only in textbooks but also in literature and reading materials that students encounter in daily life. Therefore, teachers can use real-life reading materials to enhance vocabulary development.

Students are likely to encounter many unknown, or partially known, words as they read literature and textbooks. Teachers generally find it impossible to teach all the unknown words that students will encounter. If an assignment has

■ ■ ■ EXAMPLE 3.7   *Identifying Troublesome Words*

The Physical Evidence

Shigemura uses <u>physics</u> and math to reconstruct an accident, charting the precise path the vehicles must have taken before the crash to end up as they did. For example, he uses the formula $S = \sqrt{30df}$ to <u>calculate</u> a car's minimum speed S in miles per hour at the moment the car begins to <u>skid</u>. In the formula, d = the length in feet of the skid mark left by the car and f = the <u>coefficient</u> of <u>friction</u>. The coefficient of friction is a measure of the slipperiness or stickiness of the road. Shigemura finds d with a tape measure, and determines f with a special device. The <u>matrix</u> at the right shows speeds calculated for several different combinations of d and f.

Calculated Speed S

		d	
	76	98	123
f **0.40**	30.19	34.29	38.41
0.80	42.70	48.49	54.33
1.20	52.30	59.39	66.54

$\sqrt{30 \cdot 123 \cdot 0.40} = 38.41$

If d = 123 and f = 0.40, the car was traveling about 38 mi/h when it began to skid.

Source: Miriam A. Leiva and Richard G. Brown, Algebra 1 Explorations and Applications. *Boston: McDougal Littell, 1997, p. 238. Photograph courtesy of Nathan S. Shigemura Illinois State Police.*

twenty-five or thirty unfamiliar words and a teacher devotes one minute to each word, twenty-five to thirty minutes have been spent in vocabulary development, which cuts into other instructional time. Since time and energy constraints make it impossible to devote this amount of time to vocabulary instruction on a regular basis, teachers need to focus on words that are essential to comprehension of the major points in the selection.

Research indicates that teaching *key words,* or those words essential to understanding concepts developed in a text, prior to reading a selection enhances understanding (Beck, Perfetti, and McKeown, 1982; Kameenui, Carnine, and Freschi, 1982). Students need to learn words they are likely to encounter in subsequent reading in the subject area (high-utility words). Key words are combined to form main ideas and important supporting details. In content area reading, key words are often technical terms whose referents are central to understanding the concepts of the content area. Teachers should examine textbook reading assignments carefully to determine whether the author has assumed that students know words that are actually unknown. After identifying these words, teachers can provide direct instruction focusing on them.

Literary material presents a somewhat different vocabulary problem than does exposition, because literature includes more symbolic, abstract meanings. Chase and Duffelmeyer (1990) explain that literary text requires a higher level of student involvement than exposition. They want students to realize that knowing a single word can help them accomplish such things as visualizing a character, comprehending a character's motivation, perceiving a theme, and understanding an author's point of view. To achieve this, they created a strategy, VOCAB-LIT, to teach the significant words like *ingratiating* as used to describe Brother Leon in *The Chocolate War* (Cormier, 1974). This type of word is one that, when fully understood, would reveal an important aspect of the novel. The students complete study sheets (see Example 3.8) that require them to reflect on their personal levels of word knowledge, write the sentence in which the word appears, make connections with content, look the word up in a reference, and discuss what they have learned about the word. After the students learn this strategy, they are each assigned a day for presenting a word to the group. This program has been quite successful.

■ ■ ■ EXAMPLE 3.8   *Samples from VOCAB-LIT Study Sheets*

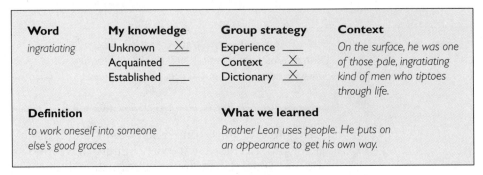

Word	**My knowledge**	**Group strategy**	**Context**
ingratiating	Unknown X	Experience ___	*On the surface, he was one*
	Acquainted ___	Context X	*of those pale, ingratiating*
	Established ___	Dictionary X	*kind of men who tiptoes*
			through life.

Definition	**What we learned**
to work oneself into someone	*Brother Leon uses people. He puts on*
else's good graces	*an appearance to get his own way.*

Source: A. Chase and F. Duffelmeyer, "VOCAB-LIT: Integrating Vocabulary Study and Literature Study." Journal of Reading, 34 (November 1990): 188–193. Reprinted with permission of Ann Chase and the International Reading Association.

■ Instructional Activities

Once specific words have been chosen for a selection, teachers have many options for actually teaching them to students. For instance, a teacher could ask students to write about an experience to illustrate a concept, to write a nonexample for the concept, and, finally, to compose word meanings. As mentioned, teachers first need to examine reading assignments carefully to determine whether the author has assumed that students know certain concepts that they actually do not know. Example 3.6, for instance, shows some questions that will help students think about conceptual relationships in exploring business concepts. The "Meeting the Challenge" vignette on pages 61–62 illustrates the need for focusing on conceptual connections as the means for genuinely learning (rather than merely memorizing) specific words.

A number of the activities presented here could have been discussed under the "Conceptual Reinforcement Instructional Activities" section because they develop concepts and relationships among concepts. We have chosen to highlight them here instead, however, because they are particularly well suited to the instruction of *specific* targeted words and terms.

Association activities can help students relate concepts to the words that represent them. Unknown words are learned by connecting them with known words that have similar meanings. Students can learn vocabulary for a field trip by viewing a video, listening to a speaker, or reading text. Students preparing to visit a local courthouse may encounter such terms as *attorney, litigation, defendant,* and *prosecutor.* Teachers can introduce appropriate words on the chalkboard, pronounce them, and discuss their meanings, thus giving students opportunities to associate the visual forms of the words with the pronunciations and the meanings. In addition to discussion (see p. 57), association activities include matching exercises, in-depth word study, crossword puzzles, analogies, sorts, and graphic organizers, which can be used for prereading activities or for review. Example 3.9 is an association activity based on a science

---

■ ■ ■ EXAMPLE 3.9   *Science Association Activity*

Directions: Draw a line to connect the words in Column A with the words and phrases that have almost the same meaning in Column B.

A	B
combustion	pushes forward
thrust	burn
propellant	supplying oxygen
oxidizer	pushing force
propels	burning chemicals or expanding gases

chapter on rockets; Example 3.10 is based on a science chapter entitled "States of Matter"; and Example 3.11 is based on a chapter on disease in a biology textbook.

■ ■ ■ EXAMPLE 3.10   *Science Association Activity*

Directions: Write *S* on the line beside a set of terms if they have the same meaning. Write *D* on the line if the terms have different meanings.

_____ hardness—rigidity
_____ brittle—will shatter
_____ tensile strength—can be pulled apart easily
_____ matter—gas
_____ malleability—lumpiness
_____ ductility—can be drawn into wires

■ ■ ■ EXAMPLE 3.11   *Science Association Activity*

Directions: Write each term from the list below on the line beside its meaning.

_____ the science of disease
_____ departure from a state of health
_____ noninfectious disease
_____ biologically inherited disease
_____ signs of illness
_____ germ disease
_____ resistance to disease

pathology	hereditary disease
disease	symptoms
immunity	infectious disease
deficiency disease	

Describe an in-depth word study.

In-depth word study increases knowledge of word meanings through association. Students using this strategy study all aspects of a word along with words that are related to it. The content teacher may identify specific words for such study or ask students to identify words they feel they need to study in greater depth. Students can use their textbooks, a dictionary, and a thesaurus to obtain the necessary information. This activity is illustrated in Example 3.12, which is an in-depth word study of the word *economy,* selected from a social studies text.

■ ■ ■ EXAMPLE 3.12   In-Depth Word Study

Economy: "The management of the resources of a country, community, or business: the American economy."

Related Words and Meanings

economy: (a second meaning) The careful or thrifty use or management of resources; freedom from waste; thrift.

economics: The science of the production, distribution, and consumption of wealth.

Word Forms

economic, economical, economically, economics, economize, economization, economizer

Opposing Concepts	*Related Concepts*
liberal	frugal
generous	thrifty
wasteful	save
careless	accumulate
bounteous	amass
beneficent	chary
munificent	miserly
improvident	parsimonious
lavish	penurious
extravagant	curtail
impoverished	retrench

How do analogies develop students' vocabulary?

Analogies show a relationship or similarity between two words or ideas. Analogy activities are conceptual and associational, comparing two similar relationships. On one side of the analogy, the two objects or concepts are related in a particular way; on the other side, the objects are related in the same way. For example, in the analogy *triangle : three :: square : four,* the relationship is "geometric figure is to number of sides." An analogy has equal or balanced sides similar to those in a mathematical equation.

Content teachers can construct analogy exercises for students. After learning how to form analogies, students can create their own. This kind of study is especially helpful for college-bound students, who will discover that analogies are popular items on college entrance examinations. Secondary school students are often unfamiliar with the format of analogies; therefore, teachers should explain that the colon (:) represents the words *is to,* and the double colon (::)

represents the word *as*. The teacher can provide examples of analogies for the entire class to work through in preparation for analogy practice activities. When working through an analogy example, students should identify the relationship, complete the analogy, and explain their reasoning. Example 3.13 shows an analogy example prepared for a science textbook chapter.

■ ■ ■ EXAMPLE 3.13   *Science Analogy Exercise*

Directions: Select the answer that completes each analogy. Identify the relationship expressed in the analogy and be prepared to explain your answer.

1. water : dehydration :: vitamins : (mumps, deficiency diseases, jaundice, appendicitis)
2. taste buds : tongue :: villi : (mouth, stomach, small intestine, colon)
3. pepsin : protein :: ptyalin : (oils, fats, starch, sucrose)
4. liver : small intestine :: salivary glands : (mouth, stomach, small intestine, colon)
5. mouth : large intestine :: duodenum : (esophagus, jejunum, ileum, cecum)
6. protein : organic compound :: magnesium : (peptide, vitamin, mineral, salt)
7. pancreas : pancreatic fluid :: stomach : (water, saliva, gastric juices, intestinal fluid)
8. saliva : ptyalin :: pancreatic fluid : (trypsin, amylase, lipase, peptones)

What two kinds of sorts may be used for vocabulary development?

Sorts are categorization activities in which items are sorted according to common characteristics. The most common sorts are closed-ended and open-ended. In closed-ended sorts, the common properties of category members are stated at the outset and the identified category gives students a basis for including or excluding a class of concepts. In open-ended sorts, no category is stated in advance and no examples are given. Students seek to identify the relationships among the concepts, grouping them together and defining the connection that has served as a basis for inclusion in or exclusion from that category.

Examples 3.14 and 3.15 present closed-ended sort categorization activities: the feature that all words in a group must share is stated in advance. Examples 3.16 and 3.17 present open-ended sorts.

■ ■ ■ EXAMPLE 3.14   *Closed-Ended Sort for Social Studies Content*

Directions: Draw a line through the name in each group that does not belong. The common characteristic of each group is identified by the word in parentheses.

1. Bob La Follette, Jane Addams, Upton Sinclair, Theodore Roosevelt, Jacob Riis (progressives)

2. Edward Bok, Joseph Pulitzer, Carl Schurz, Samuel Gompers, Ole Rölvaag, Benjamin West (immigrants to the United States)

■ ■ ■ EXAMPLE 3.15   *Closed-Ended Sort for Home Economics*

Directions: Sort the list of words into the following categories: protein, carbohydrates, calcium.

fish	nuts	bread	apples
spaghetti	cheese	kale	broccoli
eggs	sugar	peaches	milk
potatoes	cereal		

■ ■ ■ EXAMPLE 3.16   *Open-Ended Sort for Biology*

Directions: Draw a line through the word in each group that does not belong and identify the common characteristic (category) of the remaining items.
1. intestinal juice, gastric juice, maltose, pancreatic juice
2. amylase, gastric proteinase, lipase, polypeptides, peptidases, disaccharidases
3. fats, amino acids, maltose, glycerol, simple sugars

■ ■ ■ EXAMPLE 3.17   *Open-Ended Sort for Secretarial Office Procedures*

Directions: Classify the following list of words into groups and identify the common characteristic of each group.

sales invoice	multicopy
purchase order	purchase invoice
bills	horizontal spaces
sales order	binding space
credit memorandum	credit approval
purchase requisition	vertical line
business firm heading	

Which strategy gives students a structure for incorporating new concepts with existing concepts?

Graphic organizers or structured overviews can illustrate hierarchical and/or linear relationships among the key concepts in a content textbook, chapter, or unit. Graphic organizers are based on Ausubel's (1978) theory that an orderly arrangement of concepts helps students learn them. A graphic organizer gives students a structure for incorporating new concepts with existing concepts, thus helping them anticipate the words and concepts in a content selection.

Hierarchical graphic organizers are used when the relationships portrayed fit into a subordinate-superordinate array. The social studies content in Example 3.18 and the biology content in Example 3.19 fit into hierarchical arrays.

■ ■ ■ EXAMPLE 3.18   *Graphic Organizer for Social Studies*

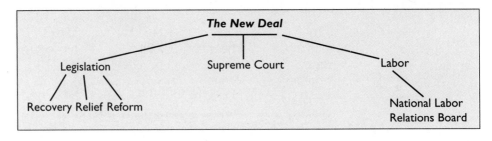

■ ■ ■ EXAMPLE 3.19   *Graphic Organizer for Biology*

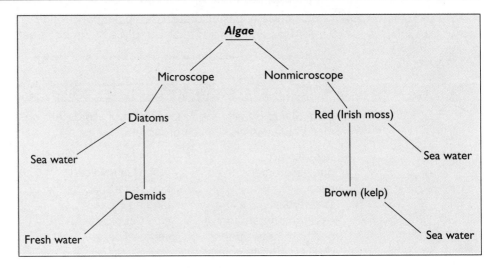

Barron (1969) recommended the following steps for developing structured overviews:

1. Identify the words (concepts) that are important for students to understand.

2. Arrange the words (concepts) into a structure that illustrates the interrelationships among them.
3. Add to the structure words (concepts) that the students understand in order to show the relationship between the specific learning task at hand and the discipline.
4. Analyze the overview. Are the major relationships shown clearly? Can the overview be simplified and still communicate the important relationships?

The relationships in a structured overview are usually arranged in the following manner:

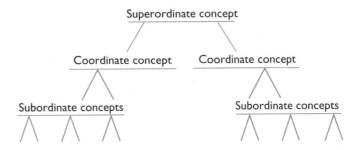

Linear arrays are created on a horizontal line, showing gradations of meanings for related terms. This is illustrated in Example 3.20.

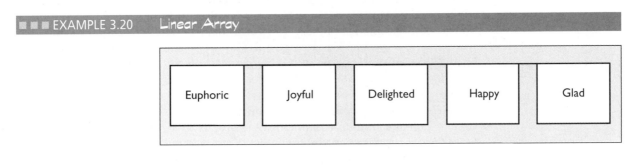

■ ■ ■ EXAMPLE 3.20   Linear Array

| Euphoric | Joyful | Delighted | Happy | Glad |

■ ■ **Additional Strategies for Students' Vocabulary Learning**

These additional strategies focus on giving students autonomy in acquiring word meanings. They include morphological analysis, using references, expanding definitions, and computer instruction.

■ Morphological Analysis

What is morpho-logical analysis?

Nagy and others (1989) found that **morphological analysis** contributes to students' vocabulary growth (White, Power, and White, 1989; Ruddiman, 1993). Morphological knowledge enables students to identify words more rapidly and accurately. A root carries the base meaning of the word. Affixes, primarily prefixes and suffixes, change the base meaning. *Graph* is a root that means "write," as in *autograph*. Prefixes are word parts added to the front of roots, and *suffixes* are word parts added to the end of roots. Many of the roots used in content area writing originated in Greek or Latin. Morphological analysis is especially valuable when used in combination with context clues, which help students determine the correct meaning of an affix. Many affixes have multiple meanings, so all meanings that occur frequently should be taught. For example, the suffix *ways* in the word *sideways* can mean "course," "direction," or "manner." When a multiple-meaning affix occurs, students can use context clues to determine which meaning is appropriate. Students can practice using morphological analysis through building new words by combining prefixes and suffixes with various root words. For instance, the word *construct* can be changed in a variety of ways, some of which are illustrated here:

construct	constructing	reconstruct	reconstructing
construction	constructed	reconstruction	

To develop morphological analysis, teachers can pose questions that will stimulate students to examine the structural aspects of words. Sample questions that might be used to develop vocabulary in a science class follow:

1. If *thermos* means hot, what is a *thermostat?* a *thermometer?*
2. If *hydro* means water, what do these words mean: *dehydrate? hydrophobia?* How is *hydroplane* related to *hydrant?*
3. If *tele* means far, what are the meanings of these words: *telescope? television?*
4. If *zoo* means animal, what is the meaning of *zoology?* Who is a *zoologist?*
5. If *tome* is the act of cutting, what is an *appendectomy?*
6. If *micro* means small, what is a *microscope?*
7. Why would you call *dynamite* and *dynamo* first cousins?

Students can create a web of words (a type of graphic organizer) structured upon a root. Webs may be developed by groups of students or by students working alone. Example 3.21 illustrates a web for the root *migr*.

■ Using References

References such as dictionaries, thesauruses, and encyclopedias, either printed or computer-based, are useful for developing word meanings. Students can use

A Web Graphic Organizer

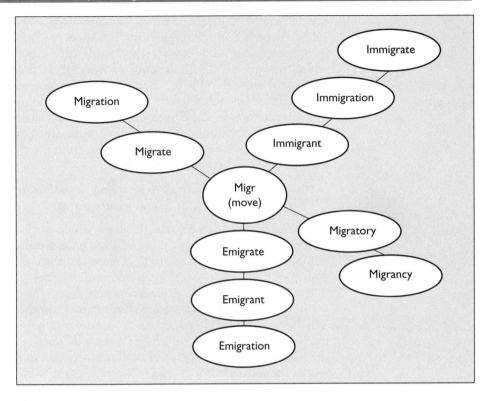

these references in conjunction with experience, context, and morphological analysis to build understanding. The following guidelines are useful when teaching the use of references in content classrooms:

1. Help students select the appropriate dictionary definition by using the context in which the word appears. The multiple meanings included in dictionaries can create problems for students because they find it difficult to choose the appropriate meaning from those listed in the dictionary. With practice, most students can learn how to use content context to identify the appropriate meaning.

2. Identify only a few key concepts for dictionary study. It is perfectly legitimate for teachers to tell students the meanings of unknown words. Secondary students generally are more willing to use the dictionary when they need it if the teacher has not forced them to use it on a constant basis.

■ Expanding Definitions

Learners need to integrate newly taught words with other knowledge (Nagy, 1988). As stated elsewhere in this book, comprehension is based largely on prior experience and knowledge. Words are understood and retained best when they are related to existing knowledge. Definitions alone provide only superficial word knowledge. Looking up words in a dictionary or memorizing definitions does not reliably improve reading comprehension (Nagy, 1988). Many teachers who have tried this method with their students can attest to its failure. A strictly definitional approach to teaching word meanings fails for a variety of reasons. First, many definitions are not very clear or precise, as illustrated in the following examples:

sedimentary: Of, containing, resembling, or derived from sediment.
hogweed: Any of various coarse, weedy plants.

These definitions are accurate, but they would not help a person who did not already know the word meanings. Most of the words in a definition should be familiar to students if they are to understand the definition. In addition, using a form of the defined word in its definition further obscures the meaning, and this occurs in both of the preceding examples.

A second reason that strictly definitional approaches fail is that students may have difficulty choosing the correct definition for a particular context from the several definitions that are given in a dictionary or glossary. Third, many definitions often do not give enough information to help students understand words for concepts with which they are unfamiliar. Fourth, definitions do not help learners use a new word. Research shows that students have difficulty writing meaningful sentences utilizing new words when given only definitions of those words (Miller and Gildea, 1987).

Definitions that students themselves generate help them relate new words to prior experiences. Thus, defining activities like the one shown in Example 3.22 are useful in developing students' understanding.

■ ■ ■ EXAMPLE 3.22   *Defining Words in Different Ways*

1. Use the word in a sentence that shows its meaning.
   Magnanimous—A magnanimous person would give you the shirt off his back.
2. Give a synonym for the word.
   magnanimous—generous
3. Give an antonym for the word.
   magnanimous—selfish
4. State a classification for the word.
   Magnanimity can be classified as a quality of mind and soul.
5. Provide an example of the word. Either draw an illustration or locate a picture to illustrate it.

6. Make a comparison of the word with another word.
Magnanimity is like generosity, but it implies more noble unselfishness.

■ Computer Instruction

Computer programs that can help students to develop extensive word understanding are available. Such programs can be motivational learning tools for students, and students can use them independently. The most common types of computer software for vocabulary instruction are cloze passage programs; structural analysis programs; homonym, synonym, and antonym programs; computer dictionaries; and computer thesauruses. The specific software selected depends both on the type of computer available and on the instructional objectives. Software and computers are constantly being changed and upgraded; therefore, it is difficult to recommend specific materials. We do recommend that teachers read this chapter carefully to establish criteria for the vocabulary software they wish to use and evaluate available materials based on their own requirements. You will also find it helpful to read the article, "Computer-assisted Vocabulary Instruction" (Wheatley, Muller, and Miller, 1993). Many computer companies and/or salespeople will provide demonstration disks of software to potential customers for examination before purchase. It is wise to take advantage of this opportunity.

Summary

Students who have large stores of word meanings comprehend content materials better than students who have limited vocabularies. Since many of the words used in content materials are labels for concepts, concept development is also an important goal of content area instruction. Knowing a word means understanding the concept it represents. Vocabulary in content materials falls into three general categories: general, specialized, and technical. Because content materials frequently contain a high proportion of unknown words, it is impossible for teachers to teach students every word they do not know. Therefore it is important for teachers to focus on key vocabulary. Research shows that direct teaching of vocabulary increases students' word knowledge and that students need practice to develop their fluency in applying vocabulary skills.

Discussion Questions

1 Why is experience central to vocabulary instruction?
2 What does it mean to know a word?
3 What are the weaknesses of a definitional approach to developing vocabulary?
4 Explain the meaning of "concepts" in your own words.

5 What are the strengths and weaknesses of context clues in deriving word meanings?

6 Why do you think practice is so important in developing students' ability to derive meaning from context?

Enrichment Activities

1 Prepare a categorization activity, as illustrated in Examples 3.14 through 3.17, for a chapter from a content area textbook or nonfiction trade book of your choice.

2 Prepare seven activities to develop vocabulary for a particular trade book or textbook.

3 Select a chapter in a content area book and identify the vocabulary you would teach to a class. Plan ways to teach the chosen terms. Following is a list of content areas and the key concepts that might be found in a chapter in each area.

Auto mechanics: thermostat, radiator, carburetor, armature, commutator, alternator, oscilloscope, polarize, camshaft, valve-tappet

Music: choreographer, prologue, prompter, score, overture, prelude, libretto, aria

Health: bacteria, virus, protozoa, metazoa, fungi, carbuncle, psoriasis, shingles, scabies, eczema

Foreign language: masculine, feminine, gender, predicate, cognates, singular

Art: introspective, murals, appreciation, technique, expression, properties, exhibitions, contemporary, interpret

Driver education: awareness, controlled emotions, maturity, irresponsibility, behavioral patterns, compensate, fatigue, carbon monoxide, medication, alcohol, depressants, visual, auditory

Psychology: learning curve, plateau, hierarchies, massed practice, feedback, frame, negative transfer, retention, overlearning

Government: delinquent, incorrigibility, omnibus, exigency, indeterminate, adjudicated, arbitrariness, interrogation, formulation, juvenile

4 Develop a procedure for in-depth study of a word.

5 Make a graphic organizer for a selection in a content area textbook or a non-fiction trade book.

6 Prepare an analogy exercise sheet (similar to the one in Example 3.13) for a chapter or unit in a content area text.

4

The Process of Constructing Meaning in Texts

Overview

Comprehension is a reflective process in which the reader integrates his or her prior knowledge with the author's cues to construct meanings appropriate to the reader's specific context (Irwin, 1991). Three major components are involved in this complex process: the reader, the text, and the context. Active, strategic thinkers integrate new knowledge with prior knowledge to infer meaning (Tierney, 1990). Moreover, understanding involves readers' responses to their literacy experience and the ability to monitor their own cognitive processes (metacognitive ability). In this chapter, the first of two chapters that address the process of constructing meaning in texts, the goals are to develop your understanding of the comprehension process as well as to present strategies for refining your students' understanding. Chapter 5 focuses on comprehension strategies employed before, during, and after actual reading.

Purpose-Setting Questions

As you read this chapter, try to answer these questions:

1 What do we know about competent comprehenders?
2 How is reading comprehension related to content reading?
3 How is the reader's context related to reading comprehension?

■ ■ What Do We Know About Competent Comprehension?

What happens during the reading process?

Reading is a process in which information from the text and the reader's knowledge act together to produce meaning. Reading comprehension involves situation-based cognition related to contexts, multiple slants, and flexibility. Tierney (1990) suggests that "information that is to be used in lots of different ways needs to be explored in lots of different ways. This suggests not limiting information to a single point of view, single interpretation, single system of classification, single slant, or single case" (p. 39). Students who read the same material for different purposes and discuss their understanding with others who have read the same text can develop multiple perspectives. They engage with and understand text, respond to text, and apply their knowledge in a variety of contexts. Competent readers develop *intertextual ties* from one reading experience to another (Tierney, 1990). Writing is significant in cultivating understanding because composing and comprehension are closely related processes.

Teachers' understanding of the comprehension process enables them to facilitate students' progress toward literacy. One way teachers can learn about the comprehension process is by examining their own reading experiences. The passage that follows can guide reflections about what occurs during reading. This example illustrates the reading experience of only one mature reader.

> The reader's eyes fell on the front-page headline of the Sunday paper that read: BRRR BOWL . . . ZIP WIN WARMS FANS. The reader realized that this headline was related to sports news because her schemata (background knowledge) provided the information that the word *Zip* referred to the University of Akron football team, "The Zips." Knowing that she was reading sports news provided her with a mental set (expectation) to read quickly and superficially because she was not deeply interested in sports. Recognizing that she was reading sports news activated a mental set for the way sports news is organized and for numbers identifying scores. The headline stating that "Zip win warms fans" suggested the University of Akron team had won the game. The language "brrr bowl" and "warms fans" also indicated that the game was played in very cold weather. Then she remembered that this was a championship game and established another purpose for reading: to find out what title the Zips had won. She learned that the Zips won the NCAA Division II championship with a score of 29 to 26 in an overtime game.

The reader did not read the first word in the headline. Instead, her eyes moved to a more meaningful word, *Zip,* a word that helped her predict the type of content and the topic. Reading a few more words enabled her to use prior knowledge to predict the article content. In this example, the reader used schemata, semantic and syntactic knowledge, and thinking skills to comprehend the information. She used strategies for understanding that included establishing purposes for reading; relating schemata to written text; thinking at literal, inferential, critical, and creative levels; and reading for main ideas and details. She integrated prior knowledge about the Zips, football, and the weather with new knowledge acquired from reading. This brief analysis reveals some of the complexities of reading comprehension and illustrates how one reader used knowledge and skills to interact with the article and construct meaning.

Research regarding meaning construction is ongoing; however previous research supports each of the following assertions, which are the basis for understanding this chapter.

Comprehension is an active, constructive process.

Comprehension is a process of making sense out of text.

Comprehension is not statically contained in a text; however, the text contributes to meaning.

Comprehension is an interactive process in which the reader, the text, and the context interact.

Comprehension is a reflective process that takes place before, during, and after reading.

Comprehension is a responsive process that involves the reader's emotional, affective, and visual involvement.

Comprehension depends on students' ability to regulate their own understanding *(metacognition)*.

Comprehension strategies enable students to understand text, learn from text, relate text to specific situations, and correct misunderstandings.

■ ■ Constructivist Theories of Literacy

What is the basis of constructivist theories of literacy?

A *constructivist perspective* focuses on how knowledge is built. **Constructivist theories** of literacy focus on how meaning is built by readers and and writers. Literacy involves manipulation of the language and the thought readers engage in when they make sense of and communicate ideas in a variety of situations. Literacy fosters the personal empowerment that results when people use their literacy skills to think and rethink their understandings of texts, themselves, and the world (Langer, 1995).

Cognitive and linguistic skills are precursors of what ability?

Current educational theory emphasizes students' underlying **cognitive and linguistic skills** as precursors of their ability to comprehend. Students learn best from *meaningful contexts* while reading for relevant purposes that link reading with listening, speaking, and writing, emphasizing that literacy is above all an act of communication (McKenna, Robinson, and Miller, 1990).

What is an example of an authentic experience?

Content area teachers guide learning through **authentic experiences** that have meaning and relevance for students, as well as encouraging reflection. Meaning is expressed differently in fiction, nonfiction, and poetry; therefore, students should have opportunities to read many different types of content and use different media (such as computers, videos, audiotapes, radio, film).

■ The Reader: Utilizing Prior Knowledge and Background Experience to Respond to Text

When readers reflect on their own cognitive processes, what abilities are they using?

Constructivists view reading as an interactive process involving the readers' use of language, schemata, and reading skills and strategies. Readers' processing is influenced by their cognitive and metacognitive abilities, their situation or context, and their affective states. Readers engage with ideas and integrate them with their existing schemata to respond to text, to address reading purposes, and to solve problems. **Metacognitive abilities** are those that students use to reflect on their own cognitive processing. Figure 4.1 shows some of the major aspects of readers' cognitive processing, and Figure 4.2 illustrates the reader's role in comprehension.

One conclusion emerging from recent research is the importance of readers' prior knowledge and background experience in facilitating comprehension. Readers draw on information from various sources concurrently to construct a representation of a text's message (McKeown et al., 1992). When readers hear or read something they have never heard or read before, it doesn't imprint on

FIGURE **4.1**

Major Aspects of Thinking in Comprehension

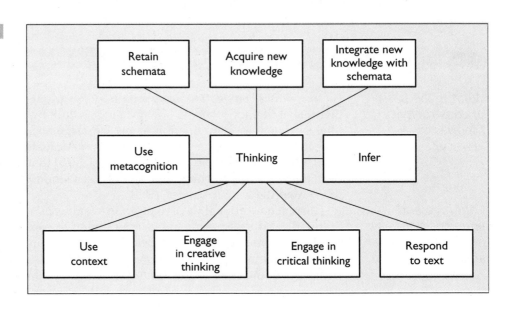

their brains directly the way print remains on paper. Instead, they respond by searching through their minds for existing knowledge and understanding to connect with the new information (Vygotsky, 1962). Students who have a high level of knowledge have a clear advantage in comprehending (Means and Voss, 1985; Dole et al., 1991), whereas lack of knowledge deters comprehension. Moreover, the extent of students' knowledge influences the *quality* of their understanding (McKeown et al., 1992).

■ Schema Theory

Why are schemata abstract rather than concrete?

Schema theory involves more than using prior knowledge and background experience to understand. **Schemata** are mental organizations of prior experiences that greatly influence how readers interpret and comprehend and what they expect from the text. Personal experiences can be organized in many categories or schemata. These mental arrangements are abstract networks of knowledge, information, and experiences. Each person's schemata are highly personal and intricately related to form an organizational structure for personal experiences and understandings. Schemata can change and grow to accommodate new information. As learning occurs, the categories within a schema are modified and new categories are built to form additional schemata within a more general schema.

The most efficient reading occurs when the schemata established in a reader's mind match the organization of the reading material. When stored knowledge relates to new information, readers can use both their schemata and the incoming information to predict language, organization, and ideas and to form hypotheses about the text. Then they read to confirm, discount, and revise their theories (Adams and Collins, 1986). These expectations about text, which increase comprehension, are discussed in the following paragraphs.

Schemata Types and Relationships

What is the basis of content schemata?

Content schemata involve knowledge of the world, which makes them extremely important for comprehension. One has only to reflect on the contrast in a sports-loving student's comprehension of the sports section of the newspaper with his or her understanding of a chapter of social studies to understand the significant role schemata play in comprehension. This student uses schemata developed from years of experience for a context, or frame of reference, just as a home economics student who has had baby-sitting experiences with younger brothers and sisters has a context for understanding a child development text.

How are content schemata different from textual schemata?

Textual schemata are based on readers' knowledge of and experience with different forms of written discourse. Using knowledge of the structural characteristics of written content enables readers to anticipate, follow, and organize reading content. Prior knowledge enables students to find information within a text and to extract that information, thus increasing comprehension (Symons and Pressley, 1993). For example, "we expect a newspaper article to have a special form, and that form is quite different from a research article" (Bowman, 1981). In a well-written research article, mature readers know where to find the parts of the study, such as the review of literature. They expect the essential information in a newspaper article to come in the first sentence. Structural knowledge like this creates links to future literary experiences.

What is the technical term for links built from one text to another?

Intertextuality is concerned with the links between the ideas gleaned from one text and those discovered in another text. Gradually, readers build a complex series of connections among the texts they have read (Carrney, 1990). Hartman (1992) says that "readers build a mosaic of intersecting texts." This mosaic greatly influences their comprehension. Research reveals that readers generate links between ideas, events, and people, although they may use these textual cues in different ways. Readers use links within a given passage as well as links between different passages. They also use textual resources such as films, videos, class lectures, conversations, and books (Hartman, 1992). Because of the impact of intertextual links, comprehension can be facilitated when reading builds on text materials that can be the source of intertextual links.

Building Schemata

Teachers can help students build the schemata that will facilitate comprehension in a variety of ways. Activities such as discussion, drama, storytelling, oral reading of all types of literature, viewing television shows and films, examining models, and participating in simulations develop schemata for content reading (Dole et al., 1991). Preteaching vocabulary, which was discussed in Chapter 3, increases background experience and conceptual development. Reading aloud to secondary students builds interest, knowledge, textual schemata, multicultural schemata, and so on. Reading aloud stories and legends like *The Corn Woman* (Vigil, 1994) develops schemata for the Hispanic Southwest with stories that secondary students enjoy. Reading aloud *Prophecy Rock* (MacGregor, 1995) expands students' schemata for Native American life. In an eleventh-grade American literature course, teachers used folklore and family sayings like those found in Benjamin Franklin's *Autobiography* and *Poor Richard's Almanac* to develop students' schemata for the United States colonial period. Then these students sought personal family materials such as letters, diaries, and photographs to build a sense of history (Renner and Carter, 1992). All of these experiences have the potential for developing students' schemata.

Langer (1981) developed the PreReading Plan (PreP), which is a strategy for assessing and developing prior knowledge. This strategy is more fully explained in Chapter 13.

Activating Schemata

Readers do not automatically *activate schemata;* however, teachers can guide them to retrieve existing knowledge related to a specific subject and/or story or text structure. When students activate appropriate schemata, they can anticipate the author's ideas and information and make inferences about content (filling in missing ideas and information), because an author cannot concretely explain all of his or her ideas. Activating schemata may be as simple as posing questions or developing vocabulary as explained in Chapter 3.

What is the function of reading guides?

What is a preview guide?

Many of the strategies and activities in this chapter are designed for activating students' schemata. For example, **reading guides,** especially **preview guides,** can help students relate what they are about to read to their own experiential backgrounds. In its simplest form, the preview guide may be a request to, for example, "list everything you already know about word processing," but it is likely to be more structured. Another style of preview guide provides students with a list of statements to review and respond to before reading; after completing the assignment, students return to the guide to verify their prior identification of the statements that are substantiated by the reading. Students may also be asked to revise statements that were proved wrong by the reading and to put question marks beside items that were not addressed by the reading. All three types of items are appropriate for class discussion; for instance, teachers can ask students to respond to items before reading and have them check their answers after reading. The highly structured preview guides are often called anticipation guides. An example is shown in Example 4.1.

■ ■ ■ EXAMPLE 4.1   *Preview Guide*

Directions: Before you read the chapter, respond to the following statements by placing a check mark beside those statements that you think will be supported by the material in the chapter. After you finish reading the chapter, check the accuracy of your responses.

1. Reference sources made available by computer technology include the Internet and CD-ROMs.

2. CD-ROMs are useful only for games.

3. A CD-ROM can hold large amounts of information.

4. A CD-ROM can store text material and sound, but it cannot store video information containing motion.

5. To use a CD-ROM, your computer must be connected to the Internet.

6. Material found on the Internet has been carefully checked by authorities, and is certified to be true.

7. Using a "search engine" is a good way to search for material on the Internet.

8. Computers connected to the Internet that hold information available to Internet users are called "servers."

9. Since Internet "addresses" are all permanent, if you find an Internet address in a textbook, you can be sure it will connect you to a server that has the material described in the textbook.
10. Since the information available through the Internet is stored on only a few computers, it is likely that all the information you need for a report will be on one server.

The Contexts of Reading Comprehension

What are the three types of context for reading comprehension?

Separating comprehension from the contextual factors influencing it is impossible (Irwin, 1991). The **contexts of reading comprehension** include the individual reader's characteristics (*reader context*), the total situation (*situational context,* e.g., audience, purpose, importance to reader), and the text being read (*text context*), all of which affect the process. These components and their relationships are illustrated in Figure 4.2.

FIGURE 4.2

The Major Components of Comprehension

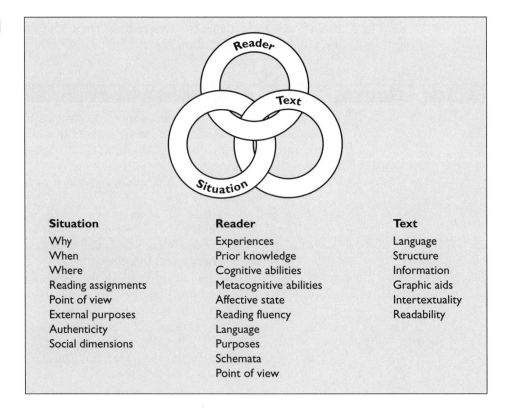

Situation	Reader	Text
Why	Experiences	Language
When	Prior knowledge	Structure
Where	Cognitive abilities	Information
Reading assignments	Metacognitive abilities	Graphic aids
Point of view	Affective state	Intertextuality
External purposes	Reading fluency	Readability
Authenticity	Language	
Social dimensions	Purposes	
	Schemata	
	Point of view	

To ensure effective comprehension, teachers need to make students aware of the situational context. Part of preparing students to read is to examine why, when, and where they are reading (Irwin, 1991). Students need to understand the purpose for reading and how to read for that purpose; according to research, many students comprehend better when they know the objectives of their reading (Irwin, 1991). The social, emotional, and physical environments during reading should facilitate comprehension.

Both the situational context and the text context are discussed later in this chapter.

■ The Reader's Context

The *reader's context* is composed of his or her attitudes, interests, purposes, predictions, prior knowledge, and skills. When content makes sense, readers actively engage in the reading process because they have some ownership of the activity (Langer and Applebee, 1987). Adolescents need to understand the relationship between what they do during reading and writing in school and what they do when reading and writing outside of school. When they understand this relationship and the relevance of reading to their lives becomes clearer, they will invest greater energy and will increase comprehension (Adams, Gullotta, and Markstrom-Adams, 1994).

Students become more active comprehenders when they have opportunities to make choices about their reading (Hansen, 1986). Teachers can give students options in choosing reading materials, scheduling reading, purposes for reading, amount of time for reading, and when and where they will share the results of their reading. The following "Meeting the Challenge" vignette illustrates how one teacher created relevant reading experiences with student options in a tenth-grade science class.

MEETING THE CHALLENGE

Steve Hargraves teaches science to tenth-, eleventh-, and twelfth-grade students using state-adopted textbooks that were selected to develop the competencies mandated by the state-adopted curriculum. He initiated the year's work by giving the students a list of the units of study they were expected to complete during the school year. Then he gave the students letters from the preceding class. These letters described the activities of the class and each student's favorite unit of study. Then the current students ranked the units as "1—very important and interesting to me"; "2—average interest and average importance to me"; and "3—little or no importance or interest to me." A portion of the ranking list looked like this:

Introduction to Earth _____
The Water Cycle _____
The Rock Cycle _____
Earth's Biography _____
Plate Tectonics _____

After the ranking, the class was divided into focus units to identify the first unit of study for the year. A recent class chose to study earthquakes, which was Unit 13 in the text and would have come at the end of the school year. But the students were very interested because many of them had just experienced an earthquake and had many concerns and questions about earthquakes. They had not realized that their community rested on a major fault and that a major earthquake had been predicted for their geographic area sometime during the next hundred years. They had read in the newspaper that their parents' homeowners insurance would probably not pay for earthquake damages.

After identifying the first unit, the teacher and students identified the questions they wished to study, the ways they wished to study those questions, and the way they wanted to present their knowledge. The students divided themselves into study groups to pursue the various questions.

Of course, incidents such as an earthquake do not occur every year for every class, but many teachers keep files of materials from newspapers, magazines, and life experiences to help students see the relevance of reading tasks to their lives.

Students may be allowed to confer and choose the order in which units are studied during the year. (© Elizabeth Crews/The Image Works)

Metacognition

Metacognition refers to the knowledge and control students have over their own thinking and learning activities (Baker and Brown, 1984; Nolan, 1991). Metacognition involves two components: (1) an awareness of the skills, strategies, and resources needed to perform a task effectively, and (2) the ability to use self-regulatory mechanisms to ensure the successful completion of the task, such as checking the outcome of attempts to solve a problem, planning the next move, or evaluating the effectiveness of attempted actions (Baker and Brown, 1984).

What is the technical term for self-monitoring?

Metacognition (metacomprehension) functions when students realize whether they do or do not understand what they are reading (*self-monitoring*) and know how to correct lapses in understanding. When students are conscious of their own thinking and comprehension, they can try different strategies if comprehension breaks down. Students who have well-developed metacognitive skills are more likely to be independent readers.

Research shows that skilled comprehenders are aware of different purposes for reading and of ways of adjusting their own knowledge to the demands of the task; they monitor their comprehension and implement corrective strategies when it fails (Baker and Brown, 1984). On the other hand, unskilled readers seem unaware that they have failed to understand material they read (Paris and Myers, 1981). Apparently, they read assignments but do not reflect on their understanding of the text. The metacognitive process is illustrated in the following example.

> Molly Rose, a secondary school student, read a selection in her mathematics text that introduced sampling, which she needed to understand as a basis for statistical analysis. She formulated questions to ascertain whether she had achieved her purpose. Answering these questions helped her realize that she understood the overall process of sampling but could not define the terms *variance*, *population*, and *population parameter*. She recognized that she needed to reread specific portions of the text to locate and study the important terms.

Students need instructional strategies to increase their understanding of their own cognitive processes, as well as ways of remedying comprehension failures. Teachers can demonstrate metacognition by modeling with content from their own subject areas. (This is discussed later in this chapter.)

Heller (1986) suggests using an exercise like that given in Example 4.2, which is based on social science content. The students fill in the topic, purpose, and section A before reading a selection. They complete sections B and C and the Answer to Purpose Question after reading the selection.

■ ■ ■ EXAMPLE 4.2   *Social Science Guide*

Topic: Imperialism
Purpose Question: How does imperialism relate to me?

A What I already knew	B What I now know	C What I don't know
Imperialism is extending power. Britain is an imperialist country.	Power can be extended through economic, military, and political means. U.S. used "dollar diplomacy" in Latin America.	Other countries that U.S. practices imperialism on. Does imperialism cause war? Is imperialism good or bad?

Answer to Purpose Question: The U.S. practices imperialism and sends U.S. tax money to Latin America.

What is an example of self-questioning?

A number of researchers have demonstrated the value of **self-questioning** as a means of encouraging active reading, and they have shown that students can learn to control their own thought processes by employing this technique (Andre and Anderson, 1978; Palincsar and Brown, 1986; Nolan, 1991). Self-questioning can be initiated with questions such as "What is the main idea in this paragraph (selection)?" and "Is there anything I don't understand in this paragraph?" Teachers can teach students about the different types of questions (literal, inferential, critical, and creative) and have them work individually or in pairs to generate questions related to their readings. (See Chapter 5 for additional discussion of questions or more information about question types.)

An exercise like that in Example 4.3 is useful in guiding students to generate questions, after they are given instruction on question types.

■ ■ ■ ■ EXAMPLE 4. 3   *Guide for Generating Questions*

Directions: Read the assigned selection, then write a question about the selection at each level indicated and answer the remaining questions.
1. Literal question:
2. Inferential question:
3. Evaluative question:
4. Creative question:
5. Give an example of the concept presented:
6. What is the main idea of the selection?
7. List the things that you do not understand:

■ The Textual Context

Why are well-organized paragraphs easier to comprehend?

The quality of a text is important in the comprehension of both fiction and non-fiction (Fitzgerald and Spiegel, 1983; Buss, Ratliff, and Irion, 1985; Berkovitz, 1986). Research shows that both **text organization** and **text coherence** contribute to comprehension (Beck et al., 1991). In one research study, Beck and others (1991) found that content and content presentation in social studies texts determined whether or not readers developed coherent representations of historical periods and historical topics. The researchers identified two major flaws in the content and content presentation of these texts. First, the texts assumed that the students had a greater variety and depth of prior knowledge than was actually evidenced, providing an excellent argument for developing schemata in preparation for reading.

How can authors create coherence?

Second, the presentation was less than coherent. **Coherence** refers to the clear presentation of material, which can facilitate comprehension. Organization of text can help students follow the ideas presented without getting lost. Beck and others (1991) found that the texts tended to present many facts with little explanation. This situation makes it difficult for readers to adjust their thinking to the organization of the selection and to follow the author's line of thought. Well-developed paragraphs are easier to understand, because each of them focuses on a single major topic, and a logical sequence of sentences is used in the structure. The sentences have coherence; they are related to the paragraph topic and to one another. In contrast, a poorly organized paragraph does not establish a focus, and the sentences frequently are not related to one another and are not presented in a logical order.

The following are examples of a well-developed paragraph and a poorly developed paragraph.

Paragraph A: Flowers bloom throughout the world. They grow on high mountains at the edges of the snow. Other flowers grow in the shallow parts of oceans. Even hot, dry deserts have bright blossoms. The only places where flowers do not grow are on the ice-covered areas of the Arctic and Antarctic and the open seas.

Paragraph B: Flowers are the reproductive parts of flowering plants. Flowers bloom throughout the world. They grow on high mountains and in the oceans. Many flowers have a smell that attracts birds and insects. Flowers bloom in the hot, dry desert during the rainy season. The only places flowers do not grow are the Arctic, the Antarctic, and the open seas.

If you identified Paragraph A as the well-developed paragraph, which is easier to understand, you are correct. Notice that this paragraph sticks to the subject—the fact that flowers grow throughout the world. The ideas are presented in a logical order, and the sentences have coherence. No loosely related ideas are introduced to divert the reader's attention. On the other hand, Paragraph B does not have a clear focus because botany and geography are mixed. The sentences are not cohesive.

Critics of textbook writing also suggest that good writing with active verbs, vivid anecdotes, lively quotations, and other literary devices contribute to readers' interest and recall (Wade and Adams, 1990; Wade et al., 1993). Moreover, the quality of readers' recall for main ideas and interesting details increases when the text includes a greater number of interesting, memorable details (Wade et al., 1993). These factors seem to make texts more readable.

Readability

What term is synonymous with reading difficulty?

Giving students reading materials they can comprehend is fundamental to developing comprehension. **Text readability** refers to the reading difficulty of materials.

Even if the readability of textbooks is appropriate for the intended grade placement, many students in the grade will not learn from them. Ninth-grade students read anywhere from one to five (and possibly more) grades *below* or *above their ninth-grade placement.* Teachers are then faced with the question of how to present the material to their students in a way that will help them learn. Students reading below grade level may need alternate materials that are easier to read. A textbook may be adequate for teaching subject-matter concepts to better students, but it may seem elementary to them, so the teacher needs to locate challenging supplementary materials. Because secondary teachers frequently use textbooks for homework assignments and expect students to read complete textbooks, matching the assigned materials to students' reading abilities is particularly important (Davey, 1988).

Readability formulas are used to measure the readability of printed materials. Most of these formulas measure vocabulary and sentence difficulty. These formulas are presented and discussed in Chapter 13.

Considerate Text

Effective readers use a variety of strategies and processes to construct text meaning. They understand the components and patterns of text structure, such as paragraphs, main ideas, and story grammar. The initial sections of this chapter addressed the current emphasis on the reader's active role in comprehension. However, to read actively and responsibly, students also must understand the nature of **considerate** and **inconsiderate** text, so that they can compensate for text limitations.

What makes a text considerate or inconsiderate?

Five characteristics account for the ease or difficulty a student is likely to encounter when reading a text:

1. Organization and structure
2. Whether the text addresses one concept at a time or tries to explain several at once
3. The clarity and coherence of the explanations
4. Whether the text is appropriate for the students' reading levels and the purpose
5. Whether the information is accurate and consistent (Armbruster and Anderson, 1981)

Organizational Patterns

Students who recognize the various patterns of text structure perform better on recall, summarization, and other comprehension tasks than readers who do not

(Shannon, 1986; Sinatra, 1991). Since *text structures* are organizational frameworks, students can learn to identify them and they will have a predictable means to interpret explanatory discourse (Sinatra, 1991). The common organizational patterns found in content textbooks and nonfiction and informational writing are illustrated in the following paragraphs.

What are five common organizational patterns found in textbooks?

1. Sequential or chronological order: Paragraphs in sequential or chronological order present information in the order of its occurrence to clarify the ideas presented, as illustrated in the following example. Readers can use time or sequential order patterns to organize and remember this information. These words may signal this text organization: *after, before, begin, beyond, during, first, finally, next, now, second, then, third, until,* and *when.*

> *The Federalist Party disappears.* During Jefferson's administrations the Republican Party grew stronger. The Republicans elected the next two Presidents—James Madison, who served from 1809 to 1817, and James Monroe, who was President from 1817 to 1825. During these years, on the other hand, the Federalist Party became weaker and weaker. Finally, in Monroe's first term, it disappeared, and Monroe was re-elected without opposition. (Wilder et al., 1982)

2. Comparison and contrast. Authors use comparison and contrast to clarify certain points. Questions like the following may help readers to understand this structure: What is the author's main idea? What similarities and/or differences does he or she use to illustrate the point? Student-constructed tables that list similarities and differences also enhance understanding. Some words that may signal the use of this pattern are *although, but, yet, nevertheless, meanwhile, however, on the other hand, otherwise, compared to, despite,* and *similarly.* The next paragraph illustrates the comparison and contrast pattern.

> Some individual health policies are filled with loopholes. The average individual health policy pays out only about 50 per cent of the premiums in benefits—compared to 90 per cent for group insurance plans. Sales commissions, other costs, and profits eat up the remainder of the premiums of individual plans. (Morton and Renzy, 1978)

3. Cause and effect: Authors use this pattern to explain relationships among facts and ideas. Readers need to identify stated and implied causes and their related effects. The following words may signal the use of cause and effect: forms of the verb *cause* or *because, since, so that, thus, therefore, if, consequently,* and *as a result.* An example of a cause-and-effect paragraph follows.

> When your body produces an antibody in response to an invading pathogen, the antibody protects you against a disease. It works for your benefit. Antibodies can also be produced in response to other materials such as pollen, the yellow powder produced by the male reproductive organs of some plants. If you have an **allergy,** your body is extra sensitive to certain substances. It works against you. Antibodies react with the pollen, dust, or other substance. A

chemical called **histamine** (HIS tuh meen) is produced. Histamine causes the symptoms of allergy, including sneezing, coughing, and itching. (Rosenberg, Gurney, and Harlin, 1978)

4. Definition or explanation: This pattern explains a concept or defines terms that are essential to understanding in many content areas. An example of a definition or explanation pattern follows.

Gravitational force pulls together masses of gas and dust into clouds in many places in space. **Gravitational force** is the attraction that pulls things toward one another. You experience gravitation every day. Because of it, your pencil falls to the floor when you let it go. Gravitation brings a pole-vaulter back to Earth and makes it hard for you to learn to ride a bike. (Jackson and Evans, 1980)

5. Enumeration or simple listing pattern: Paragraphs in this pattern list items of information (such as facts or ideas), either in order of importance or simply in logical order. Clues to this pattern are the words *one, two, first, second, third, to begin, next, finally, most important, when, also, too,* and *then.* An example follows.

Chemical energy is a stored form of energy. Fuels such as coal, oil, and natural gas have chemical energy. When they are burned, the energy is released as heat and light. Batteries also have chemical energy. Cars, portable radios, and other battery-operated devices convert chemical energy to electric energy. Food, too, has stored energy. Your body changes the chemical energy in food to heat and mechanical energy. (Hill and May, 1981)

Instructional Activities for Teaching Organizational Patterns

Instruction should focus on a communication approach and involve speaking, listening, reading, and writing (Sinatra, 1991). The focus of instruction should be the actual texts and materials that students have to read. Strategies for teaching text structure include use of preview guides, graphic organizers (also called visual organizers), and questions. Pattern guides are strategies that can focus on the organizational pattern of the text. If a text is organized according to a cause-and-effect pattern, for example, the guide would highlight causes and effects. Some possible focuses for pattern guides other than cause and effect are sequence, comparison/contrast, and categorization. A pattern guide activates a reader's schema for the particular organizational patterns frequently found in various subject areas. Example 4.4 is a comparison/contrast guide for a selection from a biology text.

■ ■ ■ EXAMPLE 4.4   *Comparison/Contrast Guide*

Directions: Read the selection about flowers and animal pollinators and then fill in the chart below to help you compare and contrast flowers pollinated by bees and moths with flowers pollinated by birds.

Flowers Pollinated by Birds	Flowers Pollinated by Bees	Flowers Pollinated by Moths
Usually red or yellow		
Petals fused into a		
long tube that holds		
nectar		

Flowers and Animal Pollinators: Made for Each Other

With rapidly beating wings the hummingbird hovers over the flower. Its long bill plunges deep inside the flower to gather the sweet nectar. As the bird flies away, its head is covered with a dusting of pollen from the flower's stamens. When the hummingbird visits the next flower, the pollen on its head will be brushed off to pollinate the flower.

Because flowering plants cannot move about as animals do to accomplish fertilization, they rely on other means of transferring pollen. Many flowers are pollinated by birds or insects. Scientists are taking an interest in studying the amazing adaptations of flowers that allow certain animals to pollinate them.

Birds have a poor sense of smell, but have excellent vision. So bird-pollinated flowers rely on color to attract their pollinators. Birds' eyes are most sensitive to the red end of the spectrum, so bird-pollinated flowers are usually red or yellow. Bird-pollinated flowers include hibiscus, red columbine, and fuchsia. Bird-flower petals are usually fused into a long tube that holds large quantities of nectar. When a bird inserts its long bill to reach the nectar, pollen is brushed off the stamens onto its head or breast.

Bee-pollinated flowers are usually brightly colored blue or yellow since bees' vision is most sensitive to this end of the spectrum. Bee-pollinated flowers also give off a sweet scent since bees are attracted to sweet or minty odors. Bee-pollinated flowers are usually open only during the day when bees are flying. Many bee-pollinated flowers have at least one protruding petal that serves as a landing platform for the bees. The nectar is usually hidden deep in the flower, but many flowers have *nectar guides* that point the way to the nectar. In violets and irises the nectar guide is a series of lines; in Turk's-cap lilies it is a cluster of spots in the center of the flower. Petunias and morning glories have a starshaped pattern that surrounds the nectar opening.

But some nectar guides are not visible to humans. Bees can see them because their eyes are sensitive to ultraviolet light. To the human eye the marsh marigold flower appears solid yellow. But to the bee, only the center of the flower appears yellow. The outer part of the flower reflects a mixture of yellow and ultraviolet light called *bee purple.*

Moth-pollinated flowers are generally white or pale yellow, and are easily visible at dusk or night when moths are most active. Many moth flowers are open only during late afternoon or evening. Moth flowers have a strong, sweet scent and include orchids, evening primroses, and night-blooming cactuses. Since moths hover while feeding, moth-pollinated flowers do not have landing platforms.

The relationship between flowers and their animal pollinators is beneficial to both organisms. The animals secure food and the flowers get pollinated. Many scientists think that flowers and their animal pollinators coevolved to suit each other's needs.

Source: From SCOTT, FORESMAN BIOLOGY by Irwin L. Slesnick et al. Copyright © 1985 by Scott, Foresman and Company. Reprinted by permission.

Graphic, or visual, organizers and structured overviews (Barron, 1969) are graphic arrangements of terms that apply to the important concepts in a reading selection. They represent different kinds of thinking processes and text organizations that can be applied to listening, reading, and writing. These strategies also develop readiness for reading and writing. They help students to see what they are thinking and/or trying to understand. (See Chapter 3 for more on graphic organizers.) Clarke (1991) recommends the following four questions as guides for developing graphic organizers:

1. As I look at this content, what central facts, ideas, arguments, processes, or procedures do I want students to comprehend? (This is related to purpose and/or objectives).
2. What pattern or organization holds the material together and makes it meaningful?
3. What kind of visual organizer will show students how to think their way through the content?
4. What problems or challenges can I pose that will force students to work through the steps of a thinking process?

Teachers can use these questions as they prepare graphic organizers for students to complete. The graphic organizers and questions in Figure 4.3 can be

FIGURE 4.3

FIGURE 4.3

Graphic Organizers
for Thinkers

Items Compared	# A	# B
1st attribute		
2nd attribute		
3rd attribute		
4th attribute		

Guiding Questions

1. What is compared?
2. Why are these items compared?
3. What is the author's conclusion?
4. What is your conclusion?
   (Do you accept the author's
   conclusion? Why?)

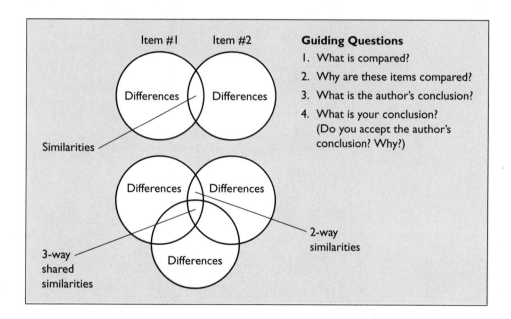

Guiding Questions

1. What is compared?
2. Why are these items compared?
3. What is the author's conclusion?
4. What is your conclusion?
   (Do you accept the author's
   conclusion? Why?)

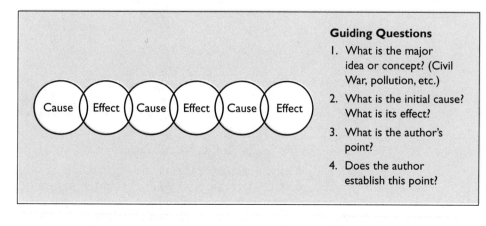

Guiding Questions

1. What is the major
   idea or concept? (Civil
   War, pollution, etc.)
2. What is the initial cause?
   What is its effect?
3. What is the author's
   point?
4. Does the author
   establish this point?

FIGURE 4.3

Graphic Organizers
for Thinkers
(cont'd)

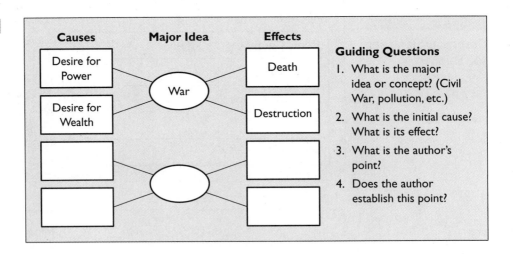

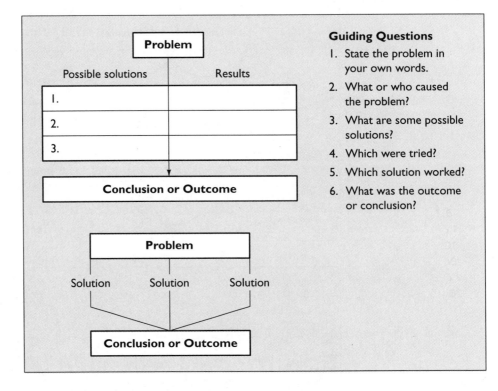

applied to most content area materials, and they are effective for main ideas and details, which are major tools for structuring information and knowledge. The questions in Figure 4.3 will help students apprehend the author's intended message (Jacobowitz, 1990).

Students can use computer graphics to create their own graphics to show their thinking and/or text organization. Our experiences indicate that students can be very creative when formulating their own graphic organizers. Student-created graphics are usually prepared as a follow-up or summary of reading content.

Wolfe and Lopez (1992/1993) suggest that the teacher develop overviews on overhead transparencies as the students watch each step and discuss it. They also suggest developing some overviews on sentence strips on bulletin boards before students work in small groups, and then individually, to develop overviews for their reading assignments. Example 4.5 shows a sample structured overview in the area of atomic structure.

■ ■ ■ EXAMPLE 4.5   *Structured Overview*

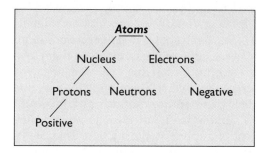

Main Ideas and Details

Why are main ideas and details so important in content reading? How are details related to main ideas?

The writing in most content area materials is structured around **details** and **main ideas;** therefore teaching students to identify the main ideas of paragraphs and entire selections is a high priority in reading programs. The main idea of a paragraph is the big idea that the author develops and supports with details throughout the paragraph. **Details** are the smaller pieces of information or ideas that are used to support this idea. *Main idea* is not a single concept; it is an umbrella term that encompasses nine specific types of important ideas (Cunningham and Moore, 1986). These types address important ideas explained in informational text, so nonfiction and content text are the appropriate content for teaching them. The nine types of main ideas are

1. Gist
2. Interpretation
3. Key word
4. Selective summary/selective diagram
5. Theme

6. Title
7. Topic issue
8. Topic sentence/thesis sentence
9. Other (unclassified responses)

Main ideas are interrelated with organizational patterns because they can be expressed in patterns such as cause and effect, contrast, sequential order, enumeration, and explanation. For example, a paragraph in a cause-and-effect pattern has a main idea and supporting details that are expressed through this pattern. The main idea of such a paragraph could be "causes and effects of erosion." The details are the specific causes and effects. Similarly, in a paragraph written with a comparison and contrast pattern, the details might be the contrasting points and the main idea the overall comparison (Palincsar and Brown, 1986).

Teachers need to go beyond simply presenting instructional strategies and *show* students how to identify main ideas and details (Reinking, Mealey, and Ridgeway, 1993). Research shows that instructions requiring students to generate the main idea of a selection or paragraph lead them to recall and understand content better than simply identifying the main idea from multiple-choice items (Taylor and Berkowitz, 1980). Therefore, students should practice writing the main idea in their own words. Palincsar and Brown (1984) found that students who learned to summarize main ideas improved their ability to answer questions and to identify important information. They also need to identify and write both stated and unstated (implied) main ideas. The telegram strategy described in the next section is useful for teaching students to identify important details that develop and support the main idea. Some authors include details that are interesting but that do not elaborate the main idea.

Main Idea and Detail Activities

Activities such as the following give students help with and practice in identifying and stating main ideas and supporting details.

1. Have students locate key words in sentences to find important details. Composing telegrams helps students focus on key words, usually nouns and verbs. The message "Mother has had a heart attack and is very ill. Please hurry home," could result in this telegram "Mother ill. Hurry home." Telegram activities can be developed with sentences selected from content textbooks.
2. Expand the activity for locating key words in sentences to finding the key words in a paragraph. After identifying the key words, students find the larger idea they point to. Readers should sum up the relationships among the key words and select the sentence that best states the main idea. If no

one sentence sums up the main idea (some main ideas are implied), students compose it. The key words are underlined in the following paragraph.

A <u>dog</u> is a <u>useful</u> animal. It <u>guards</u> our <u>homes</u> from burglars and <u>alerts</u> us when <u>guests</u> are coming. The dog will <u>warn</u> members of the <u>household</u> if <u>fire</u> breaks out in the home. Some dogs serve as <u>seeing-eye</u> dogs for <u>blind</u> people. Perhaps most important of all, dogs are loyal, loving <u>companions</u> who provide many hours of <u>pleasure</u> for their owners and families.

The main idea of this paragraph is the first sentence, "A dog is a useful animal." The key words of each sentence clearly point to this idea.

3. Have students use categorization activities to separate important from unimportant details. For instance, students can write down the details they have identified in a paragraph and categorize them as either important or unimportant to communication of the main idea. Having students state reasons that they classified details into either of these categories permits the teacher to clear up any misconceptions about the points the author stressed.

Important Details	Unimportant Details

4. Model the procedure of finding main ideas for students before asking them to locate main ideas themselves. See the examples of modeling that are included in this chapter.
5. Have students ask themselves: What is this sentence or paragraph about? What do most of the key words seem to point to? What words occur most frequently? What do these frequently occurring words relate to? What idea is related to most of the supporting details? What sentence would best summarize the frequently occurring ideas? Is the main idea stated or implied? Where is the main idea located in the paragraph (at the beginning, in the middle, or at the end)?
6. Teach students to look for words and phrases that often indicate the main idea, for instance, *first, last, the most important factor, the significant fact.*
7. Prepare blank diagrams on which students can place main ideas and supporting ideas. Following are two examples: the first example is a generic diagram; the second is a diagram developed for the following paragraph.

A mutation is a change in a gene, which is the part of the cell that determines the inherited characteristics of the offspring. The changed gene is then passed on to succeeding generations. Some mutations produce only a slight change in the offspring, whereas others produce more drastic changes.

Main Idea		A mutation is a change in a gene
Detail #1		inherited characteristic
Detail #2		passed to offspring
Detail #3		slight change
Detail #4		drastic change

8. Have students create their own diagrams for main ideas and supporting details.

9. Encourage students to write, in their own words, concise statements of main ideas.

Selection Organization

Selections are longer units of discourse composed of series of paragraphs. In content reading, we are concerned largely with expository discourse. The organizational patterns presented earlier in this chapter (sequential, comparison and contrast, cause and effect, definition or explanation, and enumeration) are found in many selections, and they are frequently combined in structuring discourse. When these patterns are identified in longer selections, they can be interpreted in the same ways as in paragraphs. However, these common patterns become parts of a macrostructure in longer discourse.

Well-written expository content—such as a content textbook chapter—begins with an *introductory section,* which previews the subject. This introduction can be compared to an inverted triangle, because it starts with a broad, general idea of the topic and narrows the topic to a more specific point. This section may be developed in a variety of ways, such as comparison and cause and effect.

The second part of a selection is the *body,* which develops the ideas that have been stated in the introduction. Each of the paragraphs that make up the body usually has a main idea and details that relate to the topic presented in the introductory section. These paragraphs may be developed through any organizational pattern the author chooses.

The chapter or selection usually concludes with a *summary paragraph* that pulls together the ideas presented in the body. A triangle can be used to illustrate this section, which begins with a specific idea and broadens and becomes more general as it develops. The pattern of the summary is the reverse of that of the introductory section. A diagram of a selection based on this pattern is shown in Figure 4.4. Content teachers can illustrate organizational patterns with the table of contents, which is discussed in Chapter 6. Textbook headings, which are helpful in understanding, remembering, and locating information, are widely used in content textbooks and nonfiction trade books (Grant, 1993).

Story Grammars. In the preceding sections we examined the common structures found in expository and descriptive text. Now consider the structural elements of narrative texts. Structure is in some ways a container for communicating a story. In a story, there are plots, characters, problems or conflicts, and

FIGURE 4.4

Diagram of a Selection

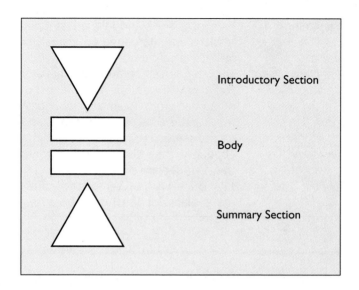

Introductory Section

Body

Summary Section

What is a synonym for story structure?

themes that revolve around characters' goals and actions. **Story structure,** or **story grammar** (*grammar* means structure), is a mental representation of the parts of a typical story and the relationships among those parts (Mandler and Johnson, 1977).

Students can identify the important elements in stories and relate these elements to one another through mapping them. Our discussion is based on the six major story elements posited by Mandler and Johnson (1977). These elements are *setting, beginning, reaction, attempt, outcome,* and *ending.* The *setting* introduces the main character and the time and place. A precipitating or initiating event occurs in the *beginning,* and the main character's response to the precipitating event is identified as the *reaction. Attempt* is concerned with the main character's efforts to attain his or her goal. The success or failure of the attempt is identified in the *outcome.* The *ending,* the last component of story structure, is the long-range consequence of the action, the final response of a character, or an emphatic statement. A story may be composed of one story grammar, or it may include a series of story grammars. In an episodic story, each episode has a story grammar. Example 4.6 shows the story grammar for the novel *The Goats,* by Brock Cole, for adolescents.

■ ■ ■ EXAMPLE 4.6   *Story Grammar*

The Goats *by Brock Cole*

Setting	A small island and the area near two summer camps—one a boys' camp and the other a girls' camp. Bryce, a camper in the boys' camp, and Julie, a camper in the girls' camp.

Beginning	As a joke, Bryce and Julie are stripped of their clothes and possessions and marooned on a small island for the night by their respective campmates.
Reaction	They join forces because they are alone and scared.
Attempt	Together they escape the island but decide that they're not going back to the camp. They find the world is dangerous and they run because no place is safe, and things are never going to be the same.
Outcome	Gradually, they discover how strong they are and how much they can depend on one another.
Ending	Julie discovers that her mother cares about her. She and Bryce make plans for the future because they can depend on one another.

Readers use their knowledge of fiction and nonfiction text structure to guide their expectations, understanding, recall, and production of text. When reading, listening, and writing, students use a structural outline of the major story and text components in their minds to make predictions and hypotheses about stories and information. These expectations focus students' attention on story events, help them understand the unfolding of time and sequence, and cue recall of text. When writing their own essays or analyses, students use knowledge of text structures to shape their discourse.

■ The Situational Context

Comprehension is usually specific to a situation (Tierney, 1990). For this reason, readers need a situational context for reading. Consider the difference in perspective among a physician, a pharmacist, and a patient reading a text. Readers need to adjust their point of view to fit the purpose and to activate schemata appropriate to the literacy experience. Situational context involves the *stance,* or *purposes,* readers have for reading, writing, and learning. It gives form to the literacy experience as well as the mode for expressing a response. Students actively engage with reading when they can see the usefulness and interconnectedness of knowledge.

Students need *authentic* purposes that they recognize as meaningful and connected to their lives. This context contrasts with a contrived purpose, which lacks meaning for readers. When giving students a reading assignment or an inquiry task that involves reading and writing, teachers guide them to identify a point of view or perspective that integrates the elements of situational context.

Readers may interpret a text in one way when reading for general understanding, but their interpretation changes when they apply ideas in real life because the situational context has changed. The reader's interpretation often changes after discussing a story with another student who has a different slant on a character or story incident. Research indicates that students' understanding appears to change over time, with readers relating ideas to a larger context and focusing on bigger ideas rather than the details that captured their interest initially (Stoodt and Amspaugh, 1994). It appears that considering various points of view and various connections among ideas helps students organize main ideas and recognize their importance relative to details. Content teachers may need to clarify purposes for students. They can give prereading questions with the instruction to "read to answer these questions." Teachers can preview the text with students, telling them what they should learn from each section. They will also want to know what will be expected of them after reading, such as an application activity, a writing activity, or a reading activity.

When students are involved in self-directed reading tasks, they need to learn how to control these situational factors for themselves. They can use the classroom model to guide their own reading. Example 4.7 shows a Point-of-View Guide for U.S. History that will help students comprehend various points of view.

■■■■ EXAMPLE 4.7   *Point-of-View Guide for U.S. History*

The New Nationalism

A Spirit of Nationalism (pp. 199–200)

1. As an average citizen of the United States in 1815, tell how you feel about your country and about being an American.
2. As a basic believer in states' rights, tell how you feel about the Supreme Court decisions in 1803, 1809, and 1824.

A Nationalist Foreign Policy (pp. 200–201)

As a member of the Monroe administration:
1. What is your reaction to General Andrew Jackson's invasion of Florida in 1818?
2. How do you feel about Russian colonization of the Pacific Northwest?
3. What effect do you think the Monroe Doctrine will have on the United States?

(Guide prepared for sections from History of the United States *by Thomas V. DiBacco, Lorna C. Mason, and Christian G. Appy. Boston: Houghton Mifflin, 1993).*

A situational context may address real-life or simulated circumstances that focus students' comprehension (Tierney, 1990). The contexts build students' motivation, curiosity, and insight because they need literacy skills to acquire information or skills to solve problems that have meaning for them. A simulated situational context for social studies could provide a student with the context of an individual who was elected to the House of Representatives. As a woman and parent of three children, she has a particular perspective. She needs to understand government, law, and the economic impact of various proposals as she debates issues.

The role of situation-based comprehension and its relationship to real-life learning will be further discussed in Chapter 5.

Summary

Successful comprehension is based on factors within the reader, the text, and the reading context or situation. Readers employ background experience, knowledge, schemata, vocabulary, metacognition, and higher-order thinking skills to comprehend. Because readers use their individual backgrounds to understand, they often construct idiosyncratic meanings when reading identical text. Research indicates that students comprehend better when they have some degree of control in the reading situation. Teachers can address this research by giving students a chance to choose what they will read, how and when they will read, and how they will share what they have understood about the subject.

In this chapter we also explored the impact of the text on comprehension, examining the organizational patterns in nonfiction and fiction. To give students reading materials they can comprehend, teachers have to consider text readability and interest in relation to students' abilities and interests. In Chapter 5 we explore additional aspects of constructing meaning in texts and strategies for developing comprehension.

Discussion Questions

1 How could reading comprehension occur without prior knowledge?
2 What are textual schemata? How do they function in reading comprehension?
3 Compare the characteristics of active readers with those of passive readers.
4 How are reading comprehension and content reading related?
5 Why are main ideas significant in content area comprehension?
6 How is intertextuality related to reading comprehension?
7 How do you think an active reader would employ metacognition?

Enrichment Activities

1 Read an article in the local newspaper and write down all the thinking processes that you use to understand what you are reading.

2 Read a current bestseller and write a brief paragraph that paraphrases the theme (main idea) of the book. Have a classmate who has read the same book analyze your comprehension.

3 Find examples of paragraphs in content area textbooks that follow organizational patterns illustrated in this chapter. Bring these examples to class to share and discuss.

4 Use the "key word" idea to analyze several paragraphs in a content textbook.

5 Choose one of the metacognitive activities presented in this chapter and plan ways to adapt it to your content area.

Strategies for Constructing Meaning in Texts

What are three major sources of comprehension data?

The goal of reading is comprehension. Readers weigh and compare data from their **schemata,** the **text,** and the **context** in which the act occurs in order to comprehend (Lewis, 1991). Making inferences, thinking critically, and synthesizing are among the reasoning skills involved in creating a coherent representation of the text. Teachers can assist this process by asking, "What did you understand?" and "What are the grounds for your understanding?" (Lewis, 1991).

Teachers can instruct students in how to implement comprehension strategies prior to reading, while reading, and after reading. Before reading, students can preview vocabulary, build background, and set purposes for reading. While they are reading, students can pause at regular intervals to monitor their understanding, to compare new information with prior knowledge, and to integrate as they read. After reading, they may choose from such strategies as summarizing information, evaluating knowledge, and making applications of knowledge. This chapter focuses on the strategic processing of text together with the techniques (strategies) and skills used.

As you read this chapter, try to answer these questions:

1 What is the meaning of the term *strategy*?

2 What is the difference between a skill and a strategy?
3 What is an authentic reading situation or context?
4 How does a reader identify appropriate comprehension strategies to use?

■ ■ The Strategic Reader

What are strategic comprehenders?

Strategic comprehenders are skilled readers who have advanced well beyond letter-by-letter and word-by-word reading. They have overlearned reading skills so that speed and accuracy are ensured. This reading fluency permits them to reason thoughtfully and consciously about prior knowledge, the text, the context for reading, and strategies for guiding meaning construction. Readers have to learn how to use comprehension **strategies,** which are specific procedures for using skills flexibly and adaptively, depending on the situation. For instance, readers use specific skills to preview a text so that they may identify key vocabulary, anticipate important ideas, activate appropriate schemata, and establish purposes for reading.

Define strategies in your own words.

Varied strategies are necessary because comprehension is not a prescribed, linear process. Strategic readers know they must implement varied comprehension strategies to address different reading contexts and different kinds of text. They activate prior knowledge, predict, question, identify contexts, make inferences, create images, relate new knowledge to existing knowledge, use the organizational framework of the text, and accommodate new knowledge. Teachers implement authentic assignments and exercises to develop students' ability to use strategies. With consistent practice, students can become confident strategy users.

Instructional approaches for strategic reading that emphasize students' awareness of their own reading strategies, alternative strategies, choosing appropriate strategies, and self-monitoring result in sizable gains in reading comprehension (Palincsar and Brown, 1986). Students learn reading strategies and skills best when the instruction is incorporated into regular subject matter classes in the context to which they will be applied (Paris, 1985; Weinstein, 1987). **Strategy instruction** should always focus on generating meaning, and skills development should support meaning development (Kucer, 1991). To acquire and integrate most cognitive processing skills and strategies, students need guided practice and feedback (Anderson et al., 1985).

What is the focus of strategy instruction?

Teachers model and demonstrate strategies; they provide guided practice and in-depth explanations. They coach, giving students assistance and encouragement, and make cognitive skills and strategies tangible through demonstra-

What is the purpose of think alouds?

tions like "**think alouds**" (see pp. 138–140). Under the teachers' tutelage, students consciously connect preexisting knowledge with future learning. Then students gradually assume responsibility for independent, strategic comprehension (Gavelek, 1986). Virtually all of the strategies introduced in this chapter begin with teacher modeling, then move to teacher coaching, and move gradually to autonomous student work.

■ ■ Fluency

How does fluency facilitate comprehension?

Fluency is based on automaticity of skills. For example, fluent word knowledge frees readers to activate prior knowledge, to focus on the text as well as the context for reading, thus facilitating comprehension. In contrast, readers whose skills are stuck at the word-by-word level must laboriously work their way through texts, so intent on getting the words right that they overlook meaning (Lesgold, Resnick, and Hammond, 1985). The following list summarizes current knowledge and research regarding reading skills and strategies:

1. Expert learners are more likely to acquire a repertoire of strategies independently as they progress through school, whereas lower-achieving students need help to acquire strategies through specifically designed interventions.
2. Both competent readers and less able readers benefit from effective instruction.
3. Effective readers know how and when to implement appropriate strategies.
4. Readers need instruction on how to transfer skills and strategies from one reading task to other similar reading tasks (Jones et al., 1986).

How does the concept of fragmentation relate to reading instruction?

5. Currently, there is considerable controversy over the **fragmentation** of reading instruction, especially in regard to skills instruction. This does not mean that skills instruction should be abandoned (Jones et al., 1986); on the contrary, explicit instruction in some skills is necessary.

What kind of reading tasks foster active learning?

Students who are less proficient seem to learn best from skills instruction that progresses from modeling and guided practice to independent learning (Campione and Armbruster, 1985; Jones et al., 1986). Skills instruction does not preclude whole language teaching philosophies nor does it preclude using a variety of reading materials and integrated units. Education for an information age calls for active inquiry, for strategies that support problem solving and communication, and for reflective reading (Calfee, Dunlap, and Wat, 1994). **Authentic reading tasks,** discussed next, foster active learning because reading materials, projects, units, and inquiries have meaning for students.

■ ■ Authentic Reading Tasks

Reading comprehension instruction should link classroom literacy activities with real-world, authentic reading and writing experiences (Brophy, 1992). These experiences help students connect the use of print with the home or the wider culture (Kucer, 1991).

Authentic reading tasks are a major aspect of the whole language philosophy of literacy development. Thematic units are one approach to developing authentic literacy tasks that integrate the language arts, as well as other curricular areas. The integrated curriculum can be authentic and can provide learning experiences more closely attuned to the way children and adults learn (Lipson et al., 1993). **Integrated units** promote higher-order thinking, concept development, and transfer of knowledge.

What processes are promoted in integrated units? Give an example of a theme that would help students discover connections among literature selections.

Integrated units make teaching and learning meaningful by interrelating content and process. In the holistic approach, **themes** give instruction a focus, create coherence across content and process, and enable students to understand what and why they are learning. Integrated units of study help students transform knowledge into the schemata and tools for learning that will be helpful throughout their lives. Themes also provide a framework for students to discover the connections among literature selections (Roser and Hoffman, 1992). To capitalize on the merits of integrated, thematic units, teachers need to serve as mediators of comprehension strategies and skills as they guide students who are discovering the connections that are the heart of integrated instruction. The role of themes, topics, and real literature in developing literacy is discussed throughout this book, and Chapter 9 focuses on literature in content classrooms. In the following "Meeting the Challenge" vignette, the integrated unit approach to using literature in the classroom is demonstrated.

MEETING THE CHALLENGE

Kyle Richards overheard his eighth-grade students discussing a news story about skiers who had survived five days without food or shelter following an avalanche. Then another student told the group about people who survived long periods of time in collapsed buildings after an earthquake. These discussions gave him an idea for a thematic unit on survival in various environments. On the basis of the students' discussion, he thought they would recognize the authenticity of this unit. Furthermore, he could integrate it with the science and social studies curriculum. An abridged version of the unit he taught follows.

Major Concepts of the Unit

1. Many survivors do not have special skills; instead they are people who refuse to give up.
2. Many survivors are ordinary people who are thrust into extraordinary circumstances that force them to find ways to solve their problems and keep on living.
3. Survivors often have to meet basic needs such as finding food, water, shelter, and protection. People who lack basic knowledge about their environment have greater difficulties in solving their problems.
4. The sources of food, water, shelter, and protection differ with the nature of the environment. For example, a person stranded on a tropical island would face different problems from those faced by one caught in a blizzard.
5. Survivors' lives are changed by the problems they faced and overcame.

Unit Initiation

Mr. Richards asked the students to brainstorm the concept of survival as it related to newspaper articles about hurricanes, earthquakes, and floods, as well as stories about individuals who had survived environmental trauma. Then he had the students map survival situations and create individual definitions of the term *survival*. The map they created is illustrated in Figure 5.1.

Following the brainstorming and semantic mapping of survival, the class studied the book *Hatchet* by Gary Paulsen. They also read newspaper and magazine articles related to survival.

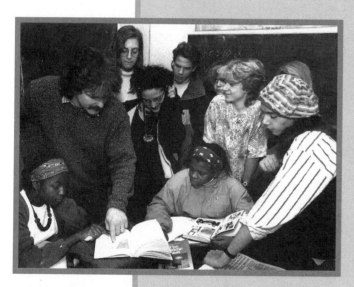

News stories may serve as the basis for thematic units.
(© Kathy McLaughlin/The Image Works)

Before Reading

1. The students identified the problems and dangers they would face if they were alone in a Canadian wilderness without assistance or equipment. They discussed the topic, and the teacher recorded their ideas on a transparency. When they finished brainstorming, they fit their ideas into categories of food, shelter, clothing, protection from animals, and so forth. They summarized these ideas in their journals and on a class chart.
2. Students were told they could choose just one piece of equipment to take into the wilderness with them. Then they wrote a paragraph or more

FIGURE 5.1

Survival Map
Created by
Students

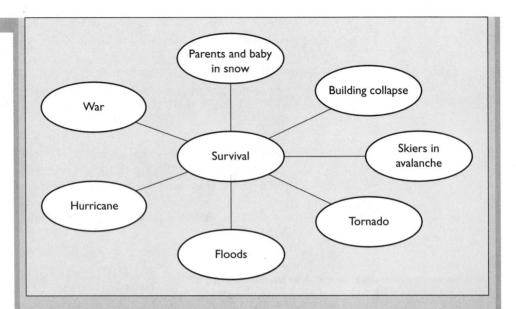

about what they chose and why they chose that particular piece of equipment. Many students cited points from newspaper and magazine articles that helped them choose their equipment.

During Reading

1. The students identified the various ways the main character in *Hatchet,* Brian, solved his problems, and they compared his strategies with those discussed in newspaper and magazine articles.
2. The protagonist in *Hatchet* was struggling with several problems throughout the book, so the teacher asked students to identify the words associated with these concepts: *divorce, fire, mistakes,* and *the secret.* They listed these words in their journal for class discussion.
3. The students identified scientific and geographic knowledge that would have helped Brian survive.

Following Reading

The students discussed the following questions:

1. "Why did Brian call the fire a 'hungry friend,' and 'close and sweet'?"
2. "What was the most valuable thing Brian invented or had in this story? Why did you choose this?"

3. "What did Brian mean when he called himself a city boy in this story? Was he complimenting himself?"
4. "Why did Brian want to tell somebody about his success in building a fire?"
5. "What did Brian learn from his experience? How did he learn this?"
6. "Who taught Brian?"

Students also did the following:

1. They identified additional figurative language that made the writing especially effective. They compared the writing style of the newspaper and magazine stories with that novel.
2. They contrasted Brian's character traits at the beginning and at the end of the story and made charts to show the contrasts.
3. They identified and discussed the theme of the book.
4. They identified the three types of conflict in the book and explained each one.
5. They discussed how this experience changed Brian's life.

Extensions

The students chose projects from the following list that could be related to the novel or a newspaper or magazine article.

1. Research flora and fauna that might exist in the Canadian wilderness that Brian could have used for food.
2. Identify other kinds of shelters that he could have constructed or found in this setting.
3. Research the concept of light refraction, which played such an important role in this book.
4. Research fire and find different ways to build fires.
5. Find a map of a similar area. Then create a map of Brian's camp and the lake.
6. Identify ways of measuring time when one lacks the usual means.

Language Arts Extensions

1. Write a script in which Brian is interviewed on a television program. The students may role-play this activity.
2. Write about Brian's first meal after returning home.
3. Compare survival situations depicted in various stories and articles. Discuss the elements to be survived, the means of survival, and the aftermaths of the situations.

4. Compare characters, character development, and character traits in various books.
5. Compare the plot lines in several books.
6. Prepare a television show or play that illustrates the survival theme.

Related Books

Slake's Limbo by Felice Holman
Julie of the Wolves by Jean George
The Goats by Brock Cole
Dogsong by Gary Paulsen
My Side of the Mountain by Jean George
Tracker by Gary Paulsen
My Daniel by Pam Conrad
Away Is a Strange Place to Be by H. M. Hoover
The Official Kids Survival Kit by Elaine Chaback and Pat Fortunato
Kid's Camping from AAAAIII! to Zip by Patrick McManus
What's Going to Happen to Me? When Parents Separate and Divorce by Edna Le Shan
Animal Ecology by Mark Lambert and John Williams
Shelters from Tepee to Igloo by Harvey Weiss
Plants That Heal by Millicent Selsam

■ ■ Thinking and Questioning

The comprehension process is one of thinking about content, and it is often stimulated by both students' and teachers' questions. Thinking about content calls on both general knowledge and specialized knowledge, as well as thinking strategies (Perkins, 1995). This view of cognitive development means students should engage in genuine problem solving, genuine inventive tasks, and genuine critical appraisal. Raising **questions** about authentic problems, projects, and tasks focuses students' thinking.

Why is raising questions significant in developing students' thinking?

More than two thousand years ago, Socrates demonstrated the power of questioning to stimulate cognitive development. Educators today know that the way a teacher structures a question influences the nature of the thinking required to respond (McTighe and Lyman, 1988). We also know that follow-up discussion strategies, such as asking for elaboration, influence the degree and quality of classroom discussion. Despite this knowledge, Goodlad (1984) reports that most classroom questions require only factual responses and that generally students are not involved in thought-provoking discussions. Thinking is more likely to flourish when ideas are valued and varying points of view are encouraged. In a thoughtful environment, students' answers and ideas are accepted, clarified, and expanded, often by the teacher's asking, "Why do you think that?"

Effective Questioning

Questioning can effectively guide and extend comprehension. In addition, asking and answering questions often reveals our thoughts and feelings, to ourselves as well as to others (Busching and Slesinger, 1995). Strategies such as providing relevant questions before students read the selection help them focus on major ideas and concepts. Asking questions that require interpretation and critical thinking stimulates higher types of cognitive processing. In contrast, focusing on literal questions that require specific correct answers limits thinking, because students can memorize the required answers. Stimulating questions are those that have several appropriate responses; such questions give students opportunities to experience success when expressing their own ideas. Good questions require multiple-word answers that foster cognitive growth. When students offer one-word answers, a teacher might say, "Can you tell me any more about . . . ?" or "Why do you think that?" or "Can you give me examples of this?" Collins (1991) suggests teaching students to ask themselves and others clarification questions such as these: "Is this what you mean _____?; "Can you give me a nonexample of _____?"; "Would you say more about _____?"; "What is the main point?" (Figure 5.2 gives examples of questions to ask and strategies to use to stimulate students' thinking.)

What could happen when you extend "wait time" after asking a question?

Giving students ample time to reflect on their answers improves the quality of the answers. Allowing three to five seconds of **"wait time"** after asking a question gives students time to process the question and formulate a response (Conley, 1987).

Questions can be posed before, during, and after reading. Questions asked before reading activate schemata and focus attention on important ideas and concepts; at this point, students can generate questions about a topic or concept. During reading, students can ask questions about how well they are comprehending. After reading, teachers can ask questions such as "Did you find the answers to your questions?" "What are they?" "Which questions are still unanswered?" "What did you learn that we didn't ask questions about?" "What did the writer do to make readers feel or think a certain way?" "How did the writer use language to convey a particular idea?" "What evidence to support a particular idea did the writer give?" (Hammond, 1983). Students who read a passage and answer questions about it generally learn more than students who only read the passage (Klauer, 1984; Tierney and Cunningham, 1984). Teaching unsuccessful readers to raise questions as they read helps them acquire the

FIGURE 5.2

Questioning for
Quality Thinking

*Source: McTighe, J.,
Lyman Jr., F. (April
1988). "Cueing
Thinking in the
Classroom: The Promise
of Theory-Embedded
Tools." Educational
Leadership 54, 7: 18–24
(Figure p. 21).*

Front	Back
QUESTIONING FOR QUALITY THINKING	STRATEGIES TO EXTEND STUDENT THINKING

Front

QUESTIONING FOR QUALITY THINKING

Knowledge — Identification and recall of
information
   Who, what, when, where, how _____ ?
   Describe _____ .

Comprehension — Organization and
selection of facts and ideas
   Retell _____ in your own words.
   What is the main idea of _____ ?

Application — Use of facts, rules, principles
   How is _____ an example of _____ ?
   How is _____ related to _____ ?
   Why is _____ significant?

Analysis — Separation of whole into
component parts
   What are the parts or features of _____ ?
   Classify _____ according to _____ .
   Outline/diagram/web _____ .
   How does __ compare/contrast with __ ?
   What evidence can you list for _____ ?

Synthesis — Combination of ideas to form
a new whole
   What would you predict/infer from ___ ?
   What ideas can you add to _____ ?
   How would you create/design a new ___ ?
   What might happen if you combined ___
     with _____ ?
   What solutions would you suggest for __ ?

Evaluation — Development of opinions,
judgments, or decisions
   Do you agree _____ ?
   What do you think about _____ ?
   What is the most important _____ ?
   Prioritize _____ .
   How would you decide about _____ ?
   What criteria would you use to assess __ ?

Back

STRATEGIES TO EXTEND STUDENT THINKING

- **Remember "wait time I and II"**
  Provide at least three seconds of thinking
  time after a question and after a response

- **Utilize "think-pair-share"**
  Allow individual thinking time, discussion
  with a partner, and then open up the
  class discussion

- **Ask "follow-ups"**
  Why? Do you agree? Can you elaborate?
  Tell me more. Can you give an example?

- **Withhold judgment**
  Respond to student answers in a non-
  evaluative fashion

- **Ask for summary (to promote active
  listening)**
  "Could you please summarize
  John's point?"

- **Survey the class**
  "How many people agree with the
  author's point of view?" ("thumbs up,
  thumbs down")

- **Allow for student calling**
  "Richard, will you please call on someone
  else to respond?"

- **Play devil's advocate**
  Require students to defend their reasoning against different points of view

- **Ask students to "unpack their thinking"**
  "Describe how you arrived at your
  answer." ("think aloud")

- **Call on students randomly**
  Not just those with raised hands

- **Student questioning**
  Let the students develop their own
  questions

- **Cue student responses**
  "There is not a single correct answer for
  this question. I want you to consider
  alternatives."

ability to comprehend complex verbal material. It appears that students who ask themselves questions engage in self-monitoring of their understanding, which leads them to independent comprehension (Hammond, 1983).

All questioning should be carefully planned to focus on important ideas and concepts in a reading selection. Poorly chosen questions and questions that emphasize insignificant details are detrimental to cognitive growth. Teachers who are preparing questions for a discussion should review the following points:

1. What are the important ideas in this selection?
2. What ideas and concepts do I want the students to remember from this selection?
3. What questions will lead students to understand these ideas and concepts?
4. What thinking abilities have the students in this group already developed?
5. What thinking abilities do the students in this group need to develop?

■ ■ Types of Thinking and Reading

Comprehension involves interpreting, analyzing, and manipulating information in response to a problem or question that requires more than a direct, one-right-answer application of previously learned knowledge. Research evidence suggests that giving students *multiple perspectives* and *entry points* into subject matter increases both thinking and learning (Sears and Marshall, 1990; Sternberg and Frensch, 1992). For instance, Gardner (1993) identified seven or more important abilities or intelligences (musical, bodily-kinesthetic, logical-mathematical, linguistic, spatial, interpersonal, intrapersonal) that are excellent entry points for integrated curricula and thematic units. (These are discussed in Chapter 3.) When using these abilities as entry points for learning, individual students apply their favored intelligences to learn concepts, ideas, and processes. Moreover, they can develop more applications of their intelligences as they learn. The various intelligences are vehicles for integrating thinking abilities such as synthesizing (putting things together), summarizing, graphically organizing, outlining, and restructuring ideas to incorporate new information. These thinking skills are teachable through demonstration and guided practice (Adams and Hamm, 1994). Thinking and problem solving are addressed in the following paragraphs.

■ Literal Thinking/Reading

What is the focus of literal thinking?

Literal thinking is concerned with directly stated facts and ideas that answer the question, "What did the author say?" Readers often quote the text to answer literal questions. The major forms of literal thinking are recognizing and recalling stated main ideas; recognizing and recalling stated details; recognizing and recalling stated sequences; following stated directions; and recognizing stated causes and effects.

The following are examples of literal-level questions based on *Nothing But the Truth* by Avi, which was a Newbery Honor book in 1991. The central characters are a student, Philip Malloy, and his English teacher, Margaret Narwin. Philip creates a problem when he sings along with a tape of the "Star Spangled Banner," to express his dissatisfaction with his English grade. He was suspended because school regulations required students to listen to the anthem in silence. However, reporters adopted the attitude that Phillip was demonstrating his patriotism, and put him in their headlines. Some literal questions for this book include:

1. What character's diary entries are presented throughout the book?
2. How does Philip Malloy describe Margaret Narwin?
3. How does Margaret Narwin describe Philip Malloy?
4. What is the primary concern of the school administrators in this story as stated in memos by the principal and superintendent?
5. How did the story end?

Students learn best when teachers model the process of answering questions. For example, to model answering the first question in a discussion of *Nothing But the Truth,* the teacher might share his or her thoughts in a "think aloud," beginning with "What character's diary entries are presented throughout the book?" Then he or she might comment on how the information sources presented are identified in the boxes in each chapter. This will alert students to the context. Students could do their own think alouds and articulate them to one another. There is a discussion on think alouds later in this chapter.

Teachers can provide students with opportunities to demonstrate their own thinking strategies. Questions that lead students to relate the text to their prior knowledge, to support their answers from the text or prior knowledge, or to apply knowledge are especially useful for encouraging them to model thinking processes. In listening to the students present their thinking, the teacher should focus on the cognitive process, as well as the answer. After students have some experience with thinking strategies, they can work in pairs modeling thinking for each other.

■ Inferential Thinking/Reading

How does literal thinking contrast with inferential thinking?

Inferential thinking is concerned with deeper meanings that are difficult to define because they involve several types of reasoning. This is further complicated by the fact that inferential questions often have more than one "correct" answer. To make inferences, readers must relate facts, generalizations, definitions, and values. Inferential questions emphasize finding relationships among elements of the written text. Essentially, making inferences involves using one's schemata to fill in information that the author assumes the reader knows. Building on readers' background knowledge is essential, due to space and time limitations. For example, in the sentence "Nancy pulled on her mittens and her parka before opening the door," the reader draws upon personal experience to infer that Nancy is going outdoors into cold weather. Students should always be prepared to support and explain their answers. Content activities such as the following can help students develop their ability to make inferences:

Comparing and contrasting historical figures
Identifying generalizations in their content textbooks.

In making inferences about reading content, readers examine the author's words, reading between the lines for implications that are not explicitly stated. To do this, readers combine information from their own experiences with text information. The main types of inferences include: *location* inferences, in which the reader infers the place; *agent* inferences, which require the reader to infer the person acting; *time* inferences, which are concerned with the time designation (e.g., when action occurs); *action* inferences, which have to do with the action occurring in the text; *instrument* inferences, which are concerned with tools or devices involved in the text; *object* inferences, which require readers to infer objects the author has implied; *cause-and-effect* inferences, which have to do with implied causes and/or effects; *category* inferences, which require the reader to infer a category to which objects mentioned in the text belong; *problem-solution* inferences, which have to do with problems and solutions implied by the author; and *feeling-attitude* inferences, which are concerned with the feelings and attitudes implied by the author (Johnson and Johnson, 1986).

Following are inferential questions based on *Nothing But the Truth:*

1. What form did the author use to tell this story? What are the advantages of this form?
2. What hints does the author include that suggest Philip may have actually enjoyed reading?
3. What are the motivations of each of the following:
   a. Philip?
   b. Margaret Narwin?
   c. The school administrators?
   d. Philip's parents?
4. What makes you think these are their motivations?
5. Why did Philip insist on singing "The Star Spangled Banner" when he didn't know it? Why didn't he know the national anthem?
6. Philip Malloy and Margaret Narwin are parallel characters. Explain how and why their character development is parallel.

7. Did anyone in this story get what he or she wanted? Why or why not?
8. What did Philip really want?
9. What did Margaret really want?

To demonstrate the inferential reasoning process, teachers can employ a think-aloud strategy that expresses their reflections regarding one of the preceding questions. For instance, in Question 6, the teacher might say, "The author portrays Philip as a student who wants to excel in track. He seems interested in the Olympics. He is caught up in a political situation because a candidate for the School Board latches onto his suspension and makes it a campaign issue. Margaret is portrayed as someone who wants to learn new teaching strategies to increase her professional skills. However, school administrators use school funds to build public support for a school levy rather than providing continuing education for Margaret. Both characters have high goals, but each is frustrated by the other. Both are caught up in a political situation that is out of their control. Both lose what they most value in this no-win situation."

■ Critical Thinking/Reading

How are literal and inferential thinking related to critical thinking?

Many educators believe that **critical thinking** is central to the curriculum because schools strive to educate minds rather than to train memories. The importance of critical thinking is well established because everyone needs to consider critically the information they receive about the world around them (Cioffi, 1992; Perkins, 1995). Critical readers recognize that they receive a limited amount of information when they read (or listen). Moreover, the information is usually presented from a particular point of view because it is filtered through the writer's perceptions. These varying perceptions lead to discrepancies in different accounts of the same incident. In order to think critically, readers must begin with an understanding of what the author is saying, so literal and interpretive thinking are necessary to critical thinking skills.

What do critical readers do?

Critical readers question what they read, suspend judgment, evaluate, and decide. Critical thinking is "reasonable reflective thinking focused on deciding what to believe or do" (Ennis, 1989). To make such judgments, the reader compares text with external criteria derived from experience, research, teachers, and experts in the field; therefore, background knowledge is essential to critical reading. Critical readers recognize the author's purpose and point of view or context, and distinguish fact from opinion. They test the author's assertions against their own observations, information, and logic. The major facets of critical reading are summarized below:

Reader is open-minded and suspends judgment until adequate data is available, thus avoiding jumping to conclusions.
Reader constantly questions reading content.

Reader has a problem-solving attitude.
Reader is knowledgeable regarding the topic.
Reader discerns author's purpose.
Reader evaluates author's qualifications.
Reader evaluates validity of material.
Reader evaluates use of propaganda.
Reader evaluates author's logic.
Reader evaluates author's use of language.

Critical reading questions based on *Nothing But the Truth* follow:

1. Was Philip motivated by patriotism? Why do you think this?
2. Is there a villain in this story? If so, who is it?
3. Is there a hero in this story? If so, who is it?
4. How did the situation escalate so quickly? Could anyone have predicted this out-of-control situation?
5. How could this situation have been prevented? How could each character have acted differently?
6. How does the "truth" differ for each important character in this story?

When modeling critical thinking, the teacher could say "To answer Question 1, you might think about patriotism and your personal definitions of this term. Also, consider the various ways people demonstrate patriotism. What do you know about patriotism?"

After some discussion, the students might suggest that patriotism has to do with loyalty to one's country or that people demonstrate patriotism when they take off their hats when the flag goes by, when they display flags, and when they play and sing the national anthem. Some students may bring up the idea that there are specific rules for displaying flags.

Then the teacher might say, "How does this information fit with the rules in the high school in this story? What do you think Philip knows about patriotism? Did anyone ask him about his patriotism? Why?"

Critical reading such as that described in the preceding paragraphs involves three major types of abilities: *semantics, logic,* and *evaluating authenticity* (Lewis, 1991). Semantics abilities include understanding the denotative and connotative uses of words, the use of vague and precise words, and the use of words in a persuasive manner. Logic skills include understanding the reliability of the author's argument and statements; recognizing the use of propaganda; distinguishing fact from opinion; and recognizing the various forms of persuasive writing. Authenticity skills include determining if adequate information is included, comparing this information with other relevant information, examining the author's qualifications, and using authoritative research sources. Critical reading in the content areas consists of explicit applications of the principles of critical thinking, which are discussed further in Chapters 10 and 11. Teaching suggestions for critical reading are given in the following section.

Semantic Learning Activities

1. Since "loaded" words play on readers' emotions, students will benefit from practice in identifying them. Words like *un-American* and *radical* call forth a negative reaction, whereas words such as *freedom, peace,* and *human rights* stimulate positive feelings. Students can practice identifying "loaded" words in newspapers, magazines, and textbooks.

2. Critical readers discover that words used in vague, general ways interfere with content clarity (e.g., the expressions "Everyone is doing it" and "They say"). Students should locate examples of vague word usage in their reading material.

Logic Learning Activities

1. Have students create syllogisms that state an author's premises and conclusions, similar to this one based on a social studies text chapter:

   PREMISES
   People with undesirable characteristics were rejected. Some "new" immigrants had undesirable characteristics.

   CONCLUSION
   Those "new" immigrants were rejected.

2. Have students verify statements found in local newspaper stories through research.

3. Have students examine sentences to identify words that signal the author's opinion such as these qualifying words: *think, probably, maybe, appear, seem,* and *believe*. The following sentences are examples:
   a. I believe this is the best cake I have ever eaten.
   b. Jane will probably come home for vacation.

4. Making a graphic representation (chart) of the facts and opinions presented by an author will help the reader examine ideas critically. Example 5.1 is a chart based on information taken from a social studies textbook.

■ ■ ■ EXAMPLE 5. 1   *Graphic Representation*

Facts	**Opinions**
"Old" immigrants from British Isles, Germany, Scandinavia	"Old" immigrants acceptable
"New" immigrants from Slavic countries, Italy, Greece	"New" immigrants unacceptable, ignorant, greedy, diseased, criminals, insane, wild-eyed, bad-smelling

---

5. Recognizing propaganda is one of the abilities required for critical reading. Discussions of propaganda techniques and methods for analyzing propaganda could be held in class. Make sure that students realize that these propaganda techniques are usually used in combination.
   a. *Bad names*—Disagreeable words are used to arouse distaste for a person or a thing.
   b. *Glad names*—Pleasant words are used to create good feelings about a person or a thing.
   c. *Plain folks*—This kind of propaganda avoids sophistication. Political candidates use this technique when they kiss babies and play with dogs.
   d. *Transfer*—This type of propaganda attempts to transfer to a person or thing the reader's respect for the flag, the cross, or some other valued symbol.
   e. *Testimonial*—This technique is like transfer except that a famous person gives a testimonial for a product or a person. Positive feelings for the famous person are supposed to be transferred to the product.
   f. *Bandwagon*—This is an attempt to convince readers that they should accept an idea or purchase an item because "Everyone is doing it."
   g. *Card stacking*—This technique utilizes accurate information but omits some data so that only one side of a story is told.
6. After learning to identify propaganda techniques, the reader should analyze the propaganda using the following questions:
   a. What technique is used?
   b. Who composed the propaganda?
   c. Why was the propaganda written?
   d. To what reader interests, emotions, and prejudices does the propaganda appeal?
   e. Will I allow myself to be influenced by this propaganda?

Authenticity Learning Activities

1. Writers should support their conclusions in the text; however, readers often need additional data to evaluate the validity of content. Ask students to consult other sources of information to evaluate the validity of the content of an article, book, or chapter.
2. Ask students to evaluate the author's qualifications for writing on the topic at hand. Questions like these will guide them:
   a. Would a lawyer be qualified to write a book on writing contracts?
   b. Would a football player be qualified to write a book on foreign policy?
   c. Would a chef be a qualified author for a book on menu planning?
   d. Would a physician be qualified to write a book on music theory?

Creative Thinking/Reading

Creative thinkers find new ways of viewing ideas, incidents, or characters that stimulate original or novel thinking or production of new materials. They strive for originality and ideas that are fundamental, far-reaching, and powerful

What is the most important aspect of creative thinking?

(Perkins, 1995). Creative thinkers are able to view their experiences from different perspectives. Good **creative thinking** always involves a measure of critical thinking, or it would be nonsensical (Perkins, 1995). Creative thinkers generate possibilities, then critically sift through and rework them. They need to be knowledgeable about a subject to think more creatively about it.

Creative thinkers/readers may come up with several ways of solving a math problem or of performing an experiment in science class. They may turn a situation from a literature selection into a puppet show, a skit, or a painting. They may make a unique table in woodshop or develop a design in home economics that surpasses those suggested in the book. To do these things, creative thinkers translate existing knowledge into new forms. Creativity is stifled when all school activities must be carried out according to the precise specifications of the teacher and if deviations from prescribed forms are always discouraged.

Creative thinking is based on knowledge about the subject and opportunities to solve problems and to respond to authentic situations. Creative thinking/reading activities related to *Nothing But the Truth* follow.

Creative Thinking/Reading Activities

1. The author stated that the truth can be discovered by only one person: the reader. What does that statement mean?
2. What is the truth, in your opinion?
3. We could say this was a failure to communicate. What other situations precipitated by failure to communicate can you describe?
4. Why was the title *Nothing But the Truth* chosen?
5. How does Philip feel when he goes to the private school?
6. How does Margaret feel when she leaves for Florida? Do you think she ever learned about newer methods of teaching? Why or why not?
7. What could Margaret have done to build Philip's interest in reading? How could you use the book *The Outsiders* to motivate him?

Strategies to Increase Comprehension

Throughout this text, strategies and activities are introduced to improve students' comprehension. These strategies focus on literacy and constructing meaning. Initially most of the strategies involve direct teacher instruction and guidance, but the universal goal is for students to use the strategies independently. Ultimately students should internalize and implement appropriate strategies.

Some of the following suggestions should be implemented before reading, some during reading, and others after reading; some strategies are used throughout the reading process. Figure 5.3 summarizes these instructional strategies and relates them to the reading process.

FIGURE 5.3

Mediated Instruction of Text: A Framework of Teaching Options for Content Area Instruction

*Source: Figure 1 from"A Framework of Teaching Options for Content Area Instruction: Mediated Instruction of Text,"
Judith C. Neal and Margaret A. Langer,* Journal of Reading, *November 1992, pp. 227–230. Reprinted with permission
of Judith C. Neal and the International Reading Association.*

	Goal	Comprehension process	Strategies	Teacher responsibility
Before reading	Readiness	Activate prior knowledge	• Questioning • Brainstorming • Posing a problem • Role playing	Initiates probes
		Predict content	• Surveying ideas • Demonstration/experiment • Semantic organizers • Building word meaning • Posing purpose questions • Structured overviews	Leads students
During reading	Understanding	Construct meaning	• Responding to purpose questions • Verifying predictions • Responding to study guide	Provides guidance for students
		Monitor understanding	• Questioning/talking about ideas • Notetaking • Student generated "quizzes"	
After reading	Retention	Process ideas	• Summarizing • Response writing • Constructing graphic organizers • Teaching others • Learning games • Discussion	Prescribes structure to promote retention of ideas
		Apply knowledge	Participation in: • Projects • Experiments • Creative work	

■ **Study Guides**

What value do study guides have?

One of the most valuable strategies for increasing students' comprehension is the **study guide.** A study guide is a set of suggestions designed to direct students' attention to the key ideas in a passage and to suggest the skills to apply for successful comprehension (Harris and Hodges, 1981). A study guide creates a point of contact between the student and the written material, showing readers *how to comprehend* content.

The instructor's goals and the students' needs determine the composition of a study guide. It may cover a chapter, a larger unit, or merely part of a long chapter. If students are given a study guide to read before they study an assignment, they can respond to the questions and activities as they read the material. Study guides may take a variety of forms. Examples of these various forms are found throughout this text.

A single study guide may set purposes for reading, provide aids for interpretation of the material, or do both. Study guides are particularly valuable when the teacher uses grouping in the content class. Each small group of students can sit together, work through their study guide individually, and then discuss their answers with one another, reconciling any differences in their answers. Handling material this way causes the students to think about the material they are reading; critical thinking is necessary as students try to reach a consensus about their answers.

Example 5.2 shows a science selection related to health and human environmental science; a study guide follows.

The teacher's instructional intent in the study guide in Example 5.2 is apparent in the overview questions, which are designed to focus on the understandings that students are expected to acquire from the selection; moreover, these questions focus the reading while requiring critical or creative reading abilities. The balance of the guide provides a series of questions and guidance statements that are arranged sequentially to parallel the ideas in the text.

■ ■ ■ EXAMPLE 5.2   *Science Selection and Study Guide*

Food Additives: A Danger, a Safeguard, or Both?

Every day suppliers deliver tons of food items to grocery stores all over the country. Most of this food has traveled hundreds of miles from farms and processing plants. Food can take days, weeks, or even months to reach your table. Did you ever wonder what kept food from spoiling on its journey?

Since many foods travel long distances before reaching the market, certain chemicals are added to prevent spoilage during shipment and storage. Other chemicals, or food additives, improve texture, prevent caking, or provide extra vitamins and minerals. Some additives make foods look more appealing by adding colored vegetable dyes.

Even though government agencies test foods and additives to be sure they are safe, some research indicates that certain food additives can cause cancer in laboratory animals.

Nitrites and nitrates are common additives in meat, fish, and poultry. At first, these chemicals were added because their interaction with bacteria made the food look fresher longer. Later, scientists found that nitrites act as preservatives. They slow down the growth of bacteria that cause botulism, a food poisoning that is often fatal.

A committee supported by the National Academy of Sciences reported in December, 1981, that the cancer risk to humans from nitrites is small but genuine. The committee recommended that the amounts of nitrites added to foods be lowered, but that enough be added to protect against botulism. One way to safely add nitrites to food is to also add vitamins C and E. Other methods to prevent botulism without adding nitrites are being tested. These methods include using ionizing radiation, which kills bacteria, adding nonpoisonous chemicals such as potassium sorbate, and adding bacteria that lower the meat's pH, inhibiting the growth of botulism bacteria.

Additives can be both helpful and harmful. If you want to eliminate additives from your diet, you might have to give up many foods. For instance, you might have to limit your diet to foods which can be grown in your part of the country. You might also have to prepare many foods "from scratch." On the other hand perhaps the inconvenience and forgoing of certain foods would be safer for us in the long run. More information is needed before definite conclusions can be drawn.

Analysis

1. What standards or criteria would you set for the use of food additives?
2. Look at labels and find out what additives are in some of your favorite foods.

Source: From Scott, Foresman Biology *by Irwin L. Slesnick et al. Copyright © 1985 by Scott, Foresman and Company. Reprinted by permission.*

Study Guide

Overview Questions: What are the positive and negative aspects of food additives? How do you feel about eating foods containing additives?

1. Read the first paragraph to find out how long it may take food items to arrive at their final destinations. What does the author mean by the phrase "to reach your table"?
2. Read the second paragraph to find out what food additives are. (Two context clues are there to help you.)
3. What are five different uses of food additives?
4. Read the third paragraph to find out the effect that food additives may have on laboratory animals.

5. Read the fourth paragraph. It tells two advantages of using nitrites and nitrates as additives. What are they?
6. What is a preservative? (Think about the root word of *preservative* and use the meaning of this word to help you decide.)
7. What is botulism? (Use the context to help you answer.) Why would you want to avoid botulism?
8. Read the fifth paragraph. Is the cancer risk to humans from nitrites real? What word tells you so?
9. How can nitrites safely be added to food?
10. What are some methods being tested to prevent botulism without adding nitrites?
11. Read the last paragraph. If you wanted to avoid additives, what two things might you have to do and why? What does it mean to prepare food "from scratch"? (The words do not mean what they usually do.)

This study guide could be used for all students who can read the textbook, with or without teacher assistance; however, if a teacher wanted to reduce the guide's length, some questions could be assigned to both groups, and other questions could be divided between the groups. For example, all students might complete items 1, 2, 4, 5, 8, and 11, which would provide some guidance through the entire selection. The other questions could be divided between the two groups as appropriate, although the items designed to aid in interpretation of the material might be best used with the instructional group. The teacher may work closely with the instructional-level group members as they discuss their assigned questions and may monitor the independent level group less intensively. The group that cannot handle the text material should be given another reading assignment in order to learn the content. This group should have its own study guide, geared to its assignment. The whole-class discussion that follows the small-group sessions with the guides will help all the students clarify their concepts and see relationships among the ideas.

A three-level study guide directs students toward comprehension at the literal level (directly stated ideas), the interpretive level (implied ideas), and the applied level (using information to solve problems) (Herber, 1978). See Chapter 9, Example 9.1 for an example of a guide designed for the short story "Man Without a Country," by Edward Everett Hale.

■ Directed Reading Lessons

What are the steps in a directed reading lesson?

A **directed reading lesson** (DRL) is a method for guiding students' comprehension of a reading selection. Directed reading approaches vary from source to source, but the following components are present in all the plans:

1. Motivation and building background
2. Skill and strategy development activities
3. Guided reading of the story
   a. Silent reading
   b. Discussion and oral reading (when appropriate)
4. Follow-up activities

Building motivation and background consists of activating students' schemata and previewing the reading selection. Research has shown that developing students' background experiences improves their comprehension (Stevens, 1982). Teachers can use videocassettes, films, filmstrips, computer programs, slides, still pictures, models, and other visual aids to build background. Discussing the topics under study helps students relate content to their own lives. Previewing the selection by reading the headings or consulting the table of contents gives students a framework for organizing the ideas acquired from reading. Examining pictures, maps, graphs, and diagrams in the reading content builds background. Structured overviews, introduced in Chapter 3, are also effective in developing students' readiness for reading.

The second step, skill and strategy development activities, includes teaching vocabulary, word recognition, comprehension, and study skills and strategies that are appropriate to the text. Instruction for difficult vocabulary words may be needed; this instruction should focus on having students use their own reading skills to determine word meanings. They should also be alerted to use glossaries.

Guided reading, the third step, includes establishing reading purposes and the actual reading of the selection. The purposes may be in the form of teacher-constructed questions or a study guide, or the students may formulate questions to guide their reading. These questions may be based on boldfaced headings, or they may be predictions about the selection. In this instance, students read to confirm or deny their hypotheses. After purposes have been set, students read silently to fulfill them. Teachers should not ask students to read orally unless they have had a chance to read the selection silently first. This avoids embarrassment that arises from inability to pronounce words or lack of familiarity with phrasing patterns. In addition, most reading at the secondary level should be silent because it is more prevalent in everyday situations.

After silent reading, students may discuss the purpose questions and any other questions that have arisen. Students may read passages orally to verify points in the discussion. Any oral rereading should be purposeful, such as reading to interpret characterization in a story. Many directed reading lessons at the secondary level do not include an oral reading component.

The fourth step, follow-up activities, includes enrichment activities related to the lesson and designed to further develop the topic. Such activities might be reading additional books on the topic or by the same author, constructing a model, writing a story related to the content, conducting an experiment, or otherwise applying concepts presented in the assignment.

Although a directed reading lesson may sound time-consuming, it involves no more time than a teacher would typically spend on a section of content text. Furthermore, after the students have been coached through these steps, they will be more likely to understand and retain the material. Example 5.3 shows a directed reading lesson that is based on an eighth-grade English textbook.

■■ ■■ ■ EXAMPLE 5.3   *English Selection and Directed Reading Lesson*

The Life of a Word

Our language constantly changes to meet our needs. We adopt words from other languages and maintain their meanings. We adapt words from languages by altering their meanings slightly. Sometimes we completely change the meaning of a word when we take it for our own. Words have origins and histories, many of which are fascinating. The study of words is called **etymology.**

Consider the word *canary,* which originally comes from the Latin word for *dog, canis.* What do dogs and canaries have in common? The Romans named a group of islands off northwest Africa, Canaria Insula, or Dog Island, because of all the dogs that they found there. Songbirds also inhabited the islands. Later, when the birds were exported to Europe, they were called canaries, after their home, the Canary Islands.

Another word that got its name from a place is *mayonnaise.* According to a legend, the town of Mahón on the island of Minorca in the Mediterranean once had a shortage of milk products. Consequently, the usual cream sauces could not be made. One chef began experimenting with eggs and oil. The result was a sauce that took the name of the city, Sauce Mahónnaise. Eventually, the word changed to *mayonnaise.*

Word change is unpredictable. For instance, the word *silly* in Old English was *seely,* meaning "blessed." The Normans were considered *seely,* because they had idle time for hunting and playing. Over time, *seely* came to mean "idle." In contrast, the word *knight* was originally the Anglo-Saxon word for youth, *cniht.* Later, it came to mean "servant," then "servant of a noble." Finally, the meaning was elevated to mean a person who served a noble with great chivalry and daring.

Many dictionaries give whole or partial etymologies. Some dictionaries list the early meanings of a word before its current meanings. Check your dictionary for its etymologies. You may also want to look at the *Oxford English Dictionary* which provides extensive etymologies.

PRACTICE

A. Create your own etymology for each of these words: *mathematics, study, gymnasium, vacation.* What are their real etymologies?

B. What is the etymology for the name of your state, the month of your birth, and the days of the week?

Directed Reading Lesson

MOTIVATION AND BUILDING BACKGROUND

1. Ask the students if they know what a *villain* is. After discussing its current meaning, tell them that it originally meant "a person from a villa" and that its meaning has changed for the worse.
2. Ask the students if they know what *nice* means. After discussing its current meaning, tell them that it once meant "ignorant" and that its meaning has changed for the better.
3. Ask the students if they know any words that have come from place names or names of people. Let them name as many as possible. Be ready to provide some examples for them, such as *pasteurization*.

SKILL DEVELOPMENT ACTIVITIES

4. Remind students that words presented in boldface print are important words for which to know meanings.
5. Review types of context clues that are often found in textbooks. Give special attention to definition clues, since there is a definition clue for the word *etymology* in the assignment.
6. Review the meaning of *-logy* (the study of). Have students name and define words ending in *-logy* (*biology, geology,* and so forth).
7. Review the meaning of the word part *un-* (not). Have students name and define words with this part (*unhappy, unwanted*).
8. Review the meaning of the word part *-able* (able to be). Have students name and define words with this part (*workable, marketable*).

GUIDED READING

9. Silent reading—Have students read the selection silently for the following purposes:
   a. Determine the meaning of the word *etymology.*
   b. Find two words whose names have come from the names of places.
   c. Determine the meaning of *unpredictable.*
   d. Find a word that had a negative meaning change over the years.
   e. Find a word that had a positive meaning change over the years.
10. Discussion and oral reading—Choose some students to read aloud and discuss the parts related to the silent reading purposes, especially if the students find the purpose questions difficult to answer.

FOLLOW-UP ACTIVITIES

11. Have the students do the two practice activities at the bottom of the selection and discuss their results in class.

12. Have the students list five words that they find that have interesting etymologies. Have a class discussion of the words.

▪ Directed Reading-Thinking Activity

How does a directed reading lesson compare with a directed reading-thinking activity?

Stauffer (1969) developed the **directed reading-thinking activity** (DRTA) to encourage students' thinking. He believed that students who are involved intellectually with the reading material, forming hypotheses, processing information, and evaluating tentative solutions become active participants in the reading process.

In a DRTA, students develop their own purposes for reading when the teacher asks them to predict what the material will be about from the title clues and the graphic aids in the text. Predictions may be listed on the board and modified or deleted as the students request. Students may change their ideas about the predictions, and they can explain their predictions during class discussion.

The teacher divides the reading material into portions that provide good prediction points. Students are asked to read to a specified point, stop, assess their previous predictions, either confirm or reject the predictions, and make new predictions if they have rejected the old ones. A discussion of the confirmation or rejection of predictions is held, and the students support their decisions by referring to information gathered from the text. This process is continued until the entire selection has been read. Students' early predictions are likely to be diverse, because the reading clues are sparse at that point, but the predictions become more convergent as the reading continues.

▪ Discussion

What are the major values of discussion in content classrooms?

Creating a social environment in the classroom promotes dialogue and discussion, as well as developing a learning community (Brophy, 1992; Wollman-Bonilla, 1994). **Discussion** is a powerful tool for developing higher-order thinking because participants interact as they present multiple points of view and listen to counterarguments (Alvermann, Dillon, and O'Brien, 1987). Students who participate in discussions learn to listen to and validate other students' perspectives. Meanings shared in discussion groups are more than a collection of individual ideas; they are part of new sets of meanings developed as members talk and listen to one another.

In a well-planned discussion, students interact with one another as well as with the teacher, and they are encouraged to make comments and ask questions that are longer than two- or three-word phrases. Such discussions offer students opportunities to enrich and refine knowledge gained from the text.

■ Question/Answer Relationships (QARs)

How do question/answer relationships (QARs) increase comprehension?

Use of **question/answer relationships** (QARs) (Raphael, 1986) is another strategy to increase comprehension. This procedure focuses on the processes for generating answers to questions and on the relationships between questions and answers. Students are encouraged to think of sources for answers to questions. The following ideas are included to guide teachers in using the procedure:

1. The first question-answering strategy is called RIGHT THERE. The student finds the words used to create the question and looks for these words in a sentence to answer the question. In this instance, the answer is within a single sentence.
2. The second question-answering strategy is called THINK AND SEARCH. This strategy involves a question that has an answer in the story, but the answer uses information from more than one sentence or paragraph.
3. The third question-answering strategy, ON MY OWN, involves a question that can be answered from the reader's own knowledge.
4. The fourth question-answering strategy, WRITER AND ME, is for inferential questions. The answer may be found by combining the reader's background with information in the text.
5. When teaching QARs, give students immediate feedback, start with short texts and work up to longer ones, and start with group activities and move to independent ones.
6. Students should learn all four strategies and how to tell the differences among them. Research shows that understanding the question-answer relationships increases student achievement.

■ K-W-L (Know-Want to Know-Learned)

What additional columns could you add to K-W-L?

The **K-W-L** strategy encourages students to activate prior knowledge and stimulates cognition and metacognition (Ogle, 1986; Carr and Ogle, 1987). Initially, the students brainstorm what they already know about the reading topic. Then they write the brainstormed information in the K (Know) column of a chart like the one shown in Example 5.4. As the students work, the teacher should encourage them to categorize the information and list their categories at the bottom of the column. The students generate questions about the text, which are listed in the W (What I Want to know) column. Additional questions may be generated as the students proceed. Finally, information learned from the text is entered in the L (Learned) column. The students map the material and use the map to write a summary.

■ ■ ■ EXAMPLE 5.4   K-W-L for Eleventh-Grade Government—"Civil Liberties":
                       The First Admendment Freedoms

K	W	L
Know	*Want to Know*	*Learned*
Freedom of speech	Does the First Amendment mean we	
Personal freedom	can do *anything* we want to? Are we	
Freedom to write	free to do things that will hurt us?	
Language		
Civil liberties		

In Example 5.4, students identified two categories in the original brainstorming (language and civil liberties). The book *Nothing But the Truth* could be used to illustrate many of the chapter concepts.

■ Think Alouds

Why do you think "think alouds" are so valuable in developing comprehension?

Think alouds are strategies that can be used to demonstrate the comprehension process or specific aspects of it. The think-aloud process makes thinking public and gives students a model for the kinds of thinking that a reader may do while reading text (Davey, 1983). Initially, teachers demonstrate think alouds to the class. After observing demonstrations, students can work in pairs, doing think alouds for each other.

When planning think alouds, teachers should select passages that contain information requiring clarification, such as contradictions, ambiguities, or word meanings. As the teacher reads the passage aloud, students follow along silently, listening to ways of thinking through each trouble spot as it is encountered. The teacher may also choose specific instances from a text to demonstrate ways of coping when comprehension breaks down.

Although think alouds generate many types of thinking, teachers should plan to focus on specific thinking abilities. For example, the teacher may choose to demonstrate the use of background knowledge to understand text and to make predictions about the reading. Describing the images the text creates helps students understand the role of visualization in thinking. Another form of thinking commonly used in think alouds is analogies, in which the reader compares prior knowledge to new information in the text. The teacher may also demonstrate strategies, such as rereading, that the student can use when he or she does not understand the text.

The think aloud in Example 5.5 demonstrates inferencing and is based on the first part of a story by Roald Dahl. To use this think aloud in a classroom, the teacher reads the story or text aloud, and the students follow along, reading the selection silently and listening to the teacher verbalize his or her thoughts as the reading progresses.

■ ■ ■ EXAMPLE 5.5   Think Aloud for Inferencing

Story Summary for "The Landlady" (Dahl, 1978)

The Bell and Dragon was recommended as cheap lodging in London, so Billy Weaver set out for this hotel. On the way there, he noticed a "Bed and Breakfast" sign in the window of a warm, inviting-looking house. The house was so attractive and well cared for that he thought it would be too expensive for him. He was about to turn away and go on to the hotel when. . . . "Each word was like a large black eye staring at him through the glass, holding him, compelling him, forcing him to stay where he was . . . and the next thing he knew, he was actually moving across from the window to the front door of the house, climbing the steps that led up to it, and reaching for the bell."

Modeling Dialogue

From the title, I predict that this story will be about an unusual landlady. The story seems quite ordinary until the description of each word staring at him "like a large black eye." These visual images are mysterious. The suspense is mounting. My experiences with television stories and previous reading make me anticipate a mystery.

The next hint of mystery occurs when the author says, "But this dame was like a jack-in-the-box. He pressed the bell—and out she popped! It made him jump." Apparently, the landlady knew Billy was at the door before he rang the bell.

The next hint of mystery comes when Billy says, "I saw the notice in the window," and the landlady responds, "Yes, I know." Billy says, "I was wondering about a room," and the landlady replies, "It's all ready for you, my dear." She talked as if she knew he was coming. The unexplained events increase the tension.

Then they discuss the price, which was less than half of what Billy expected. The landlady said, "If that is too much, then perhaps I can reduce it just a tiny bit." Why is she so willing to lower the price?

Billy thinks that she is "slightly off her rocker," "slightly dotty." He still thinks that she is harmless, but is she?

When Billy signs the guest book, he notices and recognizes the names of earlier guests, but he can't place them. The landlady assures him that he couldn't possibly know the earlier boarders, but he finally remembers that they disappeared mysteriously, and he gets worried. I anticipate danger.

Problem Solving

What kinds of thinking are stimulated in a problem-solving approach?

A problem-solving approach to reading encourages students to spend time understanding a problem before attacking it (McTighe and Lyman, 1988). In this approach the teacher introduces various methods of problem solving and poses problem situations for students to analyze. Then students identify a problem and state it in their own words, after which they brainstorm possible solutions. Critical thinking is the next stage because students have to examine the possibilities generated and eliminate the unworkable ones. Students can compare this problem with others that they know about or discuss it with another person to clarify thinking. In addition, students may gather relevant information and find out how other people have solved similar problems. A problem can be broken into parts and/or restated to expand students' understanding. Finally, writing out a problem often helps them solve it. Completing a guide similar to the one in Example 5.6, which is based on guides developed by several educators (Beyer, 1988; McTighe and Lyman, 1988; Marzano et al., 1988), is helpful for students who need practice with problem solving.

■ ■ ■ EXAMPLE 5.6   *Problem-Solving Paradigm Based on Hatchet by Gary Paulsen*

Possible solutions	Evaluate possible solutions	Support for evaluations
Eat what birds eat	+	He could eat some things birds eat, but some he couldn't.
Fish	+	Needs fishing line
Catch animals	+	Needs traps or other equipment

Solution: He used all three solutions to obtain food.

Evaluate Solution

The solution worked well, but some of the food the birds ate made Brian sick. He was able to fish and catch animals after he made equipment and found additional equipment in the airplane.

The following are examples of problems that could be used in problem-solving reading activities.

Problem-Solving Activities

SOCIAL STUDIES

1. During a Civil War unit, give students a quotation from a Southern sympathizer and one from a Northern sympathizer. Then ask them to read to determine which point of view they believe is correct, and why.

SCIENCE

2. During a unit on environmental disease, present this problem: The water purification, sewage disposal, trash, and garbage collection procedures in Greensboro, North Carolina, were completely disrupted for a two-week period as the result of a tornado and fires. What diseases could have become rampant? Why?

TECHNOLOGY EDUCATION

3. During a unit on wood types and uses, pose this problem: provide pictures of various buildings and pieces of furniture, and ask students to identify the best type of wood for each purpose and to explain their choices.

HOME ECONOMICS

4. During a unit on nutritional needs for individuals with various diseases, ask students to plan menus for individuals who have diabetes, an allergy to milk, and an allergy to wheat.

Controversial issues provide material for the problem-solving approach to content area reading. In such an approach, teachers may select issues related to assigned reading or from newspapers, news magazines, and television programs. Controversial issues that may be used follow:

1. The President's economic changes at the beginning of a new term of office (economics class)
2. The moral and/or scientific issues in genetic engineering (science class)
3. The role of computers in education and in other facets of life (social studies class)

■ Reciprocal Teaching

What are the strategies involved in reciprocal teaching?

Reciprocal teaching features "guided practice" in applying simple, concrete strategies to text comprehension (Palincsar and Brown, 1986; Rosenshine and Meister, 1994). This very successful instructional procedure consists of these four strategies:

1. Summarizing the paragraph or assignment in a sentence
2. Asking a higher-level question (one or two questions)
3. Clarifying any difficult parts
4. Predicting what the next paragraph or section will discuss

The teacher models the process and then gradually turns it over to the students while providing feedback and encouragement. This activity may be done with pairs or triads (three students, or one adult and two students).

■ Writing Strategies

Educators have recognized for some time that writing improves comprehension. Writing forces students to shape and form their responses to the text—to bring these thoughts to conscious awareness (Blatt and Rosen, 1984). Refer to Chapter 8 for additional information about writing and its relation to reading comprehension and retention.

■ Visualization Strategies

What is visualization?

Visualization is the process of forming mental images that depict reading content such as story settings, characters, story action, geographic areas, famous historical figures, scientific experiments, and steps in mathematics problems. Visualization activities like these will benefit students.

Activities

1. *Social Studies:* Develop a "You-Are-There" activity. The students could be asked to visualize Abraham Lincoln as he delivered the Gettysburg Address. They could discuss the sounds, smells, and emotions engendered by the occasion. Students could visualize a battle in a war they are studying, discussing the placement of various battle lines and giving descriptions of weapons and uniforms.
2. When working with problem-solving activities in any subject, students can be asked to visualize alternative solutions that will help them work through the various ways of solving a problem.

Summary

Comprehension is an active, constructive process based on interactions among a reader, a text, and the reading situation or purpose. Readers think before, during, and after reading text. Effective readers use strategies that are appropriate to the material and the task. Their strategies are plans for using skills to comprehend. Figure 5.4 summarizes comprehension strategies.

FIGURE 5.4

Comprehension Strategies

1. Develop a positive attitude toward reading
2. Identify important ideas
3. Identify the organizational pattern of the text
4. Identify sequence of events
5. Monitor understanding
6. Paraphrase
7. Predict
8. Question
9. Relate new knowledge to prior knowledge
10. Reread
11. Search for relationships
12. Summarize

Discussion Questions

1 Why do you think critical reading is so important for today's students?
2 What strategies and activities can a teacher use before having students start a reading assignment to aid their comprehension?
3 How is discussion related to reading comprehension?
4 What is the purpose of a think-aloud exercise?
5 How do strategies function in reading comprehension?
6 What attributes characterize fluent readers?

Enrichment Activities

1 Visit a secondary school classroom to watch questioning procedures. Notice what type of questioning is used most often. Also note how much time the students are allowed for formulating answers.
2 Select a chapter in a content textbook and make a plan to help secondary school students comprehend the chapter, using strategies suggested in this chapter.
3 Adapt one of the strategies suggested in this chapter to your content area.
4 Examine the exercises suggested in this chapter and identify those that will be most useful in your content area.

Location and Organization of Information

Overview

In this chapter we discuss location skills related to use of the library or media center, books, and computer databases. We also give attention to the organizational skills of outlining, summarizing, and note taking. These skills are important to students' success with assignments such as written reports, research papers, and class presentations in all content area classes.

Purpose-Setting Questions

As you read this chapter, try to answer these questions:

1 What location skills do secondary school students need in order to use the library effectively?
2 What location skills do students need in order to use books effectively for content area classes?
3 What skills do students need in order to use computer databases effectively?
4 What organizational skills are helpful to students who are reading material that is to be used later in some manner?

Location Skills

To take part in many study activities (primarily content area reading and writing assignments), students must be able to locate specific reading materials. Teaching students to use location aids in libraries or media centers and in books and to use computer databases will enable them to find the materials they need.

Libraries or Media Centers

Teachers and librarians/media specialists should work cooperatively to help students develop the skills needed for effective use of the library or media center (Dales, 1990). (For easy reference, the library or media center will hereafter be referred to as the library and the librarian/media specialist as the librarian, but the expanded role of this facility and these personnel in dealing with multimedia should not be overlooked.)

The librarian can help by showing students the locations of books, periodicals, card catalogs, computer terminals, and reference materials (dictionaries, encyclopedias, atlases, *Readers' Guide to Periodical Literature*, and others) in the library; by explaining the procedures for checking out books and returning them; and by clarifying the rules relating to behavior in the library. The librarian can also demonstrate use of the card catalog (either manual or electronic) and the *Readers' Guide,* and explain the arrangement of books in the library. (The Dewey Decimal System is the arrangement most commonly used in school libraries in the United States for classifying nonfiction books, although some libraries classify books by Library of Congress numbers.) Posters displayed in the library can remind students of checkout procedures, library rules, and arrangement of books, as well as how to use card catalogs (computerized or manual) and terms involved in computer searches.

The librarian can be extremely helpful to teachers. He or she may

1. help teachers locate both printed and other materials related to current units of study;
2. help teachers plan a unit on use of reference materials in the library;
3. help teachers discover reading interests of individuals and specific groups of students;
4. alert teachers to professional reading materials in their content areas;
5. give presentations to students on the availability and location of materials for particular content areas; and
6. put materials on particular content topics on reserve for a class.

If students seek material in popular magazines, the teacher may review or initially teach the use of the *Readers' Guide to Periodical Literature,* which indexes articles from popular magazines. Each article is indexed under both the subject and the author's name. Sometimes an article is also included under the title.

Social studies teachers may wish to teach students to use *The New York Times Index,* which is a subject index of articles from the *New York Times.* Since dates of publication of the articles are included, students can use this index as an aid to locating articles on the same subjects in local papers.

■ Locating Information in Books

Secondary level teachers tend not to teach textbook use to their students, possibly because they think it has been covered previously. Since elementary teachers do not always provide such instruction, possibly because they use trade books rather than textbooks in their classes, secondary school content teachers need to consider adding this component to their classes (Ratekin et al., 1985; Davey, 1988; Alvermann and Moore, 1991; Dreher, 1992).

As an indication of the need for instruction in searching texts for information, the National Assessment of Educational Progress results indicated that most young adults (ages 21 to 25) tested in 1985 were proficient in such tasks as matching one feature in a question with appropriate text information, but nearly two-thirds lacked proficiency in considering three information categories at once (e.g., finding information that required location of people, action, and situation involved in a problem) (Dreher, 1992). In a study of eleventh-grade students, Dreher and Guthrie found similar results. The students' responses showed that many started searching in an appropriate manner because they located the appropriate text pages. The responses also showed, however, that they knew highlighted terms were important in locating information, but they did not seem to be able to evaluate the appropriateness of particular terms to the question posed. This indicates a need to pay attention to metacognitive (self-monitoring) skills in classroom instruction.

In a study of college students, Dreher and Brown had similar findings, with many students locating the correct page, but not evaluating the answers chosen. Some were not able to decide on an appropriate search term and therefore were unsuccessful in their search. Help in deciding on key words when searching for information is important (Dreher, 1992). Use of computer databases and the Internet makes the need to determine appropriate search terms more critical now than ever before.

Teachers should help students locate appropriate key words because some research indicates that teachers and students do not necessarily perceive the same words as being "key words" in a particular passage (Mealey et al., 1992; Schumm, 1993).

Dreher (1992) suggests that students' search skills can be improved with more use of textbooks for varied purposes. Students who are searching texts for information need to have a plan of action; decide on text sections to examine for the information (table of contents, index, etc.); extract the needed information from the text section or sections chosen (deciding if the information makes sense in terms of the search task); integrate that information with prior knowledge; and repeat the procedure until all the needed information is found. (More information on this procedure is in Guthrie and Mosenthal [1987].)

Most informational books include special features that students can use to locate needed material. Content area teachers will find that explaining the functions of prefaces, tables of contents, indexes, appendixes, glossaries, footnotes, and bibliographies is well worth the effort in increasing students' efficiency as they use books.

Some things that teachers may wish to teach about text features are discussed next.

Preface

When a content area teacher presents a new textbook to secondary school students, he or she should ask the students to read the preface and/or introduction to decide why the book was written and discover the manner in which the material is presented.

Table of Contents

The table of contents of a textbook should also be examined on the day the textbook is distributed. Students can be reminded that the table of contents indicates the topics the book includes and the pages on which those topics begin. The teacher can ask questions such as the following during the text introduction:

1. What topics are covered in this book?
2. What is the first topic that is discussed?
3. On what page does the discussion about _____ begin? (This question can be repeated several times with different topics inserted in the blank.)

Indexes

Students need to understand that an index is an alphabetical list of the important items and/or proper names mentioned in a book, with the pages where each item or name appears. Students generally need practice in using index headings and subheadings to locate information in their books.

A preliminary lesson on what an index is and how to use it to locate information can be presented. Afterward, the teacher can use the students' own textbooks to teach index use. The lesson idea shown in Example 6.1 can be modified for use with an actual index in a content area textbook.

■ ■ ■ EXAMPLE 6.1   *Sample Index and Questions*

Sample Index

Absolute value, 145, 174–175
Addition
     of decimals, 101
     of fractions, 80–83
     of natural numbers, 15–16, 46–48
     of rational numbers, 146–148
     of real numbers, 170
Angles, 203
     measurement of, 206–207
     right, 204
Axiom, 241
Base
     meaning of, 5
     change of, 6–7

Index Questions

1. On what page would you look to find out how to add decimals? Under what main topic and subheading did you have to look to discover this page number?
2. On what pages will you find *base* mentioned?
3. What pages contain information about absolute value?
4. On what pages would you look to find out about measurement of angles? What main heading did you look under to discover this? What subheading did you look under?
5. Where would you look to find information about adding real numbers? Would you expect to find any information about real numbers on page 146? Why or why not?
6. Is there information about addition of natural numbers on pages 46–48? Is information on this topic found on any other pages?
7. Find the meaning for *base* and read it aloud. Did you look in the index to find the page number? If not, could you have found it more quickly by looking in the index?

Appendixes

Students can be shown that the appendixes in textbooks and other books contain helpful information, such as documents, maps, and tables.

Glossaries

Glossaries are often found in content area textbooks. Students need to know that glossaries are similar to dictionaries but include only words presented in the books in which they are found or terms related to a specific subject. Glossaries of technical terms can greatly help students in understanding a book's content. The skills needed for proper use of a glossary are the same as those needed for using a dictionary.

Footnotes and Bibliographies

Footnotes and bibliographies are extremely valuable aids for students doing assigned research activities. Footnotes tell the source of information in the text and can guide a student to the original source if further clarification is needed. Bibliographies may refer students to other sources of information about the subjects discussed in a book. The chapter bibliographies in textbooks are generally lists of references that the author(s) consulted when preparing the chapters and references that contain additional information about the subjects.

◼ Special Reference Books

Secondary school students are often called on to find information in reference books such as encyclopedias, dictionaries, almanacs, and atlases. Unfortunately, many students reach junior high or high school without knowing how to use such books effectively.

Prerequisites for effective use of reference books include the following:

1. Knowledge of alphabetical order of entries (Most secondary school students have mastered the principles of alphabetical order, but a few need help.)
2. Knowledge that information in encyclopedias, dictionaries, and some atlases is arranged in alphabetical order
3. Ability to use guide words (i.e., knowing the location of guide words on a page and understanding that they represent the first and last entry words on a dictionary or encyclopedia page)
4. Ability to use cross-references (related primarily to use of encyclopedias)
5. Ability to use pronunciation keys (related primarily to use of dictionaries)
6. Ability to choose from several possible word meanings the one that most closely fits the context in which the word was found (related to use of dictionaries)
7. Ability to interpret the legend of a map (related to use of atlases)
8. Ability to interpret the scale of a map (related to use of atlases)
9. Ability to locate directions on maps (related to use of atlases)

10. Ability to determine which volume of a set will contain the information being sought (related primarily to use of encyclopedias)
11. Ability to determine key words under which related information can be found

Because encyclopedias, almanacs, and atlases are often difficult to read, teachers should use caution in assigning students work in these reference books. Students will not benefit from attempting to do research in books written on a level they find frustrating. When the material is too difficult, students tend to copy the material word for word instead of extracting the important ideas.

Encyclopedias

Some secondary school students need help with the use of encyclopedias. Example 6.2 gives students practice in locating varied subjects in the encyclopedia. To complete this activity (or one modeled on it), the students decide on the key words that will help them find the specified information. For example, for "Education in Sweden" they should look first under Sweden and then find the section on education. This activity can be used to assess students' ability to locate information in encyclopedias. When used in this way, the teacher must provide follow-up explanations for students who have difficulty with the items. This activity may be modified for use as a reinforcement exercise after such explanations.

A surprising number of junior high school students and a few high school students do not realize that the name of a person in an encyclopedia is alphabetized by the last name, not the first. A student who had to write a report on James Otis came to one of the authors of this text and announced that James Otis was not in the encyclopedia. Puzzled, the author asked the student to show her how he had proceeded in looking for the name. He went to the "J" volume of the encyclopedia and began to look for "James." He seemed surprised when he was told that proper names are listed alphabetically by last name and then followed by the first name. The last three items in Example 6.2 can be used to check on or work with students' understanding of this concept.

■ ■ ■ EXAMPLE 6.2 *Activity for Using the Encyclopedia*

Directions: Look up each of the following topics in the encyclopedia. On the line beside each topic, write the letter of the volume in which you found the topic and the page number on which the topic is discussed.

1. Tennis   _____

2. Solar system   _____

3. U.S. Constitution   _____

4. Lobster   _____

5. Oleander   _____

6. Sampan   _____

7. Education in Sweden   _____

8. Computer use in library systems _____

9. Marie Curie   _____

10. Martin Luther King, Jr.   _____

11. John Paul Jones   _____

Because encyclopedias vary in content and arrangement, students should be taught to use several different sets. They can compare the entries in various sets on a specified list of topics. They may also compare different sets of encyclopedias on an overall basis, noting features such as type of index used, number of volumes, ease of reading, and date of publication.

A number of encyclopedias are now available on CD-ROM for use with computers. (See the section "Using Computer Databases" later in this chapter for more detail about electronic encyclopedias.) In schools where these electronic encyclopedias are available, students can compare and contrast them with print versions.

Dictionaries

Students frequently lack familiarity with dictionary content and use. A few have some trouble with alphabetical order. A much larger number have trouble with guide words and use of the pronunciation key, and many do not realize the variety of information that is found in a dictionary entry. Spending some time to familiarize students with dictionary use can pay dividends in their future learning.

Example 6.3 shows a page from a dictionary that is recommended for use with grades 9 through 12 and provides some instructional commentary that could be helpful to use with students who need a better understanding of the dictionary.

Dialogues similar to that in Example 6.3 can be held for other words until all of the features of the dictionary have been highlighted. For example, the teacher could read a sentence containing the word *knot* and have students decide which definition fits the context and why. Use of the dictionary to discover principal parts of verbs and degrees of adjectives should also be discussed.

knelt ● knotty   668

knelt (nĕlt) *v. var. p.t. & p.p. of* KNEEL.

Knes·set (knĕs′ĕt′) *n.* [Heb. *Kéneseth*, assembly < *kanas*, he gathered.] The Israeli parliament.

knew (nōō, nyōō) *v. p.t. of* KNOW.

Knick·er·bock·er (nĭk′ər-bŏk′ər) *n.* [After Diedrich *Knickerbocker*, fictitious author of *History of New York*, by Washington Irving.] **1. a.** A descendant of the Dutch settlers of New York. **b.** A New Yorker. **2. knickerbockers.** Full breeches gathered and banded just below the knee.

knick·ers (nĭk′ərz) *pl.n.* [Short for KNICKERBOCKERS.] **1.** Long bloomers once worn as underwear by women and girls. **2.** KNICKERBOCKERS 2.

knick·knack (nĭk′năk′) *n.* [Redup. of KNACK.] A trinket.

knife (nīf) *n., pl.* **knives** (nīvz) [ME *knif* < OE *cnīf.*] **1.** A cutting instrument having a sharp blade with a handle. **2.** A cutting edge : BLADE. —*v.* **knifed, knif·ing, knifes.** —*vt.* **1.** To use a knife on, esp. to cut, stab, or wound. **2.** *Informal.* To hurt, defeat, or betray by underhand means. —*vi.* To cut or slash a way with or as if with a knife. —**knif′er** *n.*

knife-edge (nīf′ĕj′) *n.* **1.** The cutting edge of a blade. **2.** A sharp knifelike edge <felt the *knife-edge* of criticism> **3.** A metal wedge used as a low-friction fulcrum for a balancing beam or lever.

knight (nīt) *n.* [ME < OE *cniht.*] **1.** A medieval tenant giving military service as a mounted man-at-arms to a feudal landholder. **2.** A usu. high-born medieval gentleman-soldier raised by a sovereign to privileged military status after training as a page and squire. **3.** The holder of a nonhereditary dignity conferred by a sovereign in recognition of personal merit or services to the country. **4.** A member of an order or brotherhood designating its members knights. **5. a.** A zealous defender or champion of a principle or cause. **b.** A lady's devoted champion. **6.** A chess piece moved either two squares horizontally and one vertically or two vertically and one horizontally. —*vt.* **knight·ed, knight·ing, knights.** To raise (a person) to knighthood. —**knight′li·ness** *n.* —**knight′ly** *adj.*

knight er·rant (ĕr′ənt) *n., pl.* **knights errant. 1.** A knight of medieval romance who wandered in search of adventure. **2.** One given to adventurous or quixotic conduct. —**knight′-er′rant·ry** (nīt′ĕr′ən-trē) *n.*

knight·hood (nīt′hŏŏd′) *n.* **1.** The rank, profession, or dignity of a knight. **2.** Behavior of or qualities worthy of a knight : CHIVALRY. **3.** Knights as a group.

Knight of Co·lum·bus (kə-lŭm′bəs) *n.* A member of a philanthropic fraternal society of Roman Catholic men.

Knight of Pythias *n.* A member of a secret philanthropic fraternal order.

Knights of the Round Table *pl.n.* The knights of the court of King Arthur in Arthurian legend.

Knight Templar *n., pl.* **Knights Templars.** A member of a 12th–14th cent. order of knights founded to protect pilgrims in the Holy Land during the Second Crusade.

knish (kə-nĭsh′) *n.* [Yiddish < R.] Dough stuffed with potato, meat, or cheese and baked or fried.

knit (nĭt) *v.* **knit or knit·ted, knit·ting, knits.** [ME *knitten* < OE *cnyttan*, to tie in a knot.] —*vt.* **1.** To make by intertwining yarn or thread in a series of connected loops. **2.** To unite securely and closely. **3.** To draw (the brows) together in wrinkles : FURROW. —*vi.* **1.** To make a fabric or garment by knitting. **2.** To join or grow together securely. **3.** To come together in wrinkles or furrows. —**knit′** *n.* —**knit′ter** *n.*

knit·ting needle (nĭt′ĭng) *n.* A long, thin, pointed rod used for knitting.

knit·wear (nĭt′wâr′) *n.* Knitted garments in general.

knives (nīvz) *n. pl. of* KNIFE.

knob (nŏb) *n.* [ME *knobbe*, prob. < MLG.] **1. a.** A rounded protuberance. **b.** A rounded dial. **2.** A prominent rounded hill or mountain. —**knobbed** *adj.* —**knob′by** *adj.*

knob·ker·rie (nŏb′kĕr′ē) *n.* [Afr. *knopkierie* : *knop*, knob (< MDu. *cnoppe*) + *kieri*, club < Hottentot *kirri*.] A short club with one knobbed end, used by South African tribesmen as a weapon.

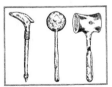

knobkerrie
Three types of knobkerries

knock (nŏk) *v.* **knocked, knock·ing, knocks.** [ME *knokken* < OE *cnocian.*] —*vt.* **1.** To strike with a hard blow. **2.** To cause to collide. **3.** To produce by hitting <*knocked* a hole in the fence> **4.** To instill as if with blows <*knocked* some sense into their

heads> **5.** *Slang.* To criticize adversely : DISPARAGE. —*vi.* **1.** To strike a blow or series of blows. **2.** To collide. **3. a.** To make a clanking or pounding noise. **b.** To undergo engine knock. —**knock around (or about).** *Informal.* **1.** To be rough or brutal with : MALTREAT. **2.** To wander from place to place. **3.** To discuss or consider. —**knock back.** *Informal.* To gulp (an alcoholic drink). —**knock down. 1.** To disassemble into parts. **2.** To declare sold at an auction, as by striking a blow with a gavel. **3.** *Informal.* To reduce, as in price. **4.** *Slang.* To receive as wages : EARN. —**knock off. 1.** *Informal.* **a.** To take a break or rest from : STOP. **b.** To cease work. **2.** *Informal.* To make, accomplish, or consume hastily or easily. **3.** *Informal.* To eliminate : deduct <*knocked* 15% off the bill> **4.** *Slang.* To kill. **5.** *Slang.* To hold up or rob. **6.** *Informal.* To copy the design or production of. —**knock out. 1.** To render unconscious. **2.** To defeat by knocking down to the canvas for a count of ten in boxing. **3.** *Informal.* To render useless or inoperative <*power knocked out* by a storm> **4.** *Informal.* To exert or exhaust (oneself or another). —**knock together.** To make or assemble quickly or carelessly. —**knock up. 1.** *Chiefly Brit.* To gain the attention of or wake up by knocking at the door. **2.** To wear out : EXHAUST. —*n.* **1.** An instance of knocking : BLOW. **2.** The sound of a sharp tap on a hard surface : RAP. **3.** A clanking, pounding noise made by an engine, esp. one in poor operating condition. **4.** *Slang.* A cutting, often petty criticism. —**knock cold.** To knock out. —**knock dead.** *Slang.* To affect strongly, usu. positively <a virtuoso piano performance that *knocked us dead*> —**knock for a loop.** *Slang.* To surprise greatly : ASTONISH. —**knock out of the box.** *Baseball.* To force the removal of (an opposing pitcher) by heavy hitting.

knock·a·bout (nŏk′ə-bout′) *n.* A small sloop with a mainsail, a jib, and a keel but no bowsprit. —*adj.* **1.** Boisterous and rowdy. **2.** Appropriate for rough wear or use <*knockabout clothes*>

knock·down (nŏk′doun′) *adj.* **1.** Forceful enough to knock down or overwhelm : POWERFUL <a *knockdown* punch> **2.** Designed to be assembled and disassembled easily and quickly <*knockdown* office furniture> —*n.* **1.** An act of knocking down. **2.** An overwhelming blow. **3.** A device or mechanism designed to be assembled and disassembled quickly and easily.

knock·down-drag·out (nŏk′doun-drăg′out′) *adj.* Marked by roughness, violence, and acrimony.

knock·er (nŏk′ər) *n.* One that knocks, as a fixture for knocking on a door.

knock-knee (nŏk′nē′) *n.* An abnormal condition in which one knee is turned toward the other or in which each is turned toward the other. —**knock′-kneed′** *adj.*

knock·off (nŏk′ŏf′, -ôf′) *n. Informal.* A usu. inexpensive copy, as of a garment <a *knockoff* of a designer original>

knock·out (nŏk′out′) *n.* **1.** The act of knocking out or the state of being knocked out. **2.** The knocking out of an opponent in boxing. **3.** *Slang.* One that is very impressive or attractive.

knockout drops *pl.n. Slang.* A solution, as of chloral hydrate, put into a drink to render the drinker unconscious.

knock·wurst (nŏk′wûrst′, -wŏŏrst′) *n. var. of* KNACKWURST.

knoll¹ (nōl) *n.* [ME *knolle* < OE *cnoll.*] A small rounded hill or mound : HILLOCK.

knoll² (nōl) [ME *knollen*, prob. alteration of *knellen*, to knell < OE *cnyllan.*] *Archaic.* —*vt. & vi.* **knolled, knoll·ing, knolls.** To ring or sound mournfully. —**knoll** *n.*

knop (nŏp) *n.* [ME *knoppe* < OE *cnop.*] A decorative knob.

knot¹ (nŏt) *n.* [ME < OE *cnotta.*] **1. a.** A compact intersection of interlaced material, as cord, ribbon, or rope. **b.** A fastening made by tying together lengths of material, as rope, in a prescribed way. **2.** A decorative bow of ribbon, fabric, or braid. **3.** A unifying bond, esp. a marriage bond. **4.** A tight group or cluster <*knots* of spectators> **5.** A difficult problem. **6. a.** A hard node, esp. on a tree, at a point from which a stem or branch grows. **b.** The circular, often darker cross section of such a node as it appears cross-grained on a piece of cut lumber. **7.** A protuberant growth in living tissue. **8.** *Naut.* **a.** A division on a log line used to measure the speed of a ship. **b.** A unit of speed, one nautical mile per hour, approx. 1.15 statute miles per hour. *usage:* Knot is a unit of nautical speed with the built-in meaning of "per hour." Therefore, a ship would properly be said to travel at ten knots (not at ten *knots* per hour). **c.** A distance of one nautical mile. —*v.* **knot·ted, knot·ting, knots.** —*vt.* **1.** To tie in or fasten with a knot. **2.** To entangle. **3.** To cause to form knots. —*vi.* **1.** To become entangled. **2.** To form a knot. —**knot′ted** *adj.*

knot² (nŏt) *n.* [Orig. unknown.] A shore bird, *Calidris canutus* or *C. tenvirostris*, related to the sandpiper.

knot·grass (nŏt′grăs′) *n.* **1.** A low-growing weedy plant, *Polygonum aviculare*, having tiny greenish flowers. **2.** A grass having jointed stems.

knot·hole (nŏt′hōl′) *n.* A hole in lumber where a knot used to be.

knot·ty (nŏt′ē) *adj.* **-ti·er, -ti·est. 1.** Tied or snarled in knots. **2.** Covered with knots or knobs : GNARLED. **3.** Difficult to compre-

---

ă **pat** ā **pay** âr **care** ä **father** ĕ **pet** ē **be** hw **which** ĭ **pit**
ī **tie** îr **pier** ŏ **pot** ō **toe** ô **paw, for** oi **noise** ŏŏ **took**

Instructional Commentary

Notice the two words at the top of the page. These words are called guide words. The first word is *knelt.* Find it in the body of the dictionary page. Where is it? (Students indicate that it is the first word on the page.) The second word is *knotty.* Find it in the body of the dictionary page. Where is it? (Students indicate that it is the last word on the page.)

Look at the bottom two lines of the right-hand column on this page and the left-hand column on the next page. (Only the first part of this is shown in the figure.) That is the pronunciation key. It has the special letter markings found in the phonetic respellings beside the entry words and a common word that has the sound each marking represents. The letter or letters that represent the sound are in bold print in the common word.

Find the word *knobkerrie* on this page. Look at its phonetic respelling in the parentheses following it. Notice that the first *k* does not appear in the respelling because it is not heard when the word is pronounced. Checking the pronunciation key, note that the *o* is pronounced like the *o* in *pot.* Looking again at the respelling, notice that the first syllable has the darkest, biggest accent mark, meaning that it gets the heaviest emphasis. Checking the pronunciation key once more, decide what sound the vowel in the second syllable has. (Students should decide that it sounds like the *e* in *pet.*) How strongly is the second syllable accented? (Students should say that it is accented less strongly than the first syllable, but more strongly than the third syllable.) How did you know? (Students should indicate that the size of the accent mark told them.) What does the final vowel in the word sound like? (Students should indicate that it sounds like the *e* in *be.*) Where did you look to find out? (Students should respond that they looked in the pronunciation key.)

Notice the *n.* just after the phonetic respelling. It tells you the part of speech of the word. What part of speech is *knobkerrie?* (If students cannot answer this question, point out the page in the dictionary that has the key to abbreviations and labels used.)

Look at the material in brackets following the *n.* It tells the etymology, or history, of the word. What does *Afr.* stand for? What does *MDu.* stand for? (If the students cannot answer immediately, refer again to the page of abbreviations.) Notice that the word is derived from words meaning "knob" and "club." Now read the definition. If, after reading the definition, you still could not decide what a knobkerrie was, you could study the illustration provided in the dictionary. Do all knobkerries look exactly alike? (After examining the illustration, students should be able to respond that they do not.)

■ Motivational Activities

Since location skills are presented to students repeatedly during their school careers, even though they may not be thoroughly learned, these skills may seem boring to students. The introduction of games, audiovisual presentations, and other motivational activities may enhance interest in the instruction. For example, paper-and-pencil scavenger hunts in the library, like the one described in the "Meeting the Challenge" vignette may be fun for the students. Cocking and Schafer (1994) have suggested library scavenger hunts to help college students learn to use many types of library resources, including CD-ROM indexes and the online search catalog.

MEETING THE CHALLENGE

Ms. MacMurray wants to check on the reference skills of the inner-city eighth graders in her English class. She confers with Mrs. Freedle, the librarian, after school the day before she has a library period. Together they pull out a variety of reference books that the students need to know how to use. Then Ms. MacMurray writes a series of questions that can be answered using each of twenty different reference books of many types, including atlases, encyclopedias, dictionaries, and almanacs. (For example: 1. What is a book by Herman Melville? [Write down its name, call number, and location.] 2. What is a catamaran, according to the *American Heritage Dictionary?* 3. What is a knobkerrie, according to the *Houghton Mifflin College Dictionary?* 4. What volume and page of the *World Book Encyclopedia* contains a discussion of catamarans? 5. What states border Colorado? 6. Who is Madame Curie?) After the questions have been constructed, Ms. MacMurray and Mrs. Freedle return the reference books to their accustomed places.

Reference skills can be checked by letting teams search for answers to a series of research questions in the library or media center. (© Michael Zide)

Back in her own room, Ms. MacMurray takes the list of students in the English class and places the students into pairs. Then she duplicates her list of questions so that each pair of students will have a copy. Choosing from among several prizes that she has solicited from local businesses, she decides which prize to give the team with the most correct answers within the time limit. (If there is a tie, the first team to finish with the highest number of correct answers wins.)

The next day, Ms. MacMurray assigns the students to their teams, gives a list of questions to each team, and escorts the students to the library. Teammates confer to choose a strategy and then begin their searches. As they intently work to win the contest, Ms. MacMurray quietly notes good and poor strategies of library use exhibited—guidance for future lessons in her class. She later uses explanations and activities such as ones described in this chapter to work on understanding and use of indexes, tables of contents, glossaries, computer databases, the card catalog, the basic library arrangement, alphabetical order, guide words, and dictionary respellings, if these prove to be problem areas.

■ Using Computer Databases

What value do computer databases have for students?

The location skills that students need in today's schools include one type that has not received much attention in the past. Students need to know how to retrieve information stored in **computer databases,** either ones that the students have compiled themselves or others that are available in the school.

A database is an organized collection of information. Conceptually, a database is like a filing cabinet (or several cabinets), with separate file folders for each article in the database. The information may be categorized by subject or by another categorization scheme and is indexed for easy access. Typically, the computer system supporting a database allows the user to construct complicated search requirements, for example, "Find all articles on distortion in optics used for telescopes published after 1980 in Sweden." Databases can be user created (student created) or preexisting, large or small, general or specific.

Ben Jonson, English actor and author, observed that there are two kinds of knowledge: what we know and what we know how to find. Increasingly, finding information is becoming a computer-oriented task involving databases. More and more occupations rely on the use of such databases, making the need for information retrieval skills and an understanding of database maintenance increasingly relevant for today's students (Oley, 1989). The variety of databases available covers agriculture, business, computers, finance, forestry, health and medicine, national and world news, and social sciences, among other topics. Access to these sources has traditionally been through trained intermediaries, often qualified librarians, but increasingly the end user has direct access to the materials via computer. Cost-effective use of these sources requires knowledge of how to construct search questions for the database system in use, of the organizational scheme of the subject matter, and of search techniques in general (Oley, 1989). The user must be able to phrase complex questions that limit the retrieval process to pertinent information without omitting any desired information.

A database can be very broad or very specific in scope, and it can be organized in a wide variety of ways. A limited database might contain the names, symbols, and basic properties of chemical compounds used in the manufacture of paper, or the names, dates of inauguration, and birthplaces of the presidents of the United States. A large database is *Who's Who in America*. The contents are the same as those in the printed volume, but its structure as a database allows searching by such things as birthplace (e.g., what famous people are from Claysville, Idaho), or profession, or college of matriculation.

Schools now have access to both local and remote databases. A local database resides on the computer system of the user, whereas a remote database resides on a computer system other than the user's. Typically, remote databases are accessed through telephone lines. Although access to large, remote databases requires some special equipment (such as a modem and a communication port on the computer), these are often available to schools. The most prevalent means of remote access is through the Internet.

A local database in a classroom might range from a small quantity of information collected as part of a class project to a complete encyclopedia. Several encyclopedias are available in computer-readable form, on CD-ROMs. Examples are *The New Grolier Multimedia Encyclopedia* (Grolier Electronic Publishing Inc.), *Microsoft Encarta Multimedia Encyclopedia* (Microsoft Corp.), and *Compton's Interactive Encyclopedia* (Compton's NewMedia). The *Encarta* is written for ages 9 to 15, but it is applicable for all ages. *Compton's Interactive* is recommended for fifth graders to adults, and *New Grolier Multimedia* is recommended for high school level to adult. Therefore, there is an electronic encyclopedia to fit the needs of any level of learner in the secondary school.

An entire multivolume encyclopedia can be contained on a single disk. Multimedia encyclopedias contain more than text; they include pictures, maps, animated diagrams, voice recordings, music recordings, and sound effects (such as sounds that animals make). Users can move around among related materials easily; for example, they might read about Bach, view his picture, and hear a recording of one of his musical compositions. They might also read about grizzly bears, see a video of one, and hear its sound. Of course, different encyclopedias have different pictures, sounds, and videos. The cost of the equipment required to read CD-ROMs can make them unavailable in some individual classrooms, but the cost is not prohibitive for a school's media center or library. Regardless of cost, the motivational aspect of using the electronic encyclopedia is high (Melnick, 1991; Krushenisky, 1993).

Since access to databases is usually limited, techniques to maximize the effectiveness of their use should be initiated. For example, a mock demonstration using slides or overhead transparencies can demonstrate the procedure for signing on to the database and the structure of search questions. Examples can be given of good and bad techniques, with emphasis on likely problem areas.

Creating small databases in the classroom can give students valuable experience in categorizing and organizing material. For this type of work on the computer, the teacher needs access to a database utility program of some kind. Examples of such programs are *FileMaker Pro* and *ClarisWorks* (for both IBM and Macintosh computers) and *AppleWorks* (for Apple IIe computers). After the information for the database has been collected and entered into the computer, the database system can be used for critical analyses, such as comparing similarities and differences (e.g., "What do rapidly growing population centers have in common? How are these areas different from declining areas?"); analyzing relationships; examining trends; and testing and refining hypotheses (Lapp, Flood, and Farnan, 1989).

What kinds of information can be found by searching Internet sites?

One important application of databases for students is the computerized card catalog in some libraries. Students access the catalog by using a computer keyboard to request information that is transferred to the student on the computer's screen. Such databases replace the traditional card catalogs, providing the traditional indexing plus complex search capabilities. Many libraries also provide access to the ERIC (Educational Resources Information Center) index of educational material, as well as to the card catalogs of other libraries and even **Internet** sites that contain electronic books and magazines and home pages that have links to a wide variety of types of information, which may include multimedia as well as text. Searching for information on the World Wide Web can be made easier by the use of a number of available search engines. Wehmeyer (1996) lists search engines that can help beginners get started. (More on the Internet is located in the Afterword of this text.)

■■ Organizational Skills

When participating in study activities such as writing reports, secondary school students need to organize the ideas they encounter in their reading. Three helpful organizational skills are outlining, summarizing, and note taking. All require recognition and recording, in an organized form, of important ideas from the materials read. The act of organizing information helps students comprehend and retain it better. Pearson and Santa (1995) found that students recalled terms in categorized lists more readily than those in random order, and they demonstrated this to the students by having class members try to learn lists of terms in each condition. Students then saw the value of organizing material in order to learn it.

What different ways can be used to outline material that is read for class?

■ Outlining

Teachers should help their students to understand that **outlining** is recording information from reading material in a way that makes clear the relationships between the main ideas and the supporting details. Before it is possible for students to learn to construct an outline properly, they must know how to identify main ideas and supporting details in reading selections. Information on how to assist students in locating main ideas and recognizing related details is found in Chapter 4.

Readiness for formal outlining tasks may be developed by having students work with **arrays,** which are free-form outlines. When constructing arrays, students are required to arrange key words and phrases in ways that show the relationships set forth by the author. They can use words, lines, and arrows to do this. It is important to use a simple, familiar story or an uncomplicated expository selection for this activity, so that the students can focus on the logical arrangement of the terms rather than worrying about the details of the story or selection. Example 6.4 shows a story array for the familiar story "Johnny Appleseed."

■ ■ ■ EXAMPLE 6.4   *Story Array*

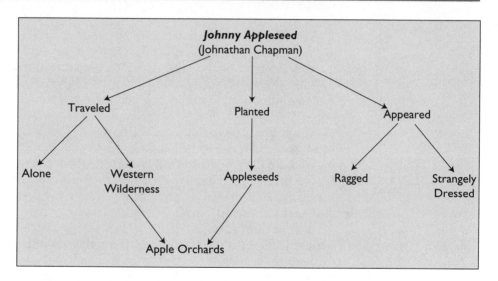

Teachers can guide students to learn how to make arrays by first supplying the words and phrases and then letting the students work in groups to complete the arrays. First the students read the selection; then they arrange the words and phrases appropriately, using lines and arrows to indicate relationships. The teacher questions students about the positioning and direction of arrows, asking for reasons for the choices made. In addition, the teacher is available to answer students' questions. Eventually, the students are expected to choose key words and concepts themselves and arrange them without the teacher's help.

Two other types of outlines that students may find useful are the **sentence outline** and the **topic outline.** In a sentence outline, each point is stated in the form of a complete sentence; in a topic outline, the points are written in the form of key words and phrases. The sentence outline is generally easier to master because the topic outline involves an extra task—condensing main ideas, already expressed in sentence form, into key words and phrases.

The first step in making an outline is extracting the main ideas from the material and listing them beside Roman numerals in the order in which they occur. The next step is locating the details that support each of the main ideas and listing them beside capital letters below the main idea that they support. These details are indented to indicate subordination to the main idea. Details that are subordinate to these details are indented still more and preceded by Arabic numerals. The next level of subordination is indicated by lowercase letters. Although other levels of subordination are possible, secondary school students will rarely need such fine divisions.

The following are two important ideas about outlining that a teacher may wish to stress:

1. The degree of importance of ideas in an outline is shown by the numbers and letters used, as well as by the indentation of entries. Points that have equal importance are designated by the same number or letter style and the same degree of indentation.
2. An outline should not incorporate unimportant or unrelated details.

Teachers can help students see how a textbook chapter would be outlined by showing them how the headings within the chapter indicate different levels of subordination. For example, in some textbooks the title for the outline would be the title of the chapter. Roman numeral headings would be centered, or major, headings in the chapter, capital letter headings would be side headings, and Arabic numeral headings would be italic or paragraph headings.

Another approach to helping students to learn to outline their reading assignments is for the teacher to supply the students with partially completed outlines of the material and then have them complete the outlines. The teacher can vary the difficulty of the activity by gradually leaving out more and more details until the students do the entire outline alone. In Example 6.5, a progression of assignments in outlining is suggested.

■ ■ ■ EXAMPLE 6.5   *Progression of Outlining Assignments*

First Assignment

Title (Given by Teacher)
    I. (Given by teacher)
        A. (Given by teacher)
            1. (To be filled in by student)

    2. (To be filled in by student)
   B. (Given by teacher)
    1. (To be filled in by student)
    2. (Given by teacher)
     a. (To be filled in by student)
     b. (To be filled in by student)
  II. (Given by teacher)
   A. (Given by teacher)
   B. (To be filled in by student)

Second Assignment

Title (Given by Teacher)
  I. (Given by teacher)
   A. (To be filled in by student)
   B. (To be filled in by student)
    1. (To be filled in by student)
    2. (To be filled in by student)
  II. (Given by teacher)
   A. (To be filled in by student)
   B. (To be filled in by student)

Third Assignment

Title
  I.
   A.
   B.
   C.
    1.
    2.
  II.
   A.
    1.
     a.
     b.
    2.
   B.

  Outlining can potentially be helpful in any subject area. A standard form of outlining, used throughout the school, will decrease confusion among the students.

■ Summarizing

What should be included in a good summary?

Good summaries of reading assignments can be extremely valuable to students when they are studying for tests. To write a good **summary,** a student must restate what the author has said in a more concise form. The main ideas and essential supporting details of a selection should be preserved in a summary, but illustrative material and statements that merely elaborate on the main ideas should not be included. The ability to locate main ideas is therefore a prerequisite for learning how to write good summaries. (Development of this skill is discussed in Chapter 4.)

The topic sentence of a paragraph is a good summary of the paragraph, if it is well written. Practice in finding topic sentences of paragraphs, therefore, is also practice in the skill of summarizing paragraphs.

Summaries of longer selections may be constructed by combining the main ideas of the component paragraphs into summary statements. Certain types of paragraphs can generally be disregarded when making summaries. Introductory and illustrative paragraphs do not add new ideas and therefore are not helpful in constructing a concise overview of the material. Students who write summaries of their reading assignments may wish to compare their summaries with the author's concluding or summary paragraphs, to make sure that they have not omitted essential details.

When writing summaries, students should try not only to limit the number of sentences they use but also to limit the number of words within sentences. Words that are not needed to convey sentence meaning can be omitted. For example:

Original sentence. A match, carelessly discarded by an unsuspecting tourist, can cause the destruction by fire of many acres of trees that will take years of work to replace.

Changed sentence. Carelessly discarded matches can result in extensive destruction of forested areas by fire.

Teachers should show students that they must delete trivial and redundant material to create good summaries. They should use superordinate terms to replace lists of similar items or actions (e.g., "animals" for "pigs, dogs, and cats"). A superordinate action can be used to replace steps in an action (e.g., "made spaghetti sauce" for "took tomato sauce, sliced mushrooms, chopped onion, oregano, and salt, . . . and placed on the stove to cook on low heat"). As mentioned above, each paragraph can be represented by an implied main idea sentence or a directly stated topic sentence. Paragraphs can then be examined to see which ones are most needed. Only necessary paragraphs should be kept, and some that are kept can be combined (Brown and Day, 1983; Brown, Day, and Jones, 1983; Hare and Borchardt, 1984; Recht, 1984).

One method of teaching summarization is discussed in Chapter 7 under the heading "Teaching Procedures." It is the Guided Reading and Summarizing Procedure described by Hayes (1989).

Practice in summarizing is most effective if it is based on material in current textbooks or other reading material for classes. The teacher may give students a textbook section to read, along with three or four summaries of the material. Then students can choose the best summary from those presented and explain why it is best. This is good preparation for independent student writing of summaries.

To write good summaries, students must identify the important material to include as well as the unnecessary material and then reorganize the material for clarity. Since ideas have to be understood, evaluated, and condensed, they are transformed in summarizing in a way that is not typical of simple recall (Hill, 1991). Therefore, retention is more likely to result when students summarize assignments.

Précis writing is a special form of summarizing that is discussed in detail in Chapter 8. Porter (1990) suggests using it with English as a Second Language (ESL) students to develop abstracting and synthesizing skills and to develop vocabulary through use of synonyms. ESL students begin by writing a précis in a group setting and continue by writing individual ones.

■ Note Taking

Taking notes on material read for classes can be a helpful memory aid. Well-constructed notes can save students time and effort. To take good notes, students must think about the material they are reading and organize it in a meaningful way; as a result, they will be more likely to remember it. It is also true that the simple act of writing ideas helps fix them in students' memories. Smith and Tompkins (1988, p. 46) point out that "the farther students move along the continuum from verbatim notes to elaborated notes, the greater the benefit they receive." This increased benefit comes from increased active mental involvement with the text. The act of organization also aids retention.

Notes on Reading Assignments

Students should be encouraged to use the form of note taking that helps them the most. Some may use semantic webs or outlines when taking notes on an assignment in a textbook. Others may write a summary of the textbook materials. Still others may wish to use what Smith and Tompkins (1988, p. 48) call structured notes: "Structured notes are graphic organizers in which the top level structure used by the author or the structure inferred by the reader is explicit in the graphic." In other words, the notes show description, time/order, cause-effect, problem-solution, comparison-contrast, and definition-examples patterns visually through the form in which the notes are taken. For example, the description pattern could have notes taken in a sunburst shape, with the concept being described in the center of the circle and the descriptive details on the rays; and the time/order pattern could have a stairstep numbered listing of events in order. Teachers should teach each pattern and the structure for notes taken in that pattern.

What are the characteristics of the Cornell Note-taking System?

Pauk (1993) suggests use of the **Cornell Note-taking System,** which he developed. With this system, the student draws a vertical line two and a half inches from the left-hand side of each page to create a cue column and a horizontal line two inches from the bottom of the page to create a summary area. Students take notes on the material in the area to the right of the cue column and above the summary area. When the students review the notes, they write questions answered in the notes in the cue column to clarify the information in their minds and strengthen their memory for the material. In the summary area of the page they sum up that page of notes in one or two sentences. This summarization helps them look at the main ideas covered instead of a collection of details. Example 6.6 shows the Cornell System in use.

■ ■ ■ EXAMPLE 6.6   *Cornell Note-taking System*

	Psych. 105 – Prof. Martin – Sept. 14 (Mon.)
	MEMORY
	Memory tricky – Can recall instantly many trivial things of childhood; yet, forget things recently worked hard to learn & retain.
How do psychologists account for remembering?	Memory Trace — Fact that we retain information means that some change was made in the brain. — Change called "memory trace."
What's a "memory trace"?	— "Trace" probably a molecular arrangement similar to molecular changes in a magnetic recording tape.
What are the three memory systems?	Three memory systems: sensory, short-term, long-term.
How long does sensory memory retain information? How is information transferred to STM?	— Sensory (lasts one second) Ex. Words or numbers sent to brain by sight (visual image) start to disintegrate within a few tenths of a second & gone in one full second, unless quickly transferred to S-T memory by verbal repetition.

What are the retention times of STM?
 	
What's the capacity of the STM?
 	
How to hold information in STM?
 	
What are the retention times of LTM?
 	
What are the six ways to transfer information from STM to LTM?
	— Short-term memory [STM] (lasts 30 seconds)
	  • Experiments show: a syllable of 3 letters remembered 50% of the time after 3 seconds. Totally forgotten end of 30 seconds.
	  • S-T memory – limited capacity = holds average of 7 items.
	  • More than 7 items -- jettisons some to make room.
	  • To hold items in STM, must rehearse -- must hear <u>sound</u> of words internally or externally.
	— Long-term memory [LTM] (lasts a lifetime or a short time).
	  • Transfer fact or idea by:
	    (1) <u>Associating</u> w/information already in LTM.
	    (2) <u>Organizing</u> information into meaningful units.
	    (3) <u>Understanding</u> by comparing & making relationships.
	    (4) <u>Frameworking</u> – fit pieces in like in a jigsaw puzzle.
	    (5) <u>Reorganizing</u> – combing new & old into a new unit.
	    (6) <u>Rehearsing</u> – aloud to keep memory trace strong.

Three kinds of memory systems are sensory, which retains information for about one second; short-term, which retains for a maximum of thirty seconds; and long-term, which varies from a lifetime of retention to a relatively short time.

    The six ways (activities) to transfer information to the long-term memory are: associating, organizing, understanding, frameworking, reorganizing and rehearsing.

Source: Pauk, Walter, How to Study in College, *Fifth Edition. Copyright © 1993 by Houghton Mifflin Company. Used with permission.*

What advantages can you see in using an I-Chart for note taking?

    Note taking for a research report can also be done in the form of I-Charts (inquiry charts) (Hoffman, 1992; Randall, 1996). An **I-Chart** is composed of a grid that has questions about the subject at the tops of columns and references consulted along the left-hand margin, providing the headings for the rows. There is also a place for other interesting facts that the students know and a summary of the findings. Hoffman (1992) wrote out the references in the right-hand column, but Randall (1996) let the students number the references and make a bibliography, and she used a separate I-Chart for each question, rather than having multiple questions on a page. Students were encouraged to paraphrase the answers to questions on their charts. Sometimes students had trouble keeping their answers focused, as you can see in Example 6.7, in which plants are mentioned in answer to a question about animals, but the charts do help students to be more organized in their note taking. Example 6.7 shows a modification of Hoffman's I-Chart (1992) used by Randall (1996).

■■■ EXAMPLE 6.7   Modified I-Chart

Name: Melanie   **Topic:** Rainforest Destruction

Subtopic: What animals live in the Rainforest?

What I already know: There are alot of birds an other animals big and small. Some of the animals living in rainforests are going extinct.

Bibliography #:	
1	Colorful birds, chattering monkeys, butterflies
2	Monkeys, squirrels, birds, jaguar, giant armadillo, plants: giant water lilies, stiltroots, strangler, and buttresses, an aerial roots, palm. Anaconda, geometrid moth, poison arrow frog, Matamata turtle, Kinkajou
3	Keel-billed toucan, rare butterflies, howler monkeys, the 3-toed sloth, tamandua (related to the anteater), jaguar, the ruby-topaz humming bird, genus Denodraba, a bird-eating spider, leaf cutter ants, and the red brocket deer.

Interesting related facts: 6% of the earth's land surface is covered by Rainforests which are a home to over half the planets species. 1/3 of earth's species are beleived to live in this rainforest, only a fraction of them have been given scientific names.

Key words: Biodeversity

New questions to research: What types of tree species live in the rainforest?

Source: Sally N. Randall, "Information Charts: A Strategy for Organizing Student Research." Journal of Adolescent and Adult Literacy, 39 (April 1996): 538. Reprinted with permission of Sally N. Randall and the International Reading Association.

Before notes are taken for a research paper, the questions that should be answered in the paper must be determined. The questions can be listed under categories important to the topic, and students can go to appropriate reference sources to find out about the categories. For example, "What types of printers exist?" and "What are some advantages of an ink jet printer?" could be categorized under the topic "Printers." All notes taken on the topic "Printers" could be labeled with this term, to facilitate organization of notes. Other categories might be "Monitors," "CPUs," and "Keyboards," for example.

Notes for a research paper can be especially effective when made on index cards that can later be sorted into topics to be covered in the paper. If note cards are used, each one should include the source of information so that the paper is well documented. Sample note cards are shown in Example 6.8. Some guidelines for note taking that may be helpful to students follow:

1. Key words and phrases should be used in notes.
2. Enough of the context must be included to make the notes understandable after a period of time has elapsed.
3. The bibliographical reference should be included with each note card or page.
4. Direct quotations should be copied exactly and should be used sparingly.
5. Notes should differentiate clearly between direct quotations and reworded material.
6. Notes should be as brief as possible.
7. Use of abbreviations can make note taking less time-consuming. Examples: $\therefore$ for therefore; w/ for with; = for equals.

■ ■ ■ EXAMPLE 6.8　　Note Cards

First reference from source:

> Herring, George C. "Indochina." *The World Book Encyclopedia,* 1991, X, 224.
>
> Indochina includes the following countries: Cambodia, Laos, Vietnam.

Source previously used:

> Herring, page 224.
>
> A variety of racial and language groups are found in Indochina, resulting in a lack of uniformity and unity among the people.

Incomplete sentences:

> Herring, page 225.
>
> Khmer tribesmen—ancestors of present-day Cambodians—empire famous for art, architecture and government.

Teachers may be able to help their students learn to take good notes by "thinking through" a textbook assignment with them orally in class, emphasizing the points that should be included in a good set of notes. This provides them with a model of the process of note taking. Students then can be encouraged to take notes on another assignment and compare them with a set of notes the teacher has constructed on the same material.

Taking Classroom Notes

What are the values derived from using the Guided Lecture Procedure?

Another way to help students develop note-taking skills is the **Guided Lecture Procedure** (GLP), devised by Kelly and Holmes (1979). The steps in the GLP are as follows:

1. Before the lecture begins, the teacher writes the lecture objectives (maximum of four) in brief form on the chalkboard, accompanied by new terms to be presented in the lecture.
2. Students copy this material from the board before the lecture begins. This gives them a purpose for listening.
3. The lecturer speaks for approximately thirty minutes while the students listen *without* taking notes.
4. The lecturer stops and gives the students approximately five minutes to write down all that they recall from the lecture. Students are encouraged to categorize and relate ideas.
5. Students are divided into small groups to discuss the lecture and organize their notes. The lecturer serves as an assistant during this phase, helping students find the answers they seek.
6. After the class, students reflect on the material and the class activities. This step helps promote long-term memory.
7. Finally, students write from memory a narrative covering the main points of the lecture and the conclusions drawn.

This procedure, which is excellent as a note-taking strategy, is also a study approach and, to a large degree, a teaching procedure. Teachers will find it helpful to use in many content classes.

Sakta (1992) suggests teaching students to use an organizational strategy for taking notes on lectures by outlining the topic, main ideas, and supporting details before class, and then explaining the organizer to the students as a preview at the beginning of class. This provides them with a framework for listening to the lecture. Sakta then suggests leaving the organizer visible during the lecture so that the students can use it as an aid to taking their lecture notes. In subsequent lessons the information included on the teacher-made organizer can be progressively reduced (in a manner similar to the progression of outlining assignments shown earlier in this chapter), moving in four steps from all information to only the topic and number of main ideas indicated. As the students become responsible for identifying more and more of the information to be included in their notes, they become more proficient note takers.

How is the Directed Note-taking Activity related to outlining skill?

The **Directed Notetaking Activity,** described by Spires and Stone (1989), includes the taking of structured formal notes in a split-page format, self-questioning to monitor involvement in the process of note taking, and direct instruction in note taking. Using the split-page method of note taking, students divide their pages into two columns and write the main ideas in the lecture in the left column and the supporting details and examples in the right column.

How are peers involved in the NOTES procedure?

Stahl, King, and Henk (1991) developed a complex procedure called **NOTES** (Notetaking Observation, Training and Evaluation Scales) to train students to be good note takers. Although it is an excellent procedure, teachers of classes other than reading and study skills classes may find it too time-consuming. (Those who would like to try the complete system can refer to the May 1991 issue of *Journal of Reading*.) Some content teachers may simply want to incorporate ideas from the longer procedure to enhance note-taking skills, without using all of the forms and cooperative learning aspects of the procedure.

When using NOTES, students do a self-evaluation of their note-taking practices before, during, and after lectures. The first step in note-taking training is for the teacher to model note taking by taking notes on an overhead transparency while a taped lecture is played, thinking aloud about the notes. Monitored practice of note taking by the students is the second major step. Next, the students receive feedback from their peers and instructor on the quality of their notes. Peer partners evaluate each other's notes, using specified evaluation criteria, and students keep a record of their progress.

Summary

Students in content area classes must be able to locate information in the library or media center; in textbooks, other informational books, and reference books; and in computer databases in order to do effective research for class presentations and written reports. To use the library, they often must know how to use the card catalog, computer terminals, and either the Dewey Decimal System or the Library of Congress system for book arrangement. To use books successfully, they need to know the parts of a book and the functions of each part.

For use of reference books, they need to know about alphabetical order, guide words, cross-references, pronunciation keys, map legends, map scales, and other location and interpretation aids. To use computer databases, they must know how to construct search questions for specific systems.

Also important to students who are writing reports are the skills of outlining, note taking, and summarizing. All these skills require the ability to recognize main ideas and supporting details. Outlining requires showing relationships among the main ideas and supporting details, whereas summarizing requires stating the important information in a more concise way. Note taking may be done to help students remember what they have read or what they have heard in lectures. Notes may be taken in outline or summary form, in the form of graphic organizers, in split-page format, on I-Charts, or in another form that the student finds useful to organize the information. Notes are frequently taken on note cards when they are being used as the basis for writing a research paper.

Discussion Questions

1 How can the librarian and the content area teacher cooperate to teach library skills that students need for research activities?
2 What parts of a book do students need to be able to use effectively if they are going to locate needed information efficiently?
3 What types of reference books need special attention from you, if your students are to do effective research for your class?
4 How can outlining help students to understand the material in the textbook for your content class?
5 What are helpful guidelines for note taking that you can share with students?
6 Which technique for teaching note taking mentioned in this chapter seems to hold most promise for your classes? What others do you know of that you could use instead?
7 What computer skills may be needed by students making use of today's libraries and media centers?

Enrichment Activities

1 Make a set of sample card catalog cards for ten or more books. Plan a lesson on use of the card catalog. Teach this lesson to a group of your classmates. *Teach the lesson in a secondary school classroom, if possible.
2 Plan a lesson on use of the index of a secondary level textbook of your choice. Teach the lesson to a group of your classmates. *Teach the lesson in a secondary school classroom, if possible.
3 Take a content area textbook at the secondary level and plan procedures to familiarize students with the parts of the book and with the reading aids the book offers.

4 Visit a secondary school library and listen to the librarian explain the reference materials and library procedures to the students. Evaluate the presentation and decide how you might make changes if you were responsible for it.

5 Make a bulletin board display that would be helpful to use when teaching either outlining or note taking. Display it either in your college classroom or in a secondary school classroom.

*These activities are designed for in-service teachers, student teachers, or practicum students.

CHAPTER 7

Reading-Study Strategies for Textbook Use

Overview

In this chapter we consider the development of strategies that enhance both comprehension and retention of information in printed material. Study methods such as SQ3R, ROWAC, EVOKER, and SQRQCQ are described, and their usefulness in helping students manage content area reading assignments is discussed. Teaching procedures such as GRASP and PSRT are also included.

Ways to help students learn to read to follow directions are suggested. How to help students learn from the graphic aids (maps, graphs, tables, diagrams, and pictures) in their content area reading materials is discussed, as well as how to help them learn to adjust their reading rates to fit their purposes and the materials to be read. The two final topics are retention and test taking.

Purpose-Setting Questions

As you read this chapter, try to answer these questions:

1 What are some study methods designed for use with content area reading selections, and how do they help?
2 What are some teaching procedures for helping students learn study skills and helping them read with more comprehension, and why are they effective?
3 How can a teacher help students of varying abilities learn to follow written directions accurately?

4 What types of graphic aids are found in textbooks, and what must students know about each one to read it effectively?

5 What are some factors to consider in instruction related to reading rate?

6 Why is flexibility of rate important to secondary school students?

7 What activities can help students retain what they read?

8 How can teachers help students read test questions with understanding?

■ ■ Preparation for Study

Secondary school students often are unaware that preparation for study is important. They think that they can simply sit down and read without preparation. This approach often results in inefficient study efforts.

Although students are not always aware of their own study styles, such knowledge can be beneficial. Two categories of study styles are strategy preferences (determined by having students try out teacher-modeled study methods and decide which are personally effective) and preferences for environmental conditions (lighting, room temperatures, noise level, presence or absence of other people, food or no food, time of day, etc.). Having students reflect on their own preferences can help them set the stage for their own study more effectively (Archambeault, 1992).

Time spent discussing effective study preparation is well spent, because it allows students to be more productive when they study. Following are some tips for teachers to pass along.

■ Looking Ahead

1. On a special page in your notebook list all the long-term (a week or longer allowed for completion) assignments that must be completed during the school term. Include deadlines.

2. Under each assignment, list component tasks (e.g., brainstorming, library research, organization, rough draft, final paper). Give yourself a deadline for completing each component task so that you will finish the entire assignment on time. Highlight dates.

3. At the beginning of every week, make a separate page for each day of that week. On the page for each day, list the tasks to be worked on that day. Check your master list for deadlines for the parts of long-term assignments and also add assignments the teacher gives during the week.

4. On each page, rank the tasks from the most to least important. Schedule the most important tasks first. Schedule these tasks for times of day when you are most alert and energetic. When tasks are equally important, schedule the harder task for your most alert, productive times. Schedule time for every necessary task. On days when not much daily work is scheduled, look at the listed long-term activities and try to get ahead on them.

■ Setting the Stage

1. Find a place to study where distractions are minimal. Consider whether music distracts you, or some types distract you and others do not.

2. Place your materials in your study area so that you have sufficient light and there is no glare that can tire your eyes prematurely.

3. Adjust the temperature so that you will be neither too hot nor too cold.

4. Gather all of your materials before you sit down to study. You will usually need pencils, pens, paper, textbooks, and reference books (especially a dictionary), although you may need more specialized material for some assignments. Check the requirements for your assignments ahead of time and assemble all the needed items.

■ Considering Your Options

1. If you work best alone, choose a time to study when your friends are not likely to disturb you, but, if you learn best in a group, consider finding someone from your class to study with you.

2. If you are a visual learner (learn best through seeing), use reading and graphic aids for studying. If you are an auditory learner (learn best through hearing), talk about the material and possibly listen to tapes of lectures. You may even want to read the material aloud to yourself. If you are a kinesthetic learner (learn best through movement), take notes on the material or find a way to use the ideas in a practical manner. In other words, take advantage of your own strengths when you study.

3. If you are a morning person, consider studying before school each day. If you are an evening person, study while you are still alert; don't let television and other distractions lure you away from your study goals.

4. Choose a study procedure that your teacher has presented that best fits your personal needs, although you may want to modify it to fit the way you think and learn.

Importance of a Study Method

According to Simons (1989, p. 419), "studies show that up to 50% of the students in secondary classrooms cannot read and learn from their content area textbooks." These students can often read narrative material effectively, but they have difficulty with expository text. Students also often do not study effectively because they *do not know how.* They have never learned how to focus on the important material, identify the organization of material, make use of graphic aids, vary reading rates and study procedures to fit the material, or connect new learning to things they already know. They often approach all content reading material with the same attention and speed used for pleasure reading of narrative material.

What are metacognitive skills, and why are they important?

Students often also fail to make use of **metacognitive skills**—that is, they do not monitor their comprehension of the material that they read as they are reading it. Metacognition involves knowing what is known already, knowing when understanding of new material has been accomplished, knowing how the understanding was reached, and knowing why something is or is not known (Guthrie, 1983). Students frequently look at or pronounce the words in a selection and feel that they have read it without checking to see if they have located important ideas and understood the content and how it fits in with information that they already know. They fail to ask, "Do I understand this point?" and "Does this make sense?" Even if they ask these questions, when the answers are negative, they may not remedy the situation by choosing and applying appropriate strategies, such as rereading, checking word meanings in a glossary or dictionary, looking for relationships among ideas, and identifying the organizational pattern of the text in order to clear up problems with meaning (Babbs and Moe, 1983). All these activities are part of effective studying.

Teachers must show students the importance of activating prior knowledge about a topic, relating new information to the prior knowledge, and realizing whether the new information makes sense in light of previous knowledge. They must also make students aware of the strategies that they can use to help them figure out meanings that are not immediately apparent. Teacher modeling of self-questioning about meaning and deciding on strategies to use when meaning is unclear is a good approach for increasing metacognitive activities among students.

Having purposes for their reading activities can increase the likelihood that students will apply metacognitive skills. If they have purposes for reading, they can check to see if those purposes were met. If they have no purposes, they may not know what to look for or what questions to ask about the material.

Study methods have been developed that help students approach content area reading material in ways that make comprehension and retention of the material more likely. These methods help students to establish purposes for reading the material and to monitor their reading to determine if they have understood the concepts. They often cause the student to look at the material more than once for different purposes, thereby making retention of the ideas more likely.

Students need to become aware of the advantages of using a study method. They need to be told how to apply each method and how to decide when to apply it. For example, neither SQ3R nor any of the other study methods described in this chapter is appropriate for use with recreational reading in fiction. Having this knowledge constitutes a metacognitive skill that is very valuable. (See Chapter 4 for more about metacognitive skills that allow students to monitor their comprehension and make adjustments when difficulties in comprehension arise.)

Students who do not know what study method to use when reading content area assignments may resort to pronouncing all the words in the selections as they read without actually thinking about the content. They may then rely on rote memorization to get them through tests on the material and, therefore, may never find meaning in the content they are studying (Clarke et al., 1989), because such memorization does not require understanding.

■ Teaching Procedures

Teachers find certain teaching procedures particularly helpful in enhancing students' study skills. GRASP, the PSRT strategy, and some recitation techniques can be useful approaches.

What goals might a teacher use GRASP to meet?

GRASP—the Guided Reading and Summarizing Procedure—is based on the Guided Reading Procedure (Manzo, 1975), with a focus on the process of summary writing. The goals of this procedure are development of a skill students can apply independently in writing reports, sharpening of their abilities to recall material they read, encouragement of self-correction, and improvement in their organizational skills. The steps in the procedure are as follows: "prepare students for the lesson, have them read for remembering details, help them group remembered details, and show them how to convert grouped details into a prose summary" (Hayes, 1989, p. 96). In the preparation phase, the teacher explains the purpose of the procedure. The selection that is given to the students to read should be 500 to 1,500 words long. The students make a list of all remembered facts. Rereading takes place to fill in information that was originally left out and to make corrections in the original listing. Then major topics in the text are determined, and the information is categorized by topic. Finally, a summary is formed by including only important information, compressing and combining information, and adding any information needed for a coherent account (Hayes, 1989).

What does PSRT stand for?

Simons (1989) suggests use of the **PSRT** strategy. The steps in this strategy are *Prepare, Structure, Read,* and *Think.* The *Prepare* step includes finding out what the students already know about the concepts in the material and, if necessary, supplementing this background information. Brainstorming about the key concepts should take place during this step. The *Structure* step involves helping students understand the text's organization through use of a graphic overview that is partially completed on the board with them. During the *Read* step, the students read the text independently for a purpose and individually complete the overview presented in the previous step. During the *Think* step, a discussion of the text is held, the overview on the board is completed as a class activity, and the students summarize the text and answer higher-order, teacher-developed questions about it. This procedure is effective because of its high levels of teacher-student interactions. It also takes into account the importance of background knowledge and text organization to reading comprehension.

Classroom recitation techniques can be used to encourage good study practices. Recitation involves saying aloud the information to be remembered. It may serve as a motivational factor for studying material because students feel the need to prepare when they may be required to make presentations in class. It also can strengthen the memory for the material, as a student must think about the information, say it, and hear the result. Some forms of recitation include paraphrasing previous contributions to the content discussion, telling something that was learned from the day's lesson, discussing answers to questions constructed by students, brainstorming about possible test questions, and responding simultaneously with the rest of the class, through signals, to true/false or multiple-choice questions. The total-class response activities allow students to respond without feeling the pressure of being singled out. They simply hold up a "true" or "false" symbol at the same time that others do. The teacher can probe for thinking behind responses when some confusion exists among the students (Rakes and Smith, 1987).

Teacher modeling of the steps in study skills procedures before students are asked to perform the steps can be a very useful technique. The teacher can move through a procedure, verbalizing the steps being used and letting the students see how each step is accomplished.

Then teachers should provide students with opportunities to practice the methods before asking them to use the methods independently. The teacher should guide students through use of each study method during a class period, using an actual reading assignment. At the teacher's direction, the students should perform each step in the chosen method. For example, with the use of SQ3R, all students should be asked to survey the material together, reading the chapter title, the introduction to the chapter, the boldface and/or italicized headings, and the chapter summary. At this time they should also be asked to inspect graphic aids within the chapter. Each of the other steps, in turn, should be carried out by all students simultaneously. This technique can be applied to any of the study methods described in this chapter.

■ Specific Study Methods

Many methods of approaching study reading have been developed. Probably the best known and most widely used, especially for social studies and science selections, is the SQ3R method, developed by Robinson (1961). ROWAC, developed by Roe, is another method that is good to use with expository texts. Other study methods have been designed for poetry, prose, and drama (EVOKER) (Pauk, 1963) and for mathematics (SQRQCQ) (Fay, 1965). Each of these methods is considered in turn. No teacher would want to use all of these methods but should choose the ones that best fit his or her classes' needs.

Study Methods for Expository Texts

With what types of printed materials should SQ3R be used?

SQ3R.   When the five steps of the **SQ3R** method are applied to a content area reading selection, a variety of reading activities must be employed. The five steps of SQ3R "are metacognitive in nature: Prior to reading, students preview the text and establish purposes for reading; while reading, they monitor their comprehension; and after reading, they summarize and review the content" (Jacobowitz, 1988, p. 127). The details related to the different steps follow.

1. *Survey.* During the survey step, the readers read the chapter title, the introductory paragraph(s), the boldface and/or italicized headings, and the summary paragraph(s). At this time the readers should also inspect any graphic aids, such as maps, graphs, tables, diagrams, and pictures. This survey provides readers with an overview of the material contained in the reading assignment and a framework into which they can organize the facts contained in the selection as reading progresses. Readers who have this knowledge about what they are going to be reading and this grasp of the structure of the text are likely to have better comprehension of the material. This step also gives the readers enough information to generate individual purposes for reading the text (Jacobowitz, 1988).
2. *Question.* During this step, readers formulate questions that they expect to find answered in the selection. The author may have provided purpose questions at the beginning of the chapter or follow-up questions at the end. If so, the students may utilize these questions as purpose questions for the reading. If not, the readers can turn the section headings into questions and read to answer self-constructed questions.
3. *Read.* This is the step in which the students read to answer the purpose questions formulated in the previous step. Notes may be taken during this careful reading.
4. *Recite.* In this step, the students try to answer the purpose questions formulated during the second step without referring to the book or their notes. This step helps to "set" the information in memory, facilitating later recall. This rehearsal process aids the transfer of information from short-term to long-term memory (Jacobowitz, 1988).

5. *Review.* At this point each student reviews the material by rereading portions of the book or by rereading notes taken during the careful reading, to verify the answers given during the previous step. This activity aids the students' retention of the material; immediate reinforcement of ideas helps them overcome the tendency to forget material shortly after reading it.

The SQ3R method, like other study techniques, seems to be learned best when taught in situations where it is expected to be used. Brazee (1979) compared the effect of *skill-centered* reading instruction (focusing on a skill apart from the situation in which it will be applied) with that of *content-centered* reading instruction (focusing on application of a skill for content learning) in social studies classes. One group of students was instructed in the SQ3R study method and rate flexibility before, and separate from, their social studies lesson; the teacher was "teaching general reading skills, assuming that such general skills would 'automatically' transfer to the content area." With this group, "at no time did the instructors indicate that the reading skills might be effectively used in the context of each social studies lesson." The other group received instruction in the same two skills, but the skills were taught within the framework of the social studies material. The material itself determined the skills to be taught, a situation that did not exist in the control group's instruction. The second group actually received less instructional time on the reading skills, but that group showed greater improvement in both rate flexibility and the ability to use the survey part of SQ3R without specific instructions to do so. This study appears to provide strong support for teaching skills in the context of content materials and during, rather than before, the content class.

Some research evidence indicates that SQ3R is not an effective method for improving literal comprehension of adolescents who have learning disabilities (McCormick and Cooper, 1991; Schumm, 1992). It is possible that any of the multistep study methods would fail to be effective with these students.

What are the differences in SQ3R and ROWAC?

ROWAC. Another general study method related to the SQ3R approach, but that utilizes the reading/writing connection and emphasizes the importance of organization more than SQ3R does, has been devised by Roe. The **ROWAC** steps are explained next.

1. *Read.* Read each heading and subheading in the assigned material. (This introduces the student to the nature of the content to be covered and helps to activate his or her background knowledge about the material.)
2. *Organize.* Organize the headings and subheadings in some way (e.g., outline or semantic web). (This gives the student a framework into which to insert the details gained from a careful reading.)
3. *Write.* Write a few paragraphs about what you predict the material will contain, based on the organizer. (This causes the student to engage with the topics to be covered in an active manner, examining connections and

sequences and making inferences. This active engagement with the topics should provide motivation and purpose for the reading of the assignment.)

4. *Actively read.* Actively read the material. (This means that the student should constantly be checking the written predictions for accuracy, questioning the reasons for variations between what was expected and what is presented, and filing information in the categories provided by the advance organizer.)

5. *Correct predictions.* Correct your original predictions by revising the paragraphs that you wrote originally. You don't have to rewrite material. Mark out words, phrases, and sentences; use carats to insert ideas; and make marginal notes. The important thing is that the final version, although not neat, is an accurate reflection of the content of the chapter. (This helps the student to integrate the new material into the organizational structure more solidly.)

A Study Method for Prose, Poetry, and Drama

For what types of printed materials is EVOKER designed?

EVOKER. This procedure should be applied when students are reading narrative prose, poetry, and drama, rather than expository text. It is a method for "close reading." The **EVOKER** steps are as follows:

1. *Explore.* Read the entire selection silently to gain a feeling for the overall message.
2. *Vocabulary.* Note key words. Look up those words with which you are not familiar. Also look up unfamiliar places, events, and people mentioned in the selection.
3. *Oral reading.* Read the selection aloud with good expression.
4. *Key ideas.* Locate key ideas to help you understand the author's organization. Be sure to determine the main idea or theme of the selection.
5. *Evaluate.* Evaluate the key words and sentences with respect to their contributions to developing the key ideas and the main idea.
6. *Recapitulation.* Reread the selection.

A Study Method for Mathematics

What content area teachers would have use for SQRQCQ?

SQRQCQ. Since mathematics materials present special problems for readers, the **SQRQCQ,** study method was developed for use with statement or word problems in mathematics. The steps are as follows:

1. *Survey.* The student reads the problem rapidly to obtain an idea of its general nature.
2. *Question.* In this step, the student determines the specific nature of the problem, that is, "What is being asked in this problem?"
3. *Read.* The student reads the problem carefully, paying attention to specific details and relationships.

4. *Question.* At this point, the student must make a decision about the mathematical operations to be carried out, and, in some cases, the order in which these operations are to be performed. The student asks what operations must be performed and in what order.
5. *Compute.* The student does the computations decided on in the previous step.
6. *Question.* The student checks the entire process and decides whether or not the answer seems to be correct. He or she asks if the answer is reasonable and if the computations have been performed accurately.

Like SQ3R, this method encourages use of metacognitive skills. Students preview the problem in the survey step, set purposes in the first two question steps, and monitor their success with the problem in the final question step.

■ ■ Reading to Follow Directions

Another skill that secondary school students need for effective study is the ability to read to follow directions. Students are constantly expected to follow written directions both in the classroom and in everyday life. Teachers write assignments on the chalkboard and distribute duplicated materials with directions written on them. Textbooks and workbooks in different content areas contain printed directions that students are expected to follow. There are also many aspects of everyday activities that require us to follow directions: reading traffic signs, recipes, assembly and installation instructions, forms to be completed, voting instructions, and registration procedures, to name a few. A traffic sign gives a single direction that is vital for a person to follow in order to avoid bodily injury, misdirection, fines, or other penalties. The other activities just mentioned involve multiple steps to be followed. Failure to complete the steps properly may result in various penalties: inedible food, nonworking appliances, receipt of incorrect merchandise, and so forth.

Many people fail at a task either because they do not know how to follow written directions or because they ignore the directions and try to perform the task without understanding its sequential steps. Almost everyone is familiar with the saying, "When all else fails, read the directions." This tendency to take printed directions lightly may have been fostered in the classroom. Teachers hand out printed directions and then explain them orally. Teachers also often tell students each step to perform as they progress through the task, rather than asking them to read the directions and point out which parts are unclear. These actions promote a general disregard for reading directions. Maybe it should not be surprising that even "good readers follow directions well only 80% of the time and poor readers are fortunate to achieve a 50% success rate" (Henk and Helfeldt, 1987, p. 603).

Following directions requires two basic comprehension skills—the ability to locate details and the ability to detect sequence. Because each step in a set of directions must be followed exactly and in the appropriate sequence, reading to follow directions is a slow and deliberate task. Rereading is often necessary. The following procedure may prove helpful:

1. Read the directions from beginning to end to get an overview of the task to be performed.
2. Study any accompanying pictorial aids that may help in understanding one or more of the steps or in picturing the desired end result.
3. Read the directions carefully, visualizing each step to be performed. Read with an open mind, disregarding any preconceived ideas about the procedure involved.
4. Take note of such key words as *first, second, next, last,* and *finally.* Let these words help you picture the order of the activities to be performed.
5. Read each step again, just before you actually perform it.
6. Carry out the steps in the proper order.

Students will learn to follow directions more easily if the presentation of activities is scaled in difficulty from easy to hard. Teachers can start with directions that have few steps and progress to longer sets of directions as the students' proficiency increases.

Some activities for developing skills in following directions are suggested below.

ACTIVITIES

1. Give students a paragraph containing key direction words (*first, next, then, last, finally,* etc.) and ask them to underline the words that help to show the order of events.
2. Prepare duplicated directions for Japanese paper-folding activities. Provide the students with paper, and ask them to follow the directions.
3. Make it a practice to refer students to written directions instead of telling them orally how to do everything. Ask students to read the directions silently and then tell you in their own words what they should do.
4. Teach the meanings of words commonly encountered in written directions, such as *array, estimate, example, horizontal, phrase,* and *vertical.*
5. Have students follow directions to make something from a kit.
6. Use activities similar to the one in Example 7.1 to make a point about the importance of following directions.

■ ■ ■ EXAMPLE 7.1   *Activity on Following Directions*

Questionnaire: Read this entire questionnaire before you begin to fill in the answers. Work as quickly as you can. You have four minutes to finish this activity.

Name _____

Address _____

_____

Phone Number _____

Age _____

What is your father's name? _____

What is your father's occupation? _____

What is your mother's name? _____

What is your mother's occupation? _____

Do you have any brothers? _____ If so, how many? _____

Do you have any sisters? _____ If so, how many? _____

Do you plan to go to college? _____ If so, where? _____

What career are you most interested in? _____

How many years of preparation past high school will be necessary if you pursue

this career? _____

Who is the person that you admire most? _____

What is this person's occupation? _____

After you have completed reading this questionnaire, turn the paper over and write your name on the back. Then give the paper to your teacher. You should have written nothing on this side of the page.

Any exercises for improving students' ability to understand details and detect sequence will also help them improve their skills in following directions. Activities in which students must integrate information from graphic aids, such as charts or diagrams, with printed information in the text will also be helpful.

Graphic Aids

How do graphic aids help students to understand content material?

Ability to interpret **graphic aids** involves visual literacy, "the ability to interpret visual messages accurately along with the ability to create such messages" (Rakes, Rakes, and Smith, 1995, p. 46). Textbooks contain numerous graphic aids that are often disregarded by students because they have had no training in the use of such aids. Maps, graphs, tables, charts and diagrams, and pictures can help students understand the textbook material better if they receive assistance in learning to extract the information from them, and they are explicitly directed to use these visual aids to help them find *specific* information (Rakes, Rakes, and Smith, 1995).

Mosenthal and Kirsch (1992) describe a procedure for searching graphic aids to find information needed to answer a given question. The steps are to decide what information is given in the question that needs to be answered by the search, to decide what type of information is needed, to search the document for information that matches the known information, and then to search for the needed information in a place related to the known information (e.g., in the same row or column or at the intersection of a particular row and column). Simply having a reliable approach to each of these types of graphic aids may be all many secondary students need to allow them to benefit from the aids in their textbooks.

Graphic aids serve different purposes in different textbooks. At times, they include information not discussed in the text, although it is related to the text discussion. Sometimes they contain information stated in the text, but present it in a more visual form. At other times, they may contain a mixture of information from the text and information not in the text, making connections apparent. Whatever their content, graphic displays have been found to improve students' comprehension. This may be because graphic aids often allow readers to scan large collections of information to see meaningful patterns and help them visualize certain kinds of information (Gillespie, 1993).

Fry (1981) developed a taxonomy of graphic aids that he believes should receive instructional time. Example 7.2 illustrates this taxonomy.

■ ■ ■ EXAMPLE 7.2   An Illustrated Version of a Taxonomy of Graphs

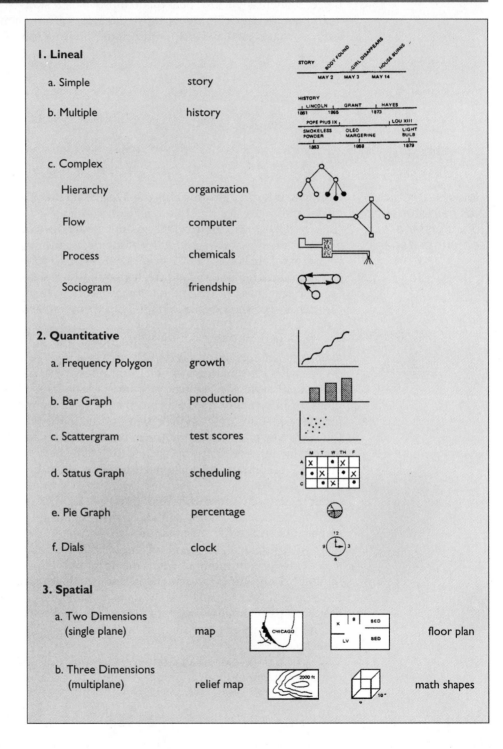

1. Lineal

  a. Simple   story

  b. Multiple   history

  c. Complex

    Hierarchy   organization

    Flow   computer

    Process   chemicals

    Sociogram   friendship

2. Quantitative

  a. Frequency Polygon   growth

  b. Bar Graph   production

  c. Scattergram   test scores

  d. Status Graph   scheduling

  e. Pie Graph   percentage

  f. Dials   clock

3. Spatial

  a. Two Dimensions
    (single plane)   map   floor plan

  b. Three Dimensions
    (multiplane)   relief map   math shapes

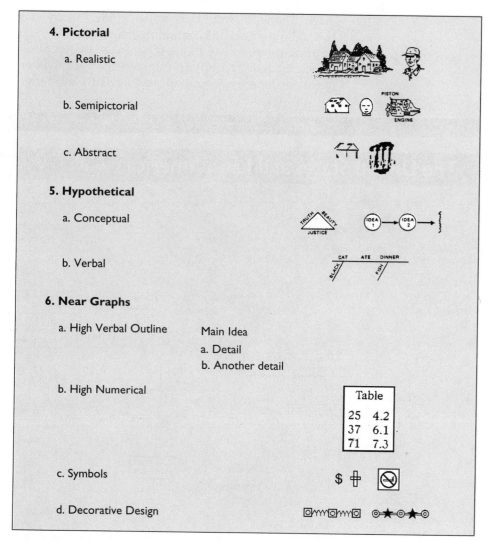

4. Pictorial

   a. Realistic

   b. Semipictorial

   c. Abstract

5. Hypothetical

   a. Conceptual

   b. Verbal

6. Near Graphs

   a. High Verbal Outline

   b. High Numerical

   c. Symbols

   d. Decorative Design

Main Idea
a. Detail
b. Another detail

Table	
25	4.2
37	6.1
71	7.3

Source: Reprinted by permission of Edward Fry.

■ Maps

Maps are found in many content area materials, although they are most common in social studies textbooks. Since maps are generally included in textbooks to help clarify the narrative material, students need to be able to read them to understand fully the material being presented.

Some students may have been taught map-reading techniques in elementary school, but many have not had any structured preparation for reading maps. Therefore, secondary school students may vary greatly in their abilities to handle assignments containing maps. A survey of map-reading skills should be administered early in the school year by teachers who expect map reading to be a frequent activity throughout the year A sample map and some useful questions for surveying map-reading skills are shown in Example 7.3.

■ ■ ■ EXAMPLE 7.3   Map of the United States and Latin America

The United States and Latin America

N. MEX.

UNITED STATES

Columbus

U.S. troops, 1916–1917

TEXAS

MISS.

LA.

ALA.   GA.

S.C.

New Orleans

FLORIDA

Santa Ysabel

Parral

MEXICO

Tampico

Mexico City

Veracruz

Americans controlled 43% of Mexican property, 1910

U.S. troops, 1914

BR. HONDURAS

GUATEMALA

HONDURAS

EL SALVADOR

NICARAGUA

COSTA RICA

U.S. troops, 1909–1910, 1912–1925, 1926–33 Financial supervision, 1911–1924

Miami

BAHAMA IS. (Br.)

Havana

CUBA

U.S. naval base, 1903–   Guantanamo

U.S. troops, 1924–1925

PANAMA

U.S. acquired Canal Zone, 1903 Canal completed, 1914

70°W   60°W

SCALE

0   300 mi

0   300 km

30°N

U.S. troops, 1898–1902, 1906–1909, 1912, 1917–1922 Platt Amendment, 1901–1934

U.S. troops, 1915–1934 Financial supervision, 1916–1941

U.S. troops, 1916–1924 Financial supervision, 1905–1941

20°N

PUERTO RICO   VIRGIN IS.

DOMINICAN REPUBLIC

HAITI

U.S. possession after 1898

U.S. warns Germany against attack on Venezuela, 1902

Caracas

VENEZUELA

COLOMBIA

Bogota

BRAZIL

10°N

100°W   90°W   80°W

GEOGRAPHY SKILLS: The United States has a long history of involvement in Latin America. Critical Thinking: Why might the Caribbean Sea have been called an "American lake"?

Questions

1. What area does this map cover?
2. What information about the area is provided?
3. What is the distance from Havana to Miami in miles? In kilometers?
4. What information does the inset map provide?
5. Which Latin American country has had the most recent U.S. involvement?
6. Where is a U.S. naval base located? Why would that location be strategically important?
7. Using degrees of latitude and longitude, what is the location of Puerto Rico?
8. In what country is Caracas located?
9. What is a canal? What canal is shown on this map?

Source for map: America's Past and Promise, by Lorna Mason, Jesus Garcia, Frances Powell, and C. Frederick Risinger. Copyright © 1995 by Houghton Mifflin Company, p. 609. All rights reserved.

After administering a survey of map-reading skills and evaluating the results, the teacher should systematically teach any of the following skills that the students have not yet mastered:

1. Locating and comprehending the map title
2. Determining directions
3. Interpreting a map's legend
4. Applying a map's scale
5. Understanding the concepts of latitude and longitude
6. Understanding common map terms
7. Making inferences concerning the material represented on a map
8. Understanding projections

The first step in map reading should be examining the title of the map to determine the area being represented and the type of information being given about the area. Map titles are not always located at the tops of the maps, as students often expect them to be. Therefore, students may overlook the title of a map unless they have been told to scan the map to find it.

Next, students should locate the directional indicator on the map and orient themselves to the map's layout. They should be aware that north is not always at the top of the map, although many maps are constructed in this manner.

Interpretation of the legend or key is the next step in map reading. The map legend contains an explanation of each of the symbols used. If students do not understand these symbols, the map will be incomprehensible to them.

To determine distances on a map, students must apply the map's scale. Because it would be highly impractical, if not impossible, to draw a map the actual size of the area represented (e.g., the United States), maps show areas greatly reduced in size. The relationship of a given distance on a map to the same distance on the earth is shown by the map's scale.

An understanding of latitude and longitude will be helpful in reading some maps. Understanding the system of parallels and meridians enables a reader to locate places on a map by using coordinates of degrees of latitude and longitude. Parallels of latitude are lines on a globe that are parallel to the equator. Meridians of longitude are lines that encircle the globe in a north-south direction, meeting at the poles.

Students need to understand many common map terms to comprehend maps fully. Among these are *latitude* and *longitude*, of course, as well as *Tropic of Cancer, Tropic of Capricorn, North Pole, South Pole, equator, hemisphere, peninsula, continent, isthmus, gulf, bay,* and many others.

Teachers should encourage students to perform more than simple location activities with maps. They should ask students to make inferences about the material represented on maps. For example, for a map showing the physical features of an area (such as mountains, rivers, lakes, deserts, and swamps), the students might be asked to decide what types of transportation would be most appropriate in that area. This kind of activity is extremely important at the secondary school level.

Students may need help in understanding different types of projections. Flat maps and globes can be compared to illustrate distortion. Inexpensive globes can be taken apart and flattened out to show one common type of projection.

It may be helpful to students to relate a map of an area they are studying to a map of a larger area that contains the smaller one. For example, a map of Tennessee can be related to a map of the United States. In this way, the position of Tennessee within the United States becomes apparent.

Further suggestions for working with map-reading skills follow.

ACTIVITIES

1. Before presenting a chapter in a textbook that requires much map reading, ask students to construct a map of an area of interest to the class (e.g., in a health or physical education class, a map of recreation facilities in the town). Help students draw the map to scale. (A mathematics teacher may be enlisted to help with this aspect.) Ask students to include a title, a directional indicator, and a legend. This exercise will give students the opportunity for direct experience with important tasks in map reading and help prepare them to read the maps in their content textbooks with more understanding.

2. When students encounter a map in a content area textbook, encourage them to use the legend by asking questions such as the following:

   Where is there a railroad on this map?
   Where do you find a symbol for a college?
   Are there any national monuments in this area? If so, where are they located?

3. Help students with map terminology by first identifying map features with examples and then asking them to point out on a wall map features such as a *gulf* and a *peninsula* when these features are pertinent to the content presentation.

4. Have each student draw a map of an imaginary place, including map features that you designate (e.g., mountains, rivers, lakes, degrees of latitude). Then have the students tell about the place, mentioning crops, industries, recreation, and so on, that fit the physical features of the area. As they incorporate knowledge about physical features of the land, climate, and land usage, they learn map skills in an enjoyable, creative way (Hayes, 1992).

5. Have students map the locations of the events in a novel or the events in a history chapter or nonfiction trade book that has no detailed map provided. Make sure they include a title, legend, directional indicator, and scale.

MEETING THE CHALLENGE

The seventh graders in Mr. Kyle's urban classroom have been having trouble learning to read maps. Mr. Kyle has come up with a creative approach to this problem. He takes heavy-grade posterboard on which he has drawn an outline map of an area and cuts it up with a knife-blade saw. He gives the puzzle pieces that he has created in this manner to his students. First, the students have to put the pieces of the map back together. Then they have to fill in the details of the area on the map (e.g., cities, rivers, landmarks, etc.). To accomplish this task, they must supply a legend with the appropriate symbols, directional indicators, and map scales, as well as place names. When they finish, they use puzzle glue to hold their production together. It can be displayed for other groups and referred to by class members as the area is studied. The students take pride in their accomplishment.

Map-reading instruction is important for students in social studies classes. (© Skjold Photographs)

■ Graphs

Graphs often appear in social studies, science, and mathematics books, and sometimes in books for other content areas. Graphs are used to make comparisons among quantitative data.

Types of Graphs

There are four basic types of graphs.

1. *Picture Graphs (or Pictographs).* Picture graphs use pictures to compare quantities. They aid in visualization of data and are often thought to be the easiest type of graph to read. Readers must realize, however, that only approximate amounts can be indicated by pictographs, making estimation of amounts necessary when interpreting them.
2. *Circle or Pie Graphs.* Proportional parts of a whole can be shown most easily through use of circle or pie graphs. These graphs show the percentage of the whole represented by each individual part.
3. *Bar Graphs.* Bar graphs are useful for comparing the quantities of several items or the quantities of a particular item at different times. These graphs may be either horizontal or vertical.
4. *Line Graphs.* Line graphs can depict changes in amounts over a period of time. They have vertical and horizontal axes. Each point that is plotted on a line graph has a value on both axes.

Representative samples of each of these types of graphs and accompanying sample questions are shown in Examples 7.4, 7.5, 7.6, and 7.7.

■ ▨ ▨ EXAMPLE 7.4   *Sample Picture Graph and Questions*

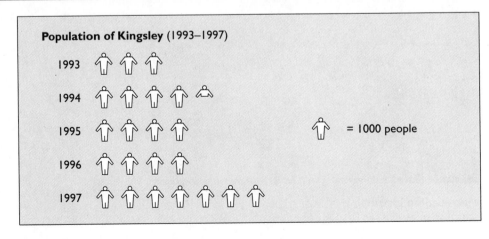

Population of Kingsley (1993–1997)

1993

1994

1995   🚶 = 1000 people

1996

1997

Questions

1. What does each symbol on this graph represent?
2. What time period does this graph cover?
3. During what year did Kingsley have the largest population?
4. Approximately how many people lived in Kingsley in 1994?

■■■ EXAMPLE 7.5   *Sample History Text with Circle Graphs and Questions*

PRESENT   ▶ A CHANGING AMERICA

CONNECTING WITH THE

If you could take a snapshot of America in 1920 and 1990 you would have two very different pictures. In 1920 the nation was at the end of a huge immigration wave. Most of those immigrants were European. Immigration was sharply reduced until the 1960s. Then waves of immigrants came from Mexico, South America, the Caribbean, and Asia.

As you can see from the charts, the 1920 Census did not even include a figure for Hispanics (people from Spanish-speaking countries). In 1990 Hispanics were the fastest-growing minority group. The charts also show that whites make up a smaller majority of Americans than they used to.

1920

89.7% White

0.4% Indian, Chinese, Japanese, all others   9.9% Black

1990

71% White

5% Native American, all others   12% Black
9% Hispanic
3% Asian

Source: U.S. Census Bureau, 1920, 1990

Source: America's Past and Promise, *by Lorna Mason, Jesus Garcia, Frances Powell, and C. Frederick Risinger. Copyright © 1995 by Houghton Mifflin Company. All rights reserved.*

[Note to readers: See how information from the text and from the graphic aid must be integrated for full understanding of the material.]

Questions

1. How has the percentage of whites in the United States changed from 1920 to 1990?
2. How has the nonwhite population of the United States changed from 1920 to 1990?
3. What are some possible reasons for the changes that occurred between 1920 and 1990?

■ ■ ■ EXAMPLE 7.6   *Sample Bar Graph and Questions*

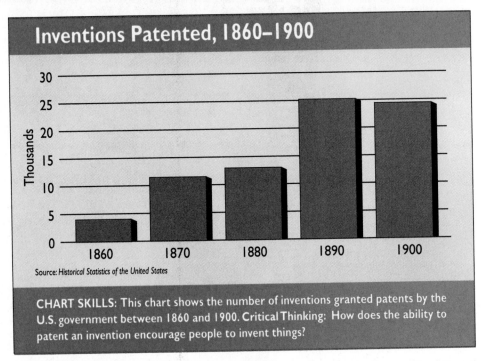

Inventions Patented, 1860–1900

Source: *Historical Statistics of the United States*

CHART SKILLS: This chart shows the number of inventions granted patents by the U.S. government between 1860 and 1900. Critical Thinking: How does the ability to patent an invention encourage people to invent things?

Source: America's Past and Promise, *by Lorna Mason, Jesus Garcia, Frances Powell, and C. Frederick Risinger. Copyright © 1995 by Houghton Mifflin Company. All rights reserved.*

Questions

1. What is the topic of the bar graph?
2. How many inventions were patented in 1860?
3. In what year shown were the most inventions patented?

4. What is the general trend in the numbers of inventions patented? What might be some reasons for this trend?

■ ■ ■ EXAMPLE 7.7   Sample Line Graph and Questions

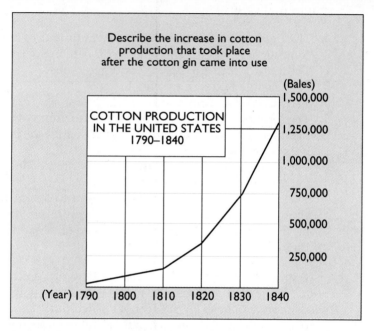

Describe the increase in cotton production that took place after the cotton gin came into use

COTTON PRODUCTION IN THE UNITED STATES 1790–1840

Source: The Free and the Brave, *by Henry F. Graff. Copyright © 1980 by Houghton Mifflin Company. Used with permission.*

Questions

1. What time period is depicted on this graph?
2. What does the vertical axis represent?
3. What does the horizontal axis represent?
4. What was the trend in cotton production over the years represented?
5. Did the invention of the cotton gin in 1793 have an effect on cotton production? Describe the effect.

(Note: If a teacher has students in the class who have directionality problems, the terms *vertical* and *horizontal* should be explained for them, since these terms are particularly difficult for these students.)

Graph Reading Skills

Students should be taught to check the title of a graph to discover what comparison is being made or what information is being supplied. They must also learn to interpret the legend of a picture graph and to derive needed information from a graph accurately.

Teachers can help students discover the following information about the graphs in their textbooks:

1. The purpose of the graph (Usually indicated by the title, the purpose becomes more evident when the accompanying narrative is studied.)
2. The scale of measure on bar and line graphs
3. The legend of picture graphs
4. The items being compared
5. The location of specific pieces of information within a graph (e.g., finding the intersection of the point of interest on the vertical axis with the point of interest on the horizontal axis)
6. The trends indicated by a graph (For example, does an amount increase or decrease over a period of time?)
7. The application of graphic information to actual life situations (A graph showing the temperatures for each month in Sydney, Australia, could be used for planning what clothes to take on a trip to Sydney at a particular time of the year.)

Fry (1981, pp. 388–389) points out that "graphical literacy—the ability to both comprehend and draw graphs—is an important communication tool that needs more emphasis in the school curriculum." He urges teachers to include graphing in their assignments, perhaps taking a section of the content textbook or an outside reading and asking students to make as many graphs as they can to illustrate ideas in the material. One of the best ways to help students learn to read graphs is to have them construct their own after the teacher has modeled how to do this. The following is a list of types of graphs students can construct to help them develop a graph schema that will enhance their understanding of the graphs found in content area textbooks:

1. A picture graph showing the number of tickets each homeroom purchased for the senior prom
2. A circle graph showing the percentage of each day that the student spends in various activities (sleeping, eating, studying, etc.)
3. A bar graph showing the number of outside readings that the student completed for English class during each grading period
4. A line graph showing the student's weekly quiz scores for a six-week period

The teacher can construct graphs such as the ones in Examples 7.4 through 7.7 and ask students to answer questions about them. Questions can also be asked about particular graphs in the students' textbooks.

Tables

Tables, which are found in reading materials for all subject areas, contain information arranged in vertical columns and horizontal rows. One problem that students have with reading tables is extracting the needed facts from a large mass of information presented.

Like the titles of maps and graphs, the titles of tables contain information about their content. Also, because tables are arranged in columns and rows, the headings for the columns and rows also provide information. Specific information is obtained by locating the intersection of an appropriate column with an appropriate row. Example 7.8 shows a sample table. The questions that follow the table are presented as models for the types of questions that teachers might ask about the tables in their students' content textbooks.

■ ■ ■ EXAMPLE 7.8   *Sample Table and Questions*

	STATE NAMES	DATE OF ADMISSION	POPULATION	NUMBER OF REPRESENTATIVES	CAPITAL	
1	Delaware	1787	658,000	1	Dover	States
2	Pennsylvania	1787	11,764,000	21	Harrisburg	
3	New Jersey	1787	7,617,000	13	Trenton	
4	Georgia	1788	6,387,000	11	Atlanta	
5	Connecticut	1788	3,227,000	6	Hartford	
6	Massachusetts	1788	5,928,000	10	Boston	
7	Maryland	1788	4,733,000	8	Annapolis	
8	South Carolina	1788	3,407,000	6	Columbia	
9	New Hampshire	1788	1,103,000	2	Concord	
10	Virginia	1788	6,128,000	11	Richmond	
11	New York	1788	17,627,000	31	Albany	
12	North Carolina	1789	6,553,000	12	Raleigh	
13	Rhode Island	1790	989,000	2	Providence	
14	Vermont	1791	560,000	1	Montpelier	
15	Kentucky	1792	3,665,000	6	Frankfort	
16	Tennessee	1796	4,822,000	9	Nashville	
17	Ohio	1803	10,778,000	19	Columbus	
18	Louisiana	1812	4,181,000	7	Baton Rouge	
19	Indiana	1816	5,499,000	10	Indianapolis	
20	Mississippi	1817	2,535,000	5	Jackson	
21	Illinois	1818	11,325,000	20	Springfield	
22	Alabama	1819	3,984,000	7	Montgomery	
23	Maine	1820	1,218,000	2	Augusta	
24	Missouri	1821	5,079,000	9	Jefferson City	
25	Arkansas	1836	2,337,000	4	Little Rock	

	STATE NAMES	DATE OF ADMISSION	POPULATION	NUMBER OF REPRESENTATIVES	CAPITAL
26	Michigan	1837	9,180,000	16	Lansing
27	Florida	1845	12,775,000	23	Tallahassee
28	Texas	1845	16,825,000	30	Austin
29	Iowa	1846	2,767,000	5	Des Moines
30	Wisconsin	1848	4,870,000	9	Madison
31	California	1850	29,279,000	52	Sacramento
32	Minnesota	1858	4,359,000	8	St. Paul
33	Oregon	1859	2,828,000	5	Salem
34	Kansas	1861	2,468,000	4	Topeka
35	West Virginia	1863	1,783,000	3	Charleston
36	Nevada	1864	1,193,000	2	Carson City
37	Nebraska	1867	1,573,000	3	Lincoln
38	Colorado	1876	3,272,000	6	Denver
39	North Dakota	1889	634,000	1	Bismarck
40	South Dakota	1889	693,000	1	Pierre
41	Montana	1889	794,000	1	Helena
42	Washington	1889	4,827,000	9	Olympia
43	Idaho	1890	1,004,000	2	Boise
44	Wyoming	1890	450,000	1	Cheyenne
45	Utah	1896	1,711,000	3	Salt Lake City
46	Oklahoma	1907	3,124,000	6	Oklahoma City
47	New Mexico	1912	1,490,000	3	Sante Fe
48	Arizona	1912	3,619,000	6	Phoenix
49	Alaska	1959	546,000	1	Juneau
50	Hawaii	1959	1,095,000	2	Honolulu
	District of Columbia		638,000	1 (non-voting)	
				435	

States

Source: America's Past and Promise, by Lorna Mason, Jesus Garcia, Frances Powell, and C. Frederick Risinger. Copyright © 1995 by Houghton Mifflin Company. All rights reserved.

Questions

1. What type of information is located in this table?
2. What are the column headings?
3. In what year were the first states admitted to the Union?
4. What was the 50th state admitted to the Union?
5. Why does the District of Columbia not have a number?
6. Why do you think the 49th and 50th states were not admitted until 1959?
7. Which state has the largest population?
8. How many representatives does California have?
9. What is the capital of New York?

■ Charts and Diagrams

Charts and diagrams appear in textbooks for many different content areas. They are designed to help students picture the events, processes, structures, relationships, or sequences described by the text. At times they may be used as summaries of text material. Example 7.9 is a chart from a history book that summarizes text material.

■ ■ ■ EXAMPLE 7.9   History Chart

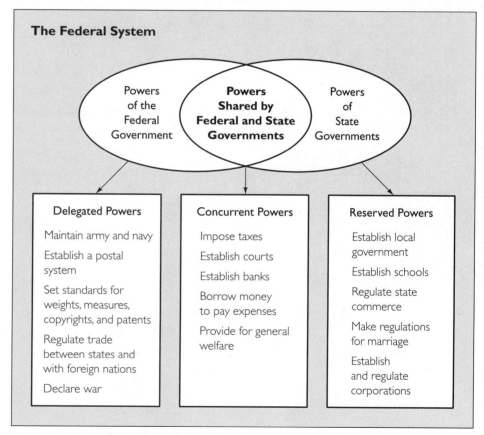

The Federal System

Powers of the Federal Government

Powers Shared by Federal and State Governments

Powers of State Governments

Delegated Powers

Maintain army and navy

Establish a postal system

Set standards for weights, measures, copyrights, and patents

Regulate trade between states and with foreign nations

Declare war

Concurrent Powers

Impose taxes

Establish courts

Establish banks

Borrow money to pay expenses

Provide for general welfare

Reserved Powers

Establish local government

Establish schools

Regulate state commerce

Make regulations for marriage

Establish and regulate corporations

Source: Jacobs, William Jay et al. America's Story, *p. 238. Copyright © 1990 by Houghton Mifflin Company. Reprinted by permission of Houghton Mifflin Company.*

Students must be made aware of the abstract nature of diagrams and of the fact that they often distort or oversimplify information. Interpretation of the symbols found in diagrams and understanding of the perspective used in diagrams are not automatic; teachers must provide practice in such activities.

Numerous types of charts and diagrams are used in the various content areas. Examples include tree diagrams (English), flow charts (mathematics), and process charts (science). Careful instruction in reading such charts and diagrams must be provided for interpretation of content material. Example 7.10 shows a diagram from a science textbook.

■ ■ ■ EXAMPLE 7.10   *Science Diagram*

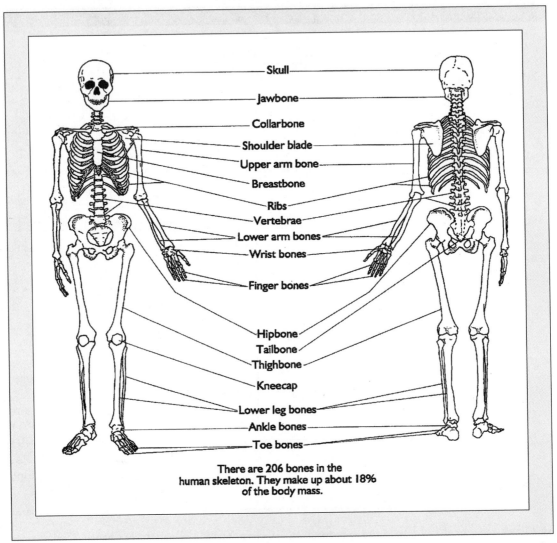

Skull
Jawbone
Collarbone
Shoulder blade
Upper arm bone
Breastbone
Ribs
Vertebrae
Lower arm bones
Wrist bones
Finger bones
Hipbone
Tailbone
Thighbone
Kneecap
Lower leg bones
Ankle bones
Toe bones

There are 206 bones in the
human skeleton. They make up about 18%
of the body mass.

Source: James E. McLaren et al., Spaceship Earth: Life Science, *p. 113. Copyright © 1981 by Houghton Mifflin Company. Reprinted by permission of Houghton Mifflin Company.*

The teacher can point out that distortions are frequently found in text-book drawings. Students can be helped to see that the diagrams in Example 7.10 are views of the human body's bone structure, which is not visible because it is covered by flesh and skin. The teacher can also identify the front and rear views and discuss the differences between them. Diagrams such as this might also appear in health textbooks. Students may be asked to label unlabeled diagrams similar to this one as a check on retention of the concepts and terminology.

Semantic maps are diagrams of the relationships among concepts in a text. Having students draw semantic maps of content material can help them comprehend it better. See Chapter 3 for detail on semantic mapping.

Diagramming the word problems presented in mathematics textbooks can help students visualize the problems and subsequently solve them (Heinich, Molenda, and Russell, 1993; Rakes et al., 1995). Such approaches to math problem solving are fairly common in elementary schools, but they often are dropped at the secondary level, even though they are still valid.

■ Pictures and Cartoons

Content area textbooks contain pictures that are designed to illustrate the material described and to interest students. The illustrations may be photographs offering a realistic representation of concepts, people, and places, or they may be line drawings that are somewhat more abstract in nature.

Students frequently see pictures merely as space fillers, reducing the amount of reading they will have to do on a page. Therefore, they may pay little attention to pictures, although the pictures are often excellent sources of information.

Since pictures are representations of experiences, they may be utilized as vicarious means of adding to a student's store of knowledge. Teachers should help students extract information from textbook illustrations by encouraging them to study the pictures before and after reading the text, looking for the purpose of each picture and its specific details. Studying pictures may help students understand and retain the information illustrated.

Example 7.11 depicts the surface of the moon on the near side and the far side. For students who have not had a chance to see a close-up view of the surface of the moon, the vicarious experience and visual imagery gained from this picture are valuable.

Cartoons are special types of pictures that contain special symbols. They often distort the things they represent in order to make a point. Students should be encouraged to read cartoons critically.

■ ■ ■ EXAMPLE 7.11   Science Textbook Illustration

*a, The near side of the moon is the side you see from the earth. **b,** The far side. How does it differ from the near side?*

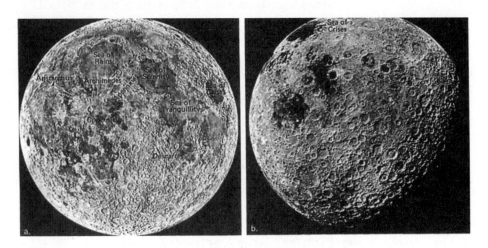

Source: Matthews, William H., III, et al. Investigating the Earth *(Boston: Houghton Mifflin Company, 1987), p. 431. Copyright © 1987 by Houghton Mifflin Company. Reprinted by permission of Houghton Mifflin Company.*

Example 7.12 can be used as an exercise in examining how a cartoon delivers a message. Teachers can help the students connect the environmental issue involved with the situation depicted in the cartoon. In the cartoon, oil spills in the ocean are referred to indirectly by equating the smell of oil, rather than fresh salt air, with the ocean.

Having students illustrate sections of content text with their own pictures or cartoons as they read engages students in deeper processing of the material and results in increased comprehension of the material. Students need to be told that their artistic ability is not being evaluated when this technique is used (Cox, Smith, and Rakes, 1994; Rakes et al., 1995).

■ ■ Adjusting Rate to Fit Purpose and Materials

Study time will be used most efficiently if students are taught to vary their reading rates to fit their purposes and the materials they are reading. Making these adjustments, which is important for good comprehension, is called

■ ■ ■ EXAMPLE 7.12   *Science Textbook Cartoon*

Source: Joseph H. Jackson and Edward D. Evans, Spaceship Earth: Earth Science, *p. 511. Copyright © 1980 by Houghton Mifflin Company. Reprinted by permission of Houghton Mifflin Company.*

What is meant by flexibility of rate?

flexibility of rate. Good readers adjust rates, thinking, and approaches automatically and are not aware that they make several changes when reading a single page.

Flexible readers are able to distinguish between important and unimportant ideas and to read important ideas carefully. They do not give each word, phrase, or paragraph equal attention but select the parts that are significant for understanding the selection. Information on familiar topics is read more quickly than information on new topics, because familiarity with a topic allows the reader to anticipate ideas, vocabulary, and phrasing. A selection that has a light vocabulary burden, more concrete concepts, and an easily managed style of writing can be read more rapidly than material with a heavy vocabulary load, many abstract concepts, and a difficult writing style. Light fiction that is read strictly for enjoyment can and should be absorbed much faster than the directions for a science experiment; newspapers and magazines can be read more rapidly than textbooks; theoretical scientific content and statistics must be read more slowly than much social studies content.

Students often think that everything should be read at the same rate. Thus, some of them read light novels as slowly and deliberately as they read mathematics problems. These students will probably never enjoy reading for recreation because they work so hard at reading and it takes so long. Other students move rapidly through everything they read. In doing so, they usually fail to grasp essential details in content area assignments, although they "finish" reading all of the assigned material. Rate of reading should never be considered apart from comprehension. Therefore, the optimum rate for reading any material is the fastest rate at which an acceptable level of comprehension is obtained. Teachers who wish to concentrate on improving their students' reading rates should include comprehension checks with all rate exercises.

Work on increasing reading rate should not be emphasized until basic word recognition and comprehension skills are thoroughly under control. Improvement in these skills often results in increased rate without any special attention to it. For best results, flexibility of rate should be developed with the content materials students are expected to read.

■ Factors Affecting Rate

Many factors influence the rate at which a person can read a particular selection, including the following:

1. Factors related to the material
   a. Size and style of type
   b. Format of the pages
   c. Use of illustrations
   d. Organization
   e. Writing style of the author
   f. Abstractness or complexity of ideas
2. Factors related to the reader
   a. Background of experiences
   b. Reading ability
   c. Attitudes and interests
   d. Reason for reading

Obviously, these factors differ with each selection. Therefore, different rates are appropriate for different materials.

Poor reading habits may greatly decrease reading rate. Poor habits include excessive vocalizing (forming each word as it is read); sounding out all words, both familiar and unfamiliar; excessive regressing (going back and rereading previously read material); and pointing at each word with the index finger. Concentrated attention to the elimination of these problems can yield good results. Often, secondary school students simply need to be made aware of the habits that are slowing them down and to be given some suggestions for practice in overcoming them. Use in a reading laboratory of the equipment described in the next section has proved helpful in correcting some of these problems.

Techniques for Increasing Rate and Flexibility

Many methods have been devised to help students increase or adjust their rates of reading. These approaches include use of special machines, timed readings, skimming and scanning techniques, and flexibility exercises.

Machines

Using special equipment to increase reading rate generally is not the content area teacher's responsibility. However, the content area teacher may have students who, despite encouragement and teacher direction, read very slowly, in a word-by-word fashion, with many regressions. These students lack confidence in their ability to read and may claim that they cannot read more rapidly. The content teacher may refer these students to a reading teacher who uses rate machines to develop students' speed. Because they cannot regress as they read and are forced to move ahead through the material when rate machines are used, students realize that they can indeed read more rapidly.

Timed Readings

To help students increase their rates of reading in material that does not require intensive study-reading, teachers may use timed readings. As is true of other study skills, techniques for improving rate may be learned best in situations in which they are actually used. In choosing appropriate selections for rate instruction, the content teacher should avoid material that includes many small details (e.g., a science experiment or a mathematics statement problem). Materials that present general background and recreational reading in the content area are more useful for this activity (e.g., the story of a scientific discovery or the biography of a mathematician).

Timed readings should always be accompanied by comprehension checks. An extremely high rate score is of no use if the student fails to comprehend the material. Teachers should encourage rate increases only if comprehension does not suffer. Some students need help in basic reading skills before they can participate profitably in these rate-building activities.

Graphs can be kept of the results of timed rate exercises over a period of weeks or months. Seeing visible progress can motivate students to continue to work on improving their rates. Comprehension charts should also be kept so rate increases can be viewed in the proper perspective.

Skimming and Scanning Techniques

When might you need to skim text? How is scanning of text accomplished?

Skimming and **scanning** are special types of rapid reading. Skimming refers to reading to obtain a general idea or overview of the material, and scanning means reading to find a specific bit of information. Skimming is faster than rapid reading of most of the words in the material because, when readers skim material, they read selectively. Scanning is faster than skimming because only one piece of information is being sought. When scanning, readers run their eyes rapidly down the page, concentrating on the particular information being sought.

Example 7.13 shows how you might go about skimming an article. Skimming techniques are used in the survey step of the SQ3R method discussed earlier in this chapter. Teachers can help develop skimming skills as they work to teach this study method.

Other skimming activities include the following:

1. Give the students a short time to skim an assigned chapter and write down the main ideas covered.
2. Ask students to skim newspaper articles and match them to headlines written on the board. Have a competition to see who can finish first with no errors.
3. Give students the title of a research topic and have them skim an article to decide whether it is pertinent to the topic.

Scanning activities are easy to design. Some examples follow:

1. Have students scan a telephone directory page to find a specific person's number.
2. Have students scan a history chapter to find the date of a particular event.
3. Have students scan a textbook to find information on a particular person.

Students need to scan for key words related to the specific facts they seek. An exercise in generating key words that are related to a specific topic may be beneficial.

Flexibility Exercises

Since not all materials should be read at the same rate, students need assistance in determining appropriate rates for different materials. The table in Example 7.14 shows three reading rates of a good reader, each of which is appropriate for a particular type of reading material.

■ ■ ■ EXAMPLE 7.13   *Skimming*

Shown below is a view of how you might skim an article. Notice that you read all of the first and second paragraphs to get an overview. By the third or fourth paragraph you must begin to leave out material; read only key sentences and phrases to get the main ideas and a few of the details. Note also that, since final paragraphs often summarize, it may be worthwhile to read them more fully.

Skimming must be done "against the clock." That is, you must try to go as fast as you possibly can while leaving out large chunks of material. Be careful to avoid getting interested in the story since this might slow you down and cause you to read unnecessary detail. Skimming is work. It is done when you do not have much time and when you wish to cover material at the fastest possible rate.

Usually the first paragraph will be read at average speed all the way through. It often contains an introduction or overview of what will be talked about.

Sometimes, however, the second paragraph contains the introduction or overview. In the first paragraph the author might just be "warming up" or saying something clever to attract attention.

Reading a third paragraph completely might be unnecessary but ... ...

the main idea is usually contained in the opening sentence ... ... topic sentence

Besides the first sentence the reader should get some but not all the detail from the rest of the paragraph ... ...

... names ... dates ...

This tells you nothing ... ...

hence sometimes the main idea is in the middle or at the end of the paragraph.

Some paragraphs merely repeat ideas ...

Occasionally the main idea can't be found in the opening sentence. The whole paragraph must then be read.

Then leave out a lot of the next paragraph ...

... to make up time

Remember to keep up a very fast rate ...

... 800 w.p.m.

Don't be afraid to leave out half or more of each paragraph ...

Don't get interested and start to read everything ...

skimming is work ...

Lowered comprehension is expected ...

... 50% ...

... not too low

Skimming practice makes it easier ...

... gain confidence

Perhaps you won't get anything at all from a few paragraphs ...

... don't worry

Skimming has many uses ...

... reports ...

newspapers ...

... supplementary ... text ...

The ending paragraphs might be read more fully as often they contain a summary.

Remember that the importance of skimming is to get only the author's main ideas at a very fast speed.

Source: Reprinted by permission of Edward Fry.

Kind of Reading	Rate	Comprehension
Slow: *Study reading* speed is used when material is difficult or when high comprehension is desired.	200 to 300 w.p.m.	80–90%
Average: An *average reading* speed is used for everyday reading of magazines, newspapers and easier textbooks.	250 to 500 w.p.m.	70%
Fast: *Skimming* is used when the highest rate is desired. Comprehension is intentionally lower.	800+ w.p.m.	50%

Source: Reprinted by permission of Edward Fry.

One type of flexibility exercise is to ask a series of questions such as the following ones and then discuss students' reasons for their answers:

1. What rate would be best for reading a statement problem in your mathematics textbook?
2. Which could you read most quickly and still achieve your purpose—a television schedule, a newspaper article, or a science textbook?
3. Is just skimming an appropriate way to read a science experiment?
4. What reading technique would you use to look up a word in the dictionary?

■ ■ Retention

Secondary school students are expected to retain much of the material from their content area textbooks. Use of study methods to enhance retention has already been discussed extensively in this chapter. Teachers can help students apply these techniques and others that will facilitate retention of material. Concentrating on material as it is read is important to retention. Some suggestions that the teacher may offer include:

1. Always read study material with a purpose. If the teacher does not supply you with a purpose, set purposes of your own. Having a purpose for reading will help you extract meaning from a passage, and you will retain material that is meaningful to you longer.

2. Try to grasp the author's organization of the material. This will help you to categorize concepts to be learned under main headings, which are easier to retain than small details and which facilitate recall of the related details. To accomplish this task, outline the material.

3. Try to picture the ideas the author is attempting to describe. Visualization of the information being presented will help you remember it longer.

4. As you read, take notes on important points in the material. Writing information down can help you to fix it in your memory. (See Chapter 5 for note-taking guidelines.)

5. After you have read the material, summarize it in your own words. If you can do this, you will have recalled the main points, and rewording the material will demonstrate your understanding.

6. When you have read the material, discuss the assignment with a classmate or a group of classmates. Talking about the material facilitates remembering it.

7. Apply the concepts that you read about, if possible. Physical or mental interaction with the material will help you retain it.

8. Read assignments critically. If you question the material as you read, you will be more likely to remember it.

9. If you wish to retain the material over a long period of time, use spaced practice (a number of short practice sessions extended over a period of time) rather than massed practice (one long practice session). Massed practice facilitates immediate recall, but for long-term retention, distributed practice produces the best results.

10. If you plan to recite the material to yourself or to another student in order to increase your retention, do so as soon as possible after reading the material. Always check your accuracy and correct any errors immediately, so that you will not retain inaccurate material.

11. Overlearning facilitates long-term retention. To overlearn something, you must continue to practice it for a period of time after you have initially mastered it.

12. Mnemonic devices can help you retain certain types of information. (For example, remember that there is "a rat" in the middle of "separate.")

13. A variety of types of writing can improve retention. Langer (1986) reported the effects of different types of writing tasks on learning from reading in the content areas. Writing answers to study questions fostered recall of isolated bits of information. Essay writing produced more long-term and reasoned learning of a smaller amount of material. Note taking fell somewhere in the middle, causing students to deal with larger chunks of meaning than did study questions, but not involving reorganization of material, as did essay writing.

14. Relate the material you are reading to things you already know. Making such connections can aid in the acquisition of new concepts and in the retention of material read (Jones, 1988).

15. Monitor your reading to determine if you understand the material. If not, reread it or take other steps to ensure understanding.
16. Avoid studying in a distracting setting.
17. Study more difficult and less interesting material when you are most alert (Memory and Yoder, 1988).
18. Anticipate what is coming next as you read a passage, and read to see if your prediction was accurate (Moore et al., 1989).

Teachers can also facilitate student retention of material by offering students ample opportunities for review of information and practice of skills learned and by offering positive reinforcement for correct responses given during the practice and review periods. Class discussion of material to be learned tends to aid retention. Emphasis on classifying the ideas found in the reading material under appropriate categories can also help.

■ ■ ■ Test Taking

Secondary school students sometimes fail to do well on tests, not because they do not know the material, but because they have difficulty reading and comprehending the test. Teachers can help by giving students suggestions for ways of effectively reading different types of tests.

Essay tests often contain the terms *compare, contrast, diagram, trace the development, describe, discuss,* and others. Teachers can explain what is expected in an answer to a question containing each of these terms and any other terms they may plan to use. This will help prevent students from losing points on the test because they "described" instead of "contrasted." Teachers can point out that, if students are asked to compare two things or ideas, both similarities and differences should be mentioned. If students are asked to contrast two things or ideas, differences are the important factors. If students are asked to describe something, they are expected to paint a word picture of it. If they are asked to diagram something, an actual drawing is required. Sample answers to a variety of different test questions utilizing the special vocabulary may be useful in helping students understand what the teacher expects. An example follows.

Question. Contrast extemporaneous speeches and prepared speeches.

Answer. Extemporaneous speeches are given with little advance thought. Prepared speeches are usually preceded by much thought and research. Prepared speeches often contain quotations and paraphrases of the thoughts of many other people about the subject. Extemporaneous speeches can contain such material only if the speaker has previously become very well informed in the particular area involved. Assuming that the speaker has little background in the area, an extemporaneous speech would be likely to have less depth than a prepared speech since it would involve only the speaker's immediate impressions. Prepared speeches tend to be better organized than extemporaneous speeches because the speaker has more time to collect thoughts and arrange them in the best possible sequence.

What are the steps in the PORPE technique?

PORPE is a technique developed by Simpson (1986) to help students study for essay examinations. The steps in PORPE are as follows.

1. *Predict.* Construct potential essay questions, based on reading of the material. Use words such as *explain, criticize, compare,* and *contrast.* Focus on important ideas.
2. *Organize.* Organize the information necessary to answer the questions.
3. *Rehearsal.* Memorize material through recitation and self-testing. Space practice over several days for long-term memory.
4. *Practice.* Write out in detail the answers to the questions that you formulated.
5. *Evaluate.* Judge the accuracy and completeness of your answers.

Simpson suggests teaching this procedure through teacher modeling and a series of group and individual activities. Many students may need help in the self-questioning portion of PORPE or in self-questioning for ordinary study purposes. Teachers should familiarize students with different types of questions and show them how to generate these questions, perhaps through think-aloud procedures. Research has shown that secondary students can be taught to generate their own questions about texts and that doing so helps low-ability students more than average or high-ability students (Andre and Anderson, 1978–1979; Gillespie, 1990).

The teacher may want to help students spread out their study for tests over several days by suggesting different activities for the days preceding the test. For example, the teacher may suggest that students reread their notes on all chapters that will be on the test on one day, apply some suggested retention enhancement techniques the next day, rewrite their notes in a more concise form the following day, and compose possible test questions and answer them on the day before the test (Strichart and Mangrum, 1993).

It is important for the students to know exactly what the test will cover and what type of test will be given, for this information will affect the study procedures used. The teacher should provide this information, but the students should ask about it if the teacher is vague about the content or fails to mention the type of test.

Students need to realize the importance of working carefully when they are taking tests and of following directions exactly They should examine the test before they begin, to determine if they have questions about what they are to do, the point values of the questions, or the manner of responding to the questions. They should answer the ones that they know well first and then allocate the remainder of their time to the harder questions (Strichart and Mangrum, 1993). They should be aware of the time available to complete the test and avoid spending too much time on items they are not likely to be able to answer. They should always check to make sure that they have not inadvertently left one or more answers blank before they turn in their papers. In general, it is wise to answer all questions with a best guess, but this suggestion is invalidated if the teacher imposes a penalty for guessing.

The student must read objective tests carefully. Generally, every word in an item must be considered. Teachers should emphasize the importance of considering the effect of words such as *always, never,* and *not,* as well as others of this general nature. Students need to realize that all the parts of a true-false question must be true if the answer is to be true. They also need to understand that all possible responses for a multiple-choice question need to be read before an answer is chosen.

Teachers can also help students improve their performance on tests by offering the following useful hints:

1. When studying for essay tests:
   a. Remember that your answers should include main ideas accompanied by supporting details.
   b. Expect questions that cover the topics most emphasized in the course, since only a few questions can be asked within the limited time.
   c. Expect questions that are broad in scope.
   d. Consider the important topics covered, and try to guess some of the questions that the teacher may ask. Prepare good answers for these questions and try to learn them thoroughly. You will probably be able to use the points you learn in your answers on the actual test, even if the questions you formulated are not exactly the same as the ones asked by the teacher.
2. When studying for objective tests:
   a. Become familiar with important details.
   b. Consider the types of questions that have been asked on previous tests, and study for those types. If dates have been asked for in the past, learn the dates in the material.
   c. If listing questions are a possibility, especially sequential listings, try preparing mnemonic devices to help you in recalling the lists.
3. Learning important definitions can be helpful for any kind of test and can be useful in answering many essay questions.
4. Apply the suggestions listed in the earlier section on "Retention."

When teachers construct tests, they should take care to avoid making the test harder to read than the original material. Otherwise, students could know the material required, but the readability level of the test could be so high that they would be unable to comprehend the questions. Students might then make low test scores because of the teacher's inappropriate test preparation rather than because of students' lack of knowledge of the concepts involved.

Summary

Reading-study skills are skills that enhance comprehension and retention of information contained in printed material. They help students manage their reading in content area classes.

Study methods such as SQ3R and ROWAC are applicable to a number of different subject areas, including social studies and science. EVOKER is a study method especially developed for use with prose, poetry, and drama; SQRQCQ is effective for use with statement or word problems in mathematics. Instructional procedures such as GRASP, the PSRT strategy, and some recitation techniques can be used to enhance the development of study skills.

The ability to follow written directions is vitally important to secondary school students. Teachers should plan activities to help students develop this important skill.

Content area textbooks are filled with graphic visual aids such as maps, graphs, tables, diagrams, and pictures. Teachers should give students guidance in interpreting these helpful text features.

Other areas to which teachers should give attention are adjustment of reading rate to fit the purpose for which the reading is being done and the material to be read, retention of material read, and test-taking skills.

Discussion Questions

1   Which of the study methods listed in this chapter is best for use in your content area? Why?
2   What is a useful procedure for teaching students to read directions with understanding?
3   What graphic aids occur most commonly in your content area? What can you do to help students interpret them effectively?
4   What is the best setting in which to offer students instruction concerning flexibility of rate? Why is this so?
5   What are some techniques for helping students increase reading rate with acceptable comprehension?
6   How can you help your students retain as much of the material that they read in their content textbooks as possible?
7   Should you give attention to helping your students develop test-taking skills? Why, or why not?

Enrichment Activities

*1 Teach one of the study methods described in this chapter to a class of secondary school students. Work through it with them step by step.

2 Collect materials that include directions that secondary level students often need to read. Discuss with your classmates how you could help the students learn to read the materials more effectively.

3 Collect a variety of types of maps. Decide which features of each map will need most explanation for students.

4 Collect a variety of types of graphs. Make them into a display that could be used in a unit on reading graphs.

5 Develop a procedure to help secondary school students learn to be flexible in their rates of reading. Use materials of widely varying types.

*6 Examine several of your old tests. Decide what reading difficulties they may present for your students. Isolate special words for which meanings may have to be taught.

---

*These activities are designed for in-service teachers, student teachers, or practicum students.

Applying Literacy Instruction in the Content Areas

Overview

The language arts are highly interrelated, and reading and writing are complementary skills. In this chapter we consider the relationships among reading, writing, and thinking in content area classes; the process approach to writing instruction; and types of writing-to-learn strategies that content teachers may employ. The goal is to help content area teachers learn to use writing to advantage in their classes. James Upton has rightly pointed out that "the emphasis must be on the quality of the content, not on language arts skills" (Sensenbaugh, 1989, p. 463).

The explanation of the process approach to writing emphasizes prewriting, drafting, revision, and publication procedures, rather than focusing only on the written product. Writing-to-learn strategies in content areas include use of the language experience approach, content journals or learning logs, dialogue journals, RAFT assignments, research reports, laboratory reports, and pen pals. The process approach to writing is useful with many types of content area writing, especially research reports and RAFT assignments, as well as creative writing endeavors.

Teachers' attempts to initiate writing across the curriculum have not been uniformly successful. Some teachers have difficulty becoming collaborators in learning with students because they hold on to the traditional role of examiner. They also have trouble looking at writing as *process* rather than *product* (Sensenbaugh, 1989). Part of the reason may be that they tend to teach the same way they were taught, and emphasis on the writing product was once common in classrooms. Focus on the product alone, however, may leave students unfamiliar with the steps needed to produce written materials that communicate well. The process approach involves the student with concern for the message and the audience for the writing from the beginning, whereas focus on the product often gives inordinate attention to the mechanics of writing without emphasizing the development of the message.

Purpose-Setting Questions

As you read this chapter, try to answer these questions:

1 What is the relationship between reading and writing activities in content area classes?
2 What are some types of writing that are useful in the content areas?
3 What are the steps in the process approach to writing instruction?

■ ■ The Relationships Among Reading, Writing, and Thinking

■ The Nature of Writing

Each incidence of writing occurs "at a particular moment in the writer's biography, in particular circumstances, and under particular external and internal pressures. In short, the writer is always transacting with a personal, social, and cultural environment" (Rosenblatt, 1989, p. 163). Writers are also transacting with the texts that they are producing, using the reservoirs of past linguistic experiences at their disposal. Freewriting (discussed later in this chapter) is a way of tapping the individual's linguistic reservoir without worry about organization or form of expression.

A writer necessarily reads what he or she has written as it is being produced. When this happens, the writer is checking to see if the writing is projecting a meaning that meets the purpose for the writing. The writer weighs words against an internal standard to see if they are right. The writer also may attempt to read the material as potential audiences will read it to see if the meaning they will construct is congruent with his or her purpose (Rosenblatt, 1989).

◼ Values of Writing in the Content Areas

Study in the content areas is designed to promote the learning of facts, principles, and procedures related to the disciplines involved. Such learning involves both literal and higher-level thinking skills and retention of material studied.

Writing is a tool for thinking. Glatthorn points out that "conscious, deliberative thought makes extensive use of symbols as a representation of reflection." Writing also is helpful in the development of thinking skills. Its "linear and structured form imposes its own sense of order on our attempts to think about relationships. And, as 'frozen speech,' it makes metalinguistic reflection more easily accomplished" (Glatthorn, 1989, p. 284). Writing can help readers explore what they know. Through writing, students come to terms with their own thoughts, solve problems, and discover new ideas. As Britton and others (1975, p. 28) explain, *An essential part of the writing process is explaining the matter to oneself. . . .* There are plenty of things we are sure we know but cannot articulate: 'tacit knowledge,' Polanyi calls it. There are many more where we may still be working towards a satisfactory understanding, and others where we surprise ourselves by only realizing after we've said or written something that we've succeeded in bringing to light an idea we thought was only half-formed." Elbow (1978) expresses a similar sentiment. He not only feels that writing enhances thinking, but he also believes that it leads to an ongoing process of self-knowledge. For reasons such as these, Jenkinson (1988b, p. 716) calls writing "a powerful catalyst for learning."

Maimon (1988) encourages the frequent use of writing activities of various types, pointing out that such activities will help students become more fluent writers. Fluency is an aspect of writing that is achieved only with practice. It is likely that the advantages of writing as a tool for thinking are more available to fluent writers than to those who are not fluent.

◼ The Relationship Between Reading and Writing in Content Area Classes

Secondary school students need both reading and writing skills for learning. Teachers of content area classes *have* generally perceived reading as a means of learning, but few have viewed writing in this way. Consequently, most content area classes exhibit a noticeable lack of writing activities; in classes studied by Applebee (1984), less than 5 percent of class time required writing at least a paragraph. This situation is unfortunate, since both reading and writing are valuable learning techniques for students in these classes.

Reading and writing have the obvious link of being written language skills. They are both concerned with communication: readers consider the author's purposes and believability, and writers the needs of their audiences (Shanahan, 1988). Because both make use of written words that represent thoughts and oral language, vocabulary development is a key ingredient in successful reading and writing activities.

Another link between reading and writing is that the construction of meaning in reading has a relationship to the organization of written material (Shanahan, 1984). Raphael and others (1986) have found that teaching students about expository text structure has a positive effect on both report writing and content area reading. (See Chapter 4 for more on teaching expository text structure.) As Konopak and others (1987) point out, the characteristics of generating, organizing, drafting, and revising ideas are common to both reading and writing. Learning to write using a particular organizational pattern has the potential to help students understand material that others write in that pattern, but students need to "have been actively involved in significant, purposeful writing before, during, or after reading" (Oberlin and Shugarman, 1988, p. 720).

We have previously stated that reading is a thinking process. Elaboration on this idea can be found in Chapter 5. This relationship to thinking is another link between reading and writing.

■ Techniques of Combining Reading and Writing Effectively

Despite the connections between reading and writing, use of random writing activities in a content course may not help students in reading. Ferris and Snyder (1986) found that use of a process approach to writing instruction (discussed extensively later in this chapter) increased writing skills, but not reading skills, for students in eleventh-grade English classes. Therefore, use of random writing assignments in an effort to improve reading performance is not advisable. Assignments must focus on the relationships between the two disciplines. For example, Shanahan (1988) suggests that after students read a selection from a text, teachers can discuss its organization in relation to the organization of some of the students' own compositions. Another suggestion is that teachers have students write explanations of a difficult text to help them understand it better and make them more aware of their levels of understanding. He also emphasizes the need for separate attention to reading and writing strategies to ensure adequate treatment of each area.

Konopak and others (1987) did find, however, that a writing treatment resulted in students' production of higher-level ideas gained from their reading and synthesis of information from various class activities. The writing treatment included making jot lists to activate prior knowledge, brainstorming and classification of ideas, preliminary writing based on the classifications, reading, and further writing.

Writing before starting the reading assignment can help students retrieve background knowledge that is needed to comprehend ideas in the written material. Activation of such knowledge can be beneficial to reading achievement. Oberlin and Shugarman (1988) suggest writing responses to prereading questions; previewing unfamiliar texts; using a short dictated excerpt from the passage to be read as the basis for prereading discussion; and making a conscious effort to tie students' existing knowledge to the content of the passage.

McGinley and Denner (1987) suggest the use of a prereading writing activity called story impressions before reading of narrative events. With this activity, the teacher constructs a series of clue words and phrases to provide the reader with the information necessary to form an overall impression of a story. The clues are systematic, designed to approximate closely the text's top-level structure. Students are asked to take the clues and construct a story of their own that would fit the information provided, thereby predicting what the story will be about. After the writing exercise, students read the story and compare their predictions with the events of the actual story. McGinley and Denner found that this procedure significantly facilitated comprehension of the stories involved, whether or not the stories that the students constructed were close to the originals. This procedure appeared to benefit remedial students more than high-ability students. An example of a set of story impressions used by McGinley and Denner and a remedial eighth grader's story prediction are shown in Example 8.1.

Cunningham and Cunningham (1987) suggest reading-writing lessons based on organizational devices, such as feature matrixes, webs, outlines, or timelines, to help students understand and retain content knowledge. The teacher first guides the students to begin filling in a class skeleton organizer (one without the information included) that is placed on the chalkboard or a transparency, using their background knowledge of the material to be studied. Then the students read the text selection on which the organizer is based, with the purpose of confirming, changing, or adding to the information in it, noting this on their personal copies of the organizer. Following this activity, the students and teacher complete the class organizer together. Disagreements are resolved by returning to the text for supporting evidence. Gaps in the information provided by the text may be used as motivational devices to send the students to reference materials. On another day, the teacher leads the group through the writing of a paragraph based on a portion of the organizer (i.e., an item on a feature matrix, a strand of a web, a main division of an outline), followed by individual or small-group writing on other parts of the organizer. Eventually students can write entire compositions from their organizers.

Example 8.2 shows an organizer both in its early stages of development during the prereading period and in completed form. This organizer was developed for information included in a chapter in *Physics: Fundamentals and Frontiers*, by Robert Stollberg and Faith Fitch Hill (Boston: Houghton Mifflin, 1980).

■ ■ ■ EXAMPLE 8.1   *Story Impressions*

Story Impressions (Prereading) Activity Based on Poe's "The Tell-Tale Heart"

Story Impressions Given to a Class	A Remedial 8th Grader's Story Guess Written from the Story Impressions
house ↓ old man ↓ young man ↓ hatred ↓ ugly eye ↓ death ↓ tub, blood, knife ↓ buried ↓ floor ↓ police ↓ heartbeat ↓ guilt ↓ crazy ↓ confession	There was a young man and his father, an old man. They lived in a house on a hill out in the bounieys. The old man hated his son because he had an ugly eye. The young man was asleep in his bedroom when he was awakened by screaming. He went to the bedroom and saw his father laying in the tub. There was blood everywhere and a knife through him. The young man found a tape recording hidden behind the door on the floor. He turned it on there was screaming on the tape. The young man started to call the police, but then he stopped and remembered what his mother had told him. She had told him that he had a split personality. So he called the police and confessed to being crazy and killing his father. His heartbeat was heavy as he called.

Source: Figure from "Story Impressions: A Prereading/Writing Activity," William J. McGinley and Peter R. Denner, Journal of Reading 31 *(December 1987), p. 250. Reprinted with permission of the International Reading Association.*

■ ■ ■ EXAMPLE 8.2   *Incomplete and Completed Organizer*

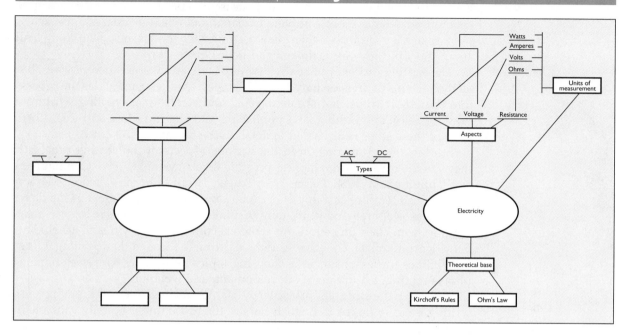

The Process Approach to Writing in the Content Areas

The process approach to writing instruction, as its name implies, gives attention to the writing process, rather than looking only at writing products. If writing across the curriculum is to be implemented by teachers, they need to know how to guide students through the writing process, regardless of the type of content. In content classes, writing has often been treated as a two-step process: (1) the writing assignment is given, and (2) the students write a paper and turn it in to the teacher. This is an inadequate and inaccurate picture of what writing in content classes should be. Students are not helped to develop their writing products, but they are graded on their effectiveness.

When a process approach to writing is used, the development of the written material is guided through various stages, with students receiving feedback from teacher and peers at each stage. Students are encouraged to think about their topics, the organization for their writing, and their audiences, for the teacher is not the only audience anticipated. The papers may be shared with peers, younger students, parents, or the community at large in letters to the editor of the local paper. Therefore, students tend to produce papers that are more coherent and have more complete explanations when a process approach is used than they produce when they assume that the teacher, who knows all about the topic anyway, is the only audience for the paper.

The writing process can be divided into steps in several different ways, but all the systems of division have multiple stages. One system divides the process into four basic steps that are *overlapping* and *recursive:* prewriting, writing a draft, revision and editing, and publishing and sharing (Ross and Roe, 1990). Each of these steps is discussed in detail in the following sections.

Students need instruction in the various aspects of the writing process if they are to achieve at the highest possible levels (Manion, 1988; Cunningham and Cunningham, 1987; Gahn, 1989; Power, 1996). In her instruction, Manion (1988) uses literature as a model of quality writing for the students. One day a week there is a three- to twenty-minute minilesson dealing with a topic in areas ranging from class procedures to sentence-combining activities that help students learn to relate, coordinate, and subordinate ideas in their writing. Other possibilities for lessons include choosing topics, techniques for revision, paraphrase writing, feature matrix development, and webbing.

Although the examples provided by Manion relate to literature, and process writing is easily linked to English classes, the procedure is equally valuable in other content area classes. Minilessons in classes such as science and social studies, for example, would be likely to focus more on choosing and delimiting topics for inquiry, on using a feature matrix for organization of related material, or on webbing of ideas than on paraphrase writing or sentence combining. They would emphasize the use of writing to express knowledge, show connections between ideas, and gain new insights into the material through organization of information from multiple sources.

Components of effective writing lessons are teacher modeling, guided practice, and feedback. Writing and conferences take place in Manion's class after the minilessons and during another complete class period each week. This process allows students to apply what they have learned from the minilessons in authentic writing experiences. Conferences are valuable opportunities for students in any content area to get feedback on the effectiveness and accuracy of their written communication. The writing teacher must be a coach and mentor. Knowledge about the craft of writing is essential. Students need the teacher's help in learning to *shape* their writing—to structure it so that it says what they want to say (Power, 1996). Romano (1996) reminds teachers that writers develop their authentic voices by crafting what they write to accomplish the language rhythms and effects that they seek. Encouraging students to attend to strategic arrangement of words and ideas and to the choice of words that convey unmistakable meaning is an important function for teachers.

Teachers should be careful to emphasize the recursive nature of the stages in the writing process. These stages are components among which students move—often in a nonlinear fashion (e.g., returning to prereading activities in the midst of writing a draft)—with different writers approaching the process in different ways (Latta, 1991).

■ Prewriting

What activities take place during the prewriting stage?

Prewriting is often neglected in content classes. This stage is used for selection and delimitation of the topic, determination of the audience for the writing, decisions about the general approach for the writing, activation of the students' prior knowledge of the subject, discussion of ideas with classmates, and organization of ideas. The topic for the writing is sometimes selected by the teacher in a content class, but the other activities can be assumed by the students. In composition classes, and sometimes in other areas, even topic selection is included in the prewriting activities.

Secondary students often do not adequately limit the scope of topics they choose. Therefore, they face researching a seemingly insurmountable amount of material on a broad topic. When they discover the scope of the task ahead of them, their response is often to inquire, "How long does the paper have to be? How many sources do we need to consult?" when they should ask themselves, "What is needed to cover this topic adequately?" A social studies student may decide to write about a topic as broad as "The Civil War" when he or she should be considering something much more specific, such as a single battle, a particular general, or a single theme related to the war. The teacher's modeling of topic delimitation can help students to perform this task effectively.

Students need to practice writing for audiences other than the teacher. The audience can be their classmates, with peers listening to and/or reading each other's drafts during the development of the drafts. Students also often have access to each other's revised writings in the form of classroom "books" composed of the collected writings of several students or of a single student, bulletin board displays, or oral sharing sessions. During peer conferences, students can learn to ask each other questions that request clarification or expansion of the information given. The peers, therefore, let each other know when the needs of the audience are not being taken into consideration. Students may find that having an audience response form to guide them in giving feedback to their classmates about the effectiveness of a piece of writing can be helpful (Aubry, 1995).

Teachers may also want to plan lessons that focus on other audiences. Letters to the editor of the local newspaper on timely subjects such as water pollution, unfairness of restrictions on youth gatherings, a local health hazard, or the drug problem in the schools give students the larger community as an audience. Students may also be asked to write simplified explanations of concepts they are studying for students in lower grades who need the information to enrich their study units, or composition students may write short stories designed for younger readers and share them with classroom teachers of lower grades. Students may write directions for carrying out procedures for their classmates to follow in class or explanations of steps in scientific experiments that other students may be curious about or want to duplicate.

Deciding on an approach to the writing may include choosing a format, such as a letter, a short story, a poem, a memorandum, or an essay. It also can include choosing the manner of presenting expository information, such as comparison/contrast, chronological order, problem/solution, cause/effect, or some other organizational pattern.

The student's prior knowledge about the topic can be activated through activities such as class discussion, brainstorming, webbing, and/or making comparison charts or feature matrixes. Students listen to the contributions of others in these class activities and remember related items to contribute. Interaction among students at this stage is extremely desirable.

Ideas may be organized through a web or map, a feature matrix, a timeline, or an outline. Students should be taught all of these techniques and be allowed to choose the one that appears to fit the task best for each assignment.

■ Writing a Draft

What takes place during the stage of writing a draft?

The stage of writing a **draft** is designed to allow the writer to put his or her ideas on paper without worrying about mechanics or neatness. Ideally, the writing time should be in an uninterrupted block, so that intervening activities do not break a student's train of thought. Some sharing of ideas with classmates may take place during this period in the form of spontaneous conversation among students seated close together. This should be allowed if it is not disruptive to the other students. Piazza and Tomlinson (1985) point out that this conversation is essentially a continued rehearsal of students' writing ideas and, as such, represents a return to the prewriting stage. Peer responses may help to shape the writing in some cases, and the interaction may make a sense of audience easier to attain. Certainly if the paper is to be a collaborative effort, the collaborators need to converse as the draft progresses.

Although Britton and others (1975) have characterized the production stage of the writing process as a lonely one, they do perceive the value of talking about the project. They feel that the relationship of talking to writing is a central one, that good talk encourages good writing, and that talk permits writers to express tentative conclusions and opinions. They say, "It is probable that of all the things teachers are now doing to make their pupils' approach to writing more stimulating, and the writing itself a more integral part of the manifold activities of the classroom, it is the encouragement of different kinds of talk that is the commonest and most productive factor" (Britton et al., 1975, p. 29).

Teachers may need to help students overcome their reluctance to take risks related to spelling and punctuation and their reluctance to produce messy first drafts by bringing in examples of their own first drafts, which are double spaced to allow for changes, with words, phrases, and sentences struck out and others inserted between lines or in margins and with some incorrectly spelled words circled to be looked up later. Students often have the impression that the draft has to be perfect from the beginning. Thus, to avoid imperfection, they substitute less exact words for ones they cannot spell without using the dictionary and substitute shorter, less complex sentences for ones they cannot punctuate without additional thought and time.

In the midst of drafting a paper, peer and teacher conferences about the writing may take place. Quick, informal teacher conferences may occur as the teacher circulates among the students to see how work is progressing. The teacher may ask students how their writing is going and, when problems are revealed, ask pertinent questions to help the writers think through the problem areas effectively. For example, if a student says, "I'm not sure what order to use to tell about these events," the teacher might say, "What order did the author of your history book use to tell about the events that came just before those events?" The student may answer, "Time order," and the teacher may ask, "Is that an appropriate order for you to use here, or do you have a reason to want to use another order? What would be the value of chronological order or some other order to your presentation?" These conferences are brief but help productive writing to continue. The teacher does not tell the student what to do with the writing but leads him or her to think in channels appropriate for the task.

In some areas, conferences between secondary student writers and university methods students are taking place online. Prospective teachers learn about the characteristics of the students that they will be teaching as they help them craft their writing through electronic mail conversations (Robbins and Fischer, 1996). More about such electronic mail partnerships, including writing and other aspects, is found in the Afterword to this book. Roe has carried out such a project in her methods courses.

Students may request peer conferences for the purpose of asking for help with some part of the writing that is giving them trouble. They may read their writing to one or more peers and say something to this effect: "I'm having trouble with this ending. What can I do to improve it?"

The peers should first respond to the piece by indicating their understanding of what it says; then they should offer positive comments on good points. Finally, they should give suggestions that they may have for improvement. Students often take suggestions better if they are couched as questions: "Would it help if you left out the last paragraph? How would it sound if you referred to the beginning statement here?" When a student has an entire first draft finished, he or she may wish to read it to a peer or several peers for further response. At this point in development, the student should read the work to his or her peers rather than having them read it. This procedure keeps the mechanical problems of the draft from interfering with a content analysis by the other students. Peers need to offer specific revision suggestions, or their comments may not be perceived as helpful. They should tell the author what they believe is good about the piece and why they think so, what parts need clarification, and what specific ways they believe the piece can be improved. Teachers may need to give some instruction in generating more specific, helpful comments. For example, they could have the students examine sample responses to a piece and tell why each comment was or was not effective (Neubert and McNelis, 1990).

■ Revision and Editing

Why is revision unnecessary for some types of student writing?

For pieces that are going to be read by others, **revision** is a necessary step, although it is not necessary for everything students write. Revision should not be expected, for example, in journals or class notes unless the student does it spontaneously.

How do revision and editing differ?

The first step in the revision process is for the student to read his or her own piece carefully, considering the criteria for writing that have been established in the class. Students should realize that revision is not just **editing** for spelling, grammar, and punctuation, although these editing aspects of writing should be considered late in the process. It involves reorganizing the material, clarifying ideas, and adding and deleting information as needed. Although revision is listed as the third step in the writing process here, it is important to realize that it is a recursive process "and can occur at any point in the writing process, embedded within other subprocesses. For example, revision may happen during planning either before or during the time pen meets paper. Or it may happen while writers review material that is either in their minds or on paper" (Fitzgerald, 1988, p. 124).

A list of criteria to use in judging students' written work may be cooperatively developed by the teacher and students, or the teacher may provide it. A set of criteria that a group might develop is as follows:

1. *Beginning*—Does it arouse the reader's interest from the start? It should get the reader "hooked" right away.
2. *Middle*—Is the information or action presented in a logical order? Is the organizational pattern evident to the reader? The organizational pattern should fit your information.
3. *Ending*—Does the ending tie up the piece satisfactorily? It should not leave the reader "hanging."
4. *Sentence structure*—Have you used complete sentences? Do your sentences make sense? Sentence fragments should be avoided, except in special cases, such as dialogue.
5. *Vocabulary*—Have you used words that say exactly what you want to say? Consider the precise meanings of the words that you used and make sure they fit the context.

6. *Point of view*—Did you maintain a single point of view in the story? Make sure that you have not shifted from third person to second person or first person, for example.

7. *Focus*—Does your piece stay on the main topic? Delete portions that stray from the main point.

8. *Audience*—Is your story appropriate for the intended audience? Read the piece with your audience in mind, and make sure that you have taken their backgrounds into consideration.

9. *Mechanics*—Have you used punctuation marks and capitalization correctly? Have you spelled words correctly? Proofread for punctuation, capitalization, and spelling. (If you wrote your piece on the computer, run the grammar and spelling check programs.)

Tchudi and Yates (1983) present another possible revision guide, shown in Example 8.3.

■ ■ ■ EXAMPLE 8.3   Revision Guide

1. As you listen to the presentation, jot down what you like best and are most interested in.

2. Write down any questions or general comments you have when the presentation ends.

3. Did you become confused or disinterested in any section? If so, identify the section and describe what happened to you.

4. Check any of the following revision methods that will help make the presentation more interesting or clearer to you:

Add more information or pictures (show where).

Take out confusing or unnecessary sections (point out).

Add an interesting fact, clue, story, or idea in the beginning that helps introduce the subject (make suggestions).

Change the order of the ideas or pictures (explain).

Add words, signals, or sentences that explain the order of ideas (show where).

Add words, signals, or sentences that help tie together your ideas and the information you present (point out where).

Give some of your own opinions, ideas, or conclusions (suggest where).

Add some interesting information or pictures at the end to reinforce your point (make suggestions).

Source: Teaching Writing in the Content Areas: Senior High School, © *1983. National Education Association. Reprinted with permission.*

Students can make their paper and pencil revisions by using carets and writing additional material between lines, marking out or erasing unwanted material, using circles and arrows to move material around, or even cutting and pasting. Their markings need to be clear, but the paper does not necessarily need to look neat.

If the piece has been written on a computer with a word processing program, the revision activity is much easier, and the final copy will be cleaner. A few keystrokes will delete material, insert material, and move material around. Papers revised in this manner never need to look messy. A computer's spelling checker can highlight suspicious words for the student to check, and other writing tools are available to check for clichés, incomplete sentences, punctuation problems, redundancies, wordiness, and other aspects of poor or mediocre writing. These tools simply alert students to potential problems in their writing and force them to look closely at their writing; they do not make changes for the students. The students must still take responsibility for making judgments about the flagged material. Many flagged parts may be perfectly acceptable, whereas some errors will not be flagged. Computers cannot consider meaning in their analyses, and therefore they make errors that a human editor is less likely to make (O'Donnell, 1979).

Students can be taught strategies to help them use spelling checkers more effectively. They can alter words that are identified as misspelled, but for which alternative spellings are not suggested, until the checker is able to offer alternatives. Different spellings for sounds must be tried in order to accomplish this. Students can also check dictionary definitions of alternatives that are offered to be sure which one fits their context. (The word processor may have a dictionary included, or there may be an electronic dictionary on the computer as a separate program.) If the checker or dictionary supports sound, the students can ask for pronunciation of the alternatives through speech synthesis. They may be able to tell from its pronunciation if the option is the one they want (Anderson-Inman and Knox-Quinn, 1996). There is some evidence that students produce better papers when they use word processors than when they use paper and pencil, particularly when they have reached a level of proficiency with word processing (Owston, Murphy, and Wideman, 1992).

After students have read and revised their papers to the best of their abilities, they may submit their work for peer editing. They may have regular partners for peer editing, certain students may act as peer editors for specified weeks, or writers may request different peer editors at different times. Peer editors read each other's papers with the class writing criteria in mind, write positive comments about the material, and make suggestions for changes or ask for clarification about parts of the writing. These comments and any marks related to mechanics are discussed with the student author. The author then decides which changes may be necessary and which ones are not desirable. This process should be modeled by the teacher before the students are expected to use it (Harp, 1988).

■ Publishing

In what ways may student writing be "published"?

The pieces that students carefully revise for sharing with others, as just described, are **"published"** in one of a number of ways. They may simply be shared orally by the student author, or they may be posted on bulletin boards, bound into a "book" to be placed in the classroom library or school library, or published in a school magazine or newspaper. Many types of writings may be "published" in various classes. Members of a shop class could develop directions for assembly of various objects. Students in a home economics class could produce meal plans for family members with special dietary needs, such as low cholesterol diets or low calorie diets. Literature students could turn a short story into a play for presentation in class or to a wider audience, and science students could write descriptions of science fair exhibits or class experiments.

Students see the reason for careful crafting of their writing when others are going to read it for information or entertainment. They get much satisfaction from seeing others reading their work, and they appreciate the opportunities to read the work of their peers.

■ ■ ■ Types of Writing to Learn in the Content Areas

Many types of writing are used in content area classes to enhance learning. The types discussed here are some of the more common ones from which teachers have reported positive results. Knowledge of the steps in the process approach to writing can help teachers to implement some of these writing-to-learn strategies more effectively.

Andrasick (1990) believes that assignments need to be both real (having the purpose of communicating with a real audience) and connected. A sequence of connected writing experiences can lead students to increased critical power. According to Andrasick (1990, p. 14), "Learning is connecting and organizing information." And sequenced writing assignments can help students make connections among information in the different sources that they read and between the text and their own experiences. Butcheri and Hammond (1994) also encourage the use of writing for real audiences, rather than make-believe ones. For example, students can write letters to authors of books they have read or to newspaper editors.

■ Language Experience Writings

Language experience writings are materials written in the students' own words. In the elementary school, language experience stories are usually

How can language experience materials be used in a content area classroom?

developed by a group of students who have had a common experience. In the secondary school, **language experience materials** may be written by a group of students who have read about a common topic and wish to summarize their findings. The teacher can record all significant contributions on the chalkboard as they are offered. At the conclusion of the discussion, the teacher and students together can organize the contributions in a logical order (e.g., chronological or cause-effect). The teacher can then duplicate the group-composed material and distribute it to the class members.

Students who can handle the textbook with ease may file the experience material to use for review for tests. A group that is unable to handle the textbook presentation may use the material more extensively. For example, the teacher may meet with this group and guide the members through the reading of the material by using purpose questions. The students are likely to succeed in reading this material because they have seen the content written on the board and because it is in the words of fellow students. Having heard a discussion of the content, the students will find it easier to apply context clues as they read. Any technical vocabulary or multiple-meaning words can be located and discussed thoroughly. These words may be written in a special notebook with accompanying pronunciations and definitions and a reference to the experience material in which they occurred. A booklet made up of experience material can serve as a reference source for these words when they are encountered again and can be used in studying for tests. At-risk and English as a Second Language (ESL) students particularly may benefit from such special word notebooks.

Experience materials may also be developed by individuals and groups who wish to record the results of scientific experiments or the periodic observation of some natural phenomena. These materials may be shared with the rest of the class in oral or written form. Such activities are extremely valuable for students who are not able to gain much information from a textbook that is too difficult for them.

Sharp (1989), Laminack (1987), Ferguson and Fairburn (1985), and Wood (1992) found the language experience approach to be effective for use with content instruction in social studies, science, and math story problems. Sharp feels that this approach motivates remedial students, builds their self-esteem, provides them with concepts that allow participation in content classes, builds reading vocabulary (including technical vocabulary), and activates and organizes the students' prior knowledge in the content areas, among other values.

Wood (1992) suggested having mathematics problems assigned to small groups of students, each of whom would solve the problem and write the processes involved in the solution. Then the students would share their solutions with the rest of the group. This type of language experience activity could be extended by having the group as a whole revise a written solution to make it clearer, more accurate, or less wordy, if necessary.

■ Content Journals, or Learning Logs

What is another name for learning logs?

Content journals, or **learning logs,** allow students to keep a written record of content area learning activities that is personal and informal. They help students to clarify their thoughts and feelings about topics under study. Students usually choose what to write in these journals, although teachers may suggest general areas of consideration and types of things they may wish to record, if appropriate. For example, the teacher may ask that the students record any questions that occur to them as they read a content chapter or listen to a class lecture and discussion, new ideas that they have gained, confusion about a topic or procedure, feelings about the subject area, predictions about the assigned reading, explanations of a recently taught concept, or some other general category—such as the answer to some broad content-related questions—at specific times. When the teacher makes a request or notes a specific thing to be recorded, journal entries may be shared by volunteers (with prior warning that sharing will be invited). At other times the students may choose among the many possibilities that arise in the classroom for their daily entries. Commander and Smith (1996) have used learning logs to promote students' metacognitive awareness. They asked questions about students' learning behaviors to which the students responded in log entries, helping them achieve insight about their learning and begin to assume responsibility for it.

The student who is doing the writing is the primary audience for the content journal, although the teacher may collect these journals and read them periodically. However, content journals are not graded in the ordinary sense; spelling and grammatical errors are not marked, for example, but sometimes extra credit is awarded for especially insightful entries (Santa, Havens, and Harrison, 1989).

When teachers take up journals, they may occasionally make encouraging comments to students in response to their entries. These comments should focus on the message the student was trying to convey and ignore problems with punctuation, spelling, and grammar. Red-penciling of journals is not allowed, no matter how tempting it may be. This frees students from the fear of writing something that they are not perfectly sure about and results in more comprehensive and creative journal entries.

Teacher comments should always be written in correctly spelled and punctuated standard English, which will serve as a model to the student for future writing. If a word has been repeatedly misspelled by the student, the teacher may write a comment in the journal with that word spelled correctly, without referring to spelling. The example can be more potent than the admonition would have been.

What is freewriting, and what purposes does it serve?

Freewriting

Some teachers have students use content journals for true **freewriting**—that is, writing that has no teacher restrictions on content. Students simply write in a sustained manner for a specified period of time. This freewriting is intended to make thinking conscious and visible (Collins, 1990).

Andrasick (1990) uses the term *freewriting* to refer to writing for a specific period of time without stopping to correct or think. This writing may be in response to reading that has been done. In content classes the teacher often specifies that the journal entries focus on a specific topic, although the students still write knowing that their writing will not be graded. Language teachers may obtain more direct benefit from true freewriting than other content teachers do, because part of their curriculum centers on self-expression. Elbow (1978, p. 67) believes, "If you are really interested in good quality writing, then you must make it your immediate goal that people write copiously, not well. Only when people begin to use writing on other occasions than when it is required—only when they have written for diverse purposes over a period of years—will they eventually come to produce good writing." Writing consistently in journals on a daily basis is valuable to development of ease in writing.

Freewriting is good for encouraging interpretation and evaluation of the material read. It may result in the discovery of alternative interpretations of the text as students strive to continue to write without pauses for correction or reflection (Andrasick, 1990).

Teachers usually designate times in class for students to write in their journals. At the beginning of a class, students may write summaries of what they learned on the previous day, or at the end of class they may write summaries of what they learned that day. They may write predictions about the lesson that they are about to begin, list everything that they think they already know about the topic, or do both. They may explain how they will apply the day's lesson in everyday life. They may record the progress of a laboratory experiment or observational study. Some teachers set aside the same time period each day for journal writing, and students are asked to write for the entire five or ten minutes about the class or observations related to the class, such as their difficulty in finding time at home to study for it. Andrasick (1990, p. 69) believes that "anything less than ten minutes is not productive."

Gordon and MacInnis (1993) provided prompts to guide students' journal writing about decimals but allowed the students to write open-ended entries about any mathematics topic that concerned them. The prompts were much like essay questions (e.g., asking how decimals are similar to and different from fractions), but the open-ended responses were simply a type of freewriting. Gordon and MacInnis made these journals into dialogue journals (discussed further in this chapter) as well, responding to all of the entries by the following week. They "found that the journals provided a window on students' thinking processes. . . . Information gleaned from the journal entries allowed guidance and instruction on a more individualized level" (Gordon and MacInnis, 1993, p. 42). The journals also encouraged students to reflect upon their mathematical understandings.

Teachers can use the journals to discover gaps in understanding and confusion that the students have. They may also gain insight into students' lives that helps explain class performance. For example, if a student writes in his or her journal, "I don't know what the chapter for last night was about. My parents left me to take care of my brothers and sisters and didn't get home until two in the morning," the teacher has an idea of the reasons behind this student's failure to answer questions in class.

Reading Response Journals

What types of entries are included in reading response journals?

Reading response journals are a type of learning log for literature classes. With these journals, typically the students read or listen to a chapter of a book and then write about it for three to five minutes immediately afterward. They comment about the characters, setting, plot, author's writing style and devices, and their personal reactions. The teacher writes while the students are writing and shares his or her entries frequently as a model for the students. Students also may share their material voluntarily. The sharing can become the basis for lively discussion. The teacher can collect the journals and comment on entries, clarifying points of confusion for the students and giving positive reinforcement to those who showed insight into the story (Simpson, 1986).

Jossart (1988) suggests a slightly different twist to the use of the reading response journal. She asks her students to select a character in the book and write a journal entry for that character at a particular point in the progress of the story when there is much descriptive action. The students try to write their entries so that each one takes on the point of view of only one character. Then they share the entries, and the other students try to guess which character supposedly wrote each one. This activity involves higher-level thinking on the part of both the writer and the listener.

Kletzien and Hushion (1992) used graphic thinking symbols, such as an arrow to indicate a prediction or a scale to indicate a judgment or evaluation, to mark examples of particular response types in the students' journals. Recalling information, giving ideas and examples, indicating causes and effects, indicating similarities and differences, making inferences, making personal identifications, using analogies, using metacognitive strategies, and analyzing authors' techniques were among the types of responses recognized and marked by the teachers. This approach resulted in responses that went beyond summaries, ones that were more varied and thoughtful. Knight (1990) used a similar marking system and found that the coded journals helped in recognizing reading comprehension difficulties.

Some teachers use reading response journals more like learning logs and have student writing before, during, and after reading. Prereading writing prompts are given to arouse curiosity about the topic, activate prior knowledge and experiences that are related, encourage personal connections with the material, and generate hypotheses about the characters and action. During reading, writing prompts may ask students to react to such features of the text as character and setting, respond personally to events or people, draw conclusions and make further predictions, or adjust previous predictions. Postreading writing prompts may lead students to apply themes to current situations; to consider the contributions of particular literary elements to the effect of the whole piece; to show changes that took place in people, places, and things over the course of the story; or to compare the work to similar works or works by the same author (Pritchard, 1993). Pritchard (1993, p. 30) indicates that the result of keeping a response journal over time is that "students will have a visible record of how their evaluations, opinions, and perceptions change over time; they may also have explicit indicators of how the literature itself has influenced that growth."

Andrasick (1990) discusses a type of journal in which students write quotations, paraphrases, or summaries of the ideas in the book on the left-hand pages of a notebook. The students use the corresponding right-hand pages to respond to the entries on the left-hand side. They may both ask questions and make comments about the material. The important thing is that they reflect on the content. Although Andrasick calls this a dialogue journal because the students are having a dialogue with the author of the text about the material, we have reserved the term *dialogue journal* for a journal in which a dialogue takes place between two people, such as a student and the teacher. The type of journal Andrasick discusses probably best fits our definition of a reading response journal. Example 8.4 shows an excerpt from such a journal (Alfred, 1991).

■ ■ ■ EXAMPLE 8.4   *Student's Journal Entries*

Dialogue Journal
Chapter Three

Andrasick, K.D. (1990). *Opening Texts: Using Writing to Teach Literature.* Portsmouth, NH: Heinemann.

What the Text Says	What I Say
p. 40 ". . . shouldn't be concerned so much with particular data as with student's ability to use data.	I'm not sure if I agree . . . The way kids are tested, e.g., ACT, other standardized tests, they must know factual data. If we can change this, then I *might* agree.
p. 40 "Many students deny the value of their experiences with texts, dismissing them prematurely.	This really bothers me. Sure, some teachers listen to students' ideas, but that's it. They say, "That's nice," and then continue with their lecture. How else can kids be expected to react?

What the Text Says	What I Say
p. 41 "When we focus on text content by asking students to respond . . . to a series of short answer questions, we deflect attention from larger textual elements and may actually interfere with students' abilities to approach thematic issues.	No way! When I read a novel, for example, I always look for specific elements that may tie into a theme. Answering . . . questions [is] a good way to increase knowledge about themes that are prevalent throughout a work.
p. 41 "Learning to discriminate between the solidity of the visible surface structure and the fluctuating, invisible text world the pages potentially contain requires practice" (Andrasick, pp. 40–41).	What a yucky sentence! Engfish! Engfish! Engfish!

Source: Suellen Alfred, "Dialogue Journal," Tennessee Reading Teacher 19 (Fall 1991): 14.

Character Journals

In what content areas would character journals be most useful?

Character journals are diaries in which students assume the role of one of the main characters in a book (Hancock, 1993). In them, the student makes first-person journal entries for a chosen character that represent one episode in each chapter. Through these entries, the students become extremely involved in the story being read, helping them attain insight into the character and his or her actions. This process also helps students examine their own beliefs, actions, and values.

Social Justice Notebooks

What kind of entries would be included in a social justice notebook?

Proctor and Kantor (1996) use **social justice notebooks** as a writing-to-learn experience. The students use their writing in these notebooks to examine controversial human rights issues. Students read and discuss news articles or editorials on the issue. Then a question about the issue is posed, and the students respond to it in writing. They are encouraged to recognize different points of view on the issue, then to take a personal stand.

The students share their writing orally, with classmates commenting and asking questions. This discussion is followed by more research on the issue, more class discussion, and rewriting. In some cases the writing leads to student-initiated action, such as letters to the editor of the local newspaper. Critical reading, enhanced by writing, results in important content learning.

Responses to Thought Questions

Thought questions resemble the essay questions that teachers use on tests. Writing responses to essay questions is probably the most traditional writing task that teachers expect of students. Teachers often assign study questions to classes for homework as study aids. Unfortunately, they may not prepare students to respond effectively to such questions, as was pointed out in Chapter 6. The students may not know the meanings of the terms used in the questions and therefore may not understand what is being asked of them (Jenkinson, 1988c). Teachers should use the procedures suggested in Chapter 6 for helping students learn to answer essay questions before asking them to respond in their journals. Teachers should define terms (such as *compare, contrast, discuss*), model answers that fit questions with each of the important terms, and provide students with practice questions for writing and discussion in class. Since the journal activity is ungraded, this practice in answering such questions is not threatening to the students, and they can be free to experiment with the technique without fear of failure.

Langer (1986) found that use of study questions did not increase students' topic knowledge as much as use of written essays or note taking on the topic. The study questions seemed to cause the students to focus on specific ideas chosen by the teacher and, therefore, "may best be used to invoke quick recall of isolated items of information" (p. 406). Teachers who use study questions as a part of journal writing should be aware that they will cause the students to focus on details of the content rather than on the overall picture.

Simpson (1986) teaches a procedure that she refers to as PORPE (Predict, Organize, Rehearsal, Practice, Evaluate) in response to her students' apprehension about essay examinations. This procedure, described in detail in Chapter 7, should result in better performance in answering study questions in journals or otherwise, as well as better performance on essay tests by many students, because of the intense involvement with text that is required.

Creative Applications

Some teachers have students use their journals for a variety of creative applications of writing in the subject area. The students may be asked to write stories about a historical period that they are studying in social studies class, making sure that they construct characters, settings, dialogues, and plots that fit the time that has been chosen. They may also write fictional interviews with historical characters, news stories about historical events, or letters to historical figures or from one historical figure to another. Dever (1992) had students role-play and write interviews of characters from novels.

Students in math classes may write their own statement problems. In a class on electronics, students can write imaginative accounts of things such as what life would be like without electron flow. Students in a home economics class can write sets of instructions for performing a specific type of task that class-mates will be asked to follow. In science class, students can write scripts for weather forecasts (Hightshue et al., 1988; Jenkinson, 1988b). To come up with other ideas for assignments, teachers may wish to refer to the list of discourse forms for content writing presented by Tchudi and Yates (1983, p. 12), shown in Example 8.5.

■ ■ ■ EXAMPLE 8.5   *Discourse Forms for Content Writing*

Journals and diaries
   (real or imaginary)
Biographical sketches
Anecdotes and stories:
   from experience as
   told by others
Thumbnail sketches:
   of famous people
   of places
   of content ideas
   of historical events
Guess who/what
   descriptions
Letters:
   personal reactions
   observations
   public/informational
   persuasive:
     to the editor
     to public officials
   to imaginary people
   from imaginary places
Requests
Applications
Memos
Resumés and summaries
Poems
Plays
Stories
Fantasy
Adventure
Science fiction
Historical stories
Dialogues and
   conversations

Children's books
Telegrams
Editorials
Commentaries
Responses and rebuttals
Newspaper "fillers"
Fact books or fact sheets
School newspaper
   stories
Stories or essays for local
   papers
Proposals
Case studies:
   school problems
   local issues
   national concerns
   historical problems
   scientific issues
Songs and ballads
Demonstrations
Poster displays
Reviews:
   books (including
     textbooks)
   films
   outside reading
   television programs
   documentaries
Historical "you are
   there" scenes
Science notes:
   observations
   science notebook
   reading reports
   lab reports

Math:
   story problems
   solutions to problems
   record books
   notes and
     observations
Responses to literature
Utopian proposals
Practical proposals
Interviews:
   actual
   imaginary
Directions:
   how-to
   school or neighbor-
     hood guide
   survival manual
Dictionaries and lexicons
Technical reports
Future options, notes on:
   careers, employment
   school and training
   military/public service
Written debates
Taking a stand:
   school issues
   family problems
   state or national
     issues
   moral questions
Books and booklets
Informational
   monographs
Radio scripts
TV scenarios and scripts

Dramatic scripts	Slide show scripts	Collage, montage,
Notes for improvised	Puzzles and word	mobile, sculpture
drama	searches	
Cartoons and cartoon	Prophecy and predictions	
strips	Photos and captions	

Source: Teaching Writing in the Content Areas: Senior High School, © *1983. National Education Association. Reprinted with permission.*

Paraphrasing and Summarizing

What is paraphrasing?

Paraphrasing and **summarizing** material learned in content area classes and from content area textbooks provides material for content journals. A surprising number of secondary school students do not know how to paraphrase the text material in their content subjects. In fact, when asked to paraphrase, many do not realize that they are simply expected to put the material into their own words. This process can just be rewording, or new forms may be used to represent the meaning of the text; for example, material from written text may be described in tabular or graphic form. Dictionaries and thesauruses are helpful tools for paraphrasing. "Research supports the view that paraphrase writing enhances reading skills and increases content comprehension and recall" (Shugarman and Hurst, 1986, p. 397). Paraphrase writing can result in improved listening, speaking, reading, and writing vocabularies (Shugarman and Hurst, 1986). Therefore, paraphrase writing in content journals can be a fruitful activity.

To teach paraphrasing, teachers should define the concept, demonstrate it for the students first with short paraphrases, offer the students guided practice in providing short paraphrases, and then provide planned independent practice. Instruction in paraphrases of longer passages can follow.

Practice in paraphrasing can be enjoyable. The teacher can present students with statements such as "A fowl in the palm is of the same value as a pair in the shrub." Students can be asked to paraphrase this sentence to produce a familiar saying. Students are permitted to refer to dictionaries and thesauruses for the activity. Later the students may be asked to locate familiar expressions, paraphrase them, and present the paraphrases to the class for decoding. Eventually, the students can be asked to locate key phrases in the textbook assignment for the day and write paraphrases in clear language. Judging of the clarity and accuracy of the paraphrases can be done in small groups, with all group members presenting their own paraphrases and participating in the evaluation of those of other students. Both paraphrasers and evaluators have to examine the text material closely in order to complete this activity. Students in math classes can paraphrase statement problems; those in social studies classes can paraphrase news articles, campaign literature, and advertisements; those in shop class can paraphrase instructions for a project; and so on for any subject area.

A form of summarizing is précis writing. Précis are abstracts of materials that retain the point of view of the original materials. D'Angelo (1983) credited skill in précis writing with improving both writing and research skills, and Bromley and McKeveny (1986) suggest that the use of précis writing enhances comprehension and recall of content material.

Students need to understand the purposes for précis writing, including vocabulary improvement and enhanced comprehension and retention. The teacher should demonstrate the process to the students, showing them how to analyze the original material, select main ideas for inclusion in the précis, reject nonessential material, and paraphrase the ideas through use of synonyms and restructuring of sentences. Encouraging the use of the thesaurus is a good technique. Taking such a close look at the content makes learning and remembering the material much more likely than if the material were processed less actively.

Group composition of a précis is a good beginning step. This can be done by having the students dictate as the teacher or one of the students records the précis. This is an application of the language experience technique described earlier in this chapter.

Bromley and McKeveny (1986) suggest that models of acceptable précis be available to students so that they can compare these models with their own products, evaluate their efforts, and perhaps revise their work. They also suggest that students save their précis for study before tests.

Students definitely need direct instruction in summary writing, which is not offered by many teachers (Hill, 1991). More information on summarizing is found in Chapter 6.

■ Dialogue Journals

What is the distinctive feature of dialogue journals?

Although **dialogue journals** *could* be content journals, they need not be. The distinctive feature of dialogue journals is that they set up a two-way written conversation between the teacher and each student. Their primary purpose is to open lines of communication. Students write about anything they choose, including both in-class and out-of-class experiences and concerns. They may offer their opinions, state grievances, provide information, make predictions, ask questions, answer questions, apologize, make promises, offer thanks, make evaluations, or give directions, among other possibilities. The written statements, questions, or observations are not evaluated by the teachers; the teachers respond to them as personal communications (Strackbein and Tillman, 1987; Jenkinson, 1988a; Bode, 1989).

Each day, time is made available for the students to write in their journals. The teachers read all the entries (generally after school) and respond to them. The responses may include recognition of what the students are saying, clarification of things about which the students are confused, answers to students' questions, questions for students to answer related to the writing or to some common interest, and sharing of personal thoughts and feelings. Grammatical and spelling errors in journal entries are never marked. The next day the students read the teachers' responses and continue the written dialogue with another entry. Strackbein and Tillman (1987) suggest that the teacher read only a specified number of journals each day if the reading load seems too great. Teachers who follow this suggestion should take care not to omit any one student's journal more often than others. Since grading is not a part of the reading, most teachers will be able to manage reading each student's journal at least every other day.

Dolly (1990) suggests the use of dialogue journals with English as a Second Language (ESL) students. She points out that such journals ensure that this reading material will be somewhat adjusted to the students' individual reading abilities, because teachers can modify their writing to fit the language proficiency of the students.

■ RAFT Assignments

How can RAFT assignments be beneficial to content area learning?

"RAFT simply stands for (R) role, (A) audience, (F) format, and (T) topic, the key ingredients for making writing assignments" (Santa et al., 1989, p. 148). **RAFT assignments** are explicit as to each of these factors: the student is told who the writer is, who the audience is, what form the writing will take, and the topic for the writing. Student roles may vary widely; they can be scientists, blood cells, trees, animals, or other animate or inanimate objects. The audiences can be classmates, younger children, or the general public. Formats can include letters, editorials, memoranda, and poems. A sample assignment might be as follows: You are the brother of a boy who is considering experimenting with cocaine (role). Through a letter (format) to your brother (audience), try to persuade him not to do this, backing up your arguments with facts about this drug (topic).

■ Research Reports

Tone (1988, p. 76) points out values of the research paper in secondary classes: "It commonly ties reading to writing. As a writing project, it usually involves the organizing and outlining of numerous facts and details. It develops comprehension that arises from synthesis and organization of information." Research papers can promote critical thinking about topics under study. They also offer practical applications of various study skills, such as library use, reference book use, note taking, outlining, and summarizing. Nevertheless, research papers should not be assigned without careful assessment of students' prerequisite skills, so that appropriate instruction can be offered if necessary skills are not in evidence. These skills should be taught as needed and connections made between the skills and the current task of answering the research questions that have been raised. Benson (1987) believes that students should be offered several note-taking, footnoting, and bibliographic forms from which to choose; this gives them a feeling of control over the project.

When content area teachers assign reports to be written for their classes, they sometimes allow students to choose their own topics. In other instances, a teacher may ask each student to write on a predetermined topic. Some educators feel that students should have a great deal of control over what they write. Britton and others (1975, p. 23) state: "But, however controlled the situation, the writer is *selecting* from what he knows and thinks . . . , and embodying that knowledge and thought in words which *he* produces, no matter how much he draws on the language of a book or of the teacher's notes." Therefore, from the perspective of Britton and others, having the teacher assign topics and guide students in writing procedures does not negate the ownership of the writing.

Davis and Hunter (1990) suggest having gifted students research the accuracy of historical novels as a project that can result in research papers that solve real problems. Anachronisms and other inaccuracies can be located by consulting reference books about the period. The students thus can have a choice of the novel to write about and a choice of focus for the paper, but they also have a well-defined task.

The process that follows can be used to help students prepare good reports. The first step listed obviously is not applicable if the teacher chooses the topic.

Step 1. Select a topic. The topic selected must be pertinent to the content area material being studied. It should be chosen because of its interest value for both the reporter and the rest of the class, if the reports are going to be shared. Ordinarily, students tend to choose topics that are much too broad for adequate coverage. The teacher needs to help students narrow their topics so that the task of preparing the report is more manageable.

Step 2. Collect information on the topic. Students should use the location skills discussed in Chapter 6 to collect information from a variety of sources. The organizational skill of note taking, covered in Chapter 6, is also essential for use at this point.

Step 3. Organize the material. Outlining or webbing the information collected is the main activity in this step. Material from the different sources used must be fused together. The sequence and relationship of main ideas and details are important considerations in forming the outline or web.

Step 4. Write a first draft. Utilizing the outline or web just formulated and the notes compiled, the students write an initial draft of the report.

Step 5. Read the first draft for revision and editing. The students read the first draft and check for organization, sentence and paragraph sense, cohesiveness of the information, appropriate usage, correct spelling, and proper punctuation. They also confirm that all material is properly documented.

At this point, peer editing may be utilized. With this approach, a peer editor carefully reads the report of his or her classmate, answering questions provided by the teacher. Some sample questions are as follows: "Does the report have a title that accurately reflects its contents? Does the report have a good beginning that sparks interest in the topic? Is the sequence in which the information is presented logical? If not, what do you think is wrong with it? Is enough information included? In your opinion, what questions remain to be answered by the report? Does the report have errors in mechanics (e.g., spelling, capitalization, punctuation)? If so, mark them for the author. Does the report have a conclusion that sums up the material adequately? Do you have any questions or suggestions for the author?" After answering these questions, the peer editor returns the report and comments to the author, who revises it, carefully considering the editor's comments. The peer editor may be asked to read and react to the report again before it is submitted to the teacher. Often two students work together, each acting as peer editor for the other.

Step 6. Revise the report. The students make needed changes in the initial draft and rewrite the report in a form acceptable for submission to the teacher. Revision is easier if the report has been written using word processing software on a computer.

The teacher can do much to help prepare students to perform effectively on an assigned written report. A procedure that a teacher might follow is described next.

1. Name a broad topic related to the course of study. Ask students for suggestions as to how the topic could be narrowed to make it more manageable. Consider a number of acceptable topics that might be derived from the original topic.

2. Choose one of the acceptable narrowed topics. Take the students to the library and have them locate sources of information on the topic. Ask each of them to take notes from at least one source and to record bibliographical information. Remind them to make use of skimming and scanning techniques as they search for information. (See Chapter 7 for information on skimming and scanning.) Encourage use of computer databases and CD-ROM encyclopedias, if they are available. (See Chapter 6 for a discussion of these resources.)

3. Return to the classroom. As a class, synthesize the notes into a single outline. (Use the chalkboard or overhead projector.)

4. Write the report from the outline as a whole-class or small-group activity, with the teacher working as the scribe or assigning a student to be the scribe.

5. Have the students read the draft for content, organization, and mechanics.

6. Make needed changes in organization, spelling, and expression on the basis of the proofreading.

The teacher who follows this procedure has essentially walked the students through the steps of report writing before asking them to attempt it on their own. Thereafter, the students will know what to expect when they are assigned individual reports to write. Help with the skills of note taking, outlining, summarizing information, and locating information should be a prerequisite for assignment of a written report if these skills have not been mastered previously. Help should also be given with composing footnote and bibliographic entries. Some dictionaries, such as the *Houghton Mifflin College Dictionary* (see sample page in Example 6.3), offer information on footnotes and bibliographic entries.

In addition to preparing students for report writing, the content area teacher should contact the school's librarian before assigning a research report. The librarian can be helpful to students as they strive to locate relevant resources.

Some computer software has been developed to help students with basic research skills. Teachers should preview these programs carefully before buying. Some are based on a single product, such as a particular set of encyclopedias, and will have little value for a teacher who does not have access to these resources.

Davey (1987) recommends having students work in teams on research reports, following steps similar to those just enumerated. She feels that research reports are less threatening and provide more active involvement when they are completed in teams of two to five students. In addition, greater learning appears to result from team reports than from individually produced reports. Teachers must monitor team work regularly and should also encourage self-monitoring of progress by team members.

Raphael and others (1988) developed the Expository Writing Program (EWP) to help students learn how to write well-organized reports with data collected from a number of sources. The EWP is designed around "think sheets" that stimulate strategy use for planning the report, gathering data, drafting, editing, and revising. The EWP Prewriting Think Sheet focuses on planning concerns such as considering the topic, things the students already know about the topic, and the audience for the paper. The Organizing Think Sheet focuses students' attention on different sets of questions that fit different text structures, such as comparison/contrast, problem/solution, and explanation. Students use the sheet that is appropriate for their chosen organizational pattern. A lined sheet of colored paper forms the think sheet for writing the first draft. Edit and Peer Editor Think Sheets provide the framework for first self-editing and then peer editing. These sheets focus on the content and organization of the paper and on planning the next step of the writing. A Revision Think Sheet encourages the students to integrate the feedback from others into a revision plan. Two types of think sheets are shown in Example 8.6. Raphael and Englert (1990) have developed a variety of examples of different types of think sheets. They also have encouraged modeling of the writing process through "thinking aloud."

■ ■ ■ EXAMPLE 8.6   *Sample Think Sheets*

Think-Sheet for Editing a Comparison/Contrast Paper

Author's name _____   Editor's name _____

Read to check information. (Authors: Read your paper aloud to your editor.)

What is the paper mainly about?

What do you like best? Put a ***** next to the part you liked best and tell why you like it here:

What parts are not clear? Put a **?** next to the unclear parts, and tell what made the part unclear to you:

Is the paper interesting? Tell why or why not here:

Question yourself to check organization.

Did the author:

Tell what two things are compared and contrasted?	Yes Sort of No
Tell things they are being compared and contrasted on?	Yes Sort of No
Tell how they are alike?	Yes Sort of No
Tell how they are different?	Yes Sort of No
Use keywords clearly?	Yes Sort of No

Plan revision.

What two parts do you think should be changed or revised? (For anything marked "Sort of" or "No," should the author add to, take out, reorder?)

1. _____

  _____

  _____

  _____

2. _____

  _____

  _____

  _____

What could help make the paper more interesting?

Talk.

Talk to the author of the paper. Talk about your comments on this editing think-sheet. Share ideas for revising the paper.

Think-Sheet for Planning

Author's name _____   Date _____

Topic: _____

Who: Who am I writing for?
Why: Why am I writing this?
What: What do I already know about my topic? (Brainstorm)

1. _____

2. _____

3. _____

How: How do I group my ideas?

Source: Taffy E. Raphael, Carol Sue Englert, and Becky W. Kirschner, "Acquisition of Expository Writing Skills," in Jana M. Mason (Ed.), Reading and Writing Connections. *Copyright © 1989 by Allyn and Bacon. Reprinted with permission of Jana Mason.*

MEETING THE CHALLENGE

Teaching students to do research papers can be approached in a number of ways. The following is a personal account of how a first-year teacher in a rural high school, Katherine Dooley, managed this challenge.

The dreaded junior research paper! The first time I taught the traditional research paper, I was distressed not by my students' lack of library skills but by the topics they chose—abortion, nuclear power, air pollution, drug abuse, teen pregnancy. Although these are important issues, they had little personal value and rarely required students to synthesize or evaluate information, resulting in papers packed with cold statistics and the excitement of bread mold. I knew if I wanted to survive reading them, I would have to direct their search, but I also knew that I could not pull that many topics out of my own head. Their papers would be interesting if they were interested in their topics. The problem was finding everyone the perfect topic.

Research papers require students to use reference skills. (© Robert Finken/The Picture Cube)

I started by having a class-long brainstorming session to answer two questions: What are you an expert at? and What do you want to know more about? For this assignment, I defined "expert" as anything they had ever done before. I started them with some examples: expert at being a son/daughter, eater, talker, teeth brusher. I also provided examples of what I want to know more about. I was thrilled with the responses. My students had tons of interesting habits, hobbies, and ideas; they just did not know it. I read their lists, circling interesting topics and writing my own brainstorming in the margin. Then I journeyed back to the library with my class, returned the papers, and held individual writing conferences to discuss ideas. My students were also surprised by their ideas. One of my "expert gum chewers" chose to write about gum and set off on what he called his "quest." Finding information was NOT easy—certainly not as easy as finding information on nuclear power. During his quest, he learned how to use a variety of types of technology and sharpened his problem-solving skills, AND he enjoyed it. Each day he came to me and said, "Yuck! Did you know gum contains . . . ?" or "Wow! Look at this, Ms. Dooley." Another student wrote she was an excellent reader of children's books to her little brother and listed sexism as something she would like to know more about. I had circled both and during the conference we had an idea. She wrote a college-quality paper looking at the portrayal of women in ten Caldecott-winning books from several decades. Again, not an easy topic because the vast majority of the information came, not from copying directly from another source, but from her own evaluation. She too had daily comments, often showing me an illustration that particularly angered her. She FELT something about a research topic, and I could feel it when I read her paper.

> With this method, I received interesting, unusual papers that had what one of my college professors called "spunk." When I allowed them to choose topics that were meaningful to them, they actually enjoyed learning about their topics.
>
> Ms. Dooley met the challenge of getting the students to write research papers by giving them some personal choice that led to motivation. Teachers in areas other than English could offer structured choices. For example, a science teacher might ask, "Which of these scientific breakthroughs or procedures has the most impact on *your* life? About which one do you have the most background knowledge? In which one do you have the most interest?" With the answers to these questions as a starter, each student could be led to choose a topic that would provide some personal motivation.

Beyersdorfer and Schauer (1992) describe a special type of research report—the personality profile. They teach about the personality profile in a two-week project. First they have students read about interesting people and decide about things that influenced their lives. Next, students select subjects to profile. Then they learn interviewing and note-taking techniques, write scripts for their interviews, and carry out the interviews. Next they make decisions based on the data collected, write the profiles, and present the profiles orally to their classmates.

■ Laboratory Reports

Secondary science classes often have laboratory components for which laboratory reports must be written. A student lab guide such as the one in Example 8.7 may be used to guide students through experiments.

■ ■ ■ EXAMPLE 8.7   *Student Lab Guide*

Purpose of This Lab: Why are you doing this lab?
Problem: What problem are you investigating?
Hypothesis: What do you think the outcome of this lab will be? Think about what you already know about the topic, and make an educated guess about the outcome.
Materials: List all materials that you will need to conduct this laboratory.
Procedure: List in step-by-step fashion the procedure you are going to use to collect the data.
Data or Results: Draw, record, or chart all detailed observations noted from the procedure above.

Analysis or Conclusion: Reread your problem statement. Did your results resolve the problem? Explain why. If the results did not help clarify the problem, explain why.

Class Conclusion: Final conclusion after class discussion. Modify your own conclusion, if necessary.

Source: Santa/Havens/Harrison, "Teaching Secondary Science Through Reading, Writing, Studying, and Problem Solving," in Content Area Reading and Learning: Instructional Strategies, *Lapp/Flood/Farnan eds., © 1989, p. 150. Reprinted by permission of Prentice Hall, Inc., Englewood Cliffs, New Jersey.*

The writing of a laboratory report can be modeled by doing an experiment and writing a cooperative laboratory report on the chalkboard or a transparency. The teacher can lead the students through each step in the process; then the students can use their lab guides to write reports independently. For students who need more support in becoming independent report writers, teachers may provide a framed report form, such as the one in Example 8.8. The sentence starters will cue the students to the information that they should be including. Use of framed reports should be phased out as the students become more adept at report writing (Santa et al., 1989).

■ ■ ■ EXAMPLE 8.8   Framed Laboratory Report

Observation: After observing [state something unexplainable], I noticed
_____ .

Problem [or question]: Why does [put observation in the form of a question or problem]
_____ .

Hypothesis: I think _____ [refer to the problem or question]
is _____ . An observation that led to this
hypothesis is _____ . I intend to prove _____
by _____ .

Materials:

1.

2.

3.

Procedure: [put in order your plan for proving your hypothesis]

  1.

  2.

Data: [Accurate detailed observations of your model and how it works are recorded here. Include visuals such as tables, graphs, mathematical operations, and pictures along with written observations.]

Analysis and/or Conclusion: [Examine the problem and your hypothesis. Did your data support your hypothesis? Explain why your results supported or did not support your hypothesis.]

My problem is _____ . The results of my investigation are

_____ . These results may be caused by _____

_____ . Therefore, these results did or did not support my hypothesis

because _____ .

Class Conclusions: After the class discussion, we concluded _____

_____ .

Source: Santa/Havens/Harrison, "Teaching Secondary Science Through Reading, Writing, Studying, and Problem Solving," in Content Area Reading and Learning: Instructional Strategies, *Lapp/Flood/Fanan eds., © 1989, pp. 150–151. Reprinted by permission of Prentice Hall, Inc., Englewood Cliffs, New Jersey.*

■ Photo Essays

Sinatra and others (1990) found that the use of photo essays and various types of semantic maps was effective for building background knowledge of culturally diverse students and for helping them to organize their thoughts into writing. The students worked in pairs initially to develop photo essays with meaningful conceptual frameworks and then reconstructed the photos on storyboards using semantic mapping formats. The images in the photos helped to bridge the language differences of the student population and to provide a common base for communication.

The procedure was to plan topics or themes, take photos to illustrate the topics, organize the pictures on a storyboard, and then write a composition on the topic with the storyboard in view. Students brainstormed ideas for photos before the actual picture taking was done. When the pictures had been developed, the student pairs worked together on the arrangement on the storyboards. The assignments elicited sequential, descriptive, and classification writing styles. Example 8.9 shows these three patterns for organizing essays.

■ ■ ■ EXAMPLE 8.9   Three Patterns of Storyboard Organization for Photo Essay and Written Composition

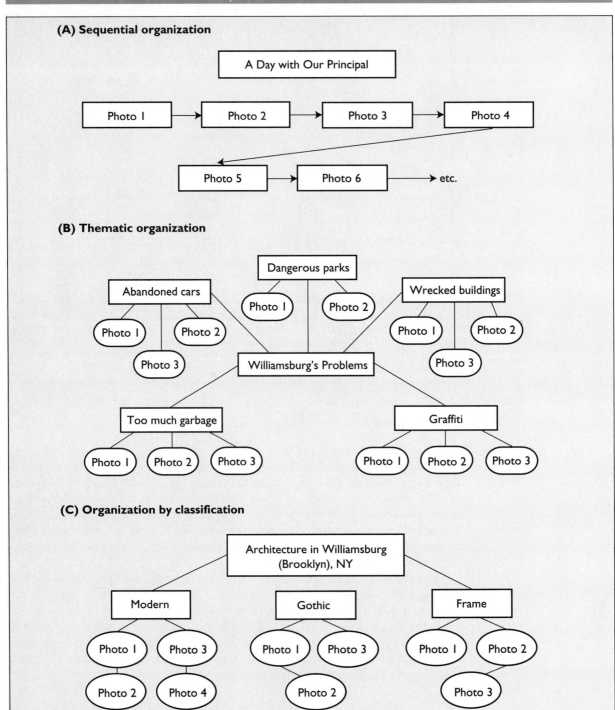

(A) Sequential organization

A Day with Our Principal

Photo 1 → Photo 2 → Photo 3 → Photo 4

Photo 5 → Photo 6 → etc.

(B) Thematic organization

Dangerous parks
Photo 1   Photo 2

Abandoned cars
Photo 1   Photo 2
Photo 3

Wrecked buildings
Photo 1   Photo 2
Photo 3

Williamsburg's Problems

Too much garbage
Photo 1   Photo 2   Photo 3

Graffiti
Photo 1   Photo 2   Photo 3

(C) Organization by classification

Architecture in Williamsburg (Brooklyn), NY

Modern
Photo 1   Photo 3
Photo 2   Photo 4

Gothic
Photo 1   Photo 3
Photo 2

Frame
Photo 1   Photo 2
Photo 3

Source: Figure I from "Combining visual literacy, text understanding, and writing for culturally diverse students," Richard Sinatra, Jeffrey Beaudry, Josephine Stahl-Gemake, and E. Francine Guastello, Journal of Reading, *May 1990, p. 614. Reprinted with permission of Richard Sinatra and the International Reading Association.*

■ Pen Pals

Writing to pen pals is a way to provide students with authentic reading and writing experiences because it involves real communication activities (Damico, 1996). A number of teachers have discovered the advantages of e-mail pen pals for motivating students to do meaningful reading and writing. Garcia-Vazquez and Vazquez (1994) paired Latino/a high school students with Latino/a university students with great success. The high school students carefully drafted their messages to their pen pals and often edited them several times before mailing them.

■ ■ Evaluation of Writing

Not all writing that students are asked to do in content area classrooms is formally evaluated. Writing in journals, for example, is done for its learning value and is not formally evaluated for a grade. Language experience writing is generally evaluated by the students who develop it as it is produced. Generally it is not graded by the teacher but is used as a learning aid in the classroom.

If the process approach to writing is used, there is much ongoing evaluation as a written piece is developed. Students elicit feedback about their writing from their peers, they proofread their own work with revision checklists in mind, and they receive feedback from their teachers during student-teacher conferences. In addition to the evaluative efforts that have gone on as materials are written, there are times when teachers must formally evaluate a final draft of a written assignment. These grading procedures may be holistic or analytic in nature.

When *holistic grading* is used, the teacher evaluates the written material as a whole. The paper is read for general impression and overall effect. It may be compared with pieces that have already been graded or scored for the inclusion of features important to the particular type of writing involved (*INC Sights*, 1989). Scoring guides, called rubrics, can be developed, which list the characteristics of high-quality, medium-quality, lower-quality, and lowest-quality papers for a particular assignment with a specified purpose and audience. This approach is referred to as primary trait scoring (Graser, 1983). Kirby and Liner (1988, p. 221) point out that holistic grading "focuses on the piece of writing as a whole and on those features most important to the success of the piece. . . . The rating is quick because the rater does not take time to circle errors or make marginal notations." Kirby and Liner suggest that teachers may use a list of criteria related to the impact of the writing, the inventiveness of the approach, and the individual flavor of the writing as a guide for their holistic grading. They refer to this type of grading as impression marking.

Analytic scales not only focus readers' attention on the features that are needed for the writing to be effective but also attach point values to each feature. The reader sums the scores for each feature in determining the overall grade. The Diederich Scale is an example of an analytic scale. It leads the scorer to assign a score of 1 (poor), 2 (weak), 3 (average), 4 (good), or 5 (excellent) to quality and development of ideas *and* organization, relevance, and movement (both of which are weighted heavier than the other considerations); style, flavor, and individuality *and* wording and phrasing (both of which are given intermediate weights); and grammar and sentence structure, punctuation, spelling, and manuscript form and legibility (all of which receive the lowest weights). Content and organization represent 50 percent of the grade; aspects of style, 30 percent; and mechanics, 20 percent. Scales such as this keep raters focused on the carefully defined criteria and keep them from being unduly influenced by surface features rather than considering all the factors contributing to the effectiveness of a piece of writing (Kirby and Liner, 1988). If students are asked to keep folders of written work over the course of a semester or year, their progress can be noted by comparing the earlier pieces with the latest ones. Students may gain more satisfaction from this type of final evaluation than from many other methods because they can see the differences in the writing and often can see that early teacher comments led to improvements in later products.

More on evaluation, especially portfolio evaluation, can be found in Chapter 13.

Summary

Writing is valuable in content area classes because it is a tool for thinking and for attaining self-knowledge and because it enhances retention of the material studied. As these benefits are gained, fluency in writing is also promoted.

Reading and writing are closely related skills. Both are written language skills, are concerned with communication, involve construction of meaning, and make use of vocabulary. Still, use of random writing activities in a content course may not help students in reading. To foster reading progress, writing assignments must focus on the relationships between reading and writing. Writing before reading can help students activate their background knowledge about a topic, enhancing reading comprehension. Reading is a thinking process, and reading comprehension requires thinking at various cognitive levels, as does writing production.

A process approach to writing tends to produce superior writing products and a better understanding of the writing process than an approach in which the teacher assigns a paper and the students write it and turn it in without process guidance. The writing process can be broken down into four overlapping and recursive steps: prewriting, writing a draft, revision, and publishing. Many types of writing-to-learn activities have been used in content classes. They include language experience writings; content journals, or learning logs; dialogue journals; RAFT assignments; research reports; laboratory reports; and pen pals.

Not all writing done in class needs to be evaluated. Journal writing is a prime example of this. Writing that is developed through a process approach is subject to ongoing evaluation as the writing progresses. Sometimes teachers need to evaluate a final draft of a piece of writing for grading purposes. When this is the case, they may use either holistic or analytic grading procedures.

Discussion Questions

1 In what ways is writing valuable in content area instruction?
2 What are some types of activities in which writing can positively influence reading achievement?
3 Which types of writing to learn would be most helpful in your content area? Why?
4 Why is the prewriting stage so important to the writing program?
5 What are some advantages to publishing and sharing students' writing?
6 What method of evaluation of final drafts seems most appropriate to you? Why?

Enrichment Activities

*1 Observe one period of a content area class. List the types of writing that the students are asked to do and the length of time spent on each writing activity.
*2 Try using one of the prereading writing activities suggested by Oberlin and Shugarman with a content reading assignment that you give. Share your feelings about its effectiveness with your classmates in written or oral form.
3 Analyze a story and prepare a story impressions clue list for it. *Try the activity with a secondary class, if possible.
*4 Try using content journals, or learning logs, in your classroom for a three-week period. Report your reaction to this technique to your classmates.
5 Make a list of creative applications of writing to your subject area.

6 With a partner from this class, role-play the use of dialogue journals for a specified imaginary class (e.g., a tenth-grade biology class). One of you write as the teacher and one as the student. Be prepared to discuss with the class your reactions to the technique.

*7 Guide a group of secondary school students through the process of writing a group report.

8 Prepare a lesson plan for using the process approach with a writing assignment. Role-play the teaching of this lesson to your classmates. *If possible, teach the lesson to a class of secondary school students.

---

*These activities are designed for in-service teachers, student teachers, or practicum students.

CHAPTER 9

Literature-Based and Thematic Approaches to Content Area Teaching

Overview

Literature has many values in the secondary curriculum, not only in English classes, where it has an undisputed place as an important subject area, but also in other content areas, where it can illuminate events and issues that are treated only briefly in textbooks. It is also valuable because it offers material on various subjects at different difficulty levels. Literature is often incorporated into thematic units in a variety of content areas. Thematic units include resources other than literature and require much planning on the part of the teacher.

Students need instruction related to reading strategies needed to approach literature and related to literary elements. Teachers can use a number of activities to encourage deeper responses to literature.

Purpose-Setting Questions

As you read this chapter, try to answer these questions:

1 How can literature enhance instruction in the secondary school?
2 How can teachers approach literature instruction?
3 What activities can be used to encourage student response to literature?
4 What four basic types of activities are part of a teaching unit?

■ ■ Values and Uses of Literature in the Secondary School Curriculum

Secondary school instruction is often highly textbook based, but textbooks by their nature cannot cover the material as well as it needs to be covered. The need to cover too many topics in a single textbook often leads to superficial coverage of each topic—often reducing it to dry facts that have little interest for students. Trade books can help to remedy this situation. Since a single trade book covers a limited amount of material—a single process, a short time period, or a single individual, for example—it has the room to elaborate on the material and use detail that brings the situations to life for the readers.

Another problem with textbooks is that, generally, all of the textbooks in a class are on a single reading level. Many students do not have the reading skill to access the information in these texts. Teachers may use alternate textbooks for some of their students, but if such materials are unavailable, teachers can use trade books for those who cannot manage the textbook reading. Trade books with various difficulty levels are available for almost any topic in the school curriculum. Some publishers supply information about readability and interest levels of many of the trade books they produce, and teachers can apply readability measures to other books of interest. However, since many factors outside of the text itself influence readability, teacher judgment may work as well as a formula in deciding what to use for particular students.

Motivation to read is a problem with many students, and trade books often offer more motivation than do textbooks. Danielson (1992) and Johnson-Weber (1989) have found that picture books serve as motivators for reading with junior high students. They also can be used to develop critical thinking skills, to make a connection between reading and writing, and to develop vocabulary, even for high school students. They add spice to content classes. Some picture books that are good for young children, such as *Jumanji* by Chris Van Allsburg (good for inferential reasoning), can be used with these students, but there are also some picture books that have themes especially appropriate for older readers, such as *My Hiroshima* by Jinko Morimoto and *Hiroshima No Pika* by Toshi Maruki, both of which make good accompaniments to a study of World War II. These books allow for application of critical reading skills and serve as stimuli for discussion and writing. Books like Graeme Base's *Animalia* and *The Eleventh Hour* could be used for vocabulary and concept development and critical thinking, respectively. English teachers might find *A Cache of Jewels, Merry-Go-Round, Many Luscious Lollipops,* and *Kites Sail High,* all by Ruth Heller, useful when discussing parts of speech, a traditionally low-interest topic for older students (Danielson, 1992).

Young adult literature selections can be used to introduce students to the various literary genres before more difficult traditional classics are tackled. Joan Lowery Nixon's excellent young adult mysteries can be used to help secondary students become familiar with the mystery genre, for example. Her writing can introduce the students to "the form of the narrative, chapters, rising action, climax, and resolution," as well as "foreshadowing, flashbacks, and point of view" (Pavonetti, 1996, p. 454). She presents a variety of characterizations, from flat to well-rounded ones, typical of the variety that students will encounter later. She thereby allows them to build the needed schemata for the genre (Pavonetti, 1996).

By pairing adolescent novels with adult novels that have related themes, styles, or other literary traits, students make a step up to more sophisticated reading and learn how to recognize connections between the works. Pairing themes is a good beginning technique. Gallagher (1995) suggests several such pairings, including the teaching of Harper Lee's *To Kill a Mockingbird* along with Nathaniel Hawthorne's *The House of the Seven Gables* for the theme of the power of love and the study of historical settings, and the teaching of S. E. Hinton's *The Outsiders* along with Herman Melville's *Billy Budd* for the theme of loneliness and isolation and the study of character development. Joan Lowery Nixon's *The Name of the Game Was Murder* can be paired with Agatha Christie's *And Then There Were None* (Pavonetti, 1996).

Young adult literature can also be used to address literacy concerns directly. Jerry Spinelli's *Maniac Magee*, Elizabeth Speare's *Sign of the Beaver,* and Cynthia Voigt's *Dicey's Song* all deal with characters who read well and ones who are struggling to learn to read.

For what types of material may teachers best use read alouds?

Read alouds by the teacher from literature that would cause reading difficulty for some students can enhance study in any content area and can entice students to read other sources. Middle school teachers find value in reading to their students daily (Sharer, Peters, and Lehman, 1995). Read alouds can broaden students' horizons, encourage listening skills, model expressive reading, engender pleasure in reading, spark writing and discussion, and invite listeners to read. High school history students could enjoy an excerpt from Lederer's *Anguished English* (Dell, 1987, p. 101) that includes these statements: "Ancient Egypt was inhabited by mummies, and they all wrote in hydrolics. They lived in the Sarah Dessert and traveled by Camelot." This material was compiled from parts of essays that students in the United States wrote. *The Phantom Tollbooth* by Juster has a good explanation of infinity that middle school math students may want to use; Proulx's *Postcards* has a description of a ground blizzard that could be used in a science class (Richardson, 1994a); and Dillard's *Pilgrim at Tinder Creek* has a description of a giant water bug devouring a frog (Richardson, 1994b). Christopher Lampton's *Endangered Species* contains a number of sections that make good science read alouds (Richardson and Breen, 1996).

What are the advantages of using audiobooks in a secondary school classroom?

An extension of the idea of read alouds is the use of **audiobooks.** Listening to audiobooks can add the dimension of hearing authentic accents, phrasing, and emphasis for characters in stories. Dialects become more manageable than they often are on the printed page. Correct pronunciations of proper names are heard. Good timing, emphasis, pause, and stress make humor more understandable for some readers. Poetry can be presented with a model of expert phrasing, accent, rhythm, and pronunciation that can enhance comprehension (Baskin and Harris, 1995). Students, especially those who cannot read at the level necessary to perform adequately in a secondary class, can read along with unabridged, single narrator audiobooks (Carroll, 1992). This can help students sense text subtleties. Such selections as Golding's *Lord of the Flies* (Listening Library; Greenwich, CT, 1977) and L'Engle's *A Wrinkle in Time* (Listening Library; Greenwich, CT, 1993) are available on tapes read by the authors, with accompanying commentary. Abridgements should be used with caution (Baskin and Harris, 1995).

The temptation to ease the reading burden on students by using films in place of the books from which they were made should be resisted in many cases. Film versions of books have simplified vocabulary, dialogue, plots, settings, themes, and characterizations. They may sometimes be used, however, to prompt an interest in reading the books. For example, teachers may have students read a book that will soon be released as a film. They may ask students to write and perhaps perform their own screenplays based on these books or to create multimedia presentations based on the literature. After the students see the films, they can compare the films with the books or write traditional reviews (Baines, 1996).

Literature Instruction

Literature instruction is designed to turn students into lifelong readers who enjoy good literature. Incorporating interesting literary selections into secondary classes helps teachers achieve these goals. These selections may be presented in a literature anthology or as trade books.

Minilessons

Teachers may teach minilessons on literary topics or reading strategies before the students begin reading, if a reading workshop approach is used in which students read, write in response journals, meet in literature circles to discuss their reading, and develop projects from the reading to share with their classmates (Noll, 1994; McGee and Tompkins, 1995). Modeling the use of a strategy through a think aloud is a good technique to use for a minilesson. When teaching a difficult piece, such as *Romeo and Juliet,* for example, the teacher may use a think aloud based on the beginning of the work to demonstrate paraphrasing, using background knowledge, predicting, visualizing, and using fix-up strategies when readers do not understand (Adams, 1995). (Think alouds are discussed in detail in Chapter 5. Paraphrasing is discussed in Chapter 8, and the other strategies mentioned are covered in Chapters 4 and 5.)

Use of Reading Guides

If the selections are related to students' schemata, they will be easier to comprehend. Reading guides, such as anticipation guides and three-level study guides, can help many students comprehend literature selections better (Lubell and Townsend, 1989). Study guides are described in more detail in Chapter 5.

A three-level guide can be especially useful with literature selections. The guide in Example 9.1 is designed for use with the short story "The Man Without a Country," by Edward Everett Hale.

The main value of reading guides is the discussion that follows their completion. Students should share their answers and their reasons for the answers.

■ ■ ■ ■ EXAMPLE 9.1 *Three-Level Study Guide*

Directions: Check the statement or statements under each level that answer the question.

LITERAL—WHAT DID THE AUTHOR SAY ABOUT PHILIP NOLAN?
_____ **1.** Philip Nolan said, "I wish I may never hear of the United States again!"
_____ **2.** Philip Nolan never actually met Aaron Burr.
_____ **3.** The court decided that Nolan should never hear the name of the United States again.
_____ **4.** Nolan was placed on board a ship and never allowed to return to the United States.
_____ **5.** Nolan was often permitted to go on shore.
_____ **6.** Nolan did not intentionally make it difficult for the people who were supposed to keep him from knowing about his country.

INTERPRETIVE—WHAT DID THE AUTHOR MEAN BY HIS STORY?
_____ **1.** Nolan never seriously regretted having denied his country.
_____ **2.** Nolan spoke against his country without realizing how much it had meant to him.
_____ **3.** Nolan never really missed hearing about his country.

APPLIED—HOW CAN THE MEANING BE APPLIED TO OUR LIVES?
_____ **1.** People should consider the consequences of their actions before they act.
_____ **2.** People can live comfortably away from home.
_____ **3.** Punishment is not always physical; it may be mental.

■ Electronic Discussions

English teachers have found that use of a networked computer lab equipped with a program such as the Daedalus Integrated Writing Environment allows students to discuss literary works by keying in responses to their classmates' comments, using a simple word processor. The Interchange program sends the comments of each student to all screens on the network. Students log in with aliases, allowing their comments to be essentially anonymous. This encourages shy students to respond more. Responses to other students' comments can be added at any time. They don't have to be keyed in immediately. They can be inserted at the appropriate places in the written discussion by scrolling the text to the appropriate points. After the written discussion, the students can get hard copies of the whole discussion. Oral class discussion based on these print-outs can follow (Craven, 1994).

The discussions are controlled through the choice of questions presented to the students. The teacher cannot control the direction of the discussions in any way that any single participant in the discussions could not. The discussions work better with only one question per conference. Several simultaneous discussions can be taking place when Interchange is used, and students can move from one to another. Craven (1994) suggests use of four conferences in a fifty-minute class, one covering a main question and others covering lesser questions.

■ Whole-Class Novel Study

What is a social constructionist perspective of learning?

Unrau and Ruddell (1995) present a Text and Classroom Context model "designed with a **social constructivist perspective** of learning in which the teacher fosters a learning environment that engages students in a meaning negotiation process" (p. 21). Example 9.2 shows a diagram of this model. This perspective emphasizes that comprehension results from assembling and transforming knowledge. Meanings evolve from interactions among the reader, the text, the classroom community, the teacher, and the context. Readers must confirm that the constructed interpretations of the text are grounded in the text, reasonably supportable by reference to the content of the text. As Rosenblatt (1983, p. 133) has said, "The process of understanding a work implies a recreation of it, an attempt to grasp completely all the sensations and concepts through which the author seeks to convey the qualities of his sense of life. Each of us must make a new synthesis of these elements with his own nature, but it is essential that he assimilate those elements of experience which the author has actually presented."

When applying this model to class study of a novel, the students can first read the novel and then write about it in their learning logs. They can write summaries or interpretations in the logs. Then they can discuss the novel in

■ ■ ■ EXAMPLE 9.2   *Text and Classroom Context*

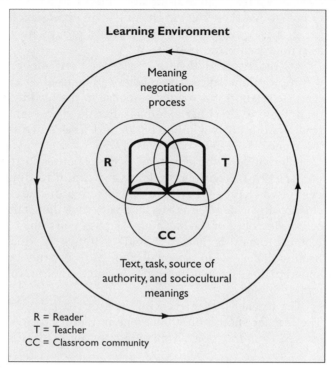

Learning Environment

Meaning
negotiation
process

R   T

CC

Text, task, source of
authority, and sociocultural
meanings

R = Reader
T = Teacher
CC = Classroom community

Source: Norman J. Unrau and Robert B. Ruddell. "Interpreting Texts in Classroom Contexts."
Journal of Adolescent & Adult Literacy 39 (September 1995): 21. Reprinted with permission
of Norman J. Unrau and the International Reading Association.

groups of three. Each member of the group is given a responsibility—recorder, reporter, or prompter (who keeps the group on task). Interpretations voiced during discussion are not seen as final but are revised as the dialogue continues. The text is fixed, but its meanings for readers change over time. Whole-class discussions can follow small-group meetings or can be guided by use of the DRTA or other strategies that encourage individual responses and group sharing (Unrau and Ruddell, 1995). (See Chapter 5 for a discussion of the DRTA.)

■ Literature Response Groups

What are the benefits of literature response groups?

In **literature response groups,** or literature circles, several students who have chosen to read the same novel read a specific number of chapters each week and meet in a group each week to discuss the reading. Students choose novels from several for which the teacher has multiple copies (preferably six to eight copies). Students can indicate their top three choices, and the teacher can form groups to read the five top choices, taking preferences into account. Each time the groups complete their novels, new groups may be formed for different selections (Simpson, 1994–1995).

As students read, they can make notes on "sticky notes" and place them on the appropriate pages. These notes can be used as a basis for the small-group discussion and for a written response to the reading that the teacher may require them to do either before or after the discussion. These responses can be read aloud at the beginning of the next week's discussion as a review of what has come before (Simpson, 1994–1995).

Alternatively, students may write responses in reading response journals. Berger (1996) asked her students to write in reading response journals after every two chapters they read. They were to include things they noticed (e.g., changes in a character or repeated patterns), things they questioned (e.g., characters' decisions or the meaning of a passage), things they felt (e.g., emotions or feelings toward a character), and/or things to which they related (e.g., connecting the events to personal experiences or other books). The teacher can respond to these journals periodically, and the entries can be shared aloud in class and discussed.

The teacher may meet with the groups, or they may meet independently. The teacher should only intervene in the discussion when the students have strayed from the topic or missed important points (Simpson, 1994–1995).

■ Sustained Silent Reading (SSR)

What are the benefits of sustained silent reading in a content area class?

Readers become more fluent in reading by actually reading. In a **sustained silent reading** program students are given a block of time to read self-selected materials for pleasure. Secondary students may be given from fifteen to thirty minutes to read without interruption and without the threat of testing or reporting that inhibits some readers. The teacher also reads self-selected material during this time. Nobody is allowed to interrupt the reading of the others. Simpson (1994–1995) points out that students can be allowed to discuss the books read during SSR, but we feel that discussion should not be required. Offering students time in class for self-selected reading shows that teachers value it.

■ Directed Reading Lessons

A directed reading lesson such as that in Example 9.3 is another way for teachers to help students read and understand books. Directed reading lessons are discussed in detail in Chapter 5.

MOTIVATION AND BUILDING BACKGROUND

1. Ask the students these questions: Do you know any good ghost stories? Have you ever sat around with a group of friends telling ghost stories? How did you feel later, particularly if you had to go some place alone? You probably felt the way Ichabod Crane felt in this story after he listened to some ghost stories and rode home alone over country roads.

2. Tell the students that the story they are going to read is a ghost story. The characters in this story include a worthy pedagogue; a rantipole hero; a ripe, melting, and rosy-cheeked maiden; and a contented farmer. After they read the story, they should try to name each of the characters listed.

SKILL DEVELOPMENT ACTIVITIES

3. Have the students match a number of words from the story with their definitions.

Words	Definitions
continual reverie	German soldiers
Hessian troopers	Bible study
spectre	constant daydream
psalmody	ghost

GUIDED READING

4. Silent—Have the students read the story silently. Tell them to think about these purpose questions as they read: What factors created an atmosphere for the ghost to appear? What happened to Ichabod?

5. Discussion—After the students have read the selection, use these questions for further discussion:
   a. How would you characterize the residents of Sleepy Hollow?
   b. Is the setting important in this story? Why?
   c. Do you think Katrina was really interested in Ichabod? Why?
   d. How are Brom Bones and Ichabod Crane alike? How are they different?
   e. What was the point of view of this story?
   f. Do you agree with the old man about the purpose of this story? What do you think the purpose was?

FOLLOW-UP ACTIVITIES

6. Have students write a paragraph telling what they would have done if they were Ichabod.

7. Ask students to read another story written by Washington Irving and compare it with the "Legend of Sleepy Hollow."

8. Have students draw a picture of the way they visualize Ichabod.

MEETING THE CHALLENGE

As a way to motivate students to read *Macbeth* and build their background for reading it, Cindy McCloud made use of a readers' theater activity. Before class, she gave a readers' theater script of the witches' scene in *Macbeth* to a selected group of students, who would take the parts of the witches and Macbeth. These students were asked to practice and polish the reading of their parts. The other students in the class were not told about this activity ahead of time.

Visualizing the setting of a story can help build student interest in reading the story. © Michael Zide

When class started, Ms. McCloud told the class to close their eyes. Then she said, "Imagine a fantastical cave filled with fog. In the entrance of the cave you see lights flickering. These lights grow dim and get brighter, then dimmer, then brighter. This piques your curiosity: you must know what these strange lights are. You walk further into the cave and spot three of the strangest looking women you have ever seen. Of course, their very appearance gives you a terrible scare, and you hide behind a rock and peer over it just enough to see what they are doing. These three cloaked, bearded figures are conjuring up a powerful spell."

As the rest of the class continued to imagine the scene, Ms. McCloud cued the designated students to take the parts they had been assigned and begin to read the scene in character. The other students were allowed to open their eyes as the selected students read the scene, acting out the part in which the witches conjure up their potion with appropriate gestures.

This interest-grabbing introduction to the play prepared the students for the subsequent reading. Students who previously had no interest in the play now saw that it had possibilities and were willing to give it a chance.

■ ■ Activities to Encourage Students' Response to Literature

Whether literature is used as the focus of study in an English class or literature selections are used as tools for study in other content areas, students need to be led to respond to the content of the selections.

■ Written Responses

Written responses are valuable tools. Reading response journals, character journals, dialogue journals, learning logs, freewriting in response to reading, paraphrasing and summarizing, and creative responses (e.g., writing letters to story characters or news stories about characters) are all written responses that have been covered in detail in Chapter 8 and/or in this chapter. Other written responses could include writing letters to the author for clarification of information, comparing and contrasting the work and other works, making time lines for the stories, or mapping the story's literary elements (setting, characters, plot, etc.).

Ollmann (1996) tried seven different reading response formats and found the hexagonal essays, in which the students responded to the literature from the perspectives of the levels of Bloom's Taxonomy, to result in more higher-level thinking. She believed that this was true because it required the students to "summarize the plot, make a personal association with text, analyze the theme, analyze literary techniques, compare and contrast with other literature, and evaluate the work as a whole" (Ollmann, 1996, p. 579).

■ Oral Responses

The most valuable oral responses to literature are the small-group and whole-class discussions that have been mentioned repeatedly as important learning tools in the classroom. Another type of oral response is the conversion of the material into a readers' theater presentation, with students dividing the material into speaking parts along content or character lines and reading the material orally with good oral expression.

Perhaps the most difficult oral response option is dramatization of the material. This dramatization can be a spontaneous reenactment of an event or scene, without written script, costumes, properties, scenery, or audience beyond the class members; or it can be a carefully planned presentation, with a student-developed script, memorized lines, costumes, properties, scenery, and an outside audience. Drama can evoke an aesthetic response to the literature. In addition, interpretation of literature is expanded through drama because it takes the students into the events to experience them vicariously. This immersion in the experience helps the students to see the points of view of the people involved in the events (Fennessey, 1995).

■ Responses Based on Multiple Intelligences

How can you incorporate activities that use multiple intelligences in your content area lessons?

Glasgow (1996) suggests a series of activities that can be used as responses to adolescent literature that are appropriate for use of **multiple intelligences.** Example 9.4 contains a list of these activities.

■ ■ ■ EXAMPLE 9.4   *Activities for Adolescent Literature Based on Gardner's Multiple Intelligences*

Intelligence	Activities
Musical/rhythmic	Create a radio or TV advertisement for an honor book. Compose a rap based on a theme of a historical novel. Compose a musical background for the reading of a poem, myth, or folktale. Compose the main character's favorite song. Compose a poem or song describing the main character of an honor book.
Visual/spatial	Make a collage of the main images in a science fiction book. Make a map of the setting for a dystopian or utopian novel. Create a model or diorama for the setting of an honor book. Market a novel by creating a magazine advertisement. Paint the setting or main character of the novel or poem. Make a story or character web of a novel. Videotape the context for realistic fiction.
Body/kinesthetic	Compose a dance expressing a theme of an honor book. Impersonate a main character from a problem novel. Mime a character from a fantasy novel. Act out a challenge facing a character in a quest. Make puppets and perform a dialogue between two or more characters in a problem-solving situation. Create a living sculpture portraying a theme of a book, play, or poem.
Interpersonal	Interview a character or an author of an honor book. Prepare dramatic dialogue of two characters in a sports novel. Write script and perform Readers Theatre for a fantasy novel.

Interpersonal (cont.)	Write a collaborative paper discussing the themes and implications of an honor book.
	Keep a dialogue journal with a friend for a problem novel.
	Do choral reading of a dialogue or poem.
Intrapersonal	Keep a reading or process log for an honor book.
	Do reader response activities such as associative recollections; character probes; most important words, passages, and aspects (Milner & Milner, 1993).
	Keep a metacognitive journal of your own reading process.
Logical/mathematical	Review a book by discussing different categories such as economics, politics, education, lifestyle, and/or religion.
	Create a timeline for a historical fiction book.
	Create a chart pairing a poem with a book, myth, or folktale.
	Map the story structure.
	Create a literature web.
	Write a critical analysis paper.
Verbal/linguistic	Compare and contrast two variants of a folktale.
	Prepare a book review.
	Do a profile of an author.
	Keep a reader response journal.
	Write a formal paper.
	Create a poetry anthology.
	Explicate a poem.

Source: Jacqueline N. Glasgow. "Motivating the Tech Prep Reader Through Learning Styles and Adolescent Literature." Journal of Adolescent & Adult Literacy *39 (February 1996): 364. Reprinted with permission of Jacqueline N. Glasgow and the International Reading Association.*

■ ■ Developing Thematic Teaching Units

What is a thematic teaching unit?

A **thematic teaching unit** is a series of interrelated lessons or class activities organized around a theme, a literary form, or a skill. Such a unit allows holistic study of the topic (Peters, Schuback, and Hopkins, 1995). Because unit activities are varied in terms of the amount of reading skill and the levels of thinking required to complete them, they offer excellent opportunities to adjust reading assignments to fit all students. Different students may complete different activities, such as reading, listening to, and/or viewing different resource materials, and share the results of these varied activities with their classmates.

Use of teaching units takes a great deal of teacher planning. The teacher must develop objectives for a unit that are in keeping with the overall goals of the class, must decide on skills to be developed, and must plan activities designed to help meet these objectives and to help develop these skills. The students may be involved in deciding on objectives and activities, within the framework of the curriculum requirements. Parents may also become involved in unit activities, if teachers will send home memos about the themes that are being studied and suggestions on how the parents can help the learning process by purchasing books related to the themes for their children or by sharing personal knowledge about the topic with their children or with the entire class.

The web shown in Figure 9.1 depicts the parts of a unit graphically. A unit generally involves four basic types of activities:

1. Introduction of the unit
2. Development of the unit
3. Organization of findings
4. Culmination activities

Introduction of the Unit

The students are introduced to the unit's theme or central idea, the literary form to be explored, or the skills to be developed. Through class discussion and/or pretests, the teacher determines the extent to which the students' backgrounds of experience in the area can contribute to the unit activities. The teacher discusses with the students what they already know about the topic under consideration and helps them to evolve questions that they need to answer and to identify areas in which they need clarification. During this discussion, the teacher helps the students relate the area of study to their own personal experiences or needs. Semantic webs of concepts or terms related to the unit theme may be effective in activating the students' background knowledge and in facilitating the discussion (Cooter and Griffith, 1989). The teacher may supply motivation for participating in the unit activities by showing a film or filmstrip or by playing records or tapes related to the subject.

Development of the Unit

The teacher begins teaching the unit by presenting core instructional material to the whole class. This material will probably consist of the textbook material and supplementary material that the teacher has carefully chosen for those students who cannot benefit from reading the text because of its difficulty level. The teacher may develop directed reading lessons (DRLs) for both the textbook material and the supplementary material.

FIGURE 9.1

Unit Development
Web

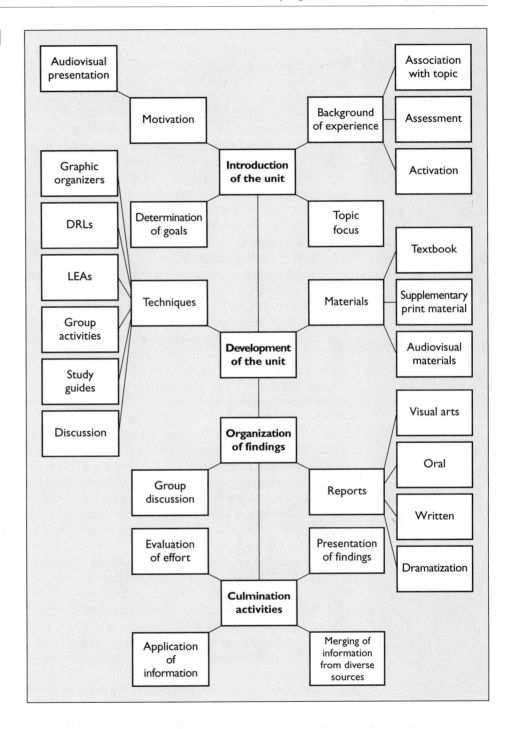

During the first step of some of the directed reading lessons, the teacher may use structured overviews to develop needed background for reading. Next, using techniques presented in Chapters 3, 4, 5, 6, and 7, he or she may teach needed vocabulary, comprehension, and study strategies and skills that are vital to the understanding of the particular passages involved. As a part of the directed reading lesson, the teacher may guide the actual student reading of the material by means of a study guide. All the students can combine what they have learned through class discussion and language experience activities. The follow-up activities will be included among the independent assignments for different research groups or interest groups formed by the teacher or by student choice after the reading of the core material has taken place.

After the core instructional presentation, the teacher may either assign areas of concern to the students or allow them to choose areas in which they have a particular interest. Self-selection may have the advantage of providing internal motivation for the unit study.

Students then form several small groups (research groups that may or may not also be interest groups) that attempt to answer specific questions, clarify specific areas of concern, or analyze particular literary works. These research groups may be formed to capitalize on the special abilities of various class members. The teacher may meet with each group to discuss the possible reference sources that are available: textbooks, library books (fiction and nonfiction), encyclopedias, other reference books, magazines, newspapers, original documents, films, filmstrips, and a variety of other audiovisual aids.

Whenever possible, books that reflect a multicultural environment should be chosen, and there should be access to large-print books, Braille materials, or audiotapes that cover the class material if there are visually impaired students in the class. Multicultural resources provide the students with a realistic picture of the world at large, even if the cultural diversity within the particular school is narrow, and they allow students whose cultural backgrounds vary from the mainstream culture to feel more comfortable and see how their culture fits into the overall picture. Godina (1996) urges integration of both selections from the traditional canon and multicultural selections into the instructional program. Materials for students with physical disabilities allow these children to participate in unit activities without undue stress and difficulty.

The teacher must be alert to the variety of reading abilities within the group and must make available books and reference aids on a number of different levels. Students then can choose books for their thematic study that are appropriate to their own reading abilities. A review of study skills such as using the card catalog, using encyclopedias, outlining, taking notes, skimming, and scanning may be helpful for some members of each research group. (See Chapters 6 and 7 for a discussion of these skills.)

Each member of each research group is responsible for collecting data. Differentiated assignments within the groups may be developed by the teacher or by group leaders, who are guided by the teacher.

■ Organization of Findings

The research groups meet after ample time has been allowed for individual members to collect data. Each group then reviews the information collected from the various sources, discusses and attempts to resolve differences of opinion, and forms the findings into a coherent report. The discussion allows the students to share the information they have discovered and find out what others have learned. The report may be oral or written and may be accompanied by audiovisual aids such as charts, tables, maps, graphs, pictures, filmstrips, or tapes. It may be in one of a number of forms, including an oral report, a panel discussion, a skit, a more complete dramatization, or a mural.

■ Culmination Activities

At the end of the unit study, the different research groups present their reports to the whole class. The class critically examines the information that is presented, merges it with the core of information learned from the textbook and supplementary materials, and determines if the purposes of the unit have been met. If the class feels that not all of the original purposes have been met, the members may regroup to finish the task.

The teacher should help the students relate the findings to events in their own lives. An activity that immediately applies the findings to real situations would be beneficial because it would emphasize the relevance of the unit.

Table 9.1 presents the steps in unit development.

TABLE 9.1

Unit Development

Introduction	Development	Organization of Findings	Culmination
1. Build background and motivation 2. Connect unit to students' experiences	1. Core lessons presented through a directed reading approach, use of structured overviews, teaching of needed skills, study guides, language experience approach 2. Research groups 3. Needs groups	1. Discussion 2. Oral or written reports	1. Merging of information from diverse sources 2. Evaluation of effort 3. Application of information

■ Sample Unit Ideas

A unit in health might be arranged around a theme such as The Food Pyramid. A discussion of the theme could reveal the background knowledge that the group has concerning the theme. A transparency of The Food Pyramid could clarify the composition of each of the four levels and six subdivisions of the pyramid. Six research groups could be formed, one for each subdivision; or four groups could be formed, one for each level of the pyramid. Additional groups might be formed to study fad diets.

Each group studying a pyramid level or subdivision could investigate the importance of the foods in its group, setting out to answer these questions: What are the benefits from eating these foods? What are the problems that could result from not eating them? Groups on fad diets could weigh the benefits and dangers of each of these diets. A variety of sources should be available, including current paperbacks, newspaper articles, and magazine articles concerned with nutrition and dieting. Textbooks and reference books, such as encyclopedias, should also be utilized.

The group reports could take a variety of forms: one possibility would be to have a student describe what happened when he or she went on a fad diet. In the whole-class discussion following the group reports, relationships among the reports should be emphasized. For example, the fad diets that sometimes have bad results often leave out some of the food groups in the pyramid.

A unit in literature might be developed around a type of literature, such as "Tall Tales of the United States." The opening discussion could include an attempt to define "tall tales" and could provide opportunities for the students to name tall tales with which they are familiar. The teacher might use a film, filmstrip, or tape during the introductory stage to clarify the nature of tall tales. Different groups could be formed to read tall tales about different superhuman individuals, for example, Old Stormalong, Paul Bunyan, Mike Fink, and Pecos Bill. Other groups could concentrate on tall tales of other types, such as Washington Irving's "Rip Van Winkle" and "The Legend of Sleepy Hollow" or Mark Twain's "The Celebrated Jumping Frog of Calaveras County." As a culminating activity, each student could write a tall tale of the general type that he or she has read. The tales could be shared in oral or written form with the rest of the class.

Guzzetti, Kowalinski, and McGowan (1992) describe a literature-based unit on China that was used with sixth graders. It included brainstorming and formation of a semantic map of knowledge held about the subject, reading aloud to students from a literature selection, use of literature selections to answer questions about China, construction of question-and-answer books by the students, and activities to encourage reflective thinking. Many of the activities could easily be used in grades 7 through 12, and some of the same literature selections, such as *Dragonwings* by Yep, could be used, particularly for seventh and eighth graders. Other selections could be replaced by ones located through one or more of these selection aids:

Anderson, George. *Asian Literature in English.* Detroit: Gale Research, 1981.

Cheung, King-Kok, and Stan Yogi, eds. *Asian-American Literature: An Annotated Bibliography.* New York: MLA, 1988.

Kim, Elaine. *Asian-American Literature: An Introduction to the Writings and Their Social Context.* Philadelphia: Temple University Press, 1982.

Ling, Amy. *Selected Bibliography of Asian-American Literature. Redefining American Literary History.* New York: MLA, 1990.

American Women: Four Centuries of Progress by Polly and John Zane (Berkeley, Calif.: Proof Press, 1989), an integrated four-part unit that examines the changing roles of women in America, can be a useful supplement to traditional history textbooks (Fox, 1989). Such supplementary material is essential until textbooks begin to reflect women's contributions to society more effectively.

All textbook presentations are by necessity brief and overly condensed. Good units provide much supplementary material that fills in gaps and fleshes out the information for students. The "Meeting the Challenge" vignette here is an excerpt from a lengthy unit on World War II, developed by two students in a graduate-level secondary reading course who realized the limited viewpoint offered to students by a single textbook presentation. This unit originally had extensive supplementary reading resources and many other activities listed, but space does not allow their inclusion. Suffice it to say that the authors of the unit found bountiful reading material that was both high in interest and pertinent to the topic. A new source by Harada (1996) would add depth to such a unit in respect to the Japanese American internment.

MEETING THE CHALLENGE

In an attempt to incorporate their knowledge of the values of student involvement in learning, multiple readings of various types, and incorporation of literature into content area study into a practical teaching plan, Bryce Stevens and Karen Claud developed the following unit plan for study of World War II.

Literature-Based Unit
World War II
INTRODUCTION
(One Day)

MAJOR CONCEPTS

1. Several factors contributed to World War II.

2. World War II involved many countries and lasted several years (1939 to 1945).

3. World War II wreaked havoc on the lives of Americans, Europeans, and Asians, as well as doing extensive damage to personal property, buildings, and valuable pieces of art.
4. The war had a creative influence on writers, artists, musicians, and even cartoonists.
5. Adolf Hitler, Winston Churchill, Joseph Stalin, Franklin Roosevelt, and Harry S. Truman are some of the important political figures involved in World War II.
6. Some of the important aspects of World War II include the involvement of Europe, America, and Asian countries in the war, and Nazi persecution.

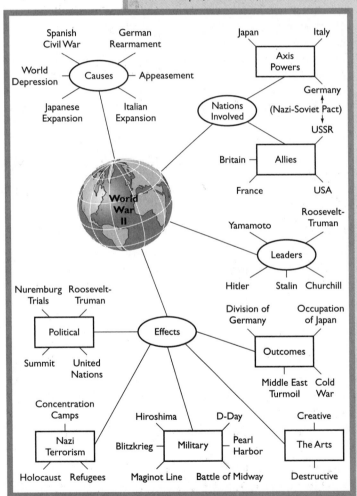

MAIN RESOURCES

TEXTBOOK
Perry, Marvin, et al. *History of the World.* Boston: Houghton Mifflin Company, 1990, pp. 684–688.

FICTION
Kerr, M. E. *Gentlehands.* New York: Harper Keypoint, 1978.

INSTRUCTIONAL ACTIVITIES

1. Review and discuss the major concepts with the students.
2. Using a world map, review the geographic setting of World War II.
3. Create a K-W-L chart during a discussion of information that students have about World War II.
4. Review the graphic organizers shown in this section to familiarize students with the outline of the text and focus points of units covered. Have students create their own graphic organizers for each topic of study. Use the one focusing on European Involvement as a guide.
5. Have students compose a class letter to the Hawaiian Chamber of Commerce requesting informational brochures or pamphlets on the battleship *Arizona* monument. The pamphlets will be used for an activity later in the unit.

6. Begin the use of literature response groups (LRGs).

7. Introduce the book *Gentlehands* by M. E. Kerr. Use this book as a read-aloud book. Plan to read aloud a couple of chapters to the class each day for the duration of the unit. See the Conclusion for a follow-up activity related to this book.

8. Extended activity: Do any of the students have war memorabilia from World War II that they could share with the class? Do any of the students have relatives or friends whom they could interview concerning their recollections of involvement with World War II? Have them share their resources with the class.

9. Make newspaper and magazine articles about World War II available for students to read in topic studies.

THREE-LEVEL READING GUIDE FOR *THE ENDLESS STEPPE*
(To be provided for use with Topic I.)

Answer the following questions for each level. Answers for Level 1 will be found from the text. Answers for Level 2 will be found through clues in the text and your interpretation of the text. Answers for Level 3 will require a response as to your interpretation of the text.

LEVEL 1: LITERAL (from the text)

1. Trace the route by which the Rudomins were sent from Vilno to Rubtovsk. Show it on the map. (Ch. 1)

2. How was the family transported? (Ch. 1)

3. How long was the train ride? (Ch. 2)

4. What work was the family assigned? (Ch. 3)

5. What is gypsum? (Consult the encyclopedia.) What is its use? (Ch. 3)

6. What is the NKVD? How do they differ from the Rubtovsk police? (Ch. 9)

7. What was Vanya the bum's name? What was his background? (Ch. 10)

8. What was killing so many people? What is the disease? (Use encyclopedia.) (Ch. 12)

9. What were the tragedies of Esther's life?

LEVEL 2: INFERENTIAL (clues in the book and personal interpretation)

1. What religion was the Rudomin family? (Ch. 1)

2. Why were the grandparents separated? (Ch. 1)

3. What is a "class enemy"? (Ch. 2)
4. Grandmother Reisa chose her moment to die, yet it was not suicide. Explain. (Ch. 2)
5. The Soviet Union was allied with Germany, then with Britain. Why were the Rudomins not freed? (Ch. 2)
6. Describe Makrinin. Why did his authority embarrass him? What kind of man was he? (Ch. 4)
7. Why do you think the Poles were not returned to Poland after the amnesty? (Ch. 6)
8. Who do you think was guilty for the missing food? Cite evidence from the book. (Ch. 8)
9. Why do you think Vanya the bum began to wash and comb his hair? Why did he disappear?

LEVEL 3: PERSONAL REACTION

1. Why was Esther's photo album so precious? Why couldn't she take it with her? What possession would you find nearly impossible to leave behind? What would you pack to take in just one suitcase?
2. Have you ever been in a position where cleanliness was no longer important compared with your other needs?
3. Describe a time when you have found humor in an unpleasant task. Compare your story with Tata's horse tale, page 59.
4. Would you have become an NKVD spy if you were in Tata's place? Why or why not?

TOPIC I:
EUROPEAN INVOLVEMENT
(Two Days)

MAJOR CONCEPTS

1. Survival was a priority for many families.
2. Many people contributed directly and indirectly to the war effort. Contributions were made by helping those who were being ostracized and also by banding together to form resistance movements.
3. The Soviet Union was not immune to Hitler's aggression, even though they were allies of Germany at the outset of Germany's expansionist policy in Europe.
4. The Germans launched a series of air raids known as blitzkriegs.
5. The Allies were the nations that were fighting against the Axis powers.

MAIN RESOURCES

TEXTBOOK
Perry, Marvin, et al. *History of the World.* Boston: Houghton Mifflin Company, 1990, pp. 688–692.

FICTION

*Hautzig, Esther. *The Endless Steppe*. New York: Crowell, 1968.
*McSwigan, Marie. *Snow Treasures*. New York: E. P. Dutton & Co., Inc., 1942.

INSTRUCTIONAL ACTIVITIES

1. Continue reading aloud from *Gentlehands*.
2. Introduce and discuss the major concepts with the students.
3. Review on the world map the European countries involved in World War II at this time.
4. Allow response groups to meet for ten minutes each day.

TOPIC II:
NAZI PERSECUTION
(Two Days)

MAJOR CONCEPTS

1. The Nazis spread terror and destruction throughout Europe during World War II. Much of their terror was directed at innocent individuals.
2. Nazi destruction and the war caused the loss of many valuable pieces of art, as well as beautiful architecture.
3. The Holocaust had a cruel and devastating effect on many people.
4. Resistance to the Nazi campaign of terror involved many individual acts of heroism by children, as well as adults.

MAIN RESOURCES

TEXTBOOK

Perry, Marvin, et al. *History of the World*. Boston: Houghton Mifflin Company, 1990, pp. 688–692.

FICTION

*Moskin, Marietta. *I Am Rosemarie*. New York: John Day, Co., 1972.
*Reiss, J. *The Upstairs Room*. New York: Crowell, 1972.

NONFICTION

Adams, Robert Martin. *The Lost Museum: Glimpses of Vanished Originals*. New York: Viking Press, 1980.

Marrin, A. *Hitler*. New York: Viking Kestrel, 1987.

Meltzer, M. *Rescue*. New York: Harper & Row, 1988.

Rogasky, B. *Smoke and Ashes*. New York: Holiday, 1988.

INSTRUCTIONAL ACTIVITIES

1. Continue reading aloud from *Gentlehands*.
2. Introduce and discuss the major concepts.

*Stories for literature response groups

3. Reproduce an excerpt (page 186) from the book *The Lost Museum: Glimpses of Vanished Originals* and distribute it to the students. What is their reaction to the first paragraph? What is their reaction to the box to the left? Was this deliberate or a misprint? Show samples of art from various artists of the World War II era.
4. Using copies of newspaper cartoons about World War II drawn during the war, divide students into groups. Give each group a cartoon and a brief biography on the artist. Have students read the biography and discuss their impression of the cartoon. Have them share this with the class.
5. Play selected samples of music from musicians and composers during the World War II era. Does their music reflect the moods of this particular time period? How might the war have affected their styles and compositions? Have students read brief biographies on a few of the musicians and composers who were notable during this time.
6. Allow response groups to meet for ten minutes each day.

TOPIC III:
ASIAN/AMERICAN INVOLVEMENT
(Two Days)

MAJOR CONCEPTS

1. The bombing of Pearl Harbor had a profound effect on Japanese Americans.
2. Japanese Americans were forced into concentration, or internment, camps because of fear among the American public that they would serve as spies and saboteurs for Japan.

MAIN RESOURCES

TEXTBOOK
Perry, Marvin, et al. *History of the World.* Boston: Houghton Mifflin Company, 1990, pp. 697–700.
FICTION
*Uchida, Yoshika. *Journey to Topaz.* New York: Scribner, 1971.
*Green, Bette. *Summer of My German Soldier.* New York: Bantam Books, 1973.

INSTRUCTIONAL ACTIVITIES

1. Continue reading from *Gentlehands.*
2. Introduce and discuss the main concepts. Use the following questions to help guide discussion:
   a. What are some differences and similarities between American and German concentration camps?

*Stories for literature response groups

    b. Was the United States justified in isolating Japanese Americans in camps?

    c. Why did we call them Japanese Americans rather than Americans?

    d. Why did the United States government not isolate German Americans or Italian Americans?

3. Introduce examples of poetry produced by Japanese Americans and Jews. Compare the poetry and art produced by individuals in German concentration camps and Japanese Americans in internment camps. Use the books *Beyond Words: Images from America's Concentration Camps* and *I Never Saw Another Butterfly: Children's Drawings and Poems from Terezin Concentration Camp 1942–1944* for art and further poetry examples.

4. Allow response groups to meet for ten minutes each day.

TOPIC IV:
FINAL RESOLUTIONS
(One Day)

MAJOR CONCEPTS

1. D-Day was an essential step in the defeat of the Axis powers.

2. The dropping of atomic bombs brought an end to the war with the Japanese.

3. War crime trials brought to light the horrors of World War II. War criminals are still sought out for punishment today.

4. World War II was one of the costliest wars in history in a number of ways. It left Europe and Asia impoverished, while spurring an economic resurgence in the United States that ended the Great Depression and led to several years of an unusually high standard of living.

MAIN RESOURCES

TEXTBOOK

Perry, Marvin, et al. *History of the World.* Boston: Houghton Mifflin Company, 1990, pp. 697–700.

FICTION

*Hersey, John. *Hiroshima.* New York: Random, 1946.

*Patent, Gregory. *Shanghai Passage.* Clarion (ISBN 0-89919-743-4).

INSTRUCTIONAL ACTIVITIES

1. Continue reading aloud from *Gentlehands*.

2. Introduce and discuss the major concepts.

3. Divide the students into three groups. Give each group one of the following assignments:

*Stories for literature response groups

Group 1: Review the materials received from writing for information on the battleship *Arizona* at the beginning of the unit. Check for portrayal of details and biases.

Group 2: Give arguments for the dropping of the atomic bombs on Hiroshima and Nagasaki in August 1945.

Group 3: Give arguments against the dropping of the atomic bombs on Hiroshima and Nagasaki in August 1945.

Have each group present their findings to the class.

4. Allow response groups to meet for ten minutes.

CONCLUSION
(Three Days)

MAJOR CONCEPTS

1. Germany and Europe were divided among major world powers following the war.
2. The division of Europe led to the Cold War.
3. World War II failed to resolve many of the problems that led to it. (Refer to present-day Balkan factionalism, the Palestinian problems, and other current events.)
4. Victory over Japan led to its occupation by America and a restructuring of its government.

MAIN RESOURCES

TEXTBOOK

Perry, Marvin, et al. *History of the World.* Boston: Houghton Mifflin Company, 1990, pp. 705–706.

INSTRUCTIONAL ACTIVITIES

1. Review the major concepts.
2. Complete the K-W-L chart. (See Chapter 5 for an explanation of K-W-L.)
3. Conduct a mock trial based on the book *Gentlehands.* Use the following guidelines to set this up:
   a. Poll the class—Who feels Frank should be prosecuted? Who would forgive and let the past remain in the past? Who is undecided?
   b. Select a student to be Frank Trenker.
   c. Select prosecution counsel and defense counsel. Allow four students on each side for research and justification. Have them choose a team leader to act as the lawyer.
   d. Select twelve people for a jury.
   e. Remaining students may serve as witnesses and as reporters who will summarize and report on daily courtroom activities, prepare classroom press releases, drawings, and so on.
4. Have the students reflect on the following questions:

a. Now that the war is over, what problems did the countries have to deal with?
b. What good and bad things resulted from World War II?
c. What factors might a politician consider when deciding to enter into a war?
d. How does World War II compare and contrast with more recent "involvements"?

5. Have the students fill in the uncompleted graphic organizer on World War II (shown on this page) in order to re-affirm knowledge gained from the study of this unit.

6. Response groups will present their books to the class. Several ways this may be done are through book reports, creating their own book blurbs, creating book jackets, bulletin board displays, dramatic presentations, or artistic displays.

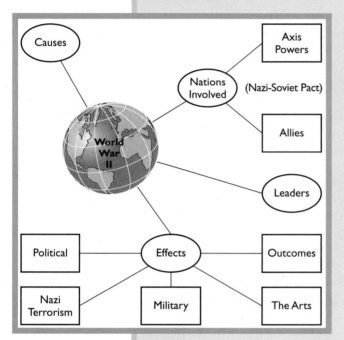

Developing a unit similar to the one in the "Meeting the Challenge" vignette would be possible in almost any content area. Both nonfiction and fiction trade books are available on a wide variety of subjects. These books can broaden the understanding of unit studies and add an element of student interest not always present when the textbook is the only reading material used. Librarians and media specialists are generally happy to work with classroom teachers in locating appropriate trade books to complement unit studies.

Summary

L
iterature is valuable for study itself and as a tool to enhance learning in other content areas. Teachers can use minilessons on reading strategies and literary elements, reading guides, directed reading lessons, electronic discussions, whole-class novel study, literature response groups, and sustained silent reading to help students learn more from and about literature that they read. Teachers can encourage students to respond to literature through written responses, oral responses, and other responses based on multiple intelligences.

Literature is an extremely important resource in thematic units in the content areas. The topics that are covered briefly in text materials are enlarged upon, and the situations depicted allow the students to experience the material vicariously.

Discussion Questions

1 How can trade books enhance content area instruction?
2 What are the values of literature response groups?
3 Which instructional techniques seem most useful for your teaching situation?
4 What types of literature could be used in your particular curricular area?
5 What types of activities can be used in your content area to encourage student response to literature?
6 How does unit teaching lend itself to differentiation of assignments?

Enrichment Activities

*1 Write out a plan for a directed reading lesson for a literature selection that you are currently using. Try it with your students and report to the class concerning the results.
*2 Develop a minilesson for a reading strategy or literary element. Use a think aloud as a part of your lesson. Try it with your students and report to the class concerning the results.
3 Choose a topic and locate trade books on a variety of difficulty levels that students could use when studying this topic.
*4 Plan a unit from your chosen subject area. Try it with students in your class. Decide how you could improve the unit if you were to teach it again.
5 Choose a short story from a literature textbook. Choose prediction points for the selection that would allow you to use it for a DRTA. Discuss the stopping points that you have chosen with your college classmates.

*These activities are designed for in-service teachers, student teachers, or practicum students.

Reading in the Content Areas: I

CHAPTER

10

Overview

Content textbooks, trade books, magazines, newspapers, and multimedia programs are used to convey the basic concepts of content area subjects (Daisey, 1993). Competent, fluent readers are able to acquire greater knowledge and understanding of subject matter (Davey, 1989). To help teachers develop competent readers, we focus on preparing them to guide students in reading and studying content reading materials in social studies, science, mathematics, English (language arts), and foreign languages. Techniques are introduced to encourage students to use strategies for developing word meanings, understanding content, and comprehending common content area writing patterns.

Purpose-Setting Questions

As you read this chapter, try to answer these questions:

1 What reading skills are necessary in fields such as social studies, science, mathematics, English, and foreign languages?
2 What common writing patterns appear in each of these content areas: social studies, science, mathematics, English, and foreign languages?
3 What unique writing patterns appear in science and mathematics?

■ ■ Introduction to Reading Content Material

Teaching any content area is concerned with helping students to read and comprehend printed materials. To learn through reading, a reader engages and interacts with a text and comprehends, interprets, and assimilates the author's ideas into the reader's framework of prior knowledge and experience. Students who recognize the important role literacy plays in learning are more likely to read assigned materials (Frager, 1993). Due to the pervasive use of textbooks in the United States, successful secondary students must be motivated to read, be able to read, and have materials they can read (Yore, 1991; Daisey, 1993).

How can multi-media contribute to multiple ways of learning?

Textbooks are not the only source for learning. The world today is available to anyone who has a computer, a telephone line, and literacy skills. Students can visit foreign countries and museums and see models or construct models that help them understand complex processes. Thus, **multimedia technology** is an important ingredient of content teaching and learning. It is a natural extension of the teacher's instructional plans (Grabe and Grabe, 1996). Educational technology includes computers, television, videodiscs and videotapes, audiotapes, and the Internet, all of which give students ways to play with ideas, to pursue inquiries about interesting topics, and to experience places, people, and times. Students can employ multiple ways of learning and knowing when using electronic media (Gardner, 1993). A constructivist approach like the one described in this book is an extraordinarily rich means of learning (Negroponte, 1995).

Successful instruction integrates electronic media with printed media and provides students opportunities to implement their learning in authentic situations. Using a wide variety of materials during class time accommodates students' diverse interests (Sanacore, 1990). The teacher's instructional role is to guide and facilitate students' explorations, to model active learning, to provide for collaborative learning, and to emphasize thinking skills and application (Grabe and Grabe, 1996). Literacy is just as essential to content learning with electronic media as with hard copy; literacy strategies strengthen instruction in all types of media.

Content teachers find that newspapers and magazines are excellent instructional aids in every subject. Newspapers and magazines are interesting, relevant, timely, and informative. They are especially useful in instruction because they are readily available and cover a wide variety of subjects. Students can read newspapers from several cities and compare the treatment of a topic in several newspapers. Newspapers and related activities can be highly motivating for students. They often find newspapers and magazines more personally relevant and readable than other types of printed materials. The organization Newspapers in Education (NIE) provides materials for teachers. In many cities throughout the United States, local newspapers have staff members who work with schools, showing teachers how to use newspapers in classrooms. Teachers can obtain newspaper teaching materials from the *American Newspaper Publishers Association (ANPA) Foundation, The Newspaper Center, Box 17407, Dulles International Airport, Washington, D.C. 20041.*

Magazines provide interesting, up-to-date content that is highly readable and motivating. In addition, magazine articles are usually short and direct. Publications are available on almost any topic that is interesting for secondary students. Computers, social science, science, psychology, and so forth are the focus of a large variety of periodicals, and they are excellent sources of content for students.

■ Content Strategies and Subject Matter

The most effective and efficient content reading instruction occurs when teachers help students read and learn content concurrently with acquiring reading strategies (Short, 1994). Content teachers have the expertise necessary to identify for their students the important ideas and concepts of the subject matter. In planning for content instruction, teachers should ask themselves, "What do I want my students to know when they finish this chapter, unit, or lesson?" For example, in a unit or lesson in geography, the content area learning objective may be for students to understand how geographic features are formed. Content area learning involves problem solving, critical thinking, conceptual development, and application. After identifying content objectives, teachers identify the learning strategies and materials their students need to achieve them. Example strategies are included in Chapters 4, 5, 6, and 7 as well as the current chapter.

Teaching strategies for software, magazines, and newspapers are like those for textbooks. Prereading or prelearning strategies are important for activating prior knowledge and building students' interest in learning experiences in all types of media. Moreover, these strategies help students understand what they are expected to do and to learn. Preparation motivates students and builds their confidence for participating (Sadker and Sadker, 1985). For instance, motivated students can understand more difficult content than those who are uninterested (Maria, 1990). Prereading activities are suggested in this chapter and in Chapters 4, 5, and 11.

Strategies implemented during and after reading can help students share and extend their comprehension (Frager, 1993). Discussions are well established as effective follow-up experiences, especially when students elaborate on their ideas and answers as they participate (Alvermann and Hayes, 1989). Writing also has proven to be a very helpful process in developing content comprehension. The suggestions in Chapters 8 and 9 will help teachers integrate writing and literature with content learning.

■ Content Text Structures

Secondary teachers see their disciplines as organized bodies of knowledge with defined methods of inquiry (Clarke, Raths, and Gilbert, 1989). However, many students do not recognize the connections among the facts and ideas they study. Instead, they attempt to learn each detail or idea as a separate entity. They overlook main ideas and their relationships to details. These students recall content as a series of memorized fragments. The "Meeting the Challenge" vignette illustrates the fallacies in this approach to comprehension. Although this instance occurred in a biology class, it illustrates that students who understand the way knowledge is structured in any subject can better understand it.

MEETING THE CHALLENGE

Matthew Smith was an average student until tenth grade. He was a diligent student who read and reread his textbooks until he knew the material thoroughly. Matthew encountered a major challenge in tenth-grade biology. First, he found that no amount of rereading made the content sink into his memory. Moreover, he did not have the time to read and reread his biology text and to read his other assignments. At the end of the first grading period, Matthew's grades were on a downward spiral and he was deeply frustrated.

Matthew made an appointment with his guidance counselor, who set up a three-way conference with himself, the biology teacher, and Matthew. After some discussion, they asked the reading teacher to join them. She asked Matthew to demonstrate his reading and study strategies through a "think aloud" and discovered that he was simply reading and rereading each sentence without addressing the overall concept of the unit and the chapter, which in this instance was "Genetics."

The reading teacher arranged four sessions with Matthew. During these sessions he learned how to use the table of contents as an overview and advance organizer. He learned to seek connections among the ideas he was reading and to connect them to his own experiences. Happily, Matthew began to grasp main ideas and supporting details, as well as the connections among ideas and concepts. He became a successful student whose grades improved throughout the school year. He finished the year with a B average in biology.

What is the advantage of learning to recognize structures found in content materials?

Five major patterns or **organizational structures** occur most frequently in content materials: chronological order, list structure, comparison-contrast, cause-effect, and problem-solution (Horowitz, 1985a). The definition or explanation pattern is another common one. These structures are found in all subjects, sometimes alone and often in combination. Among these patterns, chronological order and list structure are easiest to learn; therefore, students should examine these first (Horowitz, 1985a). Identifying these patterns in different subjects helps students achieve broader understanding and gives them a feeling of greater control over otherwise complex subject matter. After examining the easier structures, students can move on to the more challenging ones. Instruction about structure should focus on the actual materials students will read in each subject area.

A number of strategies have proved successful in developing students' awareness of text patterns (Horowitz, 1985b), including

Providing examples across topics and texts
Relating text patterns to real-life experiences
Having students identify signal words and make notes in the margins
Making visual representations of text patterns
Having students practice writing text patterns

Literature-Based Approaches to the Content Areas

What types of materials are important in developing thematic units?

Thematic units incorporating literature and media in content studies have become increasingly popular. Literature and primary sources are important in authentic approaches to learning. They can provide relevant, interesting, and intellectually provocative materials for students to develop new attitudes toward and understandings of the world around them (Guzzetti, Kowalinski, and McGowan, 1992). Electronic media can have the added advantage of making learning more concrete. Chapter 9 develops the concept of thematic units more fully.

Integrated Curriculum

What are the subjects integrated in Example 10.1?

Integrated curriculum blends subjects together. For instance, math, science, social studies, fine arts, and language arts are sometimes integrated for effective learning. The integration is based on setting curricular priorities in each and finding the overlapping skills, concepts, attitudes, and content. An example of integrated curriculum in a content text is shown in Example 10.1. The thematic unit in Chapter 9 also has many instances of curriculum integration.

4 Farm and City Life in the Middle Colonies

Section **4**

Farm and City Life in the Middle Colonies

Teaching Objective

Define the sources of prosperity in the Middle Colonies.

1   INTRODUCE

Remind students that in sections 2 and 3 they looked at the advantages and disadvantages of settling in the New England and Southern Colonies. Now have them apply what they have learned by imagining the ideal place to found a colony.
Ask: *What would it be like? What kinds of people would settle there? How would they make a living?*
(The ideal colony would have the economic resources to support a variety of econominc activities, and would be settled by hard-working people with a broad range of skills. These factors were all present in the Middle Colonies.)

SECTION GUIDE

Main Idea
The economies of the Middle Colonies benefited from good farming conditions, harbors for shipping, and the growth of manufacturing.

Goals
As you read, look for answers to these questions:

❶ Why was farming important in the Middle Colonies?

❷ What factors encouraged the growth of trade and manufacturing?

❸ What kinds of people settled in the Middle Colonies?

Key Terms
Conestoga wagon
mill

I N 1723, a seventeen-year-old runaway apprentice stepped off a boat onto the bustling streets of Philadelphia. When he was a famous old man he recalled his arrival this way:

❝I was dirty from my journey; my pockets were stuffed out with shirts and stockings; I knew no soul nor where to look for lodging; I was very hungry; and my whole stock of cash consisted of a Dutch dollar and about a shilling in copper.❞

The awkward youth was Benjamin Franklin. He had left his home city of Boston in New England to become a citzen of a very different region: the Middle Colonies.

A Wealth of Resources

In the mid-1700s a Frenchman, Michel Guillaume Jean de Crèvecoeur (krev-KUR), settled in the colony of New York. He later wrote about the colony:

❝[Here a visitor] beholds fair cities, substantial villages, extensive fields, an immense country filled with decent houses, good roads, orchards, meadows, and bridges, where a hundred years ago all was wild, woody, and uncultivated!❞

KEY TERMS

Write the key terms on the board and have students define them. Then have them draw a picture of a Conestoga wagon based on the description in the text, and ask them to list the goods it might carry. This activity is especially appropriate for Students Acquiring English.

■ Content Reading Assignments

To plan content reading instruction, teachers think through the learning task from the students' perspective, identifying the skills and strategies that will enable them to achieve the objectives and incorporating those strategies into the lesson. Content instruction is most effective when implemented with students'

The Middle Colonies

The rich farming landscape Crèvecoeur described was typical of coastal parts of the Middle Colonies—New York, New Jersey, Delaware, and Pennsylvania. Local Indians, of course, had known for centuries of the area's natural resources. The region was blessed with rich soil, a good growing season, and a number of large rivers with good harbors. New York City grew at the mouth of the Hudson River. Philadelphia was located on the Delaware River, which drained into Delaware Bay.

Many of the colonists of the region came from the farming traditions of Germany, Switzerland, and Holland. Their skills, knowledge, and hard work would yield a bounty of agricultural products—fruits, vegetables, livestock, and grain. The Middle Colonies produced so much wheat that they became known as the "bread basket" colonies. They exported wheat and other foodstuffs to the other colonies, to the West Indies, and to England.

The Pennsylvania Germans

German-speaking people contributed much to Pennsylvania's farm wealth. Most arrived as indentured servants, fleeing religious persecution. Within a generation they had made their mark on the area. "German communities could be identified by the huge barns, the sleek cattle and the stout workhorses," wrote one historian. To carry their flour, meat, fruit, and vegetables to town markets, they built **Conestoga Wagons.** The team of four to six horses that pulled the wagons often wore bows of bells. The wagons had wide wheels suitable for roads of dirt and mud. The wagon bed was curved so that contents would not spill when the wagon went up or down hills. Canvas covers protected the contents.

GEOGRAPHY SKILLS: New York, New Jersey, Pennsylvania, and Delaware made up the Middle Colonies. **Critical Thinking:** Locate the rivers that flowed through the Middle Colonies. Why might rivers have been important for settlement?

GEOGRAPHY SKILLS

Answer: The Susquehanna, Delaware, and Hudson Rivers were the main transportation routes in colonial America.

SPORTS

Tell students that country fairs (originally farmers' markets) were a major form of recreation in the Middle Colonies. Participants joined in contests to see who could run the fastest, wrestle the hardest, sing the loudest, or even catch a greased pig. They also enjoyed a variety of entertainment, from puppet shows and fortune telling to dancing bears.

2   DEVELOP

Main Idea

Have students list the sources of prosperity in the Middle Colonies, based on three categories: resources, people, economic activities.

When students have finished, have them discuss their lists.

CRITICAL THINKING: Ask: *Why would colonies benefit from having a range of economic activities, rather than just one or two?* (They would be more self-sufficient and less likely to suffer if one sector of their economy declined.)

Connections: Economics

Why were there fewer slaves in the Middle Colonies than in the Southern Colonies? (Fewer workers were needed because the grain crops grown in the Middle Colonies required only seasonal labor.)

Connections: Literature

CRITICAL THINKING: Have students restate Benjamin Franklin's sayings from Poor Richard's Almanac in their own words. *With which sayings do you agree? With which do you disagree? Why?*

current textbooks, trade books, electronic media, related printed materials, and real-life reading materials rather than using exercises that are unrelated to their actual assignments. Authentic reading activities such as simulations, taking oral histories, and solving community problems (such as selecting toxic waste sites) lead students into authentic experiences with reading, learning, and application of ideas.

Each section of this chapter introduces purposeful teaching strategies that can be adapted to various types of content, although the space constraints prohibit demonstrating every strategy with each type of content. Students who learn to use these strategies can apply them to printed materials and electronic media in their content studies.

Why are study guides useful in every content area?

As mentioned earlier, one of the most beneficial strategies for content reading is the use of **study guides.** Study guides direct students' attention to location and consideration of significant ideas (Bean and Ericson, 1989). Study guides are useful in every content subject. They may be developed to accompany textbook assignments or to focus on the concepts and ideas in trade books, magazines, newspapers, documents, film, and multimedia materials. Study guides may be completed by individuals or cooperative groups. Cooperative learning opportunities enhance content learning because a social environment enriches learning (Brophy, 1992).

What is the most important value of reading aloud to students?

Teachers who use the strategy of **reading aloud** from trade books expand and support the concepts developed in the text (Daisey, 1993). Reading aloud develops listening comprehension as well as content reading skills such as acquiring vocabulary, activating schemata, recognizing text structure, critical thinking, making inferences, developing reading interests, and applying knowledge. Read-aloud materials may include newspapers, magazines, and trade journals; information taken from the Internet; and trade books from all literary genre.

Social Studies Content

Social studies classes encompass many academic disciplines, including history, anthropology, geography, economics, political science, psychology, philosophy, and sociology. Recently, multicultural education has become an overarching theme in curriculum development. The primary objective of multicultural education is to help all students reach their potential through exploring cultural pluralism (Banks, 1981). Students learn that each culture has contributed to the culture of the United States.

Critical Thinking in Social Studies

Critical thinking has particular significance in the social sciences because understanding cause-and-effect relationships, distinguishing fact from opinion, separating relevant information from irrelevant information, and identifying and evaluating propaganda are essential skills for learning social studies (Hickey, 1990). At the center of critical thinking is the understanding that we receive a limited amount of information about a particular event (Cioffi, 1992); that is, content is presented from a particular point of view. For example, consider the 1968 Democratic Convention in Chicago; and think of the different perspectives of a Chicago law enforcement official, a convention delegate, and a peace demonstrator. When learning about unfamiliar cultures, students need schemata that enable them to understand human behaviors outside of their experiences. Teachers find that anticipation guides, study guides, and advance organizers enhance critical thinking.

Comprehension of social studies content is enhanced when readers are prepared to

1. understand the ideas and viewpoints of others;
2. acquire and retain a body of relevant concepts and information;
3. think critically and creatively, thus developing new attitudes and values and the ability to make decisions;
4. consult a variety of sources, to develop more than one perspective regarding a topic; and
5. read critically about what has happened and *why* these events occurred.

Social studies materials are written in a precise, factual, expository style which presents comprehension problems for a significant proportion of students (Sellars, 1988; Wait, 1987). However, a student must comprehend 75 percent of the ideas and 90 percent of the vocabulary of a selection in order to learn effectively from these materials and to avoid frustration (Herman, 1969). Through activities like those described in Chapter 3 and the activities that follow, word meanings are reinforced, and recall is enhanced (Stetson and Williams, 1992).

Beck and others (1991) found that revising social studies textbooks to reflect readers' cognitive processing increased their comprehensibility. Study guides are maps to cognitive processing. A study guide may cover a chapter, a larger unit, part of a chapter, or multiple materials on a topic. Students should have the study guide prior to reading an assignment, so they can reflect about it while they read. Example 10.2 illustrates a social studies study guide.

■ ■ ■ EXAMPLE 10.2   *Social Studies Study Guide*

Vocabulary

Directions: Pay attention to the words in Column A—they are important for understanding of this selection. After reading the selection, draw a line from the word in Column A to its meaning in Column B.

Column A	Column B
trade association	An organization of competing companies in one industry that sets industry standards and influences policies.
interest group	An organization designed to advance economic, social action, or other concerns of their members.
gross national product	Value of goods and services produced by a country for a given year.

Comprehension

Directions: Write short answers to the following questions.

1. What do economic interest groups try to influence?
2. What are four major categories of economic interest groups?
3. Why do economic interest groups focus on the government?
4. How do interest groups affect your life?
5. What are the positive qualities and the negative qualities of interest groups?

Directions: Write a short essay to answer this question.

6. What do interest groups for dentists and clothing manufacturers have in common?

What is a concept guide?

A **concept guide** is a form of study guide that is concerned with developing students' understanding of an important content concept. Concept guides may be developed in a number of different ways. Example 10.3 is a concept guide based on a government text chapter on civil rights. A student would complete this guide after reading the chapter. Concept guides are also discussed in Chapter 3.

■ ■ ■ EXAMPLE 10.3   *Social Studies Concept Guide*

Directions: Write a + before each term that is associated with civil rights, according to the information in your social studies textbook. Write a – before each word that is unrelated to the concept of civil rights. Be prepared to explain and support your answers by using your textbook.

_____	restrictive covenant	_____	affirmative action
_____	resegregation	_____	equality
_____	reverse discrimination	_____	Civil Rights Act of 1964
_____	segregation	_____	equal opportunity

_____ integration	_____ people's vote
_____ suspect classification	_____ open housing
_____ socialist government	_____ goods and services

■ Writing Patterns

Social studies materials are dense with ideas and facts, but they are organized around writing patterns that help readers understand the cognitive relationships of key ideas, concepts, and information. When students recognize these patterns, they are better prepared to comprehend social studies content.

Why is the cause-and-effect writing pattern common in social studies?

Cause-and-Effect Pattern

Each area of social studies is concerned with chains of causes and effects: one cause results in certain effects that become causes of other effects. The passage in Example 10.4 is written in the **cause-and-effect writing pattern.**

■■■ EXAMPLE 10.4.   *Cause-and-Effect Pattern (Social Studies)*

Beginning in the 1880s, other European groups began arriving on American shores. These groups came mainly from lands in southern Europe, eastern Europe, and the eastern Mediterranean. Except for Italy and Greece, most of these lands were controlled by the Russian Empire, the Austro-Hungarian Empire, or the Ottoman (Turkish) Empire. Within these empires were many peoples of different religions, languages, and traditions.

Starting in the 1880s, these empires allowed their people to leave. People left for a number of reasons—overpopulation, lack of jobs, and mistreatment by the government. America in turn offered jobs, opportunity, and freedom.

Eastern European Jews were one of the largest of these new immigrant groups. Next in numbers were Slavic peoples—Poles, Slovaks, Czechs, Croats, Serbs, Ukrainians, and Russians. The largest group, however, were southern Italians, like Rocco.

Source: Lorna Mason et al., America's Past and Promise. *Copyright © 1995 by Houghton Mifflin, p. 530. Reprinted by permission of Houghton Mifflin Company. All rights reserved.*

Definition or Explanation Pattern

How is the definition or explanation writing pattern an example of main ideas and supporting details?

The **definition or explanation pattern** is used to define or explain important concepts. The concept is the main idea, and the supporting details constitute the elements of the definition or explanation. To comprehend this pattern of writing, the student must identify both the concept and the author's definition or explanation. This pattern is important to the reader because the knowledge included in the definition or explanation frequently serves as a basis for learning subsequent information on the topic. This pattern is illustrated in Example 10.5.

■ ■ ■ EXAMPLE 10.5   *Definition or Explanation Pattern (Social Studies)*

Japanese Americans

The Japanese attack on Pearl Harbor created anger toward Japanese Americans. Most lived in California, Oregon, and Washington. In February 1942, President Roosevelt signed an order calling for Japanese Americans to be moved away from the Pacific Coast. About 120,000 men, women, and children were rounded up. They had to sell their homes and possessions on very short notice, usually at great loss. Since no charges were brought against them, these people had no way to prove their loyalty.

The Japanese Americans were moved to **internment camps,** areas where they were kept under guard. In the camps entire families had to live in single rooms, with little privacy. One Japanese American woman later wrote:

> "There is no way that anyone who was not in one of the camps can understand the impact it had. . . . Non-internees cannot understand the extent of our anger, the height of our outrage, the depth of our despair."

Two-thirds of the people interned were **Nisei** (nee-SAY)—Japanese Americans born in the United States. They argued that internment for racial reasons was unconstitutional. The Supreme Court, however, upheld internment throughout the war.

Source: Lorna Mason et al., America's Past and Promise. *Copyright © 1995 by Houghton Mifflin, p. 704. Used by permission.*

Chronological Order (Time Order) Pattern

What social studies writing pattern is developed through relating historical events to the reader's life?

In the **chronological order pattern,** events are arranged in order of occurrence. The teacher can help students develop a concept of time periods by having them consider time in relation to their own lives. Understanding time is necessary for comprehending social studies material, but reflecting on what one has read is more valuable than memorizing dates. Indefinite time references, such as "in the early days" or "in ancient times," may confuse the reader; therefore, the teacher needs to clarify these terms. The chronological order pattern is presented in Example 10.6.

■ ■ ■ EXAMPLE 10.6 *Chronological or Time Order Pattern (Social Studies)*

In this rivalry France was helped by the Algonquin and Huron Indians of the lands bordering the St. Lawrence Valley. Siding with the English was the **League of the Iroquois.** The five nations of the League—the Cayuga, Mohawk, Oneida, Onondaga, and Seneca—would become six when the Tuscarora joined in 1722. They joined together to end the almost constant warfare that existed among the nations.

The League would become the most powerful union of Indian nations in America. Part of its power came from its control of the only fairly easy passage between New England and the St. Lawrence Valley. This passage extended from Albany along the Mohawk River to Lake Erie. (Later it would become the route of the Erie Canal.)

By 1640 all the beaver in the Hudson Valley had been trapped. The Iroquois then began warring on their northern neighbors in an attempt to gain control of their fur trade. Within a decade they had defeated the Huron. Through conquest, the Iroquois then extended their control over an area ranging from Maine to the Ohio Valley and north to Lake Michigan. By 1670, Iroquois trappers were hauling to the trading post at Albany a million pounds of beaver skins each year.

Source: Lorna Mason et al., America's Past and Promise. *Copyright © 1995 by Houghton Mifflin, p. 159. Used by permission.*

The teacher can relate a time sequence to a student's own experience with time and help the student develop a concept of the past, present, and future. The student can relate historic occurrences to his or her own lifetime and the lifetimes of his or her parents and ancestors. For example, World War I probably occurred in the lifetime of the great-grandparents of present-day students.

Comparison and/or Contrast Pattern

When using the comparison and/or contrast pattern, an author explains social studies ideas by using likenesses and differences to develop understanding. Example 10.7 shows this writing pattern.

Two Parties Dominate American Politics

> **ACCESS**
> **The Main Ideas**
> 1. **What are the three types of party systems?**
> 2. **What barriers do third parties face in the American political system?**
> 3. **What roles have third parties played in American politics?**

Throughout its history, American politics has been essentially a **two-party system.** This idea was never stated in a law or document, but it is basic to American government. Over the years many minor or third parties have formed in the United States. Some of these third parties have influenced policies and election results. Still, two major parties have remained dominant. How did the two-party system originate and why has it prevailed? What does it reveal about American politics?

Party Systems

While the two-party system seems normal to Americans, it is not the most common political pattern in the world. Every nation's party system is unique, a part of its political culture. For simplicity, however, most countries can be classified as having one-party, multi-party, or two-party systems.

One-Party Systems

One-party systems are most typically found in nations with authoritarian governments. In such countries, the party in power *is,* in effect, the government. Only one party appears on the ballot, and the state tolerates no political opposition. Such one-party systems commonly exist where a party has gained power by force. This occurred in the Soviet Union after the Russian Revolution of 1917, and in Fascist Italy and Nazi Germany in the 1930's. Cuba and China today have one-party systems. One-party systems are often imposed in non-Communist countries after a military government takes power. Examples of this situation include Iraq and Zaire. In monarchies such as Saudi Arabia or Kuwait, a royal family holds all political power.

A different sort of one-party system can develop in a country where elections are held but one party consistently wins. There, voters have a real choice among parties, but election contests are still one-sided. This type of one-party control occurs in Mexico and Japan, for example. Some American states have had similar situations, in which either Democrats or Republicans traditionally controlled the state.

Multi-Party Systems

Political systems with many rival parties are most common throughout the world. All the democracies in Western Europe, for example, have **multi-party systems.** France and Germany each have four major parties and several minor ones. Italy has ten. Multi-party systems typically are divided along sharp ideological lines, representing the range of opinions from "right" to "left." Parties also may be linked with different religious, regional, or social class groupings.

Some nations with multi-party systems, such as Sweden, Belgium, and Germany, have very stable governments, but most are unstable. Seldom can one party capture a majority of the votes. Usually the system is held together by fragile coalitions of parties, with frequent changes in the government.

Source: Richard J. Hardy, Government in America, *p. 271. Copyright © 1993 by Houghton Mifflin Company. Reprinted by permission of Houghton Mifflin Company. All rights reserved.*

The teacher and students may develop a chart to show comparisons and/or contrasts. The following chart is based on Example 10.7.

One Party	*Multi-party*
typically authoritarian	democracies
no opposition	divide on ideological lines
typically power by force	range left to right
often based on military power	unstable coalitions

Question-and-Answer Pattern

Authors sometimes use a question-and-answer pattern to organize social studies materials. In this pattern, the author asks a question and then answers it. Readers should be able to recall the author's questions and identify his or her answers. Example 10.8 illustrates this style of writing.

■ ■ ■ EXAMPLE 10.8   *Question-and-Answer Writing Pattern (Social Studies)*

Slaves Ride the Underground Railroad

Antislavery forces did more than protect and rescue runaway slaves. In fact, they helped many slaves escape. A secret network known as the **Underground Railroad** guided some 100,000 fugitive slaves to freedom between 1780 and 1865.

What was the Underground Railroad? It was not a railroad, and it did not move underground. The Underground Railroad was a complex system of about 3,000 people—both blacks and whites—who helped transport escaped slaves. Under the cover of night, "conductors" led runaways to freedom, providing food and safe hiding places. They risked great danger in aiding slaves.

The means of transportation in the Underground Railroad varied. Slaves traveled on foot, in covered wagons, in boxes shipped by rail or in small boats gliding silently through the water by night. At the stations, slaves hid in attics, barns, cellars, and even secret rooms. Finally, at the end of the perilous journey, the runaway slave would settle in one of the 14 free states or in Canada.

Source: Beverly J. Armento, Gary B. Nash, Christopher L. Salter, and Karen K. Wixson. A More Perfect Union, *p. 333. Copyright © 1993 Houghton Mifflin Company. Reprinted by permission of Houghton Mifflin Company. All rights reserved.*

EXERCISES

1. Give the students practice exercises such as the following one to enhance learning in social studies: From the list of words and phrases below, choose a word or phrase that is associated with each of the terms in the word list.

   Words and Phrases

rules of conduct	control behavior
power to interpret and apply law	self-government
people's vote	rights of the people

   Word List

1. jurisdiction	3. autonomy
2. plebiscite	4. civil rights

2. An activity called "Possible Sentences" encourages students to learn word meanings and to predict ideas they will encounter when reading content (Tierney, Readence, and Dishner, 1990). For this activity, use the following steps:

   a. Identify important vocabulary in the reading selection and write the words on the chalkboard. Pronounce each word as you write it. The words below are taken from a social studies text chapter comparing democracy and communism

democracy	civil rights
socialism	laws

   b. Ask each student to construct sentences using at least two of the words. Record these sentences on the chalkboard, underlining the important words. Continue eliciting sentences from the students as long as the sentences are creating new contexts.

   In a <u>democracy</u>, <u>laws</u> are made by elected officials.

   c. Have students read their textbooks to verify the accuracy of the sentences they constructed.

    d. After they read the text, have the students evaluate each sentence using the text as a reference. Students may also use glossaries, dictionaries, and thesauruses. Have students modify the sentences if necessary.

3. The List-Group-Label lesson developed by Hilda Taba (1967), uses categorization to help students develop and refine concepts. This activity also encourages students to relate content to past experiences. It includes the following steps:

    a. Give students a topic drawn from the materials they are studying. An appropriate topic could be "The Geography of Georgia."

    b. Have students develop a list of words or expressions they associate with the topic. Record these words on the chalkboard until the list totals approximately twenty-five words.

Appalachian Mountains	Blue Ridge Mountains
Peanuts	Savannah River
Altamaha River	Cotton

    c. Have students group words from the large list, providing a label for each group.

Mountains	*Waterways*	*Products*
Blue Ridge Mountains	Savannah River	Peanuts
Stone Mountain	Altamaha River	Cotton
Appalachian Mountains		

4. Critical reading in social studies materials can be guided with questions like these:

    a. What was the author's purpose in writing this selection?

    b. Is the author knowledgeable and current about the subject?

    c. Is the author biased in his or her presentation? Why do you think so? An author's biases are likely to appear when causes of events are explained. The author's point of view may be affected by factors such as his or her age, nationality, religion, political views, race, family history, sex, and audience for the writing.

    d. Is the material well written and interesting?

    e. Does the author employ propaganda? If so, does the propaganda influence you?

    f. Does the author imply anything that is not directly stated? What is implied? What does the author say that leads you to this conclusion? (Hickey, 1990).

5. Technology, literature, newspapers, magazines, and field trips to museums and exhibits provide students with experiences to help build understandings of people, places, and events.

    a. A textbook chapter or unit on the western migration could be explored with a software program such as *Oregon Train II* (MECC). This classic pioneer simulation software lets students experience history as they play the roles of emigrants traveling by covered wagon to Oregon and California on the Overland trails. Literature such as *Pioneer Women: The Lives of Women on the Frontier* (Peavy and Smith, 1996) and the *Western Historical Quarterly* would enrich this study. Copies of original documents and newspapers can be obtained from state historical societies.

b. To study Vietnam, teachers could use software such as *Passage to Vietnam* (Against All Odds Prod.), a stunningly beautiful and very informative journey through Vietnam that could be used in conjunction with *Vietnam: Why We Fought—An Illustrated History* (Hoobler and Hoobler, 1990), *Portrait of a Tragedy: America and the Vietnam War* (Warren, 1990), and *Fallen Angels* (Myers, 1988). Newspapers from this period are available in most public libraries or in newspaper archives.

c. The Internet enables students to visit national parks vicariously and see sites within the parks, which helps students develop geographic concepts.

Science and Health Content

"In the past 20 years, concern over students' low levels of success in studying science, and in fact their tendency to avoid studying it whenever possible, has led to a variety of prescriptions for rectifying the situation" (Mallow, 1991, p. 325).

Studies reveal that science reading skills are important to students' success and that many students bring a range of misconceptions to science class (Mallow, 1991). These misconceptions include the belief that science vocabulary is the same as ordinary vocabulary, that science can be read as rapidly as literature, and that all science reading is of the same type and at the same level. In fact, there are at least four levels of science writing that require different reading approaches: (1) articles in the popular press (newspapers and magazines), (2) articles in popular scientific journals (for example, *Scientific American*), (3) science textbooks, (4) articles in scientific research journals. Textbooks may include a wide spectrum of writing that ranges in style from popular articles to research papers.

Written materials in health are similar to scientific materials and include a similar range of writing. Health has become an important field of study as people take more responsibility for their own health and well-being. Health education seeks to help students understand both their physical bodies and their emotional growth and development.

The process for reading a science text is the same as that used by professional scientists for reading research articles and the same as they used when they were high school students first learning science (Mallow, 1991). Readers of scientific texts must follow scientific thinking, the terse scientific writing style, and the dense content. They have to read slowly and more than once, with pencil and paper in hand, considering each new idea. Mallow (1991) recommends that students read a chapter at least three times—before a topic is covered in class, while it is being covered, and after it has been covered.

In the past, 90 percent of science teachers relied on textbooks to convey scientific content (Lloyd and Mitchell, 1989); however, today's teachers create hands-on experiences and have students conduct experiments that illustrate the importance of science in daily life. This emphasis on authentic learning experiences increases students' need for interactive reading, which means they should relate questions, experiments, and problem solving to the text. Mallow (1991) recommends that students make up their own exercises and solve them. This type of exercise could extend to experiments as well. The following strategies and activities will help teachers develop students' understanding of scientific reading and writing.

Scientific terminology can be developed with the Frayer Model, which was introduced in Chapter 3. Example 10.9 illustrates this strategy.

■ ■ ■ EXAMPLE 10.9　　*Frayer Model Activity*

Concept: Adaptation

ESSENTIAL ATTRIBUTES

1. Improves chance of survival
2. Improves genetic selection

NONESSENTIAL ATTRIBUTES

1. Seasonal changes
2. Changes that do not contribute to survival

EXAMPLES

1. Front legs of mole
2. Walrus tusks
3. Beak of black skimmer

NONEXAMPLES

1. Albinism
2. Human beings with six fingers

■ Writing Patterns

The main ideas and supporting details in scientific materials are frequently organized into classification patterns, explanations of technical processes, cause-and-effect patterns, and problem-solution patterns. Another pattern used to structure scientific content is the experimental pattern. These patterns and related strategies are illustrated in the following section.

Classification Pattern

How is informa-tion arranged in the classification pattern?

In the **classification pattern,** information is ordered under common headings and subheadings. The information sorted in this way may relate to living things, objects, or general ideas. This pattern is a type of outlining that shows a classification, the distinguishing characteristics of the members of the class, and examples (see Example 10.10). The classification represents a main idea, and the distinguishing characteristics and examples are treated as details.

■ ■ ■ EXAMPLE 10.10   *Classification Pattern (Science)*

The Geologic Time Scale

13-9 Investigating the Geologic Time Scale

It took more than 200 years for geologists to put together a workable Geologic Time Scale. The Geologic Time Scale subdivides geologic history into units of time based on the formation of certain rocks.

The largest of these time units is called an **era.** Each era is divided into **periods,** and each period may be divided into smaller units called **epochs** (*EH puhks*). When placed in proper order, these time units form a geologic calendar. If you compare the divisions of the earth's history to the divisions of your textbook, an era is like a unit, a period is like a chapter, and an epoch is like a section. The chief difference between these is that the time scale divides time, and the book divides information.

The dividing lines between eras, periods, and epochs are based on recognizable changes. These include changes in kinds of plants and animals, and episodes of mountain building. For example, the extinction of dinosaurs separates the Mesozoic (*mehs uh ZOH ihk*) Era from the Cenozoic (*sehn uh ZOH ihk*) Era. The Quaternary Period is divided into an earlier Pleistocene Epoch and a later Holocene Epoch, in which we are now living. The beginning of the Pleistocene is marked by the first advance of American and Eurasian ice caps. This started the great Ice Age of the Pleistocene Epoch. The Holocene Epoch began when the Ice Age glaciers disappeared, 10,000 years ago. (The opener to Chapter 14 and Sections 15–7 and 15–8 have more information on the Pleistocene Ice Age.) However, the dividing lines between divisions of geologic time are never sharp ones. They are more like zones of gradual transition in time.

It is difficult to understand such long periods of geologic time when a human's life span may be only 70 years. You may think of ways to help yourself visualize large numbers of things, such as pebbles. Can you do the same with large numbers of years? One way to help is to set up a demonstration that will compare a few years to millions of years.

Source: William Matthews III, Chalmer J. Roy, Robert E. Stevenson, Miles F. Harris, Dale T. Hesser, William A. Dexter, Investigating the Earth, *4th ed., pp. 312–313. Copyright © 1991 by Houghton Mifflin Company. Reprinted by permission of Houghton Mifflin Company. All rights reserved.*

Outline of Example 10.10

I. Geologic Time Scale
    A. Subdivides geologic history based on rock formation
    B. Era
        1. Largest time unit
        2. Eras can be subdivided by recognizable changes
    C. Period
        1. Subdivision of an era
        2. Periods can be subdivided by recognizable changes
    D. Epoch
        1. Subdivision of a period
        2. Based on recognizable changes

Definition or Explanation Pattern

The definition (or explanation) pattern occurs frequently in scientific content and health-related materials (see Example 10.11). This pattern may explain processes that are biological (the digestive process) or mechanical (the operation of an engine). It also may provide definitions for scientific terms, such as *atmosphere*. Diagrams often accompany this kind of pattern, so the reader must integrate written content information with the diagrams.

■ ■ ■ EXAMPLE 10.11   Explanation Pattern (Health)

Insomnia (*ihn SAHM nee uh*), or having difficulty sleeping, takes several forms. Some people have a very hard time falling asleep, or they wake up much earlier than they want to. Others may not be able to sleep more than a few hours at a time without waking up. People who have insomnia sometimes feel that they don't sleep at all, but actually they drift in and out of sleep without realizing it. They probably get more sleep than they think they do.

Exercises to help students comprehend the explanation of a process follow.

EXERCISES

1. Have students attempt to restate an explanation in their own words.
2. Have students reread the explanation to check their comprehension.
3. Have students study the sequence of steps in a process and attempt to explain the process by recalling the steps in sequence.
4. Mask the labels in a diagram that accompanies a process explanation and have students insert appropriate labels.

Cause-and-Effect Pattern

The cause-and-effect pattern often occurs in scientific or health-related materials. Study guides can be developed to help students read this pattern. Example 10.12 presents a study guide built on a health text passage.

■ ■ ■ ■ EXAMPLE 10.12   *Cause-and-Effect Pattern (Health) and Study Guide*

Being active is not just a way to improve an already healthy body—to become stronger or more attractive, for example. The fact is, if you are not regularly active, you don't just stay the same. Your health actually goes downhill.

Constantly inactive muscle fibers become smaller, and they store less energy. They exert less tension for a task, and they tire quickly. When inactive muscles are overworked, they often feel stiff and sore for a few days afterwards. Unused joints become stiff and less flexible, and can become sore if moved too far or too fast. A lack of stress regularly exerted by muscles makes bones eventually become softer and more easily broken.

The effect of regular exercise is to make muscles and joints stronger and more flexible. Tendons and bones also become harder and stronger. Well-used muscles do not tire as quickly as flabby muscles do, even though they do more work. This is because trained muscles can take up and use glucose and oxygen from the blood at a faster rate. They also get rid of waste products faster. And trained muscles are also more efficient at turning food energy into work.

Cause-and-Effect Study Guide

Directions: Read the assigned selection and identify all of the causes and effects in the selection. After reading the selection, read the list of effects and the list of causes. Then place the letter of the cause in the blank before the effect with which it is associated.

CAUSES

a. smaller muscle fibers
b. overworked, inactive muscles
c. unused joints
d. regular exercise
e. trained muscles
f. lack of muscle stress

EFFECTS

_____ **1.** Less energy is stored.
_____ **2.** Muscles tire easily.
_____ **3.** The individual feels stiff and sore.
_____ **4.** Muscles and joints become stronger.
_____ **5.** Tendons and bones become harder, stronger.
_____ **6.** Food energy is turned efficiently into work.
_____ **7.** Bones become softer.

The following exercises can be used to provide practice with the cause-and-effect and other writing patterns.

EXERCISES

1. Writing (composition) can be used to reinforce reading comprehension in any content area or of any writing pattern. In the following paragraph, the student writer connected the earth science content he read to his own experiences.

The climate is the average pattern of weather in a place. The climate affects the habitat, which includes the water, rocks, soil, and air that all living things need. Since the plants and animals need certain things to live, they exist in places where the habitat provides these things. The kinds of water, rocks, soil, and air that are available make a difference in the kinds of plants and animals that live in that place. Woodpeckers and sapsuckers live in North Carolina forests because they eat the insects that live in the pine trees growing in this state.

2. Ask students to write questions about the content they read. For example,
   a. Why do some animals become extinct?
   b. If Guilford County became a desert, what animals would become extinct?

For additional teaching suggestions, see the social studies section.

Problem-Solution Pattern

Explain the problem-solution pattern of writing.

The **problem-solution pattern** of writing is used in scientific and health-related materials to describe a real or hypothetical problem and its actual or suggested solution. For example, a writer might use this style of writing to explain how a vaccine was developed for polio.

To teach students to read and understand the problem-solution style of writing, the teacher may use the following techniques.

EXERCISES

1. Ask students to identify the problem presented in a passage and to state it in their own words.
2. Ask students to locate the solution or solutions suggested by the author.
3. Ask students to prepare a problem and solution statement similar to the following:

   Problem: Why don't bacteria grow and divide in the region surrounding bread mold?
   Solution: Fleming found that mold gave off a chemical that killed the bacteria. He isolated the chemical and tested it against bacteria. He tested the chemical on animals with bacterial disease and on sick human volunteers.

Experimental Pattern

How is literal comprehension related to reading the experimental pattern?

The **experimental pattern** of writing is frequently used in scientific materials because experiments are the basis of scientific knowledge and advancement. The reader must be able to read experiment directions and translate them into action. The reader must carry out the directions precisely and observe the outcomes carefully. The purpose of an experiment is comparable to a main idea, and experimental directions are comparable to details. Example 10.13 presents this pattern of writing.

Following are the steps a reader should use when reading and conducting an experiment.

1. Ask the following questions:
   a. What am I to find out?
   b. What materials are needed?

   c. What processes are used?

   d. What is the order of the steps in the experiment?

   e. What do I expect to happen?

2. Perform the experiment.

3. Observe the experiment.

4. Compare the actual outcomes with predicted outcomes. (Success or failure of an experiment is determined by the learning that takes place.)

5. Ask: How is this experiment related to the topic I am studying?

■ ■ ■ EXAMPLE: 10.13 *Experimental Pattern (Science)*

Clouds and Rain

2-13 Investigating Cumulus Cloud Formation

In many parts of the country, cumulus clouds appear in the sky on a warm afternoon or on a cold, windy day after a rain. When they first form, cumulus clouds look like large heaps of cotton. The flat base of the clouds marks the level where condensation begins.

If you know the temperature and the dew point at the earth's surface, you can calculate the height at which the two become equal. This is approximately the height of the flat bases of the cumulus clouds.

FIGURE 2.17

Finding the dew point in a classroom.

Procedure

Find the dew point by slowly adding small pieces of ice to a can of water.

Finding the dew point in a classroom.
Gently stir the mixture with a thermometer. (See Figure 2.17.) Record the temperature when drops of water begin to condense on the outside of the can. Repeat this several times to make sure of the temperature.

You can find the dew point indirectly by using the sling psychrometer as described in Appendix B.

Discussion
1. Compare the results obtained with the psychrometer and can methods. How close should they be? What could cause differences in the results from the two methods?
2. When air rises it cools about 10°C for each kilometer it rises. The air's dew point also decreases, as it rises, at the rate of about 1.7°C per kilometer. At what height will cumulus clouds form on the day of your observations? (See Figure 2-18 to find out how to make your determination.)

FIGURE 2.18

Sloping lines show how the temperature and dew point of dry (unsaturated) air change when it rises in the atmosphere. You can estimate the height at which cumulus clouds will form by finding where the surface temperature and the dew point lines intersect. In the example, the ground temperature is 20° and the dew point is 10°.

Source: William Matthews, Chalmer Roy, Robert Stevenson, et al., Investigating the Earth, *4th ed., pp. 61–62. Copyright © 1984 by Houghton Mifflin Company. Reprinted by permission of Houghton Mifflin Company. All rights reserved.*

What pattern does an "analogical study guide" help students understand?

Comparison

The **comparison writing pattern** also appears in science materials. In some content, writers use comparisons in the form of analogies to help readers understand scientific content. Example 10.14 illustrates an analogical study guide that was developed to help students read this writing style.

■ ■ ■ EXAMPLE 10.14   *Cell Structure-Function Analogical Study Guide*

Structure	Main Functions	Analogy (comparing the cell to a factory)
cell wall	support; protection	factory walls
cell membrane	boundary, gatekeeper	security guards
cytoplasm	site of most metabolism	the work area
centrioles	cell reproduction	?
chloroplasts	photosynthesis	snack bar
endoplasmic reticulum	intracellular transport	conveyor belts
golgi bodies	storage, secretion	packaging, storage, and shipping
lysosomes	intracellular digestion	clean-up crew
microfilaments	movement	?
microtubules	support; movement	?
mitochondria	cellular respiration	energy generation plant
nucleus	control; heredity	boss's office, copy machine
ribosomes	protein synthesis	assembly line
vacuoles	storage	warehouses

Source: "Cell structure-function analogical study guide." Thomas W. Bean, Harry Singer, and Stan Cowan "Analogical study guides: Improving comprehension in science." Journal of Reading, December 1985, p. 249. Reprinted with permission of Thomas W. Bean and the International Reading Association.

Additional Skills

In addition to understanding technical terminology and the organizational patterns featured in scientific materials, the reader of science must have mathematical understandings and knowledge. He or she must know and be able to apply the abbreviations, equations, and symbols that appear in scientific content.

■ ■ Mathematics Content

Mathematics is a style of thinking involving modeling and abstraction (Silver, 1995). Mathematics has important applications in many areas of work and study, and students should explore these applications. Literacy is critical to mathematical reasoning and to exploring applications of mathematics. The standards developed by the National Council of Teachers of Mathematics (1989) point out that "all students need extensive experience listening to, reading about, writing about, speaking about, reflecting on, and demonstrating mathematical ideas." They also state that teachers should continually encourage students to clarify, paraphrase, or elaborate. Students need to develop extensive applications of mathematics concepts, as well as connections to everyday life. Current mathematics instruction emphasizes the use of **"real-world" mathematics problems** and materials and of computer capabilities to make conceptual understanding (National Council of Teachers of Mathematics, 1989). Current textbooks acquaint students with people who use math in their professions and businesses. Moreover, mathematics instruction builds connections with other subjects, and many teachers are striving to develop a broad, integrated mathematics curriculum in the middle school (Silver, 1995). Teachers are striving to engage a diverse student population in a variety of interesting and meaningful activities that are structured to develop critical thinking and problem solving (Seeley, 1993).

Describe "real-world" mathematics problems.

These current trends are illustrated in Example 10.15, taken from an Algebra I text.

■ Words and Symbols

Mathematics is a highly compressed system of language in which a single symbol may represent several words; for example, the symbol > represents the words *greater than*. Writing in mathematics is generally denser and contains more ideas in each line and on each page than writing in the other disciplines.

In mathematics, as in some science material, words and symbols are mixed; comprehension depends not only on words and word relationships but also on the relationships between words and symbols. Students have to read symbols, signs, abbreviations, formulas, equations, geometric figures, graphs, and tables as well as words.

Vocabulary knowledge is essential to understanding mathematics. Exactness in word knowledge is important because reading one word incorrectly can alter the meaning of an entire passage. Moreover, the reader has to integrate words and symbols into thought units. Some words, such as *count*, *odd*, and *power*, have meanings in mathematics that are quite different from their meanings in everyday conversation. Students can keep mathematics journals in which they note key vocabulary terms and steps in solving various kinds of mathematics problems and patterns.

Four types of definitions are commonly used with mathematics terminology: formal definition, listing of characteristics, simulated examples, and real-world examples (Earle, 1976). Following are examples of each type of definition:

1. *Formal definition.* A square is a parallelogram that has four right angles and four sides of equal length.

■ ■ ■ EXAMPLE 10.15   *Critical Thinking in Math*

How Much Is Enough?

The number of calories that a particular athlete should consume depends on many factors including age, height, and activity level. The graph shown can help an athlete figure out how many calories from carbohydrates to include in a daily diet. Once the athlete's daily calorie needs are known, the number of calories from carbohydrates should be within the shaded region of the graph. As you will learn in this chapter, the graph represents a system of inequalities.

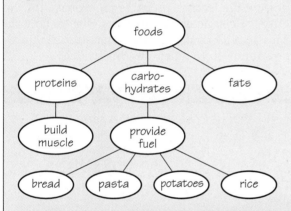

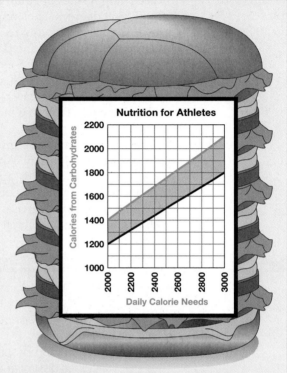

EXPLORE AND CONNECT

1. **Writing** According to the graph, if an athlete needs to consume 2200 Cal each day, about how many should come from carbohydrates? If another athlete needs to consume 1700 Cal from carbohydrates each day, about how many total calories does that athelete need?

2. **Research** In physics, a calorie is defined as a unit of heat. What is the relationship between calories used in physics and food calories? Find out how the numbers of calories in foods are determined.

3. **Project** The other 30–40% of an athelete's daily calorie intake should come from proteins and fats. What kinds of foods are high in proteins and fats? Create a poster showing how carbohydrates, fats, and proteins help the body to function.

Mathematics & Nancy Clark

In this chapter, you will learn more about how mathematics is related to sports nutrition.

Related Examples and Exercises

Section 7.1
• Example 1
• Exercises 34–36, 38

Section 7.5
• Exercises 29–31

Section 7.6
• Exercises 15–18

2. *Listing of characteristics.* Several things are true about any square. It has only two dimensions—length and height. It has exactly four sides, all of which are straight lines of equal length. It has four interior angles, which total exactly 360 degrees. Each angle is a 90-degree angle.
3. *Simulated example.* Squares can be drawn on a chalkboard, cut from paper or other material, or pointed out in drawings or pictures.
4. *Real-world example.* These can be natural occurrences that exemplify square formulation or manmade objects that utilize squares as industrial, architectural, or decorative features. Real-world examples of squares might include the shape of a field, a windowpane, a room, or a table top.

Many of the strategies introduced in Chapter 3 will help students acquire mathematics terminology. Another useful strategy involves defining concept characteristics. To use this approach, the teacher prepares an exercise for the students and asks them to identify the characteristics that describe each mathematical term in the exercise. This activity could be used after students finish reading a mathematics chapter. Example 10.16 illustrates this strategy.

■ ■ ■ EXAMPLE 10. 16   *Mathematical Terms Exercise*

Directions: Check the characteristics that describe the term. A set

_____ is a collection of objects.
_____ has members.
_____ has common properties.
_____ includes dissimilar objects.
_____ can be an empty set.
_____ has fractional numbers.

■ Reading Mathematics

It is important for teachers to emphasize that mathematics content is different from other types of content. The reading involved in problem solving is particularly difficult, because of the variety of cognitive processes that must be employed. Both linguistic and mathematics schemata are significant in understanding mathematics (Thomas, 1988). The following procedures are recommended for guiding mathematics comprehension.

Since the reading rate for mathematics is slower than that for other content areas, students should preread a section of the text at a moderate rate to get the general idea of the concept being introduced. On the second reading, they should go more slowly, taking notes and copying important information. As they read, students can paraphrase the content and devise questions relating to the assignment. Finally, they should reread any passages that are unclear and write questions regarding the information they need in order to clarify the material and focus attention on any illustrations (Henrichs and Sisson, 1980).

A directed reading lesson gives students a guide that can help them understand mathematics texts. The following set of steps can be used for directing the reading of a mathematics chapter:

1. *Introduce the new terms, using them in sentences.* Sentences from the text may be used. Give students an activity such as constructing a mathematics dictionary. Students may use their texts to help work out the meanings of the words.
2. *Ask students to preview the chapter and identify the topic.*
3. *Provide students with two or three silent reading purposes.* This step may be varied. If students have some background knowledge about the topic, they can help formulate silent reading purposes.
4. *Have students read the text silently.* Students should take notes on the content and formulate questions while reading.
5. *Work through examples and ask questions to clarify understanding.*
6. *Discuss the silent reading purposes and the questions students formulated in Step 4.*

◼ Writing Patterns

The writing patterns that occur most frequently in mathematics are the problem pattern and the demonstration pattern. In addition, graphs and charts are often used in math content reading.

Verbal Problems

Solving word problems (verbal problems) is a very sophisticated task. Many readers have significant difficulties reading and understanding word problems, which are mathematical situations stated in words and symbols. Even when they can read the words and sentences with facility, students have difficulty choosing the correct process (operation) to solve the problem. Knifong and Holtran (1977) found that 95 percent of the students they studied could read all the words correctly in word problems; 98 percent knew the situation the problem was discussing; 92 percent knew what the problem was asking; yet only 36 percent knew how to work the problem.

Kress (1989) recommends a technique similar to SQ3R for helping students solve word problems. This approach to solving verbal problems helps students identify the appropriate process or processes for solving a problem. A mathematics reading technique similar to Kress's follows. Immediately after the description of the technique, the process is modeled as it would be applied to the mathematics problem in Example 10.17.

TECHNIQUE
1. *Survey.* Read the problem out loud. Try to visualize the situation.
2. *Question.* What is the problem asking me to find? This step gives students a purpose for reading the problem. It helps them know why they are reading.
3. *Question.* What is the correct process? (e.g., addition, subtraction, division)
4. *Read.* Read the problem aloud again.
5. *Work.* Work the problem.

■ ■ ■ EXAMPLE 10.17   *Verbal Problem (Mathematics)*

Converting Customary Units to Metric Units

Objective: To convert customary units to metric units.

Because most other countries use the metric system, many United States companies convert the customary measurements of their products into metric units before exporting them. You can do this type of conversion using a chart like the one below.

When You Know	Multiply By	To Find
inches	2.54	centimeters
feet	0.3	meters
yards	0.91	meters
miles	1.61	kilometers
ounces	28.35	grams
pounds	0.454	kilograms
fluid ounces	29.573	milliliters
pints	0.473	liters
quarts	0.946	liters
gallons	3.785	liters

Example: Anderson Architects designs buildings worldwide. They recently designed a house that might be built in both the United States and Canada. The United States plans show that the length of the house is 57 ft and the width of the house is 33 ft. What are the length and width in meters that should be shown on the Canadian plans?

Source: Francis J. Gardella, Patricia R. Fraze, Joanne E. Meldon, et al., Mathematical Connections, *p. 84. Copyright © 1992 by Houghton Mifflin Company. Reprinted by permission of Houghton Mifflin Company. All rights reserved.*

Modeling the Process of Reading and Solving Mathematics Problems (as applied to Example 10.17, which was taken from an algebra book)

1. *Survey.* The question sentence in this problem is: What are the length and width in meters that should be shown on the Canadian plans?
2. *Question.* What is this problem asking me to find? (Correct conversion of feet to meters.)
3. *Question.* What is the correct process? (Requires multiplication.)
4. *Read the problem aloud.* Read the written problem aloud. Refer to Example 10.17.
5. *Work the problem.* To convert feet to meters, multiply by 0.3.

57 ft. (0.3 m per ft.) = _____   60 ft. (0.3 m per ft.) = 18 m
33 ft. (0.3 m per ft.) = _____   30 ft. (0.3 m per ft.) = 9 m

Estimate the answer.

Another valuable approach to reading verbal problems was suggested by Earle (1976). In this technique, the teacher uses a series of steps to guide students through the written language of the problem. The following steps are based on those suggested by Earle:

1. Read the problem quickly to obtain a general understanding of it. Visualize the problem. Do not be concerned with the numbers.
2. Examine the problem again. Identify the question you are asked to answer. This question usually comes at the end of the problem, but it may occur anywhere in the problem.
3. Read the problem again to identify the information given.
4. Analyze the problem to see how the information is related. Identify any missing information and any unnecessary information.
5. Compute the answer.
6. Examine your answer. Label the parts of the solution to correspond with the question that the problem asks you to solve. Is your answer sensible?

See also the discussion of SQRQCQ in Chapter 7.

Demonstration Pattern

The demonstration pattern is usually accompanied by an example that illustrates operations and concepts. This writing pattern is important in mathematics materials because it shows students how to work problems. Following are exercises to help students understand the strategies that they can use while reading the demonstration pattern.

EXERCISES

1. The student should work through the example to determine whether he or she understands the process. If the student does not compute the same answer as shown in the example, he or she should work slowly through the example again, rereading each step carefully to determine the point in the process at which he or she erred.
2. The reader should paraphrase the process in his or her own words.
3. The student should apply the process to other situations.

Example 10.18 shows the demonstration writing pattern.

■ ■ ■ EXAMPLE 10.18   *Demonstration Pattern*

Integers on a Number Line

Objective: To recognize and compare integers and to find opposites and absolute values.

Terms to Know

- integers
- positive integers
- negative integers
- opposites
- absolute value

Data Analysis

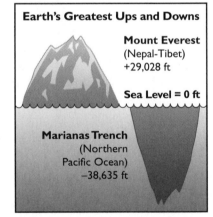

Earth's Greatest Ups and Downs

Mount Everest
(Nepal-Tibet)
+29,028 ft

Sea Level = 0 ft

Marianas Trench
(Northern
Pacific Ocean)
−38,635 ft

The diagram at the right shows information about the highest and lowest points on Earth. The positive sign on $^+29.028$ tells you that the top of Mount Everest is 29,028 ft *above* sea level. The negative sign on $^-38,635$ tells you that the bottom of the Marianas Trench is 38,635 ft *below* sea level. Sea level is represented by 0. The numbers $^+29,028$, $^-38,635$, and 0 are examples of *integers*.

An **integer** is any number in the following set.

$\{\ldots, ^-4, ^-3, ^-2, ^-1, 0, ^+1, ^+2, ^+3, ^+4, \ldots\}$ ← The braces { } mean *the set that contains.*

Integers greater than zero are called **positive integers.** Integers less than zero are called **negative integers.** Zero is neither positive nor negative. To make notation simpler, you generally write positive integers without the positive sign.

Another way to show the integers is to locate them as points on a number line. On a horizontal number line, *positive integers* are to the right of zero and *negative integers* are to the left.

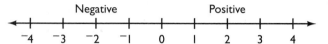

Numbers that are the same distance from zero, but on opposite sides of zero are called **opposites.** To indicate the opposite of a number *n,* you write −*n.* You read −*n* as "the opposite of *n.*"

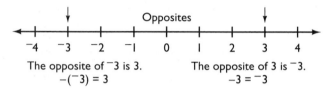

The opposite of ⁻3 is 3.   The opposite of 3 is ⁻3.
−(⁻3) = 3   −3 = ⁻3

On the number line above, you see that the symbols −3 and ⁻3 represent the same number, negative three. To make notation simpler, this textbook will use the *lowered* sign to indicate a negative number. From this point on, you will see negative three written as −3.

The distance that a number is from zero on a number line is the **absolute value** of the number. You use the sumbol | | to indicate absolute value. You read |*n*| as "the absolute value of *n.*"

Example I	**Find each absolute value.**
	a. |3| b. |−4|

Solution

3 is 3 units from 0, so |3| = 3.

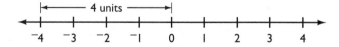

−4 is 4 units from 0, so |−4| = 4.

Check Your Understanding
1. Name another integer that has an absolute value of 3.
2. What is the absolute value of 0?

When you compare numbers, you may want to picture them on a number line. On a horizontal number line, numbers increase in order from left to right.

Example 2   **Replace each __?__ with > , <, or =.**

a. 1 __?__ −3   b. −4 __?__ −2

Solution

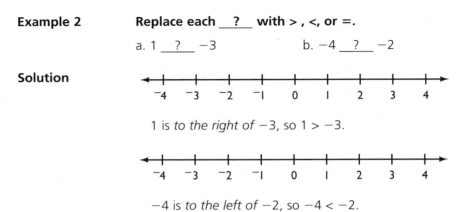

1 is *to the right of* −3, so 1 > −3.

−4 is *to the left of* −2, so −4 < −2.

Source: Francis J. Gardella, Patricia R. Fraze, Joanne E. Meldon, et al., Mathematical Connections, *p. 94. Copyright © 1992 by Houghton Mifflin Company. Reprinted by permission of Houghton Mifflin Company. All rights reserved.*

Graphs and Charts

Graphs and charts are often used to represent mathematical concepts in math materials as well as in other content textbooks, in newspapers, and in magazines. The graph in Example 10.19 appears in a mathematics textbook. The questions that follow can be used to guide students' reading of charts and graphs.

Symbols, Signs, and Formulas

Students of mathematics must learn to read and use the special symbols, signs, and formulas found in mathematics textbooks. This is illustrated in Example 10.20. First, they need to realize the importance of knowing symbols, signs, and formulas. Then they must focus on the meaning of each and learn each in relationship to its meaning and application.

■ Teaching Mathematics Content

Teachers can use vocabulary strategies to introduce the important terms and concepts in meaningful contexts. Brainstorming will help students associate mathematics terms with previous experiences. Comprehension of mathematics content is facilitated with advance organizers, structured overviews, study guides, concept guides, and directed reading lessons to focus attention on understanding while reading. Example 10.21 illustrates a mathematics reading guide based on the textbook selection in Example 10.17.

■ ■ ■ EXAMPLE 10.19   *Graphing Equations*

SECTION

7.1

Learn how to...
• **write and graph equations in standard form**

So you can...
• **solve problems with two variables, such as nutritional planning or telecommunications problems**

Using Linear Equations in Standard Form

Nancy Clark recommends that runners replace their muscles' energy stores after a marathon. A runner should eat at least 0.5 g of foods containing carbohydrates for each pound of body weight within 2 h after the race. The athlete should eat at least this amount again 2 h later.

EXAMPLE 1 **Interview: Nancy Clark**

Leon should eat at least 70 g of carbohydrates after running a marathon. One cup of apple juice contains **30 g** of carbohydrates, and 1 oz of pretzels contains **23 g**. Write and graph an equation showing combinations of pretzels and juice that provide 70 g of carbohydrates.

SOLUTION

Step 1 Write an equation.
Let j = number of cups of juice.
Let p = number of ounces of pretzels.

$$\begin{array}{ccc} \text{Carbohydrates} & + & \text{Carbohydrates} & = 70 \\ \text{from juice} & & \text{from pretzels} \end{array}$$
$$30j \quad + \quad 23p \quad = 70$$

Step 2 Graph the equation.

j	p
0	3.0
1.0	1.7
2.3	0

First make a table of values.

Then graph each point and draw a line though the points.

Combinations of Pretzels and Juice Containing 70 g of Carbohydrates

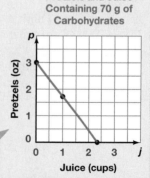

THINK AND COMMUNICATE

1. Why does the graph in Example 1 only make sense in the first quadrant?
2. How would the graph in Example 1 be different if you put cups of juice on the vertical axis?

BY THE WAY

After the Boston Marathon, runners eat snacks such as pretzels and bread supplied by their sponsors. Ten small pretzels weigh about one ounce.

■ ■ ■ EXAMPLE 10.20   *Symbols*

Graphing Inequalities on a Number Line

Nearly $\frac{1}{8}$ of the world's surface is desert and receives a yearly rainfall of less than 10 in.

The yearly amount of rainfall in deserts can be represented by an inequality.

Let *r* represent the number of inches of yearly rainfall.
The rainfall is less than 10 in.

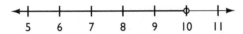

    r   <   10 ◄——⎢The < symbol indicates an inequality.⎢

You can illustrate the inequality with a graph.

   r < 10   The open circle indicates that 10 is not included.

```
  ◄——+———+———+———+———+———Φ———+——►
      5   6   7   8   9   10   11
```

The solid line represents the numbers that are
a solution to the given inequality.
(Assume numbers greater than zero in the solution.)

Some solutions are 6, 8, and 9.5.

The rainfall could have been 6 in., 8 in., or 9.5 in.

Think Aloud. Name three other possible solutions greater than zero. Include some decimal numbers.

Another example:
The amount of rainfall (*r*)
is greater than 5 in.

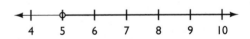

```
  ◄——+———Φ———+———+———+———+———+——►
      4   5   6   7   8   9   10
```

    r   >   5

Some solutions are 7, 5.5, and 90.5.

Think Aloud. Name three other possible solutions.

Guided Practice

Name three possible solutions greater than zero for each inequality.

1. *x* > 5   2. *w* < 32

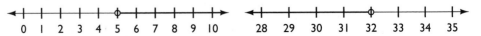

```
 ◄+—+—+—+—+—+—Φ—+—+—+—+—+►   ◄——+———+———+———+———Φ———+———+———+——►
  0 1 2 3 4 5 6 7 8 9 10        28  29  30  31  32  33  34  35
```

In Your Words. Explain the reason for your answer.

3. Is 5 included on the graph?   4. Is 3.5 included on the graph?

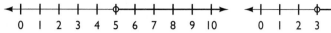

■ ■ ■ EXAMPLE 10.21   *Mathematics Reading Guide (based on Example 10.17)*

Part I: Facts of the Problem

Directions: Read the problem. Then in Column A, check the statements that contain the important facts of the problem. You may refer to the problem to verify your responses. In Column B, check the statements that will help you solve the problem.

A   *B*

_____   _____   **1.** Anderson Architects designs buildings worldwide.
_____   _____   **2.** These architects have been in business for five years.
_____   _____   **3.** They recently designed a house for construction in the United States.
_____   _____   **4.** This house can also be built in Canada.
_____   _____   **5.** The United States plans show the length of the house is 57 feet.
_____   _____   **6.** The United States plans show the width of the house is 33 feet.

Part II: Mathematical Ideas and Interpretations

Directions: Check the statements that contain mathematical concepts related to the problem. You may go back to Part I to review your responses.

_____ **1.** Canadians measure in meters.
_____ **2.** In the United States, measurement is generally stated in feet.
_____ **3.** Canadians could convert meters to feet in order to interpret the house plans.
_____ **4.** To convert feet to meters, multiply the measurements in feet by 0.3.
_____ **5.** People in the United States are using metric measurement more frequently now than 25 years ago.

Part III: Computation

Directions: Below are possible mathematical calculations. Check those that apply to this problem. You may refer to Part I and Part II to verify your responses.

_____ **1.** 57 ft + 33 ft = 90 ft
_____ **2.** 57 ft − 33 ft = 24 ft
_____ **3.** 57 ft (0.3 m per ft) = 17.1 m
_____ **4.** 33 ft (0.3 m per ft) = 9.9 m
_____ **5.** 57 ft ÷ 0.3 m per ft =

■ ■ Computer Literacy Content

What does computer literacy mean?

Computer literacy is a basic skill for today's students, and the goal for secondary teachers is to help students become intelligent users of computers. In some schools, computer literacy is a separate course; in others it is integrated with content classes because the purpose of developing computer literacy is to apply it to subject matter and problem solving. The instruction introduces concepts, and students practice with hands-on applications. The concepts introduced may include operating systems (e.g., DOS, Windows), word processing, spreadsheets, databases, management systems, systems analysis and design, software packages, and the effects of computers on society. Students need to read manuals, computing magazines, tutorial materials, and textbooks.

To become computer literate, students need to know computer terminology, how to read technical information, and how to integrate information from instructional manuals and tutorial texts with actual computer use. Using software to solve problems; to write reports, memos, and letters; to locate information in databases; and to manage accounting and budgeting applications are components of computer literacy.

The writing patterns in computer materials are much like those in science and mathematics and include the definition or explanation of a technical process pattern, the classification pattern, the cause-and-effect pattern, the problem-solution pattern, and following directions. Many graphic aids are used along with these writing patterns. Learning computer terminology and careful, precise reading of text are basic to computer literacy because overlooking the smallest detail means computer failure. The strategies introduced in science and mathematics will help students comprehend computer materials. In developing students' computer literacy, a teacher might choose to use an instructional sequence similar to the following one:

Subject: Computer Literacy
Topic: Starting and exiting word-processing software, using the mouse
Before Reading: Question students:

- "What is software?" "What kind of software is this?" (Hold up the box or documentation.) "What is the purpose of this software?" "What does *mouse* mean as it relates to computers?" Explain that students will be reading about these topics and using what they learn on a computer.
- Introduce and explain these terms: software, word processing.
- Demonstrate starting the computer and accessing the software.

During Reading: Students should be alert for the terms introduced and their context. Encourage students to look at each diagram, visualize each step, and locate the actual computer hardware that will be used.
After Reading:

- Have students summarize what they have learned.
- Then they can turn on the computers, access the word-processing software, and write a paragraph or two explaining how they could use this software. Students should use the mouse to move around in their documents.

English (Language Arts) Content

The language arts are concerned with communication, which involves listening, speaking, reading, writing, and thinking. A command of English is essential to effective communication; therefore, study of the language arts is involved primarily with effective use and appreciation of the English language. English has the most varied subject matter of all the content subjects. Study of English requires readers to work with grammar, composition, and many forms of literature—novels, short stories, poetry, biographies, and autobiographies.

Vocabulary Development

Vocabulary development is an important aspect of English instruction because students who have a large store of word meanings at their command are better communicators. Exploring changes in word meanings is one way to expand students' vocabularies.

Changes in Word Meanings

What examples can you suggest for the various types of changes in word meanings?

Studying **etymology** shows students that meanings of certain words have changed over time. For example, the word *marshal* once meant "one who held horses," not quite as impressive as its present-day meaning. Daily use of words over the years leads to gradual change in their meanings, which can be systematically analyzed as illustrated in the following list:

1. *Amelioration.* The meaning of the word has changed so that the word means something better than it once did. For example, a person who was called *enthusiastic* was once considered a fanatic. Currently, enthusiasm is considered a desirable quality.
2. *Pejoration.* Pejoration indicates that the word has a more derogatory meaning than it did earlier in its history. For example, a *villain* once was a feudal serf or a servant from a villa. Currently, a villain is considered to be a scoundrel.
3. *Generalization.* Some words become more generalized in meaning. When generalization operates, the meaning of words is broadened. Earlier in history, *picture* meant painting, but now picture may mean a print, a photograph, or a drawing. In fact, a picture may not be representational at all, because in art a picture may not have a distinct form.
4. *Specialization.* The opposite of generalization is specialization. In this case, word meanings become more specific than they were in the past. At one time, *meat* meant any food, not just lamb, pork, or beef.
5. *Euphemism.* This term indicates the use of an affectation to convey elegance, or the use of a more pleasant word for an unpleasant one. For example, a *janitor* is often called a "custodian" or "maintenance engineer," and a person does not *die* but rather "passes away."
6. *Hyperbole.* This is an extreme exaggeration. For example, a man who is tired might say that he could "sleep for a year." Exaggeration is being used to make the point of extreme fatigue. Many people currently use the word *fantastic* to describe almost anything unusual, although *fantastic* means strange, wonderful, unreal, and illusory.

Activities such as the following can be used to develop word meanings through etymology.

EXERCISES

1. Give students a list of words with instructions to determine the origin of each term and the types of changes that have occurred in its meaning. Words such as the following could be used in this activity: *city, ghetto, manuscript, lord, stench.*
2. Ask students to identify the origins of the names of the months and/or the days of the week. For example, *October* is from the Latin *Octo* (eight), be-

cause it was the eighth month of the Roman calendar. *Monday* means "day of the moon."

3. Encourage students to determine the origins and meanings of their first names and surnames. For example, *Susan* means "lily." Many surnames are related to occupation or geographic origin. The surname *Butler* means a bottle maker; the surname *Hatfield* refers to a wooded field.

Types of Words

Word knowledge can be increased by exploring some of the unique characteristics of different types of words. Activities that involve acronyms, oxymorons, and homonyms, for example, will develop students' vocabularies. Following are definitions of some special types of words:

1. *Acronyms.* Words composed of the first letters or syllables of longer terms, such as *SNAFU*, which means "situation normal, all fouled up." This is a Navy term that originated during World War II.
2. *Oxymorons.* Two incongruous words used together, such as *cruel kindness*.
3. *Homonyms*—also known as *homophones*. Words that sound alike but are not spelled alike, such as *to, too, two; pare, pair; sum, some*.
4. *Heteronyms* Words that have different pronunciations and meanings, although they are spelled exactly the same, such as:

   Don't *subject* me to that experience.
   What is the *subject* of your book?

5. *Coined words.* Words invented to meet specific needs. Words are often coined by using previously existing words and word parts. *Gerrymander, curfew, motel,* and *astronaut* are examples of coined words. Many product names are coined words, for example, *Pream, Tang, Jello,* and *Bisquick*.

Denotative and Connotative Meanings of Words

Compare a denotative word meaning with the connotative meaning of the same word.

The *denotative* and *connotative* meanings of words can be introduced through literature. **Denotation** is the literal definition of a word as defined by the dictionary. **Connotation** refers to the ideas and associations that are suggested by a term, including emotional reactions. For instance, the word *home* denotes the place where one lives, whereas it may connote warmth, love, and family. Readers must learn to recognize the connotations of words in order to comprehend a selection. By definition, *cunning* and *astute* are very similar, but when the word *cunning* is used to describe a person, it usually implies a negative quality, while describing a person as *astute* is complimentary.

Students can look for examples of both connotative and denotative uses of words in the literary selections they read. In addition, the following activities will increase understanding of denotation and connotation.

EXERCISES

1. In each pair, select the word that you would prefer to use for describing yourself. Tell why you chose the word.
   a. *creative* or *screwball*
   b. *stolid* or *easygoing*
   c. *Conceited* or *proud*
2. Provide students with a list of words similar to the preceding list and ask them to write a plus (+) beside each positive word, a minus (−) beside each negative word, and a zero (0) beside each neutral word.

Figurative language is connotative use of language. The author implies ideas through figurative language, and this expressive application of language makes written language more interesting to readers. You can refer to Chapter 3 for suggestions to aid in instruction related to figurative language.

■ Whole Language

Constructivist theories of learning posit that people learn through actively formulating their own knowledge as they read, write, and discuss (Beach, 1993). These activities enable them to truly understand. Lasting learning occurs as the result of an active process of meaning-making rather than the more passive process of filling in blanks, repeating information, or recopying information presented by the teacher (Weaver, 1990).

Do you agree that "whole language" is an important philosophy in your content area?

The **whole-language philosophy** is an application of these theories. In applying this philosophy to secondary instruction, teachers emphasize the processes of listening, speaking, reading, and writing as ways of learning (Hobson and Shuman, 1990; Johns and Palumbo, 1991). Whole-language instruction is often based on units of study that cut across curricular areas, and it provides ample opportunities for students to listen, speak, read, and write as they think critically about basic concepts and integrate the knowledge they acquire. As students formulate their own knowledge, they learn about the interdependence that exists among various bodies of knowledge (Hobson and Shuman, 1990). However, beyond these basic ideas there is little agreement about the specific applications of the whole-language philosophy.

Whole-language instruction is based on having blocks of time for reading and discussing, as well as time for teachers to read aloud to students (Frew, 1990). Blocks of instructional time permit students and teachers to integrate the language arts in ways that are impossible when scheduling is based on instruction in separate subjects. Thematic units are often used as organizational structures for integrating instruction (Sanacore, 1993). These units incorporate readings and discussion related to various subjects. Popular units for secondary students have addressed themes such as courage, freedom, and disasters, although there are no limitations beyond students' interest. Units can provide the organizational structure that guides curriculum integration, materials selection, and instructional strategies.

In Chapter 9, strategies for integrating literature in content instruction are suggested. Literature and its relationship to content literacy is explored in depth, and an example thematic unit is provided. This chapter includes examples of literature, as well as teaching ideas that illustrate the role of literature in learning.

Literature

The goal of teaching literature is to develop in readers a lifelong interest in and appreciation for literature. Having students read and respond to interesting literary selections helps teachers achieve these goals. When students read material that is related to their interests and background experience, their schemata will enable them to read with greater comprehension. Many students need guides that will help them comprehend literature, such as anticipation guides, advance organizers, and three-level study guides (Lubell and Townsend, 1989).

Novels and Short Stories

Reading novels and short stories is basic to the study of literature. A literature selection is an imaginative expression of a writer's ideas: the author shares an experience with the reader by relating incidents through a story. The longer form of the novel permits an author to develop literary elements such as characterization in greater depth than is possible within the form of the short story.

Response is concerned with the readers' reactions and feelings about reading content. Researchers have identified eight processes that are involved in a student's response to literature (Cooper and Purves, 1973). These processes are as follows:

1. *Description.* Students can restate in their own words what they have read.
2. *Discrimination.* Students can discriminate among different writings on the basis of type, author, theme, and so forth.
3. *Relation.* Students can relate to each other several aspects of a piece of literature. For example, students could discuss the relationship between a story's setting and plot or could compare the plots of two different stories.
4. *Interpretation.* Students can interpret the author's ideas and support these interpretations.

5. *Generalization.* Students can use what they have learned in one piece of literature to understand another one.
6. *Evaluation.* Students can apply criteria to evaluate a piece of literature. For example, they might evaluate the quality of the element of characterization.
7. *Valuing.* Students can relate literature to their own lives.
8. *Creation.* Students can respond to literature by creating their own art, music, writing, drama, or dance.

When teaching novels or short stories, teachers activate students' schemata. Then they have students read through the story, although the reading may extend over several class sessions. Reading the entire selection enables students to understand the entire plot, character development, setting, and theme. If the reading of a selection is broken into chapters or smaller parts, the reader may not grasp the entire selection or the way the components of the selection fit together.

In addition to using the eight processes of responding to literature to guide instruction, the teacher asks students to support answers to questions with material from the selections they have read. Students may be asked to diagram story structure in the following manner:

		Title	
Setting	*Theme*	*Plot*	*Characters*
Place	Symbols	Episode #1	Main character
Time	Incidents	Episode #2	Supporting character
		Episode #3	

Poetry

Poetry is a condensed form of writing that expresses in a succinct fashion the writer's thoughts and emotions and stimulates the reader's imagination. Frequently, a poet can inspire a reader to perceive familiar things and ideas in a new way. Poets use rhythm, rhyme, imagery, and many other devices to make a reader see or feel what they are expressing.

Teachers may use the following techniques with poetry:

1. Poems should be read aloud.
2. Poems should be read in their entirety for full appreciation of them.
3. Poems should usually be read twice for full appreciation.
4. Prose and poetry on the same topic may be compared in order to understand the succinctness of poetry.

Drama

Drama is literature that is written to be acted. In drama, the characters tell the story. Drama includes stage directions needed to understand the plot. The reader should pay attention to all information in parentheses and italics. The name of the speaker is printed before his or her lines, and the reader must be alert to the names of the speakers in order to determine who is speaking and how the action unfolds.

The following teaching procedures help students understand drama:

1. Ask the students to visualize story action.
2. Have the students read the speeches aloud to aid comprehension.
3. Have the students act out described actions to arrive at a better understanding of the action.
4. Have the students write a play and act it out as described.

Essays and Editorials

What type of writing is found in essays, editorials, and position papers?

Essays, editorials, and position papers are **expository forms** of writing. Exposition is used to explain information from a particular point of view. The author is usually trying to convince readers to accept his or her argument. Exposition contains a greater amount of information than fiction does. The strategies suggested in this chapter (and in Chapters 4, 5, and 11) for guiding the reading of content materials aid the teacher in teaching exposition. Following are activities that teachers can use to help students comprehend expository materials.

1. Identify the author's purpose.
2. Identify the author's perception of his or her audience.
3. Identify the author's argument.
4. Identify the details the author uses to support his or her argument.
5. Identify the author's organization of details.
6. Identify the details that are emphasized.
7. Identify the sequence of details.
8. Identify the author's attitude toward the topic and toward the audience (Finder, 1970).

The preceding activities can be used for discussions and study guides.

■ Grammar and Composition

Textbooks are used in many language arts classes to teach grammar and composition. They explain the grammar and punctuation of the English language, using technical vocabulary words such as *complex sentences, interrogative,* and *adjective.* These textbooks and handbooks may follow an expository pattern: a concept or idea is explained and illustrated, a definition or generalization is developed, and application exercises are provided. Many details are packed into a page, and students need to skim and scan to find the specific information they need. Frequently the material is almost in outline form, requiring readers to identify supporting details and main ideas. Some of the models and examples used in language arts textbooks are written in a narrative style, so that the reader must switch from expository to narrative style. Example 10.22 shows content from a grammar and composition text that is written in a definition or explanation pattern.

■■■ EXAMPLE 10.22   *Content from a Grammar and Composition Text*

Prepositional Phrases

A preposition is usually followed by a noun or a pronoun, which is called the **object of the preposition.** The preposition, the object, and the modifiers of that object form a *prepositional phrase.*

    prep.   obj.
There are deep cracks **in the moon's surface.** [The prepositional phrase consists of the preposition, *in,* the modifiers, *the* and *moon's,* and the object of the preposition, *surface.*]

In some sentences the preposition comes *after* the object. This arrangement often occurs in questions, as in the following example.

    obj.   prep.
Which state are you **from?** [**Think:** From which state are you?]

A prepositional phrase may have more than one object, as in the following sentence.

                        prep. obj.
The moon's surface is covered **with rocks and dust.**

Prepositional phrases usually act as modifiers. A prepositional phrase functions as an adjective if it modifies a noun or a pronoun. A prepositional phrase functions as an adverb if it modifies a verb, an adjective, or an adverb.

Used as an Adjective

                        prep. phrase
I still have to paint the other side **of the house.** [*Of the house* tells which side.]

Used as an Adverb

                        prep. phrase
Max *hit* the golf ball **into the pond.** [*Into the pond* tells where Max hit the ball.]

Source: Ann Brown, Jeffrey Milson, Fran Shaw, et al., Grammar and Composition: Second Course, *pp. 31–32. Copyright © 1986 by Houghton Mifflin Company. Reprinted by permission of Houghton Mifflin Company. All rights reserved.*

Many teachers use their text as a handbook or have students obtain handbooks to use as a reference. Students find handbooks such as the following helpful: *The Deluxe Transitive Vampire: The Ultimate Handbook of Grammar for the Innocent, the Eager, and the Doomed* (Gordon, 1993); *Checking Your Grammar* (Terban, 1993); *How to Achieve Competence in English* (Johnson, 1994).

Focusing on paraphrasing and finding applications for grammar, spelling, punctuation, and capitalization instruction help students retain the information. Advance organizers, study guides, and concept guides are especially useful for teaching the conventions of language. The Internet offers web sites for grammar, spelling, and punctuation.

■ ■ Foreign Languages

The ability to read and speak foreign languages is a valuable skill in today's world because of increased travel and communication among the people of the world. Current approaches to foreign language study include meaning-centered activities with a cultural focus that emphasizes functional language use.

Learning to read a foreign language is very similar to learning to read one's native language. The teacher exposes students to oral language to develop their readiness for learning the new language. Listening comprehension of language precedes reading comprehension; and foreign language tapes, computer programs, and foreign language broadcasts on radio and television develop listening comprehension.

Prior to reading, students need to learn about the concepts and hear the vocabulary used in the assigned selections. Discussion and practice of common phrases and expressions are useful in developing readiness to read, as is using the context to understand words and expressions. In addition, the teacher should provide questions to guide the students' silent reading.

Reading for global meaning in a foreign language is more effective than translating word by word through a page or passage. Students who have to stop several times on each line to check English equivalents are not actually reading, because they are not able to access the ideas from the written language (Carlson, 1984). Students should have opportunities to listen to, speak, read, and write the language. These activities will help them learn both the semantics and the syntax of the language. Teachers can use the same methods in teaching students to read a foreign language that they use in teaching them to read English.

Following are some specific activities useful for helping students develop comprehension of a foreign language.

EXERCISES
1. Teach students to use a foreign language dictionary.
2. Encourage students to write their own ideas in the language being studied.

3. List words in English that are derived from the language studied.
4. Ask students to describe a basketball, football, or soccer game in the language they are studying.
5. Provide students with direction cards written in English. Have them state the directions in the foreign language. For example, directions for finding the children's department in a department store could be provided.
6. The above activity can be reversed, with the directions printed in a foreign language and the students stating them in English.
7. Have students write, in a foreign language, an advertisement to sell an automobile.
8. Provide students with grocery advertisements and ask them to write the foreign word for each item in the advertisement.
9. Provide students with objects to categorize by form, function, color, or texture in the foreign language.
10. Demonstrate a "think aloud" for a foreign language reading selection, then have the students create their own think alouds for content they are reading in a foreign language.
11. Access foreign language sites on the Internet.

Summary

This chapter focuses on reading strategies for helping secondary students read content materials in social studies, science and health, mathematics, computer science, English (language arts), and foreign languages. Written materials in each of these content areas have characteristic patterns of language and organizational patterns that students can use to increase comprehension. Strategies for comprehending content materials include study guides, concept guides, and directed reading lessons.

Integration of curricula is increasing in secondary schools. In addition, electronic media, trade books, magazines, and newspapers are being used to guide students' learning.

Discussion Questions

1 How are social studies content and mathematics content alike? How are they different?
2 Why is critical reading important in social studies content?
3 How are reading and mathematics instruction changing?
4 How can teachers help students comprehend mathematics content?
5 What are the characteristics of science materials?

Enrichment Activities

1 Develop a directed reading lesson for a chapter in a social studies or science textbook.

*2 Prepare a study guide for a chapter in a social studies or science textbook. Use it with a secondary class.

*3 Prepare a study guide for a verbal problem in a mathematics textbook. Use it with a secondary class.

*4 Develop a bibliography of trade books that could be used to enrich a textbook chapter. Let secondary students use books from this list as they read the chapter.

5 Prepare a cause-and-effect chart for a topic in a content area text.

6 Check professional journals such as *Social Education, Science Teacher, Mathematics Teacher,* and *English Journal* for articles dealing with reading of content material. Share your findings with the class.

7 Check the readability level of a textbook and/or supplementary material used for one of the subjects treated in this chapter. See Chapter 13 for details.

8 Review computer software that could be used to teach one of the content subjects in this chapter.

---

*These activities are designed for in-service teachers, student teachers, or practicum students.

CHAPTER

11

Reading in the Content Areas: II

Overview

The focus of this chapter is vocational and performance-based content areas. In recent years, the lines between academic and vocational education have become increasingly blurred as educators have recognized that all students need active involvement in constructing meaning and connecting learning to the world outside of school (Christ, 1995). Further major changes are taking place in vocational education to develop students' job skills, because today's high school diploma provides access to fewer and fewer stable jobs (Stern and Rahn, 1995). Regardless of students' goals following graduation, they all need to be competent in such academic areas as communicating, computing, problem solving, group living and economic self-sufficiency, understanding relationships among groups, understanding the natural world, and maintaining wellness (Imel, 1993). These real-life competencies are essential to career success.

Accordingly, high schools, two-year colleges, and postsecondary technical institutes are providing more training for specific occupations than in the past. Each year, about half a million students participate in cooperative education or other vocational arrangements where specific learning objectives are met through part-time employment in office occupations, retailing, and other vocational fields. Vocational classes engage tens of thousands of students each year in school-based enterprises, where they build houses, run restaurants, repair cars, operate retail stores, provide print services, staff child care centers, and provide other such services (Stern and Stone et al., 1994). Our goal in this chapter is to explore strategies that will help vocational students develop the competencies they will need for life-long learning.

Purpose-Setting Questions

As you read this chapter, try to answer these questions:

1 What reading skills help students understand content information in technological education, business education, human environmental science, and agriculture?
2 What reading skills increase comprehension of content information in physical education?
3 What reading skills are required in music and art?
4 What strategies are useful for helping students comprehend the content and applications of vocational and technical materials?

■ ■ Literacy for Career-Related Education

Work-based learning plays a key role in the newer models of vocational education, with greater emphasis on basic skills and practical applications of them as well as higher-order thinking skills (Imel, 1993). Today's students will make more career changes than previous generations, due to the rapidly changing economy (Grubb, 1991; Kakela, 1993). An organized, comprehensive approach is needed to address the changes in the work force and national priorities and policies (Kerka, 1994). One strategy that addresses work force changes is the requirement of The Certificate of Initial Mastery, a document that students must earn in a growing number of states. This document shows that students have what it takes to graduate and succeed in the real world (Rothman, 1995). High school seniors in these programs are expected to work at least 60 hours on their projects.

However, the history of vocational education in this country shows that such programs also must keep the four-year college option open to students in a high school vocational curriculum; otherwise it will be difficult to attract ambitious students and to avoid acquiring a second-rate image. The 1990 Perkins Act and the 1994 School-to-Work Opportunities Act (Stern and Rahn, 1995) supported new educational options for vocational students.

Unlike cooperative education or school-based enterprises tied to vocational classes, the new programs also relate students' work experience to nonvocational subjects, including math, English, science, and social studies (Stern and Rahn, 1995). In many instances, career-related education ensures that students satisfy the course requirements for admission to four-year colleges and universities. For example, a high school curriculum that deals with health careers can provide a start for students who aspire to become doctors, nurses, or medical researchers while simultaneously preparing students who may want to enter a period of full-time employment immediately after high school as nursing assistants or physical therapy assistants. Students who are involved in such programs need a broad array of literacy strategies.

Real-world problems do not fit neatly within the bounds of any one subject area. Therefore, work-based learning is most beneficial when connected to an interdisciplinary curriciulum in which academic and occupational content are combined. For example, teachers in academic courses can integrate the health care theme into their lessons. The math teacher in one program encourages such projects as analyzing forces and angles in physical therapy, designing a building to house a health clinic, and determining how much money a medical assistant must save in five years to pay for full-time college attendance.

Describe interdisci-plinary curriculum as it relates to work-based instruction.

Although such thematic integration into content classes does not require any change in a high school schedule, some schools choose an **interdisciplinary approach** that involves teachers working in pairs. For example, the biology teacher and the health technology teacher could team to combine a study of the physiology of the heart with training in cardiopulmonary resuscitation. Of course, such an approach requires significant curriculum restructuring (Stern and Rahn, 1995). Students in work-based learning need literacy strategies like those presented throughout this text.

Literacy in vocational and technical education requires extensive use of expository and descriptive prose. Students must read textbooks, reference books, and sets of complex instructions. In most required reading, students need to study carefully and learn the information presented in the text, graphics, and text/graphic formats similar to those found at the job sites. An essential part of work-based learning is reflection. In career-related education, students reflect as they write about what they have seen and done in the workplace, and they discuss their writing in class. This process allows them to see how the problems they have confronted at work may relate to the subjects they have studied in school (Stern and Rahn, 1995). Students also need writing skills to report observations and data collected, to fill in job cards, and to complete projects.

Literacy is an integral part of technical and managerial jobs. People in these positions read to analyze problems, propose solutions, and carry out research. Managers and supervisors read to review, advise, assign, and develop organizational procedures and policies. They write materials such as letters, memos, policies, and training materials. Managers may have to create training programs when new equipment, such as a new type of cash register or a new version of accounting software, is installed. Business applications of software must often be updated and business files of customers, clients, and patients have to be systematically examined to ensure that they are current.

Aspects of Vocational Literacy

Since the amount of written material used in vocational subjects appears to be less than that required in other subjects, students and teachers may misjudge the difficulty of these materials. Many vocational materials are written in a concise expository style with technical vocabulary and are dense with information. Even brief vocational reading selections demand precise, careful reading. Students must be able to follow directions and to apply ideas and words to actual situations; thus, misreading could be costly.

Technical and Specialized Terminology

Each vocational subject includes a great deal of specialized vocabulary that represents essential concepts. For example, the word *credit* has a special meaning in bookkeeping, where it refers to a bookkeeping entry that shows money paid on an account. ("You should place this entry on the *credit* side of the ledger.") In vocational subjects, technical terms usually represent concrete concepts. For example, in human environmental science, *sauté* represents a particular way of cooking food that can be demonstrated.

The precise meaning of a technical word usually cannot be derived from context clues or dictionary definition. Technical material often does not provide the necessary clues to help a reader define a term, and many dictionaries do not include vocational terms. Therefore, vocabulary instruction is especially important in vocational subjects, and teachers need to develop word meanings as they teach these subjects. Teaching vocational and performance terminology means pointing out and defining new terms before assigning reading materials. Instructors can demonstrate the concrete meanings of many technical terms by showing students the objects or activities the words represent. Students can develop a dictionary of technical terms by entering vocabulary in a notebook. This activity will help them learn word meanings and spellings. Pictures or drawings can be added to the terms to vary this activity. The teacher should give the students quizzes on these words every other week to check vocabulary development. Additional suggestions for developing word meanings are presented in Chapter 3.

Following Directions

Every technical and vocational subject requires the student to read directions and translate them into action. For example, students of technological education must read directions for operating and repairing various pieces of equipment. In business education, students read directions for operating business machines and for setting up bookkeeping systems. Reading directions is a slow, precise process. Students often need to reread and apply strategies such as SQ3R to achieve complete understanding. They will find the following questions useful for building comprehension:

1. What am I trying to do? (What is the task?)
2. What materials are required?
3. Do I understand all of the terms (words) used in these directions?
4. What is the sequence of steps?
5. Have I omitted anything?
6. Am I ready to perform the task?
7. Was I successful in accomplishing the task?

These questions can be incorporated into study guides. Additional suggestions for developing study guides are included later in this chapter and in Chapters 5 and 10. Suggestions for following directions are also found in Chapter 7. Example 11.1 is a set of directions from a human environmental science textbook. The reader could apply the preceding questions to this example.

■ ■ ■ EXAMPLE 11.1   *Directions from Human Environmental Science*

Spiced Apple Muffins (makes 6)

⅔ c flour
3 tbsp sugar
1½ tsp baking powder
⅛ tsp salt
⅛ tsp cinnamon
⅓ c milk
1 tbsp beaten egg
1½ tsp butter or margarine, melted
⅓ c raw apples, finely chopped

1. Grease a 6-muffin pan.
2. Mix together flour, sugar, baking powder, salt, and cinnamon.
3. In a separate bowl, combine the milk, egg, and melted butter or margarine.
4. Add the dry ingredients to the liquid ingredients and mix. (Batter will be lumpy.)
5. Fold in apples.
6. Fill muffin pans two-thirds full.

Topping:

2 tsp sugar
⅛ tsp cinnamon

1. Preheat oven to 425°F.
2. Combine sugar and cinnamon.
3. Sprinkle mixture over top of unbaked muffins.
4. Bake 20 minutes or until toothpick inserted in middle comes out clean.
5. Remove from pan and cool on a cooling rack.

Source: Reprinted from Teen Guide *by Valarie Chamberlain, with permission of Glencoe/ McGraw-Hill, A Macmillan Company. Mission Hills, California, Copyright © 1990, p. 445.*

■ Technology

What computer applications can you add to those suggested here?

There are many important **computer applications** in vocational and perform- ance-based fields, including ones for securing up-to-date information and solv- ing problems. For example, in performance-based fields, students of dance can choreograph on computers; art students can explore art on the Internet, as well as create art on a computer; and musicians can compose on computers.

Likewise, computers are used in vocational fields, for example, to diagnose automotive problems or provide support in the business arena. Applications of computers, fax machines, conference calls, and the Internet are nearly univer- sal today.

■ Graphic Materials

What types of graphic materials do vocational and technical students have to read?

Vocational and technical students have to read a variety of **graphic materials,** such as blueprints, drawings, cutaways, patterns, pictures, and sketches. They must be able to visualize and interpret the scales and legends that accompany many graphic materials in order to understand both the illustrations and the textual materials.

Teachers should give students many opportunities to convert written direc- tions, drawings, and blueprints into models and actual objects. Students must coordinate the text with any illustrations (e.g., match blueprints and diagrams with pictures of the finished products). These activities help students develop the ability to visualize written ideas. Having students prepare directions, dia- grams, and blueprints for classmates to follow will help them to become more adept at understanding these written materials themselves.

Example 11.2 shows a diagram from a human environmental science text, and Example 11.3 shows graphic material from a physical education text.

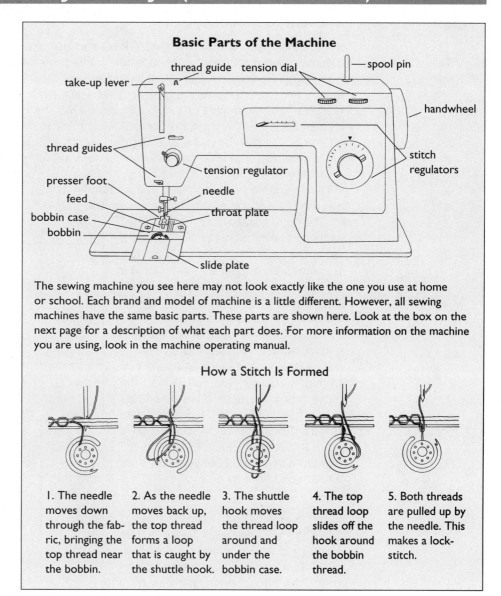

Basic Parts of the Machine

The sewing machine you see here may not look exactly like the one you use at home or school. Each brand and model of machine is a little different. However, all sewing machines have the same basic parts. These parts are shown here. Look at the box on the next page for a description of what each part does. For more information on the machine you are using, look in the machine operating manual.

How a Stitch Is Formed

I. The needle moves down through the fabric, bringing the top thread near the bobbin.

2. As the needle moves back up, the top thread forms a loop that is caught by the shuttle hook.

3. The shuttle hook moves the thread loop around and under the bobbin case.

4. The top thread loop slides off the hook around the bobbin thread.

5. Both threads are pulled up by the needle. This makes a lock-stitch.

Source: Reprinted from Teen Guide *by Valarie Chamberlain, with permission of Glencoe/ McGraw-Hill, A Macmillan Company. Mission Hills, California, Copyright © 1990, p. 335.*

The Game of Volleyball

In 1895 William C. Morgan, a YMCA director in Holyoke, Massachusetts, invented a game called *mintonette* in an attempt to meet the needs of local businessmen who found the game of basketball to be too strenuous. The new game caught on quickly because it required only a few basic skills, easily mastered in limited practice time and by players of varying fitness levels. The original game was played with a rubber bladder from a basketball. Early rules allowed any number of players on a side. In 1896 the name was changed by Alfred T. Halstead, who, after viewing a game, felt that *volleyball* would be a more suitable name due to the volleying characteristic of play.

As the game has progressed, many changes in play have occurred. For example, the Filipinos are credited with adding the spike.

The game's status has changed from its being a recreational activity to being recognized as a strenuous sport as well. The Japanese added the sport to the Olympic Games program in 1964; this contributed to the fast growth of volleyball in the last 25 years.

The exciting aspect of volleyball is that it attracts all types of players—recreational to competitive, little skilled to highly skilled—and all ages. The game has great appeal because it requires few basic skills, few rules, few players (from two to six players on a side), and limited equipment, and it can be played on a variety of surfaces, from a hardwood floor to a sandy beach.

Playing a Game

The game of volleyball is played by two teams each having two to six players on a 30-foot square (9-meter square) court, the two courts separated by a net. The primary objective of each team is to try to hit the ball to the opponent's side in such a manner as to prevent the opponent from returning the ball. This is usually accomplished by using a three-hit combination of a forearm pass

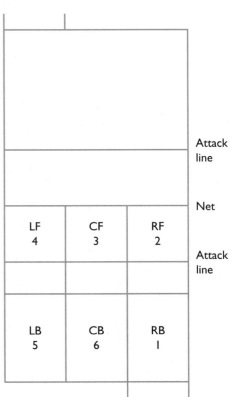

FIGURE A

Players arranged in proper rotational positions.

to a setter, followed by a set to an attacker, who spikes the ball into the opponent's court.

When there are six players on a side, three are called *forwards,* and three are called *backs.* The three players in the front row are called *left forward* (LF), *center forward* (CF), and *right forward* (RF). The three players in the back row are called *left back* (LB), *center back* (CB), and *right back* (RB). Players need to be in their correct *rotational positions* until the serve is executed. This means that players cannot overlap positions from front to back or from side to side (see Figure A). After the serve, players are allowed to play in any position on or off the court, with one restriction: back row players cannot leave the floor to hit the ball when in front of the attack line.

Source: Barbara L. Viera and Bonnie Jill Ferguson, Volleyball Steps to Success, *p. 1. Champaign, IL: Leisure Press. Copyright © 1989 by Leisure Press. Reprinted by permission of Human Kinetics Publishers.*

◼ Reading Rate

Why do vocational students have to make many rate adjustments when reading?

Readers of vocational and technical materials must adjust their **reading rates** according to purpose, type of content, and familiarity with the subject. Vocational materials are often problem oriented and include many directions that require students to adjust their reading rates to accomodate variations in reading content. In vocational studies, students read a wide variety of materials that require frequent rate adjustments. Teachers can facilitate rate adjustment by having students identify appropriate rates for each type of content.

◼ Problem Solving

In vocational and performance-based subjects, the goals are to increase the students' ability to think on the job and to perform job-related tasks. Meeting these goals is facilitated when students bring real-life problems to class discussion and to reading. Students who have opportunities for work-based learning have an advantage because they can contribute actual experiences and problems to class discussions and problem solving.

What is an example of problem-solving materials that could be used in vocational classes?

A **problem-solving approach** and student questions create a mental context for reading and thinking. The following problems were selected from problems posed by or for students in various content areas:

1. List the financial records and documents necessary for a businessperson who operates one of the following: a restaurant, a computer repair shop, an electronic sales company. The problem could be designated as a small business

with under ten employees or a larger business with the number of employees specified.

2. Detail the materials and equipment needed to take a corn crop from planting to harvest.
3. List the tools you need to build a chair.
4. Identify the materials needed to build a specific item or machine.
5. Prepare menus for nutritionally balanced meals for a week for a family of three based on a specified budget.
6. Set up an office mailing system for a company.

The problem-solution writing pattern is common in vocational materials. These materials also include presentations of factual information and how-to-do-it directions. Reading instruction should focus on these types of content materials.

Writing

Writing is an asset in retaining and understanding content materials (Gahn, 1989). Writing helps students clarify personal understandings of text (Shugarman and Hurst, 1986). Through writing activities, students expand their understanding of technical and vocational language and their ability to express ideas effectively. Writing activities also develop students' knowledge of technical vocabulary, sentence structure, paragraph organization, and sequencing. However, vocational and technical teachers need to model writing, provide guided practice, and give students feedback to guide their applications of writing in vocational subjects (Gahn, 1989). In Chapter 8, suggestions for content area writing activities are given.

Utilizing Motivation

Motivating students is a responsibility of vocational and technical education teachers. Because some students are personally motivated to learn about these subjects, their interest can stimulate them to read. Students frequently are able to read materials with higher readability levels than usual because of their interest in the reading content (Diehl and Mikulecky, 1980). The classroom library should include trade periodicals and Internet access, which provide information about new products, materials, and techniques. Periodicals also include general information about the various trades and careers. A recent issue of *Career World* discussed agribusiness, political careers, chefs, and physicians, as well as career guidance and interviewing strategies. Teachers can use these materials to develop their students' reading interests and understanding of the content area, thereby increasing students' ability to predict content and, conse-

What would you choose as the most important motivational strategy suggested?

quently, to comprehend content materials. Following are some suggestions for using **motivational strategies** to increase comprehension of content materials:

1. Display subject area books, magazines, and related materials appropriate to student interest and reading levels.
2. Suggest additional readings in magazines, newspapers, periodicals, books, and Internet sites.
3. Review and refer to relevant books.
4. Use learning activities such as field trips, movies, records, computer programs, and radio and television programs to build background and to stimulate a desire for further information.
5. Provide time in class for reading materials related to class topics.
6. To develop interest and critical reading ability, compare and contrast the way two or more authors have treated a topic.
7. Encourage students to discuss their readings with each other in pairs or cooperative learning groups.
8. Permit students to work together so that good readers can help less able ones.

■ The Textbook as a Reference

Teachers should make a particular effort to explain and demonstrate the use of textbooks and real-life printed materials as reference works, since vocational teachers use a wide variety of materials in a problem-solving format and students often are not acquainted with this approach. Instruction that familiarizes the students with the wealth of information provided in printed materials will help them to use these materials for acquiring knowledge and solving problems.

■ Reading Strategies

How does reading-to-learn contrast with reading-to-do?

Teachers need to prepare students to read vocational materials prior to reading, support them during reading, and follow up after the reading. Reading-to-learn and reading-to-do are both kinds of reading that vocational and technical students are often required to do. Sticht (1978) discussed these two categories of reading tasks. **Reading-to-learn** is a reading task in which an individual reads with the intention of remembering and applying textual information. **Reading-to-do** is a reading task in which an individual uses the material as an aid to doing something else. In the latter situation, the materials often serve as "external memories," because the individual may refer to them to check information rather than to specifically learn the content. Sticht found that most on-the-job reading is a type of reading-to-do, which may demand the following reading strategies:

1. *Read/rehearse,* which involves repeating the information or reading it again.
2. *Problem solve/question,* which involves answering questions posed by the text and/or searching for the information necessary to solve a specific problem.
3. *Relate/associate,* which is associating new information with the individual's existing store of information.
4. *Focus attention,* which involves reducing the amount of information in some way, such as by underlining, outlining, or taking notes.

Why do you think directed reading lessons help vocational students comprehend?

Directed reading lessons are also useful in helping vocational students learn to read textual materials. Following is an example of a directed reading lesson based on human environmental science content (Example 11.4).

■ ■ ■ EXAMPLE 11.4   *Directed Reading Lesson (Human Environmental Science)*

MOTIVATION AND BUILDING BACKGROUND

1. Ask students the following questions: What kind of fabric is used in the clothing you are wearing today? What is your favorite kind of fabric? Here is a box of various types of fabric. Look at each piece and try to determine the contents of each piece of fabric.

SKILL DEVELOPMENT ACTIVITIES

2. Discuss and pronounce each of the following vocabulary words. Be certain students have a concept for each type of fabric by giving them labeled samples of each to examine.

wool   brocade
synthetic fabric   lamé
satin   velvet
cotton

GUIDED READING

3. *Silent*—Provide students with *silent reading purposes* such as the following: How do you choose a suitable fabric to make a dress? How are synthetic fabrics different from natural fabrics? Have the students *read the lesson silently.*
4. *Discussion*—Discuss the silent reading purposes and ask discussion questions such as the following: Do you prefer natural or synthetic fabrics? Why? What are the advantages of natural fabrics? What kind of dress pattern would you choose for a brocade fabric?

FOLLOW-UP ACTIVITIES

5. Have students reread as necessary to solve the problem of selecting an appropriate fabric for their next garment.

After students read a chapter and complete a study guide similar to the one in Example 11.6, which is based on vocational materials shown in Example 11.5, they should have an opportunity to discuss their answers and should be prepared to explain and support them by citing the text.

■ ■ ■ EXAMPLE 11.5   *Sample Writing in Vocational Materials*

Painting and Enameling

Paint and enamel are protective and decorative coatings for the less expensive woods for which a transparent finish may not be desirable. Either paint or enamel can be used satisfactorily as a colorful finish on furniture and cabinets.

Paint is generally applied to exterior surfaces or to projects which are used out of doors. Enamel is suitable for interior trim and for projects used in the home. It comes in a gloss, a semigloss, or a dull (flat) finish. Enamel usually produces a harder finish than paint because varnish is an ingredient in enamel.

Both paint and enamel are available in many colors. Both can also be bought either in white or tinted with colors ground in oil. Each of the many paints and enamels has its own recommended thinner. Read the instructions on the container for the method of thinning and for the manufacturer's suggestions for applying.

Mixing and Applying Paint or Enamel

1. Prepare the surfaces for painting or enameling. They should be properly planed, scraped, and sanded.

2. Read the directions on the container before opening it. Each manufacturer of paint and enamel recommends how it should be mixed and applied. The container also specifies the drying time required.

3. If the directions call for a primer coat, apply it first.

4. Shake the can thoroughly. Remove the lid, and pour off some of the top liquid into another container.

5. Stir the base mixture with a paddle. Add the top liquid to the base mixture a little at a time, and stir them until they are thoroughly blended.

6. Add turpentine, linseed oil, or the thinner recommended on the can, if needed.

7. Select a suitable high-quality brush.

8. Dip the brush into the paint so that about three-fourths of the length of the bristles absorbs paint. Wipe the surplus paint or enamel on the edge of the can as you remove the brush.

9. Apply the paint or enamel to the surface with long, even strokes. A little practice helps to determine the proper amount to apply. It should cover the surface smoothly and evenly. Do not allow it to run.

10. Allow the coat to dry thoroughly according to the time given in the directions. Sand smooth with a fine sandpaper. Wipe the surface with a clean cloth.

11. Apply a second and a third coat if needed. Do not sand the final coat, because it will dull the finish.

Source: Chris H. Groneman, General Woodworking, *5th ed. (New York: McGraw-Hill, 1976), pp. 247–248. Reproduced by permission of Glencoe/McGraw-Hill Educational Division.*

■ ■ ■ EXAMPLE 11.6   *Study Guide for Selection on Painting and Enameling*

Introduction

This selection discusses the value of paint and enamel as finishing materials. Directions are given for preparing a surface for paint or enamel and applying that finish.

Vocabulary

Give examples for each of the following terms: paint, enamel, transparent, gloss, semi-gloss, dull, flat, tinted, sandpaper.

Comprehension

Directions: Put the following steps for painting in the correct sequence by numbering them. Refer to the text.

LITERAL

■ Apply a primer coat first, if needed.
■ Dip three-fourths of the length of the bristles into the paint. Wipe the surplus on the edge of the can.
■ Prepare the surface by planing, scraping, and sanding.
■ Read the directions on the container. Note drying time.
■ Apply the paint or enamel with long, even strokes.
■ Stir the paint or enamel.
■ Shake the can.
■ Apply a second and a third coat if needed.
■ Allow to dry thoroughly, sand smooth with sandpaper, and wipe clean.

Directions: Write a short answer to each of the following questions:

INTERPRETIVE

1. Does varnish provide a hard finish? How do you know this?
2. Which coating—exterior paint or enamel—is probably more waterproof? Why?
3. What would happen if you did not shake the can of paint or enamel thoroughly?
4. Why does the author recommend a high-quality brush?
5. What might happen to a cabinet if you gave it only one coat of paint?

APPLIED

6. Give an example of an item that you would finish with enamel rather than paint. Why did you choose enamel for this item?
7. Give two examples of substances that could be used for thinning paint. What is the best way to choose the right thinner?
8. Can you mix paint and enamel? Why or why not?

Applications of Literacy Strategies

The sections that follow discuss how specific literacy skills and strategies can be applied to particular subject areas. However, the skills and strategies that are demonstrated can be used interchangeably in the various subject areas. In addition, the activities included in Chapter 10 can be used with the content areas discussed in this chapter.

Technology Education

Technology content includes materials written about machine operation, woodworking, auto mechanics, drafting, and electronics repair. Obviously, these areas have large technical vocabularies that students must understand. Example 11.7 shows a selection from a general woodworking text.

EXAMPLE 11.7   *Technology Education Content*

Recognizing Good Design

Recognizing the factors that constitute good design helps create a well-designed product. When you go to a store to buy furniture, you look for certain characteristics.

One of the first is *pleasing appearance*. Does the piece of furniture have a graceful or pleasing shape? Is the color suitable? Will it fit well with other furniture in the room? These are some of the questions that will help in determining whether or not the customer thinks the product being considered for purchase has a pleasing appearance.

You consider *function* when you decide whether the product or object fulfills the role for which it was originally planned and designed. If the design problem calls for a bookcase to hold 50 books, and there is room for only 30, the product will not do the job for which it was intended and is therefore not useful.

High-quality craftsmanship is essential to good design. No one wants to buy a piece of poorly constructed furniture. Tight joints, smooth finish, and precise cutting and fitting of parts are a few of the important considerations in selecting a well-designed and well-constructed product.

Source: Chris H. Groneman, General Woodworking, *5th ed. (New York: McGraw-Hill, 1976), p. 22. Reproduced by permission of Glencoe/McGraw-Hill Educational Division.*

Readers must understand the following essential words in order to understand the preceding selection: *joints, function, appearance, craftsmanship, finish, shape, surface decorations.*

Many of the technical terms that are used in technology education classes are related to tools and equipment. Demonstrating and labeling tools and equipment clearly in the classroom can help students learn to recognize these terms when they appear in textbooks.

Many reading tasks in technology education involve the students' ability to read and implement directions. For example, students must know how to follow step-by-step directions for operating equipment, constructing furniture, or installing a carburetor. They must learn to follow the directions on "job sheets," used in technology education classes to assign daily work. Safety rules also are important reading content for technology education. Teachers should prepare study guides to help students comprehend and carry out complicated written instructions.

Business Education

Business education encompasses a wide variety of studies, including shorthand, typing, bookkeeping, computer courses, general business, business mathematics, business law, management, economics, and business communications. Each of the courses in business education has considerable written content. According to Heinemann (1979, p. 239), "Courses in business have traditionally relied heavily on reading as an important part of instruction." Many people in business face an increasing volume of transactions and the accompanying paperwork due to the heavy use of computers and facsimile machines. Nevertheless, businesspeople, like those in other occupations, underestimate the reading demands of their occupations.

Many of the written materials used in business and industry are complex and have a high readability level (Razek, Hosch, and Pearl, 1982). These materials are often filled with specialized concepts and loaded with information (Stoodt, 1985). However, business education textbooks probably do not reflect the diversity apparent in business reading materials. Generally, these textbooks fall into two categories: how-to-do-it manuals and informational books. Students must acquire the reading skills, not only to read the textbooks that are often the basis of classroom instruction, but also to read the other business materials that will be important to their careers.

Business education students and people who work in business commonly apply literacy skills such as the following:

1. Reading directions/instructions and implementing them. Workers who have to stop others to ask for instructions or who complete tasks incorrectly slow down others and themselves.
2. Skimming and/or scanning to locate needed information. These skills may be used to locate materials needed in problem solving and report writing.
3. Reading and identifying main ideas and details in newspapers, magazines, and professional journals to learn about current trends in the business world.
4. Reading memos. Memos are organized differently from other types of written communication, and they often inform employees of changes in existing practices or policies in a business situation; therefore, the receiver must read these communications and remember the details.
5. Reading and responding to business letters. Business letters are organized differently, use more technical vocabulary, and use different semantics from social correspondence. Thus they require different reading skills.
6. Reading invoices to check their accuracy.
7. Reading computer printouts to locate needed information. These printouts may be used for problem solving or as a basis for planning programs to meet specific needs.
8. Reading reference materials such as interest tables, financial handbooks, and handbooks of business mathematics. Students must interpret and apply this information.
9. Reading and interpreting textbooks in order to complete class assignments that enable students to learn business skills.
10. Reading technical vocabulary. Researchers have identified both general and specific vocabulary lists for secretaries, account clerks, and others (Rush, Moe, and Storlie, 1986).

Example 11.8 contains a selection from a business education textbook. Note the technical terminology, including *real estate, personal property tax, assessor, assessment, revenues,* and *tax base.* The preview guide, shown in Example 11.9, should be completed by students before they read the selection; it helps readers anticipate the selection content, thus increasing comprehension. After students have completed the preview guide and read the chapter, they should have an opportunity to discuss, ask questions, and support their answers.

■■■ EXAMPLE 11.8   *Business Education Content*

Property Tax

Local governments get a major share of their revenues from property taxes. This includes counties, cities, towns, townships, and school districts. About one-third of all revenues at this level comes from property tax. The state and federal governments have almost no revenue from this tax.

A **real estate property tax** is one on the value of land, and anything on the land such as houses, barns, garages, or other buildings. A second tax is the **personal property tax,** a tax applied to movable items such as automobiles, furniture, and machinery used by businesses. Because of the ease with which personal property can be hidden, the personal property tax is being used less and less. Real estate has thus become the most important property tax base and source of revenue for local communities.

The amount of real estate taxes is determined by first estimating the value of the property, and then multiplying the tax rate by the value. The amount at which the property is valued is called an **assessment,** and the government official who does the valuation is called an **assessor.**

Source: Betty Brown and John Clow, General Business: Our Business and Economic World, *p. 231. Copyright © 1982 by Houghton Mifflin Company. Reprinted by permission of Houghton Mifflin Company.*

■■■ EXAMPLE 11.9   *Preview Guide*

Directions: Place a check mark under the Yes column if you believe the selection will support the statement. Place a check under the No column if you believe the text will not support the statement. After you read the selection, review your responses.

Yes	*No*	
_____	_____	**1.** Property tax is levied on real estate and personal property.
_____	_____	**2.** Property tax is not levied on any personal property that can be bought and sold.
_____	_____	**3.** Personal property tax is applied to movable items.

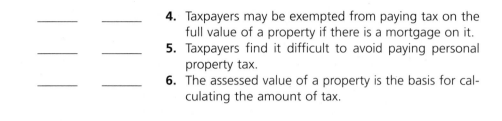

_____ _____ 4. Taxpayers may be exempted from paying tax on the full value of a property if there is a mortgage on it.

_____ _____ 5. Taxpayers find it difficult to avoid paying personal property tax.

_____ _____ 6. The assessed value of a property is the basis for calculating the amount of tax.

What is an example of a way that business students combine skimming or scanning with close reading?

Business students need to combine skimming and scanning with close reading after they locate the text they need to examine carefully. First, they should **skim** for the main idea or **scan** for specific information they need to solve a problem, to compose a letter or memo, or to write a report. Then they should carefully and accurately read **(close reading)** the section or sections of content containing the information they need. Close reading for details and main ideas is important because in many situations even a small error can have serious consequences. For example, a bookkeeping error can make a company appear profitable when it is actually losing money; a secretary's error in typing and proofreading a business letter can change the entire meaning of an important communication or a contract; and a tiny error in a computer program may result in a program that will not run, or accidental erasure of the data or program.

Chapters 3, 4, and 5 include suggestions for teaching students how to read for meaning. Teaching strategies such as preview guides, study guides, and directed reading lessons can help business education students refine vital comprehension skills. Each of these strategies can be applied to a specific area of business education.

A Reading Strategy for Business Education Materials

Explain the PRC strategy in your own words.

Students who must read the many kinds of materials identified earlier in this section can improve their reading comprehension by using a strategy like **PRC** (Stoodt, 1985). Its three phases are *prereading, reading,* and *consolidation.*

Prereading. The prereading phase of the business reading process is the limbering up part. The readers survey the reading material to identify the type of content (e.g., memo, letter, report, text) and to set the stage for remembering it. During this phase, the readers identify topics around which they can cluster the ideas that are in the selection. They also identify the author's organization; knowing how the material is organized will help them pinpoint the main ideas when reading. During the prereading phase, the readers establish questions that will guide their reading, such as the sample questions that follow:

1. What does this selection tell me?
2. What is the main point?

3. What are the important details?
4. What questions will I be asked about this reading?

Reading.   The students read carefully if close reading is necessary or scan if that is adequate. If they are reading to gather data to write an important report, close reading is in order. However, if the students are reading to locate specific pieces of information and those details are all that is needed from the content, then scanning is appropriate.

Consolidation.   During this phase, readers consolidate the information acquired from reading. Processing the information helps them organize it for long-term memory and for implementing the ideas presented when that is necessary. Readers may take notes to aid remembering and should ask themselves questions similar to the following:

1. What is it that I don't understand?
2. How does this information relate to what I already know?
3. What other examples can I think of?
4. How does this information change or alter what I already know?
5. How can I implement this information?

Business education teachers need to link their classroom activities to real-world requirements. The Meeting the Challenge vignette below shows how one teacher did this. The guide that Ms. Carruthers developed was effective in helping the students link new information from the class to real-life needs.

MEETING THE CHALLENGE

Lori Carruthers teaches business education courses in a large high school. Many of her students are employed in after-school and weekend jobs while enrolled in her classes. Although these students have opportunities to apply what they are learning in class, Lori has found that they do not relate their jobs to textbook assignments. When she asks questions in class discussion that should lead them to reflect on these relationships, the students look blank.

She decided to develop an application/reading guide that would lead them to apply the text to their experiences. The following study guide is the first one she developed.

Teachers can help students apply text materials to experiences. (© Billy E. Barnes / STOCK BOSTON)

Application Guide

1. How are the accounts receivable in your place of business similar to those described in this chapter? How are they different?
2. Does every business have to have financial records? Why or why not?
3. Does the business where you work have financial records? What kinds of records are kept?
4. Does the business where you are employed have computerized financial records? What are the advantages of computerized financial records? What are the disadvantages of computerized records?
5. What source documents are used for the financial records in your place of employment? How are the source documents similar to those discussed in this chapter?
6. How will understanding the process of recording charge sales, payments, and returns help you in other jobs that you might have in the future?

■ Human Environmental Science (Home Economics)

Why is human environmental science considered a multidisciplinary field?

Human environmental science is a **multidisciplinary field** that emphasizes a synthesis of knowledge in the social and behavioral sciences. This content area focuses on child and family behavior, technological innovations, health, foods and nutrition, clothing and textiles, design, management, housing, home furnishings, and personal growth and development. Secondary students pursue these studies for both vocational and avocational purposes.

These students find that literacy plays an important role in studying the complex materials used in human environmental science. Effective teaching strategies include guided reading lessons, study guides, and preview guides. Students have, in fact, requested that teachers provide them with such assistance. Students learn best from their reading when teachers guide them as they read a passage.

Human environmental science content includes many technical terms, for example, *developmental stages, teachable moment, top sirloin, kinship networks,* and *French seam.* Example 11.10 presents a selection from a textbook in this area. Notice that the reader must understand the following terms: *warm colors, cool colors, tertiary colors, primary, secondary, analogous,* and *complementary.* The study guide in Example 11.11 that follows the selection will help students check their understanding of these terms and of the content.

■ ■ ■ EXAMPLE 11.10   *Human Environmental Science*

Whether or not you like a garment depends very much on its color, texture, pattern, and lines. These factors are called design elements. The way that these elements work together in any one garment has much to do with how that garment looks on you. The way a garment looks on you has a great deal to do with how much you want to wear it.

A Splash of Color

Color is important to how you feel. Some colors make us happy; others tend to put us in a sad mood. Color in clothing is also important to how you look. It can make you look larger or smaller, healthy or unhealthy, or even happy or unhappy. Color can change the look of your skin. It can also change the look of other colors you wear. Try putting blue next to red. Both colors will look slightly different from the way they look alone. Now put the blue next to your face; then, the red. You may see a difference in how you look with each color.

How Colors Are Classified

Understanding how color is classified, or put into categories, makes it easier to choose what colors go together and look good on you.

Colors, themselves, are sorted into three basic groups: primary, secondary, and tertiary. Other terms having to do with light and heat are also associated with colors.

Primary Colors.   The place to start in sorting out colors is with primary colors. There are three **primary colors:** red, yellow, and blue. All the other colors are made by combining these three colors. Look at the color wheel on page 297, and use it to find the colors discussed in this section.

Secondary Colors.   The colors orange, green, and violet are **secondary colors.** They are made by combining equal amounts of primary colors. Red and yellow, for example, make orange. Blue and red make violet. Yellow and blue make green.

Tertiary Colors.   The next group is called the **tertiary colors.** This group of six colors is made by combining secondary colors with primary colors. For example, blue, a primary color, combined with green, a secondary color, makes blue-green. Look on the color wheel to see the other tertiary colors. In the name of a tertiary color, the primary color is always used first.

Other Colors and Terms

The color wheel on page 297 has 12 colors in it. As you can see by just looking around you, there are many more colors than the 12 you see in the wheel. Where do other colors come from? These other colors come from adding black or white to the primary, secondary, and tertiary colors. A color that white has been added to is called a **tint.** A color that black has been added to is called a **shade.** Navy, for example, is a shade of blue, and pink is a tint of red. Shades and tints are also referred to as color values. A color that has a dark value is a shade, or a color to which black has been added. A color that has a light value is a tint, or a color to which white has been added.

Color is also defined in terms of intensity. **Intensity** refers to the brightness or dullness of a color. For example, rust, dark brown, and tan are dull colors, while light blue and pale peach are considered bright colors.

The last way colors are described is in terms of warmth or coolness. Colors that have red and yellow in them are referred to as warm colors. Colors that have blue in them are considered cool colors. Aqua, which contains blue, is a cool color, and gold, which contains red and yellow, is a warm color. Blue is the color of sky and water. Yellow and red are the colors of the sun. These facts help to explain why these colors are considered warm or cool.

We also think of colors as being complementary to each other. **Complementary colors** are those opposite each other on the color wheel. Red and green are complementary colors as are yellow-orange and blue-violet. A pair of complementary colors is always made up of one warm color and one cool color. This contrast creates excitement.

Source: Reprinted from Teen Guide *by Valarie M. Chamberlain, with permission of Glencoe/McGraw-Hill. A Macmillan/McGraw-Hill Company. Mission Hills, California, Copyright © 1990, pp. 294–295.*

■ ■ ■ EXAMPLE 11.11   *Study Guide for Selection on Colors*

Introduction

This selection discusses color, color classifications, and the relationships among colors. The classifications include primary colors, secondary colors, and tertiary colors. Some of the relationships consist of shades and tints of colors, intensity, and complementary relationships.

Vocabulary

Find an example for each of the following terms:

primary colors   shades
secondary colors   tint
tertiary colors

Comprehension

Directions: Place a + beside each statement that is supported by the reading selection and a – beside each item that is not supported by the selection.

LITERAL

_____ **1.** Intensity refers to brightness.
_____ **2.** Colors are sorted into two basic groups.
_____ **3.** Complementary colors are contrasting colors.
_____ **4.** All secondary colors are made by combining primary colors.

INTERPRETIVE

_____ **5.** Wearing green and red together has a soothing effect on the wearer.
_____ **6.** Special effects in decorating can be created by individuals who understand the effect that colors have on people.
_____ **7.** Large areas in the home should be covered with the color red.
_____ **8.** If we block off any color in the spectrum, the remaining colors form its complement.

Directions: Write short answers for the following questions.

APPLIED

9. Identify three ways in which you can use the ideas in this article for interior decorating.
10. What are your best colors? Why?
11. What color relationship is formed by your school colors?

How are graphic aids related to literacy in human environmental science?

Human environmental science students need to learn to read **graphic aids,** such as diagrams, patterns, drawings, graphs, and charts. Example 11.12 shows a chart from a human environmental science textbook. Interpreting the pictures and the arrows is important to understanding this chart. Example 11.13 shows a different type of chart.

■ ■ ■ EXAMPLE 11.12   *Human Environmental Science Chart*

How a Bank Uses Your Money as a Resource

When you deposit your money in a bank, the money is put to work in a number of ways. The bank lends deposited money to individuals who need it to buy goods or to pay for services. For example, if someone wants to buy a car or needs to pay for a college education and does not have enough money, the bank will make that person a loan. The bank also lends money to companies. For example, it may lend money to help build a new factory.

Each borrower pays interest to the bank for the use of the bank's money. In this way, the bank uses your deposit as a resource to make more money for itself.

You benefit, too.

The bank receives $100.00 from the depositor. It makes loans and receives $110.50 back. It pays the depositor $105.25. Thus, the bank's profit is $5.25 on the loan it made.

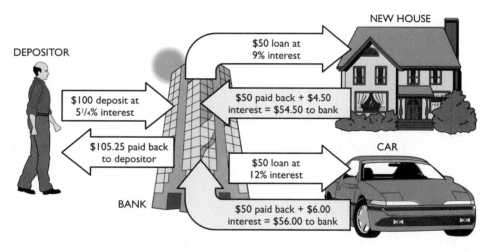

Source: Teen Guide *by Valarie Chamberlain, with permission of Glencoe/McGraw-Hill. A Macmillan/McGraw-Hill Company, Mission Hills, California, Copyright © 1990, p. 190.*

■ ■ ■ EXAMPLE 11.13   *Human Environmental Science Chart*

Accidents and Emergencies Guide

If a healthy family wants to stay healthy, it must be prepared to deal with accidents and emergencies.

What Can Happen	**What to Do**
■ A family member has a simple accident.	■ Use first aid. A child who is alone should notify the parents. Never give medicine unless the parents or a doctor directs you to do so.
■ A family member is bleeding badly, vomiting, or has a very high temperature.	■ Apply direct pressure and elevate the wounded, bleeding area. Call a doctor at once. If the doctor suggests taking the victim to a hospital emergency room, call the police. They will send an emergency car. A child who is alone should call the parents while waiting for the emergency car. The child should ask a neighbor to care for the other children.
■ A family member burns herself or himself.	■ Submerge the burned area in cold water until the pain goes away. Cover the burn with a thick, dry, sterile bandage to keep air out. Get medical help. A child who is alone should notify the parents.
■ A family member gets a dangerous substance in his or her eye.	■ Wash the eye thoroughly with water for 15 minutes. Hold the eyelid open and pour the water from the inside corner of the eye out. Put a pad over the closed eyelid. Get medical help. A child who is alone should notify the parents.
■ A family member swallows something you think may be poisonous.	■ Do not take for granted antidote on label. Much of the information may be outdated and incorrect. Call the poison-control center or hospital emergency room nearest you for instructions. A child who is alone should notify the parents.
■ A family member chokes on something.	■ If the victim is breathing, do not try to remove the swallowed item by slapping the back. Ask the child to cough up the item. If necessary, use the Heimlich maneuver (see page 271).
■ A fire breaks out in the house.	■ Get yourself and the children out of the house immediately. Go to a neighbor's house to telephone the fire department. Do not go back into the house for any reason.

Source: Teen Guide *by Valarie Chamberlain, with permission of Glencoe/McGraw-Hill. A Macmillan/McGraw-Hill Company, Mission Hills, California, Copyright © 1990, p. 110.*

Human environmental science students should know how to interpret labels for specific information, for example, the labels on foods, fabrics, and cleaning products that tell exactly how much of each item or ingredient is contained in the package. They also should know how to interpret directions for use of products. Teachers can prepare students for reading directions through directed reading lessons, study guides, and other instructional strategies suggested in Chapters 5 and 10.

■ Agriculture

According to the agricultural education division of the Wisconsin Department of Public Instruction, agriculture is America's largest and most basic industry, employing about 22 million people in more than 200 agriculture-related occupations (Doerfert, 1993). Agriculture is a complex, multidisciplinary field, and agricultural literacy courses introduce students to the depth, breadth, and diversity of agriculture in our world today, including its impact on daily lives. The recommended topics of study include (Matteson and Jensen, 1994):

- agriculture science/production management
- agriculture processing/food and fiber
- agriculture supplies and services
- agriculture mechanization/engineering and technical support services
- agriculture resources management
- professional employment in agriculture

This wide variety of subject matter creates a literacy challenge for students: each of these content areas involves a different technical vocabulary and its own characteristic patterns of organizing content. These patterns include cause and effect, problem solving, comparison, experiment, directions, and chronological order. In addition, authors often use graphs, charts, diagrams, and pictures. Following is an example of agricultural content. Example 11.14 shows scientific content. Example 11.15 shows a mapping activity based on the content in Example 11.14.

■ ■ ■ EXAMPLE 11.14   *Scientific Content*

What Are the Causes of Diseases Among Farm Animals?

A *disease* is considered in a broad sense to be any disorder of the body. (When the word is analyzed, it really means "lack of ease," which is probably its original meaning.)

Improper Feeding as a Cause of Diseases

Some diseases are caused entirely by improper feeding methods. The disease called *rickets*, in which the bones of an animal fail to develop properly, is due to improper amounts of certain minerals and vitamins. Young animals are sometimes born with enlargements in the throat region. This ailment, which is known as *goitre*, or "big neck," is caused by insufficient amounts of iodine in the ration of the mother animals during the period previous to the birth of the young. *Colic* in horses and *bloat* in cattle and sheep are usually caused by improper methods of feeding.

Animals may be poisoned by lead, which they can get through licking paint pails or freshly painted surfaces. They may also consume feeds that have a poisonous effect on their bodies. Poisonous weeds such as loco weed and white snakeroot are examples. The latter weed, if eaten by dairy cows, may injure not only the cows themselves but also the people who drink the cows' milk. Halogeton is a weed that has spread rapidly in semidesert areas; at times, it has caused the death of many sheep in some western states. Other plants that have a poisonous effect on livestock are alsike clover, when eaten wet; bouncing Bet, cocklebur, and corn cockle roadside plants; bracken fern, found in dry and abandoned fields; buttercup, when eaten green; larkspur; ergot; horse nettle; jimson weed; Johnson grass; nightshade; hemlock; milkweed; and wild cherry.

Ornamental plants toxic to goats include oleander, azalea, castorbean, buttercup, rhododendron, philodendron, yew, English ivy, chokeberry, laurel, daffodil, jonquil, and many members of the lily family. Even tomatoes, potatoes, rhubarb, and avocadoes contain toxic substances. Goats may also be harmed by toadstools, mushrooms, mistletoe, and milkweed.

Source: From Alfred H. Krebs, Agriculture in Our Lives, *5th ed. (Danville, Ill.: The Interstate Printers and Publishers, Inc., 1984), p. 405.*

■ Physical Education

Physical education is a popular area of study today. The growing national interest in physical fitness has created a parallel surge of interest in physical education in the schools. The content of physical education studies can be used to motivate reluctant readers; students who may not be interested in reading other materials often willingly read physical education materials.

Reading serves four purposes in physical education:

1. Physical education topics can motivate students to read, and reading can motivate students to become involved in athletics.
2. Students can learn game rules and signals by reading.
3. Reading can be used to increase and refine skills.

■ ■ ■ EXAMPLE 11.15   *Mapping Activity for Cause and Effect in Agricultural Content*

Improper feeding causes disease

Causes	Effects
Lack of iodine	*Goiter*

Causes	Effects
Improper feeding methods	Colic Bloat

Causes	Effects
Lead Weeds Ornamental plants	Toxic (poison)

4. Reading can increase understanding of a sport and thus can enhance the spectators' or participants' enjoyment.

Physical education is frequently taught without textbooks, but students still need reading skills to read rules and directions for playing games and to read books and magazines to improve their techniques in various sports. For example, many books and magazine articles are available to help people improve their golf swings and tennis strokes.

Reading physical education material requires a number of reading skills. There is extensive specialized vocabulary in this reading content. Each sport has a separate set of terms to be learned (e.g., *love, touchdown, foul,* and *guard*). Notice that the word *love* from tennis and the terms *foul* and *guard*, which apply to several sports, are multiple-meaning terms for which students have other uses in their everyday vocabularies.

What terms would you include in an inventory of soccer terms?

The team and individual sports taught in physical education classes require much special equipment. To learn the names and functions of the various pieces of equipment, students could illustrate each piece of equipment, label it, and describe its function. A notebook could be maintained for this purpose, in which the equipment for each sport is categorized and alphabetized. Teachers may wish to develop **inventories of terminology** related to each sport studied. These inventories can be used both as preparation to introduce the sport and, after study, as a means to review students' understanding of this vocabulary. Students can supply synonyms or define terms in their own words and may develop an illustrated dictionary of sports terms. Following are examples of inventories of sports terms (Example 11.16).

■ ■ ■ EXAMPLE 11.16   *Sports Term Inventories*

Directions: Define the following terms in your own words.

Tennis	*Basketball*	*Volleyball*
racket	dribble	court
backhand	field goal	forearm pass
forehand	foul	setter
love	free throw	set
serve	pass	attacker
net	pivot	spike
game point	press	forwards
deuce	rebound	backs
match	shoot	rotational positions
fault	traveling	net
double fault	violation	attack line
volley	backboard	serve
lob	basket	dink
slice	drive	
chop	dunk	
overhead smash	charge	

Critical (evaluative) reading is also important in physical education materials. Critical thinking is developed when students evaluate the strategies and/or equipment suggested by different authors. This is a good thinking activity, since various authorities suggest widely different approaches to a sport. Critical thinking also comes into play when students evaluate exercises and equipment for physical fitness. For example, recent television commercials recommend some equipment for exercising specific parts of the body, although many physical fitness authorities consider the equipment useless.

Example 11.17 shows an example of physical education text, and Example 11.18 shows a study guide based on this text.

■ ■ ■ EXAMPLE 11.17   *Physical Education*

Step 8   Attack

There are three methods of attack in volleyball, each of which can be very effective. The first to learn of the three methods is the *dink*. It is often looked upon as a defensive maneuver to be performed when the conditions are not right for a more powerful attack. However, the dink is also an extremely effective offensive technique used to disrupt the timing patterns of the defensive team.

The *off-speed spike* is a second option for the attacker. As indicated by its name, less than maximum force is imparted at contact. Like the dink, it is an extremely effective offensive technique used to disrupt the timing patterns of the defensive team.

A third attack method is the *hard-driven spike,* the most exciting play in volleyball. It is also one of the most difficult of all sports skills to learn. In order to make a successful spike, you must jump into the air and sharply hit a moving object (the ball) over an obstacle (the net) so that it lands within the bounded area (the court). Due to the many variables associated with spiking, its timing is difficult and its success requires hours of practice.

Why Is the Attack Important?

When your opponents have mastered the timing of your attack, the dink can catch the opponents off-guard. It is much more difficult to cover the court defensively when a team effectively mixes the speed of their attack. A well-placed dink often "breaks the back" of the opposition and may help improve the momentum of the offense.

The attacking team attempts to have as many different options available to them as possible. The off-speed spike is similar in effect to the dink, but it is hit deeper into the opponent's court. When the off-speed spike is executed, placement is the emphasis, rather than power. The attacker hopes to force the defensive player to move from the starting defensive position and make an error in attempting to play the ball.

The hard-driven spike is the primary offensive weapon in volleyball. Most teams gain a majority of their points on successful spikes. The spike takes very little time to travel from the attacker's hand to the floor; therefore, there is little time for defensive players to move to the ball, and the defensive team must locate its players on the court in strategic positions before the ball is contacted on the spike. The hard-driven spike adds a great deal of excitement to the game and, thus, has tremendous spectator appeal.

How to Execute the Dink

The approach to all three types of attack is the same. It is important because it increases the height of your jump and increases the force you are able to impart on the ball. For a high set, you, the attacker, begin on the attack line, wait for the set to be half the distance to you from the setter, and then move toward the set. Approach the net attempting to cover the distance with as few steps as possible. The last two steps are the most important. Make a two-footed takeoff by planting your right foot heel first and closing with your left foot (bringing the left foot to a position even with the right foot) or taking a hop onto both feet. As you plant both feet heels first to change forward momentum into upward momentum, swing your arms to prepare for a jump. Swing forward both arms and reach high toward the set as you jump straight up into the air. Draw your hitting arm back, your elbow high and your hand close to your ear. As you swing at the ball, your non-hitting hand drops quickly to your waist. Gently contact the ball by using the upper two joints of the fingers of your hitting hand, slightly in front of your hitting shoulder at full arm extension. Contact the ball slightly below the center back. Direct the ball upward enough to barely clear the block but still drop quickly to the floor. Return to the floor with a two-footed landing (see Figure 8.1).

PREPARATION PHASE

1. Wait on attack line
2. Watch setter
3. Eyes on ball after set
4. Weight forward
5. Anticipate approach to the net

FIGURE **8.1**

Keys to Success:
Dink

EXECUTION PHASE

1. Begin approach to net when ball is at peak of its trajectory
2. Cover distance with few steps
3. Last two steps right, close left or step to jump
4. Arms swing back to waist level
5. Both arms swing forward
6. Both arms swing high toward ball
7. Contact ball in front of hitting shoulder
8. Contact with upper two joints of fingers
9. Contact on lower back half of ball
10. Contact with full arm extension

Error	Correction
1. The ball goes into the net.	1. Contact the ball just in front of your hitting shoulder; the greater the distance the ball is in front of you, the lower it drops before contact and the greater the chance of its being hit into the net.
2. The ball does not clear the block.	2. Make contact on the back lower half of the ball with your arm fully extended.
3. You stop your approach and wait for the ball.	3. You should not begin your approach until the ball is half the distance to you from the setter.
4. You contact the net.	4. The set must be at least 1 foot from the net; you must execute a heel plant to change horizontal momentum into vertical momentum.
5. You hit the ball too high, and it takes too long to hit the floor.	5. Contact the ball in front of your hitting shoulder.

Dink Keys to Success Checklist

When performing the dink, keep in mind that your attack needs to go over or by the opponent's block in order to be successful. Your body must be behind the ball so you can direct the ball to the most advantageous area of the opponent's court. Also, be aware that officials will usually call you for improper technique if you attempt to change the direction of the ball during dink performance. This causes your hand to be in contact with the ball too long, which is a held ball.

FOLLOW-THROUGH PHASE

1. Hand follows ball to target
2. Land on both feet
3. Bend knees to cushion landing

Detecting Dink Errors

Most dink errors are associated with improper hand position in relation to the ball and poor timing during the approach. Dinking success is closely associated to your ability to disguise the fact that you are going to dink. Up until hand contact, your approach should be exactly the same as that for a spike.

Source: Barbara L. Viera and Bonnie Jill Ferguson, Volleyball Steps to Success, *pp. 81 and 83. Champaign, IL: Leisure Press. Copyright © 1989 by Leisure Press. Reprinted by permission of Human Kinetics Publishers.*

■ ■ ■ EXAMPLE 11.18   *Study Guide for the "Attack in Volleyball"*

OBJECTIVES

1. Students should know:
    a. The three methods of attack;
    b. The importance of attack;
    c. The three phases of the methods of attack;
    d. How to explain the execution of the dink in relation to footwork;
    e. How to explain the execution of the off-speed spike in relation to hand and wrist;
    f. How to demonstrate the execution of the hard-driven spike in relation to the hand, arm and wrist.

LITERAL

1. Why is the dink an important tactic when attacking your opponent?
2. Why is the hard-driven spike the primary offensive weapon in volleyball?
3. What are the most important steps in the footwork relative to the dink?
4. When you snap your wrist and roll your fingers over the top of the ball in the off-speed spike, what type of spin develops?

INTERPRETIVE

1. What would happen if you contacted the underside of the ball with the heel of the open hand in the hard-driven spike?
2. What would happen if your footwork was incorrect in the dink?
3. Why is the footwork important in the dink?
4. What direction does the ball move when it is in a topspin?
5. Is the topspin useful in a volleyball game? Why or why not?

APPLIED

1. What steps could you take to improve your hard-driven spike?
2. What step would you take first to improve your hard-driven spike?
3. Practice the footwork for each of the three attacks described in this reading and write a description of each in your own words.
4. Practice the hand and wrist movements described in the text so that you can show them to a classmate.

■ Art

Art students use and study the media of artistic expression more frequently than they use and study textbooks. The study of art does not involve as much textbook reading as many other content areas, and fewer textbooks are available in this subject than in other areas. Nevertheless, art students need to have well-developed reading skills because they read many types of written content for a variety of purposes. For example, they read to acquire information about artistic techniques, art history, and the lives of important artists. Following is a summary of the reading strategies art students commonly use:

1. *Reading for information in materials such as reference books, art history books, biographies, and magazines.* Art students often read about exhibitions, artists, and techniques. They read to identify art styles or movements. They read such magazines as *Arts and Activities, School Arts, Popular Photography,* and *Craft Horizons* to obtain current ideas. Reading for information involves identifying main ideas and supporting details.
2. *Reading to follow directions.* Art students must read and follow steps in sequential order. This kind of reading would occur when they read about topics such as new media and new techniques or how to make a woodcut.
3. *Reading to interpret charts and diagrams,* such as a color wheel. For example, art students need to learn about complementary colors.
4. *Reading critically.* The art student uses this skill when evaluating reviews of art shows or the impact of a medium or a style.
5. *Reading to implement information or directions.* After reading about a particular medium or style, an art student may experiment with it.
6. *Reading and organizing information for reports.* Art students may be required to write reports on the lives of artists, styles of art, or ways of interpreting moods and feelings in art. This reading task requires that the reader identify main ideas and details.
7. *Reading technical vocabulary related to art.* This vocabulary includes words like *linear, hue,* and *perspective.*

Study guides, preview guides, and vocabulary activities are particularly helpful to art students. In addition, many of the other strategies presented in Chapters 3, 4, 5, and 10 can be used to help art students develop appropriate literacy skills. Examples of art reading activities follow, including a vocabulary activity, a preview guide, and a study guide.

Example 11.19 includes material from a textbook used for teaching art. As you read this brief selection, note the many technical words and expressions used (e.g., *linear perspective, diminishing contrasts, hue, value, intensity of color, texture, two-dimensional surface, infinite concept, atmospheric perspective, pictorial composition, theme, picture plane, volume of deep space, softening edges of objects, scale,* and *middle ground*). Following the selection are two reading guides that are based on the passage (Examples 11.20 and 11.21).

■ ■ ■ EXAMPLE 11.19   *Art Content*

Problem 1

In conjunction with linear perspective, artists of the past frequently used diminishing contrasts of hue, value, and intensity of color and texture to achieve deep penetration of space on a two-dimensional surface. This is known as the infinite concept of space or atmospheric perspective.

Create a pictorial composition based on the theme "Objects in Space." Conceive of the picture plane as the near side of a volume of deep space. Use the indications of space suggested in the opening paragraph, plus softening edges of objects as they are set back in depth. The human figure may be used to help suggest the scale of objects in space. Foreground, middle ground, and deep space may be indicated by the size of similar objects.

Source: Otto Ocvirk, Robert Bone, Robert Stinson, and Philip Wigg, Art Fundamentals: Theory and Practice *(Dubuque, Iowa: William C. Brown Company, 1975), p. 114.*

■ ■ ■ EXAMPLE 11.20   *Preview Guide*

Directions: Check *Yes* if you believe the reading selection will support the statement; check *No* if you believe the selection will not support the statement.

Yes	No	
_____	_____	**1.** The infinite concept of space and atmospheric perspective are the same thing.
_____	_____	**2.** Artists of the past used diminishing contrasts of hue, value, and intensity of color to achieve atmospheric perspective.

_____   _____   **3.** Students should conceive of the picture plane as the far side of a volume of deep space.

_____   _____   **4.** Trees are used to suggest scale.

■ ■ ■ EXAMPLE 11.21   *Study Guide*

Introduction

This selection poses a problem for art students to solve. If you have questions after you have read the problem, refer to books and articles in the bibliography on linear perspective.

Vocabulary

Provide an example for each of the following words: linear perspective, diminishing contrasts, hue, value, intensity, texture, two-dimensional surface, infinite concept, atmospheric perspective, pictorial composition, theme, picture plane.

Comprehension

Directions: Write a short answer to each question.

LITERAL

1. What does this selection ask you to do?
2. What concept is explained in the first paragraph?
3. What is the theme of the pictorial composition that the student is to create?

INTERPRETIVE

4. Why does the author suggest that a human figure may be used to suggest scale?
5. Will color play an important role in this composition?
6. What similar objects might be used to indicate foreground, middle ground, and deep space?

APPLIED

7. What materials will you need to complete this problem?
8. Can you create another composition that has the same title but uses a different object to show scale? If so, what could you use?

■ Music

Learning music is similar to learning a language. Both tasks depend on the student's ability to perceive likenesses and differences in sounds, shapes, and symbols (Badiali, 1984). Reading words and reading music are both done left to right and top to bottom. The goal of instruction in both instances is understanding the text, and both tasks depend on students' ability to remember the meaning of symbols (Elliott, 1982).

Many music teachers choose not to use textbooks in their instruction; however, they must remember that each piece of music can be considered a text (Morgan and Berg-O'Halloran, 1989). In studying music, students must be able to read the words, the music, and the technical language.

To help secondary students with the task of reading music books, teachers may use the following strategies:

1. Anticipate students' problems before they read. Standardized reading tests and teacher-made inventories can provide data regarding students' reading skills. Observing students' performance in reading music is very helpful in isolating their strengths and weaknesses.
2. Teach the necessary vocabulary before students read a selection.
3. Develop and use illustrated dictionaries of musical terms.
4. Teach students how to study and prepare assignments (see Chapter 7). Demonstrating these techniques with music content can be helpful.
5. Use strategies such as study guides, directed reading lessons, structured overviews, preview guides, and vocabulary study to help students read and understand music content.

Music instruction often requires a high level of reading ability, including knowledge of notes, lyrics, and music theory. Students must be able to understand material that is written about music in order to interpret the music. Music students must be able to read and understand the following types of content (Tanner, 1983):

expository and narrative materials about composers
critiques, reviews, and descriptions of performances
exposition—music history
reporting—current events related to music
references— research, reviews
types of media—books, magazines, newspapers, scores

Music students read and interpret a large number of musical terms, such as *sonatina, spiritoso, andante,* and *allegretto.* In addition, special symbols are used in music books and scores. These symbols aid the student in interpreting the music. Students must be able to recognize symbols for elements such as treble clef, bass clef, notes (whole, half, quarter, etc.), rests (varying values corresponding to note values), sharps, flats, crescendo, and diminuendo. The teacher must frequently demonstrate the musical terms and concepts. For example, the teacher might demonstrate *pianissimo* by playing a song softly and show *forte* by playing the same song loudly; or he or she might illustrate a *crescendo* followed by a *diminuendo*.

Hicks (1980) points out that in instrumental music, the reading process involves recognizing the notes, which represent pitch; the meter symbols, which indicate time; and various other interpretive and expressive markings. At the same time, an instrumentalist must physically manipulate valves, bows, slides, and keys. Hicks suggests that teachers present the early stages of music reading as a problem-solving activity involving simple duple and triple meters. He suggests presenting all songs in the same key, emphasizing continuity and repetition and using materials that have repeated patterns and a narrow range. He also recommends including familiar elements in each new activity. This activity could include such elements as the following:

1. Provide background information about the song.
2. Present the words of the song in poem form on a duplicated sheet (to avoid confusion that may result from all the accompanying signs and symbols on a music sheet).
3. Discuss any words that may not be recognized or comprehended, as well as the overall meaning of the lyrics.
4. The teacher and students should divide the words into syllables cooperatively. A duplicated sheet may again be prepared with words in this form.

After the musical aspects of the song are taught, the students can use the duplicated sheet (with divided words) to sing from. Later, they may use the music books that contain syllabicated words along with the notes and other symbols.

When preparing to perform a composition, music students must ask themselves a number of questions regarding the composition and their performance. Michael Tanner asked a saxophone player in a high school band to identify the questions he had before playing a piece of music, and he produced a list similar to the following one:

1. What will playing this exercise show me?
2. What skills should I learn or develop?
3. What does this piece tell me about the composer?
4. What mood is conveyed?
5. What is the key signature?
6. What is the meter (time signature)?
7. What rhythms does the composer use?
8. What intervals are used?
9. What form does the piece have?
10. How long are the phrases?
11. How did the composer want the piece played?
12. What dynamic markings are shown and why?

13. How many motives did the composer have?
14. Is this music challenging to play?
15. Can I play this successfully?
16. Do I want to play this piece?
17. Is this music too hard?
18. How can I play better?
19. Would it help me if I heard the song played by someone else?
20. Would it help me if I heard the lyrics? (Tanner, 1983)

The music selection "Chumbara" is presented in Example 11.22. Example 11.23 is a study guide based on this selection.

■ ■ ■ ■ EXAMPLE 11.22   *Selection from Secondary School Music Textbook and Study Guide*

Source: Beth Landis and Lara Haggard, Exploring Music (New York: Holt, Rinehart and Winston, Publishers, 1968), p. 150. Reprinted by permission of the publisher.

Introduction

"Chumbara" is a Canadian college song that illustrates the use of nonsense words as lyrics. This music is versatile and is especially adapted for percussion instruments.

Vocabulary

Explain the meaning of each of the following terms or phrases: brightly, autoharp, chords C and C7, transposing to the key of C, percussion patterns, maracas, wood block.

Comprehension

Directions: Place a plus (+) beside statements that are supported by the selection and a minus (–) beside any statements that are not supported by the selection.

LITERAL

_____ **1.** The tambourine, triangle, and sticks can be used to play an accompaniment for this song.

_____ **2.** The ♩♩♩♩ pattern is suggested for the triangle.

_____ **3.** The ♩♩♩ pattern is suggested for the maracas.

INTERPRETIVE

_____ **4.** This song could be sung at a football rally.

_____ **5.** Nonsense words are used in this song to make it difficult to understand.

Directions: Write a short answer or follow the specific directions for each item below.

APPLIED

6. Can you think of another musical composition that is similar to this one?

7. What instruments (that are not mentioned) could be used to play this music?

8. Transpose this song into the key of C.

9. Make up your own patterns for different parts of the song.

Example 11.24 illustrates another type of content that music students read.

Structure of the Classical Sonata

Just as the Classical symphony is a sonata cycle for orchestra, the Classical sonata is a sonata cycle for piano, or for piano and another instrument. The number of movements in the cycle varies from three to four. The first movement is always in sonata form although it is sometimes preceded by a slow introduction. The second movement may be in sonata, ternary, or theme and variations form. In a four-movement work, the third movement is generally a minuet and trio, while the last movement is in rondo or sonata form. Sonatas with only three movements omit the minuet.

Major Composers of Classical Sonatas

Haydn's most important works for piano are sonatas. Mozart too wrote sonatas for solo piano and sonatas for piano and violin. In the early years of the nineteenth century, Franz Schubert (1797–1828) also emerged as a major composer of solo piano sonatas. While many of their works are of fine quality, it is in the sonatas of Beethoven that the epitome of the genre is reached. His works form a bridge between Classical and Romantic styles and foreshadow many later nineteenth-century developments.

Beethoven: Piano Sonata in C Minor, Op. 13

One of Beethoven's finest and best-loved works is the *Piano Sonata in C Minor, Op. 13* (the "Pathétique"), which was published in 1799, quite early in his career. The work is in three movements.

First Movement: Grave; Allegro di molto e con brio; in Sonata Form.   The first movement begins with a slow, ominous introduction. This contrasts dramatically with the main part of the movement, which is marked Allegro and cast in sonata form. The structure of the sonata form is clear, but it is further clarified by the return of the slow introductory material between the exposition and the development, and again after the recapitulation. Dramatic contrasts of theme, key, and dynamics are much greater here than in piano works written earlier in the Classical period.

Listening Guide for Beethoven's Piano Sonata in C Minor, *First Movement*

Timbre:	piano
Melody:	dotted motive prominent in introduction; first theme stresses rising motion; second theme more lyrical
Rhythm:	duple meter; tempo of introduction Grave (very slow); main tempo of movement Allegro di molto e con brio (very fast, with spirit)
Harmony:	mainly minor mode; begins in C minor, modulates most significantly to E♭ major, ends in C minor
Texture:	mainly homophonic
Form:	sonata form preceded by slow introduction

Source: Daniel T. Politoske, Music, *2nd ed. © 1979, pp. 204, 205. Reprinted by permission of Prentice-Hall, Englewood Cliffs, New Jersey.*

■ Dance

Dance textbooks focus on helping students understand movement and the elements of movement and to translate their understanding into action. The dance text excerpt shown in Example 11.25 illustrates this characteristic, and the study guide in Example 11.26 demonstrates one approach to helping readers comprehend and apply written text in dance.

■ ■ ■ EXAMPLE 11.25   *Dance Text*

2. An understanding of the body parts and their movement potential makes more intelligent movement possible.

You will experience your body as a whole and also in its separate parts. You know your nose from your toes, and have since earliest childhood, so a discussion of the parts of the body may seem superfluous. In dance, however, there are certain parts that need specific attention. These need to be clarified, so that you will speak not of the back, but of the lower, middle, or upper spine, and not of the hip bone when you really mean the hip joint.

The spine is basic to all human movement. It is a long series of bones extending from the base of the head, at about ear level, to the coccyx, or tailbone. It consists of 24 separate bones, or *vertebrae,* and two others, the *sacrum* and *coccyx.*

The spine has natural curves in it—a forward curve at the neck, a backward curve at the ribs, another forward curve at the waist, and a backward curve below the waist. These curves are meant to be there, but are not meant to be exaggerated. Fluidity of motion in the spine is a desirable asset to the dancer, and many of the things you will be asked to do are designed to give more mobility to the spine by working the curves opposite to their normal direction.

For convenience, you can speak of the spine in three sections. The *upper spine* extends from the base of the head to just below the shoulder blades. The *middle spine* continues from there to waist level, and the *lower spine* includes the remaining vertebrae, the sacrum, and the coccyx. Each of these areas can be trained to operate independently of the others, or together as a totality.

Learning Experience

Locate the 3 spinal areas on a friend or in yourself with your side to a mirror. Breathe into the upper spine while rounding it forward. Now deepen the curve by rounding the middle spine; now bend forward from the hip joint and breathe into the whole length of the spine and any place in the back or legs that feels tight.

Rounding in 3 areas of the spine.

The area of the hips is often a confusing one. The *hip bones,* first of all, are the prominent bones found on the front of the body, about three inches below the waist and about shoulder width apart. The *hip joint* is where the leg is attached to the torso.

Learning Experience

Put the heel of your hand on your hip bone and extend your fingers downward. Your palm will cross your hip joint. Lift your thigh forward and feel the break in your hip joint.

Later, when you read "hips forward," this is the part of your hip that is directed forward—the whole area you just covered with your hand. The *side of your hip* is at the same level as your hip joint and can be felt as prominent bones on the sides of your body.

Source: Gay Cheney, Basic Concepts of Modern Dance, *3rd ed. (Princeton, NJ: Princeton Book Company Publishers, 1989), pp. 22–23.*

■ ■ ■ EXAMPLE 11.26   Study Guide for Dance Text

Directions: Think about the following questions and exercises as you read this text. Try to visualize the various ideas the author introduces. Perform the learning experiences in the text and those in the application section of the study guide.

LITERAL

1. What part of the body is basic to all human movement?
2. Where are the hip bones?
3. Where is the hip joint?

INTERPRETIVE

1. Why do you think the author identified the hip area as a confusing one?
2. Why should dancers work spinal curves in different directions?
3. Visualize fluid movements. Describe fluid movements in your own words. You may have to do these movements to work out your descriptions.

APPLIED

1. Locate the three areas of your spine with the aid of a mirror.
2. Locate your hip bones, your hip joint, and the side of your hip.
3. Create a movement that will work the spine in a different direction and be sure to breathe with the movement.

Summary

Efficient literacy is a prerequisite for successful learning. Our economy has changed, so that more and more people have changed their vocational goals and have sought retraining. These individuals need literacy skills to facilitate their life changes. Although many people believe that the literacy demands of vocational subjects are less rigorous than those of academic programs, literacy is equally important in these fields of study. Moreover, the current emphasis is on transferable skills and work-related learning that presents writing tasks as well as the need to implement technology.

Vocational and performance materials are written and organized to impart information, give directions, and provide solutions to problems. Teachers should use vocabulary strategies, advance organizers, study guides, preview guides, directed reading materials, mapping, and study methods to help students comprehend these materials. Systematic literacy instruction as a part of content instruction will improve students' learning in these courses.

Discussion Questions

1 How is literacy for work-related education changing?
2 How and why is vocational education changing?
3 What kinds of literacy tasks do students encounter in vocational and technical studies?
4 What strategies can teachers use to help students comprehend vocational materials?
5 Discuss the increased integration of vocational education and academic education.
6 How can teachers effectively teach the variety of content in human environmental science and agriculture?
7 Why is literacy increasing in importance for contemporary students?

Enrichment Activities

1 Select a set of directions from a subject treated in this chapter and rewrite the directions in simpler language for poor readers.
2 Develop an annotated bibliography of materials that could constitute a classroom library in one of the subjects treated in this chapter. Indicate readability levels whenever possible.
3 Make a dictionary of terms for use in one of the areas treated in this chapter. You can use drawings and pictures from magazines, catalogs, and newspapers to illustrate the dictionary.
*4 Collect pamphlets, magazines, newspapers, and library books that could be used to develop understanding of vocabulary and concepts in a subject treated in this chapter. Use them with secondary school students.
5 Select a section in a textbook on a subject treated in this chapter and make a reading lesson plan for it.
6 Prepare a presentation, describing how you would help teach a student to read one of the following: (a) an invoice or balance sheet; (b) a contract; (c) a tax form; (d) a physical education activity or game; (e) a critical review of art or music; (f) a specialized handbook; (g) a reference source.

7 Examine materials from technology education, business education, and human environmental science textbooks. Locate examples of the common reading problems.

*8 Prepare a vocabulary activity to teach new terms in a textbook chapter. Use it with a group of secondary school students.

*9 Prepare a study guide for a selection from one of the subjects discussed in this chapter. Use it with a group of secondary school students.

10 Use a readability formula and compute the readability level of a textbook for one of the content areas discussed in this chapter (see Chapter 13 for a discussion of readability formulas).

11 Identify new applications of technology in your chosen field of study.

*These activities are designed for in-service teachers, student teachers, or practicum students.

Instruction and Assessment of All Learners

CHAPTER 12

Diversity in the Secondary School Classroom

Overview

S econdary students reflect an amazing range of diversity and variability that can make teaching and learning exciting. A school is a microcosm of society (Webb, 1994). It is within the social group that many of life's important lessons are learned. Today's educators instruct an extremely diverse student population whose individuality arises from several sources. Cultural variability is apparent in the many immigrants who have come to the United States to escape political, economic, and social ferment throughout the world. Families, such as the Japanese families who work in a Toyota plant in Kentucky, come from around the world for business and work in the United States. Moreover, students whose families have lived here for generations and preserved their cultural heritage may reflect cultural diversity.

Another source of diversity is students from low socioeconomic backgrounds and the homeless. Socioeconomic status is a most powerful predictor of school failure (Flores, Cousin, and Diaz, 1991). Students who live in impoverished circumstances may suffer from poor nutrition, abuse, lack of medical care, exhaustion, and lack of motivation. They often drop out of school because they have fallen so far behind the other students in their classes. To help these individuals, schools must address the whole student.

Another chief source of diversity in secondary schools is learning variabilities; students who are gifted learners may need challenges to succeed, whereas others require educational adjustments to facilitate literacy learning. Some students need special education to enhance their quality of life. Learners with disabilities are more prevalent in regular classrooms than they were in the past due to social and legislative changes, so content area teachers are very likely to regularly instruct such students.

No matter what the source, individual differences are just that—*differences.* Such differences are respected in sound educational programs. Encouraging each individual to realize his or her potential and to achieve a satisfying quality of life are major goals of our educational system. People with limited literacy skills are often isolated, disenfranchised, and dependent on programs of social support for survival (Harris and Sipay, 1990). In this chapter, you will learn about the challenges diversity creates in secondary classrooms, the issues involved in addressing individual needs, effective practices, classroom settings, and instructional activities that will motivate diverse learners to achieve success.

Purpose-Setting Questions

As you read this chapter, try to answer these questions:

1   What are the major sources of diversity in secondary classrooms?
2   Why has student diversity increased in recent years?
3   What are some useful intervention strategies for assisting students such as these: a student who is learning English as a second language; a student who lives in an urban ghetto; a student who is learning disabled.

■ ■ Diversity in Student Populations

What are sources of student diversity in school?

What students do you think are most in need of individualization?

Diversity in the student population enriches school life; however, for some students diversity means having different educational needs. Therefore, teachers must know how to instruct students who demonstrate wide variability in their command of literacy, which is fundamental to all learning.

Diversity in the student population creates a greater need for **individualization** of instruction to meet students' needs. Three groups within the student population have the greatest need for individualization: immigrant students from varied cultural backgrounds, high-risk students (educationally disadvantaged), and students with disabilities. The diversity among these groups and within them is extensive. We prefer to avoid labeling students, because classifying students may interfere with efforts to meet individual needs. In the following sections, we consider the descriptions and needs of these individuals.

■ ■ Cultural and Language Diversity in the Student Population

The United States is one of the most pluralistic nations in the world. In a large city school, students from a multitude of ethnic and linguistic backgrounds from throughout the world are visible. Since culture contributes so greatly to student diversity, educators who are sensitive to their own cultures as well as those of their students can better understand their students' contexts for learning. Teachers who value diversity, respect different philosophies of life, and accommodate individuality in teaching and learning styles have insights that can help them to develop students' literacy skills.

Cultural background and language are critical to learning because learners gradually appropriate the language patterns they hear (Banks, 1993). Ethnic group members often use *alternative* forms of language; these are not *inferior* forms of language, but they differ from the language used in textbooks and in teaching. In this section, we discuss students who are learning English as a second language **(ESL students)**.

What are some challenges that ESL students face?

Students' patterns for integrating knowledge into their schemata are influenced by their personal, cultural, and social factors even when they are studying in a specialized discipline. Students' cultural backgrounds impact on their ways of thinking, as well as their schemata, which determine how they interpret and mentally organize the world (Robinson, 1985). This is especially important because readers have to relate their backgrounds to text in order to comprehend.

■ Cultural Diversity

Educators seek to embrace cultural pluralism, and they assume that every culture has its own logic, no culture is inherently better, and all people are somewhat culture bound (Biehler and Snowman, 1997). Students' cultural contexts develop out of their countries of origin, homes, schools, and communities. From these sources, they learn attitudes, values, customs, language, and thinking skills. **Culture** is how a group of people tends to perceive, believe, think, and behave, but group members differ in both verbal and nonverbal communication (Biehler and Snowman, 1997). Culture also shapes students' attitudes about reading and writing and the value they attribute to these abilities (Field and Aebersold, 1990). Some ethnic group members' heritages may differ substantially from the values that so strongly influence the activities of our public schools, causing adaptation problems for both teachers and students.

What is culture?

The challenge of helping students from diverse cultural backgrounds acquire literacy is a significant one, because variations in language and reading abilities are significant sources of learning difficulties in schools. Reading ability, more than any other, empowers students to learn and develop in directions that enable them to realize their full potential.

■ Language Diversity

How are cultural schemata related to literacy?

Students whose cultural backgrounds differ from that of the dominant culture find it necessary to continually interact with information outside their own **cultural schemata** (Sadaker and Sadaker, 1991). They often need to build new schemata to understand concepts that authors assume are a part of their background knowledge. For example, students may lack knowledge about famous Americans that is assumed in textbooks. Another area that is commonly problematic for readers is use of figurative expressions in American English. Because of these types of problems, many students prefer to read stories and articles about their own cultures, and they comprehend better when reading these materials (Nelson, 1987). Teachers and media specialists can work together to identify literature, videos, and Internet resources for these students.

Students whose families speak little or no English often have no help with schoolwork at home. Moreover, their families may need the assistance of an interpreter to understand the educational system and the schooling process. Teachers should make a special effort to include families in the planning process and to keep them informed of their children's progress (Fitzgerald, 1993). The following "Meeting the Challenge" illustrates this difficulty.

MEETING THE CHALLENGE

Carmen was born in New York City, the daughter of a Puerto Rican mother and a South Carolinian father. Carmen's mother gradually became an alcoholic after her husband was killed in an automobile accident. Carmen's Puerto Rican grandmother, who lived in a Spanish-speaking community and spoke no English, raised Carmen in the Puerto Rican–American culture. Although she was very proud of her granddaughter, who was the first member of her family to attend high school, she could not discuss Carmen's progress with teachers nor could she offer assistance with homework. She really did not understand the educational system or the demands it made on her granddaughter. The situation was further complicated because Carmen had become her grandmother's interpreter, reading letters and notes, shopping for her, and generally helping her grandmother survive.

In tenth grade, Mrs. Daniels, an English teacher, recognized that Carmen was capable and motivated, but struggling to learn. After reading Carmen's permanent record and conferring with her, Mrs. Daniels asked if she could visit Carmen's home. Carmen was the interpreter during the visit. Mrs. Daniels complimented Carmen's grandmother on Carmen's maturity and ability. Then she asked about family life and education in Puerto Rico and explained the curriculum and expectations of the school Carmen attended. Later she persuaded the grandmother to visit Carmen's class. Over time she was able to make suggestions to Carmen and her grandmother about how to obtain a library card, how to study, and how to prepare for tests. She also encouraged Carmen to write about her life in the Puerto Rican community. Carmen gradually developed confidence in her literacy abilities and subsequently graduated from high school and college. She became a teacher and a volunteer interpreter in her community.

Teaching ESL Students

The language usage gap between children whose first language is not English and their nonminority, English-speaking peers grows wider throughout their school experience (Goldenberg and Gallimore, 1991). Low levels of language achievement are problematic because literacy skills enable students to achieve other goals in school. Students in ESL classes are expected to develop cognitively as well as linguistically. Moreover, they need to acquire the skills and knowledge set forth in curriculum guides and in courses of study, which creates pressure to move quickly into academic and abstract uses of English (Allen, 1991).

Research reveals a wide range of differences in the ways students learn second languages (Wong Fillmore, 1982). For example, it shows that Hispanic students developed speaking and comprehension skills best when they had opportunities to interact with English-speaking peers. Chinese students, on the other hand, found interactions with the teacher more beneficial. Hispanic students did well when the teacher's instructions were clear and the lessons well organized, but they became inattentive when the teacher was unclear. In contrast, the Chinese students became even more attentive when understanding was difficult. Information like this can help teachers plan instruction and support the culturally different learner (Allen, 1991).

The cultural background of the students must be considered in planning educational experiences. ESL students frequently have different experiences from those of students who are part of the dominant culture; therefore, teachers should clarify cultural terms or concepts. These cultural references may encompass information from the fields of art, music, and drama. Many ESL students lack a command of oral English to form a basis for reading and writing English. Their inability to converse in English inhibits both their educational and social development. Language learning develops in a social context, so the inability to converse in English inhibits students' language growth. Limited communication ability also contributes to low self-esteem.

Teachers can help alleviate communication problems with oral and visual prompts as they talk with students. Prompts such as pictures, signs, ads, and video clips help students understand their social world and how to communicate with others. Students who are strongly interested in socializing with English-speaking peers make the most progress. Moreover, teachers can encourage oral activities with cooperative activities that enable ESL students to become more actively involved in the classroom.

Researchers have learned that the amount of time required to become a proficient user of a second language has been greatly underestimated (Wong Fillmore, 1982). This research revealed that most students require four to six years to become competent users of English. For some students this process may take as long as eight years. Factors such as opportunities to converse, to learn, to read, and to write in English influence the number of years required to achieve competence.

Generally speaking, ESL students use several strategies in learning English (Allen, 1991):

1. They assume that what people are saying relates to the present situation.
2. They start talking by using a few stock expressions.
3. They look for recurring patterns in the language around them.
4. They make the most of the language they have acquired.
5. They focus on communicating meaning.

When students are learning English as a second language, teachers should consider these concepts:

1. Cognitive organization is related to culture and affects metacognition and schemata; therefore, teachers need to find ways to reach out to students'

families so that they can help parents understand classroom interaction, methods, and materials. Examples are parent conferences (with interpreter if necessary), inviting parents into the classroom, and home visits. As teachers communicate with parents they learn more about the cultures of their students.

2. Second-language reading is subject to interference from first-language knowledge; students tend to impose their existing knowledge on materials they read. For example, students from India who read about a North American wedding tended to distort the text to make it consistent with their knowledge of weddings in India (Fitzgerald, 1993).

3. Students need a grammatical and lexical base for second-language learning that is developed through language activities. Immersing students in reading and writing situations (Fitzgerald, 1993) develops a grammatical and lexical base for language acquisition. As students interact with others in a literate environment, they can acquire understandings of the conventions of print. Their experiences should be structured to emphasize the functions and purposes of reading and writing experiences.

How can dialogue journals be beneficial to ESL students?

Writing experiences, such as keeping **dialogue journals,** are especially useful in this situation. A dialogue journal is an ongoing conversation between a teacher and a student or two students. First, the student writes an entry into a notebook; those who have limited use of written English can make brief notes and/or drawings to express their thoughts. Teachers may find it necessary to prompt entries through conferencing with the students and drawing them out with questions. After entries are completed, students may exchange the journals with one another, and each may respond to the other's entry.

ESL students, like the regular classroom students, should write about content area understandings and questions. The teacher's responses to their entries stimulates the students' writing and creates a model for writing in their dialogue journals. As the students progress, this format can be changed. Partners (or teachers) can question, react, disagree, or respond in ways that express their own thoughts about the entry. Journals should be exchanged at least once a week. (Refer to Chapter 8 for additional information.) ESL students may prefer to read their journals orally to a peer until they grow more secure with spelling, grammar, and so forth.

4. Direct instruction and extensive reading are important in developing the linguistic base for second-language learning. Fitzgerald (1993) recommends the following teaching behaviors to ESL teachers:
   a. Encourage students to experiment with language and to "play" with it.

b. Use praise and encouragement to reward students' efforts to understand and communicate.
c. Downplay mistakes.
d. Be patient and allow students plenty of time to read words silently or aloud and to express thoughts in speaking and writing.
e. Encourage students to talk with English-speaking students. Before these interactions, explain to the English-speaking students how they can be supportive and encouraging to ESL students. Cooperative learning strategies are especially useful.

5. Reading and writing develop concomitantly, so it is not necessary to wait until a student reads to initiate writing. Reading instruction in first or second languages should always focus on meaning. Combining reading and writing in realistic situations capitalizes on the interrelated nature of speaking, listening, reading, and writing (Rigg, 1990).

6. Immerse students in reading and writing across the curriculum. Students need to experience a variety of genres to become competent and fluent in reading various types of content. Teachers should read aloud from fiction, nonfiction, and poetry, building on students' prior knowledge and developing appropriate background knowledge and schemata.

Fitzgerald (1993) recommends the group reading conference as another way of immersing ESL students in reading and writing. In this experience, groups of four to eight students meet with the teacher and read a text together. Afterward, the teacher asks questions such as: What was the book (article, story) about? What did you like about it? If the author were visiting, what would you say to him or her? The teacher should encourage students to participate in oral language, pointing to text or pantomiming when necessary.

Selecting ESL Materials

Texts prepared for students in this country are commonly based on the Aristotelian essay form that presents a thesis in the introduction, which is supported by arguments and is reinforced in the conclusion (Reynolds, 1993). This pattern is unfamiliar to students from some other cultures, such as the Chinese, whose rhetoric tends to be circular. The following criteria, which were adapted from Reynolds (1993), will assist teachers in selecting ESL materials for all content areas:

1. The materials should include fiction, nonfiction, and poetry readings that are good models of writing. The reading materials should be highly motivating to the students, and the characters should serve as role models and develop positive attitudes in the students (Hudley, 1992).

2. The text should stimulate students to read more about the topic and thus expand their universe of knowledge, which will help them to write about the topic.

3. The materials should provide models that include well-organized examples of English literature and samples of rhetorical forms from different cultures (Reid, 1989).

4. The text should contain samples of useful grammatical structures that address problems in grammar as the students encounter them.

5. The text should help students see that writing in a second language involves more than sentence writing and grammar. Writing should be presented as part of whole language or natural language in which listening, speaking, reading, and writing are combined in activities that are meaningful and enjoyable (Reynolds, 1993).

6. Text materials should develop students' sense of audience.

7. Text materials should encourage thinking and problem solving.

Students with Dialect Differences

How should dialect differences affect literacy instruction?

Students with **dialect differences** use a language pattern of a subgroup of language speakers. Students who grow up in a specific cultural group may speak a dialect of English used in their environment, such as Appalachian or Black English Vernacular (BEV). However, not all African-Americans use BEV, nor do all residents of the Appalachian region speak the same dialect. Within each dialect region there are many variations, including standard English. Alexander (1985) identifies three facts about BEV that will help teachers understand and work with it in the classroom: (1) African-Americans who use a form of dialect do not use all of the BEV features at all times; (2) their use of these features varies from sentence to sentence; and (3) the type of Black English used is determined by sex, age, socioeconomic status, the geographic areas in which the speaker spent his or her formative years, and the speaker's purpose, setting, topic, and audience. Black English dialect is a legitimate linguistic system with its own complex set of rules.

Most research indicates that BEV speakers are not seriously hampered in reading standard English (Holloway, 1985). Students who speak a different dialect have many opportunities to hear and understand standard English through television and movies. They are also exposed to books written in standard English in elementary school and to the general print media (e.g., newspapers and magazines). By the time these students reach secondary school age, they can comprehend written and spoken standard English, although they may not use it in their own communication.

Teachers of students with dialect differences should respect the students' languages and cultures in the same way they respect the languages and cultures of students who are learning English as a second language. Teachers who have negative feelings about their students' language may find it difficult to work with these students in an objective manner. Therefore, teachers must confront their own reactions and work to eliminate any negative feelings about their students' dialects.

Students with Special Literacy Learning Needs

What reasons can you suggest to explain the relationship between socioeconomic status and school achievement?

Students enter school expecting to learn to read and write, but failing over and over again may cause them to give up (Coley and Hoffman, 1990). **Socioeconomic status** is the single best predictor of students' reading achievement. Through no fault of their own, many students of low socioeconomic status are "at risk" of failing to learn and of failing to complete high school. Other risk factors commonly associated with school dropouts include low achievement, retention in grade, behavior problems, poor attendance, and attendance at schools with large numbers of poor students (Slavin, 1989; Polloway and Patton, 1993). Pellicano (1987) describes at-risk students as those whose poverty, family instability, or social backgrounds make them likely candidates for school failure—often falling victim to crime, drugs, teenage pregnancy, or early entry into the ranks of the unskilled unemployable.

Socioeconomic Factors

The major indicators of educational disadvantage are all based in the environment: minority racial/ethnic group identity, living in a low-income household, living in a single-parent family, having a poorly educated mother, and having a non-English language background (Hodgkinson, 1985). More recently, homelessness has been added to these indicators. Since the early 1980s there has been a substantial increase in homelessness with estimates that up to 3 million are homeless. More than a third of the homeless are families with children (Children's Defense Fund, 1988).

Homeless families endure great difficulties in obtaining basic literacy skills for their children because they are unable to provide adequate shelter, food, or clothing (Eddowes and Hranitz, 1989). Living in a car or on the streets is unsafe, and homeless shelters limit the amount of time they can stay. Homeless children are often excluded from public schools because of state and local enrollment requirements for residency status, proof of age, immunization and health records, and proof that the student has attended school. The following "Meeting the Challenge" illustrates the difficulties of students who have lived in poverty and experienced abuse.

MEETING THE CHALLENGE

Fourteen-year-old Mary Ann is an example of an individual who had given up. When her social worker/teacher first met her, Mary Ann was in a juvenile detention center. She was the oldest of the five children of alcoholic parents and was expected to take complete care of her siblings, which meant that she attended school erratically and was unable to do homework. Her low achievement contributed to her already low self-esteem.

Mary Ann reached the breaking point when an alcoholic family friend sexually abused her. When her parents refused to protect her, Mary Ann fled her home and lived on the streets until she was picked up by juvenile authorities. At this point Mary Ann refused to attend the classes provided in the juvenile facility and refused to talk with a therapist.

Since the social worker/teacher had several individuals with similar experiences in the facility, she decided to attempt a literature discussion group. She selected the book *When She Hollers* (Voigt, 1994), which she read to the five girls over a three-day period. The first day, the girls were suspicious and there was little discussion, but on the second day one girl began sobbing and this broke the ice and the girls began talking and comparing experiences. Then the instructor asked the girls to predict what the heroine would do and the outcome of the story, which generated a lively debate. After the story was finished, the girls asked if they could read another book like this one. The instructor selected *The Pinballs* by Betsy Byars and *The Girl Who Lived on the Ferris Wheel* by Louise Moeri.

Certainly, Mary Ann did not change overnight, but she began to take tentative steps to talk with other girls and eventually to a therapist. As a result she has experienced a better quality of life and eventually plans to graduate from high school.

Students' home environment exerts a powerful influence on their cognitive growth, intelligence, and language development. Many students must cope with family moves, divorce and separation of parents, death of close relatives, and leavetaking of older siblings (Richeck, List, and Lerner, 1989).

Low socioeconomic status students experience more failure and lower achievement than students from middle-class homes. Moreover, projections indicate that the number of children living in poverty will dramatically increase in the future; therefore public schools are likely to serve a much larger disadvantaged population in the future. Students live and grow in different environments that have a strong impact on their desire and ability to learn. A student's total environment includes the home, the school, the social group, and the culture.

Parents and teachers can work together to help students cope with these challenges. When parents demonstrate the value of reading skills and give children access to reading materials, they are helping them become successful. Families who can create a stable environment with adequate nutrition and rest, and who show interest in and support for their children, give them enormous advantages.

To address the problems of diverse students, new strategies must be developed. Many educators recommend that schools become more aware of and involved in the family and community contexts of their students, both to understand the problems and to learn to draw on the strengths of families and communities to enrich the education of students (Pallas, Natriello, and McDill, 1989).

◼ Instructional and School-Related Factors

Students who are unable to read competently have low achievement levels in most school subjects because they cannot read well enough to comprehend the concepts in their textbooks. These students often lack prior experience and knowledge that would permit them to learn from textbooks. They may have difficulty learning through traditional means or within traditionally structured environments, and they may require more directive, intensive, and highly individualized instruction to reach their potential (Polloway and Patton, 1993). Often their problems are not limited to academic areas; their personal adjustment may be inadequate, thus contributing to poor self-concepts and social adjustment (Quandt and Selznick, 1984; Bristow, 1985).

How does anxiety affect school performance?

Less competent readers usually realize they cannot keep up with their classmates, but they do not know to overcome their literacy problems. As a result of their reading difficulties, they manifest school-related anxiety. They become stressed and anxious when asked to read textbooks and ancillary materials they do not understand (Gentile and McMillan, 1987). **Anxiety** has a debilitating effect on school performance because anxious students tend to divide their attention between the task at hand and worry about how well they are doing (Willig et al., 1983; Wigfield and Asher, 1984).

When teachers help students acquire the strategies and reading fluency needed to deal successfully with content textbooks, they help the students reduce the stress and anxiety they normally experience in reading situations. Teachers' attitudes toward students' learning are a major factor in developing fluent readers (Wigfield and Asher, 1984).

■ Special Education Issues

Contrast inclusion with main-streaming.

Increasing numbers of challenged learners, who were once taught in special education classes, are now enrolled in regular classrooms through **inclusion** and **mainstreaming** programs (Slavin, 1989). This component of diversity arises from the special needs of individuals who are mentally retarded, learning disabled, educationally handicapped, emotionally disturbed, and behaviorally disabled (Pallas et al., 1989; Polloway and Patton, 1993). In content classrooms, diversity is increasing because of reforms in both regular and special education.

Exceptional students differ from average students in a variety of ways (see the following list). "These differences must be to such an extent that the child requires a modification of school practices, or special educational services, to develop to maximum capacity" (Kirk and Gallagher, 1993, p. 5).

Exceptional students include those with the following individual variations:

Intellectual differences, including students who are intellectually superior and students who are slow to learn

Communication differences, including children with learning disabilities or speech and language impairments

Sensory differences, including children with auditory or visual impairments

Behavioral differences, including children who are emotionally disturbed or socially maladjusted

Multiple and severe handicapping conditions, including children with combinations of impairments (e.g., cerebral palsy and mental retardation, deafness, and blindness)

Physical differences, including children with nonsensory handicaps that impede mobility and physical vitality (Kirk and Gallagher, 1993).

Students who have disabilities often receive a portion of their education in public school classrooms since the Education for All Handicapped Children Act (EHA) was passed. This law protects the rights of each child identified as having a handicapping condition and ensures the "free, appropriate public education of all handicapped children." Congress reaffirmed the federal commitment to students with disabilities in 1983 with the passage of legislation that extended this act to focus on secondary education, parent training, and preschool children. The 1990 amendments to this law (PL101-476) changed the name of the EHA to the **Individuals with Disabilities Education Act (IDEA).**

What is the purpose of the IDEA?

Why is participation in regular classrooms increasing for special education students?

In recent decades, advocates for students with learning problems have actively pursued increased integration of students with disabilities into the regular classroom. The Regular Education Initiative (REI) calls for **full inclusion** of disabled students in the regular classroom (Thousand and Villa, 1990), thus increasing the likelihood that many students with disabilities will receive all or a significant portion of their instruction in the regular classroom. In such programs, the special education teacher collaborates with the classroom teacher

*What is the pur-
pose of an IEP?*

about the student's goals, achievement, and appropriate instruction. Then the classroom teacher integrates the student with special needs into the regular classroom.

Each student identified as handicapped must have an **individualized education plan (IEP)**, which includes a description of the student's problem, the program's long-term goals as well as its short-term objectives, the special education services needed for the student, and the criteria for assessing the effectiveness of the services. Classroom teachers serve on the committees that develop IEPs for students who are mainstreamed, but not every content teacher will be on the IEP committee.

■ ■ Literacy Instruction for a Diverse Population

Educators now understand that parental involvement is a critical factor in the reading success of students. Researchers have found compelling evidence regarding the role of parental involvement. Parents' educational level is another significant factor in developing literacy. Recent research shows that the children of parents with less than a high school education are at a distinct disadvantage in the classroom (National Center for Education Statistics, 1996). Educating parents pays off for students because they start school better prepared, stay in school longer, and do better while they are there. Family literacy helps students become more literate; as parents acquire or improve their literacy, their children improve and the parents get more and more involved in their children's education, which also contributes to their achievement.

Teachers must understand the individual needs of diverse students to intervene in their learning experiences to prevent the downward spiral that can begin in the early grades and continue throughout their school careers. Reading is a complex cognitive process and therefore subject to a variety of influences. Rarely is a single factor responsible for individual differences in reading ability. The following student descriptions illustrate some kinds of variability in students' reading skills that secondary teachers may encounter in the classroom.

READING CASE 1

John is a tenth-grade student who is passing with only the minimum grade in all subjects that require reading. John's listening comprehension is high average for his grade placement, and the teacher's observations indicate that John has average ability. However, scores on reading achievement tests show he is reading at the middle of eighth-grade level. John's written assignments are poorly organized and written. His speaking and writing vocabularies are limited, and his scores on the vocabulary sections of reading achievement tests are low.

John appears to require assistance in vocabulary, organization of content, and study skills. These areas can be handled best by the various content teachers because they know the particular needs of their content subjects. John can probably be helped by classroom teachers because he has shown that he is capable of learning and because his reading difficulties seem to relate in part to a lack of experiences promoting concept and vocabulary development. Reading-study skills and organizational skills can be learned from systematic instruction that a content teacher can provide. Strategies such as those discussed in Chapters 3–7 should help John.

READING CASE 2

Mary is a tenth-grade student who is unable to pass any of the courses that require reading skills or to read any of her textbooks with understanding. Listening comprehension tests indicate that she has below-average listening comprehension for her grade, and reading achievement test scores show that she is reading at a third-grade level. The teacher's observations also indicate she has below-average ability.

Mary requires assistance from a remedial reading teacher because she is unable to progress in school. A classroom teacher could not provide adequate help in this case. Because Mary reads far below her grade placement, a classroom teacher would not have the time (or perhaps the expertise) to provide the extensive diagnosis and individualized instruction she sorely needs.

Mary's reading problems probably have several sources. She may lack the experiences that would help her construct the meaning of the language she reads, or she may come from a cultural background that differs in values, attitudes, and educational expectations from those in the school. Since she reads at such a low level, she may lack basic word knowledge skills that would permit her to read fluently.

Some students acquire basic reading abilities but lack the higher levels of comprehension necessary for learning content through reading. Therefore, content instruction must be modified for those who have not yet developed the requisite reading, language arts, and thinking abilities. These students need the underlying conceptual readiness that makes comprehension possible. Each reading assignment demands a certain level of prior knowledge to facilitate understanding. When this knowledge is missing, teachers must develop it. When it is present, teachers must activate it.

Strategies like those presented throughout this text will help students acquire the needed strategies. Some students who cannot read textbooks and related materials need remedial reading instruction that is beyond the scope of classroom teachers, but the strategies suggested in the next section are ones that classroom teachers find particularly helpful in working with at-risk readers.

■ Adapting Instructional Practices

Educationally challenged students require instruction that is adapted to their needs. The following process can help educators determine the best educational program for their students. First, consider the students' present and future needs. For instance, secondary students who plan to go to college or pursue postsecondary education need skills such as composition writing, reference reading, organizational strategies, and oral presentation. For secondary students who are not headed for postsecondary education, however, a life skills theme that focuses on living comfortably may be helpful. Such a program could focus on learning words that appear in the everyday environment, learning how to write job applications, reading package labels, and reading bus schedules.

Special needs students' academic, linguistic, and personal/social abilities must be considered carefully in planning for them. For example, ESL students may need the assistance of an ESL teacher to complete assignments; if an ESL teacher is not available, the classroom teacher may need to consult with a specialist who can offer suggestions for helping students. Effective instruction is founded on knowing students well enough to identify their individual strengths and weaknesses in learning, as well as their interests and experiences. Teachers need to know what to expect of students who are in their classes as mainstreamed or included students. This knowledge enables teachers to choose materials and to plan effective instruction that motivates and actively involves all students. Classroom teachers and special education teachers can use this knowledge to select the curricular areas that can be addressed in the classroom and those that special education teachers can handle.

The regular classroom situation must be considered. For instance, the competencies and attitudes of the classroom teacher affect the accommodations possible in the regular classroom. These accommodations are influenced by the teacher, the number of students in the classroom and their needs, and the number of mainstreamed or included students. In addition, the availability of support personnel in the school greatly affects the placement of special needs students. Support personnel include resource teachers (special education), consultative teachers, speech and hearing specialists, subject matter specialists, ESL teachers, counselors, and school psychologists. Outside resources are important to students' educational progress as well. Many challenged students need outside resources such as tutorial assistance, role models, and people who have similar kinds of special needs to encourage them. Peers can provide assistance in peer tutoring, modeling, and cooperative learning.

■ Guidelines for Effective Instruction

Adaptive instructional practices are important to secondary teachers because these teachers deal with a tremendous diversity of students, as well as large numbers of students. They often instruct from 100 to 200 students each day, for normal teaching loads consist of five or six daily classes and two to four daily preparations (Moore and Murphy, 1987). In addition to planning for large numbers of regular students, teachers must involve special needs students with their peers in the classroom. The checklist in Table 12.1 can guide special education teachers and classroom teachers in preparing for mainstreaming students.

TABLE **12.1**

Preparing for Mainstreaming: A Special Education Teacher's Checklist

1. Disabled Student

Yes	No	
☐	☐	Is familar with rules and routine of the regular classroom?
☐	☐	Follows verbal and written directions used in the regular classroom?
☐	☐	Remains on-task for adequate time periods?
☐	☐	Has expressed a desire to participate in the regular class setting?
☐	☐	Reacts appropriately to teasing, questions, criticism, etc.?
☐	☐	Student's IEP objectives match instructional objectives in regular classes?

2. Regular Class Teacher

Yes	No	
☐	☐	Has been given rationale for mainstreaming activities and asked to cooperate?
☐	☐	Has information about disabled student's needs, present skills, and current learning objectives?
☐	☐	Has been provided with special materials and/or support services as needed?
☐	☐	Has prepared class for mainstreaming activities?
☐	☐	Has acquired special helping skills if necessary?
☐	☐	Will be monitored regularly to identify any problems that arise?

3. Nondisabled Peers

Yes	No	
☐	☐	Have been informed about disabled student's participation and about disabling condition (if appropriate with the opportunity to ask questions)?
☐	☐	Have been asked for their cooperation and friendship toward disabled student?
☐	☐	Have learned helping skills and praising behaviors?

4. Disabled Student's Parents

Yes	No	
☐	☐	Have received verbal or written information about mainstreaming situation?
☐	☐	Have been asked to praise and encourage child's progress in regular as well as special education class?

5. Nondisabled Student's Parents	6. School Administrator

Yes	No		Yes	No	
☐	☐	Have been informed about mainstreaming activities at PTA meeting or conferences or through other vehicle, and asked for their cooperation?	☐	☐	Has been informed about specifics of mainstreaming activities?
			☐	☐	Has indicated specific steps she or he will take to encourage and support these activities?

Source: From "Helping Teachers Integrate Handicapped Students into the Regular Classroom" by J. C. Dardig, 1981, Educational Horizons, 59, p. 129. Copyright 1981 by Educational Horizons. Reprinted with permission from Educational Horizons, quarterly journal of Pi Lambda Theta, International Honor and Professional Association in Education, 4101 E. Third Street, Bloomington, IN 47407-6626.

Successful teachers consistently demonstrate certain teaching behaviors when instructing academically challenged students:

1. They give frequent positive feedback to students. Students with learning problems, like all students, must have a reason to learn and benefit from individualized motivation and reinforcement.
2. They provide sustaining feedback and supportive responses to students. They are supportive and encouraging to students in general.
3. They give supportive responses to problem behaviors that indicate a learning problem (as distinguished from a disciplinary problem).
4. They provide each student with opportunities to succeed, which includes asking questions students can answer correctly and providing learning tasks students can accomplish with a high rate of success.
5. They use classroom time efficiently by planning and organizing materials in advance, and avoiding student off-task time. They reduce the amount of time lost in student transitions and noninstructional activities.
6. They provide variety in their teaching methods, approaches, and materials. Change is often essential to maintaining students' interest.
7. They provide structure and direct instruction to guide children. Classroom routines and structure are important features of the instructional program.

Specific Strategies and Instructional Procedures

Reading is a constructive process for all readers, and the nature of this process is not altered when students are challenged by their special needs. The greatest opportunities for success are offered by an approach that emphasizes reading, writing, listening, and speaking. This type of instruction incorporates daily opportunities to read highly motivational, interesting material that encourages students to read frequently, thus developing their fluency.

However, many students need direct instruction to develop vocabulary, comprehension, content reading skills, higher-order thinking skills, and study skills. Teachers cannot assume students will absorb these skills as a result of numerous exposures to literature, although many opportunities to respond to various forms of literature are essential to literacy development.

Activating Schemata

Reading strategies should involve inferential thinking, problem solving, and critical thinking. Some teachers tend to stress literal-level thinking with less able students; however, these students can think at higher cognitive levels when they have appropriate background knowledge and work in collaborative, supportive groups. Therefore, adapted reading instruction should provide for building and activating schemata in a diverse classroom population. As we explained earlier, schemata are the products of background experiences (see Chapters 3, 4, and 5).

Teachers help students activate appropriate schemata and build the experiences that will help them comprehend content reading materials. They may use photographs, videotapes, models, and guest lecturers to develop schemata. Special needs students other than gifted students will probably benefit more from concrete experiences than from vicarious ones. Advance organizers and preview guides, which are discussed in Chapters 3, 4, 10, and 11, expedite schemata activation and development. Previewing text involves examining the title, photographs, headings, and introduction to help activate students' schemata. In addition, teachers who are instructing students whose native language is not English can help them by providing previews of the text in the students' native language. Teachers who do not speak the students' native languages can have someone else make audiotapes to use in previewing content. In fact, many special needs students will benefit from listening to audiotapes of previews, vocabulary development, and content reading assignments. The audiotapes should be paced slowly enough for students to follow the text. Additional strategies in this area are included later in this chapter.

Direct Instruction

Low-achieving students show greater academic achievement when their teachers follow a consistent pattern of demonstration, guided practice, and feedback, regardless of curriculum (Rosenshine and Stevens, 1984). Several studies have found direct instruction is superior to other instructional approaches in developing literacy for students with academic handicaps (Patching, Kameeuni,

What type of instruction has often been found to help low-achieving students?

Carnine, Gersten, and Colvin, 1983; Carnine and Kinder, 1985). **Direct instruction** refers to initial instruction that involves explicit teaching, flexibility in addressing students' needs, opportunities for application of learning, opportunities for practice, and periodic review of previously learned concepts.

Students who are academically challenged generally benefit from direct instruction that presents learning tasks with a small number of elements, some of which are familiar to the students. These familiar ideas or concepts provide a springboard or point of contact for the new ideas presented. Teachers can give a series of minilessons, which should be very brief because these students often find it difficult to sustain concentration and effort. Teachers can also arrange learning in a series of small steps and give students immediate positive feedback as they achieve each step. Frequent review helps build *overlearning* into lessons, which aids retention; students enjoy frequent review because it includes learned material with which they feel more secure.

Using Computers and Multimedia

One medium for providing students with individualized instruction is the computer. Computers have an obvious appeal for adolescents and give them a sense of control in the learning situation that helps build self-confidence. Properly written computer programs are not judgmental about mistakes and exhibit unlimited patience, while permitting students to work at their own paces. Additionally, when a student doesn't know a word, he or she does not have to reveal this to the teacher or to the other students. The student receives immediate feedback and reinforcement from computers. Computer instruction is often more gamelike than more traditional instruction, making drill and practice more interesting. CD-ROMs and hypertext provide students with an interactive approach to learning. Use of computers and multimedia can also encourage risk-taking by the students. Many computer programs have branching capabilities that ensure individualized instruction according to the students' needs. Branching programs offer tutorials or different sets of information depending on the students' answers; therefore, each student completing the program may encounter different information. The spell checker, thesaurus, and grammar checker offer students tools that will help them develop literacy skills.

How do cooperative learning strategies help meet the needs of a diverse student group?

Cooperative Learning Strategies

Classroom **cooperative learning techniques** involve students working together in teams of two to five students. Cooperative techniques encourage active student involvement and give special needs students opportunities to interact with peers. This approach encourages students to take responsibility for their own learning and to work collaboratively with peers. They develop independence and confidence in their own abilities and a more positive attitude toward school. Considerable evidence exists that cooperative learning experiences are more effective in promoting positive relationships between disabled and nondisabled students than competitive and individualistic ones (Slavin, Karweit, and Madden, 1989). Academically challenged and ESL students can make significant contributions to group discussions when they are encouraged.

When implementing a cooperative learning strategy, teachers should explain the process and its purpose to their students. Students must be assigned specific tasks or roles and understand why it is important to stay with a task and avoid socializing. The cooperative process includes the discussion and sharing of ideas with students as active participants. Students should understand exactly what is expected of them during group activities. The teacher assigns students to groups, which are formed prior to giving out assignments, and specifies the time limits for assigned tasks. Observations can help teachers know when and how to adjust group membership and group activities.

Many activities are appropriate for cooperative learning. Students may engage in activities such as guided independent reading, asking and answering questions, paraphrasing content, retelling content, outlining, mapping, summarizing, completing study guides, and dramatizing stories or historical events. Students who participate in cooperative learning often are involved in incidental peer tutoring because they have opportunities to learn from one another.

Peer Tutoring

Describe a peer tutoring session.

Studies of peer tutoring programs show that **peer tutoring** has positive effects on the academic performance and attitudes of those tutored. Handicapped students made appreciable gains toward regular education curriculum objectives when tutored by trained students who were themselves successful learners (Slavin et al., 1989).

In delineating the components of successful peer tutoring, Jenkins and Jenkins (1985) identified the following: having highly structured and carefully prescribed lessons with content based on the classroom curriculum and immediate teacher goals; requiring mastery to be demonstrated; having a continuous program of moderate duration (fifteen to thirty minutes daily); and providing specific tutor training for giving clear directions, encouraging and praising, confirming correct responses, correcting errors in a nonpunitive fashion, and avoiding overprompting.

The following "Meeting the Challenge" illustrates the value of peer tutoring for students who are educationally challenged.

Classwide Peer Tutoring System (CPT).   The Classwide Peer Tutoring System (CPT) demonstrates one application of peer tutoring developed to improve instruction for special needs students by increasing direct teaching and student

MEETING THE CHALLENGE

Marcus, a 16-year-old student who is educationally challenged, attended an urban high school. He was the oldest of five children who lived with their divorced mother. She worked two jobs, one cleaning office buildings at night and the other cooking in a restaurant during the day. Marcus was responsible for taking care of his siblings and getting them to school, which meant that he was often tardy, and he didn't have time to read assignments and do homework. Moreover, his mother was unable to confer with his teachers because of her employment.

Marcus was functionally literate (he could read and learn with assistance) and enjoyed successful experiences with individualized instruction in the resource class of his high school. He found it difficult to read assigned materials and to prepare written assignments when he was mainstreamed into the regular classroom. These problems persisted even though his teachers adjusted their expectations to his abilities. His teachers

**Peer tutors can often help students overcome difficulties.
(©Susie Fitzhugh)**

believed that he was capable of functioning in settings other than the resource room and that it was especially important that he interact with students in the regular classroom.

The classroom teacher and the special needs teacher collaborated to discover ways to help Marcus reach his potential. They arranged a telephone conference with his mother and were pleased that she wished to see Marcus achieve success in the regular classroom. She approved of their suggestions of using direct instruction in the regular classroom to help Marcus develop a larger vocabulary, achieve an understanding of main ideas, and develop his ability to focus on the task at hand by stopping periodically to reflect on the ideas he had read. The teachers asked various students in Marcus's classes to function as peer tutors while he learned to concentrate on the teacher's directions and ways of organizing his classwork, so he could complete his work in a reasonable period of time. His mother agreed to talk with him about his schoolwork and to praise his successes. Marcus's schoolwork gradually improved as he gained confidence in his ability to function in the classroom.

motivation, as well as increasing their opportunities to respond and their active engagement in lessons (Delquadri, Greenwood, Whorton, Carta, and Hall, 1986). This method was predicated on selection of skill activities for tutoring that were closely related to the desired curriculum goals. Students were given reinforcement for correct responses by being given social and token reinforcement. Team activities to earn points in competition with other teams were also used in this project. The teachers systematically reviewed and reinforced students' progress. Students received daily and weekly feedback about their progress. These techniques have been found to improve active student responses, reduce spelling errors, and increase the number of words read by students who are educationally disabled.

Project ACHIEVE

Teachers and administrators in Reidsville, North Carolina, schools and faculty at the University of North Carolina at Greensboro used cooperative learning strategies and peer tutoring as two cornerstones of a successful program for helping at-risk middle school and secondary school students. This multifaceted project called Project ACHIEVE (Baber et al., 1990) included a literacy component, a mathematics component, a guidance component, and parent involvement based on techniques that had been demonstrated as successful in a variety of research projects. Here we will focus on the literacy component of Project ACHIEVE (Stoodt, 1990).

At the outset, carefully selected classroom teachers were prepared to provide the at-risk students with direct instruction, to monitor their progress, and to guide the tutors' work with these students. The tutors were prepared with strategies, materials, and techniques to use with the at-risk students. The overall philosophy of the literacy component was to provide an integrated speaking, listening, reading, and writing program coupled with appropriate direct instruction. Literature, including poetry, fiction, and nonfiction, was incorporated into the project.

The tutors learned to use storytelling and discussion with the students to expand their oral language skills as a basis for reading and writing. These activities help students understand and remember the shape of stories and also build confidence in their own abilities. Storytelling affords teachers a rich resource for multicultural education. *The Story Vine* by Anne Pellowski (1984) is an example of a fine multicultural resource for a storytelling program. *Storytelling Activities*, a book by N. J. Livo and S. A. Rietz (1987), provides stories, sources of stories, and ideas for story presentations. It includes many interesting and motivating storytelling activities for developing a sense of story, sequence, vocabulary, and thinking skills. The project activities included taping the students' storytelling sessions. The scripts were typed for the students to read and reread.

Discussion played an extremely important role in teaching the at-risk students because they often acquired more information and understanding from talking and listening than through reading. Through discussion, teachers introduced the main ideas of a lesson and reviewed the important ideas from a preceding lesson to create a context for learning new material. At the end of a lesson, summarizing and recapping important ideas by the teacher or the students facilitated understanding and remembering. The at-risk students often discussed issues related to their own lives because these were of current concern and the students had the necessary schemata to create lively discussions.

Newspaper stories addressing local issues were used for many activities because they provided a good beginning for content area studies in social studies, science, mathematics, and language arts. The students learned process writing, activities for understanding and writing main ideas and supporting details, and study methods. They learned how to use the listening study guide in Example 12.1 and the directed listening-thinking activity (DLTA) in Example 12.2. Newspapers and the role of newspapers in education are discussed in Chapter 10. These were meaningful activities because listening plays a large role in teaching at-risk students, who need to listen with pen or pencil in hand. Taking notes makes students more attentive and accurate in recalling material. Listening study guides and the directed listening-thinking activity are approaches that help all secondary students, particularly at-risk students.

■ ■ ■ EXAMPLE 12.1   Listening Study Guide

Directions for Students

1. List date and class (e.g., social studies, English, home economics).
2. What is the topic (e.g., Egypt, gerunds, nutrition)?
3. How was the content organized? (Any of the patterns discussed in Chapters 4, 5, 10, and 11 may be used, such as cause and effect, examples, or comparison/contrast.)
4. Did the instructor or discussants stick to the point?
5. Do you agree with the ideas or information given?
6. Why do you agree or disagree?
7. Write the main points in no more than three sentences.

■ ■ ■ EXAMPLE 12.2   Directed Listening-Thinking Activity (DLTA)

Directions for Teacher

1. Select a story that has a strong plot. The story should include conflicts or problems to be overcome.
2. Read through the story and identify places to stop reading. These stopping places should occur just before an important event in the story so the listeners can predict what will happen next. Avoid stopping too frequently because this will fragment the story. The number of stops depends on the story length, but two to four stops work best.

3. Introduce the story by telling the students the title and author and by showing them the cover or the early illustrations in the book. If any students have already heard or read the story, ask them to keep the outcome a secret until the other students have heard it.

4. Read the story, stopping at each point selected. When you stop, ask the students to tell what has happened up to this point (briefly), to predict what will happen next, and to explain why they think so.

Stories such as the following are especially appealing for many at-risk students.

Holman, Felice (1974). *Slake's Limbo.* Alladin Books/Macmillan.

Hyde, Dayton (1986). *Don Coyote.* Ballantine.

Mowat, Farley (1956). *Two Against the North.* Scholastic.

Paulsen, Gary (1987). *Hatchet.* Puffin.

Paulsen, Gary (1991). *The River.* Dell.

One of the literacy strategies used in Project ACHIEVE was daily journal writing. Journal writing started slowly with these students, but its values became more apparent as they continued writing. Dialogue journals in which students write and the teacher responds in writing are especially valuable with diverse students because the teacher provides a model for writing ideas and reflecting on experiences. This learning exercise is easily adapted to various content subjects by writing about concepts and experiences related to each content area.

In Project ACHIEVE, the students read and were read to daily. Their reading materials were selected from highly interesting, well-written books that were easy for the students to read. The books selected for read alouds met the same criteria except they were more difficult to read. Both the read alouds and the read alones were previewed with students; then the students read or listened, and follow-up activities gave them opportunities to respond to the books. Example 12.3 shows a preview activity designed to activate schemata and build background for reading, and Example 12.4 shows a plot chart for students to complete after reading the story; the books mentioned in the examples were used along with books like the following recommended ones.

Read Alones

Byars, Betsy. (1988). *A Blossom Promise.* Delacorte. (There are several books about the Blossom family that students will enjoy.)

Byars, Betsy. (1981). *The 18th Emergency.* Penguin.

Byars, Betsy. (1979). *The Pinballs.* Harper & Row.

Klass, Sheila. (1991). *Kool Ada.* Scholastic.

Gardiner, John. (1980). *Stone Fox.* Harper & Row.

George, Jean. (1989). *Shark Beneath the Reef.* Harper Trophy.
Giblin, James. (1982). *Chimney Sweeps.* Harper & Row.
Myers, Walter Dean. (1992). *The Righteous Revenge of Artemis Bonner.* Harper-
    Collins.
Myers, Walter Dean. (1992). *Mop, Moondance, and the Nagasaki Knights.* Delacorte.
Myers, Walter Dean. (1991). *The Mouse Rap.* HarperCollins.
Paterson, Katherine. (1978). *The Great Gilly Hopkins.* Harper Trophy.
Taylor, Mildred D. (1987). *The Friendship.* Bantam-Skylark.
Taylor, Mildred D. (1987). *The Gold Cadillac.* Bantam-Skylark.

Read Alouds

Baylor, Byrd. (1978). *The Other Way to Listen.* Scribners.
Carson, Jo. (1989). *Stories I Ain't Told Nobody Yet.* Orchard.
Freedman, Russell. (1983). *Children of the Wild West.* Clarion.
Greenfield, Eloise. (1991). *Night on Neighborhood Street.* Dial. (Any of Green-
    field's books are appropriate read alouds.)
Hahn, Mary Downing. (1988). *December Stillness.* Clarion.
Ho, Minfong. (1991). *The Clay Marble.* Farrar, Straus, Giroux.
Janeczko, Paul B. (1988). *The Music of What Happens.* Bradbury.
McKissack, Patricia and Frederick. (1989). *A Long Hard Journey.* Walker.
Myers, Walter Dean. (1991). *Now Is Your Time.* Harper Trophy.
Rylant, Cynthia. (1991). *Appalachia.* Harcourt Brace.

■ ■ ■ EXAMPLE 12.3   *A Preview Activity for The Friendship by Mildred Taylor*

Whom do you have friendships with?
How do you know they are your friends?
Make a list of things that friends do for one another.
How are friends and enemies alike? How are they different?
Have you ever been in a country store? If so how are they different from city
    stores? (Students could draw a picture of the inside of a country store.)

■ ■ ■ EXAMPLE 12.4   *Plot Chart to Complete After Reading a Story*

Title	Problem	Main Character/s	How Was the Problem Solved?	Good Solution?

Write a short paragraph about the story problem.
Why do you think this story was titled *The Friendship?*

Motivational Strategies

Students with the individual differences and needs described in this chapter must be motivated to read and write and to experience success in these processes. Literacy must be exercised. The more students read, the better they read; and the better they read, the more they want to read. Thus, increased reading enhances both fluency and the desire to read. The same is true of writing. However, students must be motivated to read and write in order to activate this cycle. The following interventions are particulary helpful in secondary classrooms:

1. Have newspapers and magazines in the classroom for students to read. These publications can also provide models for writing. The more pictures in these publications, the better they will work. Students are motivated to read such materials. (Refer to Chapter 10 for newspaper teaching ideas.) Students are more likely to read materials that are displayed on counters or tables rather than being shelved.

2. Set aside time each day to read aloud and to do book talks about books the students might enjoy. You may choose to read poems, newspaper or magazine articles, books, or excerpts from books. When giving book talks, teachers should briefly discuss the main character, plot, and theme of a story but not reveal its resolution. In giving book talks about informational books, highlight the important, new, and unusual ideas and relate them to the students' existing knowledge. You may select a group of books that relate to a single theme or topic or a wide range of books that appeal to a variety of interests.

3. Make the book review section of the local newspaper available to students.

4. Create bulletin boards and book displays to encourage reading.

5. Invite local authors to discuss their writing.

6. Provide incentives for students to read. These incentives may take the form of adding points to a grade for the course or gift certificates for records, food, or clothing for a certain number of titles read. In some schools, parent organizations or local businesses may donate money or certificates for incentives. At-risk students may be more motivated by the more concrete rewards, at least in the early stages.

7. Have regular reading conferences with students. These individualized discussions are highly motivating for many students. Some categories of at-risk students receive little individualized attention from adults and may respond especially well to the conferences.

What is SSR, and why might content area teachers use it?

8. Develop a **Sustained Silent Reading (SSR)** program. You may begin with one or two days a week and gradually extend the number of days. Start with five minutes and gradually extend the time to fifteen minutes. Students may read anything they choose. Keep a selection of reading materials in the classroom in case students forget their own. In many schools, the SSR program involves everyone in the school reading at the same time.

9. Provide audiotapes of stories and poems that the students can listen to while following the text. These tapes can be highly motivational for many students. Other students in the school may make the tapes for the students who are educationally handicapped. Many students find it helpful to have tapes of the textbooks used in the regular classroom.

10. Read aloud regularly to secondary students from fiction, poetry, and non-fiction selections. As a result of their poor reading abilities, many students who are at risk have not had opportunities to read and enjoy fine literature; therefore, they do not really know what books have to offer. Furthermore, they do not know how books are supposed to sound.

Study Strategies

Example 12.5 describes various study strategies for students from diverse backgrounds. Teachers also can use strategies such as those in the following paragraphs that have proved helpful for adolescents who lack the academic skills required by secondary schools. These strategies and other similar ones are discussed throughout this book. Useful strategies focus on helping students learn how to read, write, study, and learn rather than memorize specific content. For instance, an assistance program should focus on ways to organize the material in preparation for a biology test rather than on the specific questions on the test.

Advance organizers establish a mindset for readers, encouraging them to relate new material to previously learned material before reading. Advance organizers may have a variety of focal or starting points, such as general concepts to be explored in the content, linkages of new material to previously learned ideas, or an introductory paragraph that explains the material to be read.

The Prereading Plan (PReP) (Langer, 1982, 1984) is a way of activating students' prior knowledge that involves associations, reflections about associations, and reformulation of knowledge. PreP also is discussed in Chapter 13 as an approach to assessment.

1. *Initial association:* The teacher identifies a word, phrase, or picture relating to the key concept. Then the students discuss the word, phrase, or picture and how it is related to the key concept, for example, how the 28th parallel is related to the Korean War.

2. *Reflection:* Students explain their associations.

3. *Reformulation:* Students explain new knowledge they have acquired about the topic, for example, knowledge about the Korean War.

Search strategies help students scan text before they answer questions. The goal is to reduce impulsive, thoughtless answers and to encourage thoughtful responses. Students learn to stop, listen, look, and think—to consider alternative answers and solutions before responding.

■ ■ ■ EXAMPLE 12.5   *Combined Use of Study Strategies*

Strategy	Key Words	Visual Cue	Instructions
Active processing Coping Rehearsal	Stop and think	STOP	Students were asked to remember when "look before you leap" has been valuable to them. Also discussed are the benefits of reflection.
Active processing Evaluation Rehearsal	The five Ws	WHO WHAT WHY WHERE WHEN	Students are led to use these elements in their self-questioning exercises. Also discussed are ways to elaborate upon them.
Analogy Rehearsal	Practice	PRACTICE	The benefits of "practice makes perfect" and rehearsals are discussed. Analogies to previous experiences are elicited.
Active processing Evaluation	Check your work	✓	The benefits of self-monitoring and evaluating are discussed. Ways that students can assess accurately are discussed.
Coping Evaluation Organization	Break it into smaller parts		Students are shown how to group information into smaller pieces and discuss the benefits of taking smaller bites. Also discussed is how to put things back together.
Active processing Rehearsal	Make notes		Students are led to use self-generating visual cues or notes as aids in questioning, rehearsing, and organizing information.
Analogy Organization	Organize		The benefits of organizing information are discussed using analogies from students' own experiences. The students think of their minds as houses and how keeping things in particular rooms/places facilitates access.
Active processing Coping Rehearsal	Take time/ takes time		Students are reminded that learning and development take time. Cultural differences in time use and biorhythms are discussed as well as the effective use of time.

Analogy Organization	Look for patterns **X O X O** _ _ _	The benefits of identifying and using patterns are discussed. Students are shown how to make analogies in using patterns. Patterns learned in students' own languages and cultures are used to illustrate transfer and flexibility.
Analogy Coping	Think about other things you know about the topic	Students are led to generate questions that will elicit prior knowledge about the topic.

Source: From Cognitive Learning Strategies for Minority Handicapped Students *(pp. 50–51) by C. Collier and J. J. Hoover, 1987, Boulder, CO: Hamilton. Copyright 1987 by Hamilton Publications. Adapted by permission.*

Verbal rehearsal (think aloud) helps students learn to state comprehension problems to themselves as a way of clarifying their understanding. There are three stages for developing this strategy: (1) the instructor models verbalization of the problem; (2) the students practice verbalizing aloud; and (3) the students verbalize independently and silently.

Metacognition (self-monitoring) requires active reading as students learn to monitor their own understanding of text. When students become aware of comprehension and exert control over it, their understanding improves. Students need direct instruction in using this strategy so they can develop the ability to monitor their own understanding and become conscious of errors or answers that do not make sense.

Self-questioning is a metacognitive strategy that encourages active reading. In this approach, students develop their own comprehension questions. They ask themselves general questions such as, "What did the author say to me?" "Why am I reading this passage?" "What is the main idea?"

Summary

The diversity in student populations is increasing and will continue to do so. Some factors contributing to diversity in the student population are students with diverse cultural backgrounds, educational handicaps, and various disabilities. More and more students with educational handicaps are attending school in regular classrooms because of changes in the way we educate exceptional students, such as through total immersion and mainstreaming programs.

Literacy processes are complex, and their complexity contributes to the wide range of individual differences in secondary classrooms. Much of the student diversity found in secondary classrooms arises from students' varying background experiences and concept development, and these factors are extremely important in reading comprehension. Many students learn to read and write, but not well enough to learn from their content textbooks. A common problem encountered by these readers is a lack of knowledge needed to anticipate and understand the ideas expressed in written language.

Parental involvement with education and parents' level of education are important factors in students' achievement and literacy. Students whose parents are more involved in schools and whose parents graduated from high school tend to be higher achievers.

Teaching strategies must help students develop literacy at the higher levels demanded by contemporary life. The specific instructional techniques directed at meeting individual needs, including the needs of special needs students and at-risk students, are developed throughout this text.

Discussion Questions

1 How is culture related to reading and writing?
2 Discuss the pros and cons of mainstreaming in content classes.
3 What steps can a teacher take to help students from another culture learn to read and write English?
4 Describe a disabled reader you might encounter in a secondary school classroom.
5 Describe a competent reader you might encounter in a secondary school classroom.
6 How do you think education will change in the future if an increasing proportion of students live in conditions of poverty?

Enrichment Activities

1 Interview disabled readers at the secondary level; ask them what their reading problems are and why they think they have reading problems.
2 Interview the parents of a disabled reader about the development of his or her reading problems and their possible causes.
*3 Discuss the reading problems of students with teachers of various content areas. How are the reading problems of their students alike and how are they different?
*4 Observe an ESL classroom, if possible. What problems do you anticipate these students will encounter in the content area that you intend to teach?
5 Use the guidelines in this chapter and analyze an ESL text. Identify its positive qualities and its weaknesses.

---

*These activities are designed for in-service teachers, student teachers, and practicum students.

Classroom Literacy Assessment

Overview

A major purpose of this chapter is to assist the content area teacher in determining whether students possess the literacy and study skills necessary to deal successfully with course materials. To perform this evaluation, the content teacher must be aware of the literacy and study skills appropriate to the particular subject. Salvia and Ysseldyke (1995, p. 5) describe educational assessment well when they say that it is "a multifaceted process that involves far more than the administration of a test. When we assess students, we consider the way they perform a variety of tasks in a variety of settings or contexts, the meaning of their performances in terms of the total functioning of the individual, and the likely explanations for those performances. Good assessment procedures take into consideration the fact that anyone's performance on any task is influenced by the demands of the task itself, by the history and characteristics the individual brings to the task, and by the factors inherent in the setting in which the assessment is carried out." Such assessment is data collection designed to help teachers determine problem areas and make instructional decisions.

Literacy assessment procedures are changing. Newer assessments are focusing more on processes (strategies used to understand text or revise written work) than on products (specific knowledge the student has acquired). Students are asked to produce or do something meaningful. The activity generally involves higher-level thinking and problem solving. Real-life problems and authentic techniques for solutions are featured (Herman, Aschbacher, and Winters, 1992). Because of this focus on process, many assessments appear much like regular classroom instruction, and they serve to move instruction forward instead of causing it to pause for the assessment. Because of the difficulties of developing norm-referenced measures that will reveal such processes, many of the new assessment procedures are classroom based. There is also a recent focus on more self-assessment by students, making them active participants in the assessment process.

Many types of assessment are needed to obtain a complete picture of students' abilities and possibilities. Herman, Aschbacher, and Winters (1992, p. 9) point out that "while performance assessments may tell us how well and deeply students can apply their knowledge, multiple-choice tests may be more efficient for determining how well students have acquired the basic facts and concepts. A balanced curriculum requires a balanced approach to assessment."

Instructional material often is not written at its designated difficulty level. Teachers need to know whether their students can read at the level on which the textbook is written; to discover this, they need to know what this level actually is. Additionally, teachers need to understand the factors that influence readability and how to use readability formulas and other measures for determining the difficulty of materials.

In this chapter we discuss norm-referenced tests, criterion-referenced tests, classroom-based tests, assessment of the readability of printed materials, and computer applications to assessment. They are not all mutually exclusive measures; for example, criterion-referenced tests may be either norm referenced or classroom based.

Purpose-Setting Questions

As you read this chapter, try to answer these questions:

1   What are the functions of norm-referenced tests?
2   What changes are occurring in literacy assessment today?
3   What are criterion-referenced tests?
4   What are some classroom-based assessments of reading and writing achievement, and how can the results of each be used to help teachers plan instructional programs?
5   What is meant by portfolio assessment?
6   How are computers being applied in the area of assessment?
7   How is an understanding of the readability levels of textbook materials important to a teacher?

■ ■ Norm-Referenced Tests

What types of information can norm-referenced tests give teachers?

Content teachers may administer and interpret certain types of **norm-referenced tests,** especially survey achievement tests, to check student performance in a wide range of literacy areas: reading, writing, language, reference skills, and others. Test results indicate the relative achievement of the groups tested in these areas. Teachers can compare a student's performance on a subtest in one subject with his or her performance on other subtests in a test battery. Teachers also can learn how a student's performance on a test compares with his or her earlier or later performance on the same test. Scores from two different kinds of norm-referenced tests on the same topic (e.g., reading or writing) are not likely to be comparable.

■ Scores on Norm-Referenced Tests

What are the pros and cons of these four ways of reporting results of norm-referenced tests?

Results of norm-referenced tests may be reported as (1) grade scores or **grade equivalents,** (2) **percentile ranks,** (3) **stanines,** and (4) **normal curve equivalents.**

Grade equivalent indicates the grade level, in years and months, for which a given score was the average score in the referencing sample. For example, if a score of 25 has the grade equivalent of 8.1, 25 was the average score of pupils in the norm group who were in the first month of the eighth grade. If a student (not in the norm group) who is in the first month of the eighth grade were to take the same test and score 25 correct, his or her performance would be "at grade level," or average for his or her grade placement. If that student's score had a grade equivalent of 9.1, he or she would have scored as well as the typical ninth grader in the first month of the school year.

Some words of caution need to be offered about grade equivalents. Grade equivalents do not indicate the appropriate grade placement for a student. A score of 9.0 indicates only that the average student in the norming population who was just beginning the ninth grade had a certain number of items correct; it does not mean that another student who had that number of items correct can necessarily read 9.0 grade level material.

Another problem is that "because the average reading level of the population flattens out during junior high school (Grades 7–9), grade equivalents have almost no meaning at these grade levels" (Lewandowski and Martens, 1990). Moreover, the grade equivalents from grade level to grade level (e.g., from 9.0 to 10.0) are partly hypothetical and are arrived at statistically, since tests are usually standardized at only one or two places within each grade. Because of these and other misinterpretations, some test publishers are discouraging the use of grade equivalent scores. The Board of Directors of the International

Reading Association, after noting the serious misuses of grade equivalents, has recommended that grade equivalent interpretations be eliminated from tests.

Using percentiles, stanines, or normal curve equivalents is generally more acceptable than using grade equivalents to interpret test results. Therefore, content area teachers need to understand these types of test results in order to apply the information gained from tests to classroom practice. Explanations of these methods of reporting results follow.

Percentile rank expresses a score in terms of its position within a set of 100 scores. The percentile rank indicates the percentage of scores of the norm group that are equal to or lower than the given score. Thus a result ranked in the 35th percentile is regarded as equivalent to or surpassing the results of 35 percent of those in the norm group. A student who scores in the 83rd percentile according to the local school's norms may only score in the 53rd percentile if his or her score is based on national norms because of the differences in the sample populations on which the norms were based.

A *stanine* ranks a test score in relation to other scores on that test. It is expressed as a value from one to nine on a nine-point scale. Thus, the mean score of the standard population has a stanine value of 5. A stanine of 9 indicates the highest performance on the test; stanines 7 and 8 are above average; stanines 4 to 6 are considered average; stanines 2 and 3 are below average; and stanine 1 indicates lowest performance. Stanines and percentiles may be compared as follows:

Stanines	*Percentiles*
9	96–99
8	90–95
7	78–89
6	60–77
5	41–59
4	23–40
3	11–22
2	5–10
1	1–4

Normal curve equivalents (NCEs) are used in some states and school systems. NCEs are represented on a scale of 1 to 99 with a mean of 50. They have many of the characteristics of percentile ranks but have the additional advantage of being based on an equal-interval scale. This scale allows a meaningful comparison to be made between different achievement test batteries and/or different tests within the same test battery. For example, if a student receives an NCE score of 62 on the mathematics test of a battery and an NCE of 53 on the reading test, it would be correct to say that the mathematics score is nine points higher than the reading score. Tables that show the conversions of test scores to NCEs are usually supplied by test publishers.

Readers interested in further study of measurement concepts can read Salvia and Ysseldyke (1995).

■ Criteria for Choosing Norm-Referenced Tests

A norm-referenced test that is selected for use should meet certain criteria. Its norms should be based on a population similar to the population being tested, and it should have high **reliability** and **validity.**

Why are the reliability and validity of norm-referenced tests important?

A test is inappropriate if the sample population used to establish norms is significantly different from the class or group to be tested. A description of the norm population is usually contained in the test manual.

Some people feel that students who are different in some ways from the majority of the population have an unfair disadvantage in taking many tests because the tests contain a cultural bias. Any time the background experiences of a group of students differ from those of the sample population on which the test was standardized, the test's norms are inappropriate for that group, and relying on the results of this test may lead to incorrect educational decisions (Salvia and Ysseldyke, 1995).

The concepts of validity and reliability need to be understood thoroughly by teachers who use tests. A valid norm-referenced reading test represents a balanced and adequate sampling of the instructional outcomes (e.g., knowledge and skills) that it is intended to cover. Face validity can be judged by comparing the test content with the related courses of study, instructional materials, and educational goals of the class. Evidence about validity is nearly always given in the test's manual of directions or in a technical information pamphlet; such information may be checked against the impartial opinions of educational professionals and should be carefully inspected to see if the test is designed to measure what the teacher wants to measure.

In addition to measuring the skills it claims to measure (validity) and having subtests that are long enough to yield reasonably accurate scores, a test should not result in a chance score with students obtaining high scores by luck, guessing, or other factors (reliability). The reliability of a test refers to the degree to which the test gives consistent results.

When measuring the level of achievement of an individual student, only a test of high reliability should be used, since it is necessary to find that student's specific, not comparative, level of achievement. To be considered reliable, tests should have internal consistency reliability coefficients of .85 or above and test-retest reliability of .70 or above (Lewandowski and Martens, 1990). Although a test of low reliability cannot be valid, high reliability does not guarantee that a test is valid.

Readers who are interested in more detailed descriptions of particular tests can consult the following collections of reviews on reading tests.

Conoley, Jane Close, and James C. Impara, eds. *The Twelfth Mental Measurement Yearbook.* Lincoln, Neb.: Buros Institute of Mental Measurements, 1995.

Impara, James C., and Jane Close Conoley, eds. *Supplement to the Twelfth Mental Measurements Yearbook.* Lincoln, Neb.: Buros Institute of Mental Measurements, 1996.

Murphy, Linda L., Jane Close Conoley, and James C. Impara, eds. *Tests in Print IV.* Lincoln, Neb.: Buros Institute of Mental Measurements, 1994.

Keyser, Daniel J., and Richard C. Sweetland, eds. *Test Critiques, Vols. I–VI.* Kansas City, Mo.: Test Corporation of America, 1992.

Compton, Carolyn. *85 Tests for Remedial and Special Education.* Belmont, Calif.: David S. Lake Publisher, 1989.

SilverPlatter Information Services offers a *Mental Measurements Yearbook Database on SilverPlatter* that contains the text of the *Tenth, Eleventh,* and *Twelfth Mental Measurements Yearbooks* on CD-ROM, hard disk, or via the Internet. In addition to these sources, useful articles about testing often appear in professional journals (e.g., the *Journal of Adolescent & Adult Literacy* and *Educational Leadership*).

■ Norm-Referenced Tests of Reading Achievement

What is the difference in the information obtained from a survey test and that obtained from a diagnostic test?

Norm-referenced reading tests yield objective data about reading performance. They are designed so that each response to a test item is subject to only one interpretation. The types of norm-referenced reading tests that content teachers are most likely to hear about are **survey tests** and **diagnostic tests.**

Reading survey tests measure general achievement in reading. The results can show how well students are performing in relation to others who have taken the test. Looking at scores of all students in a class gives an indication of the range of reading achievement in the class.

A single score on a survey test represents the student's overall reading achievement and does not reveal how the student will perform on specific reading tasks. However, some reading survey tests designed for secondary school students have separate sections on vocabulary, comprehension, and reading rate. Such tests yield separate scores for each section. A wise teacher is not merely concerned with a student's total achievement score but wants to determine if the student is equally strong in all areas tested. Furthermore, a careful examination of student responses to individual test items might provide the teacher with information about more specific reading needs. One way to learn more from testing is to go over the test items with the student to see if he or she can explain his or her responses. It is possible that correct responses were reached in inappropriate ways or that a student guessed at a number of the answers.

Diagnostic reading tests are used most frequently by special teachers of reading, but content teachers need some basic information about this type of test in order to discuss test results with special reading teachers. Diagnostic reading tests help to locate specific strengths and weaknesses of readers. Such tests often include subtests for comprehension, vocabulary, word identification skills, and rate of reading. Group diagnostic tests are usually given by reading specialists but sometimes are given by classroom teachers. Reading specialists usually administer individual diagnostic reading tests because they have the required experience and training. Additionally, time constraints generally make the use of diagnostic tests in the content area classroom impractical.

■ Concerns About Traditional Standardized Reading Tests

In general, traditional standardized reading tests do not reflect what we now know about the reading process and reading comprehension (Farr and Carey, 1986). Traditional tests treat reading as if it were simply skill mastery of a variety of skills (a product) rather than a constructive, strategic process in which readers make use of their prior knowledge and techniques for unlocking meaning in the text in order to understand its message (a process). Valencia and Pearson (1987) call attention to the dangers of looking at reading from the new perspective but continuing to assess students' achievements and needs from the old one. They also mention that teachers who want their students to score well on the traditional testing instruments may allow the test to influence the curriculum, resulting in inappropriate instruction in light of the current understanding of the reading process. Wittrock (1987, p. 736) explains to teachers that process-oriented comprehension measures "will not tell what your students have learned about a text passage. Nor will they tell you where your students' reading achievement lies in relation to that of other students. But process-oriented tests will tell you about the strategies your students use to make sense out of the text they read in your class. They will provide a way for you to understand the instruction in comprehension your students need."

Sternberg (1991) points out that reading from traditional tests is different from reading in real life in these ways: recall on the tests is immediate and entirely intentional; the passages have tight reasoning; students are asked to evaluate, but not construct, arguments; the passages are emotionally neutral and often uninteresting; and distractions are minimized.

Figure 13.1 is a chart from Valencia and Pearson (1987) that helps to put the problem of the mismatch between current theory about reading and current assessment techniques into perspective.

FIGURE 13.1

Contrasting Views
of the Reading
Process and
Assessment
Practices

Source: Chart from
"Reading Assessment:
Time for a Change,"
Sheila Valencia and
P. David Pearson, The
Reading Teacher, April
1987, p. 731. Reprinted
with permission of
Sheila Valencia and the
International Reading
Association.

A Set of Contrasts Between New Views of Reading and Current Practices in Assessing Reading

New Views of the Reading Process Tell Us That . . .	Yet When We Assess Reading Comprehension, We . . .
Prior knowledge is an important determinant of reading comprehension.	Mask any relationship between prior knowledge and reading comprehension by using lots of short passages on lots of topics.
A complete story or text has structural and topical integrity.	Use short texts that seldom approximate the structural and topical integrity of an authentic text.
Inference is an essential part of the process of comprehending units as small as sentences.	Rely on literal comprehension test items.
The diversity in prior knowledge across individuals as well as the varied causal relations in human experiences invite many possible inferences to fit a text or question.	Use multiple choice items with only one correct answer, even when many of the responses might, under certain conditions, be plausible.
The ability to vary reading strategies to fit the text and the situation is one hallmark of an expert reader.	Seldom assess how and when students vary the strategies they use during normal reading, studying, or when the going gets tough.
The ability to synthesize information from various parts of the text and different texts is hallmark of an expert reader.	Rarely go beyond finding the main idea of a paragraph or passage.
The ability to ask good questions of text, as well as to answer them, is hallmark of an expert reader.	Seldom ask students to create or select questions about a selection they may have just read.
All aspects of a reader's experience, including habits that arise from school and home, influence reading comprehension.	Rarely view information on reading habits and attitudes as being as important as information about performance.
Reading involves the orchestration of many skills that complement one another in a variety of ways.	Use tests that fragment reading into isolated skills and report performance on each.
Skilled readers are fluent; their word identification is sufficiently automatic to allow most cognitive resources to be used for comprehension.	Rarely consider fluency as an index of skilled reading.
Learning from text involves the restructuring, application, and flexible use of knowledge in new situations.	Often ask readers to respond to the text's declarative knowledge rather than to apply it to near and far transfer tasks.

■ Changes in Some Commercial Reading Tests

Currently some publishers are attempting to develop commercial reading tests that reflect newer views of the reading process, but they face many difficulties. Prior knowledge of test takers is difficult to assess in a concise paper-and-pencil format; whole selections sometimes take unrealistically long periods of time to read; appropriate answers to questions involving different backgrounds of experience are hard to determine; reading strategy assessment is a more abstract concept than assessment of mastery of facts; reading fluency is difficult to assess; and construction of items that require higher-level thinking is more difficult than construction of test items at the literal level of thinking. Wixson and others (1987, p. 751) have been involved in developing statewide reading tests in Michigan that "evaluate reading in a more holistic manner" without the attempt to set up "a one to one correspondence between each stated objective and individual test items." Both Wixson and others (1987) in Michigan and Valencia and Pearson (1987) in Illinois have worked out ways to assess background knowledge. The two techniques being used in Illinois for background assessment are having students predict if particular ideas are likely to be found in a selection on a certain topic and rating the relatedness of vocabulary terms to a central concept of a selection.

Wixson and others (1987) have chosen representative classroom materials and used complete selections from them. The reporting of results from these tests will "describe a reader's performance under specific conditions (for example, with a certain level of topic familiarity, a certain type of text, a certain level of interest in the text)" (p. 752). The types of test items that Valencia and Pearson (1987) have worked on include items to test summary writing skills and metacognitive judgments and items with more than one acceptable response. For example, to evaluate summary writing, students pick the best summary of the selection that they have read from three or four written by other students. They may be given a list of summary features and be asked to check off their reasons for choosing one as the best. To check metacognitive judgments, students may have to rate the helpfulness of several retellings of a selection that they have read to a variety of audiences, such as a teacher, a classmate, or a younger child.

As test items are developed to assess comprehension, producers of such tests must be aware of some research findings related to testing of students in grades 5 through 12. Some pertinent information from studies reported by Davey (1989) follows:

1. Poor readers are much slower than good readers in test completion times, adding a rate factor to a comprehension assessment that is to the disadvantage of some students.
2. Multiple-choice question scores are generally higher than free response scores, and free response questions are more difficult for poor readers than for good readers, although multiple-choice items are not.

3. Testing that allows students to look back at the passage when answering questions appears to enhance free recall responses but not multiple-choice responses, but good readers benefit more than poor readers from look-back opportunities. Good readers appear to integrate specific text information with their background knowledge and to reason about the material when they are allowed to look back. Poor readers benefit from looking back when answers are directly stated in the text but fail to use inferential strategies.

Some commercial publishers are now providing new assessments that reflect current literacy theory. *Integrated Assessment System* (Roger Farr and Beverly Farr, The Psychological Corporation, 1990) has two components: Language Arts Performance Assessments and Language Arts Portfolios. The Language Arts Performance Assessments are reading passages called "prompts," accompanied by guided writing activities used to assess the reading comprehension, composition skills, and higher-level thinking of the students. The tests have longer text samples than traditional tests and sometimes offer more than one type of text about a topic, to allow the students to synthesize information from all of the texts. Students are guided through the planning, drafting, and revision phases for their written products. More than one response is acceptable with these open-ended tasks. A standard scoring rubric is provided for each prompt/writing activity to guide assessment of the products (Werner, 1992; Commeyras, 1992).

The Language Arts Portfolios include student folders, a storage box, a teacher's manual, and an optional videotape. A variety of work is selected by the students and teachers to be placed in the portfolio with reading and writing logs, checklists, and anecdotal records. Portfolio content evaluation information, as well as information about student conferences and reporting to parents and administrators, is included in the teacher's manual (Werner, 1992).

Integrated Literature and Language Arts Program (Riverside Publishing) provides scores for listening comprehension, fictional reading comprehension, and nonfictional reading comprehension as well as scores related to prior knowledge/predicting content, reading strategies, vocabulary, constructing meaning, and composing. There is also an interest and experience survey associated with the test. The program uses passages that are intact literature selections from a variety of genres, and the exercises require a variety of response types.

Written Language Assessment (J. Jeffery Grill and Margaret M. Kirwin, Academic Therapy Publications, 1989) is designed to evaluate the written language competence of students from ages 8 to 18. The assessment is based on whole pieces of text written by the students. Each student writes an expressive, instructive, and creative essay, which is scored both qualitatively and quantitatively (Spaulding, 1989).

■ ■ Criterion-Referenced Tests

What is the difference between norm-referenced tests and criterion-referenced tests?

Whereas norm-referenced tests compare the test taker's performance with that of others, **criterion-referenced tests** (CRTs) check the test taker against a performance criterion, which is a predetermined standard. Thus a criterion-referenced test might read: "Given ten paragraphs at the ninth-grade reading level, the student can identify the main idea in eight of them." In short, a CRT indicates whether or not the test taker has mastered a particular objective or skill rather than how well his or her performance compares with that of others. A norm-referenced test, on the other hand, may indicate that the student can identify the main idea of a paragraph better than 90 percent of the test takers in his or her age group.

The results of criterion-referenced tests can be used as instructional prescriptions; that is, if a student cannot perform the task of identifying the main idea in specified paragraphs, the need for instruction in that area is apparent. These tests are therefore useful in day-to-day decisions about instruction.

However, there are a number of unresolved issues related to criterion-referenced tests. For example, the level of success demanded is one issue. Often the passing level is set arbitrarily at 80 or 90 percent, but there is no agreement as to the nature of mastery or how to measure it. Additionally, many criterion-referenced tests give the appearance that hundreds of discrete reading skills must be mastered separately, overlooking the fact that the skills are highly interactive and must be integrated with each other if effective reading is to occur. Some question exists about whether CRTs can measure complex domains such as critical/creative reading skills, reading appreciation, or attitude toward reading. CRTs may also be questioned in terms of reliability and validity. Any type of test *may* measure only knowledge of rules, rather than ability to use them, and a short set of items over a particular reading objective can be less than reliable, particularly in terms of individual assessment.

It seems likely that both criterion-referenced tests and norm-referenced tests will continue to be important reading assessment tools, serving different purposes. In fact, both kinds of interpretation—individual and comparative—are offered by a number of tests. Content teachers may make frequent use of certain CRTs. They may construct these measures themselves, using banks of criterion-referenced test items that are available for all subject areas from some state educational departments or from places such as Educational Testing Services, in Princeton, New Jersey. Teachers may choose appropriate items from such collections to construct tailor-made CRTs, or they may construct their own items.

For many years, content teachers have been using their own criterion-referenced measures to assess the results of instruction. In such cases, definite instructional objectives are tested, and there is a definite standard of judgment or criterion for "passing." Example 13.1 shows an objective that is measured by five items on a test prepared by a teacher. The criterion for demonstrating mastery of this objective is set at four out of five; that is, the student must answer four out of five items correctly to show mastery.

Note that each question in Example 13.1 is related to the objective. The criterion level for "passing" must be determined by the teacher. Results give the teacher precise information concerning what each student can or cannot do; therefore, the test results can be used to improve classroom instruction.

■ ■ ■ EXAMPLE 13.1   *Criterion-Referenced Test*

Objective. Utilizing the information found on the content pages of the almanac.

Directions. Find answers to the following:
1. Who was the fifteenth president of the United States?
2. Who holds the world record for high diving?
3. What was the Academy Award winner for the Best Picture of 1996?
4. What are the names of the Kentucky Derby winner of 1995 and the jockey who rode the horse to victory?
5. Where is the deepest lake in the United States?

■ ■ Classroom-Based Assessments

The term *classroom-based assessments* refers here to informal, primarily teacher-constructed assessments used daily in classrooms. Informal tests (tests not standardized against a specific norm or objective) are valuable aids to teachers. Most of them are constructed by teachers themselves. Other informal measures, such as observations, interviews/conferences, performance samples, and portfolio assessments provide much information. At present such measures are necessary in order for a teacher to assess outcomes of currently endorsed instructional procedures in reading, because most current norm-referenced tests are not designed to do so.

■ Informal Tests of Achievement

Several informal tests of reading achievement can be useful to the teacher in revealing student reading achievement. Six of these measures are discussed in the sections that follow: (1) assessment of background knowledge, (2) group reading inventory, (3) written skill inventories, (4) informal reading inventories, (5) cloze procedure, and (6) gamelike activities.

MEETING THE CHALLENGE

Creative teachers have always found ways to adapt assessment techniques to their particular teaching situations. Katherine Dooley, an English teacher in a rural high school, worked out classroom-based assessment techniques to meet her students' needs. Here is her account of her experience:

Assessment methods may include performance measures.
(© Richard Pasley / STOCK BOSTON)

In my first year of teaching, I quickly learned my expectations for a unit often could not be evaluated in one fifty-minute period; therefore, I divided tests into objective and subjective (essay-type) questions and gave the test over two days or allowed students to work on the essay part at home. I assumed (I should have known better than to assume) that they would HATE the idea of taking a longer test, and actually I think at first they did hate it. When I returned the tests, I noticed lots of smiles (something I thought was strange because the grades were average at best). Our discussion of the test turned into an evaluation of my evaluation of them. They loved the two-part test. Almost everyone had made a grade they were pleased with on at least one part of the test. Instead of receiving one mediocre grade, they had one great grade, and that made them feel good. In subsequent units, I continued the practice of at least two-part assessments.

The Shakespeare unit formed a new challenge. Shakespeare is my favorite, and more than anything I wanted to transfer my love of the Bard to them. In our pre-unit discussion, I discovered their negative feelings toward Shakespeare would make that difficult. In assessment, I was locked into several things by virtue of unwritten department policy. They would have to take an objective test, take a test over quotations, write an essay, and memorize the *Macbeth* dagger soliloquy; however, those things alone would only compound their dislike of Shakespeare. I wanted them to play with the play and I knew a group of my students had been videotaping their parties and club meetings since elementary school. The solution was the fact that my students were video babies. I added a video assignment to their growing list and prepared for the groaning, complaining, and whining. But they were not upset about the workload as much as the instructions for the video project: "Videotape something related to *Macbeth* (act out scenes or do a newscast or ???). It should be at least seven minutes long." They begged for more directions; I refused. I wanted them to be creative, but I was secretly petrified that the project was going to bomb. A week before the due date, they became excited and secretive. One group refused to let me near them when they were discussing the video. Everyone guarded their groups' ideas for sports stories and funny commercials.

This project was the biggest success of the year. The videos, most of which were newscasts, were loaded with lines from the play and complex puns. My favorite was a live remote from the local Taco Bell where Fleance (one of my students in lovely purple tights) was "making a run for the border" after the murder of Banquo. Students told me this was the most fun they had had all year; parents, many of whom worked the camera or did makeup, called and sent gifts saying they "had a blast" helping with this assignment. After we watched all the videos, we voted, dressed up, and gave out the Doolies (huge pieces of minerals) for best actor, actress, cinematography, and picture. In their mandatory acceptance speeches, some thanked parents, some made political or social statements, but all said they would never forget *Macbeth.* I don't think they realized it, but that was the whole idea!

Assessment of Background Knowledge

Since the background knowledge of the students plays a vital role in their comprehension of reading material (see Chapters 4 and 5), it is wise to assess background knowledge about a topic before asking students to read about that topic. When prior knowledge of the topics covered in the reading passages is lacking because students with diverse home backgrounds and mental capabilities have acquired different sets of background information, teachers should develop the missing concepts before assigning the reading. Students with varying backgrounds will often have difficulties with concepts in different content fields.

Background knowledge may be assessed in several ways. Oral methods of assessment may be better for less advanced students because they may actually know more than their writing skills allow them to express.

Holmes and Roser (1987) suggest five ways to assess prior knowledge: free recall, word association, structured questions, recognition, and unstructured questions. *Free recall* involves asking students to tell or write down all the facts they know about a topic. It is a time-efficient method, but it is more successful with older skilled readers than with younger students and less skilled older readers, who do not appear to be able to retrieve their knowledge as easily. *Word association* involves giving the students words that are subtopics of the main topic, one at a time, and asking them to tell everything they can think of about the terms as they relate to the main topic. This technique usually provides more information about prior knowledge than does free recall. The teacher may prepare *structured questions* about subtopics of the main topic to probe prior knowledge, but this approach requires expertise in question formulation and time for preparation of questions. Structured questioning offers the largest amount of information of the five types of assessments suggested by Holmes and Roser, and it provides the largest number of facts per minute of administration time. When a *recognition* task is used, questions about the subtopics of the main topic with a modified multiple-choice format are used. There may be more than one correct answer to each question. This method is relatively efficient and effective in assessment of prior knowledge. *Unstructured discussion* of the students' prior experiences with a topic is the least effective of the five approaches mentioned.

Langer (1981) developed the PreReading Plan (PReP) technique to help teachers to assess students' background knowledge about a content area topic and to activate prior knowledge they possess about the topic before they are asked to read the material. The PReP is a discussion activity for a group of approximately ten students, in which the teacher selects a key word, phrase, or picture about the topic to start the discussion. First, the teacher has the students brainstorm about the presented stimulus by saying something like, "What do you think of when you hear (the particular word or phrase) or see (the selected picture)?" The responses are recorded on the board. Then the students explain what made them think of the responses they gave, which develops an awareness of the networks of ideas they have in their experiential backgrounds and exposes them to the associations that their classmates have made. Finally, the teacher asks students if they have any new ideas about the word, phrase, or picture related to the topic of the content passage before they begin to read the text. The opportunity to elaborate on their prior knowledge often results in more refined responses, since they can use input from others to help in shaping responses.

After the PReP discussion ends, the teacher can analyze the responses to discover the students' probable ability to recall the content material after they have read it. Students who have much prior knowledge about the topic under discussion usually respond with superordinate concepts, definitions, analogies, and comparisons with other concepts. Those with some prior knowledge about the topic generally respond with examples or attributes of the concept. Those with little prior information about the topic usually make low-level associations, offering word parts (prefixes, suffixes, and/or root words) or sound-alike words or sharing not quite relevant personal experiences. Initial responses may fall into one category, and responses during the final elaboration may fall into a higher category of knowledge, showing that the process may activate knowledge as well as assess it. Langer states that responses that show much or some prior knowledge indicate that the students will be able to read the text with sufficient understanding. Responses that show little prior knowledge indicate that the students need direct instruction related to relevant concepts before they are asked to read the material.

Group Reading Inventory

What kind of information can a group reading inventory yield?

The content teacher may administer a **group reading inventory** (GRI) before asking students to use a particular text for study. A GRI of content material involves having students read a passage of 1,000 to 2,000 words from their textbooks and then asking them certain types of questions. This procedure can give some indication of how well students will be able to read a particular textbook. Content books to be studied should be written on a student's instructional or independent reading level (instructional for material to be worked on in class with the teacher's assistance; independent for material to be used by the students outside of class); trade and supplementary books should be on a student's independent level, since they are generally used for outside reading assignments. Therefore, by using a group reading inventory, the content teacher can decide whether or not to use material from a particular book for in-class or homework assignments and can decide which materials are inappropriate for use with particular students at any time.

The selection used in an inventory should be material that has not been read previously by the students. The teacher introduces the selection and directs the students to read it for the purpose of answering certain kinds of questions. As students read, the teacher writes the time on the chalkboard at 15-second intervals; each student writes down the last time recorded when he or she finishes reading the passage. Later, a words-per-minute score is computed by dividing the time into the total number of words in the passage. For example, if the passage is 1,000 words long and the student reads it in 4 minutes, the student would divide 4 into 1,000 to get a 250-words-per-minute score. When he or she is finished reading, the student closes the book and answers a series of questions of such types as

1. Vocabulary (word meaning, word recognition, context, synonyms, antonyms, affixes)
2. Literal comprehension (main ideas, significant details, sequence)
3. Higher-order comprehension (inferential and evaluative)

A sample GRI from a secondary level history textbook is provided in Example 13.2.

Materials are suitable for instructional purposes if the student can comprehend 75 percent of what he or she reads, as indicated by performance on well-constructed comprehension questions. If students can comprehend 75 percent of what they read, their comprehension will probably increase if teachers introduce specialized vocabulary words, help with comprehension, teach a study method, and provide specific purposes for reading. Of course, students have many different reading levels, depending on their interests and the background information they possess on any specific topic. Thus, a GRI must be applied to the text in each specific content area. When the student comprehends 90 to 100 percent of what he or she reads, the material can be classified as being on his or her *independent* reading level. When the student comprehends 50 percent or less of what he or she reads, the material is on his or her *frustration* level. Students scoring 70 percent or below on a set of materials should be given an inventory on easier material; those who score 90 percent or above should be given an inventory on more difficult material.

■■■ EXAMPLE 13.2   *Sample Group Reading Inventory*

Name _____ Date _____

Motivation Statement: Read to find out why the Confederation Congress was unable to settle its foreign problems.

Selection: *Dealing with Other Countries*

The men who represent one country as it deals with other nations are called diplomats. Their work is called *diplomacy,* or the *foreign relations* of their country. The foreign relations of the Confederation were not very successful. Congress did not have the power to make the states or the people follow the agreements that it made with other countries. Under these conditions other nations had little respect for the United States.

The British had promised in the Treaty of Paris to leave the territory they had agreed was now part of the United States. Instead, they remained in their forts along the Great Lakes. They also used their Indian friends to keep settlers out of the Northwest Territory. There was much fighting between the frontiersmen and England's Indian allies.

Why did the English hold these forts? They hoped to keep their fur trade and the control it gave them over some Indian tribes. They even hoped to set up an Indian nation north of the Ohio River. Suppose the American government failed to last. Some British leaders thought that they could then move back into control of their former colonies. The reason they gave for keeping their grip on the Northwest was that the United States had not kept its treaty promise to help British creditors collect their debts in America.

In 1784 Congress tried to settle some of its problems with England. It sent John Adams to London. He tried to get the British to give up the forts on American soil and to increase trade with the United States. The British refused to give up the forts until American debtors had paid the money owed to British creditors since before the Revolutionary War. They refused to make any kind of trade treaty. Adams tried for three years, but could not get the British to change their minds.

Congress also tried to settle its troubles with Spain. In the Treaty of Paris, England had given Americans the use of the Mississippi River and the right to store their goods at New Orleans. This agreement was most important to the people who had moved into Kentucky and Tennessee. They had to use the Mississippi to get their goods to market. They also needed the right to deposit, or keep, their goods in New Orleans until a ship could load them for the trip across the ocean.

Spain held the lower Mississippi and New Orleans. Its rulers would not accept the agreement made by the British and Americans. They also hoped the new nation would not succeed so they could take part of it. Spanish officials urged the settlers south of the Ohio to secede, or take their territory out of the United States. They could then join the Spanish empire. Spain would give them the use of the Mississippi and New Orleans. Spain was still a strong nation. It proved this by getting Indians to attack the pioneers who settled near Spanish territory, and by holding onto Natchez, in American territory.

But Spain was willing to discuss such problems. In 1785 Don Diego de Gardoqui became the first Spanish minister to America. He and John Jay, the American Secretary of Foreign Affairs, soon began to bargain. By this time Spain had closed the lower Mississippi to American trade. Jay was told by Congress that he must get Spain to allow such trade. Don Diego was willing, but only if Spain would control the Mississippi, most of what is now Alabama and Mississippi, and parts of Tennessee, Kentucky, and Georgia. Spain claimed this land because it had held part of it while fighting the British as allies of the United States during the Revolutionary War. Don Diego also asked that Spain should hold all lands south of the thirty-fifth parallel.

John Jay refused to accept such claims. He insisted that the United States would accept only the terms of the Treaty of Paris, which made the thirty-first parallel the boundary between Florida and the United States. Businessmen in the North and East wanted to build up their trade with Spain. In August, 1786, Congress changed its position. It told Jay that he could give up American rights on the Mississippi River for 25 years, if Spain would in turn agree to allow more American trade in Spanish ports. This would have helped the businessmen of New England, but would have hurt the farmers and settlers in the South and West. There was a bitter debate in Congress, and the men who represented seven of the states voted for this plan. This was two states less than the nine that had to agree before Congress could make a treaty. The talks between Spain and the United States then ended. The problems between the two countries were not settled until the Pinckney Treaty of 1795.

Relations with France were also poor. Thomas Jefferson became our minister to France. He wrote that the French showed him little respect. The leaders of the French government were angry because the United States could not repay its wartime debts. However, Jefferson did get them to agree to allow more trade by American ships. The Confederation had no army, and could not do much about Indian attacks. It could not open up the Mississippi, build up trade with Europe, or make needed agreements with foreign governments. More people began to wonder why they had to have such a weak national government.

Source: Boyd Shafer, et al., A High School History of Modern America, *3rd ed., pp. 104–105. Copyright 1977. By permission of LAIDLAW BROTHERS, A Division of Doubleday and Company, Inc.*

Inventory Questions

Directions: Write a short answer to each question.

VOCABULARY

1. What is meant by the term *diplomacy?*
2. Define *secede.*
3. Define *allies.*
4. What is a synonym for the word *treaty?*
5. Write the definition of the word *relations* as used in the passage.
6. What did the author mean by "keeping their grip on the Northwest"?

LITERAL COMPREHENSION

1. What job did John Jay have in the Confederation government? (Detail)
2. Why did the English remain in forts along the Great Lakes? (Detail)
3. Why was the Treaty of Paris important to the people of Tennessee and Kentucky? (Detail)
4. List, in order, the sequence of steps in the discussion of problems with Spain. (Sequence)

INTERPRETIVE AND CRITICAL COMPREHENSION

1. Do you agree with the directive of Congress to Jay in 1786? Why or why not? (Evaluation)
2. What do you think the people began to want from their national government? What makes you think this? (Inference)
3. Why did the U.S. have so much difficulty in dealing with other nations as described in this selection? (Conclusion)

Written Skill Inventories

Content teachers may want to know if students have developed the specific reading skills necessary to understand textbooks and other printed materials in their particular content areas. When teachers are preparing to teach particular chapters or units that involve reading content area materials, they should be aware of the nature of the assigned reading material. Teachers can prepare and administer skill inventories based on textbook chapters or units, modeling them after the skill inventories presented in this section. On the basis of the results, the teachers will become more aware of what activities are needed to prepare students to read and understand the assigned materials.

Skill inventories may serve as a part of the total assessment program; that is, part of a test by a science teacher may require students to read a table or graph that appears in the text; questions about interpretation of a map that appears in the text might be used as part of a social science teacher's chapter or unit test; symbol knowledge and diagram-reading ability might be included in a mathematics teacher's test; questions on vocabulary words may be used to check understanding of the special terms in a content chapter or unit; assignments in outlining or note taking or adjusting reading rate to purpose and degree of difficulty may be included in tests by all content teachers. The ultimate purpose of skill inventories is that students master and comprehend the content found in their textbooks and in other printed materials used in the classroom. The following skills are common to all content areas:

1. Understanding and using parts of textbooks (table of contents, index, list of illustrations, appendices, bibliography, glossary)
2. Interpreting maps, tables, charts, graphs, diagrams, cartoons
3. Comprehending specialized vocabulary
4. Using reference materials (encyclopedias, dictionaries, supplemental reference books)
5. Recognizing special symbols, formulas, and abbreviations

Other necessary general skills are using study methods, outlining, taking notes, and reading at a flexible rate. Of course, general comprehension skills are involved in all content areas, as suggested in the GRI. The following items may be used to prepare skill assessments:

1. *Parts of textbooks:* Have students make use of different elements in their textbooks, such as preface, index, vocabulary lists, and appendices.
2. *Maps, tables, charts, graphs, diagrams, cartoons:* Use examples from the students' textbooks and ask students to answer questions you have prepared.
3. *Specialized vocabulary:* Use words from the glossaries of textbooks or supplemental materials.

4. *Reference materials:* Use the reference materials that are available for your content area and develop questions to see if students know the various reference sources and how to use them.

5. *Symbols, abbreviations, and formulas:* See if students can recognize the most frequently used symbols and abbreviations in the content material.

The following examples (Examples 13.3 through 13.6) provide some sample reading skill tests.

■ ■ ■ EXAMPLE 13.3   Using Parts of a Textbook—Skill Inventory

Directions: Below are two columns of words or phrases. Match the expression from the righthand column with the one that means the same, or almost the same, thing in the lefthand column.

_____ Index	**1.** Name of book
_____ Table of Contents	**2.** Part of book giving additional information, such as notes and tables
_____ Bibliography	**3.** Introduction
_____ Appendix	**4.** List of books for further reading
_____ Glossary	**5.** Alphabetical list of topics with the page on which each is found
_____ Preface	**6.** Year when book was published
_____ Title	**7.** List in front of book with chapter headings or topics in sequence and page on which each begins
_____ Copyright date	**8.** List of words with their meanings

Directions: Use your textbook to answer the following questions:

1. What is the title of your book?
2. When was it published?
3. Who wrote the book?
4. What are the titles of the first three chapters?
5. How are the chapters arranged or grouped?
6. On what page does Chapter 4 begin?
7. Find the meaning of the term _____.
8. On what page is there a chart showing _____?
9. What does the map on page _____ tell you?
10. On what page does the book explain the construction of a _____?
11. What index entries are given for _____?

■ ■ ■ EXAMPLE 13.4   Reading Graphs—Skill Inventory

Directions: Look at the graph and answer the questions about it.

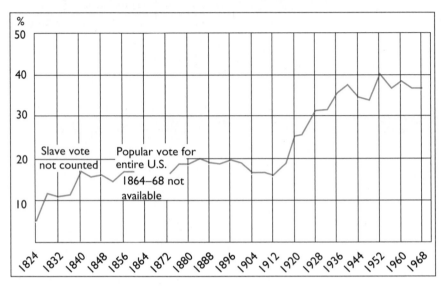

Source: Historical Statistics and Statistical Abstract.

Questions

1. Was there a steady growth of voters from 1824 to 1860? Why do you think so?
2. Around what year was there a sudden increase in popular votes cast in presidential elections?
3. Does the graph show the percentage of voting-age citizens participating in presidential elections?
4. For what years are complete data not provided?
5. About what percentage of Americans voted in the 1972 presidential election?

■ ■ ■ EXAMPLE 13.5   Using Reference Sources—Skill Inventory

Directions: Answer the following questions (based on English classroom reference sources).

1. What library aid will tell you the library number of a book?
2. What is a biography?
3. What is the difference between fiction and nonfiction?

4. Describe the content of *Dictionary of American Biography.*
5. Describe the content of *Granger's Index to Poetry.*
6. Where could you find an alphabetical listing of words with synonyms and antonyms instead of definitions?
7. What information may be found in the *Readers' Guide to Periodical Literature?*
8. Where might you find short stories listed by title, author, subject?
9. What information may be found in the *Book Review Digest?*
10. What information may be found in *Cumulative Book Index?*
11. Where might you go to find the answer to the question, "Is Steinbeck's *The Grapes of Wrath* considered to be one of his better works?"

Directions: Find the following words in a dictionary and list the guide words and numbers of the pages on which they fall.

Word	*Guide Words*	*Page Number*
anachronism		
epigram		
foreshadowing		
irony		
soliloquy		

Directions: Examine a set of printed encyclopedias. Then answer the following questions.
1. What is the purpose of an encyclopedia?
2. What are the meaning and purpose of the guide letter or letters on the cover of each volume?
3. What are guide words?
4. What is meant by cross-reference?
5. What is the purpose of the bibliographies at the ends of articles?
6. Where is the index located in the encyclopedia?

■ ■ ■ EXAMPLE 13.6   *Vocabulary—Skill Inventory*

Directions: Study the terms listed below. (The source of these vocabulary items is Chapter 27, Parts 1 and 2, "An Industrial Society" and "New Scientific Ideas," in *History of the World,* by Marvin Perry and others, Boston: Houghton Mifflin, 1990.) Use your knowledge of meanings of any of the word parts to help you understand the meanings of the whole words.

vaccination
pasteurization
radiation
evolution
genetics
sociology
psychology

Directions: Answer the following questions about the above terms:
1. What are the root words of the following words: *vaccination, pasteuriza-tion, radiation, evolution,* and *genetics?*

   If you know the meanings of the root words, use these meanings to help you determine the meanings of the new words.

   How is the word *pasteurization* different from the others? Does know-ing the root word for this word help you? Why, or why not?

   Does being familiar with common suffixes help you figure out the meanings of these words?
2. What are the combining forms that make up the words *sociology* and *psy-chology?* If you know the meanings of these combining forms, use them to help you determine the meanings of the new words. Notice how knowing the meaning of one combining form can help you with two different words.

Directions: Define the italicized words.
1. When a person has been given a *vaccination,* an injection of a solution of weakened germs, he or she may be protected from contracting the disease.
2. The process of *pasteurization* of milk was invented by Louis Pasteur when he realized that bacteria could be killed by heat.
3. Uranium gives off *radiation* that is similar to X-rays.
4. The *evolution* of living things over time could result in one species slowly evolving into another, according to Darwin.
5. Genes carry the traits that are passed from parents to their children. Mendel did work that established the foundation of the science of *genetics.*
6. When searching for a set of laws under which human society operates, Comte invented the term *sociology* to describe his scientific study.
7. Those who wish to learn more about the mind and behavior may wish to major in *psychology.*

A skills chart can be developed for recording the instructional needs of stu-dents. Skills charts include a list of skills down the left side of a page and a list of students' names across the top of the page. The teacher places a check mark beside a skill under the name of a student who successfully achieves the skill. A glance at the chart provides a guide as to which students need special help in developing a required skill. If most students need help with a particular skill, the teacher may plan a total class instructional session around that skill. If only certain students lack a skill, the teacher may set up a small skill group to help students who need it. Skill groups are temporary groups in that they are dissolved when the members have mastered the skill. A skills file (collection of materials, equipment, and supplies) may provide the needed practice activities for some students.

A sample record-keeping chart is provided in Example 13.7.

■ ■ ■ EXAMPLE 13.7   *Sample Skills Record*

Student Names

Skills

1. Parts of textbook
2. Interpretation of maps, table, charts, diagrams, etc.
3. Specialized vocabulary
4. Reference sources
5. Special symbols/abbreviations
6. Study methods
7. Outlining/taking notes
8. Flexibility of rate

Key. Pupil Performance Code

I — needs introduction and teaching
R — needs review and reinforcement
S — satisfactory (regular instruction adequate)
M— has mastered (no more practice needed)

Informal Reading Inventory (IRI)

What information can informal reading inventories provide for teachers?

Commercial **informal reading inventories,** which are compilations of graded reading selections with questions prepared to test the reader's comprehension, are used to gauge students' reading levels. These types of inventories are often administered by the special or remedial reading teacher to students identified as problem readers, but they can also be used by regular classroom teachers for special situations. According to Bader and Wiesendanger (1989, p. 403), "If we examine the definitions of *informal* (not prescribed or fixed) and *inventory* (appraisal) we realize that the intention behind these devices is to provide a window on the reading process. The reader's confidence, willingness to risk error, ability to make semantically and syntactically sound substitutions, fluency, perception of organization, and a host of other understandings and abilities can be observed." They further point out that it may be inappropriate to expect reliability coefficients for alternative forms of informal reading inventories because of "the effect of content on attention, understanding, and recall." Professional judgment is needed to make decisions when greater prior knowledge about or interest in the content of a particular passage results in unusually high performance on that passage or when limited prior knowledge or interest in the content of a passage results in unusually low performance on that passage.

A chief purpose of these inventories is to identify the independent, instructional, frustration, and capacity reading levels of the student. Such inventories are valuable in that they not only provide an overall estimate of the student's reading ability, but they also make possible identification of the specific strengths and weaknesses of the reader. They are helpful in determining what books a student can read independently and how difficult assigned reading can be if it is to be used as instructional material. Although a reading specialist might give a student an entire series of inventory selections and locate all four of these levels, the content teacher may give a similar inventory based on textbooks used in a particular class to find out if students can benefit from using those books.

Although it is time-consuming, it is possible for the teacher to construct and administer an informal reading inventory. The steps below are suggested for this procedure:

1. Select a set of books (or other materials) used at various grade levels (such as seventh, eighth, ninth, tenth, eleventh, and twelfth), preferably a series used in the class.
2. From each book, select one passage to be used for oral reading and one passage to be used for silent reading (each of 200 words or more).
3. Make a copy of each of the passages from each book. (Later, as the student reads from the book, the teacher marks the errors on the copy.)
4. Make up approximately ten questions for each passage. The questions should be of various types, including main idea, detail, vocabulary, sequence, inference, and cause and effect.
5. Direct the student to read the first passage orally. Mark and count his or her errors, using a system that allows you to identify types of errors, such as re-

fusal to pronounce, mispronunciation, omission, insertion, reversal of word order or word parts, and repetition. Mispronounced proper names and differences attributable to dialect should not be counted as errors. This, of course, requires the teacher to be familiar with the dialects spoken by the students in order to score the inventory properly. Some teachers have found it effective to tape a student's oral reading, replaying the tapes to note the errors in performance.

Then ask questions prepared for the oral reading. Count the number of questions answered correctly.

Direct the student to read the second passage silently. Ask questions prepared for silent reading. Again, count the number of questions answered correctly.

6. Count the number of errors in oral reading. Subtract the number of errors from the number of words in the selection. Then figure the percentage correct by dividing by the number of words in the selection and multiplying the result by 100.

Total the number of correct answers to questions for both the oral and silent reading passages. Then figure the percentage correct by dividing by the number of questions and multiplying the result by 100.

7. Read higher levels of material aloud to the student until you reach the highest reading level for which he or she can correctly answer 75 percent of the comprehension questions. (The highest level achieved indicates the student's probable *capacity*, or potential, reading level.)

The following chart will help the teacher in estimating the reading levels of the reader:

Level	Word recognition		Comprehension
Independent	99%	and	90%
Instructional	95%	and	75%
Frustration	<90%	or	<50%
Capacity			75%

Various writers in the field suggest slightly differing percentages relative to independent, instructional, frustration, and capacity levels. Originally, the criteria to establish the levels were developed by Betts (1946). The set of criteria for the reading levels is basically the one proposed by Johnson, Kress, and Pikulski (1987). An example of an informal reading inventory selection is found in Example 13.8.

■ ■ ■ EXAMPLE 13.8 Informal Reading Inventory Selection

◆◆11 PASSAGE ━━━ FORM A ━━━ TEACHER 11◆◆

MOTIVATIONAL STATEMENT: Read this story to find out some things Johnny Appleseed did.

There is some disagreement concerning the way in which Johnny went about planting apple trees in the wild frontier country. Some say that he scattered the seed as he went along the edges of marshes or natural clearings in the thick, almost tropical forests, others that he distributed the seeds among the settlers themselves to plant, and still others claim that in the damp land surrounding the marshes he established nurseries where he kept the seedlings until they were big enough to transplant. My Great-Aunt Mattie said that her father, who lived in rather a grand way for a frontier settler, had boxes of apples brought each year from Maryland until his own trees began to bear, and then he always saved the seeds, drying them on the shelf above the kitchen fireplace, to be put later into a box and kept for Johnny Appleseed when he came on one of his overnight visits.

Johnny scattered fennel seed all through our Ohio country, for when the trees were first cleared and the land plowed up, the mosquitoes increased and malaria spread from family to family. Johnny regarded a tea brewed of fennel leaves as a specific against what the settlers called "fever and ague," and he seeded the plant along trails and fence rows over all Ohio.

Source: Louis Bromfield, "Johnny Appleseed and Aunt Mattie," in *Pleasant Valley* (New York: Harper and Row, 1945)

COMPREHENSION QUESTIONS

_____ main idea

1. What is the main idea of this story? (Johnny Appleseed planted apple trees and fennel seed.)

_____ detail

2. In what kind of country did Johnny plant trees? (wild frontier country; marshes; thick forests)

_____ vocabulary

3. What does the word "distributed" mean? (handed out to different people)

_____ vocabulary

4. What are the nurseries mentioned in the story? (places where trees, shrubs, and vines are grown until they are large enough to transplant)

_____ inference

5. Was Great-Aunt Mattie's father rich or poor? (rich) What in the story caused you to answer that way? (He lived in a grand way for a frontier settler and had boxes of apples brought from Maryland until his own trees began to bear.)

_____ detail

6. What did Great-Aunt Mattie's father save for Johnny? (seeds from his apples)

_____ sequence

7. Name, in order, the two things Great-Aunt Mattie's father did with the seeds. (He dried them on the shelf above the kitchen fireplace and then put them in a box.)

_____ cause and effect/inference

8. What caused the spread of malaria through Ohio? (The increase in mosquitoes when the trees were first cleared and the land plowed up.)

_____ inference

9. What did the settlers call malaria? (fever and ague)

_____ inference

10. What did Johnny believe would help malaria sufferers? (a tea brewed of fennel leaves)

SCORING AID

WORD RECOGNITION

% MISCUES	
99	3
95	12
90	22
85	33

COMPREHENSION

% ERRORS	
100	0
90	1
80	2
70	3
60	4
50	5
40	6
30	7
20	8
10	9
0	10

217 WORDS (for Word Recognition)

217 WORDS (for Rate)

WPM
13020

Source: Betty D. Roe, Burns/Roe Informal Reading Inventory: Preprimer to Twelfth Grade, 4th ed., p. 100. Copyright © 1993 by Houghton Mifflin Company. Reprinted by permission of Houghton Mifflin Company. Excerpt shown: "Johnny Appleseed and Aunt Mattie" from PLEASANT VALLEY by Louis Bromfield. Copyright 1945 by Louis Bromfield, renewed 1972 by Hope Bromfield Stevens and Harper & Row, Publishers, Inc. Reprinted by permission of HarperCollins Publishers, Inc.

Cloze Test Procedure

How is a cloze test procedure administered?

An alternative method of assessment that can provide information similar to that provided by the informal reading inventory is the **cloze test procedure** (Taylor, 1956; Bormuth, 1968). This test is easy to construct, administer, and score, and it takes much less time to administer than the informal reading inventory. For these reasons, content area teachers are likely to find the cloze procedure more attractive for classroom use than the informal reading inventory.

For a cloze test, the student is asked to read selections of increasing levels of difficulty and to supply words that have been deleted from the passage. A sample cloze passage is given in Example 13.9.

Following are the steps used for constructing, administering, and scoring the cloze test:

1. Select a set of materials typical of those used in your classroom; from each level of these materials, select a passage of about 250 words. The chosen passages should be ones the students have not read previously.
2. Leave the first sentence intact, and then delete every fifth word until you have about fifty deletions. Replace the deleted words with blanks of uniform length.
3. Ask the student to fill in each blank with the exact word that has been deleted. Allow time to complete the test.
4. Count the number of correct responses. Do not count spelling mistakes as wrong answers; do not count synonyms as correct answers.
5. Convert the number of correct responses into a percentage.

The following criteria may be used in determining levels when cloze tests are used:

Accuracy	*Reading level*
57% or greater	Independent reading level
44–57%	Instructional reading level
Below 44%	Frustration level

A student who achieves a percentage of accuracy at or above the instructional level is asked to complete the next higher-level cloze test until that student reaches his or her highest instructional level. The teacher can probably assign instructional reading of tested material to any student who achieves a score of between 44 and 57 percent on that material. A score of 57 percent or better on any passage means the teacher can use the material from which the passage was taken for independent reading. A score of less than 44 percent accuracy on a passage would indicate that the material from which the passage was taken is probably not suitable for that particular student.

■ ■ ■ EXAMPLE 13.9   *Sample Cloze Passage*

Rocks exposed to the atmosphere slowly change. Air, water, and materials _____ living things can react _____ minerals in rock to _____ or even remove them.
(1)   (2)   (3)

_____ is the process by _____ rocks change to soil. _____ may result from both _____ and physical action on _____ .
(4)   (5)   (6)
(7)   (8)

In a common form _____ chemical weathering, minerals containing
(9)
_____ are broken down. Iron _____ to moisture and air _____ a red-brown
(10)   (11)   (12)
coating or _____ . The iron combines with _____ and becomes a new
(13)   (14)
_____ , iron oxide (rust). Similar _____ occur in rocks exposed _____ air
(15)   (16)   (17)
and water. Some _____ are more easily changed _____ than others. In the
(18)   (19)
_____ of air and moisture, _____ , for instance, changes to _____
(20)   (21)   (22)
minerals. Quartz, however, is _____ to chemical changes.
(23)

Physical _____ acting on rocks cause _____ *weathering.* In mechanical
(24)   (25)
weathering, _____ are broken down by _____ forces as windblown
(26)   (27)
sand, _____ water, and temperature changes _____ cause rocks to
(28)   (29)
shrink _____ expand.
(30)

Plants also weather _____ . Simple plants called lichens _____ grow on
(31)   (32)
unweathered rocks. _____ the lichens weather the _____ , other types of
(33)   (34)
plants _____ themselves. Plants remove chemicals _____ developing soil.
(35)   (36)
Living and _____ plants may also add _____ such as acids to _____ . Besides
(37)   (38)   (39)
their chemical effects, _____ roots may act upon _____ physically. Some
(40)   (41)
plant roots _____ work their way into _____ and crevices and split _____
(42)   (43)   (44)
apart. Plants also have _____ great effect on soil _____ it is formed.
(45)   (46)
Soil _____ might otherwise be carried _____ by wind or water _____ be
(47)   (48)   (49)
held in place _____ a dense mat of plant roots.
(50)

Answers:
1. from, 2. with, 3. alter, 4. Weathering, 5. which, 6. It, 7. chemical, 8. rocks, 9. of, 10. iron, 11. exposed, 12. develops, 13. rust, 14. oxygen, 15. substance, 16. changes, 17. to, 18. minerals, 19. chemically, 20. presence, 21. feldspar, 22. clay, 23. resistant, 24. forces, 25. mechanical, 26. rocks, 27. such, 28. moving, 29. that, 30. and, 31. rocks, 32. can, 33. As, 34. rocks, 35. establish, 36. from, 37. decaying, 38. chemicals, 39. rocks, 40. plant, 41. rocks, 42. can, 43. cracks, 44. rocks, 45. a, 46. after, 47. which, 48. away, 49. can, 50. by.

Source: Norman Abraham et al., Interaction of Earth and Time, *2nd ed. (Chicago: Rand McNally Co., 1976), pp. 262–265.*

Students should be given an explanation of the purpose of the procedure and a few practice passages to complete before a cloze test is used for assessment. Students need to be encouraged to use the information contained in the material surrounding each blank to make a decision about the correct word to place in the blank; otherwise they may simply guess without considering all of the available clues. Some students exhibit anxiety with this form of test, but practice may help alleviate this anxiety.

Although use of the traditional fifth-word deletion pattern is most common, some educators use a tenth-word deletion pattern, as suggested by Burron and Claybaugh (1974). This pattern is intended to compensate for the denseness of concepts and technical language in content materials.

Another modification of the cloze test has been proposed by Baldauf and others (1980) for lower secondary school ESL students. This is a "matching" cloze: students select from the five words randomly ordered in the margin and copy the correct ones into the five blank spaces for one set of sentences of the passage, continuing this procedure for other sections of the passage.

Teachers who wish to discover the ability of their students to use semantic and syntactic context clues effectively may wish to administer the cloze test and accept as answers synonyms and reasonable responses that make sense in the passage. To obtain very specific information about students' use of particular types of context clues, a teacher may wish to delete specific categories of words in specific contexts, rather than every nth word (Johnston, 1983). For example, only nouns or only adjectives might be deleted. Of course, such modifications would make determination of reading levels according to the criteria indicated in this section inappropriate, but they would allow the teachers to see how the students process language as they read.

According to Johnston (1983, pp. 62–63), a cloze test does not present "a normal reading task because often one must hold an empty slot in memory until one can locate information to fill it and construct a meaning for the segment.

This places quite a demand on short-term memory, and there are search skills involved." Therefore, because of the short-term memory demands, some students may not score as well on a cloze test as they would on another type of test.

Gamelike Activities

Some teachers use games to test students informally on the content just covered. Some base the games on the formats of popular television shows like *Jeopardy* or competitions like *College Bowl*. Others use self-created formats such as that described in the following "Meeting the Challenge" vignette.

MEETING THE CHALLENGE

Nancy Barrett, a teacher in an inner-city middle school, uses an assessment technique that she calls the Test Game. Here is her description of the technique:

This technique is an alternative to traditional written tests. It allows students to compete and interact. It is a very effective component of cooperative learning.

The teacher prepares twenty-five test questions (fill-in-the-blank) and answer sheets. Questions should be objective with clear-cut answers. Also needed are eight envelopes containing pieces of paper numbered from 1 to 25 and eight sets of test questions and answer sheets.

Next, students are divided into groups of four. (Eight groups are the maximum that I can manage.) Each group *rotates* the following jobs:

READER—reads question
CHOOSER—selects question by drawing question number
CHECKER—checks answer
ANSWERER—answers question

Groups may be arranged by homogeneous ability grouping or by random draw. I've found that homogeneous grouping based on previous test scores works best for me.

The CHOOSER draws a question number from the envelope and gives the number to the reader. The READER reads aloud that question from the test questions. The ANSWERER answers the question. The CHECKER checks the answer. If correct, the ANSWERER *keeps that question number.* If incorrect, the ANSWERER surrenders the number, and it goes back in the envelope.

Then the jobs rotate clockwise. The CHOOSER becomes the READER; the READER becomes the ANSWERER; the ANSWERER becomes the CHECKER; and the CHECKER becomes the CHOOSER.

The Test Game usually lasts about forty-five minutes. Scores are based upon the number of questions each player gets right. We simply count how many question numbers each one holds. My students really enjoy it!

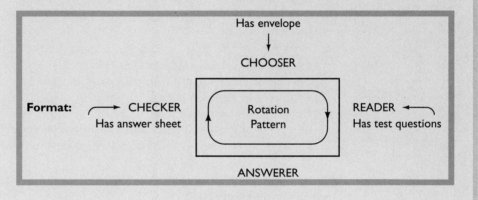

■ Observation

Systematic daily observation of students' reading performances can provide teachers with clues for planning effective instruction (Wolf, 1993). Johnston (1987) points out that most decision-making in the classroom takes place on a moment-to-moment basis as the teacher observes classroom activities. Teachers, then, need to know how to look for patterns of behavior and to keep records related to the patterns observed. Without documentation, the teacher will forget much of what he or she has seen or remember it inaccurately (Wolf, 1993). Various record-keeping devices that teachers use with observation, such as checklists, logs, class forms, and anecdotal records, can help them systematize observation and document results, but teachers should have a part in developing the forms used (Chittenden, 1991).

Teachers should try to observe students reading in instructional, recreational, interactive, individual, and formal test-taking settings in order to develop a complete picture of reading behaviors (Glazer and Searfoss, 1989). Every reading activity the students engage in provides a possible source of diagnostic information that can be recorded for analysis. Over a period of days or weeks, patterns of student development will become apparent, and consistent needs can be noted. Teachers have a unique opportunity to observe these patterns (Carroll and Carini, 1991; Zessoules and Gardner, 1991). Teachers do need to be cautious about conclusions drawn from their observations because many biases can creep in. For example, people often base assessments on early evidence and ignore later evidence if they think that they are observing a stable characteristic, and they are more likely to think a poor paper is worse than it is if they see it just after a good one (MacGinitie, 1993).

The teacher should keep questions such as the following in mind during observation of each student:

1. Does the student approach the assignment with enthusiasm?
2. Does he or she apply an appropriate study method?
3. Can he or she find answers to questions of a literal type (i.e., detail questions)?
4. Does he or she understand ideas beneath the surface level (answering inferential- and critical-level questions)?
5. Can he or she ascertain the meanings of new or unfamiliar words? What word recognition skills does the student use?
6. Can he or she use locational skills in the book?
7. Can he or she use reference skills for various reference sources?
8. Is he or she reading at different rates for different materials and purposes?

In addition, when a student gives an oral report or reads orally, the teacher has the opportunity to observe the following:

Oral report	*Oral reading*
pronunciation	methods of word attack
general vocabulary	word recognition problems
specialized vocabulary	rate of reading
sentence structure	phrasing
organization of ideas	peer reactions
interests	

During use of computer programs, teachers can observe students to evaluate their progress. When drill-and-practice or tutorial programs are used, they may look for such things as whether the student responds well to the rewards offered for successful responses, understands that particular commands cause particular responses, recognizes repeated language patterns presented in the programs, becomes more successful with practice, remembers new information that is presented, uses study strategies when working with the lessons, or needs repetition of the information before it is understood. They may also note whether the student chooses to use the software voluntarily, is enthusiastic about using the program, or becomes frustrated when using the program. These observations may provide information about the student, or they may reflect the quality of the software. When problem-solving/adventure programs (e.g., simulations, gaming programs, interactive fiction, and creative art programs) are used, the teacher may observe to see whether the student uses previously learned problem-solving strategies, organizes information for later recall, predicts solutions to the problem based on information provided in the program, relates personal experiences to the situation, and follows directions and hints provided (Shannon, 1989).

The validity of observations for assessment can be high because they exist in the context of actual reading and are a natural part of regular classroom lessons. Reliability can be high because the assessment goes on over an extended period, and patterns of responses in real reading situations have time to form (Readence and Martin, 1989).

▥ Interviews/Conferences

Interviews and teacher-student conferences can yield much information about literacy skill. Interviews are particularly good for collecting information about interests and attitudes. They are also useful for discovering why students have chosen particular strategies in their reading and writing activities. Teacher-student conferences about portfolios are discussed later in this chapter, and teacher-student conferences about students' writing pieces are discussed in Chapter 8.

▥ Performance Samples

Performance samples can be either written or oral. Both can yield valuable data.

Written work designed to meet authentic purposes can be evaluated for effectiveness, and sometimes can also be analyzed for ideas, organization, voice, style, and mechanics. Similarly, teachers may ask students to react in writing to narrative passages to discover whether they are attending to surface level plot structures, underlying universal themes, or character development (Purves, 1968; Readence and Martin, 1989). This can be a form of written retelling of the story, which has the advantage over oral retelling of not requiring the individual attention of the teacher during the retelling. This written retelling can be a valuable piece to include in a student's portfolio. Later retellings can be added to demonstrate progress.

What value does retelling have as an assessment technique?

Assessing comprehension of material read by having students retell a selection in response to the reading can be effective (Glazer and Brown, 1993), but **retelling** is time-consuming, and it may be difficult for remedial readers (Young and Bastionelli, 1990). Readers construct a text in their minds as they read a particular selection. The texts constructed by better readers are more complete and accurate than those constructed by less skilled ones. The retelling technique shows what the students consider important in the text and how they organize that information rather than showing if the students remember what the adults doing the testing consider important. A selection to be retold should be read silently and then retold to the teacher without interruption. When the retelling is completed, the teacher may request elaboration on some points, for the students may know more about the material than they can produce in a free recall situation. Teachers should listen for such things as identification of major characters, characteristics of the characters, the story's problem and solution, and an accurate sequence of events in retellings of narrative texts. They should listen for main ideas and important supporting details in expository texts (Richek, List, and Lerner, 1989). The retellings are a type of window to the reading comprehension process that goes on within a student and can be highly valuable in selected settings. Morrow (1989) cautions that retelling is difficult for students and suggests that teachers offer students guidance and practice with retelling before it is used for evaluation. She also stresses that students should be told before they read a story that they will be expected to retell it, and they should be given a purpose for the reading that is congruent with the information the teacher is looking for in the evaluation.

Retellings can be evaluated by counting the number of idea units included (probably weighted for importance) and checking for appropriate sequence. Retellings can also be checked to determine such things as inclusion of literal and implied information, attempts to connect background knowledge to text information or to apply information to the real world, affective involvement with the text, appropriate language use, and control of the mechanics of spoken or written language (Clark, 1982; Morrow, 1989).

How are think alouds used to assess reading comprehension and strategy use?

Glazer and Brown (1993) suggest the use of oral **think alouds** about reading that is in progress. Wade (1990) describes the use of a think-aloud procedure for comprehension assessment. With this procedure, students read short segments of passages in which they cannot be certain what the topic is until they have read the last segment. After reading each segment, they think aloud about the passage's meaning, generating hypotheses about the meaning from the clues in the segment just read. At the completion of the passage, the reader retells the complete passage. The activity can be recorded for later analysis as to how the reader generated hypotheses, supported them with text information, related information to background experiences, integrated new information with existing knowledge, and so on. Such recordings can be included in students' portfolios.

Use of the think-aloud procedure can reveal students who are good comprehenders, those who overly rely on bottom-up (text-based) or top-down (knowledge-based) processing, and those who fail to integrate information in the different segments of the passage. Knowing these approaches to reading can help the teacher plan appropriate instruction, such as focusing on developing or activating prior knowledge to help students understand the text; helping them to understand the function of background knowledge in comprehension; helping them link information from various sentences to form a unified, coherent idea; helping them develop flexibility in interpretations; and helping them learn to use metacognitive skills.

Baumann (1988) points out that the cloze procedure is a type of process assessment because readers have to respond *while* they are working on figuring out the text. The readers use the semantic and syntactic clues in the supplied text to construct a meaningful whole text. The cloze procedure is described fully earlier in this chapter.

Brozo (1990) makes a case for interactive-assessment for at-risk readers that resembles a directed reading lesson. First, there is a diagnostic interview to collect background information about the student's ideas about reading purposes and his or her reading strategies and ability, interests, and attitudes. Then passage placement in an informal reading inventory is determined by letting the student work through the word lists, providing assistance with difficult words and strategies for unlocking them. Activation and expansion of prior knowledge of the topic of the passage, preteaching of vocabulary, and purpose setting for the reading are used to prepare the student to read. The student reads silently first and then orally. As the student reads orally, the teacher observes use of strategies, asks questions about strategies, and models effective strategies as needed. After the reading takes place, the student retells the material. The teacher may probe for additional information through questions, allowing the student to look back through the passage to find answers. Comprehension is then extended through activities that connect the student's prior knowledge with the new content. A number of techniques found in this text—for example, semantic mapping and anticipation guides—may be used in both the preparation for reading step and this final step. This procedure is obviously time-consuming, but it has the potential for uncovering a student's actual ability to perform in classwork, rather than his or her ability to perform independently.

Dynamic assessment is also suggested for at-risk readers by Kletzien and Bednar (1990). They suggest initial assessment and strategy analysis to establish the student's reading level and to determine his or her strategy knowledge and use. They also suggest an informal reading inventory for this purpose. The teacher observes the student's strategy application and questions the student about reading strategies used. Then the teacher plans a mediated learning mini-lesson to determine the reader's capacity for modifying his or her approach to reading. The teacher discusses the student's initial performance with him or her, stressing both strengths and limitations. Then a strategy is chosen to be taught, using independent level materials. The student is taught how, when, and why the strategy can be used. The teacher models the strategy directly through a think-aloud procedure and then offers the student guided practice and independent practice. The teacher observes the student's attempts to learn the strategy. A postassessment and strategy analysis follows, using another form of the informal reading inventory that was used initially. Comparing the student's performance on the two assessment measures helps the teacher to determine his or her ability to integrate the targeted strategies into the reading process. This approach also takes quite a bit of time, although it yields useful information.

What are transfor-mative tests?

Rea and Thompson (1990) call for **transformative tests,** which are learning activities teachers use for testing. Such tests are performance-based, authentic tests for testing holistic reading/writing skills in the context of whole stories. Such tests involve beginning with a complete story and asking literal questions to serve as a basis for interpretation, interpretive questions that require predictions and drawing of conclusions about the themes introduced through the literal questions, and applied questions that ask the students to connect the interpretations made to personal life situations.

Having students work problems and explain their thought processes as they work them is a good type of performance assessment. Write-ups of conclusions about laboratory exercises can also be used to assess performance.

There are some special problems in the secondary school in using alternative assessments: classes often have very limited time frames; there is pressure to cover many specific concepts; and there are often large numbers of students to be assessed by a single teacher (Moje and Handy, 1995).

■ Portfolio Assessment

What types of items belong in a literacy portfolio?

Use of **portfolios** of students' work can be an effective way of accomplishing authentic classroom-based assessment of literacy skills. Portfolios allow teachers to examine real products of instruction, rather than a limited sample found on a test. In addition, portfolios can serve as an integral part of classroom instruction as the teacher and student confer about the contents and what the contents say about the student's literacy. Portfolios can be important, not only for teacher assessment, but also for self-assessment by the students, and they can aid the development of metacognition (Belanoff and Dickson, 1991; Condon and Hamp-Lyons, 1991; Mills-Courts and Amiran, 1991; Stock, 1991; Sunstein, 1992). Such assessment is especially appropriate in the analysis of writing, because, as Elbow and Belanoff (1991) indicate, an adequate picture of a student's writing proficiency cannot be obtained without examination of several pieces of writing produced on different days in a variety of genres. Belanoff and Dickson (1991, p. xx) point out, however, that portfolio assessment is "messy, bulky, nonprogrammable, not easily scored, and time-consuming (though . . . it's not as bad in these areas as its detractors paint it)."

Portfolios are collections of materials that should reflect "personal literacy histories" (Sunstein, 1992, p. xii). Wolf and Siu-Runyan (1996, p. 31) say, "A portfolio is a selective collection of student work and records of progress gathered across diverse contexts over time, framed by reflection and enriched through collaboration, that has as its aim the advancement of student learning." Each student's portfolio should include materials showing that student's accomplishments as a reader and a writer (Wolf, 1989). These materials can vary widely, depending on the function that the portfolio assessment is intended to serve. Possible purposes are "to promote student self-assessment, to document student learning, to guide teaching, to communicate with parents about their child's progress, or to provide administrators and policy makers with information about the impact of the school's or district's instructional program" (Wolf and Siu-Runyan, 1996, p. 32). Some examples of materials that might be included are (Au et al., 1990; Camp and Levine, 1991; Stock, 1991; Winograd, Paris, and Bridge, 1991; Cooper and Brown, 1992; Graves, 1992; Milliken, 1992; Murphy and Smith, 1992; Seger, 1992; Calfee and Perfumo, 1993; Grace, 1993; Farr and Tone, 1994; Gillespie et al., 1996; Wolf and Siu-Runyan, 1996):

1. Writing samples judged to be the student's best efforts—either current samples or those chosen for the portfolio at regular intervals in order to show progress.
2. All prewriting materials and drafts for a piece that has been developed through to the publication stage, to show the process that was followed.
3. Audiotapes of a student's best oral reading (done with prior preparation), either current samples or those collected at regular intervals to show progress.
4. Written responses to literature that has been read and discussed in class (which can be analyzed for inclusion of information on theme, characters, setting, problem, events, solution, application, and personal response).
5. Journal entries that show analysis of literacy skills or that show interest or engagement in literary activities.
6. Functional writing samples (letters, lists, etc.).
7. Reading logs that show the number and variety of books read in various time periods.
8. Videotapes of group reading discussions, audience reading activities, reading/writing conferences, or literacy-based projects (creative dramatizations, readers' theater presentations, etc.).
9. Photographs of completed literacy-based projects with attached captions or explanations.
10. Examples of writing to learn in the content areas activities.
11. Informal written tests.
12. Checklists or anecdotal records made from observations.
13. Questionnaires on attitudes toward reading and writing.
14. Questionnaires on reading interests.
15. Student's written explanation of portfolio contents and assessment of personal literacy achievements based on this evidence.

Teachers or administrators must decide the purpose the portfolios are to serve, the criteria for inclusion of materials, and who will place materials in the portfolios. If the portfolios are to be used by the administration or outside agencies, this decision-making may be entirely out of the hands of teachers and students. If the portfolios are for the teacher to use in making instructional decisions or keeping parents informed of the student's progress or for the teacher and student to use in observing and documenting the student's progress and characteristics as a literate person, the student may make many or all of the decisions alone or in collaboration with the teacher. If the portfolios are primarily for evaluation or documentation for outside individuals, including parents and administrators, the teacher may take a more active role in the decision-making than if the portfolios are only for classroom instructional purposes.

Ideally, the students will participate in the selection and evaluation of materials for their portfolios. They may need guidance, however, as to the criteria for inclusion because otherwise they may either put everything or very little into their portfolios. Including too much may obscure the information that is most helpful. Including too little may not offer sufficient input for decision-making. They also need to know what scoring criteria will be used, for well-defined scoring criteria let students (and parents) know what is being judged and the standards for acceptable materials. If the scoring criteria are vague, it will be difficult for the teacher to give a fair and consistent assessment (Herman et al., 1992). Students should participate in developing the criteria for evaluation when feasible (Gillespie et al., 1996). Collaborating with teachers to choose portfolio items that represent their progress over time and their current levels of achievement helps students to feel ownership of the learning process. Reflection about their learning activities not only leads them to choose assessment items but also helps them understand their strengths and weaknesses. It helps them understand what they need to do in the future as well (Wolf and Siu-Runyan, 1996). Murphy and Smith (1992, p. 14) believe that "the benefits of portfolios lie as much in the decision-making processes they initiate as in the range of products they contain," and Farr and Tone (1994, p. 18) think that "students learn so much from it that it serves as instruction itself, expanding the effective use of language."

Teachers may want students to keep separate portfolios for different purposes. The types of materials selected depend on the purpose of the portfolio (Wolf and Siu-Runyan, 1996). For example, one portfolio might focus on a student's best work in a variety of areas, whereas another portfolio might focus on the range of genres they have experienced and experimented with in reading and writing. Still another portfolio might show the process used in developing written pieces or in evaluating reading selections. Some teachers may want evidence of all these varying literacy aspects in the same portfolio, which makes organization of the material essential. Students should have the opportunity to organize their portfolios in ways that help them best display their literacy products and processes. Labeling the materials and indicating what criterion or criteria they meet can enhance clarity (Milliken, 1992; Rief, 1992). Rief (1992, p. 45) indicates that she sets the *external* criteria for her students' portfolios—"each student's two best pieces chosen during a six-week period with all the rough drafts that went into each piece, trimester self-evaluations of process and product, each student's reading list, and, at year's end, a reading-writing project." However, her "students determine the *internal* criteria—which pieces, for their own reasons."

Graves (1992), on the other hand, asks students to decide which pieces have particular value to them by asking them to label pieces that they like, that they found hard to write, that surprised them as they were writing, that made them realize that they were learning something about the writing, that helped them learn about the content they were writing about, that helped the reader picture the written ideas, that had good opening lines, that need reworking, and so on. Then the students can analyze the pieces for inclusion in the portfolio with a view as to what they show about the writer and his or her ability to produce pieces that exhibit good quality. Students may attach written explanations to materials in their portfolios, telling why each item was included, what criterion it meets, when the work was done, how long it took to complete, how they would evaluate its qualities, and so on (Simmons, 1992).

Students may be asked to rank their products from best to worst, arrange pieces chronologically to show a picture of literacy activities for the period, choose pieces to show a range of genres in their reading and writing experiences, or describe the development of a long-term project. Ballard (1992) expressed surprise at the students' insight into their own strengths and weaknesses and their honesty in self-evaluation.

A portfolio can reflect the ability to understand and express ideas, recognize and use organization, understand and choose appropriate words, manage mechanics of writing, carry through to completion the reading/analysis or the writing of a work, produce quality written products, revise, gain insight into material read, and perform self-evaluation. It can also indicate a student's work habits, preferences, strengths and weaknesses, attitudes, and range of reading and writing activities (Simmons, 1992). Teachers can base portfolio grades on "effort, improvement, commitment to the task, content of the work, mechanics, and volume" (Grace, 1993, p. 27), among other criteria decided on by teachers individually or in collaboration with students. Elbow (1991, p. xiv) feels that "the use of portfolios exerts a subtle pressure against holistic grading and in favor of analytic grading, against single measures of intelligence or skill and in favor of the idea that humans have multiple intelligences and skills."

Portfolio conferences can be opportunities to learn more about the process behind the development of the portfolio materials from the students. The students should explain why they included what they did and what these items show about them as literate people. The students can tell what they have learned, using the portfolio pieces as documentation, and then the teacher and students can plan future activities to work on any evident weaknesses or gaps in literacy achievement. The teacher can listen to the students' self-assessments, point out areas of growth and evidence of literacy skills, and ask questions to clarify points that the students made (Milliken, 1992; Rief, 1992).

Portfolio assessment is a criterion-referenced, rather than a norm-referenced, approach. Instead of expecting students to end up distributed along a bell-shaped curve, users of this type of assessment would expect all students to pass eventually because they have had enough time and assistance to do what they have been asked to do (Elbow and Belanoff, 1991).

◾ Self-Assessment

Self-assessment may also take place during whole-class or small-group discussion, as students discuss the strengths and weaknesses of their writing or the extent to which they understood the reading materials. Peer conferences about reading and writing can also be the basis for self-analysis.

Involving students in self-assessment makes them partners in evaluation and helps them to separate true assessment from grading (Schwartz, 1991).

Some self-assessment techniques include:

1. *Discussion.* Self-assessment may focus on a single topic, such as word recognition, meaning of vocabulary, comprehension, study strategies, or problems in reading a particular textbook. With guiding questions from the teacher, the students can discuss, orally or in writing, their strengths and weaknesses in regard to the particular topic.
2. *Structured interview or conference.* After the student has written a reading autobiography (see the section on "Attitude Measures" in this chapter), such questions as the following may be asked:
   a. How do you figure out the pronunciation or meaning of an unknown word?
   b. What steps are you taking to develop your vocabulary?
   c. What do you do to get the main ideas from your reading?
   d. Do you use the same rate of reading in most of your assignments?
   e. What method of study do you use most?
   f. How do you organize your material to remember it?
   g. What special reference books have you used lately in the writing of a report?
   h. How do you handle graphic aids that appear in the reading material?
   i. How do you study for a test?
   j. What could you do to become an even better reader?
3. *Self-rating checklist.* A sample checklist is provided in Example 13.10. It deals with several broad areas. Similar checklists could be prepared that focus on particular skills, such as reading to follow directions.
4. *Learning logs.* Students keep up with daily progress and learning that takes place in learning logs.
5. *Written reflections about work.* Portfolios often include students' written analyses of the materials included.

■ ■ ■ EXAMPLE 13.10   *Self-Rating Checklist*

Name _____ Date _____

Subject _____

Please rate yourself on these items:

	Good	Average	Need help
1. Pronouncing and knowing the meaning of most of the words in your content book	_____	_____	_____
2. Using parts of textbooks	_____	_____	_____
3. Using the dictionary	_____	_____	_____
4. Using strategies to help increase vocabulary	_____	_____	_____
5. Answering questions that call for critical thinking	_____	_____	_____
6. Being flexible in reading rate	_____	_____	_____
7. Knowing a good study method	_____	_____	_____
8. Outlining, summarizing, and taking notes	_____	_____	_____
9. Locating materials in books and reference sources	_____	_____	_____
10. Writing a report	_____	_____	_____
11. Following printed directions	_____	_____	_____
12. Interpreting graphic aids	_____	_____	_____
13. Remembering material	_____	_____	_____
14. Test taking	_____	_____	_____

Self-evaluation can lead to the use of metacognitive strategies when students are reading. They ask themselves if they understand the material, and if not, what they can do to understand it better.

■ Attitude Measures

Students' affective responses to reading selections have a critical influence on whether or not the students will become willing readers. Additionally, attitude is a determinant of whether students will read in specific content area textbooks or other content-related materials (Alexander and Cobb, 1992).

Therefore, a measure of students' attitudes toward reading experiences in general and in specific content areas is an important aspect of the total assessment program. Reading takes many forms and means many different things to different students. One student might enjoy reading the sports page but be bored or even dislike reading a library book to complete an English assignment, whereas another student might prefer the library book.

Observation, interviewing, techniques in which reading is compared with another activity, sentence completion activities, questionnaires, summated rating scales (which involve having students respond to statements on a Likert-type scale), and semantic differentials (which involve having students choose descriptive adjectives to rate the items) have all commonly been used to assess attitudes in the United States. Multiple measures may be advisable because single measures may give an incomplete picture (Alexander and Cobb, 1992).

Whether or not a student likes reading depends on what he or she is reading and for what purpose. Therefore, perhaps the most valid measure of a student's attitude toward reading would be his or her oral or written responses to individual selections.

Students are not expected to respond positively to all their reading experiences, but if the majority of their responses indicate negative attitudes toward reading, something is amiss. A profile of individual scores may be kept as an ongoing assessment of each student's attitude toward reading. Content teachers should be concerned about the attitudes of students toward reading material; students who have negative attitudes may not comprehend well and will probably need additional motivation for reading. An assessment of this type carried out near the beginning of the school term should be valuable to content teachers.

To undertake a more comprehensive study of the student's reading, some authorities suggest the use of the reading autobiography—a developmental history of a student's reading experiences. Some accounts give details about the student's early reading experiences, when and how he or she was taught, the range and variety of his or her reading, home background, and use of available resources. Other autobiographies reveal the writer's attitude toward reading, special reading interests, and perhaps reading difficulties. Sometimes they include the writer's ideas about ways to overcome the difficulties that he or she has recognized.

Interest Assessments

In reading, as in other areas, interest is often the key that unlocks effort. Consequently, study of students' reading and other interests is an important part of the teaching process. Teachers should plan ways to motivate students and show how a subject is related to their personal lives.

Content area teachers need to know the *specific* interests of each student in order to capitalize on them in recommending reading materials. One of the ways to learn a student's reading interests is through observation in daily classes. The teacher can note the books the student chooses to read, the degree of concentration and enjoyment with which he or she reads them, his or her eagerness to talk about them, and the desire expressed to read more books of similar nature or books by the same author.

More detailed information about reading interests may be obtained from an interest inventory. An inventory should include both general and reading interests. A sample inventory is presented in Example 13.11.

■ ■ ■ EXAMPLE 13.11   *General and Reading Interests Inventory*

Name _____ Grade _____ Age _____

General Interests

1. What do you like to do in your free time?
2. What are your favorite TV shows?
3. What are your favorite hobbies?
4. What games or sports do you like best?
5. What clubs or other groups do you belong to?
6. Do you have any pets? If yes, what kinds?
7. What is your favorite type of movie?
8. What is your favorite school subject?
9. What is your most disliked school subject?
10. What kind of work do you think you want to do when you finish secondary school?

Reading Interests

1. How often do you go to the public library?
2. What are your favorite books that you own?
3. What things do you like to read about most?
4. Which comic books do you read?
5. Which magazines do you read?
6. What are some books you have enjoyed?
7. What parts of the newspaper do you read most frequently?
8. Do you like to read?

■ ■ Assessing Readability of Printed Materials

What effect does readability of text-books have on content area instruction?

Readability of printed materials is the reading difficulty of these materials. Selections that are very difficult to read are said to have high readability levels; those that are easy to read are said to have low readability levels.

Textbooks are sometimes written at higher levels of difficulty than the grade levels for which they are designed. Teachers need to know whether or not this is the case, because students will not learn content from textbooks that are too difficult for them to read with comprehension.

Since secondary school teachers frequently use textbooks for independent homework assignments and often expect that the students will read the complete textbooks, matching the textbooks assigned to students with the students' reading levels is particularly important (Davey, 1988). Just getting a book that fits the curriculum at a particular level will not necessarily result in an appropriate text. Kinder, Bursuck, and Epstein (1992) found that books designed for the same purpose may differ greatly in difficulty. They found the readability levels of ten American history textbooks published since 1985 to vary in difficulty from ninth- to fifteenth-grade level.

Textbook users often overlook the fact that different sections of the same textbook may have different readability levels, some topics may require more difficult language for their presentation, or different sections may be written by different authors with writing styles that vary in complexity or clarity. English teachers, in particular, should be aware of the wide differences in readability levels of selections in literature anthologies, because different authors have written the materials. Stetson and Williams (1992) point out that social studies textbooks sometimes contain material that varies four or more years in difficulty from passage to passage.

Many factors influence the level of difficulty of printed materials. Some of these are vocabulary, sentence length, sentence complexity, abstract concepts, organization of ideas, inclusion of reading aids (such as underlining, boxing of information, and graphic aids), size and style of type, format, reader interest, and reader background. Concept load seems to be particularly important. If many new or technical concepts are introduced on each page or in each paragraph of text or if many of the concepts presented are abstract rather than concrete, the readability will be more difficult. Of the factors identified that influence the level of difficulty, two are directly related to the uniqueness of the reader: interest and background. A piece of literature may be of great interest to one student and yet have little appeal for another. A reader's areas of interest may be related to his or her background of experience. This background enables readers to understand easily material for which they have experienced vocabulary and concepts either directly or vicariously. (See Chapter 4 for a discussion of background experience as one area in which students exhibit individual differences.)

Although all the other factors mentioned obviously affect difficulty, vocabulary and sentence length have been found by researchers to be the most important in predicting readability.

■ Readability Formulas

Various formulas have been developed to measure the readability of printed materials. Most contain measures of vocabulary and sentence difficulty. Some of the most frequently used formulas are the Dale-Chall Readability Formula (Dale and Chall, 1948), the Flesch "Reading Ease" Formula (Flesch, 1949), the SMOG Grading Formula (McLaughlin, 1969), and the Fry Readability Graph (Fry, 1968; 1978). Teachers should be aware that these formulas have been developed for use with connected prose; their use with other types of text, such as mathematics calculations, is inappropriate and will result in inaccurate scores.

The Dale-Chall Readability Formula is a well-validated formula but is relatively difficult to use. Its vocabulary measure requires checking words in the text against a word list to determine whether or not they are "hard" words, which can be a tedious procedure. The Flesch "Reading Ease" Formula is also somewhat complex. The main difficulty in using it is that, when counting sentences, the user must treat each independent unit of thought as a sentence, a process that requires many decisions for each sample. Both of these formulas were revised by Powers, Sumner, and Kearl (1958). Both are fairly time-consuming unless a computer version is used to perform the calculations. Therefore, they may not be selected by secondary classroom teachers for use on a regular basis unless computer assistance is available. Many computer programs can calculate these formulas, as well as a number of others.

The SMOG Grading Formula requires the user to count each word of three or more syllables in each of three 10-sentence samples. The approximate square root of the number of such polysyllabic words is calculated (by taking the square root of the nearest perfect square); to this figure the number three is added to give the SMOG Grade. This formula takes less time to calculate than the Dale-Chall and Flesch formulas, and it may be chosen for use by some secondary teachers. It produces a score that reflects an independent reading level, meaning that a student reading at the indicated level could read the tested material with complete understanding.

The Fry Readability Graph is another relatively quick readability measure (Fry, 1972). To use the graph, one needs to select three 100-word samples and to determine the average number of sentences and the average number of syllables per 100 words. (The number of sentences in a 100-word sample is determined to the nearest tenth of a sentence.) With these figures, it is possible to use the graph to determine the approximate grade level of the selection. Fry's Graph and the instructions for using it are reprinted in Figure 13.2. The Fry

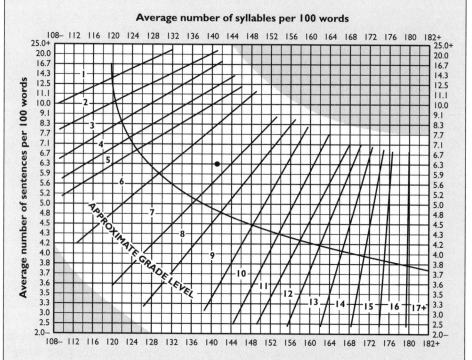

Expanded Directions for Working Readability Graph

1. Randomly select three (3) sample passages and count out exactly 100 words each, beginning with the beginning of a sentence. Do count proper nouns, initializations, and numerals.
2. Count the number of sentences in the hundred words, estimating length of the fraction of the last sentence to the nearest one-tenth.
3. Count the total number of syllables in the 100-word passage. If you don't have a hand counter available, an easy way is to simply put a mark above every syllable over one in each word, then when you get to the end of the passage, count the number of marks and add 100. Small calculators can also be used as counters by pushing numeral 1, then push the + sign for each word or syllable when counting.
4. Enter graph with *average* sentence length and *average* number of syllables; plot dot where the two lines intersect. Area where dot is plotted will give you the approximate grade level.
5. If a great deal of variability is found in syllable count or sentence count, putting more samples into the average is desirabe.
6. A word is defined as a group of symbols with a space on either side; thus *Joe*, *IRA*, *1945*, and & are each one word.
7. A syllable is defined as a phonetic syllable. Generally, there are as many syllables as vowel sounds. For example, *stopped* is one syllable and *wanted* is two syllables. When counting syllables for numerals and initializations, count one syllable for each symbol. For example, *1945* is four syllables, *IRA* is three syllables, and & is one syllable.

Note: This "extended graph" does not outmode or render the earlier (1968) version inoperative or inaccurate; it is an extension. (REPRODUCTION PERMITTED — NO COPYRIGHT)

Graph reflects an instructional reading level, the level at which a student should be able to read with teacher assistance. The authors of this text have found that, in many cases, secondary classroom teachers are more comfortable with this formula than with the other three discussed here. For that reason, it is presented in more detail. There is no implication that it is superior to the other three, and teachers should use their own judgment in choosing a suitable formula to use.

The formulas already discussed are designed for use with long passages. Fry (1990) has also developed a formula for use with passages from 40 to 300 words long. The passage should contain at least three sentences. The user selects at least three key words needed to understand the passage, looks up the grade level of each key word in *The Living Word Vocabulary* (Dale and O'Rourke, 1976), and averages the three hardest key words to find the Word Difficulty. Then he or she counts the number of words in each sentence and gives each sentence a grade according to a sentence length chart. An average of the grade levels of all sentences produces the score for Sentence Difficulty. The average of the Word Difficulty and Sentence Difficulty gives the readability estimate. This formula is designed for grades 4 through 12.

Some educators prefer to use the more lengthy and complicated formulas, which they think are more accurate. Considering the number of factors that formulas fail to take into account, however, no formula can provide more than an approximation of level of difficulty. For this reason, the quick formulas should not be scorned. Determination of the relative difficulty levels of textbooks and other printed materials can be extremely valuable to a teacher. It has been demonstrated that estimating reading difficulty by using a formula produces much more consistent results than estimating without one.

If you are daunted by the prospect of counting syllables, words, sentences, and unfamiliar words and you have access to a computer and appropriate software, you can use one of these valuable aids to save you time and effort in making calculations (Judd, 1981; Kretschmer, 1984; Gross and Sadowski, 1985). A number of programs can analyze the readability levels of texts according to a variety of readability formulas (Geisert and Futrell, 1995). A number of grammar and style checker programs, including *Grammatik 5* (Reference Software International, San Francisco, 1992) run the Flesch Reading Ease, the Gunning Fog Index, and the Flesch-Kincaid Grade Level formulas. These programs perform the calculations that teachers would ordinarily have to do manually. Teachers just have to type in the passages to be analyzed and read an on-screen menu that allows them to choose such things as which formulas to run.

Cautions and Controversies

All teachers should be familiar with at least one readability formula so that they can check the printed materials used in their classes. Then perhaps students will not be asked so frequently to read textbooks or supplementary materials that are too difficult for them. However, because of the limitations of the available formulas, teachers should always combine results obtained from the formulas with judgment based on personal experience with the materials and knowledge of the abstractness of the concepts presented, the organization and writing style of the author, the interests of the students in the class, the backgrounds of experience of the students, and other related factors such as size and style of type and format of the material. Because sampling procedures suggested by several formulas result in limited samples, teachers should be very cautious in accepting calculated grade levels as absolutes. They also should remember that textbooks vary in difficulty from section to section and should interpret samples with that in mind.

Readability formulas do not have any measure for abstractness or unfamiliarity of concepts covered. Familiar words, such as *run* and *bank,* do not always have their familiar meanings in school materials. A social studies text might discuss a "run on the banks," which would present a less familiar situation than reading about "fast movement by a person on the shore of a stream," which may be the meaning of these words that comes to mind immediately.

Authors may organize materials clearly or they may have very poor organization, and the clarity of their writing styles may vary immensely, with some choosing to construct sentences in less common ways and others choosing familiar sentence structures. Readability formulas contain no measures for organization or style.

The cohesive structure of a text (the interrelationships of ideas) also affects readability (Binkley, 1988). Standard formulas do not measure this cohesion.

Factors within individual students help determine the readability of particular material for those students. Material that is interesting to students is easier for them to read because they are more motivated to read it. Other people with similar reading skills may find the material uninteresting and, thus, much more difficult to read. Likewise, readers who have had much experience related to the topic will find the material easier to read than those who have had little experience related to it. No formula has the power to foresee the interests and backgrounds of particular readers.

Formulas also do not contain measures for mechanical features such as size and style of type and format of the printed material. Type that is too small or too large may adversely affect readability, and some styles of type make reading the material more difficult than do other styles. Additionally, closely packed type, unrelieved by sufficient white space or illustrative material, can make reading more difficult.

■ Other Methods of Readability Assessment

There are means other than readability formulas of assessing the appropriateness of printed materials for specific students. Some of these are discussed next.

Checklists

A checklist approach to assessing readability has been presented by Irwin and Davis (1980). Their excellent checklist is based on accepted psychological research and includes many considerations not covered by readability formulas. Items included in the checklist cover understandability and learnability. Example 13.12 presents the checklist developed by Irwin and Davis.

■ ■ ■ EXAMPLE 13.12   Readability Checklist

This checklist is designed to help you evaluate the readability of your classroom texts. It can best be used if you rate your text while you are thinking of a specific class. Be sure to compare the textbook to a fictional ideal rather than to another text. Your goal is to find out what aspects of the text are or are not less than ideal. Finally, consider supplementary workbooks as part of the textbook and rate them together. Have fun!

Rate the questions below using the following rating system:

5—Excellent
4—Good
3—Adequate
2—Poor
1—Unacceptable
NA—Not applicable

Further comments may be written in the space provided.

Textbook title: _____
Publisher: _____
Copyright date: _____

UNDERSTANDABILITY

A. _____ Are the assumptions about students' vocabulary knowledge appropriate?
B. _____ Are the assumptions about students' prior knowledge of this content area appropriate?
C. _____ Are the assumptions about students' general experiential backgrounds appropriate?
D. _____ Does the teacher's manual provide the teacher with ways to develop and review the students' conceptual and experiential backgrounds?
E. _____ Are new concepts explicitly linked to the students' prior knowledge or to their experiential backgrounds?
F. _____ Does the text introduce abstract concepts by accompanying them with many concrete examples?
G. _____ Does the text introduce new concepts one at a time with a sufficient number of examples for each one?

H. _____ Are definitions understandable and at a lower level of abstraction than the concept being defined?

I. _____ Is the level of sentence complexity appropriate for the students?

J. _____ Are the main ideas of paragraphs, chapters, and subsections clearly stated?

K. _____ Does the text avoid irrelevant details?

L. _____ Does the text explicitly state important complex relationships (e.g., causality, conditionality, etc.) rather than always expecting the reader to infer them from the context?

M. _____ Does the teacher's manual provide lists of accessible resources containing alternative readings for the very poor or very advanced readers?

N. _____ Is the readability level appropriate (according to a readability formula)?

LEARNABILITY

Organization

A. _____ Is an introduction provided for in each chapter?

B. _____ Is there a clear and simple organizational pattern relating the chapters to each other?

C. _____ Does each chapter have a clear, explicit, and simple organizational structure?

D. _____ Does the text include resources such as an index, glossary, and table of contents?

E. _____ Do questions and activities draw attention to the organizational pattern of the material (e.g., chronological, cause and effect, spatial, topical, etc.)?

F. _____ Do consumable materials interrelate well with the textbook?

Reinforcement

A. _____ Does the text provide opportunities for students to practice using new concepts?

B. _____ Are there summaries at appropriate intervals in the text?

C. _____ Does the text provide adequate iconic aids such as maps, graphs, illustrations, etc., to reinforce concepts?

D. _____ Are there adequate suggestions for usable supplementary activities?

E. _____ Do these activities provide for a broad range of ability levels?

F. _____ Are there literal recall questions provided for the students' self review?

G. _____ Do some of the questions encourage the students to draw inferences?

H. _____ Are there discussion questions that encourage creative thinking?

I. _____ Are questions clearly worded?

Motivation

A. _____ Does the teacher's manual provide introductory activities that will capture students' interest?

B. _____ Are chapter titles and subheadings concrete, meaningful, or interesting?

C. _____ Is the writing style of the text appealing to the students?

D. _____ Are the activities motivating? Will they make the student want to pursue the topic further?

E. _____ Does the book clearly show how the knowledge being learned might be used by the learner in the future?

F. _____ Are the cover, format, print size, and pictures appealing to the students?

G. _____ Does the text provide positive and motivating models for both sexes as well as for other racial, ethnic, and socioeconomic groups?

READABILITY ANALYSIS

Weaknesses

1. On which items was the book rated the lowest?
2. Did these items tend to fall in certain categories?
3. Summarize the weaknesses of this text.
4. What can you do in class to compensate for the weaknesses of this text?

Assets

1. On which items was the book rated the highest?
2. Did these items fall in certain categories?
3. Summarize the assets of this text.
4. What can you do in class to take advantage of the assets of this text?

Source: "Readability checklist," from Judith W. Irwin and Carol A. Davis, "Assessing readability: The checklist approach," Journal of Reading, November 1980, pp. 129–130. Reprinted with permission of Judith W. Irwin and the International Reading Association.

User Involvement Techniques

Some techniques involve trying out representative portions of the material on prospective users. These techniques take into account reader interest, reader background, author's writing style and organization, abstractness of concepts, and, except for the cloze test, they also may consider format and type size and style. Three of these techniques are cloze tests, group reading inventory selections, and informal reading inventory selections, all discussed earlier in this chapter.

Chance (1985) found the cloze procedure to be a quick and reliable way to determine the readability of specific material for individual students. He also verified that subject matter teachers find it easy to construct cloze tests and use them for determining readability.

▪▪▪ Computer Applications to Assessment

Some attempts have been made to apply computer technology to the area of assessment. The most appealing possibility to many educators may be on-computer testing, but most tests given on the computer are limited in form to objective questions that have definite single answers, limiting the scope of testing and the quality of items possible.

More commonly used are programs that enable teachers to easily construct multiple-choice, true-false, fill-in-the-blanks, and essay questions, store them, and allow various tests to be formed from different arrangements of the items. Additionally, when mark-sensitive answer sheets are used for responding to objective items, some tests can be computer scored when the answers are read by a special scanner or optical card reader.

As Bitter, Camuse, and Durbin (1993, p. 91) point out, computers "may never be able to match the perception of a human teacher when evaluating essay answers." In these days of stress on authentic testing, objective tests are often not viewed positively.

Summary

Teachers at the secondary school level often need to interpret norm-referenced reading test results to learn about individual student's reading abilities and about the range of reading abilities within the classroom. Survey and diagnostic tests can both be useful.

Traditional achievement tests do not generally reflect current views of the reading process as a constructive strategic process in which readers make use of their prior knowledge and techniques for unlocking meaning in the text. Work is being done to develop standardized assessment procedures that reflect these views, however.

Criterion-referenced tests, which check the test taker's performance against a performance criterion as a predetermined standard, can also be helpful in assessment. Results of criterion-referenced tests can be used as instructional prescriptions, making them useful in decisions about instruction.

Perhaps more useful to content teachers are informal tests, such as the group reading inventory (GRI), which gives an indication of how well students read a particular textbook; the informal reading inventory, which provides an overall estimate of a student's reading ability as well as a picture of some of his or her strengths and weaknesses; the cloze procedure, which provides the teacher with two types of information—an overall view of the student's reading ability and the appropriateness of text material for the student; and gamelike activities.

The type of assessment measure used most frequently by secondary school content teachers is the skill inventory, which provides information about whether students have developed the specific reading skills necessary to understand content material in the teacher's particular area.

Since teacher judgment enters into decisions about the level of each student's performance, the classroom teacher must carefully observe students as they perform daily tasks with printed materials. Retellings, written responses to writing, and portfolios for students are all informal procedures that, along with more common informal testing procedures, can facilitate assessment.

Student attitudes toward the reading experiences in the content classroom are an important aspect of the overall assessment program. Besides observation and discussion, there are teacher-made devices, self-evaluation devices, and other instruments available to show attitude. Similarly, since interest is often the key that unlocks effort, content teachers who know the general and reading interests of students can plan ways to motivate the students and can capitalize on these interests when selecting and using materials.

In order to adjust reading assignments to fit all students, teachers need to know the difficulty levels of classroom reading materials so they can match the materials to the students' reading levels. Difficulty levels can be determined by using readability formulas or other readability measures in conjunction with teacher judgment.

Discussion Questions

1 What do you consider to be the major strengths and weaknesses of each of the major assessment procedures discussed in this chapter?

2 Which way of reporting results of norm-referenced tests do you think is the most helpful? Why?

3 What are some of the major strengths and weaknesses of CRTs?

4 In what ways may a group reading inventory be useful to a content area teacher? An informal reading inventory?

5 Which reading skill inventory do you think would be most helpful to you as a content area teacher? Why?

6 Why might secondary teachers find the cloze test procedure easy to use?

7 Do you think a self-assessment checklist would help you learn more about a student's reading of a content area textbook? If so, prepare a self-rating checklist that would be most appropriate in your classroom. If not, explain why not.

8 How would you revise the general and reading interests inventory to be most appropriate to your specific content area?

9 Are the newer types of norm-referenced reading tests likely to be more helpful to teachers than traditional standardized tests in planning for reading instruction? Why or why not?

10   What are some effective uses of portfolios for evaluating different literacy concerns?

11   Why should teachers be concerned about the readability of content area reading materials?

Enrichment Activities

*1   If feasible, administer a norm-referenced reading test to a student and interpret the results.

*2   Prepare a group reading inventory, using content area reading materials. Administer your inventory to a student, record your results, and share the findings with the class.

3   Using a textbook of your choice, develop at least two sample questions on each of the book parts listed. (If a particular book part is not included in your text, select examples from supplemental materials.)

a. Preface, Introduction, or Foreword

b. Table of Contents

c. Index

d. Appendix

e. Glossary

f. Unit or Chapter Introduction and/or Summary

*4   Prepare a reading skills inventory for a content area textbook. Administer it to a student, record your results, and share the findings with the class.

*5   Secure a published informal reading inventory and administer it to a student. Report the results to the class.

*6   Prepare a cloze procedure test for a passage of content area reading material. Administer it to a student. Report the results to the class.

*7   Read the article "Using Think Alouds to Assess Comprehension" by Suzanne E. Wade in the March 1990 issue of *The Reading Teacher.* Try using this procedure to assess a student's comprehension skills. Tell the class your conclusions about the comprehension instruction needed by this student.

*8   Administer an interest inventory to a student. What information may be utilized in the instructional program?

*9   Prepare an interest checklist on one topic of study in your content area. If feasible, administer it to a student.

*10   If possible, administer a criterion-referenced test to a group of secondary students.

11   Assemble a portfolio that represents your own literacy skills and features. Describe the criteria you used for including items in your portfolio.

---

*These activities are designed for in-service teachers, student teachers, and practicum students.

Use of Technology for Literacy Learning in a Technological Age

Overview

Students today are immersed in technology daily. They encounter it in store checkout lanes, as well as in popular video games. They watch the news on television instead of reading it from a daily newspaper. They buy videocassettes from which to learn new skills, rather than buying instructional books.

Classrooms reflect this technological environment as well, but many classrooms are not nearly as thoroughly equipped as many students' homes and environments outside school. Cost, of course, is a factor, as is the fact that some educators did not grow up in such an environment and did not have training that covered some of the newer technologies. Nevertheless, today's educators must learn how to harness technology for the benefit of their instructional programs.

Literacy learning naturally accommodates the use of technology. Teachers find that everything from overhead projectors, audiotape recorders, and television to computers, videotape recorders, and videodisc players have applications to the literacy curriculum.

Building on Past Experiences with Technology

For many years now, teachers have generally had access to overhead projectors, televisions, and audiotape recorders as enhancements to their instruction.

■ Overhead Projectors

Use of chalkboards and on-the-spot writing and drawing of complex materials gave way to the use of transparencies displayed on overhead projectors, and the many artistically challenged teachers breathed a sigh of relief and bought sets of well-prepared transparencies to help them illustrate their classroom explanations of various topics. Writing instructional points on blank transparencies also allowed teachers to present material without having to turn their backs to classes, one way to discourage wandering attention in a classroom. Today many schools have equipment that will make transparencies out of material that teachers have typed and/or illustrated themselves at a more leisurely pace than is possible when trying to produce materials in class. Many computer programs, such as *Microsoft PowerPoint* and *mPower* (Multimedia Design), allow teachers to design transparencies with a variety of fonts, colors, and appropriate graphics. These make customizing the presentation materials that are used much less labor intensive than was true in the past.

Overhead transparencies may be used to advance literacy learning in a number of ways. When describing the stages in developing a written product, for example, the teacher can use a series of transparencies with overlays that show each succeeding step as he or she describes it. Transparencies can allow the teacher to record ideas for writing that result from a brainstorming session held before the students are expected to write. Students can then organize the recorded ideas, and various ones can volunteer to put their organizational arrangements on other transparencies to share with the class. Transparencies can allow teachers to display students' work for class analysis of accuracy, clarity, and organization of ideas. Student permission for use of the work should be obtained in advance, or the teacher could use work from classes other than the one in question, with identifying labels deleted, in order to highlight problems that are common to the current class. In addition, students can make individual or group transparencies that illustrate their understanding of content area concepts.

Transparencies can be used before reading about any topic to record semantic webs of prior knowledge about the topic or entries for a K-W-L chart. After reading, they can be used to elaborate the chart and fill in the last stage of the K-W-L chart.

■ Televisions

Televisions are found in many classrooms, and most classrooms have access to them when needed. Public broadcasting programs may fit in with the curricula of teachers in many different disciplines. Scheduling can be a problem, however, since a program that you want to use with a class may not be broadcast during the scheduled time for the class. Videotaping programs to show later for educational purposes is often a possibility, but teachers must be careful to adhere to copyright laws.

Sometimes television programs contain historical or scientific information that can fit into unit study. Students who watch television for this purpose will need to use their note-taking skills to record useful information to add to the information gathered from other sources. Sometimes movies that were made from books that are being studied in the class are available. In this case, students may also take notes, in order to compare and contrast the story in the book and the story as presented in the movie. Movies based on literature selections that the students have not read may be watched and critiqued, and students may be encouraged to read these selections for extra credit or personal enjoyment and report back to the class on the experience. Sometimes newscasts or news specials highlight a class topic—an ongoing military action somewhere in the world, a current election campaign, or a new archaeological discovery, for example. Once again, note taking will be important. Critical analysis of the information presented could take the form of reports that compare the information obtained from this source with information gathered from primary sources, such as military personnel, participants in the campaign, or archaeologists and current print media, such as newspapers or news magazines.

■ Audiotapes

Audiotapes can be used for prerecorded information on a topic, but they are probably most useful when they are used to record group discussions for later review, interviews with primary sources for use in writing reports, or findings from experiments being done in science class. Students can use them to record themselves practicing oral reports that they must give in class, so that they can play the tapes back and critique their performances. Many students have their own audiocassette recorders, used mainly for listening to music, but this resource could be tapped to improve classroom performance. Much material that lends itself to audiotaping now is being videotaped instead, as classrooms obtain more videotaping equipment.

Teachers may want to let students use their tape recorders to tape class lectures and discussions. This will allow the students to take notes at home, use the tapes as review tools, or replay the tapes to double-check ideas that were presented.

■ ■ Technology Tools and Applications for Literacy in Today's Classrooms

The prevalence of technology in classrooms will continue to increase in the future, and teachers will need to integrate it into their curricula. Technology should be a tool for learning needed material.

■ Computers

Computers are the key to the future in most walks of life. Not only are computers found in businesses for communications, record keeping, and accounting, they also are found in cash registers of retail stores and restaurants, in household appliances, and in children's toys and games. They have many potential functions in literacy education.

Word Processing

What are some advantages of having students use word-processing programs to write creative works or research reports?

The writing of student papers, both creative efforts and research reports, is an obvious application of computers to literacy education. The ease of revision and editing that **word-processing programs** provide makes students more likely to reconsider content, organization, wording, and mechanical aspects of their papers and to make changes after a draft has been completed. Spelling checkers and grammar checkers alert students to spellings and syntactic constructions that may need to be changed. Students then have to make their own decisions about the correctness of their material and the best ways to change it. These programs do not merely serve as crutches; they stimulate thought about the writing and initiate decision making. This revision and editing process often results in better written products and offers a learning experience as students see the benefits of trying different organizations and approaches. Word-processing software often includes a dictionary and a thesaurus. The dictionary can be used to decide if the chosen word has the correct meaning for the context. The thesaurus can be used to choose a synonym when a word has been overused in a selection or to pick a word with just the right connotations (Grabe and Grabe, 1998). More on word processing is found in Chapter 8.

Writing Development Software

There are some electronic outliners that help students organize the content of a paper by enabling them to put ideas in outline format. When an outline has been created, the student can easily add or delete items, as the program reconfigures the material to fit the new contents (Geisert and Futrell, 1995). Anderson-Inman and Horney (1996–1997) point out that concept maps, or semantic maps, are often developed as a result of brainstorming as a prewriting activity. They recommend *Inspiration®*, an outlining and diagramming program, for creating semantic maps. A projection device or large monitor can be used with the computer to allow the class to see the development of the map. Symbols can be dragged around the screen to organize them. New symbols can be inserted as labels for categories that are formed, as the material is organized. More ideas or categories can be added, graphics can indicate the importance or order of ideas on the map, and specific instructions can be added to the map. Such mapping allows students to record information from multiple sources on a single map to aid in synthesizing information. It is also possible to link items on the map, clarifying the relationships among the terms. *Inspiration®* can have multiple layers of smaller maps that are hidden until the user accesses them, keeping the screen from becoming crowded and confusing.

Some programs, intended for use as instructional tools, provide prompts to stimulate thought during writing (Geisert and Futrell, 1995). *Process Writing Package* (EduQuest/IBM) offers writing help to students during the prewriting, drafting, revising, editing, and publishing stages. *SEEN*, which contains six tutorials for critical reading; *Writer's Helper Stage II*, a collection of activities to help students write and revise their essays; and *Write ON!*, a library of writing activities, all have uses during the prewriting phase. *Microsoft Works* and *Write ON!* are useful during the drafting stage. *American Heritage Dictionary, Correct Grammar, Correct Writing, Microsoft Works,* and *Writer's Helper Stage II* are useful during the revising stage; and the first four are useful for the editing stage. *Express Publisher, Link Way,* and *Microsoft Works* are good for the publishing phase. The nine programs in the *Process Writing Package* are coordinated to promote writing, reading, and presentation skills for middle and secondary students (Ayers and Wilson, 1994).

Conference and Collaboration Software

What are some examples of conference and collaboration software, and what are the advantages of each type?

Special software is also available that allows students to conference electronically about their reading and writing in any area. *CommonSpace™* (Sixth Floor Media), *The Daedalus Integrated Writing Environment* (The Daedalus Group), *Norton Textra Connect* (Ann Arbor Software), and *Aspects Simultaneous Conference Software* (Group Logic) all allow students to hold networked real-time conferences about reading and writing that they do for class. Chat programs and educational MOOs (multiuser environments used on the Internet) can be used to connect students in geographically diverse locations for real-time written conversations. MOOs are text-based virtual reality environments, some of which have been shaped into virtual classrooms. Computer-mediated discussions of reading among students allow students to participate as often as they like, take as much time as they need to compose responses, and respond directly to each other (Medwin and O'Donovan, 1995; Anderson-Inman, Knox-Quinn, and Tromba, 1996; Jody and Saccardi, 1996).

CommonSpace™ also allows annotation of student writing by teachers and/or student collaborators. Annotations can be linked to the original document or to other annotations. *CommonSpace™* allows a user to insert sound comments, but such comments use a lot of computer memory and cannot be printed. It also facilitates comparison of two drafts of a document by displaying them side-by-side (Sixth Floor Media, 1995). *Personal Journal* (Scott-Foresman) is a program that allows students to write in computerized journals about topics that correlate to each of the seven titles in the *Points of Departure* (ScottForesman) elective literature series.

The Daedalus Integrated Writing Environment (DIWE) has an electronic mail function that allows both private and public messages, a class assignment feature that allows the teacher to send messages to the group, a feature that asks writers for bibliographic information and formats the works in MLA or APA style, a feature that serves as a prewriting prompt for ideas, and a feature that lets students examine on-line drafts of peers' papers, while guiding them through an evaluative process (The Daedalus Group, 1995). Daedalus MOO offers DIWE users a virtual classroom where collaborative writing projects can be undertaken (Anderson-Inman, Knox-Quinn, and Tromba, 1996).

Norton Textra Connect lets a teacher give assignments, collect, grade, and return papers over the network; join the electronic discussion of any work group; and comment over the network to work groups or individuals. It lets students post their papers, comments, and messages to the network and read assignments, comments, and messages from the teacher and other students; revise and re-post their papers after reading peer comments; and create collaborative documents (Tuman, 1994).

Desktop Publishing

What are some applications of desktop publishing programs that could be useful in your content area?

Desktop publishing programs allow for integration of text and graphics (Heide and Henderson, 1994). Generally users can flow text around graphics, choose from a variety of styles and sizes of type, format text into columns, and set up special formats (such as greeting cards, business cards, and banners). Creating posters, flyers, and class newsletters and magazines are the most common uses of desktop publishing for literacy and content development.

Databases and Spreadsheets

What are some applications of database programs in your content area?

A database is an organized collection of data. **Database programs** make possible a search of the database by the computer. The information in a database is filed so that it can be retrieved by category (Bitter, Camuse, and Durbin, 1993; Heide and Henderson, 1994; Grabe and Grabe, 1996). Many commercial databases are available for students to use in their research, and students can form their own databases of information that they collect when doing personal research. Students in American history classes might develop databases of facts related to various states; students in biology classes, ones of the characteristics of certain species; students in English classes, ones of characteristics of particular literature selections; and so on. Creating databases helps students see how to decide what data are relevant to particular topics, and they learn to analyze and synthesize large amounts of information (Heide and Henderson, 1994). Many libraries have their holdings in a computer database that students can search by author, title, and subject. More on databases is found in Chapter 6.

For what content areas are spreadsheets most useful?

Spreadsheets also organize data into a pattern, using a grid of rows and columns. They are ordinarily used to store and manipulate numerical data. Spreadsheet programs often make it possible for data to be presented in chart and graph form (Heide and Henderson, 1994; Grabe and Grabe, 1996). The reading and production of meaningful charts and graphs are important parts of literacy in today's society. Science, economics, and business math teachers may choose to have students use and interpret spreadsheets.

The Internet

What types of resources are available on the Internet that can be used by classroom teachers?

The **Internet** is a "network of networks" that involves tens of thousands of computers throughout the world. Information in the form of text, sound, video, and graphics can be obtained from the Internet. Different "server" computers supply different material, including software, graphs, maps, movies, still pictures, sound, and databases. Communication is the most common use of the Internet. The World Wide Web (WWW) is a portion of the Internet that makes use of hypertext links to allow users to click a mouse on special words or symbols that will automatically connect them to related web locations. This makes accessing information for research quicker and easier than it would be if each individual location had to be separately addressed (Mike, 1996; Ryder and Graves, 1996–1997). Many students are quite comfortable in using the Internet. They can search for information to use in research papers and other class assignments. Some students, however, will need to be assisted with learning of appropriate search strategies.

Much information is available on the Internet about any topic that is studied in school. One problem, however, is that not all of the information is accurate. If students are to use the Internet as a research source, they have to learn to check the credentials of the authors of information found on the net, to double-check information in print or other sources when possible, and to look for documentation of information presented. Anonymous information, accompanied by no documentation, must be approached skeptically. Some sites are known to be reputable, such as the Smithsonian site (http://www.si.edu), the Library of Congress site (http://www.loc.gov), and the *National Geographic* site (http://www.nationalgeographic.com), and can be used with confidence as sources. In some instances, the teacher may wish to supply the students with a list of sites to use in their research. The materials in parentheses in the previous sentence are Uniform Resource Locators (URLs), or Internet addresses. One of the problems with specifying sites on the web to students or in a book such as this one, is that, because the World Wide Web is changing so rapidly, a site that you used yesterday may not be there tomorrow.

Finding information on the Internet is facilitated by a browser, such as *Lynx* (a text-based browser) or *Netscape Navigator* or *Microsoft Internet Explorer* (both graphic browsers). In addition, there are many search engines, such as Lycos and WebCrawler, that allow you to do keyword searches. A group or individual doing a research project might complete the first two sections of a K-W-L about the topic and use the "W" (What I Want to Learn) column to generate key words to guide an Internet search. The results of the search would go in the "L" (What I Learned) column. Scavenger hunting for specific information on school topics on the Internet is fun and educational (Cotton, 1996).

The teacher can also download files to be used for class. Sharon Bailey is a high school teacher in New Mexico who teaches English and history. She downloads such materials as science fiction and bestsellers, novels from Project Gutenberg, book reviews, authors' biographies, and interviews. She, for example, "retrieved the archive for *Zlata's Diary*. Zlata became known to many as the Anne Frank of war-torn Sarajevo. There was a chat on the Scholastic Network, . . . where she discussed her book, her experiences in Sarajevo, and her fears for her family, friends, and country" (Serim and Koch, 1996, p. 40). The Scholastic Network is available on the World Wide Web. This material, of course, was pertinent to both an English class (novel study) and a history class (study of war, violence, and racism).

In Kathleen Litkey's seventh-grade English class, students researched the life and writings of Mark Twain, with some guidance from the teacher. They located information on the Internet, copied it to a word-processing file, and answered the questions the teacher had posed. Then they impersonated Mark Twain, answering the teacher's interview questions as they thought he would have. The language skills used in the project included Internet search skills, writing of descriptive paragraphs, punctuation of quotations, and using proper attribution in the final product (Serim and Koch, 1996).

Ken Hartman, a high school chemistry teacher, had his students use the Internet to research the topic of solid waste. Groups worked to collect data on six aspects of the issue. They published their findings on a server for use by others (Serim and Koch, 1996).

What kinds of information might a student or a class put on a home page?

Many classrooms or individual students now have their own **home pages** on the WWW. Although a discussion of home page development is beyond the scope of this section, students can learn to use HyperText Markup Language (HTML) to code the material for their own home pages (Cotton, 1996). Text, graphics, photographs, and even animations may be included. Classes may wish to develop web pages to display class newspapers, students' creative writing or written reports, students' art work, and so on. The importance of careful composition and proofreading and editing become evident when writing is going to be displayed to the world on the Internet.

Electronic Communications

Electronic mail (E-mail); subscriptions to electronic mailing lists (called LIST-SERVs); posting to electronic bulletin boards (newsgroups); and electronic videoconferencing are all ways of communicating by way of the Internet, although not all electronic mail nor all electronic videoconferencing is done over the Internet.

What are some ideas for using videoconferencing in your content area?

Few classrooms will likely have the cameras and software necessary for **videoconferencing** at the present, but the future may hold more opportunities to have students conference over the Internet with someone who can be seen on the computer's monitor and heard through its speakers. This would offer students opportunities to interview such people as authors of literary selections, scientists, historians, mathematicians, and businesspeople who could shed light on a current area of study. The students could compile interview questions; conduct the interview, taking notes; and write up a report of the findings, which then might be integrated into a larger project's report. In Dade County, Florida, advanced computer students use CU-SeeME videoconferencing to converse with students in other countries ("Wired Education," 1996).

What is a potential application of electronic mail in your content area?

Electronic mail has many potential benefits for the classroom. Students can E-mail students in schools in other parts of the world to discuss such things as current study topics, current events, differences in their schools and environments, and literature that is being studied. In the Kentucky Telecommunications Writing Project, for example, students in different Kentucky schools read the same books and use E-mail to communicate with each other about their reading (Bell et al., 1995). Students also can E-mail experts in various fields to get answers to questions that they need for class studies. In the Kentucky Authors Project, for example, students interact with published authors; "students share personal information as well as their works-in-progress. Authors provide feedback to each student's work, share their own ideas and approaches to writing, and, on occasion, offer direct instruction. . . . Students also have a chance to read and discuss each author's work directly with the author through on-line 'literature conferences'" (Paeth et al., 1995, p. 1). The focus of the project is on improving student writing (Paeth and others, 1995). Secondary school students can E-mail college students in methods courses to discuss matters related to the content of their curricula. A number of E-mail connections have been set up between college students and public school students to discuss books that both were reading (Moore, 1991; Bromley, 1993; Roe and Smith, 1996; Roe and Smith, 1997). The following "Meeting the Challenge" describes the project that Roe and Smith developed.

MEETING THE CHALLENGE

An entire section of Betty Roe's undergraduate reading methods students, plus graduate students in reading and language arts methods courses who chose this activity as a class project, were paired with the seventh graders in Barbara Vaughn's and Melinda Beaty's homerooms. Both the university students and the seventh graders read the book *Bridge to Terabithia*

E-mail exchanges about literature can promote analysis of the literature selections. (© Joel Gordon)

on a predetermined schedule and exchanged E-mail messages about the reading on a weekly basis. They discussed literary elements of the book and connections that they could see between the book and their lives. Both groups also viewed a video based on the book; then in an E-mail exchange, the partners compared and contrasted the book and the video. In addition, the university students posted comments about the literary elements in the book to a campus discussion group (newsgroup) four times during the semester. The seventh graders produced an *mPower* multimedia presentation based on the book to show the university students. At the end of the project, the partners met on the university campus and discussed the experience.

Seventh-grade students, university students, the two seventh-grade teachers, and the university professor involved all felt the project was beneficial and enjoyable. One seventh grader wrote to Betty Roe: "Dear Dr. Roe, I liked reading the book. I thought it was a good learning experience. I liked the feeling that I'm not the only one who sometimes doesn't understand something that I read. She helped me understand it. It was like she was my sister. I talked to her all the time. Your friend, Angie Adkins." The two seventh-grade teachers wrote, "Reading the book *Bridge to Terabithia* and E-mailing their thoughts concerning the book improved our seventh graders' reading, writing, and communicative skills. Our students were very enthusiastic about the project and really enjoyed the trip to TTU to meet their E-mail partners. We have found our students continuing to communicate with their partners even though, technically, the project is concluded for this semester. We also noticed a marked improvement in some students' self-expression. Over time, the letters became longer and more focused on the book's contents. This positive association with older students, responsible for the same work, enhanced our seventh graders' self-esteem. Some students felt that they were 'almost doing college work.'" University student Stacy Webb said, "I think it gives students a sense of responsibility and promotes the idea of discussing and enjoying what they read. It was also helpful for me in the sense that I was able to practice responding and interacting with the kind of students I will be teaching one day." Noel Roberts, another university student, said, "I read *Bridge to Terabithia* through the eyes of a child." The university students appeared to enjoy the E-mail interactions. Two major disk crashes made the postings to the discussion group less positive experiences. The *mPower* presentation developed by the seventh graders was extremely well done, and the university students were impressed. Betty Roe feels that the project was beneficial to all concerned, and she hopes to continue it indefinitely.

Stivers (1996) had college students in junior-year methods courses paired with children with special learning needs for E-mail exchanges. Some letters were general conversation, and some were lessons in which the college students modeled a skill, explained it, and then led the middle-school students to use it in their writing. The middle-school students responded well to the attention the college students paid to them, and even the college students showed evidences of increased self-esteem because of the young students' positive responses to the correspondence.

How may electronic mailing lists be used for assignments?

Electronic mailing lists send out messages to a group of interested readers. Readers "subscribe" to a particular list and thereafter receive all communications to the other members in the list until they "unsubscribe" to stop the flow of mail. Although the subscriber may be interested in the topic, the volume of mail that comes through some mailing lists is too difficult to handle. It must be read and deleted on a regular basis, generally daily. Mailing lists of interest may be subscribed to when a topic is being studied and dropped after the study is completed.

What are newsgroups?

Electronic bulletin boards, or **newsgroups,** have messages "posted" to a network location. Interested readers can read these messages electronically if they know the address of the newsgroup. Messages may be posted and read by people from all over the world (Grabe and Grabe, 1996).

Electronic Reference Works

Dictionaries, thesauruses, encyclopedias, atlases, and specialized area reference books are available on disk and CD-ROM for use with computers. Many references can also be found on the Internet. More on electronic reference works is found in Chapter 6.

What types of computer-assisted instructional programs exist, and what is the value of each type?

Computer-Assisted Instruction (CAI)

Computer-assisted instructional programs are generally of four types: drill-and-practice, which offer practice on skills that teachers have already taught; tutorial, which offer actual instruction; simulations, which set up situations that simulate reality and give students the opportunity to use decision-making and problem-solving skills; and educational games, which take a variety of formats to give students experiences related to educational goals. Any of these types of programs may be used to enhance the instructional program, but some programs are not pedagogically sound, so they must be evaluated carefully before they are used with students. CAI programs need to be focused on a legitimate educational objective; be appropriate for the maturity levels of the students; be user friendly; and be manageable, timewise, in the classroom.

Many drill-and-practice, tutorial, and game programs focus on such skills as vocabulary development, parts of speech, punctuation, and spelling. Simulation programs for any content area are good to encourage critical reading and thinking and problem solving, areas in which students have not shown proficiency on the National Assessment of Educational Progress. Although it is beyond the scope of this text to identify software for each application, representatives of simulation software can show you the types of programs that may be helpful; for example, *Capitol Hill* (The Software Toolworks) for social studies simulates the experience of a new member of the House of Representatives. *Operation Frog* (Scholastic) for science simulates a dissection; and *Ecological Simulations 1 & 2* (Creative Computing), *Three Mile Island* (Muse Software), and *Earth Watch: Weather Forecasting* (Learningways) can also enrich science lessons. *The Math Shop Series* (Scholastic) for math has the students solve problems in everyday situations related to customer services provided for stores. Any one of a wide variety of interactive fiction story programs can be used as recreational reading in an English class.

■ Videotapes

Videotapes on many topics can be used to enhance learning in those areas, just as films did in years past. They can be used to illustrate text materials for the less proficient readers or for students with limited experiential backgrounds; for example, they may be used to help bring a literary selection to life for students or to make a process (such as pasteurization) that is discussed in their text more comprehensible. Videotape recorders are easy to use, and prerecorded tapes on a multitude of topics are available for purchase, for rental from video stores, or from libraries. Students can view these tapes, take notes, and use the information for classroom discussion, reports, and projects. Videotapes based on literature selections are often available for use in English classrooms. Students can compare and contrast the video presentations with the books. When the students described in the preceding "Meeting the Challenge" did this comparison, they decided that the book was much more effective than the video.

Students can also make their own videotapes of class presentations or field trip activities. They can prepare special video presentations for which they write scripts and practice polished presentations, such as simulated newscasts.

◼ CD-ROMs and Videodiscs (Laser Discs)

What are the advantages of using CD-ROMs and laser discs?

CD-ROMs and videodiscs are both large-capacity storage media (Grabe and Grabe, 1996). Entire reference books or novels may be stored on them. They provide high-quality images and sound. Some are interactive, in that words can be selected to be pronounced, defined, or pictured, and nonlinear sequences of presentation can be followed. Information on a **CD-ROM** may be selected through keystrokes or mouse clicks. Information on a **laser disc** is often selected with a remote control unit or a bar code reader. Videodiscs can be under the control of a computer. Both types of media work well for instructional purposes.

◼ Multimedia Applications

What is meant by multimedia?

Multimedia refers to the mixing of different media. A multimedia presentation may include text, photographs, line drawings, video clips, sounds, and animated figures. The sounds and images may be drawn from videotapes, videodiscs, audiotapes, and clip art available on disks. Images may be scanned in from printed documents. "Multimedia computer systems are being produced by most computer companies. The multimedia platform usually consists of the ability to combine text, graphics, animation, music, voice, and full-motion video controlled by a microcomputer" (Bitter, Camuse, and Durbin, 1993, p. 200). These systems have interactive capabilities. Multimedia encyclopedias are common in schools today, and they allow students to read text, see video clips, hear audio clips, or see still pictures related to the subject being accessed.

Students can develop their own multimedia presentations with special software, as the students in the preceding "Meeting the Challenge" did with *mPower* (Multimedia Design). Such a presentation takes much organization, composition, and critical reading and thinking. It is truly a good literacy activity.

The use of multimedia in a unit on *Huckleberry Finn* by Mark Twain is suggested by Willis, Stephens, and Matthew (1996). One resource for the unit could be the electronic version of *Huckleberry Finn* by Bookworm, which uses graphics, audio recordings, and movies to bring the text alive. In such a unit students may plan a debate about whether the book should be banned or not. Groups of students could research their arguments and write persuasive essays using *Aspects* (Group Technologies), a writing program that allows two or more students to work on a single document from different computers. Then the students could use these essays as the basis for a debate. One group might use KidsNet, an electronic telecommunications service on the Internet, to conduct a poll of other eighth graders about their opinions of censorship or racial issues. Others might search for information about Mark Twain, the time period in which the novel is set, and public reactions to the novel when it was published. This could be partially done on the Internet. Some students might want to write poems or short stories based on their findings. These could be written with a word-processing program. A class presentation might be developed using *Microsoft Powerpoint*. The project's culminating activity could be a newsletter produced with a desktop publishing program, such as *The Student Writing Center* (The Learning Company).

■ ■ Perspective on Technology Use for Literacy Learning Tomorrow

Technology has been important in classrooms for many years, but today a much wider range of technology is available. Teachers should not abandon the good aspects of such older technology as overhead projectors, audiotape recorders, and televisions, but they should also embrace newer technology, such as computer applications, CD-ROMs and videodiscs, and videotape recorders. They must choose the tool that best fits classroom needs from the whole spectrum of possibilities. It is their responsibility to decide what to use, when to use it, and how it fits into the class structure. To do this, they must understand the capabilities and limits of each piece of hardware and each technological application.

Teachers are familiar with tools such as overhead projectors, audiotape recorders, and televisions, and their knowledge of the strengths and weaknesses of these tools in the curriculum can help them look at newer technologies analytically, avoiding the use of technology as an "add-on," and fully integrating it into the curricular program.

Present technological tools such as computer applications, CD-ROMs, videodiscs, and videotape recorders provide a range of learning opportunities for students. Computer technology allows not only CAI applications but also use of word processing, writing development programs, conferencing and collaboration software, desktop publishing, database and spreadsheet applications, Internet research sources, electronic communications, electronic reference works, electronic publishing on the Internet, and multimedia presentations. Therefore, teachers can incorporate applications as low level as drill-and-practice programs or as high level as development of multimedia presentations by the students, as their classroom needs dictate.

The incredible pace of emergence of new technology makes several things clear:

1. Technology is here to stay. It won't go away.
2. Schools can't keep up with the cutting-edge applications, but they will continually be advancing to higher levels of applications.
3. It is impossible to know what new technologies will evolve into educational tools. Virtual reality applications are already making some advances, and much effort is being expended to offer greater access to telecommunica-

tions. Web-based courses (instruction via the World Wide Web) are likely to spread in the future.

Teachers may wish to learn more about technological applications but may not know where to turn. Today there are many resources for teachers to help them learn about and have successful experiences with today's literacy learner. The technology section of most large bookstores and the magazine racks in a variety of stores provide many publications that will explain emerging technologies at various levels of sophistication. (See Figure A.1.) Professional organizations, such as the International Reading Association (IRA) and the National Council of Teachers of English (NCTE), which offer increasing numbers of sessions on technology at their conferences and conventions each year, are good resources. The locations of these conferences and conventions varies from year to year, so one may be within easy reach in the near future. The Technology, Reading and Learning Difficulties Conference focuses on technology and literacy; the National Educational Computing Conference, managed by the International Society for Technology in Education (ISTE), is more general; and EdMedia: World Conference on Educational Media and Hypermedia, an Association for the Advancement of Computing Education (AACE) conference, covers multimedia (Willis et al., 1996).

FIGURE A.1

Some Technology References

(Full bibliographic information on these books can be found in the References at the end of this book.)

1. *Education on the Internet: A Student's Guide*, by Andrew T. Stull
2. *Integrating Technology for Meaningful Learning*, by Mark and Cindy Grabe
3. *The Internet for Dummies: Quick Reference*, by John R. Levine and Margaret Levine Young
4. *Internet for Educators*, by Randall James Ryder and Tom Hughes
5. *The Internet Roadmap*, by Bennett Falk
6. *More Internet for Dummies*, by John R. Levine and Margaret Levine Young
7. *The Multimedia Home Companion*, edited by Rebecca Buffum Taylor
8. *NetLearning: Why Teachers Use the Internet*, by Ferdi Serim and Melissa Koch
9. *The Online Classroom: Teaching with the Internet*, by Eileen Giuffré Cotton
10. *Teachers, Computers, and Curriculum*, by Paul G. Geisert and Mynga K. Futrell
11. *The Technological Classroom*, by Ann Heide and Dale Henderson
12. *Technology, Reading, and Language Arts*, by Jerry W. Willis, Elizabeth C. Stephens, and Kathryn I. Matthew
13. *10 Minute Guide to the Internet and the World Wide Web*, by Galen Grimes
14. *Welcome to . . . Internet: From Mystery to Mastery*, by Tom Badgett and Corey Sandler
15. *The Whole Internet*, by Ed Krol
16. *Your Windows® 95 Internet Surfboard*, by Allen Wyatt

IRA and NCTE also include articles about integrating technology into the classroom in their journals: *The Reading Teacher* (focus on elementary and middle school) and the *Journal of Adolescent & Adult Literacy* (focus on middle school through adult)—both are IRA journals; and *Language Arts* (focus on elementary and middle school) and *English Journal* (focus on middle school through senior high)— both are NCTE journals. ISTE has many helpful publications, including *The Computing Teacher* and *Telecommunications in Education*. AACE has several journals also, including *Journal of Computers in Mathematics and Science Education* and *Journal of Educational Multimedia and Hypermedia* (Willis et al., 1996).

The World Wide Web is a treasure trove of resources, but, unfortunately, the locations of the treasures are anything but stable, since web addresses change constantly. Figure A.2 shows a few sites that you may wish to check. Use of a search engine, such as AltaVista, will help you find many more.

FIGURE A.2

Some Web Sites of Interest

(Remember that Web addresses change frequently.)

Amazon Online Bookstore—http://www.amazon.com
Ask ERIC—http://ericir.sunsite.syr.edu
The Complete Works of William Shakespeare—http://the-tech.mit.edu/Shakespeare/works.html
Children's Literature Web Guide—http://www.ucalgary.ca/~dkbrown
EdWeb—http://k12.cnidr.org:90/resource.cntnts.html
Eisenhower Clearinghouse for Mathematics and Science Education—http://www.enc.org
Houghton Mifflin's Educational Place—http://www.hmco.com
Library of Congress—http://lcweb.loc.gov
NASA's Internet in the Classroom—http://quest.arc.nasa.gov/interactive.html
NASA's Spacelink—http://spacelink.msfc.nasa.gov
National Science Foundation—http://www.nsf.gov
Northwest Regional Educational Laboratory—http://nwrel.org
Sea World Teacher Guides—http://monarch.bio.ukans.edu
Southwest Regional Educational Laboratories—http://www.swrel.org
Smithsonian—http://www.si.edu
U.S. Geological Survey—http://info.er.usgs.gov
WebMuseum—http://sunsite.unc.edu/louvre
Welcome to the White House—http://www.whitehouse.gov

References

Aaron, Ira E., Jeanne S. Chall, Dolores Durkin, Kenneth Goodman, and Dorothy S. Strickland. "The Past, Present, and Future of Literacy Education: Comments from a Panel of Distinguished Educators, Part I." *The Reading Teacher* 43 (February 1990a): 302–311.

———. "The Past, Present, and Future of Literacy Education: Comments from a Panel of Distinguished Educators, Part II." *The Reading Teacher* 43 (February 1990b): 370–380.

Adams, D., and M. Hamm. *New Designs for Teaching and Learning: Promoting Active Learning in Tomorrow's Schools.* San Francisco: Jossey-Bass, 1994.

Adams, G., T. Gullotta, and C. Markstrom-Adams. *Adolescent Life Experiences.* Pacific Grove, Calif.: Brooks/Cole, 1994.

Adams, M., and A. Collins. "A Schema-Theoretic View of Reading." In H. Singer and R. Ruddell (eds.), *Theoretical Models and Processes of Reading.* Newark, Del.: International Reading Association, 1986, pp. 404–425.

Adams, Pamela E. "Teaching *Romeo and Juliet* in the Nontracked English Classroom." *Journal of Reading* 38 (March 1995): 424–432.

Alexander, C. F. "Black Dialect and the Classroom Teacher." In C. Brooks (ed.), *Tapping Potential: English and the Language Arts for the Black Learner.* Urbana, Ill.: National Council of Teachers, 1985, pp. 20–29.

Alexander, J. Estill, and Jeanne Cobb. "Assessing Attitudes in Middle and Secondary Schools and Community Colleges." *Journal of Reading* 36 (October 1992): 146–149.

Alfred, Suellen. "Dialogue Journal." *Tennessee Reading Teacher* 19 (Fall 1991): 12–15.

Allen, V. G. "Teaching Bilingual and ESL Children." In *Handbook of Research in Teaching the English Language Arts.* New York: Macmillan, 1991, pp. 356–371.

Alvermann, D. E., and D. Hayes. "Classroom Discussion of Content Area Assignments: An Intervention Study." *Reading Research Quarterly* 21 (1989): 305–335.

Alvermann, D. E., and D. W. Moore. "Secondary School Reading." In R. Barr, M. L. Kamil, P. Mosenthal, and P. D. Pearson (eds.), *Handbook of Reading Research.* Vol. 2. New York: Longman, 1991, pp. 951–983.

Alvermann, D., D. Dillon, and D. O'Brien. *Using Discussion to Promote Reading Comprehension.* Newark, Del.: International Reading Association, 1987.

"Analyzing the NAEP Data: Some Key Points." *Reading Today* 11 (December 1993–January 1994): 1, 12.

Anders, P., and C. Bos. "Semantic Feature Analysis: An Interactive Strategy for Vocabulary Development and Text Comprehension." *Journal of Reading* 29 (April 1986): 610–616.

Anderson, R., and B. Nagy. *The Vocabulary Conundrum.* Champaign: University of Illinois, Center for the Study of Reading, 1993.

Anderson, R., E. Hiebert, J. Scott, and I. Wilkinson, eds. *Becoming a Nation of Readers: The Report of the Commission on Reading.* Washington, D.C.: National Institute of Education, 1985.

Anderson-Inman, Lynne, and Carolyn Knox-Quinn. "Spell Checking Strategies for Successful Students." *Journal of Adolescent & Adult Literacy* 39 (March 1996): 500–501.

Anderson-Inman, Lynne, Carolyn Knox-Quinn, and Peter Tromba. "Synchronous Writing Environments: Real-time Interaction in Cyberspace." *Journal of Adolescent & Adult Literacy* 40 (October 1996): 134–138.

Anderson-Inman, Lynne, and Mark Horney. "Computer-Based Concept Mapping: Enhancing Literacy with Tools for Visual Thinking." *Journal of Adolescent & Adult Literacy* 40 (December 1996/January 1997): 302–306.

Andrasick, Kathleen Dudden. *Opening Texts: Using Writing to Teach Literature.* Portsmouth, N.H.: Heinemann, 1990.

Andre, M., and T. Anderson. "The Development and Evaluation of a Self-Questioning Study Technique." *Reading Research Quarterly* 14, no. 4 (1978–1979): 605–622.

Applebee, Arthur N. *Contexts for Learning to Write: Studies of Secondary School Instruction.* Norwood, N.J.: Ablex, 1984.

Archambeault, Betty. "Personalizing Study Skills in Secondary Students." *Journal of Reading* 35 (March 1992): 468–472.

Armbruster, Bonnie B., and Thomas H. Anderson. *Content Area Textbooks.* Reading Education Report No. 23. Champaign: University of Illinois at Urbana-Champaign, July 1981.

Ashabranner, B. *To Live in Two Worlds: American Indian Youth Today.* New York: Dodd, 1984.

Au, Kathryn H. *Literacy Instruction in Multicultural Settings.* Fort Worth, Tex.: Holt, Rinehart and Winston, 1993.

Au, Kathryn H., Judith A. Scheu, Alice J. Kawakami, and Patricia A. Herman. "Assessment and Accountability in a Whole Literacy Curriculum." *The Reading Teacher* 43 (April 1990): 574–578.

Aubry, Valerie Sebern. "Audience Options for High School Students with Difficulties in Writing." *Journal of Reading* 38 (March 1995): 434–443.

Ausubel, D. *Educational Psychology: A Cognitive View.* 2d ed. New York: Holt, Rinehart and Winston, 1978, pp. 523–525.

Ayers, Phyllis, and Jamelle Wilson. "Do It Write: IBM's Process Writing: Defining Ourselves in a Changing World." Paper presented at the National Council of Teachers of English Convention, Orlando, Florida, November 21, 1994.

Babbs, Patricia J., and Alden J. Moe. "Metacognition: A Key for Independent Learning from Text." *The Reading Teacher* 36 (January 1983): 422–426.

Baber, C., et al. *Project Achieve.* Greensboro: University of North Carolina at Greensboro, 1990.

Bader, Lois A., and Katherine D. Wiesendanger. "Realizing the Potential of Informal Reading Inventories." *Journal of Reading* 32 (February 1989): 402–408.

Badgett, Tom, and Corey Sandler. *Welcome to . . . Internet: From Mystery to Mastery.* New York: MIS Press, 1993.

Badiali, B. "Reading in the Content Area of Music." In M. Dupuis (ed.), *Reading in the Content Areas: Research for Teachers.* Newark, Del.: International Reading Association, 1984, pp. 42–47.

Baines, Lawrence. "From Page to Screen: When a Novel Is Interpreted for Film, What Gets Lost in the Translation." *Journal of Adolescent & Adult Literacy* 39 (May 1996): 612–622.

Baker, L., and A. Brown. "Metacognitive Skills and Reading." In P. D. Pearson (ed.), *Handbook of Reading Research.* New York: Longman, 1984, pp. 353–394.

Baldauf, Richard B., Jr., et al. "Can Matching Cloze Be Used with Secondary ESL Pupils?" *Journal of Reading* 23 (February 1980): 435–440.

Ballard, Leslie. "Portfolios and Self-Assessment." *English Journal* 81 (February 1992): 46–48.

Banks, J. "The Canon Debate, Knowledge Construction and Multicultural Education." *Educational Researcher* 22 (1993): 4–14.

———. *Education in the 80's: Multiethnic Education.* Washington, D.C.: National Education Association, 1981, pp. 42–53.

Barron, R. "The Use of Vocabulary as an Advance Organizer." In H. Herber and P. Sanders (eds.), *Research in Reading in the Content Areas: First Year Report.* Syracuse, N.Y.: Syracuse University Press, 1969, pp. 29–39.

Barry, Arlene L. "The Staffing of High School Remedial Reading Programs in the United States Since 1920." *Journal of Reading* 38 (September 1994): 14–22.

Baskin, Barbara H., and Karen Harris. "Heard Any Good Books Lately? The Case for Audiobooks in the Secondary Classroom." *Journal of Reading* 38 (February 1995): 372–376.

Baumann, J., and E. Kameenui. "Research on Vocabulary Instruction: Ode to Voltaire." In J. Flood, J. Jensen, D. Lapp, and J. Squire (eds.), *Handbook of Research on Teaching the English Language Arts.* New York: Macmillan, 1991, pp. 604–632.

Baumann, James F. *Reading Assessment: An Instructional Decision-Making Perspective.* Columbus, Ohio: Merrill Publishing Company, 1988.

Beach, R. *A Teacher's Introduction to Reader-Response Theories.* Urbana, Ill.: National Council of Teachers of English, 1993.

Bean, T., and B. Ericson. "Text Previews and Three Level Study Guides for Content Area Critical Reading." *Journal of Reading* 32 (January 1989): 337–341.

Beck, I., C. Perfetti, and M. McKeown. "Effects of Long-Term Vocabulary Comprehension." *Journal of Educational Psychology* 74 (1982): 506–521.

Beck, I., M. McKeown, G. Sinatra, and J. Loxterman. "Revising Social Studies Text from a Text-processing Perspective: Evidence of Improved Comprehensibility." *Reading Research Quarterly* 29 (1991): 251–481.

Belanoff, Pat, and Marcia Dickson, eds. *Portfolios: Process and Product.* Portsmouth, N.H.: Boynton/Cook, 1991.

Belanoff, Pat, and Peter Elbow. "Using Portfolios to Increase Collaboration and Community in a Writing Program." In Pat Belanoff and Marcia Dickson (eds.), *Portfolios: Process and Products.* Portsmouth, N.H.: Boynton/Cook, 1991, pp. 17–30.

Bell, Nancy, Debbie Cambron, Kathy Rey-Barreau, and Beverly Paeth. "Online Literature Groups." Handout at the National Council of Teachers of English Convention, San Diego, California, 1995.

Benson, Linda K. "How to Pluck an Albatross: The Research Paper without Tears." *English Journal* 76 (November 1987): 54–56.

Berger, Linda R. "Reader Response Journals: You Make the Meaning . . . and How." *Journal of Adolescent & Adult Literacy* 39 (February 1996): 380–385.

Berkowitz, S. "Effects of Instruction in Text Organization on Sixth Grade Students' Memory for Expository Reading." *Reading Research Quarterly* 21, no. 2 (1986): 161–178.

Bernstein, Harriet T. "The New Politics of Textbook Adoption." *Phi Delta Kappan* 66 (March 1985): 463–466.

Betts, Emmett A. *Foundations of Reading Instruction.* New York: American Book Company, 1946.

Beyer, B. "Developing a Scope and Sequence for Thinking Skills Instruction." *Educational Leadership* 45 (April 1988): 26–31.

Beyersdorfer, Janet M., and David K. Schauer. "Writing Personality Profiles: Conversations Across the Generation Gap." *Journal of Reading* 35 (May 1992): 612–616.

Bieler, R., and J. Snowman. *Psychology Applied to Teaching.* (8th ed.) Boston: Houghton Mifflin, 1997.

Binkley, Marilyn R. "New Ways of Assessing Text Difficulty." In Beverley L. Zakaluk and S. Jay Samuels (eds.), *Readability: Its Past, Present & Future.* Newark, Del.: International Reading Association, 1988, pp. 98–120.

Bitter, Gary G., Ruth A. Camuse, and Vicki L. Durbin. *Using a Microcomputer in the Classroom.* 3rd edition. Boston: Allyn and Bacon, 1993.

Blachowicz, C., and B. Zabroske. "Context Instruction: A Metacognitive Approach for At-Risk Readers." *Journal of Reading* 33 (April 1990): 504–508.

Blatt, G., and L. Rosen. "The Writing Response to Literature." *Journal of Reading* 28 (October 1984): 8–12.

Bode, Barbara A. "Dialogue Journal Writing." *The Reading Teacher* 42 (April 1989): 568–571.

Bormuth, John. "Cloze Test Readability: Criterion Reference Scores." *Journal of Educational Measurement* 5 (Fall 1968): 189–196.

———. "The Cloze Readability Procedure." *Elementary English* 45 (April 1968): 429–436.

Bowman, M. "A Comparison of Content Schemata and Textual Schemata or the Process of Parachuting." *Reading World* 21 (October 1981): 14–22.

Brazee, Ed. "Teaching Reading in Social Studies: Skill-Centered Versus Content-Centered." *Colorado Journal of Educational Research* 18 (August 1979): 23–25.

Bristow, P. "Are Poor Readers Passive Readers? Some Evidence, Possible Explanations, and Potential Solutions." *The Reading Teacher* 39 (December 1985): 318–325.

Britton, James, Tony Burgess, Nancy Martin, Alex McLeod, and Harold Rosen. *The Development of Writing Abilities (11–18).* London: Macmillan Education Ltd., 1975.

Bromley, Karen. *Journaling: Engagements in Reading, Writing, and Thinking.* New York: Scholastic, 1993.

Bromley, Karen D'Angelo, and Laurie McKeveny. "Précis Writing: Suggestions for Instruction in Summarizing." *Journal of Reading* 29 (February 1986): 392–395.

Brooks, Bruce. *Midnight Hour Encores.* New York: Harper & Row, Junior Books, 1986.

Brophy, Jere. "Probing the Subtleties of Subject-Matter Teaching." *Educational Leadership* 49 (April 1992): 4–9.

Brown, A. L., and J. D. Day. "Macrorules for Summarizing Texts: The Development of Expertise." *Journal of Verbal Learning and Verbal Behavior* 22, no. 1 (1983): 1–14.

Brown, A. L., J. D. Day, and R. Jones. "The Development of Plans for Summarizing Texts." *Child Development* 54 (1983): 968–979.

Brozo, William G. "Learning How At-Risk Readers Learn Best: A Case for Interactive Assessment." *Journal of Reading* 33 (April 1990): 522–527.

Burron, Arnold, and Amos L. Claybaugh. *Using Reading to Teach Subject Matter: Fundamentals for Content Teachers.* Columbus, Ohio: Merrill Publishing Company, 1974.

Busching, B., and R. Slesinger. "Authentic Questions: What Do They Look Like? Where Do They Lead?" *Language Arts* 72 (September 1995): 341–351.

Buss, R., R. Ratliff, and J. Irion. "Effects of Instruction on the Use of Story Starters in Composition of Narrative Discourse." In J. Niles and R. Lalik (eds.), *Issues in Literacy: A Research Perspective.* Rochester, N.Y.: National Reading Conference, 1985, pp. 55–58.

Butcheri, Jan, and Jesse J. Hammond. "Authentic Writing Makes the Difference." *Journal of Reading* 38 (November 1994): 228–229.

Calfee, R., K. Dunlap, and A. Wat. "Authentic Discussion of Texts in Middle Grade Schooling: An Analytic-Narrative Approach." In R. Horowitz (ed.), *Classroom Talk About Text: What Teenagers and Teachers Come to Know About the World Through Talk About Text.* Newark, Del.: International Reading Association, 1994: 38–43.

Calfee, Robert C., and Pam Perfumo. "Student Portfolios: Opportunities for a Revolution in Assessment." *Journal of Reading* 36 (April 1993): 532–537.

Camp, Roberta, and Denise Levine. "Portfolios Evolving: Background and Variations in Sixth- Through Twelfth-Grade Classrooms." In Pat Belanoff and Marcia Dickson (eds.), *Portfolios: Process and Product.* Portsmouth, N.H.: Boynton/Cook, 1991, pp. 194–205.

Campione, J., and B. Armbruster. "Acquiring Information from Texts: An Analysis of Four Approaches." In J. W. Segal, S. Chipman, and R. Glaser (eds.), *Thinking and Learning Skills: Relating Instruction to Research, vol. 1.* Hillsdale, N.J.: Erlbaum, 1985.

Carlson, J. "Reading in the Content Area of Foreign Language." In M. Dupois (ed.), *Reading in the Content Areas: Research for Teachers.* Newark, Del.: International Reading Association, 1984, pp. 23–32.

Carnine, D., and D. Kinder. "Teaching Low Performing Students to Apply Generative and Schema Strategies to Narrative and Expository Material. *Remedial and Special Education* 6 (1985): 20–30.

Carr, E., and D. Ogle. "K-W-L Plus: A Strategy for Comprehension and Summarization." *Journal of Reading* 30 (1987): 626–631.

Carrney, T. "Textuality: Infectious Echoes from the Past." *The Reading Teacher* 43 (March 1990): 478–484.

Carroll, David, and Patricia Carini. "Tapping Teachers' Knowledge." In Vito Perrone (ed.), *Expanding Student Assessment.* Alexandria, Va.: Association for Supervision and Curriculum Development, 1991, pp. 40–46.

Carroll, Pamela Sissi. "'i cant read i wont read': Will's Moment of Success." *English Journal* 81 (March 1992): 50–52.

Catterall, James S. "Standards and School Dropouts: A National Study of Tests Required for High School Graduation." *American Journal of Education* 97 (November 1989): 1–34.

Chance, Larry. "Use Cloze Encounters of the Readability Kind for Secondary School Students." *Journal of Reading* 28 (May 1985): 690–693.

Chase, A., and F. Duffelmeyer. "VOCAB-LIT: Integrating Vocabulary Study and Literature Study." *Journal of Reading* 34 (November 1990): 188–193.

Children's Defense Fund, *What Every American Should Be Asking Political Leaders in 1988.* Washington, D.C.: Author, 1988.

Chittenden, Edward. "Authentic Assessment, Evaluation, and Documentation of Student Performance." In Vito Perrone (ed.), *Expanding Student Assessment.* Alexandria, Va.: Association for Supervision and Curriculum Development, 1991, pp. 22–31.

Christ, G. "Curriculums with Real-World Connections." *Educational Leadership* 52 (May 1995): 32–35.

Cioffi, G. "Perspective and Experience: Developing Critical Reading Abilities." *Journal of Reading* 36 (September 1992): 48–53.

Clark, Charles H. "Assessing Free Recall." *The Reading Teacher* 35 (January 1982): 434–439.

Clarke, J. "Using Visual Organizers to Focus on Thinking." *Journal of Reading* (April 1991): 526–534.

Clarke, John H., James Raths, and Gary L. Gilbert. "Inductive Towers: Letting Students See How They Think." *Journal of Reading* 33 (November 1989): 86–95.

Cocking, Terry S., and Susan A. Schafer. "Scavenging for Better Library Instruction." *Journal of Reading* 38 (November 1994): 164–170.

Coley, J., and D. Hoffman. "Overcoming Learned Helplessness in At-Risk Readers." *Journal of Reading* 33 (April 1990): 497–502.

Collins, C. "Reading Instruction That Increases Thinking Abilities." *Journal of Reading* 34 (April 1991): 510–516.

Collins, Norma Decker. "Freewriting, Personal Writing, and the At-Risk Reader." *Journal of Reading* 33 (May 1990): 654–655.

Colt, Jacalyn M. "Support for New Teachers in Literature-Based Reading Programs." *Journal of Reading* 34 (September 1990): 64–66.

Commander, Nannette Evans, and Brenda D. Smith. "Learning Logs: A Tool for Cognitive Monitoring." *Journal of Adolescent & Adult Literacy* 39 (March 1996): 446–453.

Commeyras, Michelle. "Commercially Available Language Arts Performance-Based Assessments." *The Reading Teacher* 45 (February 1992): 468–470.

Condon, William, and Liz Hamp-Lyons. "Introducing a Portfolio-based Writing Assessment: Progress Through Problems." In Pat Belanoff and Marcia Dickson (eds.), *Portfolios: Process and Product*. Portsmouth, N.H.: Boynton/Cook, 1991, pp. 231–247.

Conley, M. "Teacher Decisionmaking." In D. Alvermann and D. Moore (eds.), *Research Within Reach: Secondary School Reading*. Newark, Del.: International Reading Association, 1987.

Cooper, C., and A. Purves. *A Guide to Evaluation*. Lexington, Mass.: Ginn and Co., 1973.

Cooper, J., S. Garrett, M. Leighton, P. Martorella, G. Morine-Dershimer, D. Sadker, M. Sadker, R. Shostak, T. TenBrink, and W. Weber. *Classroom Teaching Skills*. 5th ed. Lexington, Mass.: D. C. Heath, 1994.

Cooper, Winfield, and B. J. Brown. "Using Portfolios to Empower Student Writers." *English Journal* 81 (February 1992): 40–45.

Cooter, Robert B., Jr., and Robert Griffith. "Thematic Units for Middle School: An Honorable Seduction." *Journal of Reading* 32 (May 1989): 676–681.

Cormier, R. *The Chocolate War*. New York: Pantheon, 1974.

Cotton, Eileen Giuffré. *The Online Classroom: Teaching with the Internet*. Bloomington, Indiana: ERIC Clearinghouse on Reading, English, and Communication, 1996.

Cox, G. C., D. L. Smith, and T. A. Rakes. "Enhancing Comprehension Through the Use of Visual Elaboration Strategies." *Reading Research and Instruction* 33 (1994): 159–174.

Craven, Jerry. "A New Model for Teaching Literature Classes." *T.H.E Journal* 22 (August 1994): 55–57.

Cunningham, J., and D. Moore. "The Confused World of Main Idea." In J. Baumann (ed.), *Teaching Main Idea Comprehension*. Newark, Del.: International Reading Association, 1986, pp. 1–17.

Cunningham, Patricia M., and James W. Cunningham. "Content Area Reading-Writing Lessons." *The Reading Teacher* 40 (February 1987): 506–512.

Daisey, P. "Three Ways to Promote the Values and Uses of Literacy at Any Age." *Journal of Reading* 36 (March 1993): 436–440.

Dale, E. *Audiovisual Methods in Teaching*. 3d ed. New York: Holt, Rinehart and Winston, 1969.

Dale, Edgar, and Jeanne S. Chall. "A Formula for Predicting Readability," *Educational Research Bulletin* 27 (January 21, 1948): 11–28

———. "A Formula for Predicting Readability: Instructions," *Educational Research Bulletin* 27 (February 18, 1948): 37–54.

Dale, Edgar, and Joseph O'Rourke. *The Living Word Vocabulary*. Elgin, Ill.: Dome, 1976.

Dales, Brenda. "Trusting Relations Between Teachers and Librarians." *Language Arts* 67 (November 1990): 732–734.

Damico, Natalie W. "Portfolio Reflections—10 Activities to Promote Reflective Thinking." *Notes Plus* (March 1996): 3–4.

D'Angelo, Karen. "Précis Writing: Promoting Vocabulary Development and Comprehension." *Journal of Reading* 26 (March 1983): 534–539.

Danielson, Kathy Everts. "Picture Books to Use with Older Students." *Journal of Reading* 35 (May 1992): 652–654.

Davey, B. "Active Responding in Content Classrooms." *Journal of Reading* 33 (October 1989): 44–49.

———. "Assessing Comprehension: Selected Interactions of Task and Reader." *The Reading Teacher* 42 (May 1989): 694–697.

———. "How Do Classroom Teachers Use Their Textbooks?" *Journal of Reading* 31 (January 1988): 340–345.

———. "Team for Success: Guided Practice in Study Skills Through Cooperative Research Reports." *Journal of Reading* 30 (May 1987): 701–705.

———. "Think Aloud—Modeling the Cognitive Processes of Reading Comprehension." *Journal of Reading* 27 (October 1983): 44–47.

Davis, Susan J., and Jean Hunter. "Historical Novels: A Context for Gifted Student Research." *Journal of Reading* 33 (May 1990): 602–606.

Delquardi, J., C. R. Greenwood, D. Whorton, J. J. Carta, and R. V. Hall. "Classwide Peer Tutoring." *Exceptional Children* 52 (1986): 535–542.

Dever, Christine T. "Press Conference: A Strategy for Integrating Reading with Writing." *The Reading Teacher* 46 (September 1992): 72–73.

Diehl, W., and L. Mikulecky. "The Nature of Reading at Work." *Journal of Reading* 24 (December 1980): 221–227.

Doerfert, D. L. *What Is Your Agricultural Vision?* Madison, Wis.: Department of Public Instruction, 1993.

Dole, J., S. Valencia, E. Greer, and J. Wardrop. "Effects of Two Types of Prereading Instruction on the Comprehension of Narrative and Expository Text." *Reading Research Quarterly* 26, no. 2 (1991): 142–159.

Dolly, Martha R. "Integrating ESL Reading and Writing through Authentic Discourse." *Journal of Reading* 33 (February 1990): 360–365.

Dreher, Mariam Jean. "Searching for Information in Textbooks." *Journal of Reading* 35 (February 1992): 364–371.

Duin, A., and M. Graves. "Teaching Vocabulary as a Writing Prompt." *Journal of Reading* 32 (December 1988): 204–212.

Earle, R. *Teaching Reading and Mathematics.* Newark, Del.: International Reading Association, 1976.

Eddowes, E. A., and J. R. Hranitz. "Educating Children of the Homeless." *Childhood Education* 65 (Summer 1989): 197–200.

Eeds, M., and W. Cochrum. "Teaching Word Meanings by Expanding Schemata vs. Dictionary Work vs. Reading in Context." *Journal of Reading* 28 (March 1985): 492–502.

Elbow, Peter, and Pat Belanoff. "State University of New York at Stony Brook Portfolio-based Evaluation Program." In Pat Belanoff and Marcia Dickson (eds.), *Portfolios: Process and Product.* Portsmouth, N.H.: Boynton/Cook, 1991, pp. 3–16.

Elbow, Peter. "Foreword." In Pat Belanoff and Marcia Dickson (eds.), *Portfolios: Process and Product.* Portsmouth, N.H.: Boynton/Cook, 1991, pp. ix–xvi.

———. "Why Teach Writing?" In Philip L. Brady (ed.), *The Why's of Teaching Composition.* Washington State Council of Teachers of English, 1978, pp. 57–69.

Elliott, C. "The Music-Reading Dilemma." *Music Education Journal* 59 (February 1982): 33–34.

Ellman, Neil. "The Impact of Competency Testing on Curriculum and Instruction." *NASSP Bulletin* 72 (February 1988): 49–52.

Ennis, R. "Critical Thinking and Subject Specificity: Clarification and Needed Research." *Educational Researcher* 18 (April 1989): 4–10.

Falk, Bennett. *The Internet Roadmap.* San Francisco: Sybex, 1994.

Farr, Roger, and Bruce Tone. *Portfolio and Performance Assessment.* Fort Worth: Harcourt Brace, 1994.

Farr, Roger, and Michael A. Tulley. "Do Adoption Committees Perpetuate Mediocre Textbooks?" *Phi Delta Kappan* 66 (March 1985): 467–471.

Farr, Roger, and Robert F. Carey. *Reading: What Can Be Measured?* Newark, Del.: International Reading Association, 1986.

Farrell, Ellen. "SSR as the Core of a Junior High Reading Program." *Journal of Reading* 26 (October 1982): 48–51.

Farstrup, Alan E. "Point/Counterpoint: State-by-State Comparisons on National Assessments." *Reading Today* 7 (December 1989–January 1990): 1, 11–15.

Fay, Leo. "Reading Study Skills: Math and Science." In J. Allen Figurel (ed.), *Reading and Inquiry.* Newark, Del.: International Reading Association, 1965, pp. 93–94.

Feathers, Karen M., and Frederick R. Smith. "Meeting the Reading Demands of the Real World: Literacy Based Content Instruction." *Journal of Reading* 30 (March 1987): 506–511.

Fennessey, Sharon. "Living History Through Drama and Literature." *The Reading Teacher* 49 (September 1995): 16–19.

Ferguson, Anne M., and Jo Fairburn. "Language Experience for Problem Solving in Math." *The Reading Teacher* 38 (February 1985): 504–507.

Ferris, Judith Ann, and Gerry Snyder. "Writing as an Influence on Reading." *Journal of Reading* 29 (May 1986): 751–756.

Field, M., and J. Aebersold. "Cultural Attitudes Toward Reading: Implications for Teachers of ESL/Bilingual Readers." *Journal of Reading* 33 (March 1990): 406–414.

Finder, M. "Teaching to Comprehend." *Journal of Reading* 13 (May 1970): 611–636.

Fitzgerald, J. "Literacy and Students Who Are Learning English as a Second Language." *The Reading Teacher* 46 (May 1993): 638–647.

Fitzgerald, J., and D. Speigel. "Enhancing Children's Reading Comprehension Through Instruction in Narrative Structure." *Journal of Reading Behavior* 15 (1983): 1–17.

Fitzgerald, Jill. "Helping Young Writers to Revise: A Brief Review for Teachers." *The Reading Teacher* 42 (November 1988): 124–129.

Flesch, Rudolf. *The Art of Readable Writing.* New York: Harper & Row, 1949.

Flores, B., P. T. Cousin, and E. Diaz. "Transforming Deficit Myths about Learning, Language and Culture. *Language Arts* 68 (1991): 369–379.

Fox, Dana L. "Women's Roles in American History: Materials for a Unit." *English Journal* 78 (November 1989): 78–79.

Frager, A. "Affective Dimensions of Content Area Reading." *Journal of Reading* 36 (May 1993): 616–622.

Frayer, D. A., W. C. Frederick, and H. J. Klausmeier. *A Schema for Testing the Level of Concept Mastery.* (Technical Report No. 16). Madison, WI: University of Wisconsin, R & D Center for Cognitive Learning, 1969.

Frew, A. "Four Steps Toward Literature-Based Reading." *Journal of Reading* 34 (October 1990): 213–220.

Fry, Edward. "A Readability Formula for Short Passages." *Journal of Reading* 33 (May 1990): 594–597.

———. "Graphical Literacy." *Journal of Reading* 24 (February 1981): 383–390.

———. *Fry Readability Scale (Extended).* Providence, R.I.: Jamestown Publishers, 1978.

———. "Fry's Readability Graph: Clarifications, Validity and Extension to Level 17." *Journal of Reading* 21 (December 1977): 242–252.

———. *Reading Instruction for Classroom and Clinic.* New York: McGraw-Hill, 1972.

———. "A Readability Formula That Saves Time," *Journal of Reading* 11 (April 1968): 513–516, 575–578.

Gahn, S. "A Practical Guide for Teaching Writing in the Content Areas." *Journal of Reading* 32 (March 1989): 525–531.

Gallagher, Janice Mori. "Pairing Adolescent Fiction with Books from the Canon." *Journal of Adolescent & Adult Literacy* 39 (September 1995): 8–14.

Garcia-Vazquez, Enedina, and Luis A. Vazquez. "In a Pen Pals Program: Latinos/as Supporting Latino/as." *Journal of Reading* 38 (November 1994): 172–178.

Gardner, H. *Multiple Intelligences: The Theory in Practice.* New York: Basic Books, 1993.

Gardner, H. *Multiple Intelligences: The Theory in Practice.* New York: HarperCollins, 1998.

Gavelek, J. "The Social Contexts of Literacy and Schooling: A Developmental Perspective." In T. Raphael (ed.), *The Contexts of Literacy and Schooling: A Developmental Perspective.* New York: Random House, 1986, pp. 3–26.

Geisert, Paul G., and Mynga K. Futrell. *Teachers, Computers, and Curriculum: Microcomputers in the Classroom.* 2nd edition. Boston: Allyn and Bacon, 1995.

Gentile, L., and M. McMillan. *Stress and Reading Difficulties: Research, Assessment, Intervention.* Newark, Del.: International Reading Association, 1987.

Gillespie, Cindy S. "Reading Graphic Displays: What Teachers Should Know." *Journal of Reading* 36 (February 1993): 350–354.

Gillespie, Cindy S., Karen L. Ford, Ralph D. Gillespie, and Alexandra G. Leavell. "Portfolio Assessment: Some Questions, Some Answers, Some Recommendations." *Journal of Adolescent & Adult Literacy* 39 (March 1996): 480–491.

Gillespie, Cindy. "Questions About Student-Generated Questions." *Journal of Reading* 34 (December 1990): 250–257.

Glasgow, Jacqueline N. "Motivating the Tech Prep Reader Through Learning Styles and Adolescent Literature." *Journal of Adolescent & Adult Literacy* 39 (February 1996): 358–367.

Glatthorn, Allen. "Thinking, Writing, and Reading: Making Connections." In Diane Lapp, James Flood, and Nancy Farnan (eds.), *Content Area Reading and Learning: Instructional Strategies.* Englewood Cliffs, N.J.: Prentice Hall, 1989.

Glazer, Susan Mandel, and Carol Smullen Brown. *Portfolios and Beyond: Collaborative Assessment in Reading and Writing.* Norwood, Massachusetts: Christopher-Gordon, 1993.

Glazer, Susan Mandel, and Lyndon W. Searfoss. "Re-examining Reading Diagnosis." In Susan Mandel Glazer, Lyndon W. Searfoss, and Lance M. Gentile (eds.), *Reexamining Reading Diagnosis: New Trends and Procedures.* Newark, Del.: International Reading Association, 1989, pp. 1–11.

Godina, Heriberto. "The Canonical Debate—Implementing Multicultural Literature and Perspectives." *Journal of Adolescent & Adult Literacy* 39 (April 1996): 544–549.

Goldenberg, C., and R. Gallimore. "Changing Teaching Takes More Than a One-Shot Workshop." *Educational Leadership* 49 (1991): 69–72.

Goodlad, J. *A Place Called School.* New York: McGraw-Hill, 1984.

Gordon, Christine J., and Dorothy MacInnis. "Using Journals as a Window on Students' Thinking in Mathematics." *Language Arts* 70 (January 1993): 37–43.

Gordon, K. *The Deluxe Transitive Vampire: The Ultimate Handbook of Grammar for the Innocent, the Eager, and the Doomed.* New York: Pantheon, 1993.

Grabe, Mark, and Cindy Grabe. *Integrating Technology for Meaningful Learning.* Boston: Houghton Mifflin, 1996, 1998.

Grace, Marsha. "Implementing a Portfolio System in Your Classroom." *Reading Today* 10 (June-July 1993): 27.

Grant, Rachel. "Strategic Training for Using Text Headings to Improve Students' Processing of Content." *Journal of Reading* 36 (March 1993): 482–488.

Graser, Elsa R. *Teaching Writing: A Process Approach.* Dubuque, Iowa: Kendall/Hunt Publishing Co., 1983.

Graves, Donald H. "Help Students Learn to Read Their Portfolios." In Donald H. Graves and Bonnie S. Sunstein (eds.), *Portfolio Portraits.* Portsmouth, N.H.: Heinemann, 1992, pp. 85–95.

———. "Portfolios: Keep a Good Idea Growing." In Donald H. Graves and Bonnie S. Sunstein (eds.), *Portfolio Portraits.* Portsmouth, N.H.: Heinemann, 1992, pp. 1–12.

Graves, M., and M. Prenn. "Costs and Benefits of Various Methods of Teaching Vocabulary." *Journal of Reading* 29 (May 1986): 596–602.

Grimes, Galen. *10 Minute Guide to the Internet and the World Wide Web.* Indianapolis, Ind.: Que Corporation, 1996.

Gross, Philip P., and Karen Sadowski. "FOGINDEX—A Readability Formula Program for Microcomputers." *Journal of Reading* 28 (April 1985): 614–618.

Grubb, W. N. "The Challenge to Change." *Vocational Education* 66 (1991): 24–26.

Guthrie, J. T., and P. Mosenthal. "Literacy as Multidimensional: Locating Information and Reading Comprehension." *Educational Psychologist* 22 (1987): 279–297.

Guthrie, John T. "Children's Reasons for Success and Failure." *The Reading Teacher* 36 (January 1983): 478–480.

Guzzetti, Barbara J., Barbara J. Kowalinski, and Tom McGowan. "Using a Literature-Based Approach to Teaching Social Studies." *Journal of Reading* 36 (October 1992): 114–122.

Guzzetti, Barbara J., Cynthia R. Hynd, Stephanie A. Skeels, and Wayne O. Williams. "Improving Physics Texts: Students Speak Out." *Journal of Reading* 38 (May 1995): 656–663.

Hammond, D. "How Your Students Can Predict Their Way to Reading Comprehension." *Learning* 12 (1983): 62–64.

Hancock, Marjorie R. "Character Journals: Initiating Involvement and Identification Through Literature." *Journal of Reading* 37 (September 1993): 42–50.

Hansen, J. *When Writers Read.* Portsmouth, N.H.: Heinemann, 1986.

Harada, Violet H. "Breaking the Silence: Sharing the Japanese American Internment Experience with Adolescent Readers." *Journal of Adolescent & Adult Literacy* 39 (May 1996): 630–637.

Hare, V. C., and K. M. Borchardt. "Direct Instruction of Summarization Skills." *Reading Research Quarterly* 20, no. 1 (1984): 62–78.

Harp, Bill. "When the Principal Asks: 'Why Aren't You Using Peer Editing?'" *The Reading Teacher* 41 (April 1988): 828–829.

Harris, A., and E. Sipay. *How to Increase Reading Ability.* (9th ed.) New York: Longman, 1990.

Harris, T., and R. Hodges, eds. *A Dictionary of Reading and Related Terms.* Newark, Del.: International Reading Association, 1981.

Hartman, D. "Eight Readers Reading: The Intertextual Links of Able Readers Using Multiple Passages." *Reading Research Quarterly* 27, no. 2 (1992): 122–132.

Hayes, David A. "Helping Students GRASP the Knack of Writing Summaries." *Journal of Reading* 33 (November 1989): 96–101.

———. "Initiate Cartographic Literacy with the MAP Activity." *Journal of Reading* 35 (May 1992): 659–661.

Heide, Ann, and Dale Henderson. *The Technological Classroom: A Blueprint for Success.* Toronto: Trifolium Books, 1994.

Heinemann, S. "Can Job-Related Performance Tasks Be Used to Diagnose Secretaries' Reading and Writing Skills?" *Journal of Reading* 23 (December 1979): 239–243.

Heinich, R., M. Molenda, and J. D. Russell. *Instructional Media and the New Technologies of Instruction.* New York: Macmillan, 1993.

Heller, M. "How Do You Know What You Know? Metacognitive Modeling in the Content Areas." *Journal of Reading* 29 (February 1986): 415–422.

Henk, William A., and John P. Helfeldt. "How to Develop Independence in Following Directions." *Journal of Reading* 30 (April 1987): 602–607.

Henrichs, M., and T. Sisson, "Mathematics and the Reading Process: A Practical Application of Theory." *Mathematics Teacher* 1973 (April 1980): 253–256.

Herber, H. *Teaching Reading in Content Areas,* 2d ed. Englewood Cliffs, N.J.: Prentice-Hall, 1978.

Herman, Joan L., Pamela R. Aschbacher, and Lynn Winters. *A Practical Guide to Alternative Assessment.* Alexandria, Va.: Association for Supervision and Curriculum Development, 1992.

Herman, W., Jr. "Reading and Other Language Arts in Social Studies Instruction: Persistent Problems." In R. Preston (ed.), *A New Look at Reading in Social Studies.* Newark, Del.: International Reading Association, 1969, pp. 5–9.

Hickey, M. G. "Reading and Social Studies: The Critical Connection." *Social Education* (March 1990): 175–179.

Hicks, C. "Sound Before Sight: Strategies for Teaching Music Reading." *Music Education Journal* (April 1980): 53–67.

Hightshue, Deborah, Dott Ryann, Sally McKenna, Joe Tower, and Brenda Brumley. "Writing in Junior and Senior High Schools." *Phi Delta Kappa* 69 (June 1988): 725–728.

Hill, F., and J. May. *Spaceship Earth: Physical Science.* Rev. ed. Boston: Houghton Mifflin, 1981, p. 102.

Hill, Margaret. "Writing Summaries Promotes Thinking and Learning Across the Curriculum—But Why Are They So Difficult to Write?" *Journal of Reading* 34 (April 1991): 536–539.

Hillerich, Robert L. *The Principal's Guide to Improving Reading Instruction.* Boston: Allyn and Bacon, 1983.

Hobson, E., and B. Shuman. *Reading and Writing in High School: A Whole Language Approach.* Washington, D.C.: National Education Association, 1990.

Hodgkinson, L. *All One System: Demographics of Education—Kindergarten Through Graduate School.* Washington, D.C.: Institute of Educational Leadership, 1985.

Hoffman, James V. "Critical Reading/Thinking Across the Curriculum: Using I-Charts to Support Learning." *Language Arts* 69 (February 1992): 121–127.

Holloway, K. "Learning to Talk—Learning to Read." In C. Brooks (ed.), *Tapping Potential: English and the Language Arts for the Black Learner.* Urbana, Ill.: National Council of Teachers of English, 1985, pp. 12–19.

Holmes, Betty C., and Nancy L. Roser. "Five Ways to Assess Readers' Prior Knowledge." *The Reading Teacher* 40 (March 1987): 646–649.

Hoobler, D., and T. Hoobler. *Vietnam: Why We Fought—An Illustrated History.* New York: Knopf/Borzoi, 1990.

Horowitz, R. "Text Patterns: Part I." *Journal of Reading* 28 (February 1985a): 448–454.

———. "Text Patterns: Part II." *Journal of Reading* 28 (March 1985b): 448–454.

Hudley, C. A. "Using Role Models to Improve the Reading Attitudes of Ethnic Minority High School Girls." *Journal of Reading* 36 (November 1992): 182–189.

INC Sights: A Teacher's Guide to Writers INC. Burlington, Wis.: Write Source Educational Publishing House, 1989.

Imel, S. *Vocational Education's Role in Dropout Prevention.* Columbus, OH: ERIC Clearinghouse on Adult, Career, and Vocational Education, 1993.

Irwin, J. *Teaching Reading Comprehension Processes.* Englewood Cliffs, N.J.: Prentice-Hall, 1991.

Irwin, Judith Westphal, and Carol A. Davis. "Assessing Readability: The Checklist Approach." *Journal of Reading* 24 (November 1980): 124–130.

Jackson, J., and E. Evans. *Spaceship Earth: Earth Science.* Rev. ed. Boston: Houghton Mifflin, 1980, p. 19.

Jacobowitz, T. "AIM: A Metacognitive Strategy for Constructing the Main Idea of Text." *Journal of Reading* 33 (May 1990): 620–624.

Jacobowitz, Tina. "Using Theory to Modify Practice: An Illustration with SQ3R." *Journal of Reading* 32 (November 1988): 126–131.

Jaeger, Elizabeth L. "The Reading Specialist as Collaborative Consultant." *The Reading Teacher* 49 (May 1996): 622–629.

Jenkins, J., and L. Jenkins. "Peer Tutoring in Elementary and Secondary Programs. *Focus on Exceptional Children* 17 (1985): 1–12.

Jenkins, J., B. Matlock, and T. Slocum. "Approaches to Vocabulary Instruction: The Teaching of Individual Word Meanings and Practice in Deriving Word Meaning from Context." *Reading Research Quarterly* 24 (1989): 215–235.

Jenkinson, Edward B. "'I Don't Know What to Write About Today': Some Ideas for Journal Writing." *Phi Delta Kappan* 69 (June 1988a): 739.

———. "Learning to Write/Writing to Learn." *Phi Delta Kappan* 69 (June 1988b): 712–717.

———. "Practice Helps with Essay Exams." *Phi Delta Kappan* 69 (June 1988c): 726.

Jody, M., and M. Saccardi. *Computer Conversations: Readers and Books Online.* Urbana, Ill.: National Council of Teachers of English, 1996.

Johns, J., and M. Palumbo. *Whole Language in Secondary Schools.* Focused Access to Selected Topics No. 54, Bloomington, Ind.: ERIC January 1991.

Johnson, D., and B. Johnson. "Highlighting Vocabulary in Inferential Comprehension Instruction." *Journal of Reading* 29 (April 1986): 622–625.

Johnson, E. *How to Achieve Competence In English.* Pittsburgh, Pa.: Dorrance Publishing Inc., 1994.

Johnson, M. S., R. A. Kress, and J. J. Pikulski. *Informal Reading Inventories.* 2nd ed. Newark, Del.: International Reading Association, 1987.

Johnson-Weber, Mary. "Picture Books for Junior High." *Journal of Reading* 33 (December 1989): 219–220.

Johnston, Peter H. "Teachers as Evaluation Experts." *The Reading Teacher* 40 (April 1987): 744–748.

———. *Reading Comprehension Assessment: A Cognitive Basis.* Newark, Del.: International Reading Association, 1983.

Jones, B. F., A. Palincsar, D. Ogle, and E. Carr. *Strategic Teaching and Learning: Cognitive Instruction in the Content Areas.* Alexandria, Va.: Association for Supervision and Curriculum Development, 1986.

Jones, Janet Craven. "Reading and Study Skills: Problems in the Content Areas." *Journal of Reading* 31 (May 1988): 756–759.

Jossart, Sarah A. "Character Journals Aid Comprehension." *The Reading Teacher* 42 (November 1988): 180.

Judd, Dorothy H. "Avoid Readability Formula Drudgery: Use Your School's Microcomputer." *The Reading Teacher* 35 (October 1981): 7–8.

Kakela, J. "The Vocational Interactive Reading Project: Working with Content Area Specialists." *Journal of Reading* 36 (February 1993): 390–396.

Kameenui, E. J., D. Carnine, and R. Freschi. "Effects of Text Construction and Instructional Procedures for Teaching Word Meanings on Comprehension and Recall." *Reading Research Quarterly* 17 (1982): 367–388.

Kelly, Brenda Wright, and Janis Holmes. "The Guided Lecture Procedure." *Journal of Reading* 22 (April 1979): 602–604.

Kerka, S. "New Technologies and Emerging Careers: Trends and Issues Alert." Columbus, Ohio: ERIC Clearinghouse on Adult, Career, and Vocational Education (1994).

Kinder, Diane, Bill Bursuck, and Michael Epstein. "An Evaluation of History Textbooks." *The Journal of Special Education* 25 (1992): 472–491.

Kirby, Dan, and Tom Liner, with Ruth Vinz. *Inside Out: Developmental Strategies for Teaching Writing.* 2d ed. Portsmouth, N.H.: Heinemann, 1988.

Kirk, S., and J. Gallagher. *Educating Exceptional Children.* Boston: Houghton Mifflin, 1993.

Klauer, K. "Intentional and Incidental Learning with Instructional Texts: A Metaanalysis for 1970–1980." *American Educational Research Journal* 21 (1984): 323–340.

Kletzien, S. B. "Strategy Use by Good and Poor Comprehenders Reading Expository Text of Differing Reading Levels." *Reading Research Quarterly* 26 (1991): 67–86.

Kletzien, S., and B. Hushion. "Reading Workshop: Reading, Writing, Thinking." *Journal of Reading* 35 (March 1992): 444–450.

Kletzien, Sharon B., and Maryanne R. Bednar. "Dynamic Assessment for At-Risk Readers." *Journal of Reading* 33 (April 1990): 528–533.

Kline, Norman. "Education and the Internet: The Evolution of the Electronic Library." *Syllabus* 8 (November/December 1994): 14–15.

Knifong, J., and B. Holtran. "A Search for Reading Difficulties Among Erred Word Problems." *Journal for Research in Mathematics Education* 8 (May 1977): 277–230.

Knight, Janice Evans. "Coding Journal Entries." *Journal of Reading* 34 (September 1990): 42–47.

Konopak, Bonnie C., Michael A. Martin, and Sarah H. Martin. "Reading and Writing: Aids to Learning in the Content Areas." *Journal of Reading* 31 (November 1987): 109–115.

Kress, Roy A. "Trends in Remedial Instruction." *Journal of Reading* 32 (January 1989): 370–372.

Kretschmer, Joseph C. "Computerizing and Comparing the Rix Readability Index." *Journal of Reading* 27 (March 1984): 490–499.

———. "Updating the Fry Readability Formula." *The Reading Teacher* 29 (March 1976): 555–558.

Krol, Ed. *The Whole Internet.* 2nd edition. Sebastopol, Calif.: O'Reilly & Associates, 1994.

Krushenisky, Cindy. "Lightening Your Load with Multimedia Encyclopedias." *PC Novice* 4 (October 1993): 62–65.

Kucer, S. "Authenticity as the Basis for Instruction." *Language Arts* 68 (November 1991): 532–540.

Laminack, L. "Mr. T Leads the Class: The Language Experience Approach and Science." *Science and Children* 24 (1987): 41–42.

Langer, Judith A. *Envisioning Literature.* New York: Teachers College Press, 1995.

Langer, J., and A. Applebee. *How Writing Shapes Thinking: A Study of Teaching and Learning.* Urbana, Ill.: National Council of Teachers of English, 1987.

Langer, Judith A. "Examining Background Knowledge and Text Comprehension." *Reading Research Quarterly* 19 (1984): 468–481.

———. "Facilitating Text Processing: The Elaboration of Prior Knowledge." In J. Langer and M. T. Smith-Burke (eds.), *Reader Meets Author/Bridging the Gap: A Psycholinguistic and Sociolinguistic Perspective.* Newark, Del.: International Reading Association, 1982, pp. 149–162.

———. "From Theory to Practice: A Prereading Plan." *Journal of Reading* 25 (November 1981): 152–156.

———. "Learning Through Writing: Study Skills in the Content Areas." *Journal of Reading* 29 (February 1986): 400–406.

Lapp, Diane, James Flood, and Nancy Farnan. *Content Area Reading and Learning: Instructional Strategies.* Englewood Cliffs, N.J.: Prentice-Hall, 1989.

Latta, B. Dawn. "In-Process and Retrospective Journals: Putting Writers Back in Writing Processes." *English Journal* 80 (January 1991): 60–66.

Lederer, R. *Anguished English.* Charleston, S.C.: Wyrick, 1987.

Lesgold, A., L. Resnick, and K. Hammond. "Learning to Read: A Longitudinal Study of Word Skill Development in Two Curricula." In T. Waller and G. MacKinnon (eds.), *Reading Research: Advances in Theory and Practice,* Vol. 4. New York: Academic Press, 1985, pp. 107–138.

Levine, John R., and Margaret Levine Young. *More Internet for Dummies.* Foster City, Calif.: IDG Books, 1994.

———. *The Internet for Dummies: Quick Reference.* Foster City, Calif.: IDG Books, 1994.

Lewandowski, Lawrence J., and Brian K. Martens. "Test Review: Selecting and Evaluating Standardized Reading Tests." *Journal of Reading* 33 (February 1990): 384–388.

Lewis, J. "Redefining Critical Reading for College Critical Thinking Courses." *Journal of Reading* 34 (March 1991): 420–423.

Lipson, M., S. Valencia, K. Wixson, and C. Peters. "Integration and Thematic Teaching: Integration to Improve Teaching and Learning." *Language Arts* 70 (April 1993): 252–263.

Livo, N. J., and S. A. Rietz. *Storytelling Activities.* Englewood, Colorado: Libraries Unlimited, 1987.

Lloyd, C., and J. Mitchell. "Coping with Too Many Concepts in Science Texts." *Journal of Reading* 32 (March 1989): 542–549.

Lubell, M., and R. Townsend. "A Strategy for Teaching Complex Prose Structures." *Journal of Reading* 33 (November 1989): 102–106.

MacGinitie, Walter H. "Some Limits of Assessment." *Journal of Reading* 36 (April 1993): 556–560.

MacGregor, R. *Prophecy Rock.* New York: Simon & Schuster, 1995.

Maimon, Elaine P. "Cultivating the Prose Garden." *Phi Delta Kappan* 69 (June 1988): 734–739.

Mallow, J. "Reading Science." *Journal of Reading* 34 (February 1991): 324–338.

Mandler, J., and N. Johnson. "Remembrance of Things Passed: Story Structure and Recall." *Cognitive Psychology* 9 (1977): 111–151.

Manion, Betty Byrne. "Writing Workshop in Junior High School: It's Worth the Time." *Journal of Reading* 32 (November 1988): 154–157.

Manzo, A. V. "Guided Reading Procedure." *Journal of Reading* 18 (December 1975): 287–291.

Maria, K. *Reading Comprehension Instruction: Issues and Strategies.* Parkton, Md.: York Press, 1990.

Marzano, R., E. Brandt, C. Hughes, B. Jones, B. Presseisen, S. Rankin, and C. Suhor. *Dimensions of Thinking: A Framework for Curriculum and Instruction.* Alexandria, Va.: Association for Supervision and Curriculum Development, 1988.

Matteson, G., and R. Jensen. *Teaching Units from Agricultural Literacy.* Madison, Wis.: The University of Wisonsin, 1994.

McCormick, Sandra, and John O. Cooper. "Can SQ3R Facilitate Secondary Learning Disabled Students' Literal Comprehension of Expository Text? Three Experiments." *Reading Psychology* 12 (July–September 1991): 239–271.

McGee, Lea M., and Gail E. Tompkins. "Literature-Based Reading Instruction: What's Guiding the Instruction?" *Language Arts* 72 (October 1995): 405–414.

McGinley, William J., and Peter R. Denner. "Story Impressions: A Prereading/Writing Activity." *Journal of Reading* 31 (December 1987): 248–253.

McKenna, M., R. Robinson, and J. Miller. "Whole Language: A Research Agenda for the Nineties." *Educational Researcher* 19 (November 1990): 3–6.

McKeown, M., and M. Curtis, eds. *The Nature of Vocabulary Acquisition.* Hillsdale, N.J.: Erlbaum, 1987.

McKeown, M., I. Beck, G. Sinatra, and J. Loxterman. "The Contribution of Prior Knowledge and Coherent Text to Comprehension." *Reading Research Quarterly* 27 (1992): 79–93.

McLaughlin, Harry G. "SMOG Grading—A New Readability Formula," *Journal of Reading* 12 (May 1969): 639–646.

McTighe, J., and F. Lyman Jr. "Cueing Thinking in the Classroom: The Promise of Theory-Embedded Tools." *Educational Leadership* 45 (April 1988): 18–24.

Mealey, D. L., B. C. Konopak, M. A. Duchein, D. W. Frazier, T. R. Host, and C. Nobles. "Student, Teacher, and Expert Differences in Identifying Important Content Area Vocabulary." In N. D. Padak, T. V. Rasinski, and J. Logan (eds.), *Literary Research and Practice: Foundations for the Year 2000.* Fourteenth Yearbook of the College Reading Association. Pittsburg, Kans.: College Reading Association, 1992, pp. 117–123.

Means, M., and J. Voss. "Star Wars: A Developmental Study of Expert Novice Knowledge Structures." *Journal of Memory and Language* 24 (1985): 746–757.

Medwin, Sherry, and Michael O'Donovan. "Computer-Mediated Discussion of Literature: An Opportunity for Collaboration, Inquiry, & Research." Paper presented at the National Council of Teachers of English Convention, San Diego, California, 1995.

Melnick, Steven A. "Electronic Encyclopedias on Compact Disk." *The Reading Teacher* 44 (February 1991): 432–434.

Memory, David M., and Carol Y. Yoder. "Improving Concentration in Content Classrooms." *Journal of Reading* 31 (Februry 1988): 426–435.

Mike, Dennis G. "Internet in the Schools: A Literacy Perspective." *Journal of Adolescent & Adult Literacy* 40 (September 1996): 4–13.

Mikulecky, Larry. "Real-World Literacy Demands: How They've Changed and What Teachers Can Do." In Diane Lapp, James Flood, and Nancy Farnan, *Content Area Reading and Learning: Instructional Strategies.* Boston: Allyn and Bacon, 1996, pp. 153–163.

Miller, G., and P. Gildea. "How Children Learn Words." *Scientific American* 257 (1987): 94–99

Milliken, Mark. "A Fifth-Grade Class Uses Portfolios." In Donald H. Graves and Bonnie S. Sunstein (eds.), *Portfolio Portraits.* Portsmouth, N.H.: Heinemann, 1992, pp. 34–44.

Mills-Courts, Karen, and Minda Rae Amiran. "Metacognition and the Use of Portfolios." In Pat Belanoff and Marcia Dickson (eds.), *Portfolios: Process and Product.* Portsmouth, N.H.: Boynton/ Cook, 1991, pp. 101–112.

Moje, Elizabeth B., and Dolores Handy. "Using Literacy to Modify Traditional Assessments: Alternatives for Teaching and Assessing Content Understanding." *Journal of Reading* 38 (May 1995): 612–625.

Moore, D., and A. Murphy. "Reading Programs." In D. Alvermann, D. Moore, and M. Conley (eds.), *Research Within Reach: Secondary School Reading.* Newark, Del.: International Reading Association, 1987.

Moore, David W., John E. Readence, and Robert J. Rickelman. *Prereading Activities for Content Area Reading and Learning.* 2nd ed. Newark, Del.: International Reading Association, 1989.

Moore, M. A. "Electronic Dialoguing: An Avenue to Literacy." *The Reading Teacher* 45 (December 1991): 280–286.

Morgan, H., and S. Berg-O'Halloran. "Using Music as a Text." *Journal of Reading* 32 (February 1989): 458–459.

Morrow, Lesley Mandel. "Retelling Stories as a Diagnostic Tool." In Susan Mandel Glazer, Lyndon W. Searfoss, and Lance H. Gentile (eds.), *Reexamining Reading Diagnosis: New Trends and Procedures.* Newark, Del.: International Reading Association, 1989, pp. 128–149.

Morton, J., and R. Renzy. *Consumer Action.* Boston: Houghton Mifflin, 1978, p. 308.

Mosenthal, Peter B., and Irwin S. Kirsch. "Document Strategies: Cycle Strategies in Document Search: From Here to There to Wherever." *Journal of Reading* 36 (November 1992): 238–242.

Mullis, Ina V. S., Jay R. Campbell, and Alan E. Farstrup. *Executive Summary of the NAEP 1992 Reading Report Card for the Nation and the States.* Washington, D.C.: Government Printing Office, 1993.

Murphy, Sandra, and Mary Ann Smith. *Writing Portfolios: A Bridge from Teaching to Assessment.* Markham, Ontario: Pippin Publishing Limited, 1992.

Muther, Connie. "What Every Textbook Evaluator Should Know." *Educational Leadership* 42 (April 1985): 4–8.

Myers, W. D. *Fallen Angels.* New York: Scholastic, 1988.

"NAEP Achievement Standards Draw Criticism." *Reading Today* 11 (December 1993–January 1994): 12.

Nagy, W. *Teaching Vocabulary to Improve Reading Comprehension.* Newark, Del.: International Reading Association, 1988.

Nagy, W., and P. Herman. "Breadth and Depth of Vocabulary Knowledge: Implications for Acquisition and Instruction." In M. McKeown and M. Curtis (eds.), *The Nature of Vocabulary Acquisition.* Hillsdale, N.J.: Erlbaum, 1987.

Nagy, W., P. A. Herman, and R. C. Anderson. "Learning Words from Context." *Reading Research Quarterly* 20 (1985): 233–253.

Nagy, W., R. Anderson, M. Schommer, J. Scott, and A. Stallman. "Morphological Families and Word Recognition." *Reading Research Quarterly* 24, no. 3 (1989): 262–282.

Nakell, Chuck, and Mona Helgott. *Inspiration® Education Idea Book.* Portland, Oregon: Inspiration® Software, Inc., 1994.

National Center for Education Statistics. "Reading Literacy in the United States: Findings from the IEA Reading Literacy Study." Washington, D.C.: U.S. Department of Education, 1996.

National Council of Teachers of Mathematics. *Curriculum and Evaluation Standards.* Reston, Va.: NCTM, 1989.

Negroponte, N. *Being Digital.* New York: Knopf, 1995.

Nelson, G. "Culture's Role in Reading Comprehension: A Schema Theoretical Approach." *Journal of Reading* 30 (February 1987): 424–429.

Neubert, Gloria A., and Sally J. McNelis. "Peer Response: Teaching Specific Revision Suggestions." *English Journal* 79 (September 1990): 52–56.

Newman, Fran. "Let's Join the Readers' Club!" *Journal of Reading* 25 (April 1982): 693.

Nolan, T. "Self-Questioning and Prediction: Combining Metacognitive Strategies." *Journal of Reading* 35 (October 1991): 132–138.

Noll, Elizabeth. "Social Issues and Literature Circles with Adolescents." *Journal of Reading* 38 (October 1994): 88–93.

Oberlin, Kelly J., and Sherrie L. Shugarman. "Purposeful Writing Activities for Students in Middle School." *Journal of Reading* 31 (May 1988): 720–723.

Oescher, Jeffrey, and Peggy C. Kirby. "The Effects of Graduation Test Policies on Student Subgroups." *Administrator's Notebook: The University of Chicago* 33, no. 5 (1989): 1–4.

Ogle, D. "A Teaching Model That Develops Active Reading of Expository Text." *The Reading Teacher* 39 (May 1986): 564–570.

Oley, Elizabeth. "Information Retrieval in the Classroom." *Journal of Reading* 32 (April 1989): 590–597.

Ollmann, Hilda E. "Creating High Level Thinking with Reading Response." *Journal of Adolescent & Adult Literacy* 39 (April 1996): 576–581.

Osborn, Jean H., Beau Fly Jones, and Marcy Stein. "The Case for Improving Textbooks." *Educational Leadership* 42 (April 1985): 9–16.

Owston, R. D., S. Murphy, and H. H. Wideman. "The Effects of Word Processing on Students' Writing Quality and Revision Strategies." *Research in the Teaching of English* 26 (1992): 249–276.

Paeth, Beverly, and others. "Kentucky Telecommunication Writing Program." Handout presented at the National Council of Teachers of English Convention, San Diego, California, 1995.

Palinscar, A., and A. Brown. "Interactive Teaching to Promote Independent Learning from Text." *The Reading Teacher* 39 (May 1986): 771–777.

Palincsar, A., and A. Brown. *Reciprocal Teaching of Comprehension Monitoring Activities.* (Technical Report No. 269). Champaign, Ill.: Center for the Study of Reading, 1984.

Pallas, A., G. Natriello, and E. McDill. "The Changing Nature of the Disadvantaged Population. Current Dimensions and Future Trends." *Educational Researcher* 18 (June-July 1989): 16–22.

Paris, S., and M. Myers. "Comprehension Monitoring, Memory and Study Strategies of Good and Poor Readers." *Journal of Reading Behavior* 13 (Spring 1981): 5–22.

Paris, S. G. "Using Classroom Dialogues and Guided Practice to Teach Comprehension Strategies." In T. L. Harris and E. J. Cooper (eds.), *Reading, Thinking, and Concept Development.* New York: College Board Publications, 1985, pp. 133–146.

Paterson, Katherine. *Bridge to Terabithia.* New York: Crowell, 1987.

Pauk, Walter. "On Scholarship: Advice to High School Students." *The Reading Teacher* 17 (November 1963): 73–78.

———. *How to Study in College,* 5th edition. Boston: Houghton Mifflin Company, 1993.

Pavonetti, Linda M. "Joan Lowery Nixon: The Grand Dame of Young Adult Mystery." *Journal of Adolescent & Adult Literacy* 39 (March 1996): 454–461.

Pearson, Jenny Watson, and Carol M. Santa. "Students as Researchers of Their Own Learning." *Journal of Reading* 38 (March 1995): 462–469.

Peavy, L., and U. Smith. *Pioneer Women: The Lives of Women on the Frontier.* New York: Smithmark Publications, 1996.

Pellicano, R. "At-Risk: A View of Social Advantage." *Educational Leadership* 44 (1987): 47–50.

Pellowski, A. *The Story Vine.* New York: Macmillan, 1984.

Perkins, D. *Outsmarting: The Emerging Science of Learnable Intelligence.* New York: Free Press, 1995.

Peters, Tim, Kathy Schubeck, and Karen Hopkins. "A Thematic Approach: Theory and Practice at the Aleknagik School." *Phi Delta Kappan* 76 (April 1995): 633–636.

Piazza, Carolyn L., and Carl M. Tomlinson. "A Concert of Writers." *Language Arts* 62 (February 1985): 150–158.

Poindexter, Candace C. "Classroom Strategies That Convinced Content Area Teachers They Could

Teach Reading, Too." *Journal of Reading* 38 (September 1994): 134.

Polloway, E. A., and J. R. Patton. *Strategies for Teaching Learners with Special Needs.* New York: Macmillan, 1993.

Porter, Dwight. "Précis Writing in the ESL Classroom." *Journal of Reading* 33 (February 1990): 381.

Power, Brenda Miller. "Nutshells, Monkeys, and the Writer's Craft." *Voices from the Middle* 3 (April 1996): 10–15.

Powers, R. D., W. A. Sumner, and B. E. Kearl. "A Recalculation of Four Adult Readability Formulas." *The Journal of Educational Psychology* 49 (April 1958): 99–105.

Pritchard, Ruie Jane. "Developing Writing Prompts for Reading Response and Analysis." *English Journal* 82 (March 1993): 24–32.

Proctor, Vikki, and Ken Kantor. "Social Justice Notebooks." *Voices from the Middle* 3 (April 1996): 31–35.

Professional Standards and Ethics Committee and the Advisory Group to the National Council of Accreditation of Teacher Education Joint Task Force. *Standards for Reading Professionals.* Newark, Delaware: International Reading Association, 1992.

Purves, A. C. *Elements of Writing About a Literary Work.* Champaign, Ill.: National Council of Teachers of English, 1968.

Quandt, I., and R. Selznick. *Self-Concept and Reading.* Newark, Del.: International Reading Association, 1984.

Rakes, Glenda C., Thomas A. Rakes, and Lana J. Smith. "Using Visuals to Enhance Secondary Students' Reading Comprehension of Expository Texts." *Journal of Adolescent & Adult Literacy* 39 (September 1995): 46–54.

Rakes, Sondra K., and Lana J. Smith. "Strengthening Comprehension and Recall Through the Principle of Recitation." *Journal of Reading* 31 (December 1987): 260–263.

Randall, Sally N. "Information Charts: A Strategy for Organizing Student Research." *Journal of Adolescent & Adult Literacy* 39 (April 1996): 536–542.

Raphael, T. "Teaching Question Answer Relationships, Revisited." *The Reading Teacher* 39 (May 1986): 516–555.

Raphael, Taffy E., Becky W. Kirschner, and Carol Sue Englert. "Expository Writing Program: Making Connections between Reading and Writing." *The Reading Teacher* 41 (April 1988): 790–795.

Raphael, Taffy E., and Carol Sue Englert. "Writing and Reading: Partners in Constructing Meaning." *The Reading Teacher* 43 (February 1990): 388–400.

Raphael, Taffy, Carol Englert, and Becky Kirschner. *The Impact of Text Structure Instruction and Social Context on Students' Comprehension and Production of Expository Text.* Research Series No. 177. East Lansing, Mich.: Institute for Research on Teaching, 1986.

Ratekin, N., M. Simpson, D. E. Alvermann, and E. K. Dishner. "Why Content Teachers Resist Reading Instruction." *Journal of Reading* 28 (February 1985): 432–437.

Razek, J., G. Hosch, and D. Pearl. "Readability of Accounting Textbooks." *Journal of Business Education* (October 1982): 23–26.

Rea, Dan W., and David K. Thompson. "Designing Transformative Tests for Secondary Literature Students." *Journal of Reading* 34 (September 1990): 6–11.

Readence, John E., and Michael A. Martin. "Comprehension Assessment: Alternatives to Standardized Tests." In Susan Mandel Glazer, Lyndon W. Searfoss, and Lance M. Gentile (eds.), *Reexamining Reading Diagnosis: New Trends and Procedures.* Newark, Del.: International Reading Association, 1989, pp. 67–80.

Reading Today 11 (October–November 1993): 1, 11.

Recht, Donna. "Teaching Summarizing Skills." *The Reading Teacher* 37 (March 1984): 675–677.

Reid, J. M. "English as a Second Language Composition in Higher Education: The Expectations of the Academic Audience." In D. M. Johnson and D. H. Roen (eds.), *Richness in Writing.* New York: Longman, 1989, 220–234.

Reinking, D., D. Mealey, and V. Ridgeway. "Developing Preservice Teachers' Conditional Knowledge of Content Area Strategies." *Journal of Reading* 36 (March 1993): 458–469.

Renner, S., and J. Carter. "Comprehending Text—Appreciating Diversity Through Folklore." *Journal of Reading* 34 (May 1992): 602–605.

"Results from the NAEP 1994 Reading Assessment—At a Glance." NAEP Home Page: www.ed.gov: 80/NCES/NAEP/y25flk/rbro.shtml, no date.

Reynolds, Patricia. "Evaluating ESL and College Composition Texts for Teaching the Argumentative Rhetorical Form." *Journal of Reading* 36 (March 1993): 474–479.

Richardson, Judy S. "A Read-Aloud for Science Classrooms." *Journal of Reading* 38 (September 1994b): 62–65.

———. "A Read-Aloud for Social Studies Classrooms." *Journal of Reading* 38 (February 1995): 402–404.

———. "Great Read-Alouds for Prospective Teachers and Secondary Students." *Journal of Reading* 38 (October 1994a): 98–103.

Richardson, Judy S., and Margaret Breen. "A Read-Aloud for Science." *Journal of Adolescent & Adult Literacy* 39 (March 1996): 504–506.

Richek, Margaret Ann, Lynne K. List, and Janet W. Lerner. *Reading Problems: Assessment and Teaching Strategies.* Englewood Cliffs, N.J.: Prentice Hall, 1989.

Richman, Charles L., Kathryn P. Brown, and Maxine Clark. "Personality Changes as a Function of Minimum Competency Test Success or Failure." *Contemporary Educational Psychology* 12 (1987): 7–16.

Rief, Linda. "Eighth Grade: Finding the Value in Evaluation." In Donald H. Graves and Bonnie S. Sunstein (eds.), *Portfolio Portraits.* Portsmouth, N.H.: Heinemann, 1992, pp. 45–60.

Rigg, P. "Whole Language in Adult ESL Programs." *ERIC\CLL News Bulletin* 13 (1990): 1.4–5.8.

Rivard, Joseph D. *Quick Guide to the Internet for Educators.* Boston: Allyn and Bacon, 1997.

Robbins, Bruce, and Kris Fischer. "Vaporizing Classroom Walls: The Writing Workshop Goes Electric." *Voices from the Middle* 3 (April 1996): 25–30.

Robinson, Francis P. *Effective Study.* Rev. ed. New York: Harper & Row, 1961, chap. 2.

Robinson, G. *Crosscultural Understanding: Processes and Approaches to Foreign Language, English as a Second Language and Bilingual Educators.* New York: Pergamon, 1985.

Roe, Betty D., and Sandy Smith. "TALK: Talking about Literature with Kids." Unpublished project description. Cookeville: Tennessee Technological University, 1996.

Roe, Betty D., and Sandy Smith. "University/Public Schools Keypals Project: A Collaborative Effort for Electronic Literature Conversations." In *Rethinking Technology and Learning Through Technology.* Proceedings of the Mid-South Instructional Technology Conference. Murfreesboro, Tennessee: Mid-South Technology Conference, 1997.

Romano, Tom. "Crafting Authentic Voice." *Voices from the Middle* 3 (April 1996): 5–9.

Rosenberg, E., H. Gurney, and V. Harlin. *Investigating Your Health*. Rev. ed. Boston: Houghton Mifflin, 1978, p. 313.

Rosenblatt, Louise. *Literature as Exploration*. New York: Noble and Noble, 1938, 1983.

Rosenblatt, Louise M. "Literature—SOS!" *Language Arts* 68 (1991): 444–448.

———. "Writing and Reading: The Transactional Theory." In Jana M. Mason (ed.), *Reading and Writing Connections*. Boston: Allyn and Bacon, 1989, pp. 153–176.

Rosenholtz, Susan J. "Education Reform Strategies: Will They Increase Teacher Commitment?" *American Journal of Education* 95 (August 1987): 534–562.

Rosenshine, B., and C. Meister. "Reciprocal Teaching: A Review of the Research." *Review of Educational Research* 64 (Winter 1994): 479–530.

Rosenshine, B., and R. Stevens. "Classroom Instruction in Reading." In D. Pearson (ed.), *Handbook of Research on Teaching*. New York: Longman, 1984.

Roser, N., and J. Hoffman. "Language Charts: A Record of Story Time Talk." *Language Arts* 69 (May 1992): 44–52.

Ross, Elinor P., and Betty D. Roe. *An Introduction to Teaching the Language Arts*. Fort Worth: Holt, Rinehart and Winston, 1990.

Rothman, R. "The Certificate of Initial Mastery." *Educational Leadership* (May 1995): 41–45.

Ruddiman, J. "The Vocabulary Game: Empowering Students Through Word Awareness." *Journal of Reading* 36 (February 1993): 400–401.

Rush, R., A. Moe, and R. Storlie. *Occupational Literacy Education*. Newark, Del.: International Reading Association, 1986, pp. 66–159.

Ryan, Mary E. *The Trouble with Perfect*. New York: Simon & Schuster, 1995.

Ryder, Randall J., and Michael F. Graves. "Using the Internet to Enhance Students' Reading, Writing, and Information Gathering Skills." *Journal of Adolescent & Adult Literacy* 40 (December 1996/January 1997): 244–254.

Ryder, Randall J., and Tom Hughes. *Internet for Educators*. Upper Saddle River, N.J.: Prentice-Hall, 1997.

Sadker, D., and M. Sadker. "Is the O.K. Classroom O.K.?" *Phi Delta Kappan* 66 (1985): 358–361.

Sakta, Cathy G. "The Graphic Organizer: A Blueprint for Taking Lecture Notes." *Journal of Reading* 35 (March 1992): 482–484.

Salvia, John, and James E. Ysseldyke. *Assessment*. Boston: Houghton Mifflin, 1995.

Sanacore, Joseph. "Creating the Lifetime Reading Habit in Social Studies." *Journal of Reading* 33 (March 1990): 414–418.

———. "Encouraging the Lifetime Reading Habit." *Journal of Reading* 35 (March 1992): 474–477.

———. "Giving School Administrators Feedback about Their Reading Leadership." *Journal of Reading* 38 (September 1994): 64–68.

———. "Guidelines for Hiring Qualified Reading Professionals." *Journal of Reading* 38 (February 1995): 396–400.

———. "Schoolwide Independent Reading: The Principal Can Help." *Journal of Reading* 31 (January 1988): 346–353.

———. "Supporting a Literature-Based Approach Across the Curriculum." *Journal of Reading* 37 (November 1993): 240–244.

Santa, Carol, Lynn Havens, and Shirley Harrison. "Teaching Secondary Science through Reading, Writing, Studying, and Problem Solving." In Diane Lapp, James Flood, and Nancy Farnan (eds.), *Content Area Reading and Learning: Instructional Strategies*. Englewood Cliffs, N.J.: Prentice Hall, 1989.

Schumm, Jeanne Shay. "Identifying the Most Important Terms: It's Not That Easy." *Journal of Reading* 36 (May 1993): 679.

———. "Content Area Textbooks: How Tough Are They?" *Journal of Reading* 36 (September 1992): 47.

Schwartz, Jeffrey. "Let Them Assess Their Own Learning." *English Journal* 80 (February 1991): 67–73.

Schwartz, R., and T. Raphael. "Concept of Definition: A Key to Improving Students' Vocabulary." *Reading Teacher* 39 (1985): 201.

Scruggs, T., and M. Mastropieri. "Reconstructive Elaborations: A Model for Content Area Learning." *American Educational Research Journal* 26 (Summer 1989): 311–327.

Sears, J., and J. Marshall. *Teaching and Thinking About Curriculum*. New York: Teachers College Press, 1990.

Seeley, C. "Increasing Access or Ensuring Failure? Policy Makers Throw a Hammer into the Wall." In National Council of Teachers of Mathematics (eds.), *Algebra for the Twenty-First Century: Proceedings of the August 1992 Conference*. Reston, Va.: NCTM, 1993.

Seger, F. Dan. "Portfolio Definitions: Toward a Shared Notion." In Donald H. Graves and Bonnie S. Sunstein (eds.), *Portfolio Portraits*. Portsmouth, N.H.: Heinemann, 1992, pp. 114–124.

Sellars, G. "A Comparison of the Readability of Selected High School Social Studies, Science and Literature Textbooks." Ph.D. dissertation, Florida State University, 1988. *Dissertation Asbstracts International* 48 (1988): 3085A.

Sensenbaugh, Roger. "Writing across the Curriculum: Evolving Reform." *Journal of Reading* 32 (February 1989): 462–465.

Serim, Ferdi, and Melissa Koch. *Netlearning: Why Teachers Use the Internet*. Sebastopol, Calif.: Songline Studios, Inc. and O'Reilly & Associates, 1996.

———. "Nature of the Reading-Writing Relationship: An Exploratory Multivariate Analysis." *Journal of Educational Psychology* 76 (1984): 466–477.

Shanahan, Timothy. "The Reading-Writing Relationship: Seven Instructional Principles." *The Reading Teacher* 41 (March 1988): 636–647.

Shannon, Albert J. "Using the Microcomputer Environment for Reading Diagnosis." In Susan Mandel Glazer, Lyndon W. Searfoss, and Lance M. Gentile (eds.), *Reexamining Reading Diagnosis: New Trends and Procedures*. Newark, Del.: International Reading Association, 1989, pp. 150–168.

Shannon, D. "Use of Top-Level Structure in Expository Text: An Open Letter to a High School Teacher." *Journal of Reading* 28 (February 1986): 426–431.

Sharer, Patricia L., Donna Peters, and Barbara A. Lehman. "Lessons from Grammar School: How Can Literature Use in Elementary Classrooms Inform Middle-School Instruction?" *Journal of Adolescent & Adult Literacy* 39 (September 1995): 28–34.

Sharp, Sidney J. "Using Content Subject Matter with LEA in Middle School." *Journal of Reading* 33 (November 1989): 108–112.

Sharp, Vicki. *Computer Education for Teachers*. Madison, Wis.: Brown & Benchmark, 1996.

Sheffelbine, J. "Teachers Decisions about the Utility of Dictionary Tasks and the Role of Prior Knowledge." Paper presented at the National Reading Conference, St. Petersburg, Fla., 1984.

Short, D. "Integrating Language and Culture in Middle School American History Classes." (Educational Practice Rep. No. 8). Santa Cruz, Cal. and Washington, D.C.: National Center for Research on Cultural Diversity and Second Language Learning, 1994.

Shugarman, Sherrie L., and Joe B. Hurst. "Purposeful Paraphrasing: Promoting a Nontrivial Pursuit for Meaning." *Journal of Reading* 29 (February 1986): 396–399.

Silver, E. "Rethinking 'Algebra for All,'" *Educational Leadership* 52 (March 1995): 30–33.

Simmers-Wolpow, Ray, Daniel P. Farrell, and Marian J. Tonjes. "Implementing a Secondary Reading/Study Skills Program Across Disciplines." *Journal of Reading* 34 (May 1991): 590–594.

Simmons, Jay. "Portfolios for Large-Scale Assessment." In Donald H. Graves and Bonnie S. Sunstein (eds.), *Portfolio Portraits*. Portsmouth, N.H.: Heinemann, 1992, pp. 96–113.

Simons, Sandra McCandless. "PSRT—A Reading Comprehension Strategy." *Journal of Reading* 32 (February 1989): 419–427.

Simpson, Anne. "Not the Class Novel: A Different Reading Program." *Journal of Reading* 38 (December 1994/January 1995): 290–294.

Simpson, M. "Alternative Formats for Evaluating Content Area Vocabulary Understanding." *Journal of Reading* 30 (January 1987): 20–27.

Simpson, Michele L. "PORPE: A Writing Strategy for Studying and Learning in the Content Areas." *Journal of Reading* 29 (February 1986): 407–414.

Sinatra, R. "Integrating Whole Language with the Learning of Text Structure." *Journal of Reading* 34 (March 1991): 424–433.

Sinatra, R., and C. Dowd. "Using Syntactic and Semantic Clues to Learn Vocabulary." *Journal of Reading* 35 (November 1991): 224–229.

Sinatra, Richard, et al. "Combining Visual Literacy, Text Understanding, and Writing for Culturally Diverse Students." *Journal of Reading* 33 (May 1990): 612–614.

Singer, Harry, Irving H. Balow, and Robert T. Ferrett. "English Classes as Preparation for Minimal Competency Tests in Reading." *Journal of Reading* 31 (March 1988): 512–519.

Sixth Floor Media. *CommonSpace User's Guide*. Boston: Houghton Mifflin, 1995.

Slavin, R. E., N. L. Karweit, and N. A. Madden. *Effective Programs for Students at Risk*. New York: Allyn and Bacon, 1989.

Slavin, Robert. "A Cooperative Learning Approach to Content Areas: Jigsaw Teaching." In Diane Lapp, James Flood, and Nancy Farnan (eds.), *Content Area Reading and Learning: Instructional Strategies*. Englewood Cliffs, N.J.: Prentice-Hall, 1989, pp. 330–345.

Smith, C. "Building a Better Vocabulary." *The Reading Teacher* 42 (December, 1988): 238.

Smith, J. Lea, and Holly A. Johnson. "Control in the Classroom: Listening to Adolescent Voices." *Language Arts* 70 (January 1993): 18–30.

Smith, Patricia L., and Gail E. Tompkins. "Structured Notetaking: A New Strategy for Content Area Readers." *Journal of Reading* 32 (October 1988): 46–53.

Spaulding, Cheryl L. "Test Review: Written Language Assessment (WLA)." *Journal of Reading* 33 (October 1989): 68–69.

Spires, Hiller A., and P. Diane Stone. "The Directed Notetaking Activity: A Self-Questioning Approach." *Journal of Reading* 33 (October 1989): 36–39.

Stahl, Norman A., James R. King, and William A. Henk. "Enhancing Students' Notetaking Through Training and Evaluation." *Journal of Reading* 34 (May 1991): 614–622.

Stahl, S. "Three Principles of Effective Vocabulary Instruction." *Journal of Reading* 29 (May 1986): 662–668.

———. "To Teach a Word Well: A Framework for Vocabulary Instruction." *Reading World* 24 (1985): 16–27.

Stauffer, R. *Teaching Reading as a Thinking Process.* New York: Harper & Row, 1969.

Stern, D., J. Stone III, C. Hopkins, M. McMillion, and R. Crain. *School-Based Enterprise: Productive Learning in American High Schools.* San Francisco: Jossey-Bass, 1994.

Stern, D., and M. Rahn. "Work-Based Learning." *Educational Leadership* 52 (May 1995): 35–40.

Sternberg, R. "Most Vocabulary Is Learned from Context." In M. B. McKeown and M. E. Curtis (eds.), *The Nature of Vocabulary Acquisition.* Hillsdale, N.J.: Erlbaum, 1987, pp. 89–105.

Sternberg, R., and P. Frensch. *Complex Problem Solving: Principles and Mechanisms.* Hillsdale, N.J.: Erlbaum, 1992.

Sternberg, Robert J. "Are We Reading Too Much into Reading Comprehension Tests?" *Journal of Reading* 34 (April 1991): 540–545.

Stetson, Elton G., and Richard P. Williams. "Learning from Social Studies Textbooks: Why Some Students Succeed and Others Fail." *Journal of Reading* 36 (September 1992): 22–30.

Stevens, K. "Can We Improve Reading by Teaching Background Information?" *Journal of Reading* 25 (January 1982): 326–329.

Stewart, Roger A., Edward E. Paradis, Bonita D. Ross, and Mary Jane Lewis. "Student Voices: What Works in Literature-Based Developmental Reading." *Journal of Adolescent & Adult Literacy* 39 (March 1996): 468–478.

Sticht, T. *Literacy and Vocational Competence.* Columbus, Ohio: National Center for Research in Vocational Education, 1978.

Stivers, Jan. "The Writing Partners Project." *Phi Delta Kappan* 77 (June 1996): 694–695.

Stock, Patricia Lambert. "The Rhetoric of Writing Assessment." In Vito Perrone (ed.), *Expanding Student Assessment.* Alexandria, Va.: Association for Supervision and Curriculum Development, 1991, pp. 72–105.

Stoodt, B. "Literacy Instruction." In C. Baber et al. (eds.), *Project Achieve.* Greensboro: The University of North Carolina at Greensboro, 1990.

———. *Literacy in an Information Age.* Greensboro, N.C.: Center for Creative Leadership, 1985.

Stoodt, B., and L. Amspaugh. "Children's Response to Nonfiction." A paper presented to the Annual Meeting of the International Reading Association, Toronto, Canada, May 1994.

Strackbein, Deanna, and Montague Tillman. "The Joy of Journals—with Reservations." *Journal of Reading* 31 (October 1987): 28–31.

Strichart, Stephen S., and Charles T. Mangrum II. *Teaching Study Strategies to Students with Learning Disabilities.* Needham Heights, Mass.: Allyn and Bacon, 1993.

Stull, Andrew T. *Education on the Internet: A Student's Guide.* Adapted for Merrill Education by Randall J. Ryder. Columbus, Ohio: Merrill, an imprint of Prentice Hall, 1997.

Sullivan, Emilie P. "Three Good Juvenile Books with Literacy Models." *Journal of Reading* 38 (September 1994): 55.

Sunstein, Bonnie S. "Introduction." In Donald H. Graves and Bonnie S. Sunstein (eds.), *Portfolio Portraits.* Portsmouth, N.H.: Heinemann, 1992, pp. xi–xvii.

Symons, S., and M. Pressley. "Prior Knowledge Affects Text Search and Extraction of Information." *Reading Research Quarterly* 28 (1993): 251–264.

Taba, H. *Teacher's Handbook for Elementary Social Studies.* Reading, Mass.: Addison-Wesley, 1967.

Taber, Sylvia Read. "Current Definitions of Literacy." *Journal of Reading* 30 (February 1987): 458–461.

Tanner, M. "Reading in Music Class." *Music Education Journal* 60 (December 1983): 41–45.

Taylor, B., and S. Berkowitz. "Facilitating Children's Comprehension of Content Material." In M. Kamil and A. Moe (eds.), *Perspectives on Reading Research and Instruction.* Twenty-ninth Yearbook of the National Reading Conference. Washington, D.C.: National Reading Conference, 1980, pp. 64–68.

Taylor, Rebecca Buffum, ed. *The Multimedia Home Companion.* New York: Warner Books, 1994.

Taylor, Wilson L. "Recent Developments in the Use of Cloze Procedure." *Journalism Quarterly* 33 (Winter 1956): 42–48, 99.

Tchudi, Stephen N., and Joanne Yates. *Teaching Writing in the Content Areas: Senior High School.* Washington, D.C.: National Education Association, 1983.

Terban, M. *Checking Your Grammar.* New York: Scholastic, 1993.

The Daedalus Group, Inc. *DGI Home Page: Products & Services: What Is DIWE?.* (http://daedalus.com/info/diwe/diwe_info.html) Austin, Tex.: The Daedalus Group, 1995.

Thomas, D. "Reading and Reasoning Skills for Math Problem Solvers." *Journal of Reading* 32 (December 1988): 244–249.

Thousand, J. S., and R. A. Villa. "Strategies for Educating Learners with Severe Disabilities Within Their Local Home Schools and Communities." *Focus on Exceptional Children* 23 (1990): 1–24.

Tierney, R. "Redefining Reading Comprehension." *Educational Leadership* 47 (March 1990): 37–42.

Tierney, R., and J. Cunningham. "Research on Teaching Reading Comprehension." In P. D. Pearson et al. (eds.), *Handbook of Reading Research.* New York: Longman, 1984, pp. 609–656.

Tierney, R. J., J. E. Readence, and E. K. Dishner. *Reading Strategies and Practices.* Boston: Allyn and Bacon, 1990.

Tipton, J. "Extending Context Clues to Composition and Cooperative Learning." *Journal of Reading* 35 (September 1991): 50.

Tone, Bruce. "Guiding Students through Research Papers." *Journal of Reading* 32 (October 1988): 76–79.

Tuman, Myron C., and Ann Arbor Software. *Instructor's Guide for Use with Norton Textra Connect: A Networked Writing Environment.* New York: W. W. Norton & Company, 1994.

Unrau, Norman J., and Robert B. Ruddell. "Interpreting Texts in Classroom Contexts." *Journal of Adolescent & Adult Literacy* 39 (September 1995): 16–27.

Valencia, Sheila. "Alternative Assessment: Separating the Wheat from the Chaff." *The Reading Teacher* 44 (September 1990): 60–61.

———. "A Portfolio Approach to Classroom Reading Assessment: The Whys, Whats, and Hows." *The Reading Teacher* 43 (January 1990): 338–340.

Valencia, Sheila, and P. David Pearson. "Reading Assessment: Time for a Change." *The Reading Teacher* 40 (April 1987): 726–732.

Vigil, A. *The Corn Woman: Stories and Legends of the Hispanic Southwest.* Englewood, Colo.: Libraries Unlimited Inc., 1994.

Vygotsky, L. *Thought and Language.* Cambridge, Mass.: The M.I.T. Press, 1962.

Wade, S., and B. Adams. "Effects of Importance and Interest on Recall of Biographical Text." *Journal of Literacy* 22 (1990): 331–353.

Wade, S., G. Schraw, W. Buxton, and M. Hayes. "Seduction of the Strategic Reader: Effects of Interest on Strategies and Recall." *Reading Research Quarterly* 28 (Spring 1993): 93–114.

Wade, Suzanne E. "Using Think Alouds to Assess Comprehension." *The Reading Teacher* 43 (March 1990): 442–451.

Wait, S. S. "Textbook Readability and the Predictive Value of the Dale-Chall, Comprehensive Assessment Program and Cloze." Ph.D. dissertation, Florida State University. *Dissertation Abstracts International* 48 (1987): 357A.

Ward, Stephen D., and Eugene J. Bradford. "Supervisors' Expertise in Reading Affects Achievement in Junior High." *Journal of Reading* 26 (January 1983): 362.

Warren, J. *Portrait of a Tragedy: America and the Vietnam War.* New York: Lothrop, Lee and Shepard, 1990.

Weaver, C. *Understanding Whole Language.* Portsmouth, N.H.: Heinemann, 1990.

Webb, N. "With New Court Decisions Backing Them, Advocates See Inclusion as a Question of Values." *The Harvard Education Letter* (July/August, 1994): 2.

Wehmeyer, Lillian Biermann. "Wide-Angle Searching on the World Wide Web." *Syllabus* 9 (June 1996): 34–37.

Weinstein, D. "Fostering Learning Autonomy Through the Use of Learning Strategies." *Journal of Reading* 30 (1987): 590–595.

Werner, Patrice Holden. "Integrated Assessment System." *Journal of Reading* 35 (February 1992): 416–418.

Wheatley, E., D. Muller, R. Miller. "Computer-Assisted Vocabulary Instruction." *Journal of Reading* 37 (October 1993): 92–102.

Whimbey, Arthur. "A 15th-Grade Reading Level for High School Seniors?" *Phi Delta Kappan* 69 (November 1987): 207.

White, T., M. Graves, and W. Slater. "Growth of Reading Vocabulary in Diverse Elementary Schools: Decoding and Word Meaning." *Journal of Educational Psychology* 82 (1990): 281–289.

White, T., M. Power, and S. White. "Morphological Analysis: Implications for Teaching and Understanding Vocabulary Growth." *Reading Research Quarterly* 24, no. 3 (1989): 283–335.

Wigfield, A., and S. Asher. "Social and Motivational Influences on Reading." In P. D. Pearson (ed.), *Handbook of Reading Research.* New York: Longman, 1984, pp. 423–452.

Wilder, H., R. Ludlum, and H. Brown. *This Is America's Story.* Boston: Houghton Mifflin, 1982, p. 238.

Willig, A. C. et al. "Sociocultural and Educational Correlates of Success-Failure Attributions and Evaluation Anxiety in the School Setting for Black, Hispanic, and Anglo Children." *American Educational Research Journal* 26 (Fall 1983): 385–410.

Willis, Jerry W., Elizabeth C. Stephens, and Kathryn I. Matthew. *Technology, Reading, and Language Arts.* Boston: Allyn and Bacon, 1996.

Winograd, Peter, Scott Paris, and Connie Bridge. "Improving the Assessment of Literacy." *The Reading Teacher* 45 (October 1991): 108–116.

"Wired Education: The Internet: A Valuable, Integral Part of the Teaching Process." *Curriculum Administrator* 30 (April 1996): 8.

Wittrock, Merlin C. "Process Oriented Measures of Comprehension." *The Reading Teacher* 40 (April 1987): 734–737.

Wixson, Karen K., Charles W. Peters, Elaine M. Weber, and Edward D. Roeber. "New Directions in Statewide Reading Assessment." *The Reading Teacher* 40 (April 1987): 749–754.

Wolak, Donna De Long. "Ways to Have Happier Secondary Remedial Reading Classes." *Journal of Reading* 33 (March 1990): 465–466.

Wolf, D. P. "Portfolio Assessment: Sampling Student Work." *Educational Leadership* 46, no. 7 (1989): 35–39.

Wolf, Kenneth P. "From Informal to Informed Assessment: Recognizing the Role of the Classroom Teacher." *Journal of Reading* 36 (April 1993): 518–523.

Wolf, Kenneth, and Yvonne Siu-Runyan. "Portfolio Purposes and Possibilities." *Journal of Adolescent & Adult Literacy* 40 (September 1996): 30–37.

Wolfe, R., and A. Lopez. "Structured Overviews for Teaching Science Concepts and Terms." *Journal of Reading* 36 (December 1992–January 1993): 315–317.

Wollman-Bonilla, J. "Why Don't They 'Just Speak'? Attempting Literature Discussion with More and Less Able Readers." *Research in the Teaching of English* 28 (October 1994): 231–258.

Wong Fillmore, L. "Instructional Language as Linguistic Input: Second Language Learning in Classrooms." In L. C. Wilkinson (ed.), *Communicating in the Classroom.* New York: Academic Press, 1982, pp. 283–296.

Wood, Karen D. "Fostering Collaborative Reading and Writing Experiences in Mathematics." *Journal of Reading* 36 (October 1992): 96–103.

Woods, Alice R., and Mary H. Topping. "The Reading Resource Specialist: A Model." *Journal of Reading* 29 (May 1986): 733–738.

Wyatt, Allen. *Your Windows® 95 Internet Surfboard.* Foster City, Calif.: IDG Books, 1995.

Yore, L. D. "Secondary Science Teachers' Attitudes Toward and Beliefs About Science Reading and Science Textbooks." *Journal of Research in Science Teaching* 28 (1991): 55–72.

Young, Petey, and Cynthia Bastianelli. "Retelling Comes to Chiloquin High." *Journal of Reading* 34 (November 1990): 194–196.

Zessoules, Rieneke, and Howard Gardner. "Authentic Assessment: Beyond the Buzzword and into the Classroom." In Vito Perrone (ed.), *Expanding Student Assessment.* Alexandria, Va.: Association for Supervision and Curriculum Development, 1991, pp. 47–71.

Index